Evaluating Educational
Television and Radio

A

Evaluating Educational Television and Radio

*Proceedings of the International
Conference on Evaluation
and Research in
Educational Television and Radio,
The Open University,
United Kingdom,
9–13 April 1976*

Edited by
TONY BATES and JOHN ROBINSON

THE OPEN UNIVERSITY PRESS

The Open University Press
Walton Hall, Milton Keynes
MK7 6AA

First published 1977

Printed in Great Britain by Sydenhams Printers, Poole, Dorset

ISBN 0 335 00045 2

CONTENTS

FOREWORD

PROFESSOR WILBUR SCHRAMM — Distinguished Centre Researcher,
East–West Centre, Honolulu

I have just had the experience of reading a large sample of the papers prepared for the Open University's conference on *Evaluating Educational Television and Radio*.

It was clearly a remarkable conference, and for a variety of reasons. Because 230 people came, from 30 countries, most of them at their own expense or that of the organizations they represented. Because they came to an English village to discuss a topic which, as recently as 20 years ago, would hardly have been mentioned in any of their homelands. Because the meeting apparently was thoughtful and thought-provoking, and fun, and operated evidently at a level of intellectual excitement uncommon for large academic conferences. And because it was so mercifully short—four days. If it had not been ended at that point, with trains leaving for London and airplanes from Heathrow, and a gavel to stop discussion, I can easily conceive of small groups of participants still at the conference scene a month later, talking their way down the fascinating highways and bypaths opened by the papers at the conference and by the exchanges they had barely been able to begin in four days.

Evaluation, as the term was used at Milton Keynes, is a newcomer to the field of applied research. As McAnany pointed out in his rapporteur's report, its academic respectability in the study of education might be dated to the appearance of Michael Scriven's theoretical paper in 1967. In the last two decades, however, there has been an increasing demand for summative evaluation to provide 'accountability', and in the last decade highly visible operations like the Open University and the Children's Television Workshop have demonstrated the usefulness of formative evaluation which has been going on, less formally and skilfully, for a long time. Now suddenly we have a two-volume *Handbook of Evaluation* selling for 50 dollars, a bulging annual review of evaluation, and Scriven's paper and several studies and programs which have attained a stature entitling them to be referred to at this conference as 'classical'. This is the first large conference devoted exclusively to the evaluation of educational radio and television. Therefore, perhaps it is not so remarkable after all that so many people came to talk about evaluation and that the exchanges were so lively.

What happened to those 230 persons at Milton Keynes? They looked at and listened to each other, and absorbed some idea of the extraordinary breadth and heterogeneity of their field. They went about the delayed business of beginning to build bridges between the islands within academia and broadcasting which the papers and the talk revealed; between broadcasters, managers, scholars; between disciplines engaged, with their own methods, in evaluation—anthropologists, sociologists, several varieties of psychologists, economists, political scientists, educators, and some of the applied manifestations of each. And, perhaps most important, between the basic and applied approaches to evaluation. Tony Bates, who had the titanic job of organizing and directing the conference, was rather regretful that so little 'basic' research was submitted in answer to the call for papers. Yet, if there is one lesson to be learned from the last decade of evaluation it is that the evaluations most useful to a given ETV or educational radio project have been the most closely applied and immediate ones. The usefulness of formative research has been easier to demonstrate than that of summative, which has usually become available too late to affect policies and procedures of the project with which it dealt and often has proved of doubtful applicability to later projects. Therefore, the people attracted to the Milton Keynes conference were not there, most of them, to talk about basic research; that has been for meetings of learned societies and seminars within disciplines. They came, rather, with eyes on the most distinctive characteristics of the field of evaluation—its practical, applied quality, and its usefulness to educational policy and to the design of materials of instruction.

Typically a field of this kind which begins without an intellectual father-model begins by trial and error, with many different kinds of contributors, each doing his own thing, before it becomes apparent that all this activity really fits into one field and the different kinds of people in it have something to contribute to one another. Out of this develops a broader and more powerful view of the activity in which they are all engaged. They have been nibbling at related problems; now their activities are ready to coalesce into a field of study.

Thus it may well be that the significance of the Open University conference on *Evaluating Educational Television and Radio* is that it took place at the very time when this process of growing together, this broadening of the evaluation concept, was happening, and gave a powerful stimulus to it. At Milton Keynes it must have become readily apparent that the sociologists had something to give the psychologists, the anthropologists to both of them, the economists to all the others and vice versa. Extremely interesting questions were discussed concerning the relationship of researchers to an ongoing broadcast activity—whether they belonged inside or out, whether broadcasting and educators should take an active part in planning, carrying out, and interpreting the research, and how research results could be fitted into policy making. Perhaps most important of all was the occasional talk of how basic research and applied evaluation fit together: how insights from formative evaluation can be gathered together and in some cases become hypotheses to be tested in more basic experiments; how the growing body of insights from basic research can be translated into precepts and guidelines to be tested again in application by formative research; and, most interestingly, how the various parts of a teaching–learning system can be studied in relation to each other, so that media choices can be related to other media choices, and both to the events and strategies of instruction. As Hooper noted, evaluation is best seen as a continuing system-monitoring, with pre-program studies of audience needs and abilities feeding into objectives and design, feedback from formative research and later observation contributing constantly to design and production, summative research guiding a review of policy, and the growing body of basic research findings contributing to the efficiency of all the rest of the process. The objective of evaluation as a whole is thus to decrease the uncertainty within which education has to be designed, materials prepared and learners invited to learn.

How does one read a book like this? I can only tell you how *I* read it. I read the introductory papers, then, in pairs, the animateurs' and rapporteurs' papers for each of the three main topics, then sampled the papers submitted under those topics. I missed the conversation that went on in the nine discussion groups, although the rapporteurs gave some of the flavor of it. But I suspect every reader will have to find his own way to read the book. I remember when I was a small boy, too small to go to the public library—indeed, too small to convince the librarians that I should be permitted to read the books I wanted to read—and I lived in a home sufficiently lacking in affluence that the purchase of even one book was an important event, that one day my father bought a twelve-volume series entitled *The Book of Knowledge.* What a wonderful gift that was for a small, curious, intellectually hungry boy! It contained literary prose, poetry, history, science, reproductions of art, pictures of distant countries, all organized in a way that must have been more obvious to the editors than to me. It was a whole library. I spent countless hours with that set of books, took it to bed with me when I was supposed to be sound asleep, read in it even after I was large and intellectually respectable enough to be allowed to use something other than children's books in the public library. I dipped into it wherever I felt like doing so, and read as long as it interested me—sometimes all night. I presume that the readers of this book will also find their own places to dip into it, and their own ways to read it, and I wish them the same kind of pleasure I derived from that experience I still so vividly remember.

Honolulu   *Wilbur Schramm*
November 1976

HOW TO USE THIS BOOK

This book is a collection of papers and presentations from an International Conference on Evaluation and Research in Educational Television and Radio (CEREB) held at the Open University, United Kingdom, in April 1976. Since there were over 80 different papers and presentations, originally totalling over 400,000 words, we have had to edit and shorten considerably many of the papers. We recommend therefore that these proceedings are used as a source or reference book, or as an indication of the 'state of the art'. We hope that readers will use the index and content lists selectively, and that readers will then follow up any papers which are found to be of interest by contacting the authors directly. (Names and addresses of all participants and authors are listed in Appendix 1, p. 393.)

The organization of the book follows the chronological order of the conference. After a short discussion of the reasons behind the conference and its significance, we present an edited version of all the papers submitted for the conference. The second part of the book contains transcriptions of the main presentations during the conference.

Readers who would like some guide to selecting conference papers from Part 1 might find it useful to read first the introductory chapter, and also the papers of the three animateurs (Palmer, Hooper and Allebeck). All papers submitted are numbered, and the full list of papers is given at the start of Part 1 (p. 1).

THE CONFERENCE: RATIONALE AND SIGNIFICANCE

TONY BATES — Chairman of the Conference Steering and Management Committees

Reasons for the conference

Why try to bring over 200 people from all round the world together for a conference on evaluation and research in educational television and radio? And why, in one of the most difficult economic years since the 1930s, were so many—230 people from 29 different countries—willing and able to come?

Educational television and radio are now major undertakings in most countries in the world. Although no official estimate exists, expenditure must be running at well over £20 million per annum in Britain alone, if one includes closed-circuit as well as open-network transmissions. In many countries television and radio are no longer novelties, no longer seen as a panacea for the problems of education. There is therefore an increasing pressure to justify the use and expense of television and radio for education.

As well as its expense, educational broadcasting has the awkward feature of separating those who plan and design the 'product' or teaching process from those who use it. Many believe that research has an important role to play in bridging this gap.

Related to this gap between designer and user is an increased awareness of the difficulty of decision-making and management in educational television and radio. Organizations responsible for decision-making in this area are becoming increasingly large and complex. Measuring educational 'output' is extraordinarily difficult in any circumstances, and the increasing integration of television and radio with other media makes it all the more difficult to relate decisions to outcomes. Evaluation and research therefore are obvious areas to look to for help in such situations.

Nevertheless, even though television and radio are extensively used for educational purposes throughout the world, the number of people involved in research in this area in any one country is very small. (In Britain, at the time of the conference, there were less than ten full-time researchers.) Hence research tends to be scattered, isolated, and unrelated, although many of the problems are similar from organization to organization. Also, many people in production and management—especially those who have had little direct experience of working with researchers—are deeply sceptical of the role and usefulness of research. At the same time, they would welcome any positive contribution to the difficult task of designing educational programmes.

There were also internal reasons for holding the conference. At the Open University, we had completed several major studies on the use of television and radio, and an international conference was seen as an ideal way of drawing attention to this work.

The Open University is for many people an outstanding example of the design of high-quality, integrated distance teaching materials, of which television and radio are important components. Even so, the tremendous pressures on the University staff that such a system imposes have tended to make people working in the University very inward-looking. I believe though that the University itself has much to learn from developments that have taken place in other organizations over the last six years, and nowhere is this more true than in the field of evaluation. Thus a conference on campus—and indeed, this was the first major conference ever held on the University's campus—would, it was hoped, provide a broader perspective to the University's own work, particularly regarding broadcasting and evaluation.

In short, then, quite apart from the usual motive of bringing together people with common interests, an underlying aim behind the conference was to increase the awareness of the potential—and limitations—of research and evaluation in educational television, and the implications of this for decision-making within organizations. At the same time, it was hoped that this would also have direct relevance to the working of the Open University itself.

Sponsoring bodies

For the conference to succeed, it needed wide backing and help, from both within and outside the University. It was decided therefore to approach officially a large number of organizations with interests in the topic. Each of the organizations approached nominated a representative to attend a meeting to assess the value of such a conference. This meeting was also attended by the Open University's senior administrator. The response was very encouraging, and as a result, the University agreed to take responsibility for organizing the conference—on a self-financing basis—in conjunction with the other organizations represented at the meeting. A Steering Committee was formed to oversee the general management of the conference, and a small Management Sub-Committee was nominated to look after the detailed organization (see Appendix 2, p. 399, for membership of both committees). The bodies represented in the organization of the conference were:

> Association for Programmed Learning and Educational Technology
> British Broadcasting Corporation
> British Council
> Centre Audio-Visuel, Ecole Normale Superieure de St Cloud
> Commonwealth Broadcasting Association
> Council for Educational Technology
> Department of Education and Science for England and Wales
> European Broadcasting Union
> Independent Broadcasting Authority
> Ministry for Overseas Development
> National Educational Closed-Circuit Television Association
> Scottish Education Department
> UNESCO

The members of the committees gave invaluable advice on the structure and organization of the conference, and provided a world-wide list of possible participants. The British Council and UNESCO particularly gave wide international publicity for the conference, and in addition, UNESCO provided a US $4,000 grant towards travel and subsistence for participants from Third World countries, and the British Council covered the cost for a further nine participants. The Open University provided a loan of £1,000 from its General Purposes Fund, and provided part-time administrative support, in the form of a Conference Secretary (Ms Lee Taylor). Otherwise costs were covered by the participants' own organization, or in several instances, by the participants themselves.

Aims of the conference

The Steering Committee were strongly of the opinion that the conference should examine very closely the relationship between research and decision-making. The aim was not to provide a forum for the exchange of academic papers between researchers, but to examine the role and limitations of research in the decision-making process. Secondly, it was recognized that, at least in Britain, educationists and broadcasters rarely met together, on equal terms, at a conference level, and that there was possibly much to learn from each of the different areas of educational television and radio. It was therefore deliberate policy to include research and evaluation in educational television and radio in *all* its forms, broadcast and closed circuit, for schools and universities, for non-formal and formal education, within the terms of the conference. Consequently, the following aims were agreed:

The main aim of the conference was to bring together at an international level managers, producers and researchers, to examine the value and implications of research and evaluation for organizations using television and/or radio in an educational system. It was hoped to do this in three ways:

(i) by identifying the main areas where research and evaluation is taking place in educational television and radio, the main results of the studies and how these results have been used, and their implications for the management and production of educational television and radio;

(ii) by examining critically the methods, processes and resources used and needed for research and evaluation in educational television and radio;

(iii) by exploring ways in which research and evaluation might contribute more fully to organizations concerned with or considering the use of educational television and radio.

A subsidiary aim was the examination of the need to provide more permanent and continuing links between those concerned with evaluation and research in educational television and radio.

Organization of the conference

To achieve these aims, it was apparent that the normal conference procedure of formal presentation of platform papers would be inadequate, for a number of reasons. For a start, this would severely limit the number of papers that could be made available, and as the proceedings were in English this would also place many overseas people at a disadvantage. More importantly, the conference was aimed as much at bringing about a better understanding between researchers and broadcasters as in providing information on research findings or problems of management. In any case, it was believed that if learning was to take place, this would occur more effectively if every participant could play a genuine and active role during the conference, rather than sit inactively through long and formal presentation of papers. At the same time, the Steering Committee wanted to ensure that as well as interpersonal contact, there was a concrete outcome from the conference, in the form of published proceedings.

These deliberations led us to opt for prior circulation of papers, the bulk of the time during the conference itself being devoted to small group discussion, but with a minimum number of plenary sessions for signposting at the beginning and summing up at the end of the group discussions. Consequently, it was decided to organize the conference around three themes, roughly equivalent to each of the aims, with one day's discussion devoted to each theme. The three themes were:

1　Evaluation and research findings
2　Methodology
3　The relationship between research and decision-making.

Participants were invited to submit papers of around 3000 words in length, with a 2- or 3-page summary on one of the three themes. The response was staggering. Eighty papers were submitted for the conference, 64 in time for distribution in summary form to all participants one month before the conference.

For each theme, an animateur read through the full papers, and prepared a list of questions. At the beginning of each day, the animateur for the theme presented in plenary session a paper elaborating on his selection of questions. The conference then broke into nine groups, of approximately 20–25 participants each, to discuss the questions. There was a chairman and group rapporteur, and each group had to come to conclusions related to the questions. The groups were deliberately mixed to provide a membership of different nationalities and a mixture of producers, researchers and others. Some groups had a preponderance of members interested in a similar area, such as schools broadcasting, while others were completely mixed, but the aim was to ensure as wide a range of background and experience as possible in the group discussions. On the final day, the discussions on each of the three themes were summarized from the group reports by a main rapporteur for each theme, in plenary session.

There was also an opening and closing presentation, and a session devoted to continuing links. (See Appendix 3, p. 400, for the conference programme.)

Editing of the proceedings

With the papers submitted in advance of the conference, with several other valuable papers brought by participants to the conference itself, and with the transcriptions of the eight plenary session presentations, we found ourselves with over 400,000 'written' words to edit. We had two choices. We could either omit almost half the papers, or we could provide most of the papers in a severely edited form.

We chose the latter course, for a number of reasons. The restriction we asked of 3000 words is in general too short to give a full description of a study, or a theoretical or methodological exposition. It was usually enough though to give an accurate idea of what the author has to say. The edited papers therefore should be seen as sources of reference, to be followed up by the reader through direct contact, if he or she wants further information. (We have listed all names and addresses of participants in Appendix 1.) Another reason why we preferred to keep as many papers in the proceedings as possible is that taken together, they give a good idea of the current state of the art, the extent of evaluation and research being carried out, its shortcomings and gaps, and the current trends in thinking.

There was also another reason for including as many papers as possible. We did not feel that we should apply strict academic criteria to the selection of papers. One of the points that came through loud and clear from the conference discussions was the need for 'quick and dirty' evaluation, for *less* academic presentation of results, for more information about what people are doing in the way of evaluation, including the difficulties and problems they are facing, and for more 'historical' and 'subjective' accounts of decision-making.

The criteria we have chosen for the inclusion of papers therefore are:

(i)   they must be directly relevant to educational television and radio;
(ii) they must be concerned with research, evaluation or theory.

For a paper to be included, it had to meet *both* criteria. Thus a very small number of papers submitted to the conference have not been included in these proceedings (although they were available at the conference) and these are listed in Appendix 4 (p. 401).

With regard to editing, we have reduced most in length those articles or papers previously published in journals easily available to English-speaking audiences. We have tended to omit statistical tables and diagrams, and occasionally sets of ancillary results. Almost all papers have been shortened in some way, and we hope authors will remember that full papers were available at the conference, and so forgive us for our very reluctant butchery.

We have however included more or less intact the full presentations during the plenary sessions, partly because these were not available before in printed form, and partly because we believe that they have between them captured extremely well the main issues that people were wanting to discuss—and did discuss—throughout the conference.

Organization of the papers

In the organization of the papers, we have departed from the three themes of the conference, and have organized the papers mainly in terms of the target audiences being aimed at by educational television and radio. This was a result of the general agreement which occurred during the conference about the danger of generalizing from one different kind of system to another. Also, we anticipated that general readers would be more interested in papers about similar kinds of organization to their own. Even so, we believe that most readers will find many of the papers in Section D ('The Context of Evaluation') of interest and relevance, irrespective of the type of target audience with which they are concerned.

Significance of the conference

To us, perhaps the most significant part of the conference was that it took place. We were

Table 1 Institutions where the main kinds of evaluation studies represented in conference papers have been carried out

(Nos refer to conference paper nos)

Target audience	Audience research	Formative research	Policy/summative research	Basic research
Schools/children	Hungarian TV and radio (68) BBC (26) Hong Kong (21) Swedish Radio (23) ATS-6 (Canada) (9) Malaysia (64)	Swedish Radio (14, 15, 54, 60) IBA (fellowship) (31) AIT (USA) (53) RT Eirann (38) CTW (USA) (76)	ETV-Maranhao (50) US Office of Education (42) (by Indiana) El Salvador (39) Mexican Tele-secundaria (49) } by Stanford Univ. Korea (27) Nicaragua (56)	Plymouth Polytechnic (55)
Non-formal adult	TRU (4) BBC (52) Brighton Polytechnic (23, 10) TELEAC (59) Ontario ECA (63) IBA (12) University of Adelaide (46)	UMA (USA) (20) SITE, India (78, 80) Film & TV School, India (45)	RTS/Promotion (19) Télé-Université (35) University of Turku (30)	
University/colleges	The Open University (7) Polish TV Agricultural School (29) Polish RTV University for Teachers (77)	The Open University (16, 34)	Leeds University (44) University of Montreal (51) Concordia University (70) Canberra CAE (43) C. College Chicago (18) The Open University (7)	Liverpool University (6) The Open University (40)
General			ATS-6 (11)	Bielefeld (22) University Paris VIII (25)

delighted at the enthusiasm and frankly surprised at the size of the response. We cannot claim that every worker in the field was present, or that every organization carrying out research or evaluation was represented. We were particularly disappointed that for different reasons there were no participants from Japan or Russia, although invited. Nevertheless, in 1976 there was clearly a felt need for such a conference, sufficient to move many people many thousands of miles to attend. We hope that we will be able to follow up and consolidate the contacts that have been made, and this is the subject for our section, 'Continuing Links'.

Because of the size of the response, I thought it might be useful to map out the areas where research and evaluation were taking place, as represented in the papers presented in these proceedings, in Table 1. The criterion for inclusion was that there must be a description of a project actually in operation or recently completed.

I have divided the vertical axis into *target* audiences; in other words, the type of audience with which the project is concerned. Perhaps more controversial are the categories on the horizontal axis. The first category I would describe as *audience research studies*. This would include studies which measure the number and kind of people watching or listening, and may also include audience ratings of the programmes. They do not however go beyond these very broad measures of audience reaction, and are *not* directly related to the design or improvement of individual programmes. The second category I have called *formative* research, in that the research is directly concerned with providing producers with information about specific programmes or programme policy, which can either affect the final form of a programme, or can be used for remaking a programme. The third category I have described as policy or summative research—studies concerned with judging a system or broad policy as a whole. Finally the fourth category I have described as *basic research*. In this category come studies which are concerned with how people learn from or process television or radio, identification of media characteristics, and general principles of production. (This categorization is derived from deliberations in a number of the conference papers about the main types of research, see for instance Richard Hooper's presentation, p. 334.)

In Table 1, I have included only institutions where results or studies of some kind have been carried out and reported, and have therefore excluded purely theoretical papers, or papers concerned entirely with methodology. Even so, the listings can be quite misleading, since some of the projects included (such as the Open University's) are comparatively large-scale and on-going, while others are small-scale and one-off (such as the University of Adelaide study). Also many will disagree probably not only with what I have left out, but also with where I have located studies that I have included. To get a full picture, one would need to read all the papers. Even so, the table does give some indication of both the extent and the balance between the different kinds of research, which I have summarized below in Table 2.

It would be foolish to assume that these figures are representative of all evaluation activities during 1976—indeed some of them are studies carried out up to four or five years

Table 2   Number of institutions carrying out evaluation studies represented in the proceedings

Target audience	Audience research	Formative research	Policy/ summative research	Basic research	Total* (institutions)
Schools/children	6	5	6	1	18
Non-formal adult	7	3	3	—	13
Universities/colleges	3	1	6	2	12
General	—	—	1	2	3
Total	16	9	16	5	46

* Some institutions are counted more than once—in all 38 different institutions are represented.

ago—but the figures do reinforce a feeling that I had in reading through all the papers of how little professional and organized research and evaluation is actually taking place. Many of the University studies for instance are on just one or two programmes, and are usually not funded, but carried out on top of the academic's other teaching activities. I find it disturbing that there were so few basic papers concerned with basic research—how learners process television and radio material. Formative evaluation may give some insight into this, but again there are very few studies of this kind. There does seem to me to be an imbalance between audience research studies ('head-counting' exercises) and studies which are directly relevant to programme making. It is interesting to note a statement made nearly ten years ago at the European Broadcasting Union's Third International Conference on Educational Radio and Television:

'Evaluation is essential in educational radio and television; without it there can be no progress in methods or in the most effective use of manpower and financial resources. It is also a means of comparing results with those of conventional educational methods. Thus evaluation forms an integral part of any educational radio and television programme and is not an isolated operation.'[1]

It seems to me that from the papers in this conference, most national broadcasting organizations in particular have a long way to go before such a statement of principle can be judged to have been made a reality.

On the other hand, comparing papers from the CEREB conference with those of ten years ago, several encouraging trends seem to be occurring:

1   There is more realism about what evaluation entails. There is a greater awareness of a whole range of factors necessary for evaluation to be effective in influencing decision-making, and a better understanding of its limitations. Expectations have been lowered, but broadened.

2   There is more experience, and more understanding of the need, of researchers and decision-makers working together. This is seen most clearly in the (still small) number of organizations experimenting with the formative evaluation of programmes.

3   There is more understanding that it is necessary to look at programmes in context, that television and radio are only part of the learning environment, and that these other factors deeply influence the way programmes are perceived and used.

4   There is a more realistic recognition of the political and interpersonal aspects of evaluation, and a consequent broadening of the areas of evaluative enquiry to more general management and financial issues, as well as to programme evaluation.

5   Consequently, there are signs of a broadening of methods—more qualitative, contextual and historical approaches being added to quantitative surveys and experimental methods.

6   Nevertheless, there is still a fundamental lack of theory in the use of television and radio in education, and a fundamental lack of understanding of the basic learning process involved when people use television and radio, which prevent both generalization and a meaningful and coherent growth of knowledge in the field.

7   There is still a fundamental lack of adequate funding for evaluation and research. The need for on-going evaluation requires on-going funding. Organizations using television and radio need to recognize evaluation as a budget head in its own right, and to fund it adequately.

These brief personal views of the significance of the conference however fail to do justice to the many profound and interesting issues discussed in the many papers in this report. I hope each reader will work through the book in his or her own way, and draw their own conclusions. Good reading!

Reference

1   EUROPEAN BROADCASTING UNION, *The E.B.U. Third International Conference on Educational Radio and Television*, Paris: O.R.T.F., 1967.

ACKNOWLEDGEMENTS

A very large number of people and organizations was responsible for the Conference taking place, and without the Conference, there would have been no papers, and no publication. We are most grateful, first of all to the members of the Steering and Management Committees, and their employing organizations, who are listed in full in the various appendices. We are above all indebted to all the contributors, who have allowed us without charge to use their papers for this publication. A number of publishers have kindly allowed us to reprint without charge papers which had already been previously published, and these have been individually acknowledged against the relevant papers.

Of the many people who have helped us in getting this book together, we would especially like to thank Lee Taylor. Not only was she secretary and main administrator to the Conference, she has also helped in the organization of this publication, and carried out the indexing. Robin Moss, Richard Sherrington, Michael Philps, Carole Haslam and Piers Pendred were very encouraging and influential in the early discussions about the organization and aims for the Conference. Larry Kern played a major part in the run-up to and during the Conference, organizing the papers and preparing and operating the audio-visual equipment. We would also like to thank Marion Archer, who assisted Lee Taylor; Tony Seward and Caroline de Paravicini, for publishing and editing assistance: Sue Cox, for organizing and doing a large part of the typing; and all those employees of the Open University—administrative assistants, secretaries, the staff of Reprographic Services and Media, porters, etc.—who have done much more to help the Conference and the production of these proceedings than we could reasonably have expected.

The Conference itself and this publication resulted from the willing co-operation of a great many people, but any mistakes, errors, or misinterpretations are solely our responsibility as editors. The views expressed in the individual papers are of course not necessarily shared or endorsed officially by any of the agencies involved in the Conference.

PART 1: PAPERS SUBMITTED FOR THE CONFERENCE

FULL LIST OF CONFERENCE PAPERS

Papers submitted in advance of the Conference

1

CONFERENCE PAPERS

2

3

SECTION A
SCHOOLS' AND CHILDREN'S PROGRAMMES

Introduction 8

Designing Evaluation Systems

Paper No	Author	Title	
14	Frey, C.	A method to study the effects of media in the classroom	9
66	Dunnett, C. W.	Methodology of evaluation: by survey or measurement	12
31	Kemelfield, G.	Some explorations in research, evaluation and decision-making in schools broadcasting ..	14
41	Mielke, K. W.	Decision-oriented research in school television	19
8	Boorsma, J.	Educational radio broadcasting: programme policy and decision research	25

Descriptions of existing systems

32	Kent, B.	Evaluation and educational broadcasting in Australia	27
79	Australian Department of Education	Research in educational television and radio in Australia	31
38	MacMahon, J.	Radio Scoile: research and evaluation ..	35
21	Haye, C.	ETV evaluation techniques in Hong Kong ..	38
68	Hanák, K.	Utilization of school broadcasting in Hungary	40
61	Thompson, R. H. J.	Evaluation and research for educational broadcasting in Kenya	42

6

Studies of Particular Projects

INTRODUCTION

Ask a hundred people in almost any country what they think is meant by *educational broadcasting* and ninety of them are likely to reply, 'Well, it means those programmes made for schools'.

This is certainly the popular view of educational radio and television; and it has been the starting area of most educational services.

So this first section of papers consists mainly of those concerned with the evaluation of school programmes. To them have been added a small number of papers concerned with programmes addressed to children in their own homes. There is a natural link between the two in that both are addressed to a broadly similar age-range. But it is also useful to observe two important distinctions between them:

1   That the decision to use school programmes is generally a decision of the teacher; so that any service of broadcasts for schools must first convince the main body of teachers that it is going to help and not to threaten their work. It is also important that they have some assurance that they will be invited to help in its evaluation. Children's programmes, on the other hand, are generally chosen by the children themselves—with encouragement or otherwise from their parents—and evaluation depends on their direct responses.

2   That school programmes need always to be seen in relation to a wider pattern of learning in the classroom and need to take account of the likely structure of that pattern in order to make their most useful contribution. Programmes for children at home are not so related to any other learning activity, so are much more free to develop in any way that the producers think worthwhile.

In terms of open and closed systems, therefore, school broadcasting systems have some of the features of each. They are open in the sense that teachers are usually quite free to use them or not use them, as they wish. There is not generally any requirement, or even expectation, that all teachers will use all the series relevant to their work. They are normally open in that they are broadcast on open networks and that there is no requirement for schools to 'register'. They are closed to the extent that they are directly addressed to a clearly defined audience in a familiar learning situation which can be identified, reached and communicated with in some depth. Programmes for children at home are, of course, wide open—though opportunities for feedback can, of course, be built into them.

So the first group of papers within this section is concerned with basic principles and possible methodologies in the evaluation of school programmes. They are extremely interesting in their comparative approaches, while also conveying a large measure of agreement. The next group provides some straightforward and detailed descriptions of existing evaluation systems for school broadcasting; and here the international comparisons are especially interesting. The third and last group provides studies of particular projects.

The papers in this section describe or are related to programmes for schools or children in the following countries:

Australia	Hong Kong	Nicaragua
Canada	Hungary	Sweden
Eire	Kenya	United Kingdom
El Salvador	Korea	United States of America
Holland	Mexico	

DESIGNING EVALUATION SYSTEMS

PAPER NO 14: A METHOD TO STUDY
THE EFFECTS OF MEDIA IN THE
CLASSROOM

Christer Frey, Head of Research, Education Department, Sveriges Radio.

In the Educational Program Department of Sveriges Radio there is a special group concerned with research and development questions. There are four full-time research posts, and within the framework of the budget of the program department the research group has its own budget for research and evaluation of radio and television in instruction. The aim of this internal research is to give producers such experience as can be of value both for the assessment of individual products and for production work in the long run.

Some Statements
As a starting point we would like to state some important principles:
- Radio and television are media that we cannot do without in modern schoolwork if we want to live up to the goals of the school, which in Sweden strongly underline international aspects, the importance of contacts with reality outside the classroom, etc.
- Radio and television are of value to the school.
- Research and evaluation must be carried out within the conditions of the school.
- Thus traditional research methods with a well worked out design and randomized sampling are generally not meaningful in this type of activity.
- Many valuable research and development projects can be carried out only if the researcher works inside the pro-

duction company and in close contact with program producers.
- Research must be integrated as a natural part of the work of developing programmes for educational radio and television.
- Research should be carried out by a professional staff but with a 'non-traditional mind'.

The present situation in the Swedish school
In the new curriculum of the compulsory Swedish school there are guidelines that steer instruction in a somewhat new direction. Students are expected to be able to influence the methods and contents of their instruction themselves. The ultimate aim is the development of the pupils both individually and socially. Thus the old traditional school, with its emphasis almost entirely on factual knowledge, has been changed.

In the schoolwork we now have to start from the students' own reality and in that way relate to what is happening in the world. In this respect radio and television can establish a valuable connection between life in the classroom and life outside the classroom.

Even if students must be able to influence teaching and learning to a large extent, it is of course true that teachers still put their stamp on what is happening in the classroom. One of the commonest ways in which teachers can influence what is happening in their classrooms is through their choice of teaching/learning aids. Indeed, through this choice they often limit also the choice of method and the way in which instruction can be carried out in other respects. Thus in reality the participation of the students is not always very influential.

9

In such a situation, it is often not possible for a researcher to jump in and steer the work in the classroom for research purposes. Thus researchers as well must adapt themselves to the situation prevailing in the Swedish school. This means that our research work has been of a less experimental kind but at the same time more adapted to reality.

A concrete example of a design

1 Internal discussion

Before the start of each budget year we discuss within the educational program department what essential projects should be evaluated. All our production teams are invited to express their wishes as to what research and evaluation projects they would like to have carried out during the year to come. In order to make it possible to judge each wish the production teams must define the research projects desired and give reasons for them, thus facilitating a possible ordering of priority for the various projects.

2 Priorities

Within the research and development group of the department, the suggestions delivered by the production teams are put in order of priority. The group contains all the researchers in the department and also representatives of production, planning and decision-making.

The wishes are ordered according to certain criteria:

● The results must be able to form the foundation for decision-making on the level concerned, e.g. decisions about the possible revision of a program or a series of programs.

● The project should improve our knowledge of how radio and television, and also to some extent printed material, work in the classroom.

● The research project should in the first place give answers to pedagogical and methodological questions.

● A distribution of research over various types of program projects should be aimed at.

● A prerequisite for the carrying out of research projects must be that they do not interfere too much with the organization of the school.

3 Defining goals and questions

If the researcher is to carry out research and evaluation in a meaningful way, it is necessary for him to be able—in cooperation with the program producers—to define the problems to be examined. It is therefore essential that the researcher works within the program department, thus getting to know well the persons involved, and that through those contacts he is close to the production work and acquires all the special know-how that this leads to.

4 Choosing an appropriate method

The generally phrased questions that are the result of contacts between the researcher and the producer and in many cases also the whole production team, are split up into a number of more concrete questions. In this step we try to define more precisely how to get answers to our questions by choosing methods to be used for the evaluation project in question. We usually try to choose such methods as mean as little interference with the daily school work as possible. As this can mean that the answers to our questions can in some cases be rather vague, we always try to cover the questions in several ways. In this phase we also construct the instruments needed for the evaluation itself. We employ the full scale of instruments according to what questions we want to have answered.

5 Selection of experiment schools

As, for practical reasons, we cannot choose schools altogether freely—incidentally we do not even think that such a selection would be meaningful—we normally make a selection that is *not* based on a randomized procedure. Instead we frame a number of criteria as to what our experimental schools should look like. After that we make our concrete selection from one of the lists of schools at our disposal.

We then make contact with the headmasters of the schools picked out and ask them whether they could persuade some specified teachers to take part in our evaluation project. It is very seldom, indeed, that schools refuse to take part in this type of evaluation and research work.

6 Carrying out the evaluation

We try to establish contact in advance with both teachers and students, so that there is as little friction as possible in the actual carrying out of the evaluation project. The most ideal situation, which of course we never obtain, would be if teachers and students used the material in exactly the same way as they would have done if there had been no evaluation work going on.

In many cases we think, though, that we have experienced a natural atmosphere in the school work that indicates that the results of our evaluation work ought not to have been influenced too much by the evaluation situation itself. But of course one can never fully get round the Hawthorne effect.

7 *Presenting data and reporting*

In writing our reports we try to express our experiences in a language that is understandable also to non-specialists. A very common mistake, at least in Sweden, is that research reports use a language that is incomprehensible to many people. We therefore leave out all specialist terms that are not absolutely necessary for the report, thus making it easier for the producers to acquaint themselves with the contents of the reports. Furthermore, in the reports we also try to corroborate conclusions and suggestions with as much concrete information as possible. We often quote all the teachers' answers to a question which are considered particularly relevant.

Although we try to simplify our reports as much as possible, we still use all the ordinary methods of processing, such as working through our material with the help of computers, and making use of the necessary statistical methods.

8 *Discussion with the producers and decision-makers concerned*

In this phase we discuss together with the persons concerned within the program department what conclusions can be drawn from our report. Quite often we have suggestions as to alterations in a program or in a program series. These conclusions are discussed and judged. The final judgement is made by the responsible producer or decision-maker. He or she cannot be ordered by the researcher to take any measures, and, of course, in making decisions about, for example, the revision of a program series, the persons concerned must also pay heed to other factors in the department, such as the availability of staff, budget, etc.

9 *Discussion within the research and development group*

With this last step we can be said to have gone all the way round. In the research and development group the results of the research carried out are discussed from more theoretical points of view. In certain cases the result of one research project may give rise to continued efforts along the same lines or to new research projects.

Some problems

It goes without saying that we do not carry out all research projects step by step in the way described above. There is a certain flexibility in our research work which makes it possible to take on quick and limited tasks which do not necessarily pass all the nine steps. In other cases maybe certain steps cannot be taken with as much care as would be desirable because of the load of work on the persons concerned. But, by and large, this design functions in a reasonably satisfactory way. It is being further developed gradually.

Our way of carrying out investigations, though, leads to certain problems. We would here like to mention some of them and also indicate our view of them.

1 *Representativity*

A common objection to our method is that the schools we select are not representative in the statistical sense of the word and that the results we achieve cannot then be generalized. Our answer to this objection usually is that every classroom with its teacher and students is unique. What we want to know through our research is not whether all teachers and students in Sweden look at our learning aids in a certain way. Instead we want to go deeper and describe how one particular learning aid or one particular program functions in a number of classes.

2 *Our methods exclude certain types of research*

Our way of work excludes experiments as a method. Also other types of projects are left aside. For example, we do not undertake comparative media studies. People often ask us whether television or radio is the better medium or how radio works as compared with the teacher, and we also meet questions like 'Do you learn as much if you watch a television program as if you read a book?' We consider those questions fundamentally uninteresting. Naturally there are situations where a certain medium works better than another medium, but it is far more interesting for us to find out how we can best use the media at our disposal to achieve as good results as possible at school. Thus, what is interesting to us is the cooperation and interaction of the media and not the competition between them.

3 The integrity of the researcher can be questioned

Because of the fact that the researcher is to be found within the production company his or her integrity can always be questioned. But, considering the type of research done in the Educational Program Department—developing further the use of and improving the knowledge about the media radio and television in instruction—we think it is necessary for the researchers to be within our own organization. We think that the integrity of the researchers mainly depends on the way they work and present their results. The right way to counteract accusations of partiality is, in our experience, to present open reports where the shortcomings of the methods used and the results arrived at as well as the uncertainty of certain conclusions are frankly pointed out.

PAPER NO 66: METHODOLOGY OF EVALUATION: BY SURVEY OR MEASUREMENT

C. W. Dunnett, Department of Education, South Australia.

Educational television and radio broadcasting surely is in a quandary. Fundamentally, programmes are created by the modern equivalent of the theatre or entertainment industry. When applied to education, this industry, for the first time, is faced with needs expressed in advance by schools, not in terms of a product sale, but in terms of the programme itself. The success or otherwise of a programme in relation to those needs will add a new parameter, and perhaps an additional one to an entertainment industry, where just the taping of the programme or the paying of the seat price is the end product.

An unsuccessful performance may well reduce an author's or programme's future popularity; but a value judgement by a critic on a performance, will still gain high ratings and be completely unrelated to the actual value of the programme. Educationally this cannot be so. The prime aim must be to meet the needs of the students whether or not the producers and teachers feel it was a 'good' programme.

The needs of the students can be expressed in similar terms to those of all resource-based learning or even programmed learning. Such statements of needs are confused with solutions which satisfy those needs. For now, as in early days, the teacher may well express the needs of the students in terms of the resources he or she needs to present the lessons to them. Clearly, again, this leads towards a value judgement of quality based on a solution rather than a problem.

The problem in evaluating such a situation must first be resolved by deciding which parameters to evaluate.

Three areas now exist:

1 The physical or purely quantitative measurement of how many programmes are being taken.
2 Measurements of whether the programmes that are taken achieve the educational aims of objectives that were designated for them.
3 Value judgements made by the receivers as to the 'quality' or professional nature of the broadcast which will be very much in the affective domain.

These three areas will intertwine considerably and most methods involved in obtaining evaluation of this kind are very heavily biased towards the quantitative parameters. In South Australia, we have in the past issued surveys and quantitatively estimated which programmes were taken and which programmes were not taken.

Any attempt to evaluate, using in the widest sense the success of a programme by measuring its achievement objectively, would also be somewhat bogus, as each 'user' would apply different measurements. In the case of the correspondence schools and the Schools of the Air, another situation exists, for their recipients are used to receiving their lessons in the normal situation by this mode, and without a teacher present. Consequently their success cannot be evaluated against a teacher in a live situation.

The proper use of a school's broadcast enriched and supplemented by follow-up materials, such as will be described later in this paper, is, in my opinion, leading us more to the truth of the whole situation. The natural progression of a programme to becoming a complete packaged resource leads to fuller understanding of the problem and to a possible evaluative procedure.

In this context I would suggest particularly that where a teacher is present in a learning situation then the television/radio broadcast must become a resource for him to use at will, integrated with other resources. It should become less and less structured, and become supportive not directive and lead to enrichment and expansion.

In many areas, particularly those of the affective domain, a broadcast performance can begin or summarize experiences, but only if a full educational objective can be satisfied should it ever attempt to take over a whole lesson unsupported, and act as a remote teacher.

The evaluation can now be applied more and more to the success and usage of the recording of that programme rather than what it achieves directly. It becomes a permanent resource, much in the manner of a book, a chart, a filmstrip or a recording rather than a means to an end achieving its success on its own merits alone.

If learning situations are to become resource-oriented then the design and use of broadcasts must enable and encourage the provision of a resource which can be recorded, stored and retrieved. In this manner supporting resources are produced and methods of evaluation can be applied in the 'usage' rather than 'value judged' areas. Also acceptability of the broadcast can be estimated as a parameter of the acceptability of the supporting resource which can take place, even in advance of the broadcast in most situations.

It still could be argued that even resources can gather dust. However, an unrecorded radio broadcast can gather nothing and is lost to eternity, so at least we must consider the use of recorded broadcasts as being paramount. However much dust is gathered by the resource of the library shelf it can always be cleaned and used again some time in the future. Future use will also be connected with flexibility. Therefore any added support material will more likely be of a flexible (and modifiable) nature and therefore support future use.

Earlier attempts at evaluation by survey or feedback questionnaires could almost be considered as an aggravation of objective principles. This aggravation would simply be caused by the survey prompting value judgements in the absence of precise measurements having been taken at the time the broadcast was being used. Our experiments have shown conclusively, and more particularly at junior primary and primary levels (from ages five to eight years), that broadcasts taken on their own, as opposed to broadcasts taken using packaged material in association with them, greatly differ in effect on the pupils. Such a statement itself could be accused of being a value judgement, but it is indeed difficult to express in other than observational terms the fact that a class of children are actively engaged for a full thirty minutes following a broadcast on such activities as are suggested in supporting guides, as opposed to other classes simply returning to ordinary lessons or carrying on an unstimulated discussion following a broadcast. The need for a young child to focus ideas upon objects and activities to practice rather than conceptualize must be considered paramount in the junior primary school. This is in contrast to students in the higher levels of upper secondary, who may well be able to usefully discuss concepts presented in radio or television broadcasts with no stimulation other than guidance by a gifted teacher.

In fact perhaps the use of the work concept summarizes the major difference between the real purposes of broadcasts aimed at the lower end of a school as opposed to those aimed at the upper end.

The more conceptual the less need for supporting resources and 'superficially' the easier an evaluation could take place in terms of the amount of discussion generated (if one could value a discussion by its length, as opposed to its content!). Conversely, in the junior primary school an activity aimed at learning more about 'The Garden' whereby a broadcast could stimulate children to use play, act, draw, and model items suggested on slides and photographs and tapes could surely be measured in terms of the product, and itself be product-oriented.

To conclude, I would stress the underlying aim of this paper is to highlight the need for a broadcast to be judged as 'part' of a learning process and not as a total learning process. Thus considered, an evaluation of the other parts of the process will surely be a measure of the total usefulness as seen and employed by the learner.

PAPER NO 31: SOME EXPLORATIONS IN RESEARCH, EVALUATION AND DECISION-MAKING IN SCHOOLS BROADCASTING

Graeme Kemelfield, Educational Research Unit, University of Papua, New Guinea.

This paper, while exploring the relationship between research, evaluation and decision-making, does so in a spirit of cheerful iconoclasm. It reflects the viewpoint of a researcher who has been involved with broadcasters in exploring the application of research and evaluation to their planning and decision-making and, having failed to separate them, suggests that the three carefully disentangled themes of the conference are in fact necessarily intertwined. It proposes that the application of research and evaluation studies to decision-making in broadcasting depends on the nature of the findings which emerge from such studies, and that these findings are in turn largely the result of the kind of methods adopted, as well as the questions initially posed.

The arguments which will be elaborated here regarding research methods and findings, and their relevance to broadcasting organizations, derive from extensive collaboration by the writer with schools broadcast producers, first at the BBC while engaged on the Schools Television Research Project at Leeds University, and subsequently as an ITA Fellow at Leeds, co-operating with the Schools Broadcasting Departments of three of the independent television companies.[1] The field encompassed, then, is research and evaluation appropriate to the day to day activities of schools television, but hopefully some of the issues raised may have wider application to educational broadcasting.

Broadcaster-researcher collaboration

The research collaboration to which I refer had as one initial aim, to find out how the skills of a researcher and the results of research and evaluation could benefit schools broadcasters. It was quickly apparent that the best people to define their needs and problems were the broadcasters themselves. More than that, any researcher who has familiarity with experienced producers at work will recognize the combination of creative and analytic skills which they bring to bear on a production, and which provide indispensable insights in probing programmes and their effects. Collaboration therefore extended beyond discussion leading to the posing of questions and hypotheses for research and the choice of programmes for evaluation, to a mutual working together throughout each stage of a research undertaking.

Such a participation by broadcasters in the preparation and execution of research and evaluation studies related to their own production activities, taking a front rather than a back seat, is an invitation to them to identify with the whole process of research, lending it a heightened interest and comprehensibility. Most importantly, by understanding what is going on, they are in a position to contribute their experience and insights to the interpretation (and criticism) of results. The likelihood of whatever relevance research and evaluation have being perceived, absorbed, and brought to bear directly or indirectly on decision-making is surely much higher under these circumstances.

Contact between researcher and broadcaster characteristically began with informal meetings in the broadcasting organizations, initially perhaps with an individual producer, or with a gathering at which the head of the Schools Broadcasting Department, education officers and producers would participate. The researcher would outline some ideas about the evaluation of schools broadcasts, the research techniques potentially available, and what kinds of things they might be able to reveal. Discussion then ranged over the concerns and preoccupations of broadcasting staff, in search of worthwhile topics for investigation with an evident practical relevance to the production of current or projected programme series, and their classroom use. Questions which seemed of more general interest, and amenable to tackling by research methods, were then selected for further consideration.

In retrospect, several recurring starting points for research studies can be identified. These arose out of:

(a) A desire to know whether the intended aims of a programme series were being met (there were sometimes nagging doubts about this), and the real value of programmes for their school audience.

(b) A desire on the part of broadcasters or researcher to test a hypothesis formulated about the effects of a particular approach to the use of TV, or a technique of programme making.

(c) Complaints, worries or uncertainties concerning the effects of programmes expressed in teachers' reports or from within broadcasting organizations.

The kinds of questions posed by schools broadcasters from each of our three starting points, the methods chosen to investigate them, the nature of the findings which resulted, and the implications for decision-making can now be illustrated with reference to some of the studies undertaken.

Questions, research findings and decision-making

1 Meeting broadcasters' aims—how children respond to TV

The first area of concern encountered, that of the desire of producers to know whether programme series were fulfilling the purposes for which they were designed, and

what their real value was in the classroom, is exemplified by two studies carried out in collaboration with independent television companies.

The series *Our Neighbours* produced by Granada Television for 10–13-year-old pupils was the choice for one investigation. Its intention was described as that of encouraging 'appreciation and tolerance of people of different creeds and races, now living in Britain, through an understanding of their background and way of life'. Granada's concern was that the programmes might not necessarily serve these ends, that they might, in fact, reinforce existing prejudices or even stimulate new ones, by creating a consciousness of racial differences not previously perceived.

The programme chosen from the series for evaluation was *Our Neighbours from Pakistan*. The programme notes indicated that 'what is common to us all will be stressed, what is unique will be explained'. Its aims could thus be defined as to foster recognition of shared humanity between viewing pupils and their Pakistani neighbours, but also a readiness to accept those respects in which the group was perceived nevertheless to be different. The research aimed to discern the state of mind in which the programme appeared to leave pupils, at the point where it ends and the classroom teacher must pick up the threads for discussion.

The programme placed much emphasis on Islamic cultural and religious customs, and the way in which they mould the everyday behaviour of Pakistani families in Britain. Thus, much of the information it conveyed was of a kind likely to engage children's feelings and opinions. We therefore sought to discover not only gains in factual knowledge, but whether this programme (and initially the TV medium itself) impressed its audience as an authoritative and credible source from which to learn, and then how pupils' prior opinions of, and attitudes towards, Pakistanis and their customs were influenced favourably or unfavourably by viewing the programme. We also decided to compare the responses of pupils in areas of high and low immigrant density, as previous research suggested this might be a crucial factor bearing on racial attitudes.

It was this last comparison which turned

up some of the most revealing findings. What affected the results was not the density of immigrants in the area in which schools were located, but rather the much higher density of immigrant pupils *within* one of the four schools selected. This greater day to day contact appeared to have a striking influence on the way pupils reacted to the programme, their previous apparently unselfconscious familiarity with Pakistani children interacting with the programme's message. While prior to viewing they had shown the most positive attitudes towards Pakistani behaviour, they were much more prone to doubt after exposure to the programme. In contrast, pupils from the other schools generally recorded more favourable evaluations of Pakistani behaviour in such features as cleanliness, dress and honesty after viewing.

> The full paper goes on to give more details of the research findings.

While overall, viewing children were favourably disposed towards the credibility of this programme and its medium, and while it proved highly effective in conveying factual information, there are clearly implications for decision-making in some of the findings. First, research had a potential bearing on the company's judgement as to the value of this kind of programme series, and the complexities involved in achieving its desired ends, and thus on general policy in opting for such a series. Second, it offered pointers for some improvements in production (a revision of the series was envisaged). Third, a striking diversity of reaction which was found between different types of schools, but also among pupils within each school (indicating that pupils had reacted to the programme in a relatively personal and exploratory manner, and not just in terms of stereotyped group reactions), emphasized the delicate role of the teacher, required to build on broadcasts likely to stir up complex thoughts and feelings in children. Such insights could be built into teachers notes to help them plan follow-up discussions, by sensitizing them to the frames of mind which might be encountered in classes after exposure to such a programme, particularly those

with a high proportion of immigrant children.*

If research of the kind described should be able to sensitize and help prepare teachers for using programmes, it can equally help to reveal to producers the complexity of the communication process, and that still largely unexplored territory of children's minds and experience which must interact with the producer's imagination and conceptualization as expressed through television productions. A brief reference to another investigation, into the Thames Television series *Patterns of Expression* for 9–12-year-olds, demonstrates the importance of awareness of this area where producer's hopes and intentions mesh with the prior experience and mental preconceptions of children.

The Thames series was intended to stimulate observation, and to encourage creative thinking and activity. The programme chosen for evaluation was *Display*, comparing some of the ways in which animals and human beings communicate and express themselves, emphasizing how display behaviour in animals is paralleled by dress and ceremony among people. The intention of the research was to look at whether pupils understood sequences of the programme in the way the producer had intended, that is, whether their way of 'seeing' things and relating them conformed to his, and then to look at their personal interpretations of the programme's ideas and how they wove together the materials presented in it.

> The full paper gives details of the findings of the research.

The results, particularly in some cases where pupils used photographs as a basis for story-telling and fantasy, provided evidence both of the imaginative license which pupils will take with a producer's organization of materials—surely desirable in a series aimed to stimulate creative activity—but also offer evidence of the careful preparation and follow-up necessary if programmes like the one studied

---

* It should be noted that only English children were included in school samples for research purposes.

here are to shake many pupils out of more familiar and stereotyped ways of looking at things. The education officer responsible for the series noted that the responses revealed by the study would be of material assistance in the preparation of future teachers' notes, as well as in designing future productions.

2 *Testing hypotheses about production techniques*

Discussions with a BBC TV producer concerning a British social history series which he was producing led to one instance when a producer's belief about his style of presentation became the starting point for a research hypothesis. We set out to test his belief that a dramatic presentation with a strong emotional impact, particularly one deriving from carefully chosen visuals, should have the greatest long-term impact on children's thinking about a subject. Images, that is, should recur and reverberate in their minds months or years after experiencing a broadcast which aroused strong feeling, and provoke thought.

The programme singled out for investigation was *The Big Cities*, portraying living conditions in the industrial cities of Britain in the mid-nineteenth century, and using vivid contemporary prints and documents to build up images of the period.

The programme was prepared in sound-only as well as the original TV versions, so as to allow us to separate the impact of the visuals. Reactions to the productions were gathered from a school audience, invited to act as journalists and critics for the day, and a number of their statements were then presented to further groups of children to agree or disagree with, after seeing different versions of the programme. By this means we gauged the strength of their feelings and opinions about the productions, as well as their retention of facts and details. This was done immediately after viewing the programme and one week later. After five months they were asked to recall the presentation and write about it.

The findings went some way to vindicating the producer's belief. It was clear that dramatic presentations, in either sound track-only or audio-visual forms, evoked significantly greater interest and feeling and remembrance of programme content than a more neutral version, which greatly reduced dramatic heightening. A more surprising result was the lack of difference in interest, strong feeling and recall between those who experienced the original television presentation, and the sound track presented without visuals. It pointed to the self-sufficiency and vividness of the sound track on its own, even though immediately after viewing the programme there was a tendency for the group who saw the TV version to feel more strongly about such statements as, 'It moved me tremendously that anyone could have lived like that', 'I became totally involved and couldn't tear myself away from it', and 'The men with the right ideas were silenced'.

Five months later, what was most striking was the evidence that the 'reverberations in the mind' anticipated by the producer resulted from the effect of precise concrete details in the presentation. The words of the closing song, for example, 'bugs live longer so I'm told', referring to child mortality, was more than once recalled. So were references to people sleeping six or seven to a bed, water polluted by dead animals, 'how one girl took her drinking water out of a sewer', or plagues of rats. Such detail was almost all contained in the sound track, although illustrated by contemporary prints. One pupil even wrote, 'the noise in the streets was louder than I thought it would be'.

The research, then, could be said in part at least to encourage the producer as to the validity of his general beliefs about his use of television and style of production, and to provide some insights into how his effects were achieved. Once again, it is the knowledge provided him of the communication process which is perhaps the most important contribution of the research.

> *The full paper gives another example of hypothesis-testing, based on a sequence of visual material.*

3 *Investigating the validity of complaints—classroom reception of TV*

Complaints received through teacher evaluation cards led to the setting up of an investigation of another BBC history series. One programme in particular, *The Swinging Sixties*, on life in Britain in the 1960s, which began with a sequence of the Beatles in concert, provoked concern that it was too much like 'entertainment' television, and that children would be distracted from any serious learning.

In order to test the validity of this complaint, we decided to show the programme to comparable groups of children in contrasting circumstances. One group would see it in a deliberately contrived 'entertainment' setting, to emphasize that aspect of the production. They were released from normal school periods, and saw Tom and Jerry cartoons before viewing the programme. Another group were told they were going to see an 'educational' film, and were asked to do a test under strict school discipline, before viewing the programme under teacher supervision. Both groups were asked to rate *The Swinging Sixties* for interest and enjoyment, were tested on the retention of information, and finally asked to write freely about the programme.

There was no evidence of any lack of comprehension of the main themes of the programme, or that the 'entertainment' group in any way learnt or understood less than the 'educational' group. Interesting differences emerged, however, when pupils' essays were rated by teachers along a number of different dimensions. The writings of those who viewed the programme under strict school conditions were rated as more impersonal, content-oriented and commonplace. They tended mainly to describe what was in the programme. Responses of children who viewed in a relaxed 'entertainment' atmosphere were rated as more personal, producer technique-oriented, and unusual. Their essays more typically began with, 'It made me think that . . .' rather than 'The programme told you about . . .', and they tended to give personalized, critical reactions to the presentation. In many ways, pupils appeared to be reacting according to what they believed was expected of them as indicated by the environment in which they were shown the programme.

> Again the full paper gives a second example, based on a Yorkshire TV series, *Meeting our Needs*.

The variable of classroom mood may seem to be outside the control and decision-making of the television producer, and yet undeniably influences how programmes communicate. In this case, teacher awareness seems the most vital need, and perhaps television education officers can play a helpful if limited role in encouraging such an awareness.

Some conclusions

It is clear that no one research formula or approach would suffice to tackle the range of different questions posed, and the variety in aim, style and content of the different productions chosen as material for research and evaluation. The greatest need was evidently for flexible and varied methods of investigation, tailored to meet specific demands. Methods used ranged from more conventional attitude scales and test of comprehension to picture sorting and grouping, and essay type responses. In some circumstances experimental methods were used, in others more open-ended approaches were seen as appropriate. Investigations might combine both experimental comparison and more qualitative analyses. Both production and audience variables were investigated, and their interaction with the viewing environment. In other words, the approach was at all times eclectic and exploratory.

Research and evaluation were inserted in a pragmatic fashion into day to day broadcasting operations, according to the immediate concerns and needs of the organizations. This does not, however, mean that the findings of research studies are necessarily 'one off', without more general implications or relevance to other programmes or series. Rather, it has been suggested that findings continually point to broad areas of influence in effective communication, and the results of particular evaluation studies—if research activities are pursued consistently by broadcasting organizations—should gradually build up a more general and comprehensive understanding of the complex, interacting factors which mediate communication between the producer and his school audience.

Some of the potentialities of research and evaluation in assisting decision-making in schools broadcasting have been suggested. These include the offering of some empirical guidance in making day to day policy decisions and judgements, in the light of pressures placed on broadcasters; some addition to the stock of producer's insights affecting decisions about the style and construction of programmes, and the diagnosis of possible weaknesses and improvements in communication; and increased understanding of the classroom use and reception of broadcasts, affecting decisions as to the content and adequacy of teacher's notes and teacher preparation.

Most importantly, research and evaluation can sensitize both producers and teachers to the range of children's reactions to programmes and the variables which influence them, and thus provide greater awareness and knowledge of the complexities of the communication process. What research and evaluation is unlikely to be able to achieve is scientific formulae for production, which will enable producers to adopt precise presentation techniques in order to obtain predictable results and reactions on the part of their audiences. The research described here would seem to indicate conclusively that the network of interacting variables—producer's style, the experience and preconceptions which children bring to a programme, classroom mood and the influence of the classroom teacher—are not amenable to strict control, nor does such an aim appear to be attractive to schools broadcasters, at least in the context of British broadcasting.

Reference

1 KEMELFIELD, G., *The evaluation of schools broadcasts: piloting a new approach*, Leeds, Centre for Television Studies, Leeds University, 1972.

PAPER NO 41: DECISION-ORIENTED RESEARCH IN SCHOOL TELEVISION*

Keith W. Mielke, Institute for Communication Research, Indiana University, USA.

* Reproduced, by kind permission of the publishers, from *Public Communications Review*, June, 1974. The full paper was a policy brief for the Agency for Instructional Television, Bloomington, Indiana. Their reaction to the policy brief follows this edited version.

A variety of talents and a series of co-ordinated decisions are required to get a television program successfully through the interlocking stages of planning, funding, production, evaluation, distribution, and utilization. This paper deals with the decisions involved in that process, and more specifically, how research and evaluation can help improve those decisions.

There are two primary objectives to this paper: 1 to review what evaluation can contribute to school television; and 2 to derive policy suggestions for such evaluation programs.

The scheme employed here uses four categories to make distinctions among several kinds of evaluation activities: 1 background research; 2 formative research; 3 summative research; and 4 policy research. These categories will be defined, and their utility in decision-making will be discussed. For each category, some dominant policy issues will be presented.

The full paper continues with a cogent argument for emphasis on 'decision-making' as an objective of evaluation. (This is summarized in the final recommendations.)

Category 1: Background research

If we were to run a survey on what school administrators instinctively think of as falling in the domain of instructural television research and evaluation, it would probably show that the activities called 'background research' would not be included. A common notion is that researchers and evaluators come into the picture after the product is completed to evaluate the performance of that product. This is far too limiting, and indeed may not even be the most significant contribution that research and evaluation can make. A clear stand should be taken to recognize and create opportunities for making better decisions as a consequence of research and evaluation inputs. Long before production is completed, indeed before production has even begun, systematic research is needed for the plethora of decisions that face the administrator at the planning stage.

The generic mission here is to reduce uncertainty in the planning process. It seems appropriate to include within the category of background research at least such activities as the assessment of needs that can be addressed properly via television, the assessment of a host of audience or student variables, the assessment of the physical system for production, distribution, and reception, and feasibility studies for tentative program ideas. These are all proper subjects for research contributions that are not tied to any particular program or product. (The many similarities to the processes of marketing research should not go unrecognized.)

It is recommended that background research covering such activities as those listed above be integrated permanently into the structure of the organization, if possible, rather than gearing up anew for each new project or each new potential source of funding. A modest but sustained effort in this area should provide a reliable information source to administrative planners on such questions as:

1 What are the perceived curriculum needs?
2 What is the condition of the distribution system?
3 Demographically, what is an accurate description of the potential audience?
4 Psychologically, what is the audience attitude structure toward topics A, B, and C?
5 What reception might we expect for a new series on subject X?

Dozens of questions of this order can be submitted to empirical treatments designed and administered by a team of researchers.

It should be affirmed here (although it applies equally to all categories of research and evaluation covered in this paper) that the data from research and evaluation efforts do not *per se* make the administrative decisions, nor do they even dictate a particular conclusion or interpretation. That is, research input is one source of information alongside several sources of information and guidance that the administrator uses. With or without benefit of research input, the administrator must make decisions; the goal is to improve those decisions through carefully designed background research.

Category II: Formative research

Formative research is the first of the four categories covered here to involve a specific program or project, and it should be initiated very early in the development phase of that program. Formative research is typically defined in comparison with summative research, as research or evaluation administered during the formative stages of a product (a television program in this case) that provides feedback to the production staff, enabling them to modify and improve the product before the final production decisions have been made. Formative research is pretesting programs early enough in the process to take corrective action. Summative research, by way of contrast, assesses the impact of a program or series as a whole, comparing observed effects with the effects desired or anticipated (as stated in the behavioural goals and objectives). Formative research is to summative research what repeated midcourse guidance and corrective tutoring is to the final grade for the course. Seen in that light, the importance of the formative research function should be readily apparent.

Continuing the analogy, one can speculate on the most rational decision in a choice situation: if you could only have one or the other, either repeated midcourse guidance and corrective tutoring, or end-of-course evaluation with final grade, which should you choose? Although one may rightly reject the imposition of such 'either-or' conditions in reality, the question is nevertheless instructive for the placement of priorities, and priorities are required when the resources for research and evaluation are limited, as they always are. The value position taken here is that once the agency has committed itself to a school television project, the top priority for research resources should go to formative research. There should always be a summative research component of some dimensions, but without an active formative research component, isolated summative research may be little more than an autopsy.

As you already know, production of television programs is a complicated process in which innumerable assumptions about audience attention, comprehension, and other reactions must be made. Expertise in the production process is needed so that a fair share of these assumptions will turn out to be correct. Experience shows, however, that expert judgements alone (that is, expert predictions of audience reactions) are frequently wrong. Ultimately, there is no substitute for a try-out of the program with representative audience members.

In formative research, as in the other categories, the way to find out where the research effort should be is, at least in large part, to work back from the decision-making needs of the person(s) to whom the research results will be addressed. This search has a logical and a human relations component. In formative research and evaluation, the consumer is the production staff and the decisions are production decisions. The production staff must be motivated to make use of the research results; they must be able to understand the research results; and the research results must address the production decisions appropriate to that group of consumers. Insights into the nature of producers and production can be used to generate guidelines (a) for motivational steps that can be taken, (b) for the form and purpose of research reports, and (c) for the type of questions for which data are sought.

Consider first the motivational issue. Above all, there must be mutual respect, understanding, trust, and goodwill between research and production. Without dwelling unduly on the theme of being 'nice' to one another, suffice it to say that this social factor is probably far more critical than any methodological or policy factor in determining success or failure of a formative research effort. Researchers should understand that producers have ego invested in their creations, and it can be threatening to have the program criticized by the research staff. There is little hope of getting good data or influencing the improvement of productions if goodwill and mutual respect are not in evidence. The essential climate of goodwill is quite fragile.

The level of specificity in formative research reports, with the focus on specific production decisions for specific programs, tends not to be very relevant to those not directly involved in the project. To make these reports interesting to 'outside' readers would require considerable rewriting and would change their function. A policy recommendation is that formative research reports retain their original purpose of serving the decision needs of production, and not be altered to meet the interests of other readers. An open information policy is recommended for all research reports, but only for reports in their original form, as prepared for their original function.

As it relates to program design and production, formative research also has a role to play in the formulation and selection of objectives. One procedure is for content experts to state in general terms what they believe are realistic goals and then for formative research personnel to translate these goals into measurable objectives, subject to approval by the original content experts. The ability or inability to devise acceptable behavioural measures for general goals may well be a significant criterion in deciding whether or not to include that goal in the mission for the program. Early pre-testing on the achievability of certain objectives could also influence the design of the program.

As will be discussed shortly, operationally defined objectives are also an essential part of the summative research operation, where the interest is not in program design and improvement, but in determining the degree to which the objectives were met. Although functionally quite distinct, there can be some interplay between formative and summative research.

In general, however, the formative research agenda should be distinct because of its improvement orientation, that is, its concentration on the domain of manipulable factors under the control of production. Of course, the production staff must be concerned with the assessment of behavioural objectives, but a final 'report card' on how well the program performed may offer no insight whatsoever on how to improve it the next time around (if there ever is to be a next time). Many formative research questions will tend to resemble closely the questions a good producer-director would be naturally considering anyway in the design and production process e.g., is this enough reference to the previous programs for the students to make the logical connections to this program? Will the students detect the subtle humor in the closing scene, or will that be confusing to them? Given a battery of such questions, it should be evident that to be responsive, considerable methodological ingenuity and variety are required on the part of the in-house formative research staff. It is recommended that both background research and formative research be conducted by in-house research staff, sensitive to the particular needs of the Agency for Instructional Television (AIT) and committed to long-term good relationships with AIT personnel. With formative research responsive to the real needs of production, production can be an enthusiastic supporter and consumer of research.

Category III: Summative research

As defined earlier, summative research assesses the extent to which a program (or series) has reached its objectives. Summative research probably resembles the most common expectation of what research and evaluation is about. It is conducted because decision-makers need overall performance data. Did I spend my money wisely? Does this program merit additional funds for revision? Should this program be scheduled for next year? These are decisions that need the summative research output.

Typically, many of the consumers of summative research are outside the organization. A recommended policy is that all summative research for outside consumers be conducted by research groups outside AIT, for reasons of detached objectivity and credibility. It is further recommended that the design and measuring instruments for all contracted summative research should be approved first by in-house AIT administrators to insure that all relevant objectives are measured in an appropriate manner. After AIT has approved the research procedures, the outside research agency should be autonomous.

Unfortunately, it is still too common to find situations where summative research is an afterthought. Researchers have had to resort to monitoring a completed program, inferring what the objectives or producer's intent must have been, and then writing summative evaluation items on that basis. This should not happen. The planning of summative research should begin as soon as the planning for the program begins. If there are to be pre-test/post-test comparisons as part of the summative research, it is obvious that the

research must be in the field before the first airing.

There are arguments for incorporating standardized instruments into summative research and arguments against. Supportive arguments include:

(a) you thereby get a measuring instrument that has been field tested;
(b) you have a common basis on which the performance of other groups can be compared; and
(c) there are national norms established for many of these instruments.

Arguments against standardized instruments include:

(a) many of them are not designed as a measure of program effects;
(b) there is some possibility that an existing instrument could influence the curriculum by tailoring the objectives to fit the instrument; and
(c) most importantly, standardized tests may have minimal overlap with the total configuration of program objectives. This hurts in two ways: for content on the test but not covered in the program, there will be no demonstrable effect of the program. For content on the program but not on the test, significant effects could go unmeasured.

The recommendation is that original instruments be used to insure precise reflection of program objectives.

Some objectives are easier to measure than others, and there may well be understandable pressure to lean toward the more readily measured outcomes in the program design. One can invoke the argument that, if the objective can't be specified, it has no place in the program or the research. Such a hard-nosed position could limit the curriculum goals to the capacity of the art and science of measurement. For television, which has a marvellous ability to communicate non-verbal information and to involve people emotionally, this would be an unfortunate limitation. Reasonable men and women should work out on a case-by-case basis the best compromise between two desirable outcomes: rigor of measurement and exploitation of the potential of the television medium. It might, for example, be reasonable to require behavioural measures for a majority of the desired outcomes, with other objectives being allowed far less rigor. Even an occasional shot in the dark with no measurement whatsoever should not be precluded. It should be noted that a greater ability on the part of researchers to measure the more elusive outcomes (affective variables, for example) would facilitate their formal incorporation into various curricula. If AIT is ever inclined, contrary to an earlier recommendation, to sponsor basic research, then such measurement research would be an excellent investment.

After recognizing and supporting completely the scientific values of rigor, clarity, precision, reliability, validity, and the like, one must also recognize that most research, even the best research, compromises downward from the lofty ideal. With great resources some compromise will be necessary, and limited resources, compromise is unavoidable. In decision-oriented research, one frequently is in the position of being able to increase the rigor of a study for a few thousand dollars more, but then deciding as a matter of priorities in resource allocation that the return is not worth the investment. How far downward one can compromise and still find utility in the data is a value judgement that should be made on a case-by-case basis. Again, the operative criterion is utility in the decision-making process. Frequently, the options available are to make the decision with no data at all or to make the decision with data that are considerably compromised from the ideal. In such a situation it is not uncommon for reasonable people to prefer some data over no data at all. The research data combine with whatever other formal and informal inputs the decision-maker can muster to influence the analysis and the conclusion.

Category IV: Policy research
Policy research, the last of the four categories of decision-oriented research to be covered here, will be easier to discuss if subdivided into two parts: (a) policy research tailored to the policy-making needs of AIT; and (b) policy research tailored to the policy-making needs of larger societal and governmental units.

The organizational machinery required for on-going background research, recommended in an earlier part of this paper, would also be ideal for serving AIT's policy-making needs. As background research, the data could help lay the groundwork for intelligent planning of specific school television materials. As in-house policy research, similar data could help provide a basis for the sustained review, modification, and creation of general AIT policy. The two uses of research data are, of course, highly interrelated. The policy research does not generate policy; it generates data that top level administrators should find useful in policy areas. The non-exhaustive agenda suggested for background research is equally well suited for policy-making needs.

In brief review, the suggested areas were assessment of needs, of audience variables (both demographic and psychological), and of physical system variables (production, distribution, reception), and feasibility studies for program ideas. At a somewhat higher level of abstraction, these activities can be thought of as a form of sustained system monitoring combined with predictive simulation models. System monitoring should yield multifaceted status reports on the system in which AIT operates. In program planning, predictive simulation models should bring to bear logic and evidence in predicting the consequences of spending resources before actually committing the resources. In policy deliberations, predictive simulation models should bring to bear logic and evidence in predicting the future status of the system.

Consider several hypothetical (but, it is hoped, plausible) policy issues. The value of research input should be self-evident.

'To what extent should AIT diversify its media products over the next fifteen years?' Predictions on the future status of the system would obviously be required here for the decision-making process. 'How will the needs of the school systems change?' 'How will technological developments affect AIT?' And so forth.

'What are the major factors, the convergence of which should cause AIT to undertake production activity and the non-convergence of which should preclude AIT involvement?' Responsibility for such blockbuster policy issues resides with the administrative decision-maker, but he or she should find it most useful to be able to check out empirically at least some of the multitude of assumptions that feed into such deliberations.

The research staff and the administrator should cooperate in breaking down the big policy questions into relevant questions that can be answered. The question 'What should a rational person know before setting policy on this complicated issue?' should generate a host of items, some of which can, and some of which cannot, reasonably be assigned to research.

The policy needs of societal units that involve AIT activities are another matter. AIT should be a cooperative participant in contributing whatever it can to these other 'outside' policy issues coming from responsible agencies, but would not actually conduct the research. Presumably, AIT would have a clear position and would serve as an advocate, for example, in government considerations of the role of educational media for the next decade. In another policy setting, AIT could share relevant experience as an expert witness (as, for example, in some state's deliberations about the pros and cons of sex education in the schools, or emotional health in the schools). In another setting, AIT may simply provide data, as for example, in response to a UNESCO survey.

Because of the impact of television and its multitude of effects (and side effects)—some of which are considered positive and some negative, some of which are intended and some unintended, some controllable, some uncontrollable—the AIT areas of activity will inevitably brush against policy issues in a variety of other agencies and organizations. These encounters offer opportunities for positive influence in a rather wide spectrum of policy.

Policy recommendations

I have tried to broaden the typical conception of the role of research and evaluation in televised instruction to include research inputs at a variety of points in the system. By going under the rubric of decision-oriented research, a variety of other elements tend to flow logically from such a starting point: identification of research problems, the channels of communication, the chain of command, the consumer of research reports, the delineation of meaningful distinctions among types of research and evaluation, and the specification of research objectives, to list a few.

Research methodology was not considered at all and a variety of terminological issues and territorial disputes were simply bypassed and left for another day. The purpose of the paper was to review/discuss the areas in which research and evaluation could make positive contributions to AIT, and to discuss some of the policy issues that relate to those potential contributions. For all such issues, there is a recommended position for your consideration and discussion.

In isolated form, here is a summary list of research policy recommendations, most of which were covered in the preceding text.

1 Each AIT activity should have a research and evaluation component.
2 AIT should restrict its research efforts to decision-oriented and product-specific research and evaluation. AIT should cooperate with but not sponsor basic or theoretical research. If, for whatever reasons, AIT does decide to invest in basic research, this research should be in areas that have high probability of practical pay-off, such as in new measurement methods to index non-cognitive effects.
3 Background research and in-house policy research should be established as a permanent and integral part of AIT, transcending specific projects.
4 Formative research should be conducted by an in-house research staff, working in the service of production, and organizationally integral with production. A prerequisite to appointing production decision-makers should be their willingness to work with formative research in the improvement of the product.
5 Once AIT is committed to a production project, top priority for research resources should go to formative research.
6 There should always be some form of summative research, but funding here is secondary to a quality formative research program.
7 All research and evaluation is to be judged by the criterion of utility in the various decision-making processes. This utility will be enhanced if the consumer can be involved in setting the specifications for the research and

evaluation projects. This holds for all four categories of research discussed in this paper.

8 Summative research for outside consumption should be assigned on contract to outside, competent, research groups. Control over the design of the summative research and the instruments used should remain in-house with AIT, but once approved the outside group should be autonomous.

9 In the vast majority of cases, original research instruments rather than standardized tests should be employed for formative and summative research.

10 Before information officers release or quote from research findings for publicity purposes (no matter whether background, formative, summative, or policy research is involved), a responsible research officer should approve the release to insure that the interpretation being conveyed is in fact correct and supported by the data.

The outcome: AIT research and evaluation policy

Reactions elicited by the preceding paper in regional meetings—and reactions solicited from individuals in the field of television evaluation—resulted in a policy statement prepared for the AIT Board of Directors. The AIT Board, composed of chief state and provincial school officers and educational television representatives from the United States and Canada, reviewed the suggested research policy and adopted the following as the research and evaluation policy for the Agency.

1 Each AIT project and activity shall have a research and evaluation component, appropriate to its goals.

2 AIT shall restrict its research and evaluation efforts to decision-oriented and product-specific research and evaluation. AIT should cooperate with, but not sponsor, basic or theoretical research. Empirical data collected for AIT projects should be made available to consumers and researchers in appropriate fields.

3 All research and evaluation shall be judged by the criterion of utility in the various decision-making processes. This utility will be enhanced if the consumer can be involved in setting the specifications for the research and evaluation projects.

4 Background research and in-house policy research shall be established as a permanent and integral part of AIT. Background research should include local, state and provincial resources for educational and telecommunications systems data. The information collected should be disseminated when it is comprehensive and pertinent.

5 Formative evaluation of AIT projects shall be conducted by an in-house research and evaluation staff, working in conjunction with the production team. A prerequisite to appointing production decision-makers should be their willingness to work with formative evaluation in the improvement of the product.

6 In production projects, formative evaluation shall receive priority allocation of research and evaluation resources. Formative evaluation designs should include learner verification of the learning objectives. Summative evaluation, in some form, should be conducted; but funding for this area is secondary to formative evaluation. Summative evaluation data on the use and effects of AIT products should be collected and disseminated by AIT.

7 If undertaken, major summative evaluation projects shall be conducted by independent research groups. Control over the design of major summative evaluation and instruments used should remain with AIT.

PAPER NO 8: EDUCATIONAL RADIO BROADCASTING: PROGRAMME POLICY AND DECISION RESEARCH*

J. P. Boorsma, Pedagogic Didactic Institute, University of Amsterdam, Netherlands.

According to a broadcasting law, Dutch broadcasting organizations have been obliged to offer a 'balanced' output, which

---

* Author's summary of the full paper submitted to the Conference.

means that there has to be a certain ratio of cultural, amusement, informative, and educational programmes. But what exactly is meant by the term 'educational'?

The two broadcasting organizations AVRO and VARA (each independent, neutral, and socialist) have founded the so-called Dutch Educational Radio-Broadcasting Foundation in 1951. Their interpretation of the term 'educational' has been the basis of the organization mentioned above; this foundation is responsible for the production of school radio series solely designed for the educational system at a primary level.

The content of this summary has to be read in the context of the programme policy of this foundation. A number of reasons are presented which indicate the relevance of research into educational radio in general, and into school radio in particular.

Reason 1   School radio might be considered as a societal subsystem, embedded within broadcasting organizations, but related to another societal subsystem, the educational system. The relevance of research is determined by the need to account for the choice of the programme policy, by analysis of school radio programme contents, in the wider perspective of school radio's societal and pedagogical significance.

Reason 2   School radio has the potential to influence the normal curriculum, as well as for revising existing curricula. This leads to an unsolved research problem: what is the relationship between basic opinions about the educational significance of curricula and its conversion into curriculum construction on the one hand, and on the other, the choice the teacher makes from the total range of school radio programmes offered?

Reason 3   School radio, considered as a multi-media teaching–learning system, is implemented in the school as a result of a decision a teacher has made in advance. How does school radio fit the needs of the existing curriculum?

Reason 4   The quantity and quality of educational radio is in itself a reason for intensifying and extending the amount of research.

It is a fallacy to assume that nowadays we are in the position to make generalizable conclusions about the effectiveness of school radio, since research carried out to date is peripheral and incoherent. Despite the fact that school radio has been in existence for some decades, only little or peripheral research has been carried out concerning those research problems that are crucial for school radio:

- What effect does school radio have on the primary educational system, if we see programmes provided by school radio as part of multi-media learning packages?
- What will happen if we change the didactic relations between the different components of the multi-media learning package?
- What exactly is the contribution which school radio could make to the construction and/or revision of curricula?
- What exactly is the relation between educational goals, instructional objectives, and the characteristics of radio itself?

Recognizing the distinction Salomon has made with regard to media research, namely 'research *with* media' and 'research *on* media', it might be reasonable to state that 'research *with* the medium: school radio' has dominated. Research *on* the medium school radio has hardly been carried out at all. It is typical of research with media that school radio researchers have paid insufficient attention to the crucial problems mentioned before.

It is an educational condition *sine qua non*, that the programme policy might be changeable. School radio research has to provide the empirical basis on which decisions should be taken. Decisions are management and design oriented. Research has to yield data which permit policy makers to take decisions concerning the choice of the subject matter, the determination of the number of components of a multi-media learning package, and the design of a series. So the content and type of research are determined by the function research has with regard to the programme policy.

By putting together the dimension (research) 'with-on', and the dimension (decision) management-design we get the following matrix:

with	(2)	(...)	(1)
	(...)	(...)	(...)
on	(4)	(...)	(3)
	design		management

26

DESCRIPTIONS OF EXISTING SYSTEMS

PAPER NO 32: EVALUATION AND EDUCATIONAL BROADCASTING IN AUSTRALIA

Brian Kent, Australian Broadcasting Commission, Melbourne, Australia.

Educational broadcasts in Australia are mainly the responsibility of the Australian Broadcasting Commission (ABC) but a strong tradition of co-operation exists between it and the various educational authorities in all aspects except perhaps that of evaluation. Each State Education Department is a large, powerful independent oligarchy with a relatively large budget and manpower strength. The ABC's Education Department is one of a number of departments within the ABC and it has nationwide responsibilities in educational broadcasting.

Its program output in both radio and television, though one of the largest within the Commission, makes, of necessity, only a minor contribution to the total educational input of any school.

Because the contribution must always be minor and because the program makers are broadcasters not educationalists, only rarely have programs been designed to directly teach. The broadcasters prefer to exercise their expertise and make full use of the technical and creative powers of the media, producing programs which are imaginative, interdisciplinary, stimulating and frequently first class in broadcast terms. Such programs bring with their creation the problems of proof of validity. The pragmatic educationalist faced by the daily problems of his classroom may sometimes be sceptical of the expressed value of broadcasts; the enthusiastic producer reacts badly when his piece of art is seen as something less.

The picture then is of enrichment programs offered by the broadcasters of a national organization to the educationalists of six separate state systems, which in terms of the numbers, manpower and finance involved can only have a peripheral impact on the formal education scene of primary and secondary schools in Australia.

Attitudes to evaluation

The relationship between the ABC and the educational communities of the States may account for lack of enthusiasms among researchers in tertiary institutions or State Education Departments to undertake either research or evaluation studies into educational broadcasting in Australia. The ABC Education Department itself has expressed little greater practical enthusiasm. It has never appointed an officer with qualifications in research or evaluation as a requirement, though its program officers must be qualified as graduate teachers, nor has it created a research/evaluation position for educational broadcast duties.

The ABCs Audience Research Department endeavours to service the Education Department's needs but is limited by other demands to periodic quantitative surveys. To offer a personal viewpoint, a further inhibiting factor in the development of a formalized, structured evaluation may be that recruits to educational broadcasting in Australia have been drawn traditionally from graduates in the fields of the humanities, rather than the sciences, and their sympathies are directed towards the former.

The development of specialized tertiary courses in education in recent years and the tendency to draw new personnel from that source, has perhaps evened the balance. But the study of the scientific method in an education course directed towards later application in the classroom, does not transfer easily to evaluation of the type of broadcast under discussion.

Professional broadcast producers by their very nature tend to grant a low priority level to the post-broadcast investigation of results of their programs, and the rapacious nature of broadcasting tends to limit their energies and time to production.

None of this is to say that the ABCs Education Department is not aware of the value of and need for, evaluation studies applied to educational broadcasts; it rather expresses an attitude towards scientifically-based investigation and a statement about priorities.

Types of evaluation

Continuously successful educational broadcasts are almost always the result of team planning. Though the production techniques, the skills and creative abilities required for educational broadcasts are those of other types of broadcasts, factors peculiar to the educative process have to be considered. These include the motivation, age and span of attention of the audience, the relevance of the content, the listening conditions, the attitude of the teacher.

An awareness of these factors is an essential pre-condition to planning. But no one individual normally possesses all the necessary knowledge. Therefore most planning is team planning.

It is at the planning stage when all the factors, including ideas, are brought together that hypotheses or theories are formed regarding the results. It is at this point that evaluation begins, at the planning stage. The post-broadcast evaluation is to test the hypotheses—that a successful educational broadcast has been produced and transmitted.

Quantitative Surveys

Planning as described above is simplified and becomes more efficient if enough is known of the factors to be considered. For this the planners should be able to draw on a data bank. And the data for this bank is collected by the simplest, and in qualitative terms the least-useful, of evaluation process, the *Evaluation Survey of Use*.

This is the type of information survey commonly used by market and audience researchers. It is intended to provide quantitative results only, though certain qualitative material can be elicited from the answers to some questions. As a quantitative questionnaire it is preferable that all schools be surveyed rather than a Random Probability Sample commonly used, when seeking to project to a total population of a community. The data sought should include: all information about audio/visual equipment, i.e. age, model, use and future plans; the size of the school; the number, experience and shortage, if any, of teachers; the number of classes and grades; purchase of printed broadcast support material such as program guides, teachers' notes, children's activity material; the numbers of qualified operating staff and servicing and maintenance facilities; electrification facilities and reception difficulties; subjects taught and proposed; past, present and future use of educational broadcasts; the requirement for pre-service or in-service training in the use of broadcasts.

Even this brief list provides not only statistical data, but by extraction of the amount and age of equipment, future plans, use of printed material and requests for training, attitudes towards educational broadcasts can be assessed, and once assessed give notice for action in providing further information, better teacher training, or improved transmission. In order that extractions can be made easily and data readily retrievable by planners, computer storing of the information is of high importance.

Proper planning and evaluating of educational broadcasting probably requires as a necessary first step a survey similar in purpose to that described above; which can also help to identify areas where the system is not working properly and suggest means of improvement. Such a survey should be repeated every three to five years depending on the availability of other sources of data provision such as school visiting by broadcasters and educationalists. If from the original survey, registration cards for each responding school are established, information is readily available to visiting officers who can add new information as the result of such visits.

Before considering other forms of evaluation the point should be made that each evaluation involves entry into a school, at least through the postal service but often by broadcasters. The vast increase in funding of education by Governments in Australia has intensified the interest of the academic and other educationalists in classroom activities and resulted in a virtual invasion by them of schools. A broadcaster may be simply another invader. To ease this problem and help ensure and maintain good communications between the broadcasters and the schools, some teaching institutions (it is the headmasters' decision in Australia) accepted the suggestion that a teacher in the school be appointed to act as a broadcasting officer. He not only co-ordinates school visits and seminars, but the completion and return of questionaires, program report cards, complaints and all matters appertaining to educational broadcasts. The effectiveness of evaluation of all kinds is likely to be increased if such positions were established as the norm.

Qualitative surveys

Given a data bank and even a broadcast officer in each school to co-ordinate evaluations, can the planning team's hypotheses be tested; can the program or series be shown to be valid? Broadcasters seek answers from their audience in the three areas of fulfilling educational objectives, obtaining guidance on the merits of the production techniques used, and planning for the future.

If the programme series were intended to teach factual matter directly, and influencing factors were controlled, standardized tests of achievement using experimental and control groups and statistical measures of difference between results may help prove the hypothesis. In fact, it has been possible to prove empirically that successful teaching through television is possible, that educational objectives can be reached and from the results, guidance on production and help in future planning should follow.

Producers of enrichment programs, and that is our concern in this paper, though seeking the same answers, present broadcast material that does not lend itself happily to measurable objective testing of success.

So broadcasters and educationalists must turn to other less conclusive methods.

Almost inevitably these depend on human observation and subsequent judgement.

Psychologists have coined a phrase to express the observational approach. They call it 'Real World Observations', which suggests that ivory castle theorizing is not as practical or useful as observations in the real world of classroom listening where unexpected staff absences, unserviceable radio sets, flat batteries, unexpected visitors, accident-prone children or numerous other minor dramas appear to beset teachers at about the time they tune into a scheduled educational broadcast.

Program appraisal questionaires

My own endeavours to reduce the built-in error of observer bias and improve the reliability and acceptance of observations has been to adapt the interview techniques of psychological testing practice and produce a *Program Appraisal Questionaire*. All questions the observers ask of the teachers, children and themselves as they watch or listen, are pre-determined and no divergence from them is permitted except for one general area when free comment and suggestion for further programs is encouraged. This insistence on keeping to the stated questions is intended to control any unconscious bias which might result under free questioning and to prevent the observer diverging because of his own personal interest into questionings on other issues.

If questionaires are well prepared, data beyond that arising from the actual broadcast itself can be obtained e.g. the teacher's pre-broadcast preparation, the use and relevance of teachers' notes, the ability and preparedness of the teacher to record the program for later use, the post-broadcast activity. Many of each observer's written answers on the questionaire can be checked against the teacher's and children's answers, e.g. interest maintained or not, the high and low points of interest, relevance of subject matter, stimulation to spontaneous activity. Frequently the general comments suggest useful program ideas and help identify class and teacher needs.

Instant appraisal

A variation on the Program Appraisal Questionaire method which is more immediate and more subjective is the *Instant*

Appraisal, so called by the executive producer who first used the system.

Only members of the planning team take part and it is meant to allow them to record mentally or in note form (no set questions are involved), immediate impressions of the effect of the program in the classroom situation. Each member watches in a different classroom or school and freely questions the students and teacher in order to obtain the best overview. After viewing (it has only been used with television) each member returns immediately to meet with other team members under the chairmanship of the executive producer. All impressions and suggestions are noted down and an analysis made from which useful key points frequently emerge.

This Instant Appraisal was first considered for and has only been used with pilot programs. Each pilot is usually seen in the above conditions three or four times after which decisions regarding future programs can be made on the basis of reliable evidence.

Small groups

Associated with Instant Appraisal is the use of *Small Groups* to obtain immediate reaction. This has been used in a limited and experimental way with groups of teachers gathered together for seminars or in-service courses. Programs are screened or heard and each member of the audience is asked to respond with his immediate reaction, as a teacher faced with such a program. The method has a further advantage in that it acts as a starter for discussion on educational broadcasting. Our experience had been that teachers in discussion or debate situations learn a great deal more about educational broadcasting and its uses in the classroom as a result of their response to each other than from the broadcasters. The broadcasters on their part gained considerable insight into teachers' attitudes to teaching and broadcasting and the particular program viewed.

Special listening posts

Schools may be prepared to act as reporting agents on educational broadcasts and it is clear that usable material will become available if schools use evaluation forms and not unstructured and informal questions which will not allow comparison with other reports. But because educational broadcasts are only one of the minor influences impinging on the comparatively well-served Australian classroom, permanent listening-post schools tend to be erratic reporters and over a long period enthusiasms may wane, which would be reflected in poor quality answers. A more satisfactory means of using listening posts is as reporters on special or new series. Schools which have assisted in the planning of the series by offering expert advice or information on pupils' interests, will almost certainly be ready-made enthusiasts for reporting, when transmissions begin. But high enthusiasm as a result of close and dedicated identification can, especially for laymen, create its own bias. But firm insistence on the use of questionaires provides some safeguard.

The future

Recent developments in closed-circuit television equipment and other audio/visual aids for use in schools has led the Advanced Colleges of Education (particularly the former Teachers' Colleges) to establish courses in the use of media. The State Education Departments taking advantage of this inexpensive, reliable, compact equipment have extended their audio/visual departments to provide television programs, and commercial interests are beginning to provide educational television software. Future developments may include these three contributions offering what each does best. The ABC Education Department, backed by the full resources of the national broadcasting service, will continue to produce programs which take advantage of these resources, the State Education Departments with less sophisticated equipment may opt to provide direct teaching programs on new syllabuses and teaching techniques, and commercial interests may prefer to accept commissioned work on behalf of the educational community.

Whatever the development, 'enrichment' programs will continue to be the more difficult to evaluate, and though those of us who work in the field are convinced of the value of our product in educational terms, the layman teacher will demand more concrete evidence than our faith.

To ensure a place as acceptable contributors, in the face of new developments, the broadcasters must sponsor or initiate research into the problem of evaluating the open transmission programs which will still be provided. Such research would improve effectiveness and offer direction for the future. The questions about educational broadcasts which seem to beg for answers that are more concrete than our present judged guesses, include matters relating to: the listening span of attention at different ages, the amount and type of learning and when in the program it takes place; the retention of learning with or without re-inforcement; listeners' recall ability of broadcast material; what in a broadcast most effectively triggers learning or recall? Does this effect vary greatly with different individuals and if so, why? Can recall be triggered effectively by a program designed for this purpose? Is post-broadcast spontaneous activity a significant pointer to learning and can it be measured? Is it true that the most significant effect of broadcasts is a change of attitude? How best can this be measured?

A lead to some of the questions posed may come from a minor experiment I set up to test the hypothesis that a radio history broadcast will cause an attitude change favourable to history, among senior primary children. Control and experimental groups were matched for intelligence and socio-economic background. Measures of attitude change, immediately after the broadcast, showed that the experimental group which received pre-broadcast preparation and, after hearing the broadcast, a follow-up lesson, showed a statistically significant change of attitude favourable to history. The first control group taking the broadcast without preparation or follow-up showed no statistically significant change nor did the second control group which did not take the broadcast, but received a normal history lesson on the same topic. One month later without further history lessons or broadcasts the situation had changed. The experimental group had reverted to the pre-broadcast position, that is, the attitude change had dissipated, the non-prepared first control group remained the same, but the second control group which had been given a normal class history lesson, now showed a statistically significant change of attitude favourable to history.

An assumption could be made that broadcasts have an immediate and significant effect but that retention is quickly lost, and the hypotheses could be stated that for both an immediate and lasting effect the teaching lesson and the broadcast are both necessary and complement each other positively. However the experiment could not be considered valid in that certain factors were not controlled firmly enough and the sample was insufficient in size. But the purpose of the experiment, to establish an experimental design for future development, was successful. That future development is yet to happen.

PAPER NO 79: RESEARCH IN EDUCATIONAL TELEVISION AND RADIO IN AUSTRALIA

Australian Department of Education, Woden, Australia.

The organization of education and broadcasting in Australia

In Australia, the provision of primary and secondary education is primarily the responsibility of the six State Governments. The Federal Government is responsible for this provision in the two Federal territories. Approximately 25 per cent of school children are enrolled at independent or non-State schools. Tertiary level institutions (universities and colleges of advanced education) operate independently of the school system.

Broadcasting services in Australia are provided by a dual system of national and commercial stations. The national network of radio and television broadcasting stations is operated by the Australian Broadcasting Commission, which is a statutory authority of the Federal Government. The national radio network covers virtually all Australia and the television network reaches in excess of 98 per cent of the population. Commercial radio and television stations provide services within technical and program standards set down by the Australian Broadcasting Control Board.

Some of these stations are grouped into networks and all are supported by revenue from advertising.

A few universities have low-powered campus radio stations which provide educational programs. Community radio and Frequency Modulation radio are in their infancy, but are expected to develop steadily.

Historical background to educational broadcasting in Australia

Provisions of radio and television programs for schools is a responsibility of the Australian Broadcasting Commission (ABC) responsible to the Australian Parliament through the Minister for Post and Telecommunications. The ABC came into existence in 1932 and took over some elementary radio programs for schools then in existence. A Federal Officer was appointed to supervise these radio broadcasts and in 1936 the first Federal Committee for School Broadcasts was called together at which four States were represented. By 1956, on the eve of the introduction of television, educational radio programs were being produced in all six States, some for use throughout Australia, others directed to meet local needs. Staff by this time totalled 27.

Television was first introduced in New South Wales and Victoria and within twelve months the first experimental educational television programs were being produced. This experimental stage ended in 1963 by which time total educational broadcasting staff had grown to 38. In 1963 new types of programs were introduced, studio and production facilities were extended and by 1975 professional staff totalled 86.

A high proportion of primary and secondary schools (90 per cent or more) now use educational radio and television broadcasts provided by the ABC. Most of these schools have audio recorders; most secondary schools and many primary schools now also have video recorders. Recording programs allows the schools greater flexibility in their use and also provides opportunities to use them more intensively. The high cost of satisfying the demand for increasingly sophisticated program production is partly offset by greater sharing of programs between States. Radiovision

programs have become widely accepted and booklets for these programs have good sales. Broadcast programs for schools are supported by pupil booklets and teaching guides which are widely used.

Since the introduction of broadcast television in Australia less than twenty years ago, usage of television in schools has grown steadily. But in spite of the availability of cheaper video cameras and video recorders, growth has almost entirely been associated with increasing the utilization of ABC school telecasts and the level of intra-school program production and other uses remains low. There has been a change in emphasis in the style of school broadcast programs, from the direct teaching and supplementary teaching formats to the broader enrichment and motivational program styles. This trend has probably been a reflection of a number of factors including the greater incidence of seconded and advisory teachers being involved in production and planning; a reduced need for teachers for the more didactic-type of programs because of the greater availability of adequate textbooks and in-service courses related to new curriculum approaches; and a broadening of curricula coupled with a trend to devolve curriculum decision-making to schools and teachers.

Throughout Australia, approximately 134 radio and 125 television programs for primary schools are broadcast by the ABC each week. The corresponding figures for secondary schools are 73 (radio) and 76 (television). Programs cover current affairs, music, drama, literature, art, mathematics, social sciences, health and religious education, and languages.

Some provision of adult or further education programs is made through broadcast services provided by tertiary institutions. Many of these programs form part of courses leading to an award, although they also serve persons taking subjects for professional continuing education.

While the vast majority of educational broadcast programs is provided by the Australian Broadcasting Commission, commercial broadcasting stations do produce programs for pre-school and kindergarten age children, and a small number of other programs are produced locally in co-operation with universities and colleges. However, actual transmission time given to educational programs averages only 30 minutes weekly per commercial station, which is approximately 0.5 per cent of total weekly transmission.

A special use of radio which has been in operation for a number of years is the 'School of the Air' service provided for children in the sparsely-settled remote areas of the continent who are unable to attend school. 'Schools of the Air' supplement these children's correspondence lessons and attempt to alleviate the disadvantage of an isolated location. Radio lessons are prepared by special teachers, and broadcast over twelve transmitters maintained by the Royal Flying Doctor Service for emergency communications.

Responsibility for research in educational broadcasting

As the organization responsible for the production of school broadcasts, the ABC maintains State Education Advisory Committees in each of the six States. Much of the information on the use of broadcasts in the schools is derived from the ABC State Liaison Officers who are State Government officers, responsible to their respective Education Departments. In some States, the ABC is involved in their selection, and provides them with offices. They have responsibility in a wide area of activities, including:

1 The gathering of information—about the needs of schools and channelling of this information to the appropriate bodies.
2 Contributing to the deliberations of the various committees in the ABC's advisory structure.
3 An involvement in program design.
4 A contribution to teacher training both in colleges and in various forms of in-service courses.
5 A significant participation in publicity and public relations.

The ABC also maintains an Audience Research Department, covering all its activities, which has periodically conducted sample surveys in schools.

The Australian Department of Education and the former Department of the Media conducted a survey of television equipment in all Australian schools in 1974. Both this and the 1972 survey by the ABC were more in the nature of fact-gathering than interpretative exercises.

Research projects in educational broadcasting may be funded within general programs of the Federally-funded Education Research and Development Committee (ERDC) and the Australian Research Grants Committee (ARGC); and the Australian Council for Educational Research (ACER) which is supported by both Federal and State Governments. An ACER-sponsored research project on the use of closed-circuit television in a number of secondary schools, known as 'The Malvern Project', was completed in 1973.

Examples of research findings

The 1972 survey conducted by the ABC's Audience Research Department collected information from samples of primary and secondary schools in each State on the following aspects: number of classes at each grade level, sizes of schools (by numbers of teachers), availability of radio and television equipment, brand of video-tape recorder, acquisition of video-tape recorders, location of television sets, school-day starting time, morning recess time, lunch time, school finishing time, use of school radio programs, use of school television programs, consumption of broadcasts in schools by programs—radio and television. The survey yielded a high response rate (e.g. 87 per cent in Victoria), and a number of results were of use in arranging program schedules. It also showed that sizeable audiences existed in schools for early school and pre-school programs. Some indications of the level of usage of individual programs was obtained and expressed as a 'program usage index' (PUI). The PUI for any particular program was 1.00 if taken regularly by all eligible classes.

In 1974 the Australian Departments of Education and the Media conducted a survey of television equipment in all Australian primary and secondary schools. The survey was intended to give accurate data relating to television equipment and was concerned with collecting detailed information on such matters as:

the distribution of equipment among different school types, school sizes,

States and urban/non-urban areas; the quality of pictures and sound reception; the brands and types of video equipment in use; and the non-broadcast use of equipment, e.g. school production of lesson material.

The survey achieved a response rate of 86 per cent from over 9,000 schools to which questionnaires were posted. It showed that nearly 14,500 receivers/monitors were in use, representing an average of nearly two receivers for each school. Of the schools that responded, nearly 7,000 (91 per cent) were equipped with television receivers, and 676 schools had no receivers. While over 60 per cent of all schools in the survey were in non-urban areas, more than 80 per cent of those without receivers were in non-urban areas.

The survey revealed that 16 per cent of urban schools had video recorders, compared with 10 per cent for non-urban schools; the overall figure for all schools being 12 per cent. Only one-fifth of the video recorders were in primary schools, which represented about four-fifths of the total number of schools in the survey. However, primary schools were in the process of becoming equipped. One school in twenty was equipped with a video replay unit and a little over one quarter of these were in primary schools.

The Malvern Project, completed in 1973, was a three-year trial of closed-circuit television production and usage in four secondary schools in the Melbourne area, with particular regard to the uses of closed-circuit televisions to aid the effectiveness of classroom teaching. The project was sponsored by the Australian Council for Educational Research. As it developed, its facilities produced supplementary audio-visual material for individual student use in association with closed-circuit television (CCTV). The project demonstrated that the individualized and specialized nature of the programs made to suit the syllabus requirements of one particular school, or sometimes one class within a school, made the possibility of schools sharing each other's work remote. Little use was made by schools of the opportunity to have students make their own programs. Moreover, few teachers felt sufficiently competent in production and direction techniques

to enable them to provide useful supervision of the students' work in this regard.

The project provided a warning that in situations in which school staff were fully committed in time and effort to current teaching loads, it would be unrealistic to imagine that even with considerable outside support they would be able to use CCTV to improve what they were doing in the classroom.

Research need areas

The informal research now done on individual school programs by producers and others might well be supported by more frequent and deeper studies. More regular surveys of the usage of available programs could be undertaken on a large number of schools. Such routine information gathering could be supplemented by *ad hoc* studies into areas such as the degree of usage of non-school broadcasts, e.g. talks, documentaries, and magazine-type programs and dramas, and methods employed by teachers in using broadcast and supplementary material.

Some studies could also look at the importance of the use of video distribution systems in increasing the level of program usage, bearing in mind the high cost of providing schools with such systems. The effects on program usage of factors such as the quality of reception and the time-tabling of broadcasts, should be examined in greater detail. There could be scope for a limited number of research studies commissioned to measure, by use of controlled experiments, the efficiency of new radio and television program styles compared with older formats or traditional lessons. Attention could also be given to studying the effectiveness of educational broadcasting in the tertiary and adult education fields and, in the case of tertiary institutions, this could usefully extend to closed-circuit television applications in such institutions as a whole.

Research has been conducted into children's use of television outside school hours and results indicate that average weekly viewing exceeds total time spent weekly in school. There could be scope for research into the relationship between home and school viewing, the kind of learning associated with each (e.g. active vs passive; incidental vs purposive; parent vs teacher vs self-directed) and the extent of the potential demand (among adults as well as children) for more educational programs out of school hours.

Research into more basic aspects of the provision of educational broadcasting could examine to what extent the various facilities provided contribute to better learning in real terms, when viewed against the various educational, economic and general social criteria.

PAPER NO 38: RADIO SCOILE: RESEARCH AND EVALUATION

John MacMahon, Education Department, Radio Telefis Eirann, Republic of Ireland.

In Ireland the schools' broadcasting service is provided by Radio Telefis Eirann (RTE), the national broadcasting network, and is funded by the Government, through the Department of Education. A schools' television service for the second-level schools only, has been available since 1964 but, until 1975, no schools radio service was available for either first-level or second-level schools. In 1973 the Minister of Education announced that a schools' radio service was to be developed and that the service would be piloted in primary schools in Irish speaking areas of the country.

Three teachers were recruited and trained by RTE as producers for schools programmes and ideas for programmes were tested intensively during the training period. Themes and approaches were based on the new child-centred curriculum which was introduced in primary schools in 1971.

In the pilot project three series dealing with various aspects of the school curriculum were transmitted:

MUSIC *Bimis ag Ceol*—Let's sing.

STORYTELLING *Ag Scaoileadh Sceoil*—Spinning a yarn.

ENVIRONMENTAL STUDIES *Rotha na Cruinne* —The Wheels of Life.

Ten weekly programmes of 15 minutes duration were broadcast in each series and every programme was transmitted twice a week. The programmes were designed for pupils in the 10–12 age group. The broadcasts were supported by a pupils' book and notes for teachers.

The pupils' book contained works and music for the songs in the music series and illustrations to support the themes of the programmes in the storytelling and environment studies series. The teachers' notes provided a brief outline of the aims and themes of the programmes and some general guidelines for utilization.

Aims and descriptions of the series

After the major function of piloting a nation-wide schools service and devising methods, infrastructure and procedures to allow for its development and evaluation in a dynamic way, the more immediate aim of the scheme was to provide suitable educational material for pupils in Irish speaking schools which do not have access to the same range of resources as schools in which English is the vernacular. These schools are situated on the Western seaboard and are predominantly rural. The majority of them are small two-teacher schools and each teacher would have an average of 20 pupils between the ages of 8 and 12.

Each series has specific objectives which were outlined in the teachers' notes. For the *Bimis ag Ceol* series the objectives were:

1 To encourage the pupils to sing and to learn new songs.
2 To present music to pupils as an activity in which they themselves could take an active part.
3 To allow children to hear and sing songs regularly, rather than to 'teach' them how to sing.
4 To make the pupils aware of some elements of musical notation and terminology.

The programmes consisted of 14 songs, almost all of them in Irish, and the children were asked to listen and to join in the singing. The songs were presented by three singers (1 male and 2 female).

The objectives of the *Ag Scaoileadh Sceoil* series were:

1 To familiarize the pupils with storytelling.
2 To enable the pupils to enjoy stories.
3 To stimulate creativity and imaginative thought in the pupils.
4 To enrich the children's language and experience.

Each programme consisted of one story presented in a dramatized and/or narrative format. Different presenters were used for each story. The stories included stories written specifically for children; stories from established Irish authors; and three classical stories (Irish, Greek, Biblical).

For the *Rotha na Cruinne* series the objectives were:

1 To help the pupil develop an understanding of himself, his relationships and his physical and social environment.

2 To encourage the pupil to obtain more information about, and greater knowledge of his environment.

This series had a conceptual unity underlying the various programmes. It examined the individual and his relationships, the family, a child in a different culture, shelter, a village community, a city centre, various aspects of service in a community and the natural environment at a lakeside. The programme on the lakeside was a radiovision programme.

Two of the final programmes were devoted to children's reactions and samples of their work which resulted from the programme.

Research and evaluation

The criteria used to evaluate the pilot scheme were developed from the stated objectives of each series. Research and data collection were directed towards:

1 The enjoyment the pupils derived from the programmes.

2 The interest the pupils showed in the programmes.

3 Which were the particular items the pupils reacted to?

4 Did the pupils learn from the programmes?

5 What did the pupils learn?

6 How did teachers use the programmes?

7 What classroom or out-of-school activity was stimulated?

Data was collected by three Educational Officers who visited the 149 participating schools to observe pupils' reactions and talk to them about the programmes. During classroom observation particular attention was paid to facial expression, movement, points of high or low interest, active participation where it was called for.

To ensure that the children's reactions were not influenced by the presence of a stranger an effort was made by each officer to visit one school regularly over the ten-week period and children quickly became accustomed to his presence.

The Education Officer generally questioned the children about the programme to obtain their impressions and to supplement the information obtained from observation. The questions were non-directive and open-ended since it was thought important not to influence the pupils' own impressions of the programme.

The teachers' observations, opinions and reactions were also obtained on visits to schools and they were requested to keep a diary in which they noted comments on each programme. A number of meetings of teachers were held in each area to provide a forum for discussion and exchange ideas.

Summary of the findings

Of the 149 schools for which information is available, 139 used the programmes, a participation rate of 93.3 per cent. Between 2,500 and 3,000 pupils listened to the broadcasts in these schools. Teachers and pupils reacted very favourably to both content of the programmes and the presence of a radio in the schools. The pilot scheme made suitable resources available for Irish speaking pupils and an infrastructure for a production—research interaction in educational broadcasting was established within RTE.

The music series was an immediate success with all pupils. The liveliness of the songs, the techniques of presentation, the enthusiasm, and continuity of the presenters all helped to develop an atmosphere of entertainment and enjoyment in the schools. The pupils joined in the singing and learned the words and music without difficulty. In many cases the songs were heard being sung in the playground and during recreation. The children became involved in making music and contributed their own verses to some songs, wrote their own songs in some cases and participated in dancing and providing percussion.

Though the series made no effort to teach music and songs in a didactic way the children learned the words and tunes without difficulty and also learned some fundamental musical theory which was provided during the programmes.

Teachers were initially unsure about their role in relation to these programmes and many felt that they should encourage the children to sing, or lead the singing themselves. After a few weeks the majority were content to relax and enjoy the music with the children, giving a lead when appropriate. The response and involvement of the pupils was strengthened when the teacher's enjoyment and involvement were obvious.

The reactions of pupils to the stories in the *Ag Scaoileadh Sceoil* series varied. The difficulties posed by various dialects may have influenced reactions since it was found that a story which was very entertaining for children in one area was virtually incomprehensible to children in another area, where the dialect was different.

Children liked simple stories of adventure, humour and fantasy and were satisfied to listen and be entertained by the programmes.

Initially, teachers seemed concerned with the content of the story and its relevance to the curriculum and were prepared to use the story as a basis for a lesson in the same way as they would use a story in a textbook. After some time teachers became more aware of the potential of radio in encouraging relaxation and enjoyment and were content if the children found the stories entertaining.

It was first thought that teachers would use these stories as a basis for various forms of classwork but the teachers' notes did not provide any specific direction. Consequently the use made of these stories varied greatly. Some teachers used the stories as a basis for creative work—drawings, paintings, simulation, dramatization, writing similar stories —and some others concentrated on asking the children to write a summary of the story or retell it in their own words. In other cases the stories were used as a basis for a formal language class e.g. grammar, words, phrases.

The *Rotha na Cruinne* series had a conceptual unity which integrated each programme into an overall plan. For the series to be successful an understanding of the underlying conceptual unity by the teachers was essential. The series was dependent on the teacher for its effectiveness in a way that the other series were not.

The reactions of teachers to this series varied, probably because of a lack of clarity about the aims and objectives of the series. The research findings emphasize the fact that if a series of this type is to be successful the objectives need to be made clear to the teachers and the fundamental theoretical basis explained in detail beforehand.

Many of the children grasped the concepts introduced in the series and realized the conceptual unity underlying the series. Since research was not directed specifically at concept formation by the children it is difficult to establish in detail what concepts the children developed from listening to the programme.

The programmes were successful in stimulating children to examine their environment and many interesting projects developed as a result of the programmes. The children liked finding out about other people and places and were pleased with the information they obtained.

Production techniques

Certain production techniques were found to generate a much better response than others. Many programmes called for overt participation by the children and this proved a highly successful technique for attracting attention and retaining interest. Most teachers thought that when children were asked to be active during the programme they enjoyed the programme far more.

Humour ranked high in the list of factors which children felt contributed most to their enjoyment of Radio Scoile. Sound effects also contributed greatly to the atmosphere of a programme and to the stimulation of the children's imagination. Music and song was found to attract the attention of the children if they had lost interest.

Most children expressed a preference for dramatization and dialogue while many teachers initially thought that the stories would have been more effective if presented in narrative form. By the end of the project most teachers felt that a balance of dramatic and narrative forms would probably be most effective in retaining interest and in stimulating the imagination.

Teachers initially had some doubts about the value and usefulness of radio programmes for schools and many expected traditional lesson-type programmes. By the end of the pilot scheme teachers' understanding of schools radio had altered and the majority of them were surprised by the programmes and enthusiastic about their potential.

The pilot scheme identified many logistical problems which may otherwise have remained unnoticed—areas of poor reception, problems of distributing supplementary materials, suitable times for transmissions etc.

The research—production interaction

The Radio Scoile pilot scheme formed the basis for the development of a dynamic research-production relationship in which research is a basic aspect of programme development. New ideas and approaches are tested before they are incorporated into a programme and programmes are continually evaluated and their impact assessed.

This type of relationship ensures that producers are continually aware of the effects of their programmes and are sensitive to any changes in the needs or reactions of his audience. Research of this nature is considered by all members of the department as an essential aspect of educational broadcasting.

Financing of research

Research formed an integral part of the Radio Scoile pilot scheme and consequently it is difficult to distinguish between research costs and other production costs. It is estimated that research costs, including travel, subsistence, salaries and publication of the report were approximately 12 per cent–15 per cent of the total costs of the pilot scheme.

Since the project was subjected to intensive research this percentage is much higher than research costs now allowed for other programmes.

Conclusion

The Radio Scoile scheme was the first step in the provision of a comprehensive schools' radio service for the whole country. Research formed an integral part of this pilot scheme and resulted in a comprehensive report and evaluation of the scheme.

For various reasons research and data collection was directed towards the overall impact of the programmes on the children rather than towards individual development in particular areas. It was first essential to provide producers with some feedback on their programmes before quantifying the effectiveness of a particular item and assessing its educational value. It is intended that future research will be directed towards the effects of particular production techniques on the children in terms of educational development and towards the production of educational programmes which will also be entertaining.

At present a production—research relationship has evolved from the Radio Scoile experience for the production of a radio series for pre-school children, an out-of-school magazine series of radio programmes for the 9–12 age group and a television series about the transition from school to work for those who finish their schooling at 15+. Many of the research findings of the Radio Scoile pilot scheme have been incorporated by the producers in the new radio series.

The results of the pilot scheme indicate that the methods used to obtain data were adequate for the objectives specified. For more specific objectives different techniques would be necessary.

As a result of the pilot scheme RTE possesses an infrastructure on which further developments in education broadcasting can be based. There also exists a number of teachers who have co-operated with researchers and producers in evaluating programmes. These teachers, it is hoped, will be a valuable asset in the development of the service.

PAPER NO 21: EDUCATIONAL TELEVISION (ETV) EVALUATION TECHNIQUES IN HONG KONG*

Colvyn Haye, Head of ETV Service, Education Department, Hong Kong.

The ETV cycle in Hong Kong begins and ends with Teachers Committees. Teachers

---

* Reproduced by kind permission of the publishers from: *Educational Broadcasting International*, December, 1973. (A Journal of the Centre for Educational Development Overseas, published by Peter Peregrinus Ltd.)

who devise ETV syllabuses play a vital part in producing ETV and then, as users of ETV, evaluate the success or failure of ETV in classrooms. Evaluation returns are carefully studied by Teachers' Committees with a view to reshaping and improving ETV each year and so the ETV cycle begins again. ETV is a dynamic, continuous process in Hong Kong and evaluation is the key to its success.

The importance of evaluation was recognized before ETV was launched in Hong Kong in September 1971 and several forms of evaluation were envisaged. Firstly, it seemed imperative to seek the views of teachers using the service. This was done by the creation of Teachers' Committees, chaired by ETV producers who were themselves teachers trained as broadcasters. These committees were drawn from a cross-section of government, government-aided and private schools and included other responsible professional opinion from the Inspectorate of the Educational Department. Broadly representative, therefore, committees devise ETV syllabuses and review ETV progress annually, but it is vital that teachers evaluate ETV in classrooms and we think they can do this in Hong Kong by using a special return form. Teachers can assess the success or failure of classroom television in three broad areas: technical reception (clarity of picture and sound), programme content (teaching aims and points, pupil interest, pace, vocabulary and presentation) and support material (teachers' and pupils' notes). The logic of this is apparent, but we know that we cannot leave it there.

With the best will in the world, teachers will be polite rather than rude. Perhaps Western tradition is blunt, but in the East teachers will frequently tell you what they think you want to hear. And so it is necessary to check and double-check classroom evaluation returns by classroom visits. Producers visit schools at least once a week during transmissions to see for themselves how their programmes are being received and utilized. They talk to teachers and pupils and learn much, but, being human, they may be prone to subjectivity in judging the impact of their programmes. Consequently, Inspectors of Schools are also asked to assess ETV programming.

Inspectorate reports take two forms. Using the standard evaluation return, Advisory Inspectors, who are subject specialists, express professional opinions of the programmes and Supervisory Inspectors give regular reports on classroom reception and utilization.

Sheer numbers in Hong Kong suggested an evaluation return designed for data processing and this is done weekly. Eight hundred questionnaires go out each week of the 30-week ETV year to teachers taking each level of ETV in primary schools. Thus, 1,600 return forms are currently despatched (800 for Primary 3 and 800 for Primary 4 classes) to a sample cross-section of teachers in schools. Two hundred teachers are asked to assess each of four subjects covered by ETV at both levels each week. A high percentage (80 per cent) make returns, which are then processed. Tabulated returns, colour-charted by ETV production teams, are a useful guide to programme success and, as has been described, returns are carefully studied by Teachers Committees with ETV curriculum reform and development constantly in mind.

There is one other form of evaluation that we in ETV Hong Kong are working towards: returns from pupils themselves. We should like to know what the children think of ETV: not only whether they find it fun, but whether it stimulates them and makes them want to find out more about life and learning. Obviously an evaluation return for pupils requires careful construction and we have asked the Research Testing and Guidance Section of the Education Department to devise one on sound psychological lines.

Finally, the main question: can we prove that ETV helps children to learn better in Hong Kong? The answer to this in terms of scientific educational research will never be known, because we have no control groups in Hong Kong and no way of controlling the other variables in a clinical test situation. We are in a sense the victims of our ambition. The universal availability of ETV in Hong Kong (the service goes out seven hours a day via our two commercial television stations and can be taken by anybody with a receiver) and the size of our target audiences (100,000 in 1971/72, 200,000 in 1972/73) preclude the research possible with small pilot projects. However, we are certain that we are succeeding. Everything we learn from our evaluation techniques tells us that children are learning better with ETV. We see a marked improvement in the attention span, concentration and ability of classes taking ETV. Happiest of all, ETV is making education fun and this, after all is the name of the game.

PAPER NO 68: UTILIZATION OF SCHOOL BROADCASTING IN HUNGARY

K. Hanák, Mass Communication Research Centre, Budapest, Hungary.

1 Some general remarks and considerations

One of the most controversial issues of our age is the following: what is the role of the school as an important institution of socialization in the age of scientific-technological revolution?

The relevant questions are different in socialist and in capitalist countries. However, despite the significant difference, there are a number of similar or common problems to tackle. To mention just a few: how far can school convey the increasing amount of knowledge? Do the results of scientific-technological revolution infiltrate into school education, and if so, do they basically transform or only modify traditional education? The discussion on the modernization of education appears to centre around two main issues, the selection and enlargement of the curriculum on the one hand, and facing the tasks of modern mass-education, on the other.

In up-to-date school and adult education, mass media have a significant role to play. In my opinion their role and significance is likely to increase in all countries and social systems. Before coming to the point of the research I have done I should like to clarify an important question of principle which is relevant in the field of mass communication research as a whole. When investigating the function and effectiveness of school broadcasting, *society-centred research should be preferred*, starting from an analysis of macro-level social process, *instead of means-centred, media-centred research*, focussing *only* on various means

of mass communication. Consequently, we should not exclusively pay attention to the tool, the medium, itself, but rather to their social role and effect. For in fact, it is only this kind of approach which is capable of yielding information not only to leaders of a society but also to producers of educational programmes. I think this principle should be valid for both short-term and long-term educational mass media research, because the basic aim is to feed back valid opinion of users to programme-makers.

2 Some information about the aims and methods of our survey

In Hungary, education through mass communication started somewhat belatedly. School radio and school television programmes aimed at the elementary and middle levels of education have been broadcast since 1962 and 1964, respectively. This also accounts for why we started investigating these programmes as late as 1973. We had to have some time and experience before setting out to take a proper account of the extent and efficiency of the utilization of educational channels.

The aim of our investigation was first and foremost to find out:

(a) about the degree of availability of broadcasts to schools;
(b) to what extent and for which subjects the educational channels are utilized;
(c) what school teachers think of the programmes; how far these programmes can serve as an aid to work at school;
(d) pupils opinions about the programmes; whether they use them.

At this point we also wanted to find out about the motivations behind home viewing and listening of school broadcasts.

We designated school as the basic unit of the survey. Schools included in the study were so sampled as to represent the condition and distribution according to the main types of localities of primary school in Hungary. On the basis of these principles, 226 schools were chosen for the sample: 165 village, 29 country town and 32 city schools.

Type and method of the study is extensive and intensive at the same time. It is extensive, since it cannot provide an answer to a lot of intricate pedagogical questions that can be approached only by means of an intensive study of effects, embracing a longer period of time and involving a control group, for comparison. Thus it excludes such problems as the effectiveness of the use of educational broadcasting, with regard to each specific subject, the role of various channels of education in the complicated process of teaching, etc. It is intensive, in that it seeks to identify and typify attitudes, opinions, relating to the channels of education, too.

The three level-structure of the research enabled us to gain a detailed picture about the utilization of educational broadcasting in primary schools.

(a) Interviews were made with the headmasters of 156 primary schools.
(b) Surveying the sub-sample of teachers:
    (i) interviews were made with 478 teachers,
    (ii) self-administered questionnaires were filled in by 533 teachers.

The sub-sample of teachers consisted of 1,011 persons, 368 of these, teaching at the lower school classes, from the first to fourth, 643, in turn teaching at the upper classes from the fifth to eighth. Teachers of the upper school classes were so sampled as to represent those teaching humanistic and physical/natural science subjects more or less proportionally.

(c) Four pupils in each school belonging to four different degrees of school achievement, attending the eighth class (14-year olds), filled in a self-administered questionnaire that contained questions mainly about how much they made use of educational broadcasting out of classes, at home. The sub-sample of pupils consisted of 587 persons.

3 Results of the research

The use of school radio at primary schools, during classes: 35 per cent of the surveyed schools use school radio during classes regularly (at least once a month) or occasionally (once in 2 or 3 months).

26 per cent of the schools use school radio during classes continually. 33 per cent of the schools use school radio out of classes (at study circles, special in-school lessons after classes).

The use of educational television at primary schools, during classes: educational television is used regularly at least once a

month (and occasionally once in 2 or 3 months) by 76 per cent of the schools. The proportion of schools using ETV at least once a month is 66 per cent.

52 per cent of the surveyed schools utilize ETV out of classes (at study circles, special in-school lessons after classes).

These data show that, though not equally, both channels of education play a major role in primary education. Differences in the degree of their utilization among schools at various types of localities can be observed only with school radio: it is used somewhat more in town schools than in village ones. As to ETV, type of locality does not seem to make any significant difference, though data of little hamlet schools stand out, reflecting their particular devotion to ETV.

The study sums up the opinions of teachers and headmasters about the use of educational broadcasting and how to adapt these channels of education to the whole teaching process.

The teachers evaluated and analysed the advantages and possible disadvantages implied in the use of educational broadcasting from quite a lot of aspects. The interviews carried out with the teachers brought valuable information also concerning their opinions about radio and television programmes directed at them. General demographic and social factors (such as sex, age, level of education, social background, etc.) proved to be irrelevant in telling whether teachers make use of educational broadcasting or not.

School radio is used during classes by 20 per cent of the questioned teachers while this percentage is much higher, 70 per cent, with educational television.

The study went further than earlier Hungarian researches, in that it identified why teachers who did not use educational broadcasting, do not use it.

The pupils' opinions about educational broadcasting
The questionnaires show that the scope of both channels of educational broadcasting goes far beyond the classrooms. Pupils make advantage of these programmes for learning and education at home, too. School radio is listened to by 40 per cent of the pupils also at home. Approximately 50 per cent of the pupils are regular home

41

viewers of the programmes of ETV. While most of the pupils listening to school radio at home are girls, there is no difference in the extent of viewing of ETV between boys and girls.

There are interesting findings about how children, from different social strata, make use of the help provided by educational broadcasting. According to the data, the children's social background (the occupation, the place occupied in the social structure by the pupils' parents) has little bearing upon the extent of the home use of educational broadcasting.

Workers' children utilize school radio and ETV at home more or less to the same extent and this can be regarded as an objective expression of the fact that educational broadcasting plays an important levelling role, in reducing the differences in the knowledge of children.

Educational broadcasting has a universal function: transmission of knowledge. Today, in Hungary this form of education plays at the same time a most important social role with its contribution in levelling differences, originating from the different places in the regional-ecological settlement (village, country town, city) and in the social structure.

4 On our plans concerning adult education

For the past few years there have been serious efforts made in Hungary to further develop not only the entire school system, but also adult education. Hungarian Television is to launch in the Autumn of 1976 its *Open University programme*, which, apart from its aim of general enhancement of education, is meant to prepare for university education. My Institute, in due course, is to launch an intensive survey, spanning many years, which is meant to find out about the extent, motivation and efficiency of collective and individual utilization of adult education programmes. We are intending to apply modern complex methods co-operating in a special team with different experts (educational programme makers, teachers, sociologists, psychologists, scholars of educational technology, etc.)

5 Means-centred or problem-centred research

I started from the assumption that mass communication is inseparable from the whole of the social system. Therefore a narrowly media-centred, means-centred approach is inevitably biased. It is evident that without media, without good technical conditions, the educational programmes do not work. So the tools, the technical conditions, the means are important but not sufficient. The most important and fruitful approach is to make social problem-centred research.

It is thus with this idea that I should like to conclude this paper. When journalists asked Professor Loeb, the very versatile scholar, if he was a neurologist, a chemist, a physicist, a psychologist, a sociologist or a philosopher, he answered, 'I solve problems'. I think that this also shows the track that we researchers of educational mass communication, in our various capacities, have got to follow, to be able to solve problems for the sake of educational broadcasting and cultural values.

PAPER NO 61: EVALUATION AND RESEARCH FOR EDUCATIONAL BROADCASTING IN KENYA

R. H. J. Thompson, Head of Schools Broadcasting, Ministry of Education, Kenya.

The need for research and evaluation in the field of educational media is generally recognized, although some people would argue that the effort would be better used in producing materials, particularly in a developing country, because the need for education and educational materials is so great that searching for perfection is a luxury that cannot be afforded. Properly orientated research which is aimed at practical objectives can point the way to improved use of resources of money, manpower and equipment and avoid wasted effort in less effective directions. Too often educational media operations have been set up with no preliminary research simply because it has been done elsewhere. Once a media operation is established it is self-generating—it needs more and more manpower, more and more equipment, more and more money. The organization wants to 'do its thing' on an even larger scale and it cannot slow down the growth process long enough to sit back and examine where it is going and why. Even in small organizations this happens until somebody calls a halt to take stock. Unless research is built into the original concept of the organization, it is difficult to graft it on later. Production has become the god and the producers do not want to listen to anybody who questions what they are doing. Many organizations find themselves in this situation and it usually requires outside pressure to make them face it.

Any research/evaluation project needs to start from what the objectives of the operation or planned operation being researched are and from there to conduct research to find out how far these objectives are being achieved, or are likely to be achieved. This means that the researchers must have carte blanche to talk to and question the members of the organization about their objectives and their ways of working towards them. They must also be able to visit and question users of the products and to conduct tests. This means that they must be given a degree of authority both within the organization and amongst the users. This is not difficult if the research is fully supported by the head of the organization and if the organization is itself part of an integrated system, such as exists where the Ministry of Education controls both the schools and the educational broadcasting organization. It will be more difficult where much looser links between makers and users exist and where the users are not organized into easily controllable units. In either case, it is probably better that where research is being grafted on to an already established organization, that initially it should be conducted by an internal unit which will concern itself with efficiency in producing and disseminating products.

This type of operation is likely to be accepted as beneficial by members of the organization and can lead on to external research which will concern the effectiveness of the organization and which may result in major re-organization. However initial projects are introduced into the system it is important that members of the organization are kept fully informed about what is going on. They must not be allowed to feel that the researchers whether internal or external are saboteurs bent upon destroying their well-established modes of operation.

The situation in Kenya

The Schools Broadcasting Service in Kenya is a section of the Chief Inspector of Schools Department of the Ministry of Education. Its basic function is to provide teachers with support materials transmitted to them through the medium of radio. It has developed other ancillary functions over the years, particularly in the field of supplementary textual and pictorial material and is becoming increasingly involved in teacher education through radio support to correspondence materials for in-servicing teachers and through the use of visual media for support to pre-service residential teacher training.

It is intended to expand the service into an Educational Media Service. Some uncoordinated basic research and evaluation of programmes has been carried out spasmodically over a period of years but in order to rationalize the future functions of the proposed Educational Media Service, an officer was appointed in September 1975 to carry out as a first task an extensive programme of research into the factors within the education system which affect the impact of the materials being offered by the present Schools Broadcasting Service, and to carry out general evaluation of the materials and the Service itself. This programme is still in its early stages but has already produced some results which, taken in conjunction with previous findings, provides evidence on which certain changes in direction and emphasis in the functions of the existing Schools Broadcasting Service can be based. Future work in this research and evaluation programme will cross-check and extend the work already done on the existing functions of the Schools Broadcasting Service, and extend outwards from the formal school system into research into the place of media of various forms in teacher education and non-formal education.

Research up to the present

Until September 1975, the only research projects which have been undertaken were an in-depth study of one series of secondary school history programmes and their atti-

43

tude changing effects; a research experiment to consider the use and value of sound effects in radio lessons for primary schools; and a brief research project on the Schools Broadcasting Service in general carried out by a management studies team from the Kenya Institute of Administration as a training exercise in 1973.

The in-depth study of the attitude changing effects of the secondary history series suggested that specific attitude changes could be induced in secondary students by the radio medium even in situations where these changes conflicted with attitudes of the teachers themselves. The research pointed out the dangers of centrally-based producers and writers disseminating material without comprehensive discussions with people in the field and of the need for material to be thoroughly checked for factual accuracy and for its attitude forming content. Conversely it indicated that radio could be used to correct prejudiced attitudes of the teaching force.

The research into sound effects showed that they could be confusing and mitigate against understanding of programme material unless they were sounds commonly heard in the child's own environment and that even then, the sound would usually have to be identified within the programme text. Even such common sounds as a Land Rover engine often cannot be identified by children, particularly in poor reception conditions unless the text makes it quite clear that a Land Rover is involved. This research has led to very controllable use of effects in Schools Broadcasting programmes and identifying text being incorporated.

The general research into the Schools Broadcasting Service concerned itself mainly with the structure and organization of the Service and has been used as supporting evidence to help bring about changes and development in the Services itself.

In addition to these specific research projects, fairly systematic evaluation has been carried out for a number of years by users and spasmodic testing and evaluation of new materials is carried out by producers.

The evaluation by users is done by completing simple printed questionnaires, which are then sent to the Schools Broadcasting Service at the end of each term. To keep the returns to manageable proportions Primary School Inspectors in the 41 Districts of

Kenya and Provincial Secondary Inspectors in the 6 Provinces are asked to send the questionnaires to a 5 per cent sample of their schools and to organize the collection of them at the end of each term. In the past these returns were passed on to the relevant programme producer for study and necessary action. In practice this usually meant a brief perusal and some stored up impressions to be borne in mind for future productions. These returns are now being handled by the Research Officer who will analyse the criticisms and comments which will be discussed at staff meetings before being passed over to producers for action. Producers also carry out testing exercises on sample programmes for new series and whenever time allows they go out to distant areas to evaluate programmes off-air. These trips are of dubious value because evaluation of programmes and their utilization tend to become confused and often the evaluation is of the system into which we are feeding, as much as of the programmes.

Phase 1 of the programme which the Research Officer has been given is, as already stated, to collect and analyse evidence about the effectiveness of the existing Schools Broadcasting Service and about the factors which affect this effectiveness. He started by analysing material already collected by the methods outlined above and prepared a schedule of visits to organizations which could provide information and data to fill in the gaps and to up-date existing information, and a schedule of visits to schools to evaluate programmes and to obtain teachers' reactions to the programmes offered to them.

The organizations which have considerable influence on the effectiveness of radio programmes for schools and the ways in which they can or should assist the Schools Broadcasting Services are as follows:

(a) *The Ministry of Education* staffing and equipping the Service.

(b) *The Inspectorate* (*Central, Provincial Secondary and Primary*) assistance in the promotion of the materials provided for schools. Assistance in the scripting of programmes. Assistance in the fostering of proper utilization of material and the evaluation of programmes.

(c) *The Kenya Institute of Education* involvement of Schools Broadcasting in the planning and development of new curriculum material and the use of radio in course structures and in promoting curricula and methodological innovation.

(d) *The Kenya Schools Equipment Scheme* prompt provision of Schools Broadcasting sale materials, radios and tape recorders to schools.

(e) *The Voice of Kenya* provision of airtime and studio facilities. Improvement of reception. Technical advice on radios and tape recorders for schools.

(f) *District Education Officers (and their Divisional Education Officers)* prompt supply of teachers' notes, timetables and other free materials to schools.

(g) *Teachers' Colleges* instruction of student teachers in the use of schools broadcasts.

Research in the future

The research which the internal research team will carry out will be largely utilization based. It will concern itself primarily with identifying and suggesting action on such things as reception, distribution of materials, timetabling, use of taping services, language, pace, content, and format of programmes, teachers need for assistance in subject areas, type and amount of support materials required, new educational areas in which media materials would be useful and so on. This sort of information is vital to the effectiveness of the organization.

When internal research and evaluation projects have been carried out and the results analysed and prepared as evidence with suggested action to be taken, the Research Officer will submit his report to the Head of Schools Broadcasting and preliminary discussion will take place between them. The officer whose section will be responsible for taking any agreed action will then be brought in and the necessity for and feasibility of the suggested action considered. When administrative or organizational action is involved, it will be taken as a result of agreement at this stage. If, however, the suggested action involves professional considerations either of an educational nature, a broadcasting nature, or both, further discussion will be necessary with Chief Inspector of Schools and/or the Voice of Kenya and with the producers. However, the Research Officer will be fully

involved in the decision-making process. He will have gathered the evidence and interpreted it into recommended courses of action and will be expected to justify his recommendations in order for decisions to be based on them.

The Schools Broadcasting Service has no specific funds set aside for research and evaluation. These internal activities are supported as part of the overall function of the Service and are at present on a limited scale. The proposed Educational Media Service will have a Research Unit which will be required to produce detailed project plans and which will probably have its own operations budget.

In a sophisticated society people are receiving messages all the time from newspapers, magazines, books, friends, the family, teachers, general radio and television and so on. This makes it impossible to crystallize out the effects of messages received from specific sources such as educational radio and television. In less sophisticated societies there are fewer message sources and in particular very few sources of educational messages and it is possible to some extent to discover the effects of specific educational messages if the proper control situations are set up. Little has been done in Kenya in this field, and in addition to the utilization-based studies, more sophisticated research is required into the very reasons for the existence of the Schools Broadcasting Service. What real impact do radio programmes have in the Kenya context, on the educative process? How effectively does radio import knowledge, affect attitudes and foster innovative educational practice? One small research project concerned with attitude changing has been carried out, but a comprehensive project to determine the real effectiveness and the cost effectiveness of radio is required. Such a project should be carried out independently of the Schools Broadcasting organization which obviously has subjective opinions as to its own worth.

The Bureau of Educational Research of the University of Nairobi is interested in such research projects and discussions are going on at present on the possibility of mounting an initial selective project. In such external research, projects should be commissioned periodically as necessary and funded separately either directly by the

Ministry of Education or some external source. It would be wrong to expect the Service itself to set money aside from its own research budget for independent research activities, as paying the piper might affect the tune. Indeed the initiative for setting up such projects should come from the Ministry of Education rather than the Service, as part of its efforts to ensure the most effective use of education funds.

External research results would be submitted to the organization commissioning them. The reports might be discussed between the researchers and the responsible officials and the Head of the Broadcasting Service might be brought into these discussions, but the researcher would not be further involved in decisions as to the action to be taken.

Research and evaluation in Kenya in the field of educational radio and television has been spasmodic, but attention is now being given to this vital area. Both internal and external projects are being set up, and the internal project has already begun to produce evidence which suggests that major shifts in emphasis in our programming, in the provision of support materials and possibly in our target audiences will be necessary. We are working in an attitude changing medium and we must ourselves be willing to change our attitudes when evidence shows that change is necessary.

PAPER NO 49: HOW EVALUATION AND RESEARCH HAVE HELPED THE MEXICAN TELESECUNDARIA

Antonio Noguez, Dirección General de Educación Audiovisual, Mexico.

In 1950, 42 per cent of the total Mexican population lived in urban areas and 58 per cent in rural ones. By 1970 the figures had directly reversed; one can see that the trend of rural people is to immigrate to big cities where they find better employment opportunities.

However, there are 83,705 towns in Mexico with a population of fewer than 500 inhabitants. This fact creates a problem for the government which has to provide education for all the boys and girls living in the rural areas, and the problem is greater due to the scattered location of the small towns. This was the reason for starting, in 1966, a project called Telesecundaria, in which the rural communities had to provide the essential school facilities, and the Ministry of Public Education was in charge of broadcasting televised secondary school lessons and hired primary school teachers who acted as classroom co-ordinators.

The Dirección General de Educación Audiovisual (DGEAV), a bureau of the Ministry of Public Education, was placed in charge of the Telesecundaria project. Up to the present school year (1975–6), there have been 49,000 graduates and the enrolment for this year in the three grades is 41,000 pupils spread throughout 1,600 televised classrooms in 16 states and the Federal District. Telesecundaria covers an area which approximates that of England and Scotland combined and the lessons are broadcast through channel 5, a commercially-owned station, and Television Cultural de México (TCM), a government network with several relay stations in the Republic.

The closed-circuit experience

In 1966, it was decided to stage a controlled experiment with the Telesecundaria to obtain enough information to facilitate the broadcasting phase.

On 5 September, four classes began to watch the television lessons; three of them had a teacher to guide the learning process and to control attendance and discipline, while the other, a class of adults, worked by itself without a teacher.

A viewing chamber allowed observation without disturbing the classroom activities. There were evaluators for each of the ten subject matters of the secondary school curriculum who rendered valuable information to television teachers, producers and other persons involved in the technical and pedagogical control of the Telesecundaria.

A few months after the initiation of the closed-circuit experiment the class of adults had to be suspended due to the high number of drop-outs and to the general feeling that a teacher was needed to co-ordinate the classroom activities and to reinforce learning.

All the students were submitted to a medical examination which revealed that

58 per cent of the pupils were healthy and 42 per cent had problems such as astigmatism, miopia, conjunctivitis, etc. At the end of the school year the students were re-examined and it was determined that constant viewing of television in the morning was not harmful to their health.

Psychological tests were given to the pupils for the purpose of accumulating data pertaining to their interests, personality and other factors affecting their achievement.

In spite of the fact that television teachers had received an orientation course on television production, studio management and selection and use of visuals, it was necessary to know how this theory was working in the actual presentation of lessons. There were also certain aspects to observe such as:

(a) What visual aids were more effective?
(b) What was the pupils' attention span?
(c) Was the pupils' participation in the studio a help or a deterrent to the job of television teachers?
(d) What was the real value of work books and study guides in the pupils' achievement and to what extent did they help the co-ordinator's job?
(e) What were the main problems of producing six 30-minute lessons every day, having only one small studio and limited production facilities?

Some initial problems

The educational programmes were experimented with over a period of three years. During the initial year the first grade lessons were channeled through closed circuit and evaluated. In the second year, the lessons for first grade pupils were broadcast on channel 5 while second grade programmes were produced for closed circuit, and so on.

Unfortunately, the observation centre was housed at a considerable distance from the production centre, so feedback was given in printed forms and the television teachers and evaluators had little or no opportunity for face-to-face discussions.

After several months of systematic evaluation, there was some resentment on the part of the television teachers when they received the evaluation forms as they had no opportunity for rebuttal. On the other hand, when the television teachers did not pay attention to some of the evaluators' observations, the latter felt frustrated and their attitude towards the lessons was hyper-critical. Under these circumstances the feedback was not always reliable. As soon as the dialogue between television teachers and evaluators was established, the feedback was improved.

Results of the observations

As educational television was a new activity in the DGEAV, new personnel had to be trained, both presenters and staff. The staff members were recruited from the commercial stations but unfortunately the salaries in educational television are low and the best people did not come. These cameramen, floor managers, switchers and camera directors had been accustomed to the patterns of commercial production, so the reports from the evaluation department helped to establish a definite criteria for educational television production.

1 There must be enough time to read the captions shown in the lessons.
2 The production staff should take into consideration that our educational messages are received in classrooms with 25 or 30 pupils, so we have to be very careful about the number of elements composing each image, the size of the letters, the composition, etc.
3 The six pupils working with the television teachers in the studio were a valuable help in setting the pace of the lesson and they were especially needed in English, Physical Education and Music, since they performed certain actions.

Classroom activities

The observation of the activities performed by the three pioneer coordinators provided a number of ideas about the job to be performed by their future colleagues. On one hand, these elementary school teachers faced the problem of learning the information given on television and the guiding of pupils' activities for 20 minutes after each televised lesson. The following year the television lessons were reduced to 20 minutes and the follow-up period was extended to 30 minutes. All the information gathered about the coordinator's activities helped the authorities to have a better idea of the orientation courses to be given to 500 teachers enrolled in the first course for Telesecundaria coordinators.

E

(Only 304 were chosen.) Photographs, slides, films and other visual aids were prepared during the closed-circuit phase and used later in the courses for new classroom coordinators.

Television teachers

Teachers have always had the desire 'to see ourselves as the pupils see us'. Video taping has now given us this possibility.

The Telesecundaria TV teachers could observe their teaching behaviour on video tape, although this was not possible very often since most of the lessons were 'live' transmissions.

The feedback sent to TV teachers covered the following aspects:

(i)   Poise in front of the cameras.
(ii) Gestures and good or bad speech habits.
(iii) Grammar failures.

At the beginning of Telesecundaria, TV teachers used the 'teleprompter', a small device with a small screen on which the script is shown to the teacher. The pupils did not like the way some of the presenters stared at the cameras as if they were hypnotized, so very soon this device was discarded as teachers learned to talk to the cameras without reading the script.

Printed materials

The classroom coordinator and the pupils had a calendar of transmissions and a study guide was a very valuable aid to recall the topics and orient the follow-up work.

There were no big corrections to the printed materials but in some subjects the content was shortened and the use of more illustrations was encouraged.

Pupils' achievement

In order to obtain information about the partial achievement, monthly exams were given to the pupils. The results at the end of the first semester were the following:

Mathematics 34% passed the examinations
Spanish   77% passed the examinations
Geography   80% passed the examinations
History   67% passed the examinations
Biology   67% passed the examinations
English   39% passed the examinations

These figures point out that Mathematics and English should be reoriented in terms of presentation, follow-up work in the classroom and variety of written exercises.

Evaluation forms

From the beginning of the closed-circuit phase it was necessary to design an evaluation form containing 6 main aspects and 26 variables.

In order to improve the quality of the feedback, the evaluation forms became more detailed and complex. The one used three years later contained 5 aspects but 57 variables. Soon, the evaluators felt they could not manipulate such complicated reports. At present we work with an evaluation form having only 3 aspects and 18 variables.

Direct feedback: pupils-television teachers

In order to provide direct feedback to TV teachers and producers, a confrontation was arranged at which pupils and coordinators had the opportunity to express freely their opinions about the programmes. Unfortunately this meeting was not very successful because there was no chairman to handle such a difficult situation and the pupils had no mature criteria from which the television teachers 'were going to be condemned by their faults'. No other meeting of this sort took place again. Instead the TV teachers visited the classrooms in the evaluation center from time to time to gain direct information from the pupils and coordinator.

Some results of the first year

1 It is absolutely essential that every classroom in the Telesecundaria project has a coordinator to guide the learning process.
2 The classroom coordinator's role is different from the role of the elementary or secondary school teacher.
3 Pupils in Telesecundaria made exam scores similar to their counterparts in the conventional system. From 52 pupils in the closed-circuit experiment, 40 passed all the examinations, 10 failed in one or two subjects and 2 failed in more than three.
4 There must be a very careful selection and training of future classroom coordinators to assure the success in Telesecundaria.
5 The technical problems related to

transmission should be solved if the broadcasting phase was to start in 1968.

6 The official secondary school curriculum should be adapted to the specific circumstances of Telesecundaria, but without changing the general objectives of this school level.

The orientation course for new coordinators

All the evaluation activities of the closed-circuit experiment formed the base for organizing the first course planned to orient and prepare the primary school teachers for their job in the TV classrooms. 304 teachers were selected among 500 who followed the short course given in three weeks in October 1967.

The subject matters included were:

(a) Organizing the teleaulas (TV classrooms) in the communities.
(b) Classroom learning activities.
(c) Adolescent psychology.
(d) Basic concepts of handling and maintenance of TV receivers.

Besides the theoretical formation, it was decided to broadcast twenty special programmes on Saturday to reinforce the topics learned in the three-week course.

Two more courses were held the following two years on the same subjects but with different contents.

Evaluation in the broadcasting phase

It was clear that the closed-circuit work was over and we needed more representative evaluation data on the main aspects of Telesecundaria, so it was decided to gather the information from the TV classrooms established in the Federal District (Mexico City and its environments).

The staff of twelve evaluators was placed under the supervision of the Technical Department of DGEAV and a plan was established for periodical and systematic visits. The job was concentrated in the Federal District due to lack of personnel in the provinces. With this scheme, feedback was gathered from about 150 TV classrooms in the urban and suburban areas.

There is now a closer relationship between evaluators and television teachers and producers since the evaluation offices are located in the building where all Telesecundaria work takes place. The real limits on time and action of TV teachers were more clear to evaluators after a short course (given in the summer of 1972), wherein they had to prepare and present short programmes. They had the opportunity to act as floor managers, cameramen and presenters in order to make them aware of the different problems a TV teacher has to go through. All the evaluators agreed that this kind of course should have been given long before. Our current evaluation reports include new terminology such as 'fast panning', 'good medium shot', 'lack of head room', etc.

The Stanford-DGEAV evaluation

In 1972, members of the evaluation department of DGEAV and some specialists of the Institute for Communication Research at Stanford University conducted an evaluation for one year. The evaluation was performed in the states of México, Morelos and Hudalgo as well as the Federal District and the following results were obtained:

1 Telesecundaria's components are substantially less costly than those of the conventional system ($150 US dollars per pupil per year against $200). Telesecundaria was about 25 per cent less expensive than the direct teaching system.

2 In the tests of comparative achievement the result was NSD (no significant difference) since pupils in both systems had similar scores. The tests were carried out in Mathematics and Spanish with a sample of third grade students.

3 The study on teacher behaviour in the classroom showed that in Telesecundaria as well as the conventional system there was a need to improve teaching attitudes as both coordinators and classroom teachers talked too much and used almost no visual aids, giving little opportunity for pupils to participate.

4 A small sample, 777, of Telesecundaria graduates was examined through a survey of 39 coordinators with these results:
—44 per cent of the 1972 graduates had continued their education,
—29 per cent were employed,
—27 per cent were unemployed or could not be traced.

This survey was carried out by mail and we received only about 10 per cent of the questionnaires sent to the coordinators.

Use and value of the Stanford-DGEAV final report

Since the beginning of the Telesecundaria the coordinators felt they were not properly located in the educational bureaucratic ranks and labor union of teachers, because they were previously working in elementary schools but knew they were doing the job of secondary school teachers.

Several times they had officially asked the educational authorities to create a new and definite job classification for them. The Stanford report about the pupils' achievement and the figures about cost per pupil per year helped to convince the authorities to set aside a special budget beginning in 1974, thus increasing the coordinators' salaries and placing them under the direct administrative control of DGEAV.

The facts and figures of the report have also convinced some of the state educational authorities to incorporate Telesecundaria in the state system.

For these new states, Professor José Angel Hermida, current Director General of DGEAV and Professor Emma López, Head of Telesecundaria, have created radical changes in the administrative policy. The state educational authorities must now take the responsibility for the construction of building as well as the teachers' salaries and the granting of diplomas to pupils.

Another positive contribution of the Stanford report was the evidence concerning the coordinator's teaching behaviour, which has been considered in the preparation of the three year multi-media course for coordinators. This course will comprise summer sessions, use of textbooks and other printed materials, and TV lessons which will train the coordinators in the new procedures, methodology and learning concepts established by the Educational Reform. The coordinators must deal with the new approach to learning in which the teacher guides the learning process by encouraging greater pupil participation.

In addition, there has been a change on the part of those national or international institutions reading the Stanford report. This is due to the fact that it was performed by a wellknown international research center working in conjunction with a Mexican bureau.

Final comments and conclusions

1 Evaluation of the Mexican Telesecundaria has played an important role in the making of procedural decisions, especially at the beginning of the pro-project in its closed-circuit phase.

2 As a result of the evaluation carried out in 1972 with the technical aid of Stanford's Institute for Communication Research, the educational authorities see the results in a more serious light.

3 Surveys carried out by mail should be preceded by a thorough explanation and motivational sessions in order to convince the participants of the importance of the final results. Classroom teachers tend to underestimate the real value of their opinions.

4 If the feedback gathered in the evaluation is not taken into consideration in changing the presentation of TV lessons, there is a feeling of frustration on the evaluator's side, so there must be a close contact between TV teachers and evaluators, bearing in mind that evaluation is a way to determine whether or not we are achieving the educational objectives.

5 Evaluation must respond to the concerns of the decision-makers so the focus of evaluation has to be identified by the authorities.

6 Evaluation must respond to the different needs of the project and it must change according to the new structures and objectives set by educational policy.

PAPER NO 2: UTILIZATION OF SCHOOL PROGRAMMES IN SWEDEN*

Ingrid Aman, Education Department, Sveriges Radio, Sweden.

With a certain regularity the research group of the Educational Programme Department measure to what extent radio and TV are used in schools. Data for the research project reported on here were collected in

---

* Author's summary of full paper submitted to the Conference.

the spring of 1975 by means of a postal inquiry, sent out to a simple random sample of teachers on the intermediate level (grades 4–6) and the upper level (grades 7–9) of the compulsory school.

It turned out that 91 per cent of the intermediate-level teachers and 59 per cent of the upper-level teachers declared that they had used one or more of the school programmes in the autumn term of 1974. By and large, those utilization figures are of the same order of a frequency count in 1970.

Particularly among the upper-level teachers we find great differences in the utilization of programmes between different school subjects. Thus, where foreign languages—English, German, and French—are concerned, between 80 per cent and 95 per cent of the teachers had used some school programmes in their teaching. Among teachers of Swedish and technology the corresponding figure was 60 per cent, while it was lower for teachers of social science and natural science.

During the term in question the intermediate-level teachers of the sample had, on an average, utilized some 10 programme series, i.e. between 30 and 40 radio programmes and some 5 TV programmes. Corresponding figures for the upper level were generally lower and varied between different school subjects, due to—among other things—differences in the output.

A comparison between different types of population districts showed that programme utilization was lowest in large cities.

It turned out that nearly all teachers had access to a sound-tape recorder in their teaching. School-radio programmes were listened to almost solely on tape recorders. The majority of teachers also had access to a black-and-white TV receiver in their teaching, and 18 per cent of the intermediate-level teachers and 64 per cent of the upper-level teachers had facilities to play back recordings of TV programmes. Of the teachers who had used TV programmes during the term in question, 84 per cent of the intermediate level teachers and 12 per cent of the upper-level teachers had resorted to only 'direct watching'. (We use the terms direct watching, watching at the moment of broadcasting, and indirect watching, watching recordings of the broadcasts.) On the upper-level no less than 80 per cent had used only recordings of TV-programmes and not watched direct at all.

PAPER NO 26: MONITORING, RESEARCH, PLANNING AND DECISION-MAKING IN SCHOOL BROADCASTING

A. Jamieson and C. Stannard, School Broadcasting Council for the United Kingdom.

The organization of policy-making

The provision of BBC broadcasts for schools follows a long and complex process of educational planning involving consultation with a wide range of advisory bodies and professional people. Basically, the educational aims and policy for school broadcasting are formulated under the aegis of the School Broadcasting Council for the United Kingdom (SBC). The Council is composed of people drawn from a wide area of educational knowledge and experience, including representatives from professional teacher organizations, local education authorities, colleges of education, universities, and the Department of Education and Science. These Councils meet regularly to review policy for educational broadcasting. The School Broadcasting Council is assisted by Programme Committees, each with an age group responsibility (up to 9, 8–9 to 12–13, and 12–13 to 18). These committees authorize fieldwork inquiries and consultations to investigate current educational developments, and advise the Council and the officers on possible BBC initiatives to meet them. Proposals for new series are carefully considered and agreed by the committees, which also review the effectiveness of current series and recommend changes as they think necessary.

The BBC has a team of professional officers, led by the Education Secretary. Their duties are to assess the changing patterns of organizational and curriculum change in schools and colleges and to advise the Council and the BBC on the likely effects of these developments upon educational broadcasting. The central SBC staff are responsible for directing research, coordinating publicity and other organizational matters. The divisional Education Officers (based in different parts of the country) visit schools and colleges to assess the effectiveness of broadcasts, to provide information about the schools' needs, and to maintain the important functions of liaison and advice between the Council and classroom.

The BBC Broadcasting Departments—School Radio and School Television, and the departments in the national regions—are responsible for acting upon the educational policy established by the Council. The Departments draw up and submit programme proposals and initiatives, and prepare and make programmes. In addition, they are responsible for the provision of accompanying publications — teachers' notes, pupils' pamphlets, booklets, filmstrips and other supporting materials. There are also throughout the UK some twenty local radio stations with an education producer responsible for the provision of local educational programmes, produced in cooperation with groups of local teachers. The great majority of ideas for programmes arise within the production departments, whose staff also have close links with schools and colleges and a wide range of consultants. The great strength of BBC schools broadcasting is founded on the close partnership that exists between the School Broadcasting Council and its staff, and the educational and technical skills of producers.

Research within the SBC

(a) *The Research Section* The Research Section of the SBC makes annual surveys of the use of broadcasts in over 3,000 schools (primary and secondary) and further education colleges. This information is collected into the annual *Survey of Listening and Viewing*. The annual survey provides audience figures for every BBC series (and some Independent Television (ITV) series) and provides information on equipment usage.

In addition, the Research Section also carries out a number of detailed surveys (about six each year) into individual series, different curriculum areas, or particular types of equipment. These surveys are arranged by means of postal questionnaires and are completed by headteachers, heads of departments, or class teachers. The questions indicate the age and ability of pupils using the series; the context of use; whether broadcasts are used 'live' or recorded; the value of the accompanying publications, and other aspects of the series that are of particular concern to the School Broadcasting Council and the BBC. The views of teachers are thus directly canvassed. Some of the postal enquiries are supplemented by visits from Education Officers to other user schools. The Education Officers report separately on the subject of the inquiry, and thus provide valuable additional evidence.

From 1975 it is intended that the inquiries carried out by the Research Section will delve more deeply into curriculum patterns and teachers' needs. Two major investigations are currently being mounted. A questionnaire on the teaching of English in primary schools is being distributed to a sample of 500 schools. This inquiry seeks to elicit the extent to which broadcasts are used in relation to English work in the classroom. The aspects of English teaching that are being investigated are pre-reading and reading skills, aural and visual discrimination, other work in language associated with broadcasts, and literature.

This inquiry, made more urgent by the recommendations of the Bullock Committee[1], is intended to provide evidence to assist the Council and the BBC in processing, developing and planning policy. The inquiry is supported by school visits and programme assessments carried out by a team of Education Officers working in the schools.

A second major inquiry, based on a questionnaire and visits to schools by Education Officers, deals with a television History series for the 13 to 16 age group. The inquiry aims to discover the courses and methods that are thought to be appropriate by teachers for this age group, and seeks advice on the form and content of programmes that would supplement these courses.

(b) *Education Officers* The Education Officers of the SBC carry out investigations in the field, and these systematic reviews of the use of programmes in schools are considered to be important features of research work. Broadcasts are reported on in regular submissions of evidence which often relate to particular questions set by the programme planners, and this evidence is analysed to provide detailed digests of teacher opinion on current series.[2]

This process of observation and report is valuable for the current series of programmes, and also assists departments in planning or modifying programmes. Education Officers therefore engage in a consultancy function by arranging meetings with teachers, advisers and other educationalists, to assess and report on curriculum change and development.

(c) *Publications* Another aspect of the BBC operation which is monitored is the provision of publications. The BBC provides, at the request of the Council, a wide range of teacher's notes, pupil's pamphlets, filmstrips and other publications to accompany the 130 or more series. Statistics of sales are obtained and this information is regularly provided for the Council.

(d) *Producer's research* Research and evaluation are not confined to the staff of the SBC. Each series has a budget allocated to it. This budget is related to direct costs of production, and if any research is to be attempted it is paid for out of the programme budget. In some cases this research may include the piloting of programmes, consultation with an educationalist, or the establishment of a reporting panel of teachers. In periods of economic restraint, the research element may be squeezed because production costs absorb the majority of the budget. Producers also visit schools to assess the effectiveness of broadcasts and keep in touch with curriculum development projects.

(e) *Classroom interaction observation* Recently, the input/outcome feature of educational research has been questioned as a suitable mode of inquiry. Researchers are increasingly turning to the study of what goes on in the classroom, and this process has been described as 'classroom interaction observation'. The emphasis has moved from externally-based, centrally-directed research projects to the impact of projects on teachers and learners. For the BBC, this kind of inquiry has been at the core of the work of Education Officers and it is interesting to note the switch to closer classroom study of the interaction of materials/teachers/learners.

(f) *External research* In the past, the BBC commissioned some research and investigatory projects by individuals and groups who operated outside the BBC and the SBC. In 1972–3, G. S. Hayter wrote a report[3] for the BBC and the Independent Television Authority (now the Independent Broadcasting Authority) into the effects and influence of broadcasts in schools and into the levels and use of equipment. A feature of the inquiry was the way in which teachers assisted in the process of assessing educational gains from the planned operation of broadcasts. Earlier, in 1969, a detailed feasibility study on the education of deprived children in relation to audio-visual materials was commissioned jointly by NCET (the National Council for Educational Technology) and the SBC.[4]

There have also been independent inquiries into (among other items) sex education in the primary school in relation to radio-vision and television series on sex education; the use and value of the *Look and Read* series; and the use of a geography series on the USA. On occasions support has been provided by the BBC to allow selected university and college lecturers to follow-up and report on particular aspects of the educational output. For instance, in the summer term of 1975 an inquiry was mounted and a report written on *Nursery-age children and broadcasts*, which referred particularly to two series, *Playtime* and *You and Me*.

Evaluation and independent research

In recent years a number of different groups and bodies that have offered evidence to the Annan Committee have drawn attention to the need for research into educational broadcasting. In addition, there was a specific recommendation in the Bullock Report[1] suggesting a similar objective: 'Ideally, what is required is the involvement of qualified educational research teams, so that evaluation can be linked closely to production'. This suggestion neatly phrases the SBC, BBC objectives, but funds to finance research have not been as easy to obtain as advice on how to mount it.

Added point has been given to these suggestions in a book that links children's reactions to television with Piagetian theory.[5]

One of the assertions of Grant Noble is that the needs of children at various ages (but particularly those in the pre-operational stage of development) have been neglected by television producers. This view is questioned by SBC and BBC staff, but the findings of the research clearly have important implications for the conceptual levels of 5 to 8 year olds in relation to broadcast sequences, and underline the need for further investigation of these issues.

The drawbacks and problems of research

There are complex difficulties associated with research into broadcasting. The existing methods of research, of pre- and post-testing, of long-term (2 or 3 or more years) in which a research programme is carried through, are not always suitable instruments for broadcasting. The decision-making, consultancy and planning process is itself a complex one, and the products, the programmes, reflect a long process of planning within the production departments. An investigation of a science series might, for instance, take three years, during which the style and content of the programmes change, so that the lessons learned from the research might be of little value because the programme-makers have moved on to fresh objectives and new programme content. Long-term research, then, if applied to a particular current series or programme, would have limitations if the findings were to be applied to current series.

Another difficulty is linked to the product itself. The staff of the production departments absorb the advice that they are given from consultants, advisers, committees and the Council, and in the making of a particular programme they will be influenced by this advice and other suggestions from senior staff and colleagues. But committees of experts are notoriously ineffective in acts of creation. The form, structure and scope of a programme is the producer's responsibility and the creative activity of making a programme will not necessarily be a direct consequence of applied research findings, but rather an intuitive response expressed in words, music, drama and other artistic ingredients. This is not to say that research into particular programmes is not valuable, but its

application is not necessarily dynamic in the sense of an immediately recognizable influence.

Another problem is associated with the reception of broadcasts in schools, not only reception in the broadcasting sense, but reception by different teachers in widely differing classroom situations. This difficulty is revealed in the reports of Education Officers, who have attempted to analyse why a programme is suitable and successful in one classroom context, but is inadequate in another. The reason, more often than not, is dependent on the teacher's attitudes and involvement with the broadcast, which suggests that teachers' reactions, opinions and use of programmes should feature as a high priority in research.

Another problem associated with programme research is the range and speed of programme-making. Over 130 different BBC series for schools are transmitted each year with more than half new series or new programmes in existing series. It may be possible to operate this process alongside a research inquiry, to put the evaluation and planning process to the test, but the contemporaneity of the programme would be affected and this is one of broadcasting's advantages. However, with a series that is not immediately affected by day to day events, such as a series on reading, it should be possible to arrange this kind of inquiry.

An even more complex difficulty is associated with the components of a programme, and the effects upon children. A programme has several functions, and may stray into several subject areas (music, language, history, etc.). In addition, the broadcast is likely to have many effects at different affective and cognitive levels: it may deal with vocabulary, but also involve understanding and interpretation of a narrative, require the appreciation of music, and appeal to the visual or oral sense in an emotional manner: these elements are difficult to isolate and distinguish.

Faced with these problems, one should persist with the question: what are the purposes of research? If the inquiries are to have a direct and calculable influence on programmes or on the system of consultancy and evaluation applied to planning procedures, the objectives should be clarified, the impossible tasks rejected, and the more limited ones investigated.

54

Possible lines of research

The SBC and BBC are convinced that their methods of seeking out advice, defining policy and monitoring series are effective. However, what have been lacking in the past are independent surveys, by qualified educational research teams, into the effects of broadcasts on learners or teachers. Research of this nature could provide evidence in five major areas. The research in this field would indicate the pupils' gains in distinctive cognitive areas, or examine changes in attitudes and interests related to broadcasts, or examine particular techniques of presentation.

(a) *Knowledge, skills and interests*
(i)   increase in knowledge
(ii)   development of comprehension and understanding
(iii)   the learning or extension of a particular skill
(iv)   areas of pupils' interests
(v)   changes in pupils' attitudes and opinions.

(b) *Individual programme gains*
(i)   gains to pupils from individual series or programmes within series
(ii)   gains from individual items in a programme package
(iii)   the value of differing production methods
(iv)   the value and effects of techniques; visual discrimination; the optimum length of sequences; the range and depth of content in relation to pupils' ages and abilities.

(c) *Individual pupils' gains* Differences in knowledge, skills and ability between differing groups of pupils, differentiated by age, ability and maturity.

(d) *Utilization in schools* The value of varied approaches to the material broadcast: VCR/VTR; repeated transmissions and recordings, etc.; utilization in relation to classroom variables.

(e) *Teachers' attitudes*
(i)   What are the needs and objectives of teachers who use school broadcasts?
(ii)   How can these objectives best be met?
(iii)   In what ways are broadcasts integrated with school, class or individual work?
(iv)   What, in teachers' views, are the most effective programmes, and what are the most effective patterns of programme use?
(v)   What are the factors influencing teacher choice of programmes?
(vi)   What are the particular strengths and weaknesses seen by teachers in broadcasting?

Funding and organization

(a) *Funding* External funding has in the past been sought for research into school broadcasting from the Department of Education and Science, but without success. Fresh approaches to external bodies are to be made shortly. The allocation of finance for programme production is the responsibility of the Heads of Radio and Television (Schools) and, as earlier comments have made clear, research or consultation has to be met from within the budget allocated for a programme. In addition, the costs of programme-making are so high that the BBC may not always be able to respond to a request from the SBC to provide a series or a request based upon research findings.

(b) *Organization* Within the SBC, it is considered essential and necessary that fieldwork inquiries and reports and investigations carried out by the Research Section should be submitted to senior management within BBC and SBC, in order to guide the policy-making decisions arranged through the Council, and thus subsequently the production departments. This information, combined with the educational experience of staff and members of Council and its committees, provide the core of knowledge on which decision-making is based.

(c) *Application* No firm opinion can be held of the most effective methods of applying external research to schools' broadcasting within the BBC because so little operational research has been made available. Internal evidence (such as the Research Section's inquiries) are provided immediately for the benefit of BBC Production departments, to be added to the other criteria which guide producers when they plan series, and to senior management in the SBC and BBC to aid them in reviewing the educational policy on which series are based.

Conclusion

Clearly, external research would be of value to broadcasters. However, for reasons already given it is apparent that long-term evaluation of a series is difficult. The greatest immediate value to aid programme-makers would be inquiries into production techniques such as the visual and verbal impact, and their efficacy in relation to educational objectives. These enquiries, connected with discrete items and techniques, could be applied to series which deal with straightforward items of information or skills, rather than with other series that seek to arouse interest or appreciation. Certainly, as this paper would indicate, research into educational broadcasting is long overdue.

References

1 BULLOCK, Sir A., *A Language for Life*, London, HMSO, 1975.
2 McQUAIL, D. and BAILEY, K. V., *Research and School Broadcasting*, London, BBC, 1965.
3 HAYTER, C. G., *Using Broadcasts in Schools*, London, BBC, 1974.
4 BBC, *The Contribution which Audio-visual Materials Might Make to the Education of Young, Deprived Children*, London, BBC, 1969.
5 NOBLE, G., *Children in Front of a Small Screen*, London, Constable, 1975.

PAPER NO 53: THE FUNCTIONS OF EVALUATION IN COOPERATIVE PROJECTS: THE AIT EXPERIENCE

Saul Rockman, Director of Research, Agency for Instructional Television, Indiana, USA.

The agency

At a time when the cost of high quality instructional television almost always exceeds the money available, cooperative production and development have become a source of salvation. When several agencies pool their money and occasionally their production resources and talents as well, each agency is able to obtain a higher quality television series than it, alone, would have been able to develop and produce. Instructional series for elementary, secondary, and higher education have been produced through these cooperative arrangements, or 'consortia'.

Among the most successful consortia for the creation of instructional television series have been those managed by the Agency for Instructional Television (AIT), a non-profit, American-Canadian organization located in Bloomington, Indiana. One of AIT's major functions is the development of joint program projects involving state and provincial education agencies.

Over the past six years, AIT has successfully developed seven consortia. The number of participant members has ranged from thirteen to forty-two state and provincial educational agencies in the United States and Canada. The cost of the projects has been as high as $750,000; no direct federal aid has been sought or received for any of them. The instructional television series developed through AIT's consortia are widely broadcast and used by schools. One of these series, *Inside/Out*, received an Emmy as the best instructional series of 1974, the only time a series designed for in-school use has ever received this award. The subjects of the consortium projects, all for elementary school use (first through eighth years of school), have included art education, career awareness, metric education, and emotional health education. The success of these consortia has stimulated other instructional development and production agencies to form local, regional, and national cooperative projects with the hope of creating widely used and effective instructional television materials.

Although the activities of the Agency for Instructional Television may be unique, these activities can serve as process models for other cooperative projects. Before the function of evaluation within the consortium model can be discussed, however, I must briefly explain the role of AIT. The Agency for Instructional Television, through its development arm, of which research and evaluation is a part, serves essentially as an executive producer or a corporate project manager. AIT creates a prospectus for potential instructional television projects after lengthy consultations with educational agencies in the United States and Canada. AIT then seeks to fund the project through the state and provincial educational and television authorities. When eventual full funding seems attainable, a content design team develops a conceptual basis for each program in a series and suggestions for the print materials accompanying it. Then the creative talents of writers/producers/directors at each production site come into play. AIT does not have any production facilities of its own. It contracts with educational television agencies that have the required production capabilities. To reduce the time required to create television programs of the highest production quality, multiple production agencies are used. The projects are produced on film for television.

The AIT executive producer, accompanied by the project's content consultant, serves to unify the work of the various production agencies by frequent site visits. The content consultant has final approval rights on content matters, as does the AIT executive producer for production. During the development of a series, the members of the consortium gather several times to review the project and its products (television programs, teacher guides, in-service training materials, etc.) and to prepare for assimilation of the series into local schools.

That, in a nutshell, summarizes the AIT consortium process—consortium formation, design, production, assimilation.

Evaluation

Neither the development process nor its evaluation component emerged fully with the first consortium effort. Both have developed and matured over the past few years. I would like to discuss the evaluation process, as opposed to a specific project, a process that has not become static, but is still changing to meet the needs of each succeeding project.

Evaluation, of course, plays different roles in successive phases of a project. The central function of evaluation for AIT's consortium projects is to provide useful data to project personnel. Data about programs and their associated project components, based on feedback from the intended audience(s), are required to improve these instructional materials. The projects' evaluations have stressed preformative and formative activities; summative evaluation has been beyond the financial ability of AIT's consortia. Without extensive support from foundations or the Federal Government, it will probably

remain so. Nevertheless, much can be learned about the potential use of a series within the framework of the formative evaluation process.

Since the writing and production of a television series takes place in various parts of the United States and Canada, it makes little sense for the formative evaluation activities to be centered in Bloomington, Indiana, a non-representative university community. So AIT arranges for local evaluation consultants to work with each production agency. These local evaluators, primarily educators, have access to students and teachers and can respond quickly to evaluation requests of writers and producers. The local evaluation consultants are requested to help writers and producers at all stages of the development of programmes. In some cases, the program theme or concept is the focus of data collection; later, script outlines form the basis of questions. As scripts are completed, student reaction to dialogue and events is studied; rough-cuts of programs are screened for student analysis. The writers and producers themselves also meet with teachers and children during the production process. All these formative evaluation activities are conducted locally, and the local evaluation consultants report directly to the production personnel. Contact is often by telephone rather than in writing, so that one day's findings can generate new material for the next day. Rapid turnaround is a requirement; the evaluator is at the mercy of the production schedule, unable to delay it.

The success of the local evaluation process depends on the relationship established between the evaluator and the creative personnel. As long as the writers and producers themselves are willing to raise questions about what they are doing, and can consider alternatives to what they have created, the local evaluation process can be successful. However, the local evaluation consultants must remember that they are neither judges of the creative process nor advocates of a particular theme or story line. Rather, they are neutral, independent middlemen between the writer/producer and the intended audience.

Had the formative evaluation been composed solely of this local evaluation component, the learner verification process would have been satisfied for a consortium developed series.[1] Each programme in a series would have had, in one form or another, review and input from the intended audience. Modifications and improvements would have taken place as a result of student and teacher reactions to the program materials. Nevertheless, the process so far described is inadequate to serve the special needs of consortium projects.

Field tests

AIT initiates a field test of the programs immediately following the formative evaluation activities. The consortium agencies can volunteer to participate in these field tests. Still perceived as formative evaluation, this field testing permits programs that have been tested in segments to be examined as a whole and modified still further by audience reactions. In addition, it allows the consortium agencies to participate in the process of creating effective instructional materials. In cooperatively developed television projects, cooperation —the opportunity to participate—can be as important as the pooling of money.[2] In AIT's experience, involving eventual users of the project helps to create allies and supporters who will seek the most effective and extensive use of the instructional television programs.

Field testing is conducted with videotaped copies of the first answer prints of the programs. Changes in the program based on the field test data are expected and budgeted for. At each field test site, AIT trains observers to take the programs into classrooms and to collect data on:

1 Students' visual attention to the program

Based on the assumption that if students are not watching they may not be learning, attention may be a necessary though not sufficient condition for optimal learning. AIT has created a simple, almost foolproof method of gathering attention data, which can be explained in a single page of written instructions. In contrast to the equipment required by the CTW distractor approach,[3] the only technology required is a pencil and a watch with a second hand. Attention is measured in 10-second intervals by two observers stationed in the classroom. The data are then plotted in relation to program segments.

2 Students' comprehension of the program and their attitudes about the characters and concepts

Many of AIT's consortia have developed television series in the affective rather than the cognitive domain, making traditional cognitive gain scores irrelevant in measuring the objectives of the programs. In seeking the impact of these programs an examination of comprehensibility is an appropriate first step. Adults, no matter how sophisticated and sensitive they are to the ways of children, are often unable to predict the extent to which children perceive, understand and remember television material.[4] Friedlander and Whetstone report[5] that less than one-half of the material in an informational program for children was comprehended by a sample of the audience. Yet most evaluations conducted on instructional television programs still seek changes in behaviour and/or performance without knowing whether the audience has understood the message. In AIT's evaluation, a series of program-specific questionnaires are used to solicit information on: the comprehensibility of the program theme and concept, perceptions of the major characters, attitude towards the concept and characters, appeal of program segments, salience of and identification with the program events, comprehensibility of language, filmic techniques, and plot. Questionnaires are cross-validated by interviews with samples of the audience.

3 The classroom discussion process that follows the viewing of programs

In many of the AIT cooperatively developed series, the objective of the lesson is not met by the television program alone. By design, post-viewing classroom discussions are necessary to clarify, focus and extend the instruction. The classroom discussion process allows observers to note the understandings and misunderstandings of both students and teachers. Close analysis of the process can help generate a model for in-service training of teachers to deal with unfamiliar subject matter, such as affective health information. It can assist in the development of teacher guides to accompany the series. AIT has developed its own classroom observation system, which requires about three hours of training to obtain 80 per cent or better inter-coder agreement. It examines the degree to which students and teachers focus on the program itself or generalize about their own feelings or actions in analogous situations. It permits observers to note the amount of teacher initiation required to maintain the discussion and the degree to which the audience deals with the decision-making process, a desired outcome. Data gathered by systematic observation are validated by a second observer who keeps a narrative account of the same post-viewing discussion.

4 Teachers' opinion and attitudes about each program and about the concept of the series

In the traditional educational setting, teachers serve as the gate-keepers of instructional materials. Teachers determine whether or not the programs will eventually be used in the classroom. Given the disruption of field testing, it is a wonder that teachers find any of the new materials worthwhile. Nevertheless, questionnaires are provided to each teacher participating in field testing. Likert-type and multiple-choice items are used to keep teacher resistance to a minimum. Teachers' guides are also 'tried out' in sample classrooms and with teacher panels.

Summary

In summary, the functions of evaluation for consortium projects fall within the framework of formative evaluation and program revision based on audience reactions and performance. These program development functions serve the consortium projects well, as the finished products attest. However, each consortium project also seeks participation by its membership, and participation extends the functions of the formative evaluation process. The willingness of consortium agencies to volunteer their time, personnel, and often financial support to the evaluation process suggests strong advantages to the participants.

First, participation in the consortium process is often its own reward. Active involvement gives a sense of ownership and a feeling of accountability for the dollars spent. Second, participation in the field test permits the consortium agency to have television materials that are not yet available to anyone else. These programs

are available for an agency's own 'political' and instructional purposes to show administrators, parent groups, and others. A third advantage lies in the opportunity to work with teachers and learn of their reactions prior to the actual introduction of a series. Based on this information, utilization specialists can begin working early to implement the series' acceptance into the educational system. Often teachers who field test materials become advocates of the programs and help generate support for the new project. Another advantage of participation is that professionals in a state or provincial education agency who do not normally consider television useful in schools can be involved in the field testing and converted to become proponents of the series and committed to its use. A fifth benefit of participation in field testing is that an agency's own personnel can be trained in evaluation techniques which may be useful to their own organization. There are also requirements and obligations for agencies participating in the evaluation process. Time and personnel must be set aside, classrooms must be obtained, facilities, equipment, and opportunities for training must be arranged, and finally data must be collected.

When completed, however, field testing results in a committed population of specialists willing to extend themselves to introduce the new television series, sufficiently experienced with it to speak knowledgeably, and frequently able to adapt evaluation procedures to locally produced materials in the future.

In addition, participation by consortium agencies in field testing also provides benefits for AIT and the formative evaluation process. There is a free and available subject pool from which classrooms can be drawn for reviewing and reacting to new television programs. In consortium projects, national and even international sampling is possible. Thirdly, evaluators and testers are provided at no cost by consortium agencies. The most important benefit to AIT is that participation results in commitment to the television series and its effective classroom use.

The evaluation process in cooperatively developed projects requires belief in people as well as in the process itself. AIT's evaluation model has worked successfully and may be applicable for other agencies and other projects. Evaluation is but a part of the cooperative development process and plays a positive role as long as the co-operative process is working well. If there is give-and-take between participants and management, as well as between evaluators and producers, then the process can have beneficial results for all.

References

1 KOMOSKI, K., *Pilot Guidelines for Improving Instructional Materials Through the Process of Learner Verification and Revision*, New York, EPIE Institute, 1975.

2 ROCKMAN, S., *School Television is Alive and Well*, Palo Alto, California, Aspen Institute (in press).

3 PALMER, E. L., *A Comparative Study of Current Educational Television Programs for Preschool Children*, Final Report, Monmouth, Oregon, Oregon State University, 1969.

4 ROCKMAN, S., *Predicting Student Response*, Presentation to the Southern Educational Communications Association, Annual Meeting, Louisville, Kentucky, 14 May 1974.

5 FRIEDLANDER, B. Z. and WETSTONE, H., Suburban preschool children's comprehension of an age-appropriate informational television program. *Child Development*, Vol. 45, No 2, 1974.

STUDIES OF PARTICULAR PROJECTS

PAPER NO 9: TELEVISION EFFECTS
ON CANADIAN ARCTIC HIGH
SCHOOL STUDENTS: A CROSS-
CULTURAL COMPARISON

Gary O. Coldevin, Concordia University,
Montreal, Canada.

The development and application of satellite television transmission systems has provided a unique opportunity within North America to profit from what might be termed a 'second chance' to examine the effects of a highly developed medium injected into previously non-accessible areas. The ATS-6 (Application Technology Satellite) deployment for example permitted a variety of American studies to be undertaken in the Appalachian region, Rocky Mountain communities and remote Alaskan villages in addition to the major work presently underway in India (Satellite for Instructional Technology Experiment). While a substantial file of television 'effects' research has accumulated during the past twenty years, for the most part these studies have been confined to examination of an entrenched medium rather than a more rigorous stance from an established baseline, now made possible through satellite distribution. Notable departures are found in the Himmelweit (1958) and Schramm (1961) studies. However the populations sampled here were within well developed communication systems with a variety of media other than television competing for audience exposure. Television thus became a major competitive rather than unique medium in its information and entertainment functions. Even though similar situations may apply to any given region or population, the degree and type of competing media provide the major background criteria. For example, while many of the remote settlements in northern Canada have access to short wave radio signals, the quality of transmission is highly dependent upon ionospheric conditions with a sporadic reception strength prevailing at any given time. It is emphasized that radio is the only other medium directly relevant in this context since the majority of natives have limited access to the press. Within these circumstances, the immediacy effects of satellite transmitted television suggest a formidable break between comparative isolation and simultaneous participation in southern entertainment and information programming.

The satellite re-broadcast system in the Canadian Arctic may be contrasted with the American and Indian experiments in two primary ways:

1 The television programming is 'full service', that is to say, similar CBC service provided to southern Canadians (approximately 16 hours per day) is beamed directly to northern re-broadcast centres.

2 The service is permanent. When the present satellite (Anik I) life is terminated, a new satellite will be re-instated. The developmental effects of television are thus ascertainable in the Canadian situation as well as inter-sample comparisons between Arctic and southern Canadian populations.

Study setting and purpose

The present study was conducted in Frobisher Bay, a community of 2,500 permanent residents situated on the south-east portion of Baffin Island. The racial composition of the community is approximately 40 per cent Euro-Canadian and 60 per cent Eskimo (Inuit). The primary importance of the centre for this study is that Frobisher Bay has a regional high school servicing the Eastern Arctic and is the only community in the area to have access to satellite television. Television service was originally introduced through the facilities of the CBC Frontier Coverage Package, a four hour, 7.00 to 11.00 pm video tape local rebroadcast service. The Frontier Package, inaugurated during the winter of 1972, was subsequently replaced by the full service Anik I satellite broadcasts in March 1973. At the same time the study was undertaken (November 1974) the full service had been in operation for one and a half years in addition to the one year run of the Frontier Package. The data gathered here are part of a fuller project analyzing the impact of the Frontier Package on native heads of households and the developmental effects of television presently in progress.

The purpose of the study was to contrast and compare television effects across three distinct types of student groupings serviced by the high school, namely, Euro-Canadian (referred to as 'white' in the community), Inuit students resident in Frobisher Bay and Inuit students from the various isolated settlements in the Eastern Arctic. The data are compared on the two primary levels of cultural/racial origin (Euro-Canadian vs Inuit) and media background (Frobisher Bay vs settlements). Specifically the following dependent variables are assessed:

1 *Television indices*
(a) Availability
(b) Exposure levels and timings
(c) Most and least preferred programs
(d) Perceived primary language for northern broadcasting
(e) Projected situational utility role in terms of information/education and community programming

2 *Social/psychological indices*
(a) Travel aspirations
(b) Occupational aspirations
(c) Preferred employment roles

3 *National Unit information levels*

4 *International Issue identification and dominant sources*

5 *National Issue identification and dominant sources*

6 *Predominant leisure time activities*

Procedures
Questionnaire development
The final questionnaire was essentially composed of open-ended questions to allow maximum latitude for responses. When decision questions were elicited, the attributes for the orientation selected were also probed.

Within the television indices section, exposure levels and timings were extracted through the 'general estimate' method separately for both weekdays and weekends. For program preferences, respondents were asked to name and provide a rationale for the selection of their three most and least favourite programs. The perceived primary language for northern broadcasting was intended to assess differential native language attachments among Inuit groupings. Situational utility roles for television were probed through questions eliciting types of information/education programs useful for personal and peer group viewing and relevant content appropriate for community information requirements.

Social/psychological indices included travel aspiration locations, projections of preferred employment roles and concomitant preferred working locations (north vs south). National unit information levels were established through a series of eight questions concentrating on Canadian geography and political structures while international and national issue identification questions focussed on major problem areas. In assessing dominant sources separately for international and national cognitions, two types of measure were employed. In the first, respondents were asked to rate available community and school sources on a four-point Likert-type scale as to utility in answering the various questions. Secondly, the one most and least important source was elicited following the scale rating tasks. Finally, subjects were asked to indicate pursuits most engaged in when not working or studying as a measure of leisure time activities.

The samples
The complete sample consisted of 190 students, representing approximately 90 per cent of the total high school enrolment. Individual groups were split as follows: Euro-Canadian 70; Inuit-Frobisher Bay 70;

Inuit-Settlements 50. While the sampling ranged across all grade levels (7 through 12) the majority of subjects were clustered in 7 through 9 categories. Sex distribution was skewed toward males for both Frobisher Bay samples (averaging 60 per cent) with male/female equivalence for settlement students.

All Inuit students recorded speaking and understanding both English and Inutitut (Eskimo). However, the proportion of those reading Inutitut (Eskimo syllabary) was significantly higher for settlement natives (88 per cent as opposed to 69 per cent for Frobisher Bay natives). Reading levels also produced significant differences between Euro-Canadian and native samplings. The vast majority of Euro-Canadian reading levels were synonomous with grade levels while both Inuit samples were primarily in the 3 to 6 year categories. The relatively poor English reading levels among Inuit students has been attributed to a cultural evaluation of the utility of this skill within the immediate environment, an orientation in turn which is reflected in generally low motivation levels toward basic subject materials. It is anticipated that television in its present format will maintain or erode these reading levels further.

Statistical analyses

Two-tailed t-tests were employed for national unit information level comparisons with Chi-square contingency tables and Fisher Exact tests where appropriate generated for social/psychological variables and international and national issue identification comparisons. In all analyses significant differences were tested at the .05 level of confidence.

Results

Salient results arising from data analysis are summarized as follows:

1 The near saturation of television in the community was evident in 100 per cent availability in Euro-Canadian homes, 97 per cent in Frobisher Bay native homes and 98 per cent in accommodations provided to settlement students. The proportion of colour sets was appreciably higher for Euro-Canadian homes (69 per cent) as opposed to Frobisher Bay native domiciles (39 per cent).

2 Frobisher Bay residents registered higher average exposure levels per day for both weekdays (between 4 and 5 hours) and weekends (between 5 and 6 hours) than settlement students. Twenty per cent of both Frobisher Bay samples reported 'all day' viewing on weekends as opposed to 4 per cent of settlement students.

3 The primary areas of similarity between Euro-Canadian and Inuit samples were found in:

(a) the uniform rating of 'dramatic series' as the most preferred program category and 'public affairs and talk shows' as the least favoured category,
(b) the dominance of television as the major source for both international and national cognitions,
(c) the primacy of television viewing as the foremost leisure time activity.

The importance of the latter finding was reflected in the closing of the cinema (which offered new billings four times per week) some two months after the introduction of full service television. The supremacy of television as the salient information source for international and national dimensions is largely taken up at the expense of school sources.

4 Major differences between cultural groupings occurred in information levels of national geographic units and political structures, international and national issue identification, travel aspiration destinations, meaningful employment roles and projected employment locations. Within these measures, Euro-Canadians demonstrated significantly higher scores on all cognitive indices, were more international in desired travel destinations, more oriented toward professional occupational roles and more inclined to opt for southern Canada as a preferred working location.

5 Differences among Inuit samples are discernible throughout the majority of variables assessed with a marked tendency of settlement students toward more traditional or localized posturing. Noteworthy examples occur in positions taken toward the inclusion of the Eskimo language within the present television program scheduling, relevant topics for community information

F

programming, preferred travel destinations and the 'urban south' as a preferred working location. Cognitive levels toward both international and national dimensions are also lower among settlement natives than their Frobisher Bay counterparts.

6 Both Inuit groupings appear to have departed considerably from classic traditional stances and it is suggested that settlement natives may have only a short catch-up period before matching their 'television' counterparts more closely.

Discussion
The superiority of the Euro-Canadians on international and national cognition levels suggests that cultural background may be a critical factor in the televised information retention process. International and national news events appear to hold limited importance to native students within the immediate environment. Conversely, however, the attitudinal changes as reflected in virtually half of the native television sample's expressed desire to work in southern urban areas points out the need to prepare natives to realistically cope with the southern environment or to re-vitalize the importance of traditional patterns in the northern life style. The existing gap appears to be widening considerably as a consequence of television in the community.

In the present study we can conclude that fundamental attitudes have been appreciably altered among native students and that the changes are directly proportional to television exposure. We will further conclude that the process of change will continue unchecked given the present programming format. It would seem therefore that if a familiarity with the traditional Eskimo life style, value structure and language are to be forwarded to future generations, critical changes are requisite in both the television format and formal educational curricula. A quote from John Goodlad although in a different context, capsulizes succinctly the dilemma facing the Eskimo culture:

> On the one hand, a powerful medium (television) has caught the attention, indeed the very lives, of our children. But it lacks sufficient substance to nurture a civilization and appears to care not, despite its protestations, whether it uplifts or

debases. On the other hand, the only institution charged specifically with the performance of educational functions fails to grip a significant portion of its cliental. Unfulfilled educational promise lies between.

A judicious application of educational television would seem particularly warranted in the circumstances, one which attempts to bridge the gap between entertainment and purposive message design within the appropriate cultural milieu. Whether this can be accomplished given the 'southern entertainment' entrenchment in the community is debatable. The 'lessons' to developing countries at similar or projected stages of programming would appear to be significant.

PAPER NO 39: INSTRUCTIONAL TELEVISION IN EL SALVADOR'S EDUCATIONAL REFORM*

Mayo, J. K., Hornik, R. C., and McAnany, E. Institute for Communication Research, Stanford University, USA.

The Central American republic of El Salvador is among the smallest and most densely populated countries of the world. With approximately 3.5 million inhabitants and an annual population growth of 3.5 per cent, the nation's limited resources must be spread thinner with each passing year.

Agriculture is the basis of the Salvadorian economy and, although agricultural production has continually improved, the country has had to increase markedly its imports of basic food commodities in recent years. Despite such imports, the most recent study of nutrition levels revealed that the majority of the population remains

* Reproduced, with kind permission of the publishers (UNESCO), from *Prospects*, Vol. V, no 1, 1975.
This article is based on four years of field research which the authors, together with Dr Wilbur Schramm and Dr Henry T. Ingle, conducted in El Salvador under contract to the Academy for Educational Development and the United States Agency for International Development.

deficient in both calories and protein consumption.

Compounding the pressure of population growth in El Salvador is a broad range of economic and social problems common to Third World nations. The most recent survey of land ownership revealed that a majority of El Salvador's productive land was controlled by less than 2 per cent of its land holders. These individuals exercise great economic and political power. Their large estates produce the nation's main export crops, coffee and cotton, and they employ many thousands of agricultural workers. All told, approximately 60 per cent of El Salvador's active work force is engaged in agriculture, although due to the seasonal basis of the work, most agriculture workers are actually underemployed.

Origins of the education reform

Educational reform emerged as an important government priority during the last decade when El Salvador's leaders decided that only through a comprehensive upgrading of the school system and the provision of new kinds of training opportunities could the nation begin to resolve its pressing economic and social problems and, at the same time, carve out a larger place for itself in world trade.

To remedy the numerous problems that had been inherited from previous administrations and to streamline an educational system whose goals and procedures had ceased to fit the needs of El Salvador, a comprehensive five-year reform plan for education was set forth in 1968. The plan was systematic and thorough in its approach, touching virtually every aspect of the educational system. The major reforms included:

1 Reorganization of the Ministry of Education.
2 Extensive teacher retraining.
3 Curriculum revision.
4 Development of new teachers' guides and student workbooks.
5 Improvements of the system of school supervision to provide 'advice' instead of inspection.
6 Development of a wider diversity of technical training programmes in grades X–XII.

7 Extensive building of new school rooms.
8 Elimination of tuition in grades VII, VIII and IX.
9 Use of double sessions and reduced hours to teach more pupils.
10 A new student evaluation system incorporating changes in promotion and grading policies.
11 Installation of a national instructional television system for grades VII–IX.

Although some of these changes were enacted immediately, most were begun with the understanding that additional planning, experimentation and adjustment would be required and that major changes could only be introduced on an incremental basis. The five-year reform timetable was nevertheless a strict one.

The catalytic effect of television

The instructional television (ITV) system was thrust immediately into the forefront of El Salvador's educational reform because it exerted a powerful and determining influence over the content of the other re-reforms and, particularly, their rate of development. By the time other elements of the reform began to take shape, the Division of Educational Television, assisted by the United States Agency for International Development, was already producing nineteen programmes a week for use in El Salvador's secondary schools (grades VII to IX). When leaders of the reform insisted that televised instruction should not be started ahead of concomitant changes in curriculum, teacher training and supervising pressures grew on other divisions of the ministry to keep pace with television's timetable.

The Salvadorians realized that if television was to be relied upon to upgrade the quality of instruction at the secondary level, the broadcast lessons would have to reflect a reformed curriculum. In the words of the Minister of Education:

The present curriculum is archaic and is not responsive to the real needs of life. Since television is only an instrument for implementing curriculum, the quality of the whole educational system depends on the quality of the curriculum. The effective establishment of instructional television requires at the very least the elaboration of new and better curricula.

Thus, from the outset of the reform, the revision of the curriculum for grades VII to IX was tied closely to television. With televised instruction and a revised curriculum destined for all of El Salvador's junior high schools, the ministry's planners further decided that classroom teachers would have to make fundamental changes in their traditional teaching styles. To ease the transition, a year's retraining course was developed and the system of school supervision was redirected away from the narrow task of inspection toward a more open and positive approach emphasizing classroom observation and counselling. Finally, the new curricula and the new teaching methods suggested the need for improved classroom materials for both teachers and students. These classroom materials were initially developed and distributed by the ITV Division.

ITV was unquestionably the most visible and highly publicized of El Salvador's educational reforms. Articles appeared in the nation's press documenting the early interest in ITV and subsequently recording the government's efforts to construct a new studio and install television sets in Salvadorian schools. The publicity given ITV overshadowed the fact that other significant changes were occurring in El Salvador's educational system. In 1970, when a sample of parents were asked to recall what they knew about their country's educational reform, most could only remember television.

Finally, ITV was the component of the reform that demanded the most foreign technical assistance. Among the forty or so foreign advisers who worked alongside Salvadorian counterparts in the reform projects, more than thirty had at least some association with the ITV system. Such a concentration of resources sustained the momentum of the project and maintained ITV's pre-eminent position.

El Salvador's experience suggests that to be an effective instrument of change, major educational innovations such as television cannot simply be appended to traditional structures; rather, they must be accompanied by multiple-changes in other areas of the educational system. As the reform progressed, most Salvadorian leaders ex-

pressed the view that the educational reform could not have been implemented without the catalytic effect of television.

ITV's effects on students

In 1968, the year the reform began, there were approximately 20,000 students enrolled in El Salvador's public seventh, eighth and ninth grades (lower secondary level). They, along with some 23,000 private school enrollees, constituted less than a quarter of the young people of eligible age (13–15) for the three grades. By 1973, more than 65,000 students were enrolled at the same level. Counting an additional 26,000 private school students, the seventh and ninth grade matriculation was elevated to 34 per cent of the 13–15 year old population. The large increase in enrolment brought on by the elimination of tuition fees also resulted in a change in average social background of students, with more students from poorer and rural homes able to register for the first time.

On a regular basis from 1969 to 1972, an evaluation team composed of researchers from El Salvador and Stanford University administered general ability and reading tests as well as mathematics, science and social studies achievement tests to three cohorts of Salvadorian secondary students. Cohort A, which began seventh grade in 1969, included students studying with television and other elements of the reform and students learning in the traditional way. Cohorts B and C, which started seventh grade in 1970 and 1971 respectively, included only students from reform classes. These groups were divided into ITV and non-ITV sub-samples.

Over three years, the ITV students gained from 15 to 25 per cent more on the general ability tests than did their non-ITV peers. The advantage was unaffected when controls for socio-economic status and for individual student characteristics were applied. On reading tests, ITV and non-ITV students gained about the same.

The results of the achievement tests were mixed: sometimes ITV students outperformed students in non-ITV classes and sometimes the reverse occurred. When the test results for three years (two years in the case of cohort C) were combined, ITV students in every cohort had an advantage over non-ITV students in each subject. In mathematics this was the result of an ITV advantage in all three grades. In social studies and science, the cumulative advantage was due to particularly strong seventh grade performances which outweighed the mixed eighth and ninth grade results.

At the outset of the reform no criteria were established to judge learning effectiveness. No one in the Ministry of Education or in any of the outside organizations providing technical assistance suggested how much extra learning should be expected to justify the investment in so many innovative programmes. Nevertheless, the educational reform and particularly its ITV component were successful in enhancing student learning. The test results revealed a clear trend: ITV learning gains were significantly greater than the non-ITV gains in most comparisons. Reform classrooms with ITV, retrained teachers, a revised curriculum, and new materials proved to be a better learning environment than either traditional classrooms or classrooms with all elements of the reform except for television.

The collection of learning data was supplemented by periodic surveys of student attitudes and aspirations. A majority of students were favourable toward ITV throughout the four years in which attitudes were surveyed. However, high initial enthusiasm declined somewhat as students progressed from seventh to ninth grade. Attitudes toward English benefited most from the introduction of ITV, a subject little liked by non-ITV students, but well regarded by ITV students. Disadvantaged children and children with low general ability were more favourably disposed toward the television series than their more advantaged peers.

Advanced schooling was regarded by students as the key to success in El Salvador. More than 90 per cent of the students surveyed in each of the three cohorts wished to continue their studies beyond the ninth grade, and approximately 50 per cent hoped to obtain a university degree.

Given El Salvador's high level of unemployment and the shortage of well-paid jobs at the middle level, it was not surprising that so many students should aspire to university careers. The students recognized that the best jobs would be awarded to university graduates, and that a good job was the best guarantee of social prestige and mobility in the years ahead. To this extent, their educational aspirations must be considered realistic. These same aspirations must be considered unrealistic, however, in terms of the students' actual chances of fulfilling them.

Unfortunately, it was not possible to determine whether the reform had produced great changes in student aspirations since there was no comparable baseline data from before 1969. Nevertheless, the data gathered in the four-year period conveyed a warning: the aspirations of students for both education and jobs were so high as to present a real problem to Salvadorian planners in the future.

ITV's effects on classroom teachers

Under El Salvador's educational reform a concerted effort was made to retrain all secondary teachers so that they could work effectively with a revised curriculum and a new ITV system. The observational evidence from the classroom indicated that as the reform progressed, Salvadorian teachers began to rely less on lecturing or rote drill and more on student activity; they asked more 'thought' questions; and they were encouraging students to ask their own questions, state their own opinions and work on individual projects. These characteristics were all observed frequently enough to suggest that El Salvador's classroom teachers were changing.

Perhaps the best way to sum up the teachers' reactions to television would be to say that the 'rosy glow' cast by ITV in 1969 faded by the end of 1972. Nevertheless, teachers remained predominantly favourable to the use of television in their classrooms. Despite disagreement with ministry officials on the way some changes had been implemented, the majority of teachers were in accord with the goals and philosophy of the educational reform.

Did the downward trend in teacher attitudes during the reform's first four years belie the wisdom of spending so much time and money on their retraining? The answer to this question depends on how one considers the teachers' grievances. What accounted for the teachers' negative attitudes was not ITV or the reform as such, but rather the poor working conditions (ever larger class sizes, gruelling double sessions, lack of classroom materials) and low pay under which they continued to labour. Given these conditions, it was not surprising that teachers were dissatisfied or that they twice went on strike.

Problems of bureaucratic integration

The teachers' strikes illustrate the severity of the problems that occurred when teachers and administration were required to accept procedures and policies they themselves had not made. Of course, some changes were integrated into the school system more easily than others. For example, a new secondary curriculum was made and accepted without great trouble. New promotion policies were accepted, but not integrated so fully.

The closing of numerous teacher-training schools was resented even though the effect of reducing teacher unemployment and the high praise eventually accorded the centralized teacher retraining programme went far toward winning teacher acceptance.

The transformation of the supervisor-inspector role into that of the supervisor-counsellor presented the greatest difficulty. The new role was a very unfamiliar one in El Salvador and the supervisors opposed it because they perceived a loss of authority and prestige. Ministry of Education bureaucrats opposed it because they, at first, did not exert direct control over it. An apparent mistake was made in putting a supervisor corps into the ITV Division instead of into the departments of the ministry that had direct charge of the schools and the teachers.

Despite these difficulties, the Salvadorian experience underscores the advantages of putting local people in charge of developing all aspects of a new ITV system instead of relying on outsiders to do it. After three years ITV was more firmly established in El Salvador, the local component of experienced television people was more firmly established, and the outlook for continuing and expanding the system was better than in other countries that have relied on foreign experts to do the actual production and tele-teaching. On the other hand, the experience also illuminated the disadvantages of relying so much on local but inexperienced production talent.

Perhaps the greatest shortcoming of the El Salvador project and one of the great complaints of the classroom teachers was the uneven quality of the television lessons. The conclusion that seems to emerge from this experience is that as a country wants to 'learn by doing' (which has advantages over the long term), it must allow enough time before going on the air to train production teams, to let them gain experience, and to test and remake as many programmes as possible.

The Salvadorian experience also suggests that beginning one grade at a time avoids many problems that a system can get into by introducing television into a number of grades simultaneously. It was also possible in El Salvador to try out the television for a year in thirty-two pilot classrooms before expanding it to the entire school system. At the end of its first broadcast year (1969), the producers were able to revise and improve the vast majority of seventh grade programmes before they were transmitted on a nationwide basis.

ITV systems never develop quite as quickly as expected and El Salvador was no exception in this regard. Among other things, El Salvador, like all other countries, found that it took more time than expected to build an adequate administrative apparatus to design and carry out such a large number of educational reforms simultaneously.

The costs and efficiency of ITV in the reform

Research on the efficiency and costs of El Salvador's use of ITV and other key elements of the educational reform produced the following results:

1 Enrolments in grades VII, VIII and IX expanded by 300 per cent (from 19,104 to 65,390) between 1968 and 1973. The increases reduced the traditional bottleneck between sixth and seventh grades, so that almost 60 per cent of the students entering sixth grade in 1971 continued on to seventh in 1972.

2 The number of dropouts and repeaters within the three grades diminished after the initiation of the reform. This increased efficiency was due to an easing of standards as well as an improvement in the quality of teaching.

68

3 Costs of the ITV system were divided into two components: fixed costs (including studio facilities, production costs, etc) which were the same no matter how many students were watching, and variable costs (television receivers, student workbooks, etc) which increased with the number of students in the audience. The total fixed costs per year (apportioning the cost over twenty-five years of the project to each year under assumptions specified in the text) were estimated to be $1.1 million. Of that sum, approximately $800,000 was the cost to the Salvadorian Government; the rest consisted of grants from USAID and other foreign agencies.

To the fixed costs must be added the variable costs and, for each student in the system, there was a yearly cost of about $1.10. Thus, in 1972 when 48,000 students were enrolled, the per student cost of ITV to the Government of El Salvador was $17.75, while the total cost (including outside loans and grants) was $24.35.

4 Knowing the number of students actually enrolled in the first seven years of the project, and projecting enrolments through year twenty-five of the project, it was possible to estimate the average cost per student during any part of that period. This approach recognized that in the early years of a project fewer students were likely to be served, but as the project matured, many more students would be included. Over the full twenty-five years, the average yearly cost per student was calculated to be $17.

5 The introduction of ITV was accompanied by an increase in the number of students per class (from thirty-five to forty-five) and an increase in teacher load (40 per cent additional classroom hours) with only a 20 per cent increase in teacher pay.

Conclusions and implications

Given the accomplishments of the first four years, what general conclusions can be drawn from El Salvador's experience with ITV, and how applicable are such conclusions to other countries?

El Salvador's educational reform, and

particularly its ITV system, accomplished what they were expected to do under the original five-year plan. The bottleneck in secondary education was widened and with each passing year more students poured into the seventh grade. A greater percentage of these students were from disadvantaged backgrounds and most were expected to complete the ninth grade. Largely because of ITV, the great expansion in enrolment did not lead to a decline in learning. In fact, just the opposite occurred; students learned more under the reform with ITV than they did under the traditional system.

Although ITV was unquestionably an expensive innovation for El Salvador, the Ministry of Education managed to offset some of its cost by increasing both classroom teachers' hours and class size. Given the projected rise in enrolments, the per student costs of instruction under the reform with ITV will eventually be less than if the reform had been introduced with traditional class size and teacher loads.

More students, better learning, and equal or lower per student costs: these are notable and impressive results. How did El Salvador achieve them when so many other countries have failed or fallen short in their efforts to introduce ITV?

The Salvadorian experience underscores the idea that ITV or any other instructional technology is best conceived in terms of broad system needs. ITV was not imposed over traditional structures; rather, it was co-ordinated with other major changes in El Salvador's educational system.

Nevertheless, ITV played a catalytic role in the reform because it magnified the need for change in numerous areas. When the government decided to invest in television, it made sense to revise the curriculum so that the broadcast lessons would carry the most modern knowledge and teaching methods. Similarly, when El Salvador introduced ITV in the classroom something had to be done to prepare the classroom teacher. Consequently, a major teacher retraining programme was organized, and so on for the reforms in supervision and evaluation and the provision of new materials for both teachers and students. Not all of these changes were successful, but such changes do not come easily in national school systems or ministries of education.

PAPER NO 27: THE COST OF INSTRUCTIONAL RADIO AND TELEVISION IN KOREA

Dean T. Jamison, Educational Testing Service, Princeton, USA. *Yoon Tai Kim*, Korean Educational Development Institute, Seoul, Korea.

Introduction

In the period 1970–1 the Republic of Korea undertook a major systems analysis of its educational sector; the purpose of the analysis was to ascertain the feasibility of improving the internal efficiency of the educational system and of making the system more responsive to Korea's economic and social needs. Two important conclusions of the analysis were that a single entity within Korea should take responsibility for educational reform activities, and that an important initial target for reform would be the elementary (grades 1–6) and middle (grades 7–9) schools. In August 1972, the Government of Korea responded to these recommendations by establishing the Korean Educational Development Institute (KEDI) under the direction of Dr Yung Dug Lee; one of the first major tasks facing KEDI was development of a reform project at the elementary and middle school levels. Another task was the development of a radio/correspondence secondary school to increase the range of options open to individuals wishing secondary education. Our purpose in this paper is to report cost information from the media aspects—television, radio and print—of these reform projects.

The elementary/middle (E/M) project is now in the course of development, and final plans for implementation remain to be decided on. The E/M project will, however, use ITV and, to a lesser extent, radio to provide instruction. Present plans call for students in grades 2 through 9 to receive about six 20-minute television lessons per week by the time the operational phase of the project begins in 1978; more intensive use of ITV will be considered if funds become available. Plans call for students in grades 1 through 9 to receive about ten 20-minute radio lessons per week. In addition to the use of television and radio, the E/M project will involve reform of curriculum and textbooks and may involve use of differentiated staffing, use of individualized instruction, and maintaining the overall student-to-teacher ratio with multiple grouping of students, such as small (30–40 students), medium (45–60) and large (60–80).

At the time of this writing (September 1975) the E/M project is at a critical juncture. The first phase of its activities—initial planning for and tryouts of the new instructional approaches—is nearing completion. Its transmission facilities and new studios are scheduled to become operational within a few months, thereby allowing the second major phase of the project—comprehensive demonstrations in 30 schools— to begin, and a third one in 45 schools. The demonstration phases will continue through February 1978. A fourth phase, that of nationwide implementation, will begin in the course of the demonstration,* and in parallel with it; implementation is planned to occur in the period 1976–80.

The KEDI E/M project is ambitious in the comprehensiveness of the reform it plans to implement and in the extent to which it will attempt to utilize research results from educational psychology in its instructional design. The project is, in addition, utilizing the most recent technical advance in transmission systems, the tethered aerostat, for signal distribution; KEDI's use of an aerostat will be the first use made of this technology for television broadcasting. For all these reasons, then, the E/M project will be closely observed and its costs will be important to ascertain. The cost information we shall present in this paper is based in part on costs that have been incurred, and in part on present KEDI plans. The results are thus tentative.

Component costs

In this section we will present information on the various components of the costs of the media aspects of the E/M project. We first discuss development and start-up

---

* Present KEDI planning calls for operational installation of 6,950 TV receivers in over 20,000 classrooms in 1976; these are in addition to 168 receivers (1 receiver per 2 classes) to be installed in demonstration schools. Final budget authorization remains to be made for the operational installations.

Table 1 System development and start-up costs

Item	Amount
System development (including book writing and curriculum preparation)	US$3,014,000
Training and technical assistance	524,000
Contingency	351,000
TOTAL	$3,889,000
Total, annualized at 0%	$194,000/yr
Total, annualized at 7.5%	$381,000/yr
Total, annualized at 15%	$621,000/yr

Table 2 Capital costs of studio facilities

1 *Construction and installation*

Land	$55,000
Construction of studios and research Center	1,910,000
TOTAL	$1,965,000

	discount rate		
	0%	7.5%	15%
Annualized construction cost (over 50 years)	$39,300	$151,500	$295,000
TV studios' share	21,000	80,300	156,400
Radio studios' share	2,400	9,100	17,700
Research center's share	16,100	62,100	121,000

2 *Studio equipment cost, including shipping*

TV studio equipment	$1,500,000
Radio studio equipment	125,000
TOTAL	$1,625,000

	discount rate		
	0%	7.5%	15%
Annualized TV equipment cost (over 10 years)	$150,000	$219,000	$299,000
Annualized radio equipment cost (over 10 years)	12,500	18,200	24,900

3 *Total costs, construction plus equipment*

	total cost	annualized cost		
		0%	7.5%	15%
TV studios	$2,540,000	$171,000	$299,000	$455,000
Radio studios	243,000	15,000	27,000	43,000

costs, then production costs, next transmission costs, and, finally, reception site costs.

(a) System development and start-up costs
Table 1 shows system development and start-up costs.

These costs total $3,889,000. We annualize capital costs by using the standard accounting annualization formula; if we are given an initial cost, C, for an item of capital (start-up activities as well as equipment are considered capital), its period of usefulness in years, n, and an interest rate on capital, r, the *annualized cost* of the capital is given by a(r,n)C. The annualization factor, a(r,n), is in turn given by:

$$a(r,n) = (r(1+r))^n/((1+r)^n-1).$$

The table shows the annualized value of these start-up costs assuming the costs to be spread over an estimated 20-year project lifetime. These start-up costs are the total estimated to be incurred during the period September 1972, through February 1978.

(b) Program production costs
KEDI is now completing the construction and installation of equipment in a large new studio and research facility. The facility will have two radio studios and two TV studios. Table 2 shows construction costs for the entire facility, and apportions those costs among the TV studios, radio studios and research center. It also shows the costs of studio equipment, including shipping. The table shows annualized values of these capital costs using KEDI's lifetime estimates and interest rates of 0 per cent, 7.5 per cent and 15 per cent. The estimated total cost of the TV studios, including equipment, is $2,540,000; that for the radio studios is $243,000.

Table 3 shows estimates of the recurrent costs per 20-minute program; these total $598 per TV program and $30 per radio program.

In order to obtain a rough estimate of the *total* cost per program, the recurrent cost per program (from Table 3) must be added to the cost per program of capital facilities. To compute this we assume that the capacity of the TV studios is 1,860 programs per year, and that of the radio studios is 9,620. The annualized capital costs of the TV and radio facilities (item 3, Table 2) are then divided by these production rates to obtain an estimate of capital costs per program. Table 4 shows the total production costs per program, i.e., the sum of the capital plus recurrent costs; assuming a 7.5 per cent

Table 3   Recurrent costs of program production per programme

1	*Television*	
	Broadcasting program development* (producers, editors, engineering and studio personnel)	$243
	Scriptwriting and actors	206
	Films, video tapes, sets	100
	TOTAL	$549

2	*Radio*	
	Broadcasting program development* (producers, editors, engineering and studio personnel)	$12
	Scriptwriting and actors	10
	Tapes and setting	5
	TOTAL	$27

* KEDI has budgeted $713,000 to the E/M project for broadcasting program development in the period 1972–8. Assuming that 14,600 radio programs are produced in this period, 2,205 TV programs are produced, and that broadcasting program development costs for TV stand to those for radio as do the other recurrent costs (i.e., 20:1), one obtains the numbers in the table.

Table 4   Total production costs per program

| | Recurrent cost plus capital costs annualized at | | |
	0%	7.5%	15%
Television	$641	$710	$794
Radio	29	30	31

discount rate, the cost per TV program is $710; the cost per radio program $31.

(c) Transmission systems costs

From the technical point of view, a principal source of interest in the KEDI E/M project is that it will be the first to use a tethered aerostat as the platform for its television and radio transmitters. An aerostat is a dirigible shaped lighter-than-air craft lifted by helium gas and the aerodynamic force of the wind. A steel tether, less than an inch in diameter, links the aerostat to the ground station; in Korea the aerostat will be tethered at an altitude of 10,000 feet. The Korean installation will have two aerostats —one for regular use, and one for immediate back-up in case of failure of the first. Each will carry two UHF TV transmitters and one FM radio transmitter. In addition to these broadcasting packages, carried for KEDI, the aerostats will also carry telecommunications equipment.

The KEDI complex in Seoul will beam the TV and radio signals to the operating aerostat at Bong Yang, 70 miles away, by a C-band (4–5 GHz) microwave link; the aerostat will receive these signals, shift their frequency, and retransmit them. Wankel motors connected to a generator will supply the power to operate the on-board electronics package; the operations crew will lower the aerostat every several days to refuel the motor and to undertake regular maintenance. Standard UHF television sets will receive the signals with an estimated FCC Grade 'A' signal quality at distances up to 60 miles from Bong Yang; a Grade 'B' signal should be obtainable at distances of 90 miles. At some additional expense (about $600) one can add a higher gain antenna and a low noise preamplifier/convertor to a standard UHF receiver, increasing the coverage radius substantially. Present plans call for installation of four

UHF relay stations to provide coverage beyond the reach of the aerostat, and transmission cost estimates here are based on that assumption. KEDI is examining the possibility of acquiring a second aerostat site as an alternative to the relay stations.

As of September 1975, the aerostats were installed at Bong Yang, and preliminary tests were under way to ascertain whether actual signal strengths would match predicted ones to various parts of Korea.

Table 5 presents the capital cost of the transmission system, including site preparation and construction. The costs in that table are based on an assignment of 47 per cent of the aerostat system costs to KEDI's broadcasting facilities; this is the figure used for Korean government accounting. While allocation of fixed costs among alternative uses of an installation is inevitably somewhat arbitrary, this allocation seems reasonable enough.

Table 6 presents current estimates of the recurrent costs of the transmission facilities; these costs include operations, maintenance and spare parts, power, and helium for the aerostats. Each aerostat uses about 190,000 cubic feet of helium, the current price for which in Korea is at present $.34 per cubic foot—substantially above the world market price. Thus the value of the helium in the two aerostats is about $130,000. The permeability of the aerostat membrane (which is extremely low), the inevitable small tears in the membrane, and occasional dumps of helium for flight control cause a steady loss of helium. Site engineers hope this loss can be kept to 200 cubic feet per aerostat per day which would result in a total cost to the installation of $50,000 per year. An earlier analysis[1] suggested that recurrent costs would be about 40 per cent higher than these estimates, which are based on the most recent KEDI planning figures. It is probably fair to say that, until KEDI has

Table 5   Capital costs of transmission system

1 *Construction and installation*				
Aerostat site, including equipment installation		$351,000		
4 relay station sites		82,000		
TOTAL		$433,000		
		annualized at		
		0%	7.5%	15%
Annualized construction cost (over 30 years)		$14,400	$36,700	$65,900

2 *Equipment, including shipping*				
Aerostat		$3,290,000		
4 relay stations, including equipment installation		82,000		
TOTAL		$3,372,500		
		annualized at		
		0%	7.5%	15%
Annualized equipment cost (over 10 years)		$337,250	$491,300	$672,000

3 *Total costs*				
	Total	annualized at		
		0%	7.5%	15%
Total capital cost	$3,806,000	$352,000	$528,000	$738,000

Table 6   Recurrent costs of transmission system

At aerostat site	$199,000/yr
At relay transmitter sites	11,000/yr
TOTAL	$210,000/yr

had several years of experience with the system, there will remain substantial uncertainty concerning the recurrent costs of the transmission facility.

Table 7 presents estimates of the costs per channel per year, based on the cost information from Tables 5 and 6. To allocate costs among the one radio and two TV channels, we allocated KEDI's fraction of the aerostat facility costs in proportion to the transmitter costs *per se*. As the TV transmitters cost $370,000 each and the radio trans-

mitters cost $203,000, the fraction of total KEDI aerostat cost allocated to the radio transmitter is 22 per cent, and the fraction allocated to each TV transmitter is 39 per cent. Half the cost of each TV relay station was then added to each television channel's fraction of aerostat costs to obtain total annual cost per television channel; at a 7.5 per cent discount rate television costs $291,000 per channel per year. At the same discount rate, the radio channel costs $156,000 per year.

Assuming that the channels transmit for eight hours a day six days a week (or 2,500 hours per year) the cost per hour of transmission of UHF television is $88 at a discount rate of zero; $116 at a discount rate of 7.5 per cent; and $150 at a discount rate of 15 per cent. The cost per hour of FM radio transmission is $48 at a discount rate of zero; $62 at a discount rate of 7.5 per cent; and $80 at a discount rate of 15 per cent.

Table 7　Total annual costs per channel per year*

| | Recurrent cost plus capital costs annualized at | | |
	0%	7.5%	15%
UHF Television (Channels 20 and 26)	$221,000/yr	$291,100/yr	$374,000/yr
FM Radio (104.9 MHz)	$119,000/yr	$156,000/yr	$200,000/yr

* The system will transmit two channels of UHF television and one channel of FM radio; the costs indicated for television are per channel, and include the costs of the four off-the-air relay stations for reaching areas in the south. The FM radio signal is planned to reach far enough to cover the south from the Bong Yang aerostat site.

Table 8　Reception site costs (television and radio)

1　Capital costs (per 3 classrooms)

UHF color television receiver	$516
Television receiver installation	27
Radio set	31
TOTAL	$574

	0%	7.5%	15%
Annualized capital cost (over 5 years)	$115	$142	$171

2　Recurrent costs (per 3 classrooms)

TV operating cost—power, spares and maintenance	$103
Radio operating cost—power, spares and maintenance (at 20% per annum of initial cost)	6
TOTAL	$109

3　Total annualized cost (per 3 classrooms)

| | recurrent cost plus capital cost annualized at | | |
	0%	7.5%	15%
for television	$212/yr	$237/yr	$265/yr
for radio	12/yr	14/yr	15/yr
TOTAL	$224/yr	$251/yr	$280/yr

Table 9   Reception site costs (print)

1 *Elementary school*

Teacher's Guide, including tests (1600 pages per teacher per year @ $.0021 per page)	$3.30 per teacher per year
Student Workbooks (1000 pages per student per year)	$2.50 per student per year

2 *Middle school*

Teacher's Guide, including tests (1300 pages per teacher per year)	$2.70 per teacher per year
Student Workbooks (1200 pages per student per year)	$3.20 per student per year

3 *Total print costs per student per year*

(class size = 60)

Elementary school	$2.60 per student per year
Middle school	$3.30 per student per year

(d) Reception site costs

There are two principal components to the reception site costs: the first is the purchase, installation, and maintenance of the TV and radio receivers, and the second is the purchase of printed materials. Table 8 shows the television and radio costs; Table 9 shows the printed material costs, based on presently planned levels of print usage.

Current plans call for three classes to share reception equipment; assuming an average class size of 60, reception equipment will be shared among 180 students. Table 10 shows annual reception site costs per student per year under this assumption. At a discount rate of 7.5 per cent these costs total $4.00 per student per year; of this amount printed materials account for 65 per cent, television accounts for 33 per cent, and radio accounts for 2 per cent. Even with the low costs per printed page that KEDI plans for, the high planned utilization of printed materials causes print to be a dominant factor in reception site costs.

Total cost functions

Based on the information presented in the preceding section, we can prepare an annualized total cost function for both the television and the radio components of the

Table 10   Annual reception site costs per student

(1 radio, 1 TV receiver for every 3 classes)	Recurrent costs plus capital costs annualized at		
	0%	7.5%	15%
Television only	$1.18	$1.32	$1.47
Radio only	.07	.08	.08
Television plus radio plus print	3.85	4.00	4.15

E/M project, as well as one for the project as a whole. These cost functions are of the following form:

$$TC(N,h) = F + V_N N + V_h h,$$

where TC = total system costs, per year,
  N = the number of students reached,
  F = fixed system costs,
  V_N = variable cost per student,
  V_h = variable cost per hour.

Table 11 shows the values of the cost parameters, F, V_N, and V_h, for the television, radio, and print components of the E/M reform, each considered separately.

For example, the cost function for only the television aspect of the reform, assuming a 7.5 per cent discount rate, can be seen from Table 11 to be:

$$TC(N,h) = \$267,000 + 1.32N + 2246h.$$

KEDI now plans to provide 70 hours of TV per year at each of eight grade levels, re-

sulting in a value of h of 560; putting this value of h into the above equation we obtain:

$$TC(N) = \$1,524,000 + 1.32N.$$

If N = 1,000,000 the average cost is $2.84 per student per year or 4.1c per student per hour. On the other hand, if N is 'only' 100,000 the average cost is $16.65 per student per year or 24c per student per hour. Similarly one can examine properties of the cost functions for radio and print.

It is also possible to construct a cost function for the reform as a whole. Here we use the 'total' entry at the bottom of Table 11 and consider separately the number of hours of television and radio programming. Let h_T equal the number of hours of TV programming and h_R equal the number of hours of radio programming. With a 7.5 per cent discount rate we then have:

$$TC(N,h_T,h_R) = \$381,000 + 4.00N + 2246h_T + 182h_R.$$

Table 11 *Total cost functions*

Television		annualized at		
		0%	7.5%	15%
Fixed system costs	F	$136,000	$267,000	$435,000
Variable cost per student	V_N	1.18	1.32	1.47
Variable cost per hour	V_h	2011	2246	2532
Radio		annualized at		
		0%	7.5%	15%
Fixed system costs	F	$41,000	$80,000	$130,000
Variable cost per student	V_N	.07	.08	0.8
Variable cost per hour	V_h	164	182	204
Print		annualized at		
		0%	7.5%	15%
Fixed system costs	F	$17,000	$34,000	$56,000
Variable cost per student	V_N	2.60	2.60	2.60
Variable cost per hour	V_h	0	0	0
Total (television + radio + print)		annualized at		
		0%	7.5%	15%
Fixed system costs	F	$194,000	$381,000	$621,000
Variable cost per student	V_N	3.85	4.00	4.15

As before, we let $h_T = 560$. KEDI currently plans to broadcast 1,095 hours of radio per year to students in grades 1–9, so the cost function becomes, in terms of N only:

$$TC(N) = \$1,836,000 + 4.00N.$$

If $N = 100,000$ the average cost per student per year is $22.36; if $N = 1,000,000$, this cost drops to $5.84. This cost includes television, print and radio. In our previous example we computed the cost per student per year of television alone to be $2.84; television costs are thus about 49 per cent of the total.

In the full paper, costs for the radio/correspondence high school are also calculated.

Conclusion

In concluding, it is perhaps worth stressing once again the preliminary status of the figures reported here. It is far too early in the E/M reform for the costs reported here to reflect actual experience; on the other hand, enough equipment has been purchased and installed for at least some of the figures reported here to reflect more than planning estimates. Jamison, Klees, and Wells[2] discussed problems of error in cost estimation in the planning and early phases of instructional technology projects, and noted an almost universal tendency for estimates to understate actual costs. Time alone will tell whether the planning estimates reported here will follow the general pattern.

References
1   LEE, CHONG JAE, *The life cycle cost analysis of the transmission systems for the educational reform in Korea*, Seoul, Korea, KEDI, 1975. (Unpublished typescript.)
2   JAMISON, D., KLEES, S., and WELLS, S. *Cost analysis for educational planning and evaluation: methodology with applications to instructional technology*, Princeton, N. J., Educational Testing Service, to be published in 1976.

PAPER NO 56: THE NICARAGUA RADIO MATHEMATICS PROJECT

Barbara Searle and Patrick Suppes, Institute for Mathematical Studies in the Social Sciences, Stanford University, California, USA.

Among the various technologies of instruction now being used around the world, ranging from programmed instruction booklets to color television and computers, radio emerges as one of the most economical. Although radio instruction has been used in various parts of the world for over forty years, it has been little studied. In a recent survey of experimental and empirical studies of the effectiveness of teaching by radio, Jamison, Suppes and Wells[1] found few in which radio carried the major burden of instruction, and none that examined the relation of curriculum structure to student achievement.

Responding to the growing use of instructional radio in developing countries and the need for research in this area, the United States Agency for International Development (AID) has funded the Institute for Mathematical Studies in the Social Sciences at Stanford University to investigate the teaching of mathematics by radio in the primary grades of a developing country. The Institute has chosen to work in the schools of Nicaragua, primarily in the rural sector.

The Radio Mathematics Project assumes responsibility for all of the mathematics instruction children receive. A daily lesson consists of a thirty-minute radio presentation, followed by approximately twenty minutes of teacher-directed activities, for which instructions are contained in a project-developed teacher's guide. Children use either printed worksheets or their own notebooks for written responses. Teachers are asked to supply simple materials, such as bottle caps and sticks, and the project occasionally provides other supplementary materials, such as rulers printed on cardboard. The focus of our research is how best to use these limited resources—the radio, student worksheets, a teacher's guide, some simple materials—to teach mathematics effectively.

In discussing the current project we have found some scepticism that mathematics can be effectively taught by means of radio. It is a primary purpose of this project to test this hypothesis. A successful outcome of this experiment gains in importance because of the low cost of radio technology. If good achievement results can be obtained, then the cost-benefit ratios for radio in the case of teaching primary school mathematics may be the best of any of the feasible technologies, including even traditional instruction with adequately trained teachers.

Application of psychological principles of instruction

Each mathematics lesson consists of two parts, the broadcast portion and the teacher-directed portion, with the broadcast designed to be presented first. During the broadcast portion of the lesson, the children are asked to respond orally, physically, and in writing, and they do so 50 to 60 times during each thirty-minute lesson. Sometimes children handle concrete materials during the broadcast—for example, counting or grouping bottle caps. After the radio transmission, the teacher continues the lesson, following the directions given in the teacher's guide.

A fundamental question facing designers of radio instruction is: how can we implement principles of good teaching using radio as the instructional medium? A list of such principles might include the following:

- instruction is more effective when children respond actively;
- reinforcement—knowledge of results—increases rate of learning;
- children's thinking progresses from the concrete to the abstract, and therefore practice with concrete materials facilitates learning;
- practice is more effective when distributed over many sessions rather than concentrated in fewer, longer sessions;
- children learn at different rates.

A good teacher uses these principles as he makes decisions about organizing classroom activities, preparing lesson outlines, and even about arranging the furniture in the classroom. We are attempting to use these principles as guidelines for determining the structure and content of radio lessons.

(a) *Active responding* We distinguish three types of responses which we ask of children:

oral, physical, and written. We will discuss each of these three response types in turn.

Characters in a radio program may talk either among themselves or directly to the listeners. We make careful distinction between these two modes. When characters are talking to each other, we expect children to listen without responding. When a character talks directly to the children, we expect and plan for the children to respond. In this way a type of dialogue can be established between a radio character and the children. Student responses are highly structured, and there is, of course, no genuine interaction; nevertheless the process engages the attention of the children.

Oral responses include such 'conversations' between the children and radio characters, and also answers to exercises presented in both free-response format and multiple-choice format. An example of an oral exercise in multiple-choice format is:

'I am thinking of two objects—a box and a ball. Which is round?'

An oral exercise in free-response format, presented directly, is:

'What is 5 plus 10?'

and presented in story form:

'Juan earned 5 centavos yesterday and 10 centavos today. How much did he earn altogether?'

As another type of oral response, children sing songs. A song is taught by having radio characters sing it several times at its first presentation and then at least once in several successive lessons. After only a few repetitions the children are able to join the singing. Almost all the songs we use are about mathematics. Lyrics are written by the project staff and set to music and recorded by Nicaraguan musicians.

Physical activity is a second kind of response that the radio characters ask of the children. They may play games—one game has the children patting their knees, their shoulders, their cheeks, a specified number of times—or they may be asked to hold up fingers, handle materials or point to pictures or numbers on the worksheet.

Finally, the children are asked to write, either on a worksheet or in their notebooks. Once again, exercises are presented in multiple-choice format or in free-response format. In the former children mark the correct choice, while in the latter they may draw pictures, or write numerals or words.

The lessons maintain a high level of student response. During a thirty-minute radio lesson, children respond on average sixty times.

(*b*) *Reinforcement* Two variables must be attended to in designing reinforcement in the context of an instructional program. These are the schedule of reinforcement (for what proportion of exercises are answers given), and is the pattern of answer presentation regular or irregular. The second variable is the time elapsing between the presentation of an exercise and the reinforcement (presentation of an answer). Our work to date suggests that with radio, reinforcement should be immediate, and irregular.

(*c*) *Concrete materials* There is almost universal agreement today that lower primary-level students should use concrete materials while studying mathematics. However, there are many obstacles to the use of materials during radio lessons. Many teachers are not familiar with using materials, and the government does not provide any. Problems also arise when children have difficulty handling materials. Notwithstanding these difficulties, we use materials during radio lessons, and have for the most part experienced success.

The use of materials during the post-broadcast segment of the lesson has fewer disadvantages because the flexibility of the classroom permits the teacher to cope with difficulties that arise. We encourage teachers to provide concrete experiences for students and use the teacher's guide to suggest materials and activities.

(*d*) *Mixed drills* The research literature on the effect of practice on learning supports the proposition that skills need to be practised regularly to be maintained, and that distributed practice is superior to massed practice. For this reason we have developed a lesson structure that provides for the inclusion of several different topics in each lesson, as well as different types of activities and different modes of responding.

A lesson is constructed from segments, each of which is based on a small bit of curriculum. Each segment description specifies the exercises, the mode of presentation, and the mode of response required. From four to seven segments are presented by radio, and from three to six by the teacher in the post-broadcast period. For example, Lesson 18 has seven radio segments and three post-broadcast segments. These are:

Radio	1	Show the addition facts 2 + 2, 3 + 2, 4 + 1, 1 + 2 using fingers. 'How much is 2 plus 2?'
Radio	2	Rote count from 1 to 20, two times.
Radio	3	Give successors orally for 5, 8, 7, 9, 10. 'What number comes after 5?'
Radio	4	Write numerals from dictation. 'Write the number 4 (3, 5, 2, 6).'
Radio	5	Write the successors to 2, 1, 4, 3, 1. 'Write the number that comes after 2.'
Radio	6	Ordinals 'first' and 'second', oral, then written, response, using drawings. 'There is a plate on the first table. What is on the second table? Circle the first table (second basket, second box, first dish).'
Radio	7	Readiness for addition, drawing. 'Draw 2 balls on the first line. Draw 1 ball on the second line. How many are there in all? (oral response) (1 + 2, 1 + 3, 3 + 2, 2 + 2).'
Teacher	8	Reading numerals from 1 to 7 (printed on worksheet). 'Circle the 3 (6, 2, 4, 7, 5).'
Teacher	9	Read numerals 1 to 9 on cards (prepared by teacher).
Teacher	10	Count objects, from 1 to 10 (materials chosen by teacher).

This outline illustrates the variety of topics and response modes that may be incorporated in a single lesson. However, as is evident from the outline, topics are not chosen at random, but in relation to one another. Segments 1 and 7 give different types of practice with roughly the same addition combinations. Segment 4 provides practice in writing the numerals needed in segment 5, and so on.

An outline like that above (with additional information concerning response modes, timing, and worksheet layout) provides the basis from which script writers produce a script for the radio lesson, curriculum writers produce the teachers' guide, and the artist prepares the worksheet.

(e) *Differential learning rates* Coping with differential learning rates is the most difficult problem facing the developer of curriculum for radio. During this first experimental year we are concerned primarily with exploring the extent of the problem. How large is the spread in achievement at the beginning of the year, and as the school year progresses? Do children who are performing very well or very poorly appear to lose interest in lessons?

We have experimented with ways of providing different levels of instruction to different children during broadcasting. We have developed exercises that had different printed materials associated with a single set of verbal instructions, allowing children who are listening to a common set of instructions to work different exercises. We have also given different instructions to two groups of children, asking them to work on different tasks at the same time. These methods hold promise for differentiating radio instruction.

Structure of the curriculum

Project lessons are based on the mathematics curriculum specified by the Nicaraguan Ministry of Education. Some changes in emphasis and some reorganization have proved necessary in constructing the radio lessons, but in general the content of project lessons meets national specifications.

The process of obtaining lesson segment descriptions from the rather general curriculum specifications of the Ministry of Education curriculum guide involves several steps. First, the mathematical content is divided into topics or strands. For first grade the strands are Basic Concepts, Number Concepts, Addition, Subtraction, Applications and Measurement. Then for each strand a set of objectives is formulated, defining the behavior expected of a student who has successfully completed the first-grade instructional program. The objectives specify only what the student should be able to do at the end of the

year, and each objective must be broken down into sub-objectives appropriate for instruction. Consider, for example, an objective that states:

> The student will count the number of objects in a set of N objects, where N is less than or equal to 25.

The first sub-objective might restrict the number of objects to five or fewer, a second might use from six to ten objects, and so on. Thus, the next step in curriculum preparation is to subdivide each objective into a series of sub-objectives, called classes. The classes of exercises must then be put in order so that for any given concept or exercise type, all those prerequisite to it come earlier in the instructional sequence.

We have now for each strand, a series of classes specifying the material that is to be taught, in units appropriately designed for instruction. For each class of exercises, students must be taught how to perform the task, they must be given opportunities to practice it, and then, later, they need further opportunities to review it. When the instructional sequence for a strand is constructed, each class appears several times, providing for these instructional tasks. The lesson segment descriptions, discussed above, are taken from these class descriptions, which characterize the entire curriculum. The class descriptions may be sampled at any time to provide test items to measure student progress in attaining curriculum objectives.

Evaluation of the program

An important component of the program is the collection of extensive student performance data, by means of frequent tests. In addition, observational data are collected regularly by project staff members. The systematic and frequent collection of data provides immediate feedback to the curriculum specialists and radio script writers and allows for much informal experimentation with teaching techniques.

During 1976 first-grade lessons will be broadcast to fifty classrooms. At the same time, initial development and pilot testing of second-grade lessons will proceed, using the same level of observation and data collection as was used for first grade. The project proposes to develop lessons for one additional grade level each calendar year.

The effectiveness of the program will be evaluated by comparing mathematics achievement in randomly selected experimental and control classrooms. Since the project lessons are based on the mathematics curriculum designed by the Nicaraguan Ministry of Education, both experimental and control classes can be expected to have studied roughly the same material during the school year, allowing for a comparison of mathematics achievement of the two groups.

The project also plans a study of repetition and dropout rates, as a component of an analysis of the economic consequences of the use of radio for instruction in this setting. We will also analyse the costs of expanding the use of radio in various configurations, to provide guidelines for Ministry of Education decisions about continuing the project and expanding the student base.

We anticipate that the results of our work will provide information about the significant variables that must be attended to in designing effective instructional radio programs, and that our results will help other countries make decisions about the use of radio for classroom instruction.

Reference

1 JAMISON, D., SUPPES, P. and WELLS, S., The effectiveness of alternative instructional methods: a survey, *Review of Educational Research, 44*, 1974.

PAPER NO 28: THE COST OF INSTRUCTIONAL RADIO IN NICARAGUA: AN EARLY ASSESSMENT*

Dean T. Jamison, Educational Testing Service, Princeton, USA.

In early 1975 a group of the Agency for International Development (AID) sponsored researchers and mathematics curriculum specialists began working with Nicaraguan counterparts in Masaya, Nicaragua, on radio programs to teach elementary school mathematics. The Radio Mathematics Project (RMP) is now completing its first year and is reaching approximately 600 first-grade students on an experimental basis. During 1976 programming will be extended through the second grade, and a carefully controlled evaluation of a large-scale implementation of the first-grade curriculum will be undertaken. Present plans call for continued expansion of curriculum coverage to higher grade levels and for implementation of the radio curriculum throughout Nicaragua. Searle, Friend, and Suppes[1] discuss in detail the RMP's activities and future plans. The purpose of this paper is to provide an early assessment of what RMP costs have been and can be expected to be.

Our cost function for the RMP will be constructed to give annualized total cost, TC, as a linear function of two independent variables—the number of lessons presented per year, and the number of students enrolled in a course, N. Each enrolled student would take the 150 lessons of a single year's course. The cost function we are assuming has, then, the following form:

$$TC = F + V_N N + V_h h,$$

where F, V_N, and V_h are parameters we can determine from cost data.

The first parameter, F, consists of all cost components invariant with respect to hours of programming or student usage, i.e., it consists of central project costs:

F = annualized starting costs + project administration costs.

Start-up costs were annualized at three different discount rates, so we have three values for F (each excluding research costs):

$$F = \begin{cases} \$75,600/\text{yr if } r = 0 \\ \$91,800/\text{yr if } r = 7.5\% \\ \$112,800/\text{yr if } r = 15\%. \end{cases}$$

The next parameter, V_h, depends on transmission costs and program production costs; it equals the annualized cost of preparing a lesson (including formative evaluation) plus the cost of transmitting it once. The annualized cost of a lesson is \$107 at a 0 per cent discount rate; \$160 at a 7.5 per cent discount rate; and \$213 at a 15 per cent discount rate. The cost of transmission is \$16. Thus we have:

$$V_h = \begin{cases} \$123/\text{yr if } r = 0 \\ \$176/\text{yr if } r = 7.5\% \\ \$229/\text{yr if } r = 15\%. \end{cases}$$

---

* Author's summary of full paper.

The final cost parameter, V_N, depends only on the cost per enrolled student per year; $V_N = \$3.83/yr$.

Our final cost equations are, then, given by (in dollars per year):

$$TC = \begin{cases} 75,600 + 120\,h + 3.8\,N \text{ if } r = 0 \\ 91,800 + 173\,h + 3.8\,N \text{ if } r = 7.5\% \\ 112,800 + 226\,h + 3.8\,N \text{ if } r = 15\%. \end{cases}$$

Three basic points emerged from this analysis of the costs of the RMP in Nicaragua:

1 The intensive efforts put into program preparation suggest that, unless careful effort is undertaken to make these programs available to many users, the cost per student of program production will be extremely high. The costs can be spread among users by insuring a long life (10 or more years) for the programs, by implementing the RMP through all or most of Nicaragua, and by attempting to use the same programs with only slight revision for Spanish-speaking students elsewhere in Latin America or within the United States.

2 The presently planned levels of classroom supervision, teacher training, and student workbook usage result in per student reception costs of $3.83 per year, or, assuming 150 30-minute lessons in a year, costs of 5.2c per student-hour. These costs are exceptionally high, suggesting the value of continued, careful experimentation with lower levels of supervision, less frequent and less intensive teacher training, teacher training by radio, and more limited workbook use.

3 It appears possible to reduce substantially the reception site costs and to spread programming costs over a large audience. Even if this be done, the project is apt to remain somewhat expensive by the standards of instructional radio projects. For this reason, principal emphasis in evaluation of the RMP must be placed on its capacity to improve the effectiveness of instruction, as indicated by its effects on mathematics achievement test scores and student repetition rates. It is too early in the project to assess its performance along these dimensions.

Reference

1 SEARLE, B., FRIEND, J., and SUPPES, P., *Application of Radio to Teaching Elementary Mathematics in a Developing Country*, Stanford, California, Institute for Mathematical Studies in the Social Sciences, 1975.

PAPER NO 3: EVALUATION OF TWO EDUCATIONAL MEDIA PROJECTS

Jan Löjdqvist and Ingrid Aman, Research Assistants, Educational Department, Sveriges Radio, Sweden.

Changes in our society necessarily lead to efforts to change also our schools. School reforms and new curricula express this attitude. In the new curriculum for the Swedish compulsory school there is stress laid on the responsibility of the school in the developing of the emotional and volitional life of the students along with the other traditional tasks of the school. Many prominent pedagogues have also stressed the importance of supporting children's creativity and pleasure in expressing themselves. We can here understand creativity in a very wide sense—making a personal contribution of your own and showing a curious questioning attitude towards the world around you. The mere fact that students freely express their own thoughts and opinions is then a form of creativity.

However, the work carried out in Swedish schools is still considerably more concentrated on the intellect and memory of the students than on their creative ability and emotional life. The introduction of a new curriculum does not automatically lead to great changes in the working methods of the teachers. Classroom work is often guided by many years' experience and is founded on the teacher training of long ago that did not stress the creative aspects of the teacher's work. We can also maintain that there is a contradiction between on the one hand, the stress laid in the curriculum on the development of the student's emotional and volitional life and critical thinking, and on the other hand traditional ideas about subject matter and division of disciplines. The contents of instruction will in practice be strongly influenced by traditional teaching aids and there is little time left over for trying new methods of work. Further, teachers often feel insecure in trying freer and more creative methods in their work. They need more guidance and support, if they are to be able to change their methods in practice.

In this connection school radio and school television ought to be able to fulfil an important function. In the Educational Programme Department of Sveriges Radio (SR) some projects have been produced with the aim of giving teachers help in introducing new subject-matter and new methods in their teaching. Those projects have also been the object of research and evaluation. One of the projects in question is *The Globe*, a television series for the low-level dealing with questions of a broadly human kind. Another project of this kind is *Rhythm and Creation* (RaC), which is an in-service training project in music for teachers of the compulsory school.

The Globe
The series called *Klotet*, *The Globe*, was produced to help the teachers of the lower-level classes to deal with the overall objectives. We knew that many teachers find it difficult to discuss matters from daily life and human problems with their pupils. Such discussions often become dull and moralizing, if the pupils are not stimulated to take an active part. The series consists of eighteen television programmes, each on a separate theme. Each programme is presented by two well-known presenters, a man and a woman. In the series they deal with different problems and situations from daily life. Examples of themes are 'friendship', 'justice', 'communication', 'fear'. Each programme presents the theme in several ways, e.g. talks between the presenters, short films, sketches and interviews. It is the aim of the programmes to stimulate classes to some kind of follow-up, e.g. a free discussion about the theme or some other creative activity like painting and drawing, playing, dramatization, singing. To help the teachers there is a teacher's guide with suggestions of ways to follow up the programmes.

Before the whole series was produced one pilot programme was tested in a region of the country. In this pre-testing more than 80 per cent of the teachers in the test region said that they would use the series, but we did not know for sure that they were representative of all low-level teachers in the country.

Therefore, when the series was broadcast for the first time in 1973, we carried out an investigation of utilization to get answers to questions like:

- can you get pupils and teachers to use regularly a series which does not go well with the traditional subjects?
- if so, to what extent did that depend on the kind of information the teachers had got about the series?
- what different types of follow-up did the teachers use after the programmes?

By asking a representative sample of 500 teachers we found out that it is possible to influence the teachers to take a greater interest in the overall objectives, but they need support in the form of stimulating material which they can use in their teaching.

More than 80 per cent of the teachers knew about the existence of the series before it started. That is a very high figure. Each programme was seen by almost 70 per cent of the teachers and their pupils in the target group. In this survey we also collected information about different methods that the teachers used in their follow-up of the programmes. In summarizing the teachers talked very positively about the series. This gave us some general information about the series. To get closer to the question of *how* the programmes were used and what effects they might have on the classes, we also made another study. By selecting seven schools and three classes in each of those schools we got a sample of pupils and teachers with whom we had a close contact throughout the series. In this way we had many possibilities to study the effects of the programmes more thoroughly than would have been possible with other methods.

We put questions like:

- how do teachers and pupils use the programmes in the daily school work?
- were the most important goals of the series fulfilled to stimulate teachers and pupils to discuss problems about human relationship?
- what attitudes do the teachers and pupils have towards the series; is it possible to notice any change during the series?
- how do the different components of the programmes function?

As a result of this investigation we could see that the positive pupils' reactions in the beginning of the series were maintained throughout the series. This is unusual for longer series. The popularity of *The Globe* series among the pupils even increased—which is even more unusual.

We could also state that work with the contents of the series very soon became a natural part of the daily school work. If the teacher sometimes forgot the broadcast he was immediately reminded by the pupils. There were also classes which saw the same programme several times. (Each programme of the series was broadcast three times.) Mostly, the teachers and the pupils talked about the contents of each programme directly after the broadcast, but many times both teachers and pupils came back to the scenes in the programmes in other contexts.

The follow-up of the programmes took different forms. Discussion about the theme was the most common form, but also painting and drawing or writing were frequent. The teachers usually tried the activities suggested in the teacher's guide. When the guide suggested plays, dramatization and other free activities, many teachers followed this. It seemed that the teachers needed support from the guide to start such activities.

The most popular components of the programmes were those which were fun and full of action. But the pupils were also quite interested in the short documentary films and in the presenters' dialogues, provided that they were not too long. Interviews with children were found to be the least popular components. It was also found that each of the eighteen programmes contained at least some part which could be used as a starting-point for a discussion. The best components in this respect were those which referred to the pupils' own experiences. The children would tell about their thoughts and experiences in a very spontaneous way, provided that the teacher did not try to correct the views that were expressed. But the teacher's help was needed to encourage all pupils to take part in the discussions.

To get even closer to the answer to the question about the effects of the programmes on the pupils' attitudes we made an intensive study on two of the programmes in the series. A number of psychologists showed the programmes to some classes and then interviewed some of the pupils individually. The interviews were recorded. Afterwards the interviews were analysed on the basis of Piaget's development theory and psychodynamic development theory.

We can state that the programmes have had effects on the pupils. In some cases parts of the programmes have been misunderstood or misinterpreted, but to quote the summary, 'Even if there are misunderstandings the pupils do react to the programmes. Few children remain disengaged'.

In the preliminary report the psychologists stress the importance of the follow-up of each programme. They say that a change of attitudes and human behavior is nothing 'that can be dealt with five minutes before lunch break'. Preparation and follow-up from the teachers are very important.

> The full paper includes a similar account of the *Rhythm and Creation* project.

Conclusion

In conclusion we would like to maintain that the results of the evaluation of both *The Globe* series and the RaC project show that those two programme projects can be regarded as examples of teaching/learning aids which have at least temporarily influenced instruction and the situation of students in a desirable direction. Through both of the projects a large number of teachers have been stimulated to try new, freer and more creative methods in their work. We now know that there is a readiness with many teachers, at least on the low level and the intermediate level, to use such methods when they are given guidance and help in stimulating their students. But there is of course a risk that many teachers will go back to their earlier behavior when a programme series or in-service training project has been finished. To bring about lasting changes there is a need for follow-up and recurrent contributions in the same fields and co-ordination with other in-service training activities.

PAPER NO 60: TRIALOGUE: A RE-SEARCH AND DEVELOPMENT PRO-JECT

Rolf Svensson, Head of Planning, Education Department, Sveriges Radio, Sweden.

To make decisions is not particularly difficult. It is considerably more difficult to make the right decisions, for which you are ready to take the consequences for some time.

In this paper we are going to look more closely at the role which research in radio and television in education plays in the decision-making process, namely the research carried out in the Educational Programme Department of Sveriges Radio. Obviously, pedagogical research is carried out in many institutions in various parts of the country, the results of which in one way or another influence decision-making in broadcasting. The same is the case with research in other countries in this field. Influence of that kind is not treated in this paper.

The decision-making process will be described through a case study, dealing with the development of an extensive multi-media project for the upper level of the compulsory school, the project being called *Trialogue*.

The development of the multi-media project Trialogue—a case study
A new curriculum for the compulsory school
Starting in 1970 a new curriculum was introduced in the Swedish compulsory school. The introduction took place gradually and was completed in the school year 1972–3. The organizational and pedagogical innovations were most pronounced at the upper level.

In its pedagogical chapters the new curriculum recommended that school work should as far as possible be along what we call work-project principles. In the first place this was true about social science and natural science, where students were to work with a number of such projects where subject matter from the traditional school subjects was grouped together in new combinations, considered to be more natural for the students and thus easier for them to handle. The curriculum underlined the importance of students having more oppor-tunities to work more independently at school, both individually and in groups. Simultaneously teachers should adopt the role of supervisor and tone down their earlier task of imparting available knowledge. Furthermore, the curriculum recommended that teachers of different school subjects should come together in teams to give each other mutual support in this kind of interdisciplinary instruction. The earlier 40-minute lessons could be prolonged to working periods of between 80 and 120 minutes.

With such an approach school work could be more problem-centered. Students could study phenomena as they appear in real life and not split up in school subjects.

Motivation, activity, concretization, individualization, and cooperation were the key words of the new curriculum. In the introductory chapter of 'Objectives and guide-lines' stress is put on the role of the school for the personality development and social development of the student and not only his intellectual growth. These so-called 'overall objectives' have ever since been at the centre of pedagogical discussion in Sweden.

The grade 7 subjects
The new curriculum was published late, only some eight months before it was to be applied. The commercial producers had no possibility of producing new learning aids quickly enough. It was in this situation that Sveriges Radio undertook to plan and to produce continually during the school year a number of products of a multi-media type to support teachers in their passing over to the new order. This gradual publication of programmes and other learning material naturally had to build on confidence in Sveriges Radio on the part of the receiving schools. As many as 24 per cent of the upper-level schools of the country took these projects, thus buying a pig in a poke. Certain projects were taken by up to 50 per cent of the target audience.

Researchers in the project group
To be carried through successfully these projects of course presupposed careful planning in a great many respects, organizational as well as pedagogical. For the planning and production of the projects we created a special project group of which

planners, radio producers, television producers, editors of printed material, and researchers were members. The first measure to be undertaken was to develop syllabuses for the sectors of the curriculum to be covered by the projects, namely social science, natural science, and Swedish. In those syllabuses it was indicated week by week, month by month, what work projects were continually produced by Sveriges Radio. Those syllabuses were developed in consultation with the National Board of Education.

Together with the National Board of Education the contents of each project were defined in special goal descriptions. In this work the researchers of the project teams made essential contributions. The goal descriptions facilitated the production and later became the foundation of tests of knowledge and skills.

The Grade 7 projects and their successors, the Grade 8 projects and the Grade 9 projects, covered all the items of the syllabuses for the target grades in the subjects concerned. However, each project could also be used separately.

The learning material was delivered gradually during the school year according to a special plan of delivery. Schools received material for about two months at a time.

Possibility of a quick feedback
The possibility of a quick follow-up of the first projects and evaluation of the result of their use in the school was a prerequisite for success. The first experiences could soon affect the continued planning and production during the first school year at the same time as it was possible to revise the first projects for the following school year.

During the first year ten upper-level schools, geographically spread all over the country, took part in a systematic evaluation of the projects. Teachers and pupils continually sent in reports on how the learning aids functioned in their daily school work. Furthermore, many conferences and meetings were organized with teachers and pupils all over the country.

Experiences
In a report on the Grade 7 projects published later the researchers summarized opinions expressed by teachers and pupils. The most important experiences were the following:

Negative
- the radio programmes were generally considered to be too long and too difficult for the pupils.
- assignments and exercises were considered to be too monotonously designed, which was to the detriment of individualization.
- the amount of time allotted to each project was not always enough.
- many teachers were of the opinion that the material directed their classroom work too much.
- working with separate projects was considered a problem in that it made it difficult for students to see the subject matter in its totality.

Positive
- on the whole the learning material functioned satisfactorily in the new situation.
- television programmes were all through judged more positively by both teachers and students.
- the fact that the material was designed as multi-media projects and that it consisted of separate pamphlets for the projects instead of a manual was generally judged favourably.
- students were of the opinion that learning was facilitated by multi-media learning aids where sound and pictures were integrated with printed material.
- the students' results in knowledge and skills were on the whole good.

From grade 7 projects to 'Trialogue'
For copyright reasons a school radio programme produced by Sveriges Radio cannot be used in a school later than three years after the day of the broadcast. Although this law really covers only sound radio the corresponding practice has also been developed for school television. Planning for the school year 1973–4 we therefore had to decide whether to give up the Grade 7 projects or to revise and broadcast them again.

The situation was now in many respects very different from what had been the case in 1970. The commercial producers had caught up and on the market there were now several teaching aids for the upper level in the subjects concerned.

From quantity to quality

The Grade 7 projects had been produced in order to meet an acute need. That reason was hardly valid any more. Many schools went over to other teaching/learning aids as they appeared on the market. About 10 per cent of the schools stuck to the Grade 7 projects, however, and that was a target audience that was large enough to justify our further developing a multi-media alternative with an unconventional pedagogical design. The production—or rather revision of the old products—could now be concentrated on questions of quality. The Grade 7 projects had been produced under extraordinary circumstances. It was therefore only natural that the material should have certain shortcomings. Through the continuous follow-up and evaluation there was fairly full documentation on the merits and shortcomings of practically every work project. During the three years when the projects had been produced we had considerably increased our knowledge of how the media should be integrated with printed material and how the products should be methodologically designed to meet the demands of the school. Thus, the prerequisites for a revision were good.

In the paper sent to the National Board of Education in the spring of 1972—according to an annual procedure—we therefore asked the question whether the material should be revised and published again. The majority of the institutions reacting on the paper were of the opinion that that should be so, and in its summarizing answer the National Board of Education wrote:

> The National Board of Education shares the opinion of Sveriges Radio that the material produced for Grade 7 should in revised form be offered to the schools for yet another period of three years. Furthermore it seems advisable to undertake a thorough follow-up study of the material revised in its totality according to the results of earlier evaluation.

In next year's budget the Minister of Education wrote:

> Furthermore, during the budget year of 1973–4 Sveriges Radio intends to investigate the various problems in connection with the use of the so-called Grade 7–9

projects. In my opinion Sveriges Radio had made valuable contributions in connection with the introduction of the new curriculum. I am also of the opinion that the efforts for the areas of schooling where there is a lack of learning material are particularly urgent as well as the investigation just mentioned.

Against this background the Educational Programme Department took the final decision to revise the Grade 7 projects and publish them for another period of three years under the name of *Trialogue*. Simultaneously it was decided that this new material which we hoped would be more elaborate than its predecessor should be the object of comprehensive research on the functions of multi-media material in the teaching/learning process.

Trialogue—project

In starting the revision work the project group asked themselves the following questions:

- how should instructional and learning materials be designed to direct classroom work also towards the overall objectives of the curriculum?
- how should study material be designed to help teachers develop the new roles described in the curriculum?
- how should instructional and learning materials be designed to make students feel that they are working with essentials that are of importance to them and engage them?
- how should the emotional effects of the presentation of the material be increased to motivate the students for the verbal and theoretical parts of the work?
- how should learning materials be designed to give support to individualization?
- how should the principle of project work be combined with the demand for continuity and comprehensive coverage of the subject matter?

The production of *Trialogue* was preceded by comprehensive planning and construction work where we discussed questions like the function of the programmes, the directive effects of learning aids, the rôles of teachers, problems of individualization, the weaknesses and merits of the principle of project work and other methodological problems. The result of all this thinking was what we called the *Trialogue* model.

The *Trialogue* model

It would in this context lead us too far to give a detailed description of the structure of the *Trialogue* model. Let us therefore limit ourselves to some main features.

Overall objectives

The overall objectives of the curriculum have systematically been integrated in each of the *Trialogue* projects with the help of a method or model that was developed within the National Board of Education in co-operation with the Pedagogical Institute of the Gothenburg University. This is a field where development has only just started, so this method must be regarded as a first attempt.

Goal descriptions

The contents of each *Trialogue* project have been defined, as earlier in the Grade 7 projects, in special goal descriptions. To what extent and in what way students are expected to master the contents is expressed by means of a special taxonomy.

Methodological design

The majority of the *Trialogue* projects have been structured according to a simple methodological model.

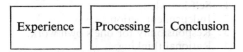

The model is based on the opinion that students should in their work projects, go from the concrete to the abstract, from the special to the general. This should make it possible for them to start from their own situation and experience.

Consequently, whenever feasible, students should acquire the experience to carry the rest of the work on through direct study of reality itself. Many work projects therefore contain suggestions for excursions, study visits, experiments and such like. Radio and television programmes are resorted to when it is not very easy to get the desirable experience through experiments, excursions etc. The programmes often take the form of case studies which present

people and their social environment in a way that is very near a first-hand experience. They are meant to arouse students' curiosity and wish to examine the matter further, i.e. to go on in the project, and the programmes certainly do not just give them ready-made opinions.

Naturally methods of work vary. The teaching/learning aids give students support in the form of assignments mainly of three kinds:

- study questions which help the students find their way through what has been described in programmes and other learning aids;
- analytical questions which help them to discover causes and effects;
- evaluation questions with the help of which the student can take a stand either by himself or together with his fellow students.

To help students with their conclusions and generalizations the printed material of each work project finishes with a summary.

Pedagogical planning

It was with this kind of pedagogical model that the *Trialogue* project group wanted to answer the questions that they asked themselves at the start of their revision work. In the production teams of the various projects there were always one or more active teachers.

Starting from the goal description and the aspects we undertook the pedagogical planning of the project, the division of labour between the various media and the methodological design.

The following questions needed to be answered *inter alia*:

- in what different ways should students be given the opportunity to work through and simultaneously assimilate the contents of the project?
- how should students be given an opportunity to put into practice what the aspects of the overall objectives stand for?
- what concrete experiences of the contents of a project should students have as a basis for assimilation and further generalization and abstraction?
- in what different ways can sound and picture media contribute to increased concretization and simultaneously pre-

sent the contents in such a way that the intended student activities are started?

● what parts of the contents should be published in the printed material and in what form?

● what is the role of the teacher?

Some hypotheses for research
Some hypotheses for research were:

● that radio and television in combination with printed material facilitate learning and conceptualization;

● that a varied and planned division of labour between teacher, student and learning aid not only facilitates the learning of knowledge and skills but also works towards the overall objectives of the school;

● that pre-planned and pre-produced learning material based on fundamental psychological experience increases the effects of school work;

● that media in combination increase and keep the student's motivation and the concretization of instruction;

● that the possibilities of individualization within the frame of the class increase if learning-aid production pays heed to the whole teaching/learning situation and not only the production itself;

● that pre-produced learning material frees the teacher for personal contact with his students;

● that radio and television open the school towards society and the world.

Research and evaluation of the *Trialogue* material will give us some answers to whether these hypotheses are correct. During the school year 1973–4 Sveriges Radio carried out comprehensive research whose results are still being analysed and worked on. A summarizing report will be published in 1976.

Conclusion
The production of the Grade 7 projects was accompanied by extensive evaluation work. This method of work confirmed what we had already been able to observe, namely the high value of evaluation and following up radio and television projects for schools. Our experience was widened in several aspects.

However, similar to what is true for other countries in the world there is a difference between the philosophical goals set up in the curricula and the reality of the classroom. Most of the teachers in Sweden still put the emphasis on the intellectual part of the development of the personality—they impart knowledge and skills, often through one-way communications *from* the teacher *to* the pupil.

The most common objection to the integration of the overall objectives is the difficulty of transferring the general and philosophical terms in which the curricula are worded into concrete teaching activities.

The lack of a concrete model of how to integrate the overall objectives in a teaching aid was one of the most important starting-points of the *Trialogue* project.

The aims of *Trialogue*
This program series was planned for the seventh grade of the comprehensive school, lower secondary level. It was designed for the major part of the lessons in religion, civics, history, geography, physics, chemistry, biology and Swedish. It is based on the multi-media principle, i.e. radio and television combined with printed material.

Techniques of making the curriculum more concrete
An analysis of the normative goals deduced from the curriculum leads us to set up a number of so-called 'aspects', eighteen in all:

1 Self-knowledge.
2 Independent action.
3 Responsibility for one's own work.
4 Rational thinking.
5 Critical evaluation.
6 Honesty.
7 Perseverence.
8 Ability to plan.
9 Development of study techniques.
10 Development of a broad outlook and a sense of totality.
11 Creativity.
12 Self-expression in free formative activities.
13 Awareness of working environment.
14 Moods and emotions.
15 Participation.
16 Cooperation.
17 Understanding of others.
18 Responsibility for others.

When planning a teaching aid the producer mostly chooses among these eighteen aspects and picks out those which are most appropriate with respect to the kind of topic to be dealt with, the content and so on. Sometimes this process develops as a co-operation between the producer and the researcher.

Evaluation of the effects of the integration of the overall objectives

To be able to evaluate the integration of the overall objectives we formulated three questions:

1 to what extent does the teaching process contain activities which go along with the overall objectives?
2 to what extent do the teaching aids suggest activities which go well with the overall objectives?
3 what are the effects on the pupils of the activities related to the overall objectives?

By establishing a rather close contact with the experimental classes, twelve altogether, we were able to follow the school work in detail throughout the school year. We tried to cover the first two questions above as thoroughly as possible in order to be able to deduce the answers to the third question from the material collected.

The first question—teaching activities
From the diaries, which the teachers filled in to describe their teaching activities, we can get a fairly good impression of what aspects of the overall objectives were covered.

According to their own judgements the teachers covered from four to nine aspects of the overall objectives in the course of a so-called work project (10–15 lessons).

Question two—suggestions in the teaching aids
The judgements from the teachers are a list of activities in the classroom. The second question must then be: to what extent were those activities a consequence of the teaching aids used? Or put somewhat differently: did the teaching aid reinforce or keep back the development of new methods?

The teachers of social sciences are the most satisfied with the coverage of the overall objectives. The teachers of natural sciences and of Swedish can be described as

rather satisfied with the teaching aid in this respect. In *Trialogue* evaluation was of more stringent kind. The so-called *Trialogue* model was studied in many respects. One aspect of the study was whether the overall objectives could be built into a pre-produced multi-media material. Another aspect was whether the general pedagogical model of the project could bring about a sufficiently varied learning process.

The experiences of *Trialogue* have—in a higher degree than those of the Grade 7 projects—given us knowledge of what steps and considerations should be part of the pedagogical planning and production of a multi-media project. This knowledge can be used in the future decision-making in at least two respects:

● in the first place, what jobs in the teaching/learning process a multi-media project can take on with a fairly good chance of success.
● in the second place, how multi-media material should be designed against the background of the needs it is intended to meet.

Of course, the future decisions need not concern projects of the size described in this paper, but the experience acquired is also necessary for minor projects.

PAPER NO 15: TRIALOGUE: A RESEARCH AND DEVELOPMENT PROJECT

Christer Frey, Education Department, Sveriges Radio, Sweden.

Overall objectives—a background

The objectives for the Swedish compulsory school (the ground school, grades 1–9) are stated in a curriculum. The final purpose with the school is to develop the pupils' personalities. In earlier times this has just meant giving the pupils knowledge and skills. In the new curriculum (1969) they also put a stress on the other part of the development of the personality—the social part.

However, similar to what is true for other countries in the world there is a difference between the philosophical goals set up in the curricula and the reality of the classroom. Most of the teachers in Sweden still put the emphasis on the intellectual part of the development of the personality—they impart knowledge and skills, often through one-way communication *from* the teacher *to* the pupil.

The most common objection to the integration of the overall objectives is the difficulty of transferring the general and philosophical terms in which the curricula are worded into concrete teaching activities.

The lack of a concrete model of how to integrate the overall objectives in a teaching aid was one of the most important starting-points of the *Trialogue* project.

The aims of *Trialogue*

This program series was planned for the seventh grade of the comprehensive school, lower secondary level. It was designed for the major part of the lessons in religion, civics, history, geography, physics, chemistry, biology and Swedish. It is based on the multi-media principle, i.e., radio and TV combined with printed material.

Techniques of making the curriculum more concrete

An analysis of the normative goals deduced from the curriculum leads us to set up a number of so-called 'aspects', eighteen in all:

1 Self-knowledge.
2 Independent action.
3 Responsibility for one's own work.
4 Rational thinking.
5 Critical evaluation.
6 Honesty.
7 Perseverence.
8 Ability to plan.
9 Development of study techniques.
10 Development of a broad outlook and a sense of totality.
11 Creativity.
12 Self-expression in free formative activities.
13 Awareness of working environment.
14 Moods and emotions.
15 Participation.
16 Cooperation.
17 Understanding of others.
18 Responsibility for others.

When planning a teaching aid the producer mostly chooses among these eighteen aspects and picks out those which are most appropriate with respect to the kind of topic to be dealt with, the content and so on. Sometimes this process develops as a cooperation between the producer and the researcher.

Evaluation of the effects of the integration of the overall objectives

To be able to evaluate the integration of the overall objectives we formulated three questions:

1 To what extent does the teaching process contain activities which go along with the overall objectives?
2 To what extent do the teaching aids suggest activities which go well with the overall objectives?
3 What are the effects on the pupils of the activities related to the overall objectives?

By establishing a rather close contact with the experimental classes, twelve altogether, we were able to follow the school work in detail throughout the school year. We tried to cover the first two questions above as thoroughly as possible in order to be able to deduce the answers to the third question from the material collected.

The first question—teaching activities

From the diaries, which the teachers filled in to describe their teaching activities, we can get a fairly good impression of what aspects of the overall objectives were covered.

According to their own judgements the teachers covered from four to nine aspects of the overall objectives in the course of a so-called work project (10–15 lessons).

Question two—suggestions in the teaching aid

The judgements from the teachers are a list of activities in the classroom. The second question must then be: to what extent were those activities a consequence of the teaching aids used? Or put somewhat differently: did the teaching aid reinforce or keep back the development of new methods?

The teachers of social sciences are the most satisfied with the coverage of the overall objectives. The teachers of natural sciences and of Swedish can be described as rather satisfied with the teaching aid in this respect.

To summarize, the teachers expressed their satisfaction of the *Trialogue* material; the method used to integrate the overall objectives functioned fairly well. By using multi-media materials the teachers were able to start new processes in the classroom. This they had not envisaged when they started using the *Trialogue* material.

Question three—effects on the pupils

The question is very difficult to answer in a straightforward way. It is impossible to measure the effects about, for example, the development of a more cooperative attitude. We therefore used answers from the teachers both in interviews and in questionnaires. They were invited to judge the effectiveness of the teaching aid in reinforcing a learning situation in accordance with the overall objectives.

If the figures are compared with those collected through other channels we can assume that *Trialogue* succeeded fairly well in establishing a basis for a new kind of learning situation in school, which has had a positive effect on the pupils' individual and social development.

We also noticed as a side effect that both the teachers and the pupils became more aware of the necessity to arrange the learning situation in such a way that it motivates the pupils not only for the lessons but for the entire school work. Maybe we can say that this side effect is the most important effect of *Trialogue*.

Conclusions

Trialogue has shown that there are great advantages in using a learning aid based on the multi-media principle to deal with the overall objectives in the curriculum. Through the radio and television media we cannot merely motivate the pupils and make a topic more concrete. We can also start new processes in the classroom, which can develop the pupil individually and socially. One way to facilitate these new processes is the use of the radio and TV media to free the teacher for tasks for which he is best suited. You can never expect emotional reactions from a TV set.

A teaching aid has a relatively short life and this is true for *Trialogue* as well. But the important principles, methods and con-crete suggestions in *Trialogue* are valid over a longer period. This is why we consider the side effect of *Trialogue*, i.e. making the teachers more aware of and willing to accept the overall objectives, to be such an important effect.

PAPER NO 54: TRIALOGUE: A RESEARCH AND DEVELOPMENT PROJECT*

Claes Rudén, Education Department, Sveriges Radio, Sweden.

The aims of *Trialogue*

This programme series was planned for the seventh grade of the compulsory school (junior high-school level). It was designed for the major part of the lessons in religion, civics, history, geography, physics, chemistry, biology and Swedish. It was based on the multi-media principle, i.e. radio and TV combined with printed material and slides.

The *Trialogue* survey

During the school year 1973–4 we conducted a comprehensive survey of the function of the *Trialogue* material in the work of the schools. The survey was conducted in six schools, spread all over the country, which use *Trialogue* in their work. The main purpose of the survey was to examine whether pre-planned teaching/learning aids of a multi-media type could facilitate an instruction along the lines of the double aims of the school—the imparting of knowledge and personality development.

Twelve classes, comprising some 300 pupils, were involved in the survey. The teachers of the classes concerned, approximately 45, have assessed the study material in various ways.

General results of the *Trialogue* survey

Teachers think that multi-media teaching/learning aids are better than ordinary aids regarding:

● stimulating and engaging students (according to 94 per cent of the teachers).

---

* Author's summary of full paper.

- concretizing difficult subject matter and giving it life (87 per cent).
- activating students over the weak performance (74 per cent).
- giving students knowledge and skills (60 per cent).

The greatest advantages of *Trialogue* according to the teachers are that the teaching/learning aid:

- provides variation so that classroom work becomes stimulating and motivates students to work well;
- contains both printed material, sound and moving pictures and that the link between the media is good.

The methodological design
The *Trialogue* material has been built on a design going from the concrete to the abstract, and you can describe the three steps of the design in this way.

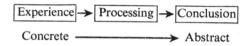

The work project normally starts with some kind of experience of what is to be studied. This can be with the help of a radio or TV programme that introduces into the classroom people or milieus, or shows processes or phenomena that it would otherwise be difficult to meet in the classroom. A strong experience of what is to be studied can also be given sometimes through texts and pictures in the students' pamphlet or through a demonstration carried out by the teacher.

The point is to start with a strong experience of what the students are to work with in the work project. The presentation should be concrete. On the other hand it need not be structured in the sense that it is strictly adjusted to the situation of the students and that conclusions are drawn.

The concrete idea of the subject matter that students have acquired through this start will then be part of the frame of reference to be used for the processing of the matter that follows. It is with particular care that we have tried to find a variety of ways of assimilating the matter. Students work with texts and pictures of various kinds.

Every work project finishes with a recapitulation, a summary which makes generalizations of the essential points of the contents. It can be described as an abstraction of the most essential of that which has been treated in the project.

The Egypt of the Pharaohs—An example of a *Trialogue* project
We shall now give you in short an example of the practical application of the methodological design—experience, processing, conclusion. The example is called 'The Egypt of the Pharaohs', a work project in social science for grade 7. Students are then about 14 years old. The project covers some 5 'lessons' of 80 minutes each, and the work is organized in a non-traditional way.

After the introductory television programme the students of the class are split up into seven groups. The students assimilate the larger part of the subject matter in the form of group work. The groups are expected to work mainly on their own and then report to each other what they have learnt. The teacher's most important role is to organize and superintend.

We can sum up the design of the project in the following figures:

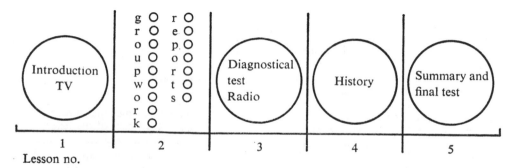

The attitude of the teachers and students to the Egypt of the Pharaohs

Let us quote some of the results of the evaluation of the project 'the Egypt of the Pharaohs'. All teachers were very positive in their assessment of the printed material of the project. The students were also very positive. Using a scale from 1–4 the mean value of the students' assessments on the scale 'uninteresting—interesting' is 3.5.

The theoretical mean value of the scale is 2.0 and the students' assessments vary between 2.0 and 2.6, with a mean value of 2.3.

The high value of the TV programme (2.6) confirms the importance of a strong experience in the beginning of the work. The judgements show that the study material engaged and motivated the students also in the processing phase. The conclusion phase got a lower mean value and of course a summary cannot be as much fun as the other parts of the study material as it has to be more verbal and thus more abstract.

To sum up

Through the TV programme about the saving of the Abu Simble Temple the students got a concrete idea of how impressive monuments the ancient Egyptians were capable of constructing 3,000 years ago. The programme aroused their interest and motivated them well for the work. The pamphlet pictures of other ancient monuments helped the students to choose themes for study. Already after one lesson they were deep in study of the chosen theme. This can be said to be contrary to earlier pedagogical planning where we used to start by giving the students a structure, a firm ground to build on before they were invited to deeper study of certain phenomena. The work with the group themes and reporting on the group work functioned well thanks to the rich picture material in the pamphlet, the slides and the rest of the extra material.

Through their reports the groups share their knowledge with their fellow students in the other groups. In this way they are made to realize their responsibility that the reports are good. The group reports were then followed by the diagnostical test. The result of the final test showed that the students had assimilated the contents of the work project in a satisfactory way.

Conclusions

The results of the *Trialogue* survey show that there are advantages in using teaching/learning material based on the multi-media principle, when we want to attain the double goals of the curriculum, i.e. both cognitive subject-matter objectives and overall objectives.

It can be maintained that in the school it is equally important to ask how to work as to ask what to learn.

A combination of different media makes it possible to offer a variety of forms of presentation and suggestions for further work.

With the radio and TV programmes we have not only motivated the students and made the contents of the instruction more concrete to them. We have also increased the possibilities for both teachers and students of varying their ways of working and of developing new teaching methods in education.

PAPER NO 76: FORMATIVE RESEARCH IN THE PRODUCTION OF TELEVISION FOR CHILDREN*

Edward Palmer, Vice-President, Research, Children's Television Workshop, New York, USA.

There is currently in the United States unparalleled interest in the systematic use of broadcast television to promote the social, emotional, and intellectual growth of young children. Support for this movement lies in the recognition that television is ubiquitous, reaching into 97 per cent of all US households; that young children are exposed to upwards of thirty hours of television fare each week; that while they learn a great deal

---

* This is a severely abridged version of a paper which first appeared in *Media Symbols: The Forms of Expression, Communication, and Education*, Seventy-Third Yearbook of the National Society for the Study of Education, Part 1, pp. 303–29, (Chicago, University of Chicago Press, 1974). We are very grateful to the publishers for allowing us to use this paper in the proceedings.

H

from what they watch, there have been far too few significant attempts to plan program content in order to address important areas of learning and development systematically; and that no other approach can promise to deliver so much to so many at so small a unit cost.

An important feature of this movement is its emphasis on 'formative' planning and research. First, important objectives are clearly identified, then systematic audience tests are carried out in order to evaluate progress toward their achievement during the actual course of a program's production. Formative research is typically contrasted with summative research, which is concerned with follow-up testing to determine the educational effect of new products and practices when actually put into use. What follows is a description of the approaches to formative planning and research taken by the Children's Television Workshop (CTW) in the production of *Sesame Street* and *The Electric Company*.

At the beginning of the *Sesame Street* project, the functions formative research could serve and the field methods it could apply were not at all clear. There were no precedents of sufficient scope and generality from either the field of educational technology in particular or the field of educational planning and research in general to provide clear guidelines. What has been learned about the formative planning and research process at CTW has come about under quite unusual circumstances, and since it is unlikely that these conditions will ever be duplicated in substantial detail, it remains to be seen what sorts of new or modified approaches will be required in different situations. What is presented here certainly cannot be construed as a dependable recipe that will assure the success of other like ventures.

Among the unusual circumstances associated with the Workshop's productions, some, no doubt, had quite a direct bearing on the effectiveness of the formative research. For instance, the two Workshop projects were well funded; each was budgeted in its first season at upwards of seven million dollars for production, research, and related activities. This level of support made it possible to utilize high-level production talent and resources and to make extensive use of expert educational

advisers and consultants. In addition, both projects enjoyed unusually long periods of time—in each case, approximately eighteen months—for prebroadcast planning and research. Time and resources were available to plan their curricula carefully and to state their educational objectives in very explicit terms. This meant that producers and researchers alike, as well as the independent evaluators who were carrying out pre-season and post-season achievement testing projects, could proceed without ambiguity of purpose and in a coordinated fashion. Had there been ambiguity in terms of either the particular objectives to be addressed or the commitment of the producers to direct each segment toward the achievement of one or more of those objectives, the formative research could not have been useful, for there would have been no clear criteria for evaluating a program segment's effectiveness.

Also unusual in the CTW case was the policy followed in production recruiting and the organizational and interpersonal relationships between the in-house research and production staffs. All of the key producers came from commercial production backgrounds. None had formal professional training in education or experience in educational television production. Yet they were given the responsibility for final production decisions. They did not work under the researchers, nor did the researchers work under them. The intended function of the formative research was to provide information which the producers would find useful in making program-design decisions relating to both appeal and educational effect.

To the extent that the formative research worked, it worked in large measure because of the attitudes taken toward it by producers and researchers alike. The producers were committed to experimenting with the cyclic process of empirical evaluation and production revision and tended to have the ability not only to see the implications of the research, but also to carry these implications through into the form of new and revised production approaches. Accordingly, the usefulness of CTW's formative research has depended not only on the qualities of the research itself, but also on the talents of those who put its results to use. Moreover, the producers never expected the research to yield full-blown decisions; they recognized that its function was to provide one more source of information among many. From the research side, because the responsibility for final production decisions resided with the producers, it was necessary to develop and apply only methods which provided information useful to the producers. Accordingly, the producers were involved from the outset in all research planning. No observational method was ever persistently applied, and no specific study was ever taken into the field without their participation.

The CTW operational model
The principal activities undertaken in the production of *Sesame Street* have come to be viewed by CTW as a model, and this model was again applied in the production of *The Electric Company*. If there is a single, most critical condition for rendering such a model of researcher-producer cooperation effective, it is that the researchers and the producers cannot be marching to different drummers. The model is essentially a model for production planning. More specifically, it is a model for planning the educational (as opposed to the dramatic) aspects of the production—and formative research is an integral part of that process. In the case of *Sesame Street* and *The Electric Company*, at least, it is hard to imagine that the formative research and curriculum planning could have been effective if they had been carried out apart from overall production planning, either as *a priori* processes or as independent but simultaneous functions. The activities included in the model are presented below in their approximate chronological order of recurrence.

(a) Behavioral goals
As the initial step toward establishing its educational goals, CTW, in the summer of 1968, conducted a series of five three-day seminars dealing with the following topics:

1 Social, moral, and affective development.
2 Language and reading.
3 Mathematical and numerical skills.
4 Reasoning and problem-solving.
5 Perception.

The seminars, organized and directed by Dr Gerald S. Lesser, Bigelow Professor of Education and Developmental Psychology at Harvard University, were attended by more than a hundred expert advisers, including psychologists, psychiatrists, teachers, sociologists, film-makers, television producers, writers of children's books, and creative advertising personnel. Each seminar group was asked to suggest educational goals for the prospective series and to discuss ways of realizing the goals on television. The output from the initial seminars was then systematically organized, refined, and made operational by the CTW staff and board of advisers. This work resulted in specific goals stated in behavioral terms. These behavioral objectives served as a common reference point for the program producers and the designers of the follow-up achievement tests. Essential coordination of production and evaluation was thus assured.

(b) Existing competence of target audience
While the statement of goals specified the behavioural outcomes which the program hoped to achieve, it was necessary to ascertain the target audience's existing range of competence in the chosen goal areas. In its initial formative research effort, the Workshop research staff therefore compiled data provided in the literature and did some further testing of its own to determine the competence range. The resulting information helped guide the producers in allocating program time and budget among the goal categories and in selecting specific learning instances in each goal area.

(c) Appeal of existing materials
To be successful, CTW had to capture its intended audience with an educational show whose highly attractive competition was only a flick of the dial away. Unlike the classroom teacher, the Workshop had to win its audience, and it had to hold their attention from moment to moment and from day to day. At stake was a potential variation in daily attendance which could run into millions. Measuring the preferences of the target audience for existing television and film materials was therefore crucial in the design of the new series.

(d) Experimental production
Seminar participants and CTW advisers

had urged the use of a variety of production styles to achieve the curriculum goals adopted. Research had confirmed the appetite of the target audience for fast pace and variety. Accordingly, the CTW production staff invited a number of live-action and animation film production companies to submit ideas. The first season of *Sesame Street* eventually included the work of thirty-two different film companies.

Prototype units of all film series produced by or for the Workshop were subjected to rigorous preliminary scrutiny and empirical field evaluation. Scripts and story boards were revised by the Workshop producers on the basis of recommendations from the research staff, further revisions were made after they had been reviewed by educational consultants and advisers, and finished films were tested by the research department with sample audiences. Some material never survived the process. Four pilot episodes were produced for a live-action film adventure series entitled *The Man from Alphabet*, but when the films were shown to children they failed to measure up either in appeal or educational effect, and the series was dropped. Sample videotaped material went through the same process of evaluation, revision, and occasional elimination.

By July 1969 a format for the program had been devised, a title had been selected, a cast had been tentatively assigned, and a week of full-length trial programs had been taped.

Completed prototype production elements were tested by the research staff in two ways: the appeal of the CTW material was measured against the appeal of previously tested films and television shows; and the CTW material was tested for its educational impact under a number of conditions. For instance, field studies were conducted to determine the effect of various schedules of repetition and spacing, of providing the child with preliminary or follow-up explanation, of presenting different approaches to a given goal separately or in combination, and the relative effectiveness of adult versus child voice over narration. Extensive observation of children watching the shows provided information about the child's understanding of various conventions of film and television techniques. When each research study concluded, the results were reported to the producers for their use in modifying the show components tested and for their guidance in producing subsequent elements. It should be noted that this progress-testing also served a formative research function for the Educational Testing Service staff by field-testing the instruments and administration procedures that were to be employed in later summative evaluation.

(e) The progress testing

The evolution of *Sesame Street* did not end with the first national broadcast on 10 November 1969. Formative research continued throughout the six-month broadcast season. During this time, it became possible to begin examining the cumulative impact of the series. Accordingly, the research staff instituted a program of testing the show's effectiveness, using the summative evaluation instruments designed by the Educational Testing Service (ETS) of Princeton, New Jersey. A sample of day-care children, predominantly four- and five-year-olds, were pretested prior to the first national telecast. One-third were tested again after three weeks of viewing the show, the same one-third and an additional one-third were tested after six weeks of viewing, and the entire group was tested after three months of viewing. Comparisons between experimental (viewing) and control (non-viewing) groups at each stage of the testing gave indications of strengths and weaknesses in both the execution of the curriculum and the production design. Other independent formative studies of program appeal and of the responses of viewing children also influenced production decisions during this period.

(f) Summative evaluation

The summative research and evaluation carried out by the Educational Testing Service on each of the program's first two seasons followed a plan developed in consultation with CTW staff and advisers. Participation of ETS representatives in all the main phases of pre-broadcast planning helped to ensure that program development and follow-up testing were coordinated.

For the first-season study, ETS developed and administered a special battery of eleven tests covering the major CTW goal areas to a sample of children from Boston,

Philadelphia, Durham and Phoenix. The groups included three-, four-, and five-year-olds from middle- and lower-income families in urban and rural settings and in both home and day-care situations. A special side study related to children from Spanish-speaking homes. Other measures assessed home conditions, parental expectations for the children, and the like. In instances where the results of the first season's summative research were fed into production decisions for the second season, they took on a formative function. For example, the summative data indicated that the children's knowledge and skills before viewing the programs had been underestimated in some goal areas and over-estimated in others. This was taken into account in programming the second season of *Sesame Street*.

(g) *The writer's notebook*

As the producers and writers began to develop scripts, animations, and live-action films addressed to particular behaviorally stated goals, it became apparent that the goal statement was not a wholly adequate reference. After having been given several successive assignments in the same goal area, they began to express the need for extended and enriched definitions which would provide creative stimulation. Gradually, through trial and error, a format for the Writer's Notebook was developed which the producers and writers found useful.

The Notebook emphasized four criteria:

1 To focus on the psychological processes involved in a particular form of behavior.
2 To exploit and extend the child's own experiential referents for such behavior.
3 To prompt the creation of various similar approaches by the producers and writers themselves by presenting them with highly divergent examples.
4 To provide suggestions free of any reference to particular characters or contexts from the television program, so that the ways in which the suggestions could be implemented would be left as open and flexible as possible.

These features of the Writer's Notebook may be highlighted through an example. In the broad area of 'symbolic representa-tion', the word-matching objective was stated as follows: 'Given a printed word, the child can select an identical printed word from a set of printed words'. To implement this objective, the Notebook encouraged the producers to use words with different numbers of letters, to vary the location within the word of the letter or letters which fail to 'match', and to present various matching strategies—such as comparing two given words letter by letter, moving word which were initially separated into physical superimposition, and spelling out each of two given words and comparing to see if one has made the same sounds both times. Another recommended approach was to make use of the 'sorting' format, already familiar to viewers, wherein three identical things (in this case, words) and one odd thing are presented simultaneously along with a standard song which invites the viewer to find the one which is different. Still another was to construct a letter-by-letter match for a given word by choosing from a large pool of letters. To encourage still other approaches, another recom-mendation was to present pairs of words which matched in one sense but not in another—for example, pairs in which the same word is presented in different type faces, or in which one of the pair is the upper- and the other lower-case version.

The producers and writers asked that similar suggestions be developed for other goal areas. Again, suggestions were solicited from advisers and consultants. In addition, the Notebook provided a place and a format for collecting the ideas of the in-house re-search staff and helped to ensure that these ideas would be seen and used.

> The full paper goes on to set out a model for research on presentational learning, describing CTW formative research on appeal, comprehensibility, activity-elicit-ing potential, and internal compatibility.

Organizational and interpersonal factors

As technologically sophisticated forms of instruction come into increasing promin-ence, it will be necessary to make increased use of production teams whose members possess a diversity of highly specialized talents. In anticipation of this trend, we need to know more about related organizational and interpersonal conditions. These conditions deserve attention in any attempt to establish a working partnership between television-research and production groups, and they play a role which is even more prominent in the formative research context than in the context of more traditional approaches to educational research.

An important factor in CTW's case has been the opportunity for the members of the two groups to learn about each other's areas of specialization during an eighteen-month pre-broadcast period. Furthermore, every new formative research approach is treated as an experiment to be continued or discontinued depending on its evaluation by the producers themselves.

The fact that CTW's researchers and producers possess not the same but complementary skills is also significant, largely because it makes for clear and distinct functions on the part of each group. Still another factor is that the producers, before joining the project, made the commitment to try to work with formative research. This advance commitment helped to support the cooperative spirit through the early, more tentative period of the effort. Also, research never takes on the role of adversary to be used against the producers in winning a point or pressing for a particular decision. On some matters, the producers must hold the final power of decision and be free to ignore research suggestions if production constraints require it.

In all, the factors consciously dealt with in the interests of researcher-producer cooperation have ranged from the careful division of labor and responsibility to housing the two staffs in adjacent offices, and from patience and diplomacy to occasional retreat.

The distinctive role and functions of formative research

Formative research is distinguished primarily by its role as an integral part of the creative production process. It is important to maintain a clear distinction between this type of research and summative research—that is, research undertaken to test the validity of a theory or the measurable impact of an educational product or practice. Research undertaken in the context of scientific validation is concerned with effects which have been hypothesized *a priori* within the framework of a broader deductive system, with the use of empirical and statistical procedures well enough defined as to be strictly replicable (at least in principle), and with the highest possible degree of generalizability across situations. While research carried out within the formative context can possess these same characteristics, it need not and typically does not. The main criterion for formative research recommendations is that they appear likely to contribute to the effectiveness of the product or procedure being developed. It is neither expected nor required that they be validated by the research out of which they grew. Establishing their validity is the function of summative research.

As this view implies, to achieve the objectives of formative research it is often necessary to depart from traditional research practices and perspectives. This is not to say that experimental rigor has no place in the formative context. However, even where strict experimental and control conditions have been maintained, there is seldom anything to be gained by using tests of statistical significance. The creative producers often prefer to work directly with information about means, dispersions, and sample size. Also, whereas matching of experimental and control groups on the basis of pre-test scores is discouraged where inferential statistics are to be used, because of the conservative effect on the usual tests for the significance of the results, such matching can be very useful in the interests of efficiency and the maximization of the reliability of information based on small samples. In the area of sample selection, it also can be useful to depart from the traditional practice of including all age and socio-economic groups for which the educational materials are intended. Time and effort may often be saved by selecting a sample of average performers, of performers from the high and low extremes, or, where the intent is mainly to up-grade the lowest performers, a sample only of those. In general, where biased methods of sampling and biased methods of testing are more efficient than unbiased methods, and where the objective is not to make accurate population estimates, it is often useful to exploit the very biases which quite properly would be avoided in other research situations.

In practice, it tends to be difficult for researchers trained and experienced in traditional approaches to adopt an appropriate formative research point of view. In the formative situation, their first responsibility is to improve a specific product or practice and not to contribute to a general body of knowledge (though the two objectives certainly are not incompatible). In such instances, studies must first address the information needs of the product designers and not the special theoretical interests of the researchers. Where it is economically impossible to cover a wide range of empirical questions and to rigorously report or establish careful experimental conditions, and where the usefulness of the results is not unduly compromised as a consequence, the former course may deserve priority. Quantitative indices, such as percentages, and highly detailed item-level data, if they communicate most effectively with the creative producers, are to be preferred over those which conform to standard practice for research reports. Broad, speculative interpretations of empirical results are typically more useful than interpretations limited to the more strict implications of a study. And, as indicated earlier, biased methods of sample selection and testing often can be employed to good advantage. However, in following these departures from standard research practice, there is a risk of producing misleading results. Accordingly, it is essential that resulting production recommendations be appropriately qualified.

Formative research, in my view, is properly eclectic and pragmatic. In these respects, it is highly compatible with the current trend toward defining instructional objectives very explicitly, then developing through systematic trial and revision instructional systems for achieving them. This approach, incidentally, in no way diminishes the traditional rôle of the behavioral sciences in education or the usefulness of existing theory and knowledge. Rather, it holds that a useful step between basic research and educational practice is additional research of a formative sort, directly concerned with specific combinations of educational objectives, instructional media, learners, and learning situations.

This is not to say that formative research is exclusively concerned with putting theory into practice. It has the equally valid function of starting with practice and transforming it into improved practice. It also has the function of providing hypotheses for further research and theoretical development. This is, incidentally, what is coming to be the dominant conception of the technology of education—a commitment not to teaching in the older audiovisual tradition, but to achieving a planned educational effect.

One long-standing point of view in education holds that theories and results growing out of the 'mother' disciplines of psychology, sociology, anthropology, and the like, will filter into effective educational practice if enough educators have been trained in these basic disciplines. While this approach has been useful to a degree, it has not produced broadly satisfactory results. Meanwhile, creators of new educational products and practices have proceeded largely without the benefits of measurement and research. This is partly because skill and training in these areas have been linked to the process of theory construction and validation, and partly because there has been an inappropriately rigid adherence to traditional research practice within the product development context. Formative research procedure promises to help in creating a mutually constructive relationship between these two overly isolated realms—the science and the technology of learning.

PAPER NO 55: CHILDREN'S PERCEPTION AND UNDERSTANDING OF TELEVISION*

Ann Searle, School of Behavioural and Social Science, Plymouth Polytechnic, UK.

Television is very widely used as an educational medium for children of all ages, but there has been practically no investigation of young children's perception and understanding of television. There is considerable

---

* Author's summary of full paper.

background information suggesting that in many ways young children's view of television is likely to be of a different nature to that of adults.

There is a great deal of perceptual research suggesting that young children's ability simply to accurately see what is on TV could be less than might be imagined. For example:

VURPILLOT (1968) and ZAPO-ROZHETS (1965) have shown that the eye movement strategies of young children are particularly haphazard or tend to fixate on a few features.

DOYLE (1975) has shown how young children are less able to focus attention and resist distraction.

POTTER (1966) showed young children take longer to recognize pictures than do adults, and that it is hard for children to recognize incomplete or indistinct forms.

GIBSON and GIBSON (1955) have argued that children's ability to discriminate between simple shapes is surprisingly poor.

ELKIND et al (1964) showed that young children tend to observe parts or wholes of pictures, not both.

Research by CARMICHAEL (1932) suggests that verbal material influences visual perception.

Evidence on memory in children is limited and at times conflicting, but the long-term memory of children is generally agreed to be poor. It has also been argued that young children have predominantly visual memories, which might suggest TV should be a particularly important educational tool. The cognitive research of PIAGET and BRUNER suggests that the child does not differentiate logical relations until the age of 7 or 8, that until this age incoherence of understanding is acceptable to the child, and that it is not until after 7 or 8 years that the child is capable of transcending what is immediately perceptually present to link past, present and future events.

Little previous research has been done in this area using TV or film. What there is conflicts, with French work suggesting that until the age of 9 or so children gain very little except enjoyment from films, whilst Swedish work has found considerable learning among children of 7 and below. This conflict seems to be due to methodological differences in research methods and materials used.

The author would argue that research should be done in this field as it would be useful to teachers, to television producers and of psychological interest. A project is just beginning at Plymouth Polytechnic concentrating on 4–9 year olds' comprehension of, and memory for, TV programmes.

SECTION B
NON-FORMAL ADULT EDUCATION PROGRAMMES

Designing evaluation systems: theories and methods

Assessing needs and interests

Studies of particular projects

INTRODUCTION

The papers in this section are all concerned with the most open of all areas of educational broadcasting—the attempt to reach adult audiences in their homes, without any requirements of enrolment.

This area poses challenging new questions in terms of problems and methodologies. To begin with, we have only an impressionistic understanding of the sections of the adult community we can hope to reach—according to the educational levels within the community, the objectives we set ourselves, the approaches we use and the transmission times and channels we have at our disposal. Then, very importantly, within these constraints we have somehow to find out what are the main needs and interests of these cross-sections of the community.

At once it is clear that social survey methods are likely to be more necessary in this area than in school, college and university systems, and we find this reflected in the papers for this Conference.

Once target audiences have been defined, there is still the problem of identifying those audiences and establishing a communication with representative sections of them. This poses further problems of social enquiry. When in turn these problems have been solved, the wide range of background and experience in almost every adult audience brings another set of problems; and the wide range of relevant subject matter brings yet one more. And all these problems have to be solved before systematic evaluation can begin.

So it is not surprising that this section of papers ranges more widely than the other sections. It begins with a number of papers that examine the special problems of studying adult audiences and the practical methods that can be brought to these problems. On the whole these papers are optimistic rather than gloomy, without in any way being self-deluding. They face the problems squarely and tackle them pragmatically. Then there is a group of three papers that are especially concerned with the study of potential needs and interests, which is clearly an important aspect of adult education broadcasting. The section again ends with studies of particular projects. The papers in this section cover the following projects:

Organization	Country
University of Adelaide	Australia
Ontario Educational Communications Authority	Canada
Finnish Broadcasting Authority	Finland
TELEAC	Holland
Satellite Instructional Television Experiment	India
TRU	Sweden
BBC	United Kingdom
IBA	United Kingdom
University of Mid-America	United States of America

DESIGNING EVALUATION SYSTEMS: THEORIES AND METHODS

PAPER NO 24: USEFUL EVALUATION DESIGNS FOR EVALUATING THE IMPACT OF DISTANCE LEARNING SYSTEMS

Robert C. Hornik, Institute for Communication Research, Stanford University, California.

Administratively, the programme operates well. Participants do the things they are supposed to do more or less on schedule. The project managers believe their objectives (teaching literacy or mathematics, or developing political consciousness) are being met. But the nagging doubt remains. How much change or learning has really occurred? How can the project's impact be established so as to satisfy not only the enthusiastic project manager but the skeptical outsider, the funding agency and others unwilling to accept enthusiasm as evidence?

The traditional answer, do an experiment, is ideal, and, as with most ideals, is often unrealistic. If a project has the resources, can manage to recruit participants for the experiment, and is convinced that the returns are sufficiently high, it is encouraged to push ahead. The rest of this paper is for those for whom the classical experiment is impossible, or simply not worth the expense.

What makes an experiment so difficult to do? By definition, the experiment requires the recruitment of a population equivalent in all ways to the people enrolled in the distance learning system. In a system whose participants are volunteers, an experimental design would require randomly selecting among volunteers and permitting only some to enroll in the system, but convincing the rest to respond to necessary tests and questionnaires. The dropout rate from such a control sample is likely to be high unless substantial rewards—cash payments, priority in subsequent years for access to the system—are offered. Also, for a system which provides itself on a first come-first serve selection process, as many distance learning systems do, this departure from that principle may be unacceptable.

For programs like Latin American radio schools or radio farm forums, an experimental design would require organizing perhaps twenty farm forums and then delaying the initiation of activities for a randomly selected ten. If the delay is long (and if one is interested in change in farm productivity, in literacy, or in political consciousness, the delay will need to be long) the problem of differential dropout from control and experimental samples is bound to arise. And again, the ethical acceptability of recruiting forum participants, and then letting them wait at a significant cost in enthusiasm and perhaps in willingness to participate in future self-improvement activities, is questionable.

For distance education that operates within the confines of an existing school system (the El Salvador, Ivory Coast, Colombia ITV projects) the opportunities for mounting experiments should be the most promising. Even there, however, the difficulties are considerable. The provision of a new service to some schools and not others, especially if the others are geographically close, as random assignment would require, is politically very difficult. Governments do not often experiment; lack of confidence in results, implied by the proposal of an experiment, is not politically tactful.

Experiments are rarely a feasible approach; but there are approximations to experiments, suitable for particular projects, which can provide adequate information for policy needs. In the following sections a series of such approximation designs is suggested. Each design controls for only those threats to valid inference which would worry a 'reasonable' observer in judging the impact of a particular type of project.

The Before-After Design

Between July and December 1972, seven hundred thousand latrines were built in Tanzania. During the first ten weeks of the same period, the government operated a radio study group campaign which addressed messages about latrines and other health behavior to two million Tanzanians. Few observers would doubt the connection between the two.

An imaginary open university teaches basic math to its first year students. At the beginning of the year they accurately answer only twenty per cent of the questions on an exam. On an end of year parallel exam, their average score is eighty per cent. Again, who would doubt the power of the math course?

For both cases (and in others, some literacy projects, some family planning projects) we realize that we cannot state with statistical rigor how much change would have occurred regardless of the project activities and how much was due to those activities. Yet the size of the change is overwhelming; we know, through substantive knowledge of the participants and the type of objectives, that the greatest part of that change was the result of project impact. There are no other reasonable explanations. Without outside intervention, latrines are not built and math is not learned in that volume and at that speed.

The approach is simple: measure before the project begins, and after it ends (or the appropriate cycle ends) and look at the difference. The difference (D) is seen as the result of two types of effects: project effects (PE) and other effects (OE), the change which would have occurred had the project not been operating (we will ignore the interaction effects). $D = PE + OE$. This design provides no entry point for statistical separation of PE and OE; attribution of all or most of the difference to the project effect depends on the subjective power of

one's argument that other causes are not likely explanations for the difference.

> The full paper goes on to discuss two limitations to the Before-After Design:
> (i) that it is only useful for projects aiming at large effects,
> (ii) that it is not appropriate where alternative influences are considerable.
> But the design can be extended by adding a time series design.

The natural control group

(a) *The mountain in the way*

Mountains have a marvellous capability for blocking radio signals. It may be that two villages (or sets of villages) equidistant from a major city, essentially similar in social characteristics, turn out to have different access to a radio signal, and thus different access to the radio school or the regular agricultural information broadcasts.

Access to the program is essentially random; that is, ability to hear the radio broadcasts is not related to any other characteristics of the village which might affect the dependent variable of interest. Analogous natural control groups might be suggested for situations in which convenient mountains were unavailable.

The central measurement activity is straightforward. Before the programs begin, each village (or set of villages) is measured on the dependent variable to verify that they are essentially similar; after measurements are used to establish difference scores for each village or set of villages. The difference score for the experimental group may be the result as before of two broad types of causes: project effects and other effects. However, in this case, it is worthwhile to partition the other effects term; common other effects (COE) are the result of causes common to both control and project samples. Specific other effects (SOE) are those which exclusively affect either the project villages or the control villages. These reflect both special events (the lava from the volcano flows into one village but not another) which occur during the time of the experiment, and original differences between the villages or sets of villages which call into question how natural a control the control group really was (was the radio-receiving village also a half-day closer to the highway into the city?)

(for project village(s))
$$D = PE + COE + SOE$$

(for control villages)
$$D = COE$$

By subtracting the difference scores of the control group from those of the project group, one can eliminate statistically the common other effects. Thus

$$D_{(PV)} - D_{(CV)} = PE + SOE.$$

The specific other effects are confounded with the project effects, and if the project and control samples have only one or a very small number of villages, statistical inference can take us no further. Once again, attribution of D to project effects must be supported by the apparent unreasonableness of alternative hypotheses attributing D to specific other effects. In general it is easier (again, subjectively, not statistically) to eliminate specific other effects hypotheses than common other effects hypotheses. The reasonable outsider might refuse to accept a given difference from a before-after design as evidence for project effect, but he/she might accept that difference as good evidence if a natural control sample showed a considerably smaller before-after difference.

(b) *Increasing sample sizes*

The specific other effects can be further partitioned, and statistical inference used to eliminate one portion of them if the number of villages is increased beyond a small number. There are specific other effects which occur within individual villages; village X has a dynamic mayor, village Y does not. If the radio signal is received in X and not in Y, the effects of the radio are confounded with those of the dynamic mayor. If the sample includes a larger number of villages, these individual village effects are reduced; each sample tends to lump together villages with and without dynamic mayors.

(c) *The last class design*

Another type of natural control group design seeks to make project/control comparison not across geography but across time. In 1973, the seventh grade in a school district studies mathematics in a traditional way; the following year the bulk of the content is taught via television. The 1974 group does a good deal better.

The logic of inference for this design is essentially the same as for the previous design. Common other effects are controlled as are specific other effects related to individual classrooms if the sample of classrooms is large enough. Once again, the one threat to valid inference not subject to statistical elimination regards possible differences between 1973 and 1974 classes other than access to televised instruction. Was there some difference in the quality of prior preparation; was one group more intelligent than the other; was there a teachers' strike one year but not another? Were the curricula and the exams used to measure learning different in a way likely to bias results?

The advantage of comparisons over time in contrast to comparisons over geography relates to the subjective ease of persuasively eliminating these alternative explanations for results. Prior preparation and intelligence are subject to direct test; teachers' strikes are noticeable events. Curricula and exams are often subject to direct manipulation by project managers. If classes, or villages, or other social units under study are changed over a short time in ways unrelated to a project, the causes of those changes are likely to be observable.

(d) *The 'They should do better' control group*

If it is impossible to locate an equivalent natural control group comparing over time or geography, the next best solution may be to make comparisons with groups one would intuitively expect to be more advanced on the outcome variable. Assume the attendees at an open university are those who could not find places in traditional universities. If, none the less, they do as well as or better than students in a traditional university on the basic economics exam, project managers may feel confident of their efforts at least with regard to the competition.

Since media-based learning systems so often represent second chance opportunities, the location of such 'they should do better' control groups is frequently possible. Whether the control group did slightly better on a secondary admission test, lives in a more urban area, or farms a more productive soil, one can say with some confidence that it should have done better, all else being equal. If, on a before test, the advantaged control group does do better, but by the end of the measurement cycle the project sample is equal or superior, an inference of project success is often legitimate.

This strategy is not for projects which expect small gains and/or can only locate substantially advantaged control groups. It will be most attractive to educational projects, projects which often have a traditional educational standard against which they are inevitably compared by decision-makers.

(e) The diluted experimental control group
Among the most troublesome aspects of mounting an experiment is the need to recruit volunteers and then randomly assign them to the program or withhold the program from them. It is difficult to prevent dropouts from the control sample, and it may be unacceptable in principle to exclude some volunteers from the program benefits.

For some projects, it may be possible to lessen these difficulties without giving up all the advantages of random assignment. Instead of recruiting volunteers and then randomly assigning some to the project and some to a control condition, a researcher might reverse the order of those steps. That is, he or she would randomly assign some social units to the project and others to a control condition, and then actively recruit participants within the social units assigned to the project.

Concretely, a radio farm forum project is seeking new villages to work in. It defines a population of twenty villages where it would like to arrange forums. The project managers randomly assign ten to the project condition and ten to the control condition. At that point, field workers begin to work in the ten project villages, actively encouraging farmers to join the forums. At the end of the appropriate cycle, agricultural innovativeness (however defined) is measured in both the project and the control villages.

Problems associated with this design are discussed in detail in the full paper.

Final comments
Limitations of these designs
These designs are all approximations to classical experiments. Each suffers from one defect or another—defects that make it difficult to estimate project effects precisely. Overall, they can be seen as appropriate for projects which expect large effects and for which results can be analyzed in the light of relatively complete knowledge about the project implementation—so that threats to inferences about project success can be confronted persuasively.

It should also be understood that for these designs effects assigned to a project can relate to any and all aspects of those projects. Classroom television may work because teachers are forced to organize teaching schedules efficiently; radio schools may work because students gather together in a reinforcing social organization. Novelty effects related to innovation *per se* may explain year to year differences in math achievement. These are inseparable parts of the initiation of the project. In the absence of experimental designs varying one aspect of a project at a time, arguments over which element counted are endless and inconclusive. What's more, they are in many ways irrelevant to project evaluation. One can rarely evaluate innovation; one can only study the innovation embedded in its social context and historical implementation, an implementation which includes aspects superficially unrelated to the essence of the innovation, but important in explaining its effects.

Relevance of these designs
These are useful designs. Policy-makers and project managers, however, may have questions for which these designs provide no answers. The decision to undertake one of these evaluations should not be taken unless the questions posed match the answers the research can provide.

It may be that policy makers do not care about the *relative* success of a given program, its advantage over alternative programs, or over no program. What they care about is whether the project achieves a criterion at an acceptable cost. If it does not reach the criterion, it is inadequate regardless of whether it has done better than a control group. If it reaches the criterion, the policy maker may not care that there exists another alternative which can reach the criterion at lesser cost. If major resources have been committed to the ongoing program, redirecting efforts may demand too much in bureaucratic and political terms; the difference in cost must be very large, as must be the probability of successful implementation of the alternative.

In that context, evaluation designed to improve the functioning of the project may be the only useful research. At times, that will include an overall estimate of project success; most often it will mean examining bits and pieces of projects from a variety of perspectives.

PAPER NO 20: A PRAGMATIC EXAMINATION OF THE USES OF RESEARCH AND EVALUATION DATA IN DECISION-MAKING

Dennis D. Gooler, Office of Research and Learning, University of Mid-America, Nebraska, USA.

Phi Delta Kappa's National Study Committee on Evaluation prefaced their report[1] with these words:

> The Purpose of Evaluation
> is not to Prove
> But to Improve

The very title of that report, *Educational Evaluation and Decision Making*,[1] captures the essence of a relationship that is the subject of this paper: evaluation is to have some positive relationship to decision-making. Stufflebeam and his colleagues on the Study Committee offered a definition of evaluation that more clearly specifies this relationship:

> Educational evaluation is the process of delineating, obtaining, and providing useful information for judging decision alternatives.

This paper represents an examination of this definition in practice. The setting is a major experiment in post-secondary education known as the University of Mid-America (UMA). The issue concerns the use of research and evaluation data in the decision-making processes of this experiment. The major intent of the paper is to explore barriers to the use of such data in decision making at UMA, thus providing a pragmatic platform from which to discuss in more general terms the relationship of formal data to decision making.

The paper is divided into four sections. The first section contains a description of the UMA context; the second a brief review of the kinds of decisions to be made in the UMA experiment; the third describes barriers discovered in the UMA context as attempts have been made to provide useful information for selecting from among decision alternatives; the fourth offers some observations on ways to deal with these barriers.

UMA is in many ways a unique setting for consideration of these issues. The uniqueness of this setting, however, should not necessarily be taken to mean that the *barriers* to uses of evaluation data are themselves unique. It is likely that such barriers confront people in most educational settings as data are generated for use in decision making.

The UMA context

The predecessor to UMA, the State University of Nebraska (SUN), was formed in 1971, in response to a University of Nebraska study of the recommendations of the Carnegie Commission on Higher Education and the Newman Task Force. During SUN's planning period, strategies for the design and delivery of mediated adult education were studied, and experimental lesson modules were developed and tested. Three market and clientele surveys of the potential audience for open learning were commissioned.

In order to broaden its economic base of operations, increase its potential target audience, and assure that its open learning program would reach the widest possible learner market, SUN investigated the formation of a regional consortium. The plan developed was thought to be both advantageous and feasible, and as a result the University of Mid-America (UMA) was incorporated on a non-profit basis specifically for the regional production and dissemination of technology-based open learning systems. Iowa State University, the

University of Kansas, Kansas State University, the University of Missouri, and the University of Nebraska were the initial participants in UMA.

UMA is in fact neither a university in the usual sense (it has no faculty or campus) nor an external degree program (it offers no degrees or credits). It is a means of providing learners, through individual state delivery systems, a rich variety of post-secondary learning opportunities which can be used to meet differing individual interests or the educational needs of specific groups of adult learners.

One primary aim of open learning is to improve access to education and thus educational benefits for all citizens, regardless of age or individual circumstances. Opening access to education means delivering education to the learner where he is, on his own terms, without requiring him to give up a job or other economic advantages in order to participate. Current advances in communications technology such as television have presented the potential for delivering education without the usual institutional and time constraints, while keeping the learner central to the process.

> The full paper then analyses this approach in greater detail.

The UMA post-secondary open learning system is thus seen to differ from the traditional educational setting in a number of ways:

1 Its learners will be different, since UMA aims to reach target audiences among those who are not now reached by traditional institutions and since its learners are not restricted by admission requirements, or by rigidities of time and space limitations.

2 Its offering of learning opportunities is intended to be different, since its curriculum will not be structured solely around rigid blocks of content called 'courses' but may be flexibly structured in units which can be put together by learners in a wide variety of ways to serve individual needs and interests.

3 UMA will work with states and institutions which use a variety of delivery approaches and personal contacts.

4 The curriculum will be non-traditional, in that learning opportunities will be offered in both discipline-oriented and in problem-or topic-oriented areas.

5 Since the open learning system might focus on learning rather than credits, it could offer a wide variety of learning opportunities which are designed solely for personal enrichment, or are 'creditable' in other than traditional ways.

6 Most importantly, the open learning system will differ from the traditional institution generally in demonstrating a readiness to meet students where they are educationally. The program will thus try to help learners meet their educational objectives, using whatever resources can be made available, including locally available courses or resource people, correspondence offerings, and independent study opportunities, credit by examinations, and such credit bank programs as the New York Regents External Degree Program.

7 The open learning system will, if the economic projections prove accurate, differ from traditional education in reaching learners at a lower total cost.

Decision points

There are a variety of decisions UMA must make as it seeks to expand and operate its program. Some of these decisions are of particular relevance to the theme of this conference, as they affect the uses of television and radio in the UMA program. Research and evaluation data have potential for impacting upon the following kinds of decisions:

Program goals/directions Before specific decisions about media selection and usage can be addressed, the organization must make some basic decisions about what it is trying to achieve. Research and evaluation data of various kinds, such as market survey data, may play a role in determining program direction.

Content selection Decisions about content must be made at both a global and course-specific level. At the global level, it is important to ascertain which bodies of content should be included in the overall UMA curriculum. At the course level, decisions must be made about which *specific* content will be included in a given course. Both levels of decisions may be informed to some extent by, for example, data concerning the needs and interests of intended participants.

Pedagogy/design UMA places a great deal of emphasis on instructional design as a means of assuring that both content and instructional strategies are carefully and thoughtfully designed with the learner in mind, according to what is known about how adults learn. Evaluation and research data are of particular importance to these kinds of decisions.

Media selection/usage Once content has been selected, and design principles agreed upon, decisions must be made about *what* media are to be used in a given multimedia course, and *how* those media are to be used. Such decisions should be informed by prior experience with the media, gathered through research and evaluation procedures.

Delivery alternatives While UMA is primarily a producer of courses, it must also be concerned with the delivery systems used to make these courses available to learners. Data about the effectiveness and efficiency of various forms of delivery should thus be useful in making delivery decisions.

Obviously, a host of other decisions must be and are made on a daily basis. Whatever the nature of the decision, the central issue of this paper is to identify those decisions that might be informed by research and evaluation data, and to describe the barriers that might prevent the application of such data.

Barriers

There are at least four primary barriers which represent potential (and often real) hindrances to the use of research and evaluation data in decision making related to instructional development in the UMA context.

(a) *Development as art*

Much of instructional development remains art, not science. In some respects, development viewed as art represents a barrier to the use of research and evaluation data. The instructional development processes used by UMA in creating courseware emphasize the need for creative and talented team members to develop interesting and educationally sound materials. While there are some rather clearly defined steps in most instructional development processes, individual members of a course team must none the less exercise their own creativity in implementing various aspects of that process. Of particular interest are the creative talents of those who work with media, particularly television. UMA seeks to employ television producers and writers who have had successful experiences elsewhere. These individuals are artists who, together with their years of experience, have some unusual creative abilities as well. Many producers and writers are unaccustomed to basing design or production decisions on empirical data. Some producers are resistant to the uses of such data, while others simply lack experience in dealing with certain kinds of evaluation data.

While this barrier never will (nor possibly should) be completely overcome, there are some things that might be done to reduce the barrier. For example, we find if we work closely with all members of the course team, right from the start of the development effort, their propensity to utilize evaluation data is much higher. Similarly, if people such as producers and writers are asked to specify the kinds of questions they have about their productions, and if an evaluation can attend to those problems, the data tend to be used much more.

(b) *The cost of precision*

A second barrier to the utilization of research and evaluation data concerns the nature of the data itself. That is, evaluative data are viewed as being imprecise, or lacking definitive qualities. The essence of this barrier is often found in the caveats that accompany evaluation data:

> The following data should be used extremely carefully. The reader should not extrapolate the findings of this study to any other setting, at any other time, or any other way. These data are based on a limited sample, possibly not representing the total population involved. The statistics used herein are valid only under certain conditions and assumptions. More studies must be done to replicate the findings of this study.

The point is that, with an array of caveats accompanying data, thus signalling its imprecise nature, how can we expect consumers to use the results?

Precision is gained at a cost. We in the research office at UMA have often been criticized for providing data at such a general level that no one can do anything with it. It is one thing to know that 48 per cent of the people like what they saw in a given television program. It is quite another to say what *caused* people to like or dislike that program, or what can be done to improve the program. To address issues of cause is to become more precise. That precision can be expensive.

An extended example is given in the full paper.

The more precise you get in your measurement or research, the more it costs, in both time and money. One has to decide when enough is enough, and when to proceed on the basis of the data at hand. Things are never precise enough, although I expect the intuition of experienced men and women counts for much in major development efforts. Designers and producers can undoubtedly improve their practice through their informed use of good data, but data alone, even precise data, do not make decisions. How precise those data ought to be, compared to what it costs to obtain the data, is an important issue, and often becomes a barrier to the effective utilization of evaluation results. Users and producers need to dialogue about what will be acceptable and usable evidence in examining the effectiveness of courses and materials.

(c) *Multiple standards*
Another barrier to the use of evaluation data is that individuals often do not agree on what data mean, and therefore are inclined not to use the data.

UMA has encountered this issue both with respect to evaluating courses it has developed, and with respect to courses being considered for possible acquisition. UMA has, for example, gathered evaluation data from learners which reveal very positive attitudes toward the course (or course segment), and simultaneously gathered data from content experts, revealing very negative evaluations of the course. Similarly, a course developed elsewhere is brought to UMA and examined for possible acquisition by designers, producers, content people, research people, and possible prospective learners. Each of these groups examines the course from different per-

spectives, and uses different standards in rendering judgements. There are few courses that make it through all those screens. In part, the 'not invented here' syndrome is at work; if we didn't do it here, it isn't good enough. Multiple standards clearly exist.

But whose standards shall prevail? UMA may wish to go ahead with a course based on positive feedback from learners, but some academic specialists may look at the course and reject it. Who is a course for? Is it for the academic scholar, or is it for the farmer in Cozad, Nebraska? There are clearly multiple audiences involved in the UMA enterprise. When tensions arise, who makes the decision about whose standards will prevail? The problem becomes increasingly difficult because funding agencies also render judgement about the course, and thus utilize their own standards.

(d) *Time*
The clock and the calendar cause havoc for evaluation within a development project like UMA. There has been much rhetoric in evaluation circles about the fact that evaluation tends to deliver too little, too late. One example from an early development effort in UMA, may be useful in illustrating this point.

In one of the first courses created by UMA, production was accomplished under great time constraints. The course consisted of television programs, a newspaper component, textbook, study guide, and some audio-cassette tapes. Initially the course was planned for development over eighteen months, but instead had to be completed in eight.

The evaluation office proposed to do what was called 'prototype testing' wherein a small group of representative learners were asked to preview all materials as they were developed. Data resulting from this review would be fed into the development process, and hopefully would shape the course before it was actually offered under real settings.

All of the course components were worked on simultaneously, but the fifteen television programs were to be filmed during three production blocks. An acting company was brought in for one week, during which the first five lessons were shot. Approximately four weeks later, the next five television programs were shot, followed by four more weeks and the remaining five television shows. It was the hope of the Office of Research and Evaluation to gather data between these production blocks, so that the second five programs produced could be informed by what was learned from the first five.

The post production period, lasting about two weeks, followed each week of taping, during which time tapes were edited and put together in final form. By the time Research and Evaluation obtained those tapes, there were only two weeks remaining before the next batch of television shows would be shot. The Office was not able (possibly through its own inexperience) to gather necessary data, and to turn those data around fast enough to have any significant impact on the development process.

With experience, however, we have begun to work on the timing barrier. For example, in a course presently being developed by UMA, data gathered by Research and Evaluation on learner evaluations of two television programs were reported to the course team within twelve hours of the collection of those data, and impacted immediately on the production of other programs being taped at that time. Other techniques have been created to generate formative evaluation data that is much more quickly available to course team members. However, there will always be pressures to constrict sharply the developmental period of a course, and thus pressures to proceed without benefit of formal evaluation data. Furthermore, it is not always certain that useful evaluation data can be collected. Time represents a formidable barrier indeed to the use of data in decision making.

Passing the barriers

Given these four major barriers, and recognizing the probable existence of many others, is there reason to suppose that research and evaluation data can be used in making decisions in an educational program such as UMA? The answer, in my estimation, is a qualified *yes*.

In the description of these barriers, some suggestions have been made as to how the barriers might be reduced. To describe in detail actual procedures for such reductions would require considerably more space than can be allotted to this paper. There are, however, some general statements that can be made about ways to reduce or circumvent these barriers, particularly decisions related to the use of television and radio in programs like UMA.

With some notable exceptions, the primary impact of research and evaluation data on the decision-making process in UMA will come in a holistic form. That is, it will be difficult to trace a one-to-one relationship between a specific bit of evaluation data and a specific impact on a specific decision. Rather, decisions in UMA will be impacted as a result of the wisdom that accrues from aggregate data and experience, developed over time. To be sure, some immediate decisions may be made based on particular data. We have seen that happen with respect to utilization of a particular kind of approach to a certain television segment. What is more likely, however, is that the whole *concept* of the uses of television will be influenced by data collected at different times, and in different ways, aggregated together in some meaningful fashion. Over time, new data become part of the conventional wisdom, infused into the overall conceptual frameworks of the organizations.

It is also clear that research and evaluation data will not be used by, for example, a course development team, if the team does not include someone who can represent those data for the team's use. Data without advocates seldom make an impact. We have established an Office of Formative Evaluation and Testing, to insure that an evaluation person is a member of each course team.

Related to the idea of an advocate on the spot is the idea that research and evaluation data are more likely to be used in decisions if use of data is regarded as standard operating procedure by key administrators in the organization. Without such institutional support, evaluative data may well go unheeded. Securing this kind of administrative climate may require some educating of top administrators as to the uses of data.

Evaluation data are also more likely to be used as both producers and consumers of those data, through experience, come to understand what is really critical in terms of variables to focus upon, and in what form data should be reported. Similarly, course teams are becoming more astute in asking the kinds of questions that will influence the ways decisions are made. There is an important interaction that must occur between producers and consumers of data. This interaction takes time to develop.

Finally, barriers to effectively using evaluation data may be lessened as we make progress in formulating theories of learning and teaching-at-a-distance. Theories and models assist in predicting and controlling. As these models or theories are tested and found to be valid, decision makers are more apt to utilize data that fit into the models, allowing decision makers to more accurately predict and control program directions and processes.

Education is so often a hit and miss proposition. Perhaps that is the way it should be. But those who seek to do research and evaluation on the technologies of television and radio, and make their findings usable and useful in improving educational programs, need to possess theories that can guide selection of *what* to evaluate or research, and how and when to report results. The questions asked in an evaluation may well be the critical determiners of its eventual use and impact. This is a considerable barrier, not susceptible to immediate solution. But steps must be taken to develop these theories. Research and evaluation may itself be the primary means whereby such theories can be developed.

Reference

1   PHI DELTA KAPPA NATIONAL STUDY COMMITTEE ON EVALUATION, *Educational Evaluation and Decision Making*, Itasca, Illinois, F. F. Peacock Publishers, 1971.

PAPER NO 13: EDUCATIONAL TELEVISION: A NEW APPROACH TO EVALUATION*

Alain Flageul, Group for Research and Education for Development (GREP), Paris, France.

Until recently, my experience in evaluation of educational television had led me to believe that most evaluations have been carried out merely to justify political or institutional decisions, and that this has warped the published results in such a way that the other functions of evaluation could not be satisfactorily realized. More recent experience though suggests that it is possible to take a different route for the evaluation of educational television.

I   Evaluation after the event, and evaluation as institutional inflexibility

Most of the time, evaluation of educational television can be crudely categorized as depicted in the diagram below.

Evaluation then is a link in the decision chain; it is evaluation after the event, because it occurs after transmission, and it is institutionalized because as a link in the chain, there are strains put on it which allow it no freedom either in its methods (which is natural) nor in its results (which is not so satisfactory).

The constraints are:

1   Evaluation after transmission will seek to justify the production organization's actions in its own eyes, and 'artistic' values will carry more weight than educational values.

---

* Translated from the original French.

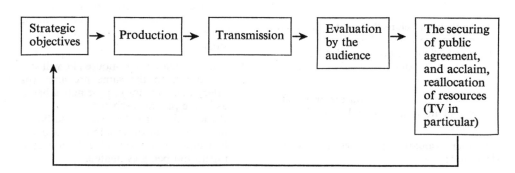

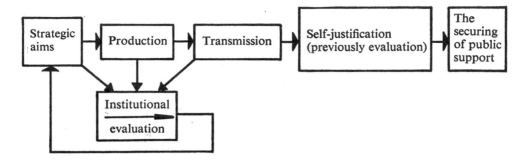

2 Evaluation after transmission is subject to external pressure from organizations which decide the fate and financing of educational television. Usually, the public nature of educational television attracts a certain amount of political risks, and the educational television organizations are well aware of this, so external pressures on the evaluation process from financers, advisors, or transmitting bodies are enormous.

II Evaluation of the public is blind evaluation

Evaluation after transmission never allows for the collection of satisfactory qualitative information. Although we might find out how many and what kind of people watch, we never know what impact the programmes have either at an intellectual level nor above all in affective or emotional terms. But these are just the kinds of questions which ought to be answered by organizations using television for education. There are viable ways of tackling this problem, developed by commercial market researchers, but generally they are impractical or unacceptable in the educational context. I believe then that another kind of evaluation should be undertaken: *a priori* evaluation.

III Evaluation before the event, evaluation as institutional flexibility

This kind of evaluation would take place *before* transmission. If classical evaluation takes the viewpoint:

'Show me the picture you are transmitting and its impact, and I will tell who you are'

the other evaluation proposes the reverse viewpoint:

'Show me who you are and I will tell you what image you are transmitting and its impact'.

IV Evaluation of the institution is open evaluation

A transmitted message is the result of a balance between fundamental ideological structures in opposition. These ideological gambits are those of the confronting institutions, and the relationships between power and money are components of this confrontation. To analyze the interplay of the relationship between power and money, it is necessary to identify the nature of the message finally transmitted and its impact on the population (the population being another confronting 'institution').

From the origination of an idea to its transmission, there will always be a number of crises: these crises provide the source of analysis. There are other methods, but my aim here is merely to suggest another possible track for evaluation:

Desirable schema

(*see diagram above*)

Classical evaluation remains (it would be suicidal to get rid of it), but now clearly as a self-justifying activity, while genuine evaluation is free of the external pressures.

This is obviously an oversimplification, and there are two major drawbacks to consider:

1 If the evaluator is 'in-house', he will still be subject to the same pressures (of salary and function) in the new schema as in the previous schema.
2 If the evaluator is 'external', and based in a funding or other interested agency, he would be an intolerable threat to the institution being evaluated.

It is necessary then that the evaluator should be from an independent organization, contracted to work within the educational television organization.

While this would still be seen as a threat, it is more one to their comfort that to their existence. But to have no independent evaluation could lead to such sterility that the absence of evaluation would lead to withdrawal of external support. So *a priori* research is probably the last chance for educational television to remain in research and not slide rapidly towards the only end of every organization: ruination.

PAPER NO 4: EVALUATION AS A POLICY-DEVELOPING INSTRUMENT AT TRU

Lars E. Amling, Head of Evaluations, TRU, Sweden.

The letters TRU stand for 'Television och Radio i Utbildningen' (Television and Radio in Education). TRU is a Commission which was appointed in 1967 to carry out experimental and development work in radio and television in various areas of education.

Educational work via radio and television is also carried out in Sweden by the Swedish Broadcasting Corporation (Sveriges Radio (SR)). In its findings published in the spring of 1975 the TRU Commission proposed an amalgamation of the educational unit of SR and TRU on 1 July 1977 to form a new, independent, unit outside SR. Parliament is expected to reach a decision on this during 1976.

The purpose of this paper is to attempt to describe how evaluation has functioned, and continues to function, as a policy-developing instrument at TRU's adult education section. A description will be given of how the methods have been changed and supplemented over the years, and how the results of evaluations have affected the directions in which work at TRU has proceeded—their effect, for instance, on course design, the presentation of study materials, forms of collaboration

with study organizations, as well as their effect on recruitment and publicity.

During the 1967 session, Parliament, at the instigation of the Government, took several important decisions affecting Swedish adult education. Following the reforms of primary and secondary compulsory education during the 50's and 60's, the 70's would be devoted to a reform of adult education. It was considered especially important to reach the large group of adults whose education consisted solely of a 6- to 7-year basic education (65–75 per cent of all adults engaged in active employment) and who hitherto had made little use of existing educational opportunities for adults. They should be given the chance to acquire the same standard of education as their children, viz. a standard corresponding to the 9-year compulsory basic schooling, with the option of a further 3 years at 6th-form level.

These objectives would be attained by, for example, encouraging local authorities to establish special schools for adults. The curricula would be the same as in the compulsory schools but the number of teacher-led lessons would be greatly reduced. A 3-year course would be covered in 3 terms. Certificates would be awarded at the end of the courses as in the ordinary school system.

The same Government proposal (and Parliamentary decision) spoke of the large part to be played by radio and television in adult education in order to realize the desired objectives. Seen against the background outlined above, it was therefore natural for TRU at this time to be given specific directives to produce examination-oriented courses at 6th-form level in accordance with the curricula for ordinary schools, but adapted to meet adult requirements. Two subjects—Business Economics and English—were dealt with in the first two courses of this kind but these were to be followed in the next few years by several others dealing with, for instance, Psychology, Social Psychology, Social Politics, as well as with Mathematics and Swedish (these last two in accordance with the syllabus for Grades 7 to 9). The courses were primarily intended for private study.

Thorough evaluations were made in connection with all these courses. The evaluations were in most cases descriptive and summative and aimed at pin-pointing the number of participants, their aims, their educational backgrounds, as well as the study results. The methods most frequently used involved postal inquiries and telephone interviews. Some of the surveys were addressed to the entire population, others to representative samples of participants or teachers.

Even if the drop-out figures in the larger surveys were in many cases high and results therefore not too reliable, it was nevertheless shown that only a minority of the target group originally envisaged had in fact been reached by the radio and TV courses. Of the people who had taken Business Economics only 25 per cent had nothing more than elementary education behind them and for the English course this figure was 11 per cent. As far as their objectives in studying were concerned, only 17 per cent of the Business Economics students were attempting to gain a certificate.

The majority took the course because they would be able to make use of their newly-acquired knowledge in their jobs or because they found it an enjoyable hobby. The drop-out figures from one term to the next (the courses covered 3 terms) were high. The total number of certificates issued at the end of the Business Economics course was 1,300—a figure which can be compared with the following sales figures for the four textbooks: Part I—63,000, Part II—28,500, Part III—27,400, Part IV —19,000.

The results of surveys made on other 6th-form level courses gave similar indications:

- It is difficult to attract people with a brief basic educational background by offering courses covering a number of terms, constructed on the basis of the ordinary school system curricula and leading to certificates.
- Only a minority of Swedish adults are interested primarily in qualifying for certificates.
- The study organizations were not particularly interested in the TV/radio courses since they had had little say in their design and had received little information about them. Consequently few local groups were formed.

With regard to the evaluation methods, it could be concluded that large-scale summative surveys had proved to be rather inexact instruments, affording somewhat unreliable data on which to base decisions.

Since, in spite of these shortcomings, the results nevertheless all pointed in the same direction and since the results were corroborated by surveys made by other organizations than TRU, it was suggested by the TRU advisory committee on adult education that new methods should be sought and that material for study in groups should be given priority.

Publicity and recruiting efforts during the first year (1968–9) had been very limited. Before the start of the academic year in the autumns of both 1969 and 1970 TRU devoted more resources to publicity. For example, publicity in the form of leaflets and course prospectuses was distributed free of charge via the study organizations. Short TV spots were also produced. Surveys were made of the effects of this publicity. It was shown that the TV spots had made the most impact but that they consistently attracted the attention of twice as many people with higher educational backgrounds as of people with only a brief basic schooling.

The full paper described five projects designed to reach the less advantaged in the adult community. These five projects are summarized below.

---

1 A recruiting campaign in pottery in Lidkoping, which doubled the number of adults engaged in TRU courses

Results of this campaign:

- A special Government Commission has carried out experimental work using various types of canvassing recruitment and good results have been achieved. Consequently, as from 1975, the Government is providing the study organizations with special grants for this type of work.
- The radio programmes in the mathematics course had been designed especially for use in a group study situation. The circle leaders had also been trained in advance to use the material methodically. Since 1970, the sound material elements of most TRU courses have been produced in two versions—one version for use in group study contexts, and

another for the individual listener taking the course by radio.

- In conjunction with most courses TRU now produces leaflets for use by the local study organizations in canvassing recruitment at places of work and in residential areas. These leaflets provide the recruiting personnel with the kind of arguments that they are likely to need, and these arguments have often been formulated by students and circle leaders who have been involved in a pre-test of the instructional materials.
- TRU now provides a circle leader 'kit' with most of its courses, consisting of training material for the leaders. The kit contains extracts from the instructional materials and provides tips on teaching method together with information on how the course designers have intended the materials to be used.
- The evaluation resources at TRU have tended more than in the early years to be directed towards formative evaluations and the pre-testing of study materials rather than towards summative evaluations.

2 An elementary course in Swedish language

During 1972 TRU began the planning of an elementary course in Swedish. It was addressed to people who found it difficult to express themselves in speech and writing and who did not resort to using the language frequently or with confidence in dealing with the authorities. The aim was to eliminate this anxiety and to encourage people to use the language at their disposal however inadequate they might feel it to be. The course also aimed at providing people with the motivation and the wherewithal to play an active part as members of the community. The instructional materials centred on concrete everyday situations. The basic material consisted of newspaper articles together with relevant language exercises. As students acquired practice in the use of the language they were also acquiring valuable information about the various organizations and institutions in the community of which it is of practical use for a person to be aware in his role as citizen. The materials were produced primarily for use in groups but a separate version was also issued for private study.

The research group thought it desirable to pre-test the design of the materials before any final decision was made as to its form and bulk. The first five (of a total of twelve) units were to be tested during the spring of 1973. The study organizations in three counties (in which TRU had for a year or two been carrying out experimental work using regional adult education advisers) were invited to take part in the experiment. The aim was to create about 20 study circles, each containing about 10 students. However, so much interest was shown that 30 study circles took part in the project.

When each unit had been completed—that is to say, after about every second week—points of view were collected from the students, by means of fairly detailed questionnaires, and from the circle leaders, who were interviewed on the telephone by the advisers using a comprehensive and structured interview formula. Results were collated centrally and presented to the project group about ten days later. The points of view could thus be put to use immediately and thus provide a basis for decisions affecting the revision of the instructional materials. These were to be ready for distribution in final form in time for the autumn of 1973.

3 Lessons learnt from evaluation

- The project group got rapid feedback information and could start on revision work straight away. (Large surveys often involve a lapse of 1–2 months before the final report comes in.)
- The study organizations could become acquainted with and try out a new set of materials before it was to be distributed and could start planning their marketing strategy. (The experimental material was also sent to the national head offices of the study organizations—for information.)
- TRU's information department also gained a basis on which to build their publicity (they were able to use the evaluation results in their presentation). For instance, 'argument leaflets', in which students and circle leaders who had been involved in the pilot scheme formulated the arguments, were printed for the use of recruiting personnel.
- Other TRU projects that were being planned at the time were fully informed of the favourable results achieved by the

media design of the language project and were able to build on the experiences thus gained.

The experiment had however one serious limitation: the students who were recruited to the experimental circles had a considerably higher level of basic education than had been envisaged in the target group. Reactions to the degree of difficulty presented by the instructional materials had therefore to be regarded as unreliable. TRU therefore decided to carry out an extensive survey together with WEA during 1973–4.

4 A further survey

The survey was to cover a representative sample of 'ordinary' study circles using the instructional materials. The sample consisted of 104 circles. The result of the survey shows, among other things, that:

● The intended target group had to a very considerable extent been reached. 80 per cent of the students had been born before 1941 and an equally large percentage were in full employment. 73 per cent had received no more than 7 years of basic schooling, 44 per cent had had no vocational training and 15 per cent had never previously taken any course at all.

● Half of the circles had followed the suggestion of spending two study sessions, a total of 180 minutes, on each unit of the course, while the rest had gone at a slower rate since the students had shown so much interest and had asked for a more thorough treatment of the material.

● Half of the circle leaders, and a slightly smaller proportion of the students, thought that the short sound tapes had provided variety and new sidelines during the study sessions. What criticism there was was devoted mainly to the poor quality of the sound tape copies.

● The students particularly liked the fact that the study materials combined instruction on Civics and Swedish. 22 per cent of the students said the materials had exceeded their expectations, primarily because the course was of such practical value and had not been as difficult as had been feared.

● At the beginning of the course the majority of the students expressed the hope that they would improve their ability to speak in front of a group and to take matters up with national and local authorities. At the end of the course most of them felt that they were no longer afraid to approach the authorities. They also had a better understanding of what was presented in the press and on radio and TV.

● More than half of the students had got to know about the course through canvassing recruitment at their place of work. 30 per cent had had their attention attracted to it by TV publicity.

● As many as 79 per cent wanted to go on to study some other subject at the completion of the course. Most interest was expressed for courses on Swedish grammar, some other language, social problems and the working environment.

5 A course in everyday law

While the course in elementary Swedish was at the pre-testing stage, planning was begun on a course in everyday law for the same target group: adults with only a short formal education. The results of the pre-testing of the Swedish course were studied and discussed by the project group working on the law course. Among other things they noted particularly the favourable results gained by using short sound tape items in group study and they developed this technique further. The necessity of linking the material to the student's everyday experiences (and of avoiding legal theorizing) was another lesson learnt, as was the division of the course into units.

Since most of the members of the project group were academics with little or no practical experience of adult education, there was some uncertainty at the outset as to the entry behaviour that could be assumed, i.e. the amount of knowledge that could be assumed on the part of the students, and the level of language that would be appropriate. It was therefore decided to produce *one* unit of the course and test it on a small number of groups, with special reference to these two problems. The data was collected by means of questionnaires to students and circle leaders as well as by holding structured 'hearings' with each of the ten groups involved in the pre-testing.

The answers to the project group's questions were thus obtained and production of the first five (of ten) units of the course was begun. These were then tested, as the

Swedish course had been, on a fairly large number of groups in the three counties involved in the earlier experiment. In this pre-test it was possible to make use of the organizational contacts established the previous year as well as to benefit from the experience as interviewers that the TRU advisers had acquired. This pre-test thus ran more smoothly than the previous one.

The information and publicity surrounding the new course on everyday law achieved results equally as favourable as in the case of the Swedish course. When the finished product was finally published it met with a particularly favourable reception and was given a wide distribution. The study organizations immediately asked for a further course on the subject.

6 Courses for the handicapped

A special problem in the matter of creating teaching materials and of the evaluation methods to be used is posed by the needs of disabled persons. A special group within TRU has been working for some years on developing and producing materials for the partially-sighted, the partially-deaf, and for people of retarded development. Close co-operation has also been established with the various organizations for the disabled.

The finished products that the project has finally been able to publish during the past year have been preceded by several years of experiment and research of a very limited nature. Here are some examples of what has been done:

For the deaf several different variants of the same TV programme have been produced, employing different combinations of sub-titles, sign language and lip-reading in an attempt to discover what mix would have the best informative effect. Special versions for deaf people studying in groups and for private study have been tried out.

For people of retarded development previously broadcast TRU programmes have been revised and several variants made with significant differences as regards the language used, the amount of information given, the pace of the programme, the type of accompanying assignments and exercises. Tests have usually been carried out at the various institutions for the developmentally retarded.

This work, of which a few brief examples have been given, has also made quite new demands on evaluation methods. The traditional methods of collecting data from participants cannot be used when their ability to communicate is seriously impaired. The evaluator has therefore to work in very close contact with the project groups, with the organizations for the disabled, and with the circle leader. It has only been possible to use questionnaires on a very limited scale and then only for the purpose of obtaining very simple basic information. Face-to-face interviews with group leaders as well as visits to groups, combined with hearings involving leaders, students, the project group and the evaluator were the techniques most often used. It has not always been possible to present the results in the conventional way in the form of statistical data but the project group has nevertheless managed, albeit with difficulty, to collect sufficient information to serve as a basis on which to make decisions affecting the design of the course, its pace, the level of the language to be used, appropriate study methods, etc.

The work of the various project groups made for disabled persons provides an exceptional and unique illustration of the fact that pre-testing and evaluation are necessary instruments in all development work in producing instructional materials. They also provide, however, an illustration of how evaluations have played an integral part in shaping a philosophy, or policy, of education.

The experience gained from the intimate evaluation procedures that were developed at the micro level in collaboration with project groups, evaluators, research workers, organizations and target groups in producing materials for disabled persons should serve as a model for future work in developing evaluation methods within TRU's general adult educational programme. The extensive surveys described at the beginning of this paper will still be needed in future, even if on a more limited scale and for very specific purposes, at the macro level. What, on the other hand, need to be developed are instruments for the micro level, instruments that can provide the project groups with speedy and reliable information and TRU's management with material on which to base policy decisions.

PAPER NO 80: SATELLITE INSTRUCTIONAL TELEVISION EXPERIMENT: A SOCIAL EVALUATION

Binod Agrawal, Research and Evaluation Cell, ISRO, Government of India

How we evolved the design

Viewing the cultural/social complexity of India, it was strongly felt that a single discipline could not provide answers for all the problems arising while evaluating SITE. Further, no ready-made theoretical framework or methodological strategies were available which could be plugged into the social evaluation of SITE. Historical factors associated with the growth and development of various disciplines of social sciences in India were also responsible for this conviction. For example the experiment was to be conducted in the 'rural areas' where historically social anthropologists-cum-sociologists have conducted most of the researches. Therefore, their assistance in the project was sought. Further, the first few to take up the responsibility belonged to three disciplines—anthropology, communication and sociology. With their theoretical bias and methodological preoccupation it became very clear that a monolithic approach for evaluating the socio-cultural 'impacts' of SITE would not be possible. Therefore, a *multi-disciplinary* approach to cover a broad spectrum of SITE impact on rural audiences was adopted. Sociologists would conduct 'KAP' studies, while anthropologists could go and live in the villages for an extended period to understand the process of rural communication and evaluate the impact of SITE.

At the same time, it was evident that one could not live within the boundaries of their own disciplines while participating in a project like SITE. This led to the foundation of an *inter-disciplinary* approach for SITE social evaluation. In this way, the 'Social Evaluation Plan' was conceived as *inter-* and *multi-*disciplinary involving many disciplines of social sciences.

Having agreed upon the research approach, the next most important question was what should be our research design and priorities for summative evaluation. After considerable discussion we felt that SITE was a rare opportunity for conducting a field experiment in social sciences. Therefore, experimental research design was conceived.

Keeping the above views in mind the first draft of social evaluation plan was prepared by inhouse social scientists in April 1974. In order to have a broad based acceptance of our research plan we had dialogues with leading social scientists and specialists in SITE instructional areas of the country. The 'Social Research Plan' was discussed at length in a two-day seminar held in May 1974 to finalize the future action of research. The final social research plan is an outcome of these discussions.

Research design

Essentially field experiment involves 'before' and 'after' study of the same groups under observation and measurement of the impact generated by the introduction of TV. In this design, we have introduced a mid-point observation and also we have taken non-SITE villages as controlled ones. The final research design for the summative evaluation is outlined in the table below.

It is hoped that the difference between a control and an experimental village over the period will allow us to measure the social impact of SITE. Accordingly, almost all summative evaluation studies have followed this design.

Keeping the two separate time slots in mind, the evaluation has been divided into two parts. In part one the morning programmes for 5 to 12 year old school children are being evaluated. In part two, the evening programmes for adult audiences are

Non-SITE villages (control)	Pre-SITE (T_0)	During SITE (T_1)	After SITE (T_2)
SITE villages	Pre-SITE (T_0)	During SITE (T_1)	After SITE (T_2)

being evaluated. The rationale for separating the two parts stems from the fact that the programmes require different treatment as they are meant for distinct target audience. However, research design remained the same.

SITE social evaluation

After having defined the general research approach and design, we divided total social evaluation activities into the following stages: 1 Context evaluation, 2 Input evaluation, 3 Process evaluation, and 4 Summative evaluation.

Context evaluation In the context evaluation we essentially took up two activities: audience profiles and need assessment studies. For the preparation of these studies we collected both primary and secondary data from the field, and analysed it in Ahmedabad. The reports were prepared for the use of producers. The basic question raised while preparing audience profiles was 'given the cultural diversities in India, is it possible to create a typical Man, family, village, countryside to project on TV, acceptable to a large audience, having dialectical regional and linguistic differences from each other?' In preparation of the audience profile, attempts were made to use 'non-technical and descriptive language' so that it can be used by the producers. In need assessment studies, efforts were focused on evaluation of the observed needs, though ideally one should also assess the felt needs of the people. These reports were sent to programme producers and also discussions were held for their proper utilization.

Input evaluation The term 'formative evaluation' has also been used for the same purpose. The aim of the 'Input Evaluation' is to examine alternative ways to meet the objectives that have either been modified or added by the decision to change. In other words, to help producers in taking programme design decisions. Many of our researchers were involved in this activity from the very beginning, and one researcher was involved full time in conducting input evaluation of children's programmes at our Bombay studio. Though these studies started as a commitment on our part, it has paid dividends in influencing the programme design decisions.

Process evaluation One of the salient aspects of this experiment is to have continuous feedback from the audience. 27 researchers are stationed in SITE villages to interview and observe every day 270 adults and approximately the same number of children. Data thus collected are quickly despatched to Ahmedabad where it is scrutinized and analysed. Rating on the selected dimensions is automatically done by computer and the results are supplied to programme producers. Qualitative trend reports are also generated periodically to help producers to make mid-core corrections in their programmes.

Summative evaluation At the moment our major thrust is on summative evaluation. The summative evaluation includes a large survey covering 72 experimental and 36 controlled villages spread over 6 clusters. In Kheda 5 experimental and 5 controlled villages are selected for the study. These surveys are only confined to adult population. The execution responsibility of surveys of 6 clusters is entirely ours. Major guidelines and research plans are designed by Survey Research Group (adults) consisting of external social scientists in their individual capacities and institutional capacities. Those involved from our side are also members of this group. Kheda survey is entirely our responsibility. The SITE impact study on children is entirely conducted by National Council of Educational Research and Training (NCERT), New Delhi. However, required manpower was supplied by us for field data collection.

Anthropological studies are being conducted in seven villages, one in each cluster, under the broad heading of holistic study. Two similar studies have been supported by us and are being conducted by A. N. Sinha Institute of Social Studies, Patna, on a parallel design as we have conceived. In addition one female anthropologist is collecting separate data on the females response to TV.

Four indepth studies are underway as a part of summative evaluation. These studies are very specific and would evaluate one of the aspects of SITE instructional areas.

In the first study we are attempting to find out which economic class gains most from SITE. This study is being conducted in one village. In the second study attempts are being made to evaluate the impact of TV on rural leadership and emergence of new leadership due to TV in two villages. In the third study our efforts are to understand what are impact of TV on family planning behaviour in one village. And in the fourth study the major question to be answered is why viewers get alienated from TV. The study is being conducted in two villages. In all these studies there is a strong emphasis on participant observation.

How are we organized

Research planning and design activities are handled by the regular research staff drawn from almost every social science discipline at Ahmedabad and in the six clusters. The staff is selected in such a fashion that *inter* and *multi*-disciplinary researchers can be handled in order to achieve the SITE goals.

One research scientist is acting as the manager of the Cell. Six research scientists belonging to psychology, sociology, anthropology and communication give the leadership to the research projects in Ahmedabad and in Bombay. In addition, one research scientist specializing in statistics and computer science and presently attached with PRL Computer Centre, Ahmedabad is also a part-time member of the cell. The research scientists are supported by ten research assistants and one research associate.

In each cluster, an associate scientist along with seven research assistants and one anthropologist form the core data collection unit. In addition, as and when need arises, we hire research assistants from a panel, permanently residing in the clusters and at Ahmedabad. Manpower loading envisages a peak period during November 1975 to February 1976 with a total strength of 99 research staff.

The whole research staff at Ahmedabad is supported by a secretarial staff having the ratio of approximately 1:2 and at the cluster 1:6. All the research staff have a minimum qualification of a masters degree in one of the branches of the social sciences and several years of research experience.

Our experience that can be shared

One of the basic handicaps, one observes in the present experiment, is the non-specification of social objectives and last minute involvement of social scientists in the experiment. Both these factors must be taken into serious consideration at the preliminary stages while designing a TV system for educational and developmental purposes. This holds true specially for third world countries where in many cases basic social data are not available for planning out decisions.

It seems that we have put too many eggs in one basket by taking the responsibilities of various kinds of evaluative studies from context evaluation to summative evaluation. Based on the observations and experiences so far, I would suggest that context and summative evaluations should be done by those who are not directly involved in input and process evaluation as far as possible. At the same time, researchers working in input and process evaluation should be closely associated with the producers and production units. This will help to have close day to day interaction between producers and social scientists. Further it may be advisable to set up separate groups or give the contract to outside groups for conducting context and summative evaluation, if such facilities are available within the country.

Given the importance and scale of the experiment, it seemed desirable to involve outside agencies for evaluating social impact of SITE. Also in doing so, we were trying to be more objective in our studies. In two projects—SITE Impact Survey (Adult) and SITE Impact Study (Children), we have involved outside agencies. We have also given two fellowships for holistic study. Our experience shows that a number of difficulties arise in collaborative studies where responsibilities are not clearly defined. Further when committees are asked to execute projects and if more than one agency is involved research decisions get delayed. However, if the total responsibility is given to an outside agency the problems are fewer.

In time-bound projects like SITE, many decisions are to be made in the field situation. However, in the existing organizational set up the decisions are taken at one point and they are executed in the field which creates time lag and sometimes it is difficult to execute the plans. In a future system I would suggest that such decisions should be left to research personnel and they should be given financial and executive powers to execute the same.

PAPER NO 52: WHAT KIND OF EVALUATION IS USEFUL TO ADULT EDUCATION BROADCASTING?

John Robinson and Neil Barnes, Educational Broadcasting, BBC, United Kingdom.

1 Evaluation and research: some definitions and criteria

In the hope of avoiding unnecessary misunderstandings, it is useful first to attempt some definitions. 'Evaluation' is quite easy to define. It is simply the estimation of a degree of value: of a work of art or a scientific discovery, or in this case the efficiency of a learning process. The criteria may be argued about; the methods may lead to endless discussion. But the purpose is clear: to assess some measure of efficiency.

'Research' presents a lot more difficulty, because this is one of those Humpty Dumpty words. In Lewis Carroll's 'Through the Looking Glass', Humpty Dumpty tells Alice (in rather a scornful tone): 'When I use a word, it means just what I choose it to mean—neither more or less'. That is how most of us use the word 'research'. At one extreme it is taken to mean that someone reads everything he can find on a subject and then produces his own summary as a research report. At the other extreme research is only accepted if it means the creation of strictly experimental conditions, as close as possible to an experiment in the physical sciences and with every factor eliminated (as far as possible) that is not directly a part of the experiment.

Between these two extremes is a whole range of useful activity that involves the systematic collection of usable evidence. In the case of educational broadcasting, this sometimes means the creation of special conditions, as in the developmental testing of programme material during the production stage; sometimes it takes the form of collecting practical evidence once the programmes have been transmitted.

For educational broadcasting, therefore, a pragmatic approach to this wide range of activity would lead to a wide definition of the *meaning* of 'research', but with strict criteria to the *value* of its results.

This would suggest a definition on the following lines:

The process of research may be taken to include all systematic collection of evidence, designed to test a hypothesis or to answer specific questions, which evidence can be used in the making of future decisions.

Clearly this is a definition of a method; and this makes it possible to distinguish in a useful way between research and evaluation. 'Evaluation' is a purpose; 'research' is a method. Very often they overlap; but it is fair to say that evaluation is a purpose that is sometimes served by research, while research is a method that is sometimes used for evaluation. This can be expressed in a simple diagram:

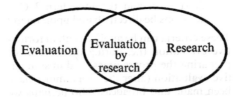

This wide definition of research still involves some important principles. First the study must be systematic. The haphazard collection of bits of evidence, such as the producer asking his friend to ask their friends to follow a broadcast series and give him their impressions, can never properly be called research. It also means that the evidence should be representative of the whole field being studied. To collect the views expressed in letters that happen to be addressed to the production team, for example, may well give an entirely unrepresentative view of the total response to a broadcast series. It may indeed be more misleading than helpful. So the collection must be systematic.

At the same time it must be usable in relation to future decisions. We have all read reports of studies which are elegant and impressive to read, but are as impractical in effect as a stage design by Gordon

Craig or Salvador Dali. We have all read reports that are technically brilliant, but as self-contained and often self-indulgent as a film by Fellini or Ken Russell. Others again take such a long time and are so expensive that they are museum-pieces before they are finished. As far as the practitioners of educational broadcasting are concerned, this kind of theoretical research just does not justify the time and money spent on it.

But there is research, often of a fairly modest kind, which fully justifies the human effort, the money used and the time spent on it. The criteria for assessing such research lie in the answers to three important groups of questions:

(a) *Objectives*
     Are these clear, practicable and likely to be useful?
(b) *Methods*
     Are these systematic, and effective in pursuit of the objectives? Are they not excessive in time and not prohibitively expensive?
(c) *Applications*
     Are these of practical value, both in the short term and the long term? Can decisions be directly based upon them?

These criteria can be applied both in formative evaluation (i.e. during the process of preparing the programmes) and in summative evaluation (after the programmes have been made and broadcast). So perhaps we have produced our own Humpty Dumpty definitions. At least we hope they are practical ones.

2 Adult education broadcasting: some characteristics

For purposes both of evaluation and research, adult education broadcasting is very different from school broadcasting. It is different at least in the following characteristics:

(a) Generally speaking it is primarily addressed to voluntary audiences situated in their own homes who are not readily identified as classes in schools can be identified. So their qualities are less easy to assess and their response to the programmes is less easy to observe. (This is not true, of course, where adults are *enrolled* as students, as in the Open University or the Telekolleg, in television-based credit courses in North America or the broad-

casting and correspondence courses in Japan.)

(b) Whether the audiences can be identified or not, they present a much greater variety of ages, previous education and life experience, than the specified age group for a school broadcast course.

(c) The audience will also be much more varied in the amount of time they are prepared to give to their study, in addition to the time spent in following the broadcasts. This means, for instance, that the broadcast material has to be presented at a pace that can be geared by the users to very different learning commitments.

(d) Adult education broadcasters can similarly assume a less regular pattern of following the programmes than a school series addressed to a particular age group. So repetition and revision must be built in to the broadcast series itself.

3 Formative evaluation: some merits, problems and examples
Merits

The principal merit of formative evaluation is that it can help to shape the learning material during the actual process of preparation. It thus has an initial effect on the nature of the material offered and at once meets the criterion of practicality.

It also brings the evaluative process much closer to the production process and it is likely in time to lead to better mutual understanding between the researcher and the producer.

Problems

The main problem of formative evaluation is that of time. It demands a considerable time for preparation and production, if pilot material is to be made, pre-tested and modified in the light of the results.

Another problem is that it is not usually possible to represent in a pre-testing situation the precise audience and circumstances that are likely to be reached when the material is actually broadcast. For example, the best that one can probably hope for in pre-testing a beginners' language course, is to find a beginners' class in an adult education centre; and this class may show significant differences from the audience eventually reached by the broadcasts. So allowance must be made for these possible differences.

Examples

Formative evaluation is particularly useful when little is known about the intended audience's response, emotional as well as intellectual; when the question is not only, 'How much will they learn?' but also, 'Will they actually be prepared to watch or listen?' Such research, therefore, tends to get carried out in innovative situations when provision is being made for a group in the community for the first time, or where a completely new style of programme is being tried for groups already provided for. In both cases no 'case law precedents' exist. Formative evaluation attempts to set some and thus give guidance to the producer in the production of the real thing.

On the Move is the title of the BBC's current television series directed to adults who have basic difficulties with reading or writing—whose various disabilities (resulting from an even more varied range of causes) tend to be hidden under the blanket term 'adult illiterate'. No previous attempt has been made in Great Britain to produce material specifically for this section of the population. In a basically literate society, illiteracy is shaming; so, because of the acute sensitivity which many adults in this situation possessed, it was essential to do nothing in or through the broadcasts which would unintentionally increase any sense of alienation or worthlessness.

For these reasons a comprehensive period of piloting took place during the year preceding the first transmission of the broadcasts (which began in October 1975). The production team initially gleaned what were thought to be the essential characteristics of the target audience—their attitudes to education and to the outside world, the motive for wanting to learn and how they might react to outside help being offered. Early in 1975 three ten-minute video-taped 'programmes' were prepared, for showing to groups drawn as near as possible from the 'target' audience. One major difficulty in gathering such groups was that the primary aim of the series was to reach out to those with reading and writing difficulties who had so far lacked the confidence to ask for help outside their own home. The aim of the intended series was to provide sufficient support and encouragement for them to feel able to do that. In the event an approximation to the target audience had to be made and the programmes were shown to adult students in literacy classes and voluntary groups in many parts of the country. Their subjective comments, sometimes pungently adverse, frequently very perceptive, about the needs of the lone adult, were reported back to the producer by the BBC field staff of Further Education Officers.

From these new reports new pilot material was produced in April and this too was tried out in a similar way—but on this occasion with far fewer adverse comments. So by the following October, when the first broadcasts were transmitted, their style and content was felt to be as near as possible to being acceptable to the needs of this diverse group of perhaps five million adults.

At the same time as the broadcast material was being piloted, similar trials were being carried out on the printed material— the BBC book which is closely linked with the television programmes. This too was adapted in the light of subjective comment.

Piloting of this kind has been done for other series—notably for series for teachers, for industrial managers and for another major project now under way, in trade union studies for active trade unionists.

4 Summative evaluation: some merits, problems and examples

Merits

The main merit of summative evaluation is that it is directly based on the real situation; it is assessing what actually happened. This is particularly valuable when a course is to be repeated, as is generally the case in BBC adult education and is always the case in the Open University (where each course is repeated for four or five years).

It usually means there is less pressure of time than there is in formative evaluation. Although the collection of data may still have to be concentrated in a fairly narrow period of time, there is more time beforehand for preparation, including selection of representative samples, and afterwards for considered assessment of the results.

Problems

The main problem is that while a lot of effort may go into this form of evaluation, the results may still be so particular to the individual course that they have little value in any future decisions. There is, therefore, a pressing need to draw more general principles from this kind of evaluation, which can have more general application.

There is also the problem of time which is the converse of the time shortage applying in formative evaluation. Here it may seem that time is so plentiful that both interest and value have been largely lost by the time the results see the light of day.

Another question particularly posed by the longer span of summative evaluation is whether the research is best carried out by the broadcasting organization itself or whether it should be encouraged in external research units, not least in educational institutions which are interested in the content of the broadcasts.

Examples
Summative evaluation has particular strength where the results can be seen to have a direct relevance to future planned projects. Such continuity of provision is illustrated in the BBC's adult education output by its regular provision of modern languages courses. Lessons learned about a beginners' course in one language are likely to have a direct application, not only to subsequent courses in that language, but also to beginners' courses in other languages.

Kontakte and *Wegweiser* are the first two stages of a three-stage multi-media course in German for beginners. *Kontakte*, the first stage, consists of 25 television and 25 radio programmes, 3 workbooks and LP records and audio cassettes, all designed for the individual home learner. Extra materials in the form of film strips and notes for teachers are also provided for use in adult language classes using the *Kontakte* course. *Wegweiser*, the second stage, consists of 25 radio programmes and books, records, cassettes and teachers' notes.

The research in this case is being carried out by the Department of Communication at the Brighton Polytechnic, with a major commitment by two senior researchers and a great deal of voluntary co-operation. It is funded within the Brighton Polytechnic by research funds drawn from a number of external sources.

The research study is divided into two main parts:

(a) to describe the use and to assess the learning effectiveness of the course when used by home-based adult learners;

(b) to describe the use and to assess the learning effectiveness of the course when used by language classes in tertiary institutions (mainly evening adult classes).

It will be seen that each part has two distinct objectives: to describe patterns of use (together with the composition of the audience); and to assess the effectiveness of the course by judging the student's progress. In the case of effectiveness, this is assessed purely in terms of the aims of this course; there is no attempt to compare it with other courses. So the objectives are clear, if somewhat broad.

Moving to methods, in the case of *Kontakte* there are basically four:

(a) A questionnaire and a series of progress charts (every 5 weeks) sent to a random sample of 750 home learners, drawn from those who volunteered by returning a pre-paid card in the first textbook.

(b) A more detailed study of 30 home learners, obtained by local advertizement in the area of the research centre, involving performance tests at regular intervals.

(c) A questionnaire to 417 institutions known to be interested in using the course in language classes, together with the same performance tests as mentioned in (b) administered by the class teacher in each case.

(d) A more detailed study of 5 language classes within the institution conducting the research, involving again the same performance tests.

What about the applications? An interim report of the *Kontakte* study has now been produced and already it is clear that cross-reference among the parts of the study will provide most useful evidence for future decisions. This includes evidence about the kinds of people who follow broadcast language courses at home and the extent to which they differ from those who attend classes, in educational background, in knowledge of languages and in other ways; whether the progress and dropout of home learners is significantly different from those in classes; whether the demands made by the course are too heavy or too light for a

128

majority of the learners; which particular aspects of the course are more successful than others. The *Wegweiser* research project should shed light on the extent to which students proceed from a first to a second stage of a broadcast language course and with what success.

All these factors can be of great use in planning similar courses in German and in other languages.

It will be noted that this research has been done by an academic team outside the BBC; and the team's co-operation has been greatly appreciated by the BBC production department. It illustrates the question already posed of whether summative evaluation should be the broadcasting organization's responsibility or whether research teams outside should be encouraged to undertake it.

Similar research has been done by Open University research teams on BBC/Open University programmes.

5 Some conclusions

This paper suggests that, in any particular circumstances, the most useful form of evaluation will be the one that gives the clearest affirmative answers to the three groups of questions at the end of Section 1. Such evaluation should provide evidence that can be learnt and applied most practically in the future.

It is also suggested that this is most likely to be achieved when the research works closely with both the production process and the future planning process and is largely in sympathy with both of them. The virtues of objectivity that are sometimes supposed to follow from a position of reserved detachment are usually grossly overrated and are more likely to lead either to irrelevance and misunderstanding or to complete indifference and nil effect. It is essential that policy-maker, manager, producer and researcher should work in the closest harmony possible. They should sound more like a barber's shop quartet than the rival crowds at a football match. All too often it is the latter that occurs.

Whether the research function is based in the same department, or even in the same organization, as the management and production function, does not seem to matter critically—it may well be useful if they are; but as long as close communication can be maintained, then harmony of working can generally be achieved.

ASSESSING NEEDS AND INTERESTS

PAPER NO 59: STUDYING AFTER FULL-TIME EDUCATION

Chris Sonnemans, Department for Research and Documentation, TELEAC Foundation, Netherlands.

Although young people nowadays have access to full-time education until they are 25, 75 per cent of the Dutch population over 15 dropped out of school when they were 15 or 16 or even younger.

The educational situation has improved of the past few years; however, for older people the situation is relatively unfavourable. After termination of full-time education, participation in education is only possible at the cost of great efforts and relatively high expenses (night classes, correspondence courses etc.).

In its initial stage, Teleac employed an 'open' way of programming; in doing so, it understandably placed emphasis on the medium of television. This open way of programming had the effect that Teleac selected topics on the basis of 'catering for all tastes'. However, recent developments in the Netherlands and abroad pointed towards a more closely defined or varied way of programming, modelled on the Telekolleg in Western Germany, or the Open University in Great Britain. This development resulted in an emphasis within Teleac on the multi-medial aspect of adult education.

Studying after full-time education

There are several ways of determining what could be Teleac's future tasks. One way is to ask a number of experts about what they think should happen in the future.

Another way is to focus on the needs of the people who take Teleac courses. It is also possible to derive a policy from the actual behaviour of people in relation to adult education. This implies that they have to be asked what they are *doing* rather than what they *want*. A prerequisite for tracing out a policy is to make an inventory of the various activities of Dutch people in the field of courses and training, after termination of their full-time education.

In 1973 the Department for Research of Teleac decided to set up a research project covering several years. This would be a research project bearing the working title 'Studying after full-time education', subdivided into four parts:

Part I   Making an Inventory
Part II   The Profile of the Teleac Course Member
Part III   An Analysis of Obstacles
Part IV   A Synthesis.

With 'making an inventory' we mean mapping out all the possible activities of Dutch people over 15 with regard to supplementing their full-time education and the type of education taken.

Undoubtedly there are Dutch people who took either correspondence courses, night classes, industrial trainings, or Teleac courses, and who met with a number of difficulties. As yet we know little about the nature of the difficulties we already noticed, and how to deal with them. This aspect is being studied in an investigation into the number of obstacles people encounter when they want to complement their full-time education.

On the basis of these investigations it is possible to formulate a number of audiences about which policy to follow.

In June 1973 we had the opportunity to put the first part of this research project into practice.

Intomart b.v., a Dutch research bureau, employs the so-called Multi-Client Investigation, i.e. an investigation in which by order of a number of clients a representative sample of the Dutch population older than 15 is interviewed. In this way it is possible to split up the fixed costs over various clients so that there are less expenses for each participating client. A similar investigation was carried out in March 1974 and February 1975.

In the meantime, the reports covering Parts I and II have been published (only available in Dutch language),[1,2] which are summarized below:

Findings of Studying after Full-Time Education, *Part 1, An Inventory over the years 1973, 1974, 1975*
Clearly it is impossible to give all the results of the investigation in this paper. We shall therefore confine ourselves to the most significant findings. In the presentation of the results in this paper, we have not taken into consideration the respondents who were still attending full-time education. The results given here consequently refer to respondents who have terminated their full-time education.

In the period ranging from 1973 until 1975, there were approximately 10,000,000 Dutch people in the Netherlands over 15. Of these, about 1,400,000 still attend full-time education. In the following table 1 per cent represents about 86,000 Dutch people. We suspected that there might be an increasing interest in taking courses or training after full-time education. A comparison of the data of the three investigations is outlined in Table 1.

It shows a distinct increase in partici-pation in one or more courses or training after termination of full-time education. The increase in 1974, compared with that of 1973, (3 per cent) is only slight, and might well be attributable to the sampling method. The increase in 1975, as compared with that of 1974 seems far less coincidental. In 1975, a significantly greater number of people took courses or training compared with 1974 ($X^2 = 14.20$ p $< .001$).

Interpreting the figures, we can see that at the end of the sixties and in the beginning of the seventies, there has been an increased interest in studying after full-time education, with an extra increase in 1974–5. A similar development has been found in calculations of the increase in the number of pupils at night schools for secondary education in the Netherlands. In 1969, there were 8,081 registered pupils. In 1973, this number had increased to 28,179.

In our society developments occur which might influence the interest in Teleac courses in the future. What we need to know is who actually took courses or training after termination of their full-time education. In order to answer this question we took the number of years of full-time education as variable.

Table 2 shows that the number of years of full-time education is highly correlated with taking courses or training.

Further analyses of the data indicates that more years of full-time education implies:
● more chance of taking courses or training.
● more chance of finishing a course.
● more chance of intending to take other courses, and
● more chance of interest in educational

Table 1   % of people over 15 taking courses or training after full-time education

Have you started taking courses or training after your full-time education?	1973	1974	1975
	%	%	%
Yes, I have started taking one or more courses or trainings	44	47	54
No, never	56	53	46
Total	100	100	100
Number or respondents	(1308)	(1318)	(1290)

Table 2   % of people in courses/training by years of full-time education

Have you started on a course or training?	No of years of full-time education									
	6 years or less		7–8 years		9–10 years		11 years or more		Total	
	'74	'75	'74	'75	'74	'75	'74	'75	'74	'75
	%	%	%	%	%	%	%	%	%	%
Yes	20	23	36	45	57	63	70	73	47	54
No	80	77	64	55	43	37	30	26	53	46
Total	100	100	100	100	100	100	100	100	100	100
Number of respondents	277	205	326	370	356	388	334	324	1318	1290

television in general and Teleac courses in particular.

Television education is one of the many possibilities in the Netherlands for studying after full-time education. A recent analysis of the training figures of Philips shows that in 1974 4,448 course members of Philips had been accomodated in 412 institutions, including Teleac. Teleac is one of the many possibilities for taking courses; this appears also from the report *Adult Education and Training in the Netherlands:*[3]

'... The total in 1971 of participants in Adult Education and Training is estimated to be somewhere about 1,200,000.'

In the season 1971–2 a total of 49,145 people took courses at Teleac; this is approximately 4 per cent of the above mentioned number. In this investigation no difference was found between one-day courses and courses ranging over several years. A small number of course members take several shorter courses in one year; thus they constitute a large percentage of the 1,200,000 participants. The Teleac investigation 'Studying after Full-Time Education', Part I, shows that in February 1975, approximately 800,000 people took a course or training of some kind (this does not include the shorter courses and training). Teleac's 'market-share' in this figure was 2 to 3 per cent (in March 1974, it was approximately 5 per cent).

With an average viewing density of 1–2 per cent, and a decreasing 'course member market-share' of 2–3 per cent, we feel that the significance for adult education of

educational television in general and Teleac courses in particular, has clearly been shown. (In Western Europe the average viewing density for educational programs is 1–2 per cent.)

Needs with regard to Teleac courses
One of the questions in the investigation was whether the respondents were at all interested in Teleac courses, and if so, what subjects Teleac should deal with in the future. Over one third (35 per cent) of the Dutch population over 15 are interested in Teleac courses, and mention one or more subjects. This means that there is an immediate 'course member-market' of 3,500,000 people.

However, here also the number of years of full-time education is the decisive factor for this interest. The more years of full-time education, the greater the chance that people are interested in taking a Teleac course, and the greater the chance that they might mention one or more subjects. Besides, this question whether people are interested in Teleac subjects does not create a new need: this need already exists. Those people who already have the intention of taking one or the other course in the future are more prompt in mentioning one or more subjects than those who do not have this intention.

All respondents interested in Teleac courses appear to be predominantly interested in language courses, subjects within the scope of humanities, and hobby courses. Only 9 per cent of the respondents showed an interest in courses within the scope of the exact sciences. This seems odd, since the total amount of time in Teleac planning given to exact sciences ranged between 20 per cent and 35 per cent over the past few years.

For all categories of courses, the main interest is centred on the starting-level. As far as subjects regarding the arts, the humanities and hobbies are concerned, the respondents show little ambition to acquire a diploma, whereas a large proportion of those respondents who mentioned exact and/or vocational subjects are highly interested in diplomas.

The main preference regarding the duration of either art or hobby courses is approximately 6 months; for exact science courses this is 12 months; for vocational courses 3 months. However, all course categories should preferably start in September or October.

Finally, it also appears that those respondents who mentioned the least subjects are housewives and old-age pensioners; those respondents who mentioned the most subjects are adolescent scholars, students, unemployed people, and people who for one reason or another have no occupation. Those respondents who have either full-time or part-time jobs are in an intermediate position.

Summary of Studying after Full-Time Education, *Part I: An Inventory over the years 1973, 1974 and 1975*
Teleac Foundation is one of over 400 institutions in the Netherlands for adult education. Teleac means something to a relatively large part of the Dutch people. There is a group of about 500,000 viewers/course members who in the course of 10 years have ordered the additional material of one course or more. They constitute the group of approximately 100,000 'hard-core' course members, i.e. people who ordered the material for 3 courses or more.

Findings of Studying after Full-Time Education, *Part II: The profile of the Teleac course member*
We shall confine ourselves again to the most significant findings. In Dutch secondary comprehensive night schools 90 per cent of the pupils are *younger* than 30 years old. Of the 'hard-core' course members of Teleac, i.e. people who ordered the

material for 3 or more courses, 90 per cent are *older* than 30 years.

The profile of the Teleac course member is as follows:

- he is of the male sex;
- his age is between 30 and 49 years; he is married with 2 children, so his family consists of 4 persons;
- he has had secondary education; his average net income is Dfl. 2,080 a month;
- he is taking or took courses after termination of his full-time education. In most cases he completed the courses or training; he intends to take more courses or training in the future;
- he is so-called 'light' viewer; he does not watch television for more than 8 hours a week;
- the Teleac course member reads nationwide newspapers, notably De Volkskrant or NRC/Handelsblad; he compares his own views with opinion-magazines, particularly Elseviers Weekblad or Vrij Nederland;
- training, income, function, and reading habits indicate to a great extent the political inclination of the Teleac course member, which is either rightish (VVD) or leftish (PvdA). In all cases he puts a solid trust in the Dutch political system;
- for the average Dutchman television is the most reliable medium of information; for the Teleac course member this is the newspaper;
- not only does the Teleac course member take courses more often after termination of his full-time education, but he finishes them more often and has a greater intention of taking other courses;
- the Teleac course member is also a more regular reader; he is especially active in church affairs and sports clubs; he is a concert, theatre and cinema goer, he visits museums, and takes Teleac courses, too;
- the well-informed are getting better informed because they are stimulated to gain more information.

Summary
In February 1975, 54 per cent of the Dutch population over 15 stated that they had taken or were still taking a course or training of some kind after termination of their full-time education. 46 per cent had not

taken any course or training after their full-time education.

Among the 54 per cent mentioned above, there is a group of approximately 100,000 so-called 'hard-core' Teleac course members, i.e. course members who ordered the material for 3 or more courses. The Teleac course member is at the top of the social ladder.

References
1 TELEAC FOUNDATION, *Studying after Full-time Education*. Parts I a-c. An Inventory of 1973, 1974, 1975. Utrecht, Department for Research and Documentation, 1974.
2 TELEAC FOUNDATION, *Studying after Full-time Education*. Part II. The Profile of the Teleac course member. Utrecht, Department for Research and Documentation, 1975.
3 HANS LINGTON, *Adult Education and Training in the Netherlands*, Amsterdam, Kohnstam Instituut, 1975.

PAPER NO 63: POTENTIAL TARGET AUDIENCES FOR MEDIA-BASED ADULT LEARNING

Ignacy Waniewicz, Director, Office of Planning and Development, Ontario Educational Communications Authority, Canada.

What is the nature and scope of deliberate involvement of adults in formal and non-formal part-time learning activities in a region containing an abundance of institutions of formal education? What is the specific contribution which educational broadcasting and, in general, educational communications media can make in an area which is probably one of the most media-saturated areas in the world? To answer the first question, a major probability sample survey was carried out by the Ontario Educational Communications Authority (OECA). The OECA operates a network of educational television stations in Ontario, Canada, and provides program services through cable systems and distribution of video tapes.

Results indicate that 30 per cent of the approximately five million adults living in the province were engaged in a deliberate learning activity. A further 18 per cent wish to undertake part-time deliberate learning.

The survey was conducted between 29 October 1974 and 10 January 1975, through personal interviews with 1,541 male and female residents of Ontario of age 18–69 not enrolled in educational institutions as full-time students. The respondents were selected in a multi-staged systematic random sample.

The findings, as well as the findings related to obstacles to learning experienced by different groups of the adult population are being used in drawing of conclusions regarding the role of the media and, in particular, the mass media, in meeting those needs for part-time learning which are not being met by the existing opportunities and facilities, on the one hand; and on the other, in removing the obstacles which hamper access to learning for those who consciously desire to enter such an educational venture. The study points, for example, to many specific areas where media support may be of help. In some cases, it identifies unserved target audiences, in other cases it implies the use of more diversified teaching/learning situations. In still others it points to the need for a new curriculum so as to make it more pertinent to learning needs which Learners and future Learners can identify as their own. The following are selected highlights of the study.

The learners and the would-be-learners
The number of Ontario adults who are actively engaged in learning can be considered by all standards as relatively high. The incidence of learning, as well as the interest in learning by those who are not yet engaged in a deliberate learning process, spreads over the entire spectrum of adulthood and early old-age. At least 1,400,000 adults are actively engaged in a systematic learning activity; 80 per cent of them have the intention of continuing systematic learning in the near future, and over 800,000 adults who currently are not engaged in such an activity—at least in their own perception—express the intention to study in the next year or two.

One of the main conclusions that may be derived from these data is that Ontario's educational opportunities are numerous and relatively accessible to many parts of the population. The educational services in Ontario are already, to a significant degree, 'open'. Judging, however, from the number of would-be-learners and their specific demographic and socio-economic characteristics, and—as it will be seen later—from the reasons why the non-learners do not participate in learning activities, the educational services in their present state are not sufficiently adapted to the needs of numerous *specific* population groups.

Among those who require a more 'open' educational system are women, particularly women of age 18–20, 25–34 and 45–49, and persons of certain types of occupations, e.g. homemakers and clerical workers.

The results of this study indicate clearly that working adults need new and a greater variety of educational services and opportunities. Anticipating findings which will be discussed later, it should be pointed out that these newly required services would have to take into account, to a greater degree than existing services, people's constraints in time, in geographic location, in ability to leave home, in ability to travel, etc. Opportunities better adapted to particular needs are also required by both the youngest adults and the middle aged.

In large urban centres, despite the high incidence of learning, more learning opportunities are needed for numerous groups of adults unable to take advantage of existing ones. More efforts are needed to make learning accessible to various ethnic groups, particularly the French speaking population of Ontario.

Income level and the level of educational attainment are closely related to participation in adult learning. The more people are educated and the more money they earn, the more actively they are interested in learning. However, the variable that is most responsible for the incidence of learning seems to be educational attainment. If the incidence of learning is higher among those with a higher personal and family income, it appears to be so because their educational attainment is generally higher.

The gap between the 'haves' and 'have-nots' in education seems to widen, though the level of educational achievement of the population in general seems to be increasing. More efforts are needed if there is

to be any change in the chronic situation in which the lower socio-economic classes are consistently 'under-represented' among adult learning participants, while those of the middle and upper groups are consistently 'over-represented'.

Among those who are in search for learning opportunities better adapted to their needs one may also identify four other significant groups: white-collar workers, unskilled labourers, rural adults and home-bound people.

Looking at the findings from the point of view of different variables, the relatively major groups of learners can be identified as:

- persons of age 18–29;
- men of age 18–34;
- women of age 18–29 and of age 45–49;
- singles;
- persons whose language most often spoken at home is English;
- those with at least some post-secondary education;
- persons who are employed full-time;
- professionals and white-collar workers;
- people with a family income of over $20,000;
- people in communities of over 500,000;
- persons residing in South Central Ontario.

The major clusters of would-be-learners comprise:

- women of age 18–34 and age 45–49;
- men of age 25–29;
- persons with children at home;
- persons with more than grade school education and less than completed high school;
- people with at least some post-secondary education;
- homemakers;
- people employed part-time;
- white-collar, clerical workers;
- unskilled labourers;
- people with a personal income below $7,500 and above $12,000;
- people living in centres of 30,000–100,000 and in rural areas;
- people living in Eastern Ontario.

Among non-learners, the most significant groups can be identified as:

- people of age 50–69 and age 40–44;
- men of age 40 and over;
- women of age 50 and over;

● persons with 5 or more children at home;
● persons who are widowed, separated or divorced;
● persons speaking languages other than English at home;
● people whose educational attainment is not higher than grade school;
● retired persons;
● farmers;
● unskilled labourers;
● persons with a family income of less than $10,000;
● people from rural areas and from centres of 10,000 to 30,000;
● residents of north-eastern Ontario.

Where do adults learn?

While 70 per cent of learners take at least one course in a formal education institution, all formal education institutions together have only a 30 per cent share of the total learning activities of adults. In other words, 70 per cent of deliberate learning takes place outside the system whose primary objective is education.

Still, taking into account the number of different individuals served, the greatest suppliers of educational opportunities throughout the Province remain undoubtedly formal education institutions. However, the share of specific types of formal education institutions varies quite substantially from area to area. For example, while in South Central Ontario, universities provide for over 17 per cent of the adult learning activities, their role in northern parts of the province is considerably smaller in this respect. Anticipating other data that will be discussed later, it is conceivable that a certain type of tele-university, i.e., a higher education institution designed specifically to meet the needs of people living in areas where universities are not easily accessible, may well fill a significant gap.

While, as the study shows, there is a considerable number of would-be-learners interested in formal learning among the population of the older age brackets, formal education institutions seem to cater more to the needs of younger persons. Also, courses available at the place of work or organized by the employer seem to be oriented rather toward the younger age brackets, leaving the occupational concerns of the older people unmet.

Very few learning opportunities seem to be offered at the place of work for unskilled workers. The study indicates that among this occupational group there are more would-be-learners than learners. The gap in educational opportunities for this group becomes more evident if we take into account the fact that their major interest is vocational education.

Nearly 40 per cent of all adult learners participate in learning for credit. However, here again, it seems that the opportunities for learning for credit are designed to fit the needs of the young. The study shows clearly that the demand for this type of learning is considerably higher among older age groups.

Self-directed learning is very popular among Ontario adults. Another form of home-based learning, learning through radio and television, also seems to be quite substantial in comparison with the relatively few opportunities for systematic study currently being offered. These factors seen in the light of the demand for more formally recognized learning schemes, as well as in the light of a number of other elements that will be mentioned later, seem to indicate the need for the introduction of a greater variety of forms for sequential and structured learning.

What do adults learn?

Occupational concerns of all kinds are undoubtedly one of the most powerful motivational forces for learning. 60 per cent of all learners study at least one subject related to their jobs and occupations, and nearly half of all learning projects are connected with this domain of interest. The intentions of would-be-learners are similar, although, as a greater proportion of them are not employed, they may be less inclined to articulate this motivation.

A substantial amount of learning takes place as a result of concerns related to personal growth, development and self-realization. The other two major stimulants are recreational interests and the interest in attaining higher levels of formal education.

Very often the nominal description of the subjects people study or intend to study may not be easily identifiable with their actual interest and purpose of learning. It is also conceivable that people may often not be in a position to recognize easily whether or not a given area is, in fact, congruent with their desires and aspirations. It seems particularly important, therefore, that educators and educational planners provide opportunities for learning that are more closely related to peoples' desires and motivations, and that educational opportunities be described in terms of the various goals they can help to achieve.

The analysis of what people learn, as well as the comparison of information related to learners and would-be-learners seem to point to a number of gaps. For example, more flexible educational opportunities are needed in the domain of vocational and professional education, particularly for persons of age 18–24, for women, and for persons with a relatively lower level of educational attainment. More flexible learning opportunities in the domain of formal education seem to be needed to meet the needs of persons of age 21–24 and 45–55, and in particular of women, of persons with some post-secondary education, and of professionals, executives, and managers. More opportunities for education in the domain of hobbies and recreation seem to be required for women of age 21–55, for persons with an educational attainment below completed high school, and for homemakers. Opportunities for personal development are in high demand by persons of age 25–29, and by persons without any secondary education.

Preferred methods of learning

We have already indicated the considerable popularity of self-directed learning, as well as the significant participation in radio and television learning relative to the number of study opportunities offered by the media in a systematic way.

The information on the methods of learning which learners and would-be-learners prefer and/or consider suitable adds additional light on the problem of home-centred learning or learning at-a-distance. On the surface it may be striking that the traditional methods of classes and lectures are still very popular among adults. The other side of the coin is, however, that hundreds of thousands of persons consider suitable and, in many cases, prefer to learn through such methods as learning by correspondence, short-term seminars and conferences, community

groups, interest groups, action groups, watching specially produced television programs accompanied by study guides, listening to educational radio programs and audio cassettes accompanied by study guides, and through self-directed learning. It seems that in a situation where hundreds of thousands of people cannot use the existing educational opportunities, there is plenty of room for initiative and plenty of promise for success for the introduction of a variety of multi-media and multi-method teaching/learning schemes and approaches designed for specific target audiences and specific subject areas.

Do adults want credits? Do adults want degrees?

Over 1,300,000 learners and would-be-learners are interested in learning for credit or some other kind of recognition of their learning effort as compared with about 500,000 persons who currently study for credit. The two most numerous groups, counting each around a half a million people, seek a written confirmation of satisfactory completion of a course of study, or a credit toward a professional or vocational certificate. Over 200,000 adults want to study for a credit toward a university degree and about 50,000 for a high school credit.

The interest in official recognition of the learning effort is not less noticeable among respondents with higher levels of educational attainment. This interest is higher among employed respondents than among non-employed and among those employed full-time rather than part-time.

The desire for credits is not limited to those who study academic or vocational subjects. A large proportion of persons interested in personal development, hobbies and recreation, home and family, and other educational purposes having very little to do with the realm of formal steps, levels, grades, etc., would, still, very much like to have some kind of an official recognition for their learning effort. One has the impression that for many people the issuing of certificates of completion of courses, of achievement, or simply of attendance, may play a motivational role in learning.

Learners and would-be-learners were asked whether they would like to get a degree or diploma if they had the opportunity within the next ten years. Nearly 70 per cent of learners and 60 per cent of would-be-learners answered in the affirmative. Among learners, seen from the numerical point of view, the most popular title is a Bachelor's degree, followed by a certificate or license to practice an occupation. The third place—in terms of frequency of expressed desire—is taken by a Master's degree. Would-be-learners are most frequently interested in occupational credentials, followed by a high school diploma and Bachelor's degree. The most popular credits through all age groups are a Bachelor's degree and an occupational license. Speaking in numerical terms, it can be estimated that about 350,000 individuals would be interested in Bachelor's degrees, which is about the same number of people who are interested in occupational certificates or licenses; over 200,000 persons are interested in Masters degrees; about 160,000 in high school diplomas; about the same number in community college diplomas; and about 60,000 in Doctors degrees.

Why Adults Learn

The establishing of reasons for which people learn, on the basis of their spontaneous replies during a survey interview, is important for the design of learning programs to meet people's needs, for the proper marketing and promotion of available learning opportunities, etc. The importance of providing learning opportunities designed in content and form to relate better to the needs and desires felt by people themselves cannot be overemphasized.

By far the two largest clusters of reasons are the desire to achieve personal goals, understood as a quest for personal growth, development and fulfillment, and the desire to achieve practical goals, understood as some kind of material benefits. These two categories of reasons are most frequently mentioned by both learners and would-be-learners, by respondents of all age groups, and of both sexes, of all levels of educational attainment and of all other demographic and socioeconomic variables. Relatively few answers reflect a desire to meet a religious or social goal. Also relatively low is the frequency of referring to the desires to meet family needs. Generally speaking, there is a high degree of congruency between the responses related to categories of learning interests, and the responses regarding reasons for learning.

Obstacles to learning

Perhaps the best way of summing up the findings about barriers to learning and reasons for not learning would be to look at the data from the perspective of the total population. Nearly two million adults in the province consider that being busy is an obstacle to learning. Nearly 700,000 persons, 15 per cent of the total adult population, consider that they can't afford learning activities, and half-a-million people consider that they are too tired to learn. Over half-a-million find it too hard to get out of the house, and for nearly half-a-million people courses are located too far away.

Nearly 400,000 people dislike schedules and exams, over 300,000 adults are not certain that the courses that are available are of value to them and a quarter-of-a-million consider that the available courses do not correspond to their interests.

Lack of self-confidence does not seem to be a major obstacle. Only about 4 per cent of all respondents are not sure that they are capable to handle learning, and about 6 per cent feel that they lack the prior education necessary for further learning.

Let's set aside such reasons as being too busy, being too tired and lack of interest in further learning, assuming—rightly or wrongly—that they belong to those about which the educational planner or administrator can do little. The major group of obstacles to which solutions have to be sought will then be those related to financial problems, mobility, and problems with adapting to existing opportunities. It might be worthwhile to have a look at how they affect the major clusters of would-be-learners and non-learners.

Women of age 18–34 and 45–49 have been identified as a major group seeking an opportunity for learning. When we look at the obstacles which respondents mentioned most often, financial and mobility problems are on the top of the list for women would-be-learners of age 18–24; for women of age 25–44, they are in second, third, and fourth place, immediately after 'being busy'. For another major cluster of would-be-learners —men of age 25–29—financial problems are the second most frequently mentioned, and those related to mobility problems are fourth on the list of obstacles.

Seen from the perspective of other variables, would-be-learners with children at home list the financial and mobility problems in second, third, and fourth place. The same three obstacles related to financial problems and mobility are on the top three or four places on the list for would-be-learners who are homemakers, for would-be-learners with only some and completed post-secondary education, for white-collar workers and unskilled labourers, and for would-be-learners living in Eastern Ontario.

The patterns are very similar for non-learners except that the problem of adaptability to existing opportunities, and problems related to the lack of self-confidence seem to be of somewhat greater importance.

The analysis of obstacles to learning and reasons for not learning seem to point once again to the great role that media-based educational systems could play in meeting the learning needs of the Ontario population, particularly if they were combined with a variety of interactive teaching/learning situations adapted to people's requirements in terms of time, location and approach. A more detailed discussion of these problems is, however, outside the terms of reference of this report.

PAPER NO 12: ASSESSING NEEDS FOR ADULT EDUCATION ON TELEVISION

P. Dannheisser and I. Haldane, Independent Broadcasting Authority, London, UK.

Both the Independent Broadcasting Authority (IBA) and the British Broadcasting Corporation (BBC) undertake to broadcast Adult Education programmes on television. The IBA broadcasts some 200 hours of these programmes each year: programmes produced by Independent Television Companies throughout Britain and approved by the Adult Education Committee of the IBA.

The full paper gives the detailed formula for such programmes.

It goes without saying, that a further important—but not all important—factor should be that programme policy should attempt to satisfy the educational interests and preferences of the viewing public. Examples could be given of programmes in the general output and in the Adult Education field which have awakened dormant interests or helped to create new interests amongst viewers. Frequently cited instances include archaeology, show jumping and yoga. Thus it is very far from the authors' intention to suggest that such needs—assessment research results are sufficient material on which programme planners can frame policy. In 1968, however, it was recognized as a necessary element in future policy-making and the research department of the Independent Television Authority designed and commissioned a survey on Viewer Preferences in Adult Education.[1] The survey was undertaken by the British Market Research Bureau.

This paper describes the results of this research. It should be understood that the objectives of the research were limited to understanding the relative interest to viewers of a number of possible topics: no attempt was made to clarify the kind of treatment of these topics, or of the kind of presentation which would be most appreciated: such an extension of aim would have made the whole operation too cumbersome and time-consuming from the respondents' point of view. Where interest was expressed in a topic, however, the research established the level at which the respondent wished the topic to be treated, either fairly elementary or more advanced. Respondents (i.e. potential viewers) were asked to express the degree of their interest in each of a list of 130 topics: they were not asked about groups of topics (or areas of interest), but subsequent statistical analysis of the data combined the topics into related fields of interest, each made up of several individual topics which together tended to be found of interest among the viewing public.

This piece of research followed an earlier study[2] carried out by a team of BBC Education Officers in 1965 and contrasts with their approach. In the BBC survey, a team of Education Officers sought to collect the views of experts in the field of Further Education in order to assess their observations of the needs of the country and the interests of potential viewers. The BBC approach was to gather—from experts and consultants—'observed' needs. The piece of research described below attempted to measure the 'felt' needs of the viewer in a indirect manner. These two methods of needs-assessment have been found complementary.

Method

As this was an area of research in which there were no established techniques or procedures it was necessary to proceed by stages. Earlier exploratory and pilot stages were designed to allow greater insight into the extent of the range of topics which should be covered, and into the most effective technical means of conducting the research.

At the earlier stages thirty non-directive discursive interviews with adults and four informal group discussions with men and women took place in London and Manchester. Arising out of these stages of the work it became clear that a very wide range of topics would have to be covered but that simple naming of these would cause no misunderstanding or problems of comprehension. The basic technical problem was how to induce a respondent to go through a list of over one hundred topics, consider each and report on the likelihood of viewing a programme dealing with it, without fatigue and with a minimum of prestige-induced bias.

The problem was solved by preparing booklets, each containing 130 topics ranging from Angling to Zoology, with one topic per page: each topic had a code number, and the respondent would, in reporting to the interviewer, use only the code number. This gave the appearance of a secret ballot, minimized prestige effects and avoided interviewer influence; at the same time it was practicable and easily workable in the interview situation.

The order in which the pages of the booklet were collated (that is, the order of presentation of the topics) was subjected to random rotation to avoid order bias, and the degree of interest in the topic was measured by asking the respondent to state his/her likelihood of viewing by choosing one of five statements from a prompt card:

I *Definitely* watch it.
II *Probably* watch it.
III *Possibly* watch it.
IV *Probably* not watch it.
V *Definitely* not watch it.

It is important to stress that at no point in the survey was the word 'educational' used. Respondents were asked to comment on 'subjects for future television programmes'. In that way any bias or expectations which may have been induced in a respondent answering questions associated with 'education' were avoided. In the interview extensive classification data were collected from respondents relating to their educational status, demographic characteristics and amount and type of television viewing. Respondents who stated that they 'would definitely watch' a topic were asked simple supplementary questions relating to that topic: these further probes were designed to give additional information about the preferred 'programme quality' for each topic, and comprised questions along three dimensions:

1 Elementary . . . advanced.
2 Single programme . . . programme series.
3 General family interest . . . personal interest only.

The sample was a quota sample with controls on sex and working status within a random selection of 100 polling districts in 96 constituencies in Great Britain. Female interviewers of British Market Research Bureau, fully trained and briefed and working under supervision, were issued with representative quotas of individuals of different categories, and were instructed to attempt interviews only in pre-selected streets. Interviewing took place within respondents' own homes. The sample design incorporated planned over-sampling in Scotland and Wales in order to provide sufficient interviews in these areas for separate analysis. Although the original total target sample size was 2,000 adults in homes with television, bad weather and widespread illness at the time of the main fieldwork reduced the achieved sample to a total of 1,850.

Results

1 *Viewers' general areas of interest*

To obtain a general indication of the subject areas which appeared to be of greatest interest to potential viewers, a 'net interest level' was calculated for each group of topics. This was the percentage of all respondents who stated that they 'would definitely watch' *at least one topic* within the group (see Table 1).

Three aspects of this general ranking of groups of topics are noteworthy. The method of calculating 'net interest' will tend to favour groups with many topics as against groups with few but it will be seen that there is no direct and obvious relationship between number of topics in group and rank of group, although the largest group stands first in rank order. Other criteria bear out the conclusion that domestic subjects are of greater public interest.

Secondly, one can observe the great difference in public interest between the sciences and the liberal arts or humanities. 'The Sciences' stand second only to domestic subjects in general interest: 'Religion, Philosophy and the Human Sciences' stand, with 'Literature' and 'Languages', at the very bottom of the list.

Thirdly, this general ranking of groups of topics conceals the fact that the different groups have interest and appeal to different sections of the public and a balanced output of programmes would have to take account not only of content and treatment but of the audience for which they are planned.

2 *Level of treatment*

Respondents were asked whether they would prefer the programme to be: (a) fairly *elementary*, so that most people watching could understand it, at least to

Table 1   Percentage of all respondents who 'would definitely watch' at least one of the topics in a group

		'Would definitely watch' %	No of topics in group
1	Home and family	82	26
	(Safety in the Home)	44	1
2	The sciences	64	16
3	History and geography	59	10
	(Travel)	42	1
4	Home maintenance	56	3
5	The arts	48	8
6	Law and government	47	12
7	Hobbies	47	8
8	Theatre	45	4
9	Careers	44	13
	(Education)	29	1
10	Current and world affairs	42	3
11	Local affairs	39	3
12	The car	39	2
13	Religion, philosophy and human sciences	35	6
14	Literature	27	5
15	Languages	13	6
			128

After Table 1, only the 'top' 5 subject groups are shown. All 15 are given in the full paper.

Table 2   Level of treatment wanted

		Fairly Elementary %	*More Advanced* %
	All respondents who 'would definitely watch' one or more topics in a group		
1	Home and family	63	37
2	The sciences	69	31
3	History and geography	64	36
4	Home maintenance	68	32
5	The arts	61	39

Groups 6–15 omitted for reasons of space

start with, or (b) more *advanced* than that (see Table 2).

In calculating these proportions a weighted average score was derived which took into account, for each group, all the topics within the group which would 'definitely be watched' by each respondent.

The proportion of the public who want to have each topic treated at an elementary, and at an advanced level, shows very little variation from topic group to topic group.

3 *Interest by different sections of the viewing public*

Up to this point the paper describes the degree of interest expressed by potential viewers *in general*. This approach can conceal large differences between the interests of specific segments of the population. These differences were examined for groups of people of different social grade, sex, age, for people educated to different levels and people who said they watched differing amounts of television. To some extent these groups are bound to overlap.

People between the ages of 16 and 24 expressed less interest in watching the topics in general than did the other sections of the viewing public (see Table 3). Women were particularly interested in 'Home and the Family' and 'Literature': and men particularly in 'Careers' and 'The Sciences'. 'Religion, Philosophy and Human Sciences' was the only topic group more attractive to the youngest age group (16–24) than to the older groups.

Table 3   Sex and age

		% Sex		% Age		
	'Would definitely watch' (one or more topics in group)					
		Men	Women	16–24	25–44	45+
1	Home and family	70	94	76	82	85
2	The sciences	72	57	64	69	60
3	History and geography	58	60	55	57	61
4	Home maintenance	60	52	37	58	61
5	The arts	45	51	45	49	48

Groups 6–15 omitted

Table 4   *Social grade*

'*Would definitely watch*' (*one or more topics in group*)

ABC1   Upper middle, middle and lower middle class (32% of population)

C2   Skilled working class (41%)

DE   Working class (27%)

		ABC1	C2	DE
		%	%	%
1	Home and family	81	83	84
2	The sciences	65	65	62
3	History and geography	63	59	53
4	Home maintenance	47	60	61
5	The arts	55	47	41

Groups 6–15 omitted

Interest was highest in general among the ABC1s and lowest amongst those in the DE social grades. The exceptions most noticeable are the topics in the groups 'Home Maintenance', 'The Car' and 'Home and the Family' (see Table 4).

Terminal Education Age Respondents were divided into 3 groups dependent on the age at which full-time education ceased, and on whether some other form of systematic study was undertaken after that age. (See Table 5.)

Those whose full-time education ended at 15 or under and who did not study after that age were least interested in the topics in general. Those who had studied at all after

that age showed over all a similar degree of interest. 'Home and the Family' and 'Home Maintenance' do not follow the general rule. Terminal Education Age groups are strongly related to social grade groups and their patterns of interest are similar.

4 *Individual topics*

Topics related to *Home and Family* had a substantial lead over all other groups (Table 6). Of course these topics may attract an artificially high expression of intent to view—a vote against such topics could literally be thought to be a vote against 'home and mother'. Respondents however used code numbers in the interview in order to minimize this effect—programme topics were

Table 5   *Terminal education age*

'*Would definitely watch*' (*one or more topics in group*)

		16 and over	15 and under	
			Studied since	Not studied since
		%	%	%
1	Home and family	76	84	85
2	The sciences	67	67	61
3	History and geography	65	62	53
4	Home maintenance	44	63	58
5	The arts	54	52	43

Groups 6–15 omitted

K

Table 6   Amount of TV viewing

		up to 2 hours	3–4 hours	5 hours or more
	'Would definitely watch' (one or more topics in group)			
		%	%	%
1	Home and family	77	82	91
2	The sciences	62	64	67
3	History and geography	58	57	63
4	Home maintenance	47	59	62
5	The arts	49	47	49

Groups 6–15 omitted

not mentioned. 'Safety in the Home', 'Health', 'First Aid', 'Cookery' and 'Care of Old People' all came high on the list of programmes that would 'definitely be watched'. Topics in the group of *Sciences* were of greater interest to men than to women. Applied and natural sciences ('Nature', 'Medicine' and 'Progress in Space') came high on the list compared with 'Physics', 'Chemistry' and 'Statistics'. In the group labelled *History and Geography*, 'Travel' was a subject of wide general interest but mostly topics in this group were of interest to the more educated sector of the audience. Inversely, topics in the group 'Home Maintenance' were of most interest to those who left school at fifteen or younger. The average level of interest for the topics in this group was higher than for topics in any other. In the group labelled *The Arts* only 4 per cent claimed they would watch programmes about 'Sculpture' in contrast to the 21 per cent who said they would be interested in programmes on 'Antiques'. Both are frequently dealt with on television. 'Taxation' headed the list of *Law and Government* topics. 20 per cent said they would watch, but on the whole problems of civics were of low interest. 'Gardening' was the most popular *Hobby*. 15 per cent said they would be interested in 'Bird Watching' programmes, but only 7 per cent wanted to see 'Ornithology', underlining the importance of simple descriptions in questionnaires of this type. The group least popular amongst respondents was *Languages*. The greatest interest was for 'French' (5 per cent of the sample) but only 2 per cent said they wanted Russian. This, in spite of the wide popularity of language classes in institutional adult education.

Conclusion

In 1969, Brian Groombridge—then the Education Officer of the ITA wrote:

It would be an abdication of responsibility to aim programmes designed for particular sections or strata of the public, solely in the regions of their present declared interest. The research indicates what is likely to be the best point at which to win a particular section of the audience to the regular viewing of purposive series. It also to some extent indicates routes through which an audience, once built, might be consolidated and led into a wider perspective of interests. Thus instead of describing, say, the working of various social and welfare services in an academically head-on way, it might be desirable to present the same material in terms of the changing needs of the family, its different members calling for different forms of community support at different ages and stages.

Without this ambition, to build on declared interest to enlarge awareness, a passive response to the research result could help create or reinforce certain kinds of educational apartheid in our society—domesticity for the workers and their wives, arts for the middle class and high politics for a still smaller élite among them.

With the benefit of hindsight, Brian Groom-bridge—now Head of Educational Programme Services, adds:

> It is gratifying that the Independent Television Companies, in their submission to the official (Annan) Committee of Enquiry, publicly acknowledge the influence of this research. There is often, however, a discrepancy between the richness of research findings and the thinness of their application, and so it proved on this occasion. The Authority and its advisers were strengthened by this research in their conviction that there were no intractable problems in the way of presenting the general audience with educational material across a very wide range of human concerns. As the note just quoted suggests, we even felt that the research might be used to guide teaching and programming strategies. In the event, the companies on the whole chose to make rather selective and superficial use of the findings—quoting them, for example, in support of programme proposals in the domestic area, and mostly ignoring them in fields such as science,

and never, to my knowledge, using them with any kind of pedagogical insight. The reasons for this are manifold. The research was commissioned by the Authority, without perhaps sufficiently involving the companies in its planning. To make better use of it would have required a structural cohesiveness in the ITV system which, in the adult education sector, it is only just achieving . . . there are clear indications now that the adult education effort of the companies is becoming less one-sided and more purposeful.

References

1 BRITISH MARKET RESEARCH BUREAU, *Viewer Preferences in Adult Education: Report on Interests and Preferences of the Viewing Public*, London, ITA, 1969.

2 EUROPEAN BROADCASTING UNION, Needs and Interests of the Adult Community in the United Kingdom, *8th Meeting of the European Broadcasting Union Study Group of Teaching by Television*. Rome, EBU, 1969.

STUDIES OF PARTICULAR PROJECTS

PAPER NO 23: THE USE OF RADIO AND TELEVISION LANGUAGE COURSES

Brian Hill and Sandra Gasser, Department of Communication Studies, Brighton Polytechnic, UK.

A considerable proportion of the air time allotted to educational broadcasting on both radio and television is devoted to language teaching. In the last academic year twenty seven language series were transmitted. Eighteen of these series were for schools and nine for further education audiences.

The variety of languages taught, the variety of series objectives and the variety of methodologies employed make any all-embracing statements regarding the use, and even more the potential, of radio and television impractical. However, there is a very real need for studies in this field and a unit of research workers and support staff has been established at Brighton Polytechnic to define those areas which can be validly investigated and to undertake specific studies.

To date, research has concentrated on three aspects—the home learner of a first stage German course *Kontakte*; the classroom exploitation of this same course in colleges; and the classroom exploitation of *Le Nouvel Arrivé*, a television series for the 13–15 year age group. The operation has lasted approximately two years and has been funded by the West German Government (approximately £2,000), the Independent Broadcasting Authority (approximately £5,500) and the Polytechnic (approximately £6,500). The BBC has co-operated fully in the collection of data, the establishment of the sample and the pro-vision of tapes and programme scripts. The projects were designed in close consultation with BBC and ITV producers and with the invaluable co-operation of the BBC's further education liaison service (*Kontakte*) and Thames Television (*Le Nouvel Arrivé*).

The purpose

All three investigations are designed along the same lines, to find out more about how the broadcast courses were actually used and to obtain some indication of their success in achieving their stated aims. In each case attention has also been paid to establishing the context in which the radio and television programmes were being used in order to obtain the information on general circumstances which might be applicable to other courses in the same area. It is hoped that the data generated can be taken into account when planning future policy.

Design considerations and methods of enquiry

Several limitations had to be taken into account in designing the research projects and in some cases these need to be considered when evaluating the significance of the data obtained. The main problems were as follows:

(a) Since we were researching programmes that were being recorded only shortly before transmission, it was difficult to assimilate the characteristics of individual programmes into planning. Nor was it possible to build into the programmes elements which might have generated information in a controlled way.

(b) In the individual circumstances in which programmes were used, a number of uncontrollable variables existed.

The variety of user characteristics made any attempt at detailed comparisons between learner performances very dangerous (both with the home learner and the classroom situation).

(c) The research was linked to specific courses and considerable care had to be exercised not to make unsupported generalizations.

(d) It was difficult in many circumstances to make the distinction between media-based and audience-based information.

(e) No attempt could be made at this stage to test the effectiveness of radio and television vis-a-vis other teaching methods.

With these factors in mind, a research strategy was developed which attempted to generate information in two ways:

(a) A broad-based national enquiry to establish the context of the learning situation and to generate data on such aspects as who was using the course, for what purposes, in what way, plus data on subjective assessment of success.

(b) An in-depth series of case studies which looked in more objective detail at learning success as defined by such factors as attainment of aural performance, attainment of oral performance, attainment of reading performance and improvement of knowledge about the country.

The specific methods used and a brief summary of the results obtained for each section are as follows:

1 *The home-based learner with* Kontakte

(a) Following a pilot run on known users of previous courses a detailed *questionnaire* was designed to establish a *profile* of the *Kontakte* audience. A serious learner was defined as someone who purchased a course book and a reply paid post card was inserted into Book 1. Of those expressing willingness to cooperate in a research project by returning the postcard, a random sample was established weighted slightly in favour of beginners, rather than those with previous knowledge of German. Completed questionnaires were received from 601 respondents out of 750 initially sent out.

RESULTS

The questionnaire produced information on the biographical background of respondents and on factors which might affect language learning behaviour. 32.1 per cent of the audience were aged between 41–65, 51.6 per cent between 22–40. 56.7 per cent were male with the majority, both male and female employed full time (64.6 per cent). The overall standard of education was relatively high. Approximately 50 per cent had experienced some form of further and higher education and a further 28 per cent listed their last establishment of full-time education as grammar or technical school.

As might be expected, an overwhelming 96.5 per cent had English as their native language, but somewhat more surprising was the number of respondents (79.2 per cent) who had already spent time learning a foreign language. The principal language previously learnt was French with some 50 per cent having formal academic qualifications ranging from 'O' level to a degree. It was also of significance that a relatively large section of the initial respondents had previously followed a course in German and were not therefore 'pure' beginners. A surprising 23.5 per cent of the random sample had actually followed a previous BBC intermediate course *Reportage*. The majority of respondents had learned their language at school and very few had experience of audio-visual or audio-lingual methods. On the other hand, approximately 80 per cent had experienced grammar-translation methods.

In attempting to gain some indication of respondents' reasons for learning a foreign language possible alternatives were provided to reflect vocational and industrial motivation as well as reasons of general interest i.e. short holidays abroad. Overwhelmingly learners were wanting to learn for personal rather than professional reasons; firstly for holidays abroad, secondly for general interest and thirdly as a hobby.

Considerable interest in Germany as a country was evident in that 73.7 per cent stated that they had already visited Germany, though the majority of this total was made up of people spending less than four weeks on holiday (as opposed to more than four weeks on business).

(b) *A progress card* was sent to each of the respondents every five weeks. This asked for information on how the programme had been used (viewing and listening hours), whether he/she had used the books/cassettes, etc., whether he/she attended classes and how he/she rated the course components on a four- or five-point scale. Returns of progress cards were:

Programmes 1–5: 596 (79.5 per cent)
Programmes 6–10: 472 (62.4 per cent)
Programmes 11–15: 372 (49.6 per cent)
Programmes 16–20: 316 (42.1 per cent)
Programmes 21–5: 287 (38.3 per cent)

It can be seen therefore that 38.3 per cent of the initial sample are known to have finished the course.

RESULTS

Information processed to date indicates that most respondents followed both radio and television. Throughout the first twenty weeks, for instance, most respondents followed one television and one radio programme a week; second most popular learning pattern was one television programme per week; third was two television with one radio and fourth two television. Other patterns such as one radio session or three television and one radio showed very low scores. An important point is that the proportion of learners using just radio tended to increase as the course progressed indicating that the demands of following both elements at the same time were considerable.

The most popular broadcast was the TV programme on Sunday mornings (38.3 per cent), followed by the Sunday radio programme (22.5 per cent), the Saturday TV programme (16.9 per cent), the Wednesday radio programme (15.6 per cent) and the Wednesday TV programme (6.6 per cent). The audience for the Sunday TV programme was virtually constant throughout the course, but the Sunday radio audience increased its percentage towards the end.

It became clear that the majority of learners were only willing to spend an average of one–two hours per week on their German, *including* following the programmes and further work by themselves. The next largest category of learners devoted two–three hours per week. An in-

significant number were willing to spend five hours or more (the target suggested as ideal by the course designers).

Learners were asked to rate the course components on a five point scale. The number of people NOT using television increased as the course progressed (from 9.5 per cent in the first five programmes to 16.7 per cent in the last five). Of those who used it, very few thought it was of no use at all (1 per cent). 10.7 per cent thought it was not very useful though this figure tended to decline towards the end. The majority thought it was quite useful (36.3 per cent) or very useful (39.7 per cent).

With radio the evidence suggested that, although fewer people overall were using it, it was rated more highly, 50 per cent stating radio was very useful as opposed to 19 per cent quite useful. The book was rated highly, with 66 per cent 'very useful' and 21 per cent 'quite useful overall'.

The most obvious point to make about the record/cassette element is that most people did not use it (70 per cent). The majority of those who did, gave it the rating 'not very useful'.

(c) A *drop-out questionnaire* was administered to most respondents who did not return their progress cards. Just over 200 were sent out and a relatively high return of 170 completed questionnaires obtained. Questions were asked as to why learners had given up the course, how they rated the course overall and whether they would follow another radio or television course.

RESULTS

It appears that most people who stopped studying *Kontakte* did so for personal reasons, rather than the fact that they were dissatisfied with the course. 88.87 per cent said that they would use a broadcast language course again.

When respondents were asked to indicate their reasons for discontinuing by ticking any of twelve different categories, the highest scores were: difficulty in finding time for preparation and follow up (48.43 per cent), pressure of work (45.91 per cent), inability to follow *Kontakte* on a regular basis (32.7 per cent). The most frequently given 'pure' course-based reason—irritation with TV studio scenes—was only ranked fifth.

(d) A local group of 29 learners was established and *tests* administered every five programmes to obtain information on their progress in aural/oral and reading skills. To do this, batteries of special tests were constructed, based on the stated aims of the preceding five programmes. Complete test results were obtained for 14 learners, the others having stopped using *Kontakte* at various stages.

RESULTS

The single most interesting point to emerge from these figures at this stage is that all scores were relatively high, even though at the time certain independent observers considered the tests rather difficult. No scores fell below 60 per cent and in the reading test 5 a score of 95 per cent was achieved. In terms of the balance between the skills of listening, speaking and reading, the only clear trend to emerge is that reading scored a considerably higher mark than the other two. This is interesting since the course presentation devoted virtually no time to the specific practice of reading. It is also worth noting that in the majority of the tests, those who were eventually to complete the course, i.e. to take all five tests scored significantly higher marks than those who were subsequently to drop out.

2 *The classroom exploitation of* Kontakte
(a) A *questionnaire* was sent to colleges known to be users of broadcast courses. Of 417 sent out, 179 were returned (42.9 per cent). Information was obtained on numbers using *Kontakte*, on methods of exploitation, and on equipment. Subjective opinions were solicited from teachers on the role of language broadcasts in formal further education teaching.

RESULTS

An overwhelming 84 per cent of institutions were using the course in connection with evening classes, for an average of 2.18 hours per week. Other uses were relatively minor, with service work (15 per cent), examination classes (14 per cent) and optional language classes (10 per cent) predominant. Only 7 per cent of institutions were using the course for businessmen's classes. (More than one answer could be ticked in this question).

When asked whether they were using the

course as core material or as a resource to be used with other courses, *68 per cent* of institutions said that they were using the course in the former mode, 11 per cent in the latter, and 20 per cent of colleges were using *Kontakte* for both purposes.

As far as classwork was concerned, 72 per cent of institutions using the course were using the broadcasts in class. Of these, 23 per cent were using just TV, 39 per cent just radio and 38 per cent both radio and television. Most colleges were using the broadcasts in recorded form (86 per cent), very few live.

When asked to indicate how they used the broadcasts in class, interesting differences emerged between radio and television, presumably as a result of hardware availability, familiarity etc. The most popular uses of the radio programme in class were the use of parts of these to act as a stimulus to oral (52 per cent of colleges) and aural (50 per cent) work. The radio programme was used in its entirety to present new material by 30 per cent of colleges and was the fourth most popular use. In the case of television, however, the playing of the TV programme whole to present material was the most popular use (35 per cent of colleges), following by stimulus for oral (27 per cent) and aural (23 per cent) work.

Users were asked to rate the effectiveness as classroom teaching aids of certain parts of the radio and TV programmes using the categories 'very useful', 'quite useful' and 'not very useful'. Most users rated the TV studio sequences as 'quite useful', filmed actuality dialogues as 'very useful', TV exercises as 'not very useful' and the gist comprehension passages as 'quite useful'. In the case of radio, most colleges deemed the studio sequences 'quite useful', the actuality dialogues 'very useful', the radio exercises 'very useful' and the 'Hoeren and Verstehen' passages 'very useful'.

Colleges were also asked to rate the other course components on the same scale. Most users considered the books to be 'very useful', the filmstrips 'quite useful', the records/cassettes 'quite useful', and the teachers' notes 'quite useful'.

The full paper gives more details of this part of the enquiry.

(b) The same *tests* were administered to five classes of users in colleges as were administered to the home sample. In all there were 68 potential respondents, but due to various technical and organizational factors very few completed all sections of all tests. The tests are being re-run this year with different classes in an attempt to achieve more satisfactory results.

RESULTS

A number of general points can be made about the test results obtained. The first is that, as with the group of home learners, the general level of proficiency achieved in the three skills as measured by our tests is very high—scores of over 90 per cent were achieved and at no point did scores fall below 50 per cent. To this extent one can say that *Kontakte* was successful in achieving its stated aims. The second point is that those students completing all tests always performed better than those who did not, hinting at the rather obvious point that attendance on a regular basis will result in good test scores.

3 *The classroom exploitation of* Le Nouvel Arrivé

(a) A *questionnaire* was sent to all schools who had expressed an interest in using *Le Nouvel Arrivé* by ordering the teachers' notes. 51 per cent were returned and information obtained on facilities available, on teachers' opinions on what should be provided for schools by the broadcasting authorities and what use was actually made of the series itself.

RESULTS

67 per cent of those replying had video-recording equipment, and a high percentage (around 90 per cent) were provided with the equipment needed in order to make use of tapes and filmstrips. 22 per cent had, in the past, used one or more TV language series for schools with pupils of different abilities. Where such series were used with only one ability level in a school, they were used predominantly with the top of the ability range.

In the second portion of the questionnaire teachers were given the opportunity to indicate what sort of schools TV language series they would like to see in future. Over 60 per cent of those replying wanted

future series to be aimed at a variety of abilities, as is the case at present.

The three main reasons stated for using such TV programmes at all were, in order of preference: the country of the foreign language can be brought alive; TV can conveniently provide experiences in the classroom which would otherwise not be possible; and the visual element is important in the learning process.

When asked about associated support materials, the majority thought it desirable to have both Teacher's Notes and Pupil's Book.

The third part of the questionnaire sought information on how teachers had used *Le Nouvel Arrivé*. It was used, by those who replied, predominantly with 14-year olds. There were 78 groups of 14-year olds, 57 of 13-year olds and 50 of 15-year olds represented. Most teachers said they used the series to support the teaching of both French language and background studies, and there were more groups of mixed 'O' and CSE candidates than any other level. Almost all teachers used the series as 'enrichment material' to support other teaching.

(b) An *objective study* of the 11 classes using the course was constructed. Tests were administered before and after to see if any changes had taken place in such factors as motivation, desire to visit France, attitudes to French people, and background knowledge of France.

RESULTS

The tests suggested that *all* the children involved had increased their background knowledge of France, the greatest gains being made by those classes where the TV programmes were more extensively followed up by the teacher. No significant changes were recorded in motivation and attitudes, though the figures did show that these were fairly high to begin with amongst all the pupils involved. There is considerable evidence to suggest that the influence of the teacher is paramount in deciding the effectiveness of a course and that the nature and extent of the television materials are less crucial factors.

The significance of this research

Although certain aspects of the investigation proved less profitable than had been hoped, and further corroboration of results is needed, a considerable body of useful information has been generated which begin to suggest a framework for the development of a coherent policy for broadcast language courses in the areas researched. Some discussions have taken place between the research teams and those responsible for producing and planning programmes. It seems likely that the more conclusive results will contribute towards policy decisions.

Plans have been made to continue investigations within the general area of broadcast language courses. Certain of the methods (the initial questionnaires, the ongoing progress chart sampling, the pre- and post-testing) have produced reliable results. Other methods (notably the testing for achievement in a college situation) must be considerably modified in the light of experience.

It must be stressed, however, that a fuller appreciation of the significance of the research, particularly that related to *Kontakte*, must await the results of a more sophisticated evaluation at present in progress. When this is finished, it is hoped to achieve some indication of the importance of such factors as previous language learning experience, educational background and reasons for starting the course. It then should be also possible to consider the body of data obtained in a broader perspective.

PAPER NO 10: THE INSTITUTIONAL USE AND EVALUATION OF A BBC MULTI-MEDIA GERMAN COURSE FOR ADULT BEGINNERS, *KONTAKTE**

Allen Cooper, Department of Communication, Brighton Polytechnic, UK.

Most BBC adult education series are designed for the home-based learner, but increasing use is being made of them by colleges and evening institutes. This paper

---

* Author's summary of full paper submitted to Conference.

describes aspects of a project being carried out at Brighton Polytechnic concerning the patterns of use and effectiveness of a BBC multi-media German course for adult beginners, *Kontakte* when used institutionally.

The project was conducted in two parts. A survey was carried out of educational establishments known to be using *Kontakte*, together with a number of colleges with experience of other BBC foreign language series for adults in the past. The purpose of the survey was to determine both the ways in which the course had been used and teachers' views on the course and more general aspects of the foreign language provision of the broadcasting authorities. In addition to this mainly descriptive work, an attempt was made to gain a measure of course effectiveness by designing and administering tests to five groups of *Kontakte* learners within the polytechnic. These tests were planned to measure student achievement in the skills of listening, speaking and reading against the expressed linguistic aims and objectives of the course.

The principal results of the questionnaire survey and the tests are summarized in an accompanying paper (no. 23). Very briefly it can be stated that student performance in the three language skills as measured by our tests was uniformly high, indicating a high level of course effectiveness. However, the college survey had shown that most use was being made of the course in the adult evening class sector, whereas our tests had been carried out with full-time students in a polytechnic. Other considerations also prompted us to look at our findings more closely: some tests were conducted with low student numbers which made generalizations hazardous, and piloting of the tests was not possible owing to the nature of the course under investigation. In general, the findings seemed to be telling us more about our own position with regard to language teaching rather than the potential of multi-media language courses.

It was therefore decided to re-run the project in the current academic year within the polytechnic to investigate further some of the institutional factors which had resulted from the first year's work. An open-access course using *Kontakte* materials was initiated and this is currently being monitored with a view to determining the most efficient teaching mode for elementary language service teaching within the poly-technic.

The research findings also raised a number of important questions relating to the problem of evaluation, particularly with regard to course effectiveness. Our college survey had shown that most use was being made of the *Kontakte* course in a sector of the educational world not covered by our tests where learners were very different to our own. The course itself was designed to be used in many different ways and special materials were available for class use. If we were in fact evaluating in order to generate information to be used in decision-making by the broadcasting authorities, we began to wonder what sort of decisions could be made on the basis of our findings which would help to improve course effectiveness. Thought was therefore given to the question of what course effectiveness means. It seemed that course effectiveness only has a meaning if the measurement is accompanied by a statement of the *level* at which the evaluation has been carried out, 'level' being defined as the amount of time spent on the course and the number of course materials used. At each level there will be a number of *learning environments* where students learn in different ways and have access to varying combinations of course materials. The degree of effective learning in any given learning environment will be influenced in turn by certain *relevant personal characteristics* of the students and learners in that environment. If this argument is correct, the resulting matrix for an evaluation of course effectiveness is very complex.

Given the complexity of the evaluation procedure, the action that can be taken by the broadcasters to improve the effectiveness of their courses would appear to be relatively limited. The elaboration of guidelines on effectiveness in terms of the acquisition of certain linguistic skills, which might suggest learning strategies and methodologies, would seem to be very complex and it may well be that criteria for effectiveness in the context of multi-purpose broadcast language courses are better expressed in non-linguistic terms.

PAPER NO 46: THE EVALUATION OF STRUCTURED NON-CREDIT RADIO COURSES AT THE UNIVERSITY OF ADELAIDE

G. P. Mullins, K. A. Conlon and G. P. McLeod, University of Adelaide, South Australia.

The aim of this report is to describe the evaluation of listener response to general interest and vocationally orientated courses presented in 1972, 1973 and 1974 on Radio University, 5^{UV}. 5^{UV} is an educational radio station administered by the Department of Adult Education, University of Adelaide, South Australia. It opened in June 1972 under a restricted licence just off the broadcast band and it was obliged to transmit solely to registered students. Music and general interest programmes (as distinct from courses) were banned. From September 1973 bridging and background music was allowed and an increased bandwidth improved transmission quality. In March 1975, the station shifted to a new frequency in the medium frequency band. It was allowed to broadcast music and virtually any material of an educational nature. The survey described below covers the period from June 1972 to December 1974. This period was characterized by the inevitable teething problems inherent in the development of the first general education radio station in Australia. These problems arose from the restrictions and variations in the licence conditions, financial problems, the difficulty of gaining public acceptance of educational radio, especially the idea of paying for courses, and the difficulty of assessing the effect of the programs on an audience scattered within 100 miles radius of Adelaide.

The evaluation was limited to structured courses—as distinct from the talks, access and music programs presented by 5^{UV}. These courses were a mixture of general interest courses (e.g. history, literature, ecology, religion), language courses (German, French and Japanese), and vocational or extension courses (e.g. nursing, management, computing). All courses were open to all members of the public; special qualifications were not required as a condition of enrolment and courses were not seen as a preparation for examination.

However some extension and language courses did assume a certain level of knowledge. Typically courses consisted of between 5 and 10 units which were broadcast weekly. Most units were 30 minutes long, although some extension programs were 45–50 minutes long. The radio programs were supplemented by a notes kit which included background material, notes and illustrations to accompany the radio lectures, references and reading lists and discussion questions. 'Live' tutorials and demonstrations sometimes supplemented the radio courses, especially language and extension courses.

The aim of the survey was to answer three simple, basic questions: who listened to the course, why did they enrol, and what was their reaction to what they heard? Radio was seen as a means of reaching sections of the community which had little contact with the already existing and fairly traditional adult education agencies; hence the interest in the characteristics of the students. It was also important to know what motivated them to enrol (and thereby pay $1–$2 per unit). The extent to which students became involved in the learning experience, and their satisfaction with what they experienced, would be taken as an indication that the courses—developed very much in the dark as far as the general interest courses were concerned —were appropriate to an Australian audience.

Method

A questionnaire was distributed to all students who enrolled for courses between June 1972 and December 1974. This involved two distributions, in the latter part of 1973 and 1974. There were 52 courses with a total enrolment of 4,666. However, some students did enrol for more than one course and so received more than one questionnaire.

Questionnaires were accompanied by return-paid envelopes and further encouragement to complete and return the questionnaires was given on air. Students were assured of anonymity. However, the rate of returns was disappointingly low— 34 per cent.

As regards the structure of the questionnaire, there were 47 questions. These covered the usual personal details, e.g. age,

educational standard, occupation. The remainder of the questionnaire focussed on the students' previous contact with adult education agencies; their reasons for subscribing to the course; their response to the radio programs and notes in terms of the style and level of presentation; and their degree of understanding, interest and participation. Most of these questions were in the form of five to six multiple choice questions. Finally details about listening habits and the quality of reception were sought for technical and administrative purposes.

Results

The data from the two distributions of the questionnaire have been combined because of the marked consistency across the two batches. What differences there were will be commented upon in the course of discussion.

The profile of 5^{UV} subscribers which emerged from the survey was a disturbing one. 54.6 per cent were in the professional, managerial or self-employed categories; as against 2.4 per cent in the categories of workers (process, shop, rural or service). 56.9 per cent had received a tertiary education and 64.7 per cent had previously attended or subscribed to some form of adult education activity. From these figures it would seem that we were educating those sections of the community which were already well educated and which could afford to pay for further education.

It may be that this restricted access to further education is closely associated with the problem of communicating what is available to those who might profit by it. In this case 30.5 per cent of the respondents heard of their course via a 5^{UV} brochure or broadcast and 79.2 per cent of those who had already done an adult education course had done so with the Department of Adult Education or the Workers' Educational Association—two closely associated agencies through which 5^{UV} publicity was channelled.

The relative youth of the students (58.4 per cent under 40 years of age and 31.4 per cent under 30) was the most striking departure from 'the traditional' adult education student. Unfortunately the sex of students was not asked: 16.6 per cent gave their occupation as home duties but this obviously underestimates the proportion of women in the sample.

Why do people enrol in courses? The most obvious question—vocational vs general interest—was not decided by the responses. 31.3 per cent enrolled because they thought the course would help them in their employment and a further 10.5 per cent did so in order to supplement other formal studies. 41.8 per cent sought to broaden their general knowledge or help themselves pursue a hobby or leisure activity.

The attitude of the respondents to their courses could be assessed under three headings: the drop-out rate, the degree of participation and the degree of satisfaction expressed in the course. On all these measures the response was very positive. 81.1 per cent listened to most or all of the units of the course. 90.6 per cent listened to at least half the units.

Apart from merely listening to the radio component of the course, students participated in the learning experience to a considerable degree. This was indicated by the 83.1 per cent who studied the notes kit and the 27.5 per cent who made their own notes in the course of the broadcast and who did at least one hour's extra study beyond the notes. 47.8 per cent read at least two of the references given by the lecturers, and 17.7 per cent took advantage of the possibility of group study by forming listening groups.

A steady two-thirds of the respondents (percentages ranged between 61.4 and 75.5) expressed their satisfaction with such aspects of the course as the rate and level of communication, the degree of interest (65.6 per cent found the presentation 'interesting' or 'very interesting'), the length of individual units and of the course as a whole and the size and usefulness of the notes kit. People's expectations seemed to be fulfilled at a reasonable level: 73 per cent believed that the course came up to their expectations and 76.8 per cent thought that they *learned* what they expected to learn. A surprising number, 62.8 per cent, believed that they absorbed most or all of the material and an incredible 94.6 per cent claimed to have understood most or all of the material. While this may be taken as an indicator of customer satisfaction, obviously it should not be treated as anything

more than a subjective impression. The ultimate test—78 per cent would enrol for further courses on associated subjects and 57 per cent tuned into 5^{UV} at times other than the course broadcast time.

Conclusions

Before discussing the conclusions which might be drawn from the above results a few reservations about the data should be expressed. The sample was undoubtedly biased in the sense that those students who completed the questionnaire were likely to be those who completed the course, and these, in turn, were more likely to express satisfaction with the course. Any comments about the degree of participation or satisfaction expressed by the respondents must be read in the light of this bias. Secondly the low rate of return of the questionnaire must be viewed with concern. This does not necessarily affect the validity of the findings, but it does leave considerable room for error in the results. Two factors probably contributed most to the low rate of return: the absence of any face-to-face contact with the students in many courses and the time lapse between completion of the course and receipt of the questionnaire. This latter factor could also affect the results in that some students were questioned about their attitude to the course very soon after completing it whereas others were not contacted until up to twelve months after completion of the course.

Future surveys will have to give much more attention to the distribution of questionnaires and to a more persistent follow-up for reluctant responders—despite the constraints of time and money.

The overall conclusions can best be stated in terms of the three questions originally posed:

Who enrolled in 5^{UV} courses?
Why did they enrol?
What did they think of the courses?

A relatively young, well educated professional or semi-professional person was most likely to hear about and enrol in 5^{UV} courses. He or she did so as often as not for general as for vocational interest. Having enrolled, the student stayed with the course and participated quite actively in it. Not surprisingly he or she was then very satisfied with the end result and was likely to come back to educational radio for further education.

The courses produced by 5^{UV} are suited, in style and content, to our present customers. We are not reaching as wide a cross-section of the community as we should. However it is not clear from this study whether this shortcoming is a result of our style of programming and production or of our publicity outlets.

A final comment concerns the need for further research to focus on at least two aspects of the courses which were not covered by the questionnaire described above. We need to know more about the degree of real information gain attributable to the courses. It is not enough to know that students *thought* they understood, absorbed or learned the content of the course. Secondly, we need to know more about reactions to and effects of specific courses and individual units within those courses. For the moment, however, it is worth reporting that the courses do seem to meet a real need in Australian adult education.

PAPER NO 30: A STUDY OF ATTITUDINAL CHANGES DURING AN OPEN AND MEDIATED IN-SERVICE TRAINING COURSE FOR TEACHERS*

J. *Karvonen*, University of Turku, Finland
O. *Nöjd*, University of Jyväskylä, Finland.

1 Background of the investigation

The comprehensive school reform which is being carried out in Finland requires the organization of extensive teachers' further training. Further training is divided into three parts: in-service training, further training courses of long duration and re-training. In-service training is intended for all teachers. The training of about 40,000 teachers is a very demanding task. In 1968 the National Board of Education started courses on comprehensive school didactics which were arranged at universities during

---

* Authors' summary of main paper submitted to the Conference.

the summer term. Because traditional in-service training proved too expensive both for course organizers and for participants and only a very small percentage of applicants could be accepted, more economical and efficient forms of training had to be considered. In the academic year 1968-9 the National Board of Education arranged a course on comprehensive school didactics together with the Finnish Broadcasting Corporation and the universities. The course contained 28 television programmes, 28 radio programmes, a handbook and seminars, arranged in different parts of the country. Practically all teachers to be trained could be reached by mass media and the educators were selected from among the best educators in universities, the National Board of Education and the Finnish Broadcasting Corporation.

2 Research methods

An attempt was made to acquire information about the changes that occur in students during a further training course. For this reason the experimental group/ control group design was applied. The measurement of dependent variables formed an extensive problem group of its own, because there were many kinds of variables to be measured. The collection of data—except for the measurement of learning results—was carried out by means of a mail questionnaire.

(a) Selection of subjects

The experimental group was drawn from among the 6,445 teachers enrolled for the course, by stratified sampling. A total of 16 groups was formed, among which the subjects were selected at random. In the group of secondary school teachers it was, however, not necessary to carry out sampling in all sub-groups because there were very few participants. In such a case all members of the group were included in the study. The control group consisted of non-participating primary school teachers among whom sampling was carried out in the same way as in the experimental group. Because of several practical difficulties it was unfortunately not possible to have a control group consisting of secondary school teachers in this study. The members of the experimental group who were included in the sample were sent a questionnaire with instructions. The instructions explained the purpose of the study and emphasized the role of each response in the successful carrying out of the study.

(b) Measurement of attitudes

(i) CONTENT VARIABLES OF ATTITUDES

In this study the following attitude objects were chosen:

- school reform process
- changes in school work
- teachers' further training
- educational research
- school democracy

Attitude objects were selected from a fairly general level, because the aim was to study the more general effects on attitudes of the further training programme. During the further training course information was given about these objects. It was hoped that the course would influence the attitudes towards these objects.

(ii) STRUCTURE VARIABLES OF ATTITUDES

In this study an attitude is defined as a response tendency system composed of the affective, cognitive and action component. Components are measured by means of the attitude differential technique. Since the units under study were groups, it was presumed that the reliability problem of the measurement would be considerably easier to solve than in studies at the individual level. For this reason and to keep the length of the questionnaire within reasonable limits an attempt was made to measure different components in the simplest possible way. The measuring device used for the affective component was the adjective pair *pleasant-unpleasant*. This adjective-pair can be considered to measure particularly the affective response tendency most logically, consistently and empirically. The cognitive component was measured with the adjective-pair *useful-harmful*. These adjectives were chosen because by means of this dimension we can evaluate the instrumental value of this attitude object to the respondee. The measurement of the action component has been most difficult in the attitude area. Firstly we have to distinguish between overt action and action tendency. Action tendency can often not turn into overt action because of various preventing factors. In this case the respondee was given a situation in which he was presumed to have an opportunity to act for the attitude object or against it. For example, when attitudes towards school reform were studied, the respondee was asked whether he would act for or against the reform, provided that he had an opportunity to influence decisions concerning the reform. Here we are not going to discuss the basic hypotheses of the attitude differential any further, because they have been described in detail elsewhere.

(c) Results

Attitudes are examined first by studying their location in the attitude space formed by the affective and cognitive component. The location is determined on the basis of the group means of the components. Secondly we study the factorial structure of attitudes, and thirdly the factorial structure of change scores. In the investigation we first study how attitudes change from the initial measurement to the final measurement, secondly the factorial structure of the attitudes of the initial and final measurement, and thirdly the factorial structure of the attitude change.

3 Summary

The attitude of secondary school leavers to the school reform became clearly more positive during the course. On the whole the attitudes of the different sub-groups within the experimental group approached each other during the course, i.e. the test group became more uniform. In the attitudes of the control group change appeared only in one area in corresponding period; the attitudes of the control group towards further training became more negative in the affective component during the course. According to the results, changes were produced in attitudes during the course on comprehensive school didactics which were in line with the objectives of the course. It was established that the influence aimed at the cognitive area of personality—dissemination of information—caused changes also in the affective area. The factorial study of attitudes showed that attitudes had differentiated during the course.

SECTION C

UNIVERSITY AND COLLEGE COURSES ('CLOSED' SYSTEMS)

INTRODUCTION

The papers in this section are concerned primarily with systems which could be designated as 'closed' systems, with regard to the intended target audience. These courses are, as Naomi McIntosh describes (paper no 37):

> aimed at groups of students who are known, or at least can be located, since they have formally to register and perhaps pay a fee for the course.

In addition, they are usually part of a system leading to some form of credit or qualification.

The papers in this section cover the following systems:

System	Country
Liverpool University	UK
Leeds University	UK
Canberra College of Advanced Education	Australia
Catholic University of Peru (CETUC)	Peru
Sir George Williams University	Canada
Université de Montreal	Canada
Chicago TV College	USA
Radio-Television University for Teachers	Poland
Television Agricultural Secondary School	Poland
Free University of Iran	Iran
The Open University	UK

Even within this group of 'closed' systems, there are enormous variations. In some systems, students watch or listen to programmes individually, without the mediation of a university or college teacher (Free University of Iran) or without even the company of fellow students (The Open University), while in other systems, students view in class situations, with their teachers present. Some students (The Open University, Free University of Iran, Chicago TV College) have no direct access to those responsible for designing the programmes, while for others, the University teachers are much more easily accessible (Leeds University, Liverpool University, Université de Montreal, Canberra College of Advanced Education).

These variations significantly affect both the transferability of results, and the way in which research and evaluation can be carried out. In a large production system like the Open University, it is possible to have a professional, full-time team of researchers. In a CCTV system such as Leeds or Liverpool University, those who do the research tend to have other responsibilities as well, either as producers, or as teaching staff in other departments (such as psychology or sociology). Therefore, as well as the organizational structures varying considerably between institutions, those carrying out or interested in research or evaluation in the different systems also have marked differences in background, responsibility, resources, and approach to the problems of research and evaluation.

Also, in this sector, as in the other two, there are differences in the degree to which research has been established or carried out. Therefore, in this section we further subdivide the papers into two groups:

L

1 Papers concerned with the methods or theories, or the development of research and evaluation, but not to any large extent describing completed research projects.
2 Papers where the emphasis is on completed research and evaluation studies.

Generally, within these subdivisions we begin with systems with ready accessibility of university or college teaching staff (e.g. Leeds or Liverpool University), moving on to more distant and more individualized or isolated learning situations (e.g. The Open University).

DESIGNING EVALUATION: THEORY AND METHODS

PAPER NO 48: IS THE ETV STYLE THE RESULT OF A COST-EFFECT-IVE POLICY?

Carl Neads, Television Producer, University of Liverpool, UK.

The difference between ETV and broadcast programmes

Universities have been producing educational television (ETV) programmes for many years—the first University Educational Television Service was set up in 1966 at the University of Leeds—and now the majority of universities in Britain have television centres. The respective television units provide programmes which have a distinct style or identity that clearly sets them apart from broadcast-produced educational programmes. I feel we must ask ourselves why it is that an ETV programme is immediately recognizable as an ETV product, a product often referred to as academic television. Also, I should like to pose the question—is it the cost-effective policy of the ETV system itself that moulds the distinctive style, or the producer, or can we isolate other factors that differentiate ETV from broadcast television? Having isolated these factors should we then continue with the present style or attempt to emulate the broadcast model?

In order to consider the ideologies of the two systems, ETV and broadcasting, I should like to imagine two programmes on the same subject matter, one programme to be made by ETV and one by broadcasting. The subject matter will be an operation on a dog with a fractured femur.

The broadcast version will form part of a series of programmes on *The Work of the Vet*. I suggest that in this version we are likely to see the following scene. The vet will outline the operation on a radiograph to the worried owners of the dog. They will then disappear to the waiting room and we will see a shot of the dog being anaesthetized, followed by a very condensed version of the operation interspersed with cutaways of the nurse and the vet. The viewer will be left with only a hazy impression of the operation but the programme would have aimed to be entertaining; the shots used will be chosen for the interest value and visual impact.

On the other hand, the university produced programme will start with the vet and radiograph and he will outline the operation and procedures to be used. We will then concentrate on the operation itself with very few cutaways—in fact cutaways could be a distraction. The shots chosen will be those that show the techniques most clearly—visual impact will be of secondary importance. These two illustrations show in a very obvious manner how the two systems would deal with similar subject matter. They reflect the two ideologies: the ideology of broadcasting being to entertain, and the ideology of ETV to educate.

The two systems tend to produce programmes with distinct identities. We can examine this question of identity by considering two dimensions:

1 Degree of arousal
2 Degree of educational information in the programme

These dimensions can be represented by the diagram on page 162.

Using these dimensions programmes can be classified and a programme like the 'Morecambe & Wise Show' is fairly high on the Arousal Scale but low on the Educational

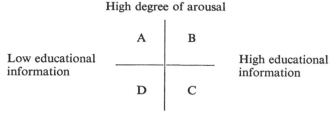

High degree of arousal

	A	B	
Low educational information			High educational information
	D	C	

Low degree of arousal

Information Scale. On the other hand, 'The Burke Special' is high on the Arousal Scale and also high on the Educational Information Scale. Broadcast programmes will tend to fall into sections A and B; each company is aiming to hold the viewers' attention and dissuade him from either operating the channel change switch, or the off-switch.

In ETV we assume, rightly or wrongly, that we have a motivated audience, which is also usually a captive audience. Thus the need to stimulate the viewer is not the prime aim of the programme; instead it aims to be educationally informative and so is high on this scale. Most ETV programmes fall within section C, that is high on educational information scale, but low on the arousal scale.

I should like to suggest that the ideologies of the two organizations force producers into quite different positions. In the course of the production of a programme a series of decisions has to be made which affect the final product. The ETV producer will put an emphasis on the educational information scale; thus when faced with a difficult decision he will play safe and move to the dimension that will result in the least criticism from his peer group. So the ideology of the organization results in the ETV producer concentrating on the educational information dimension and forgoing attributes in the arousal dimension; but for the broadcast producer the converse is true, so he will concentrate on the arousal dimension—because his ideology is one of entertainment. Another factor that may affect the direction in which a programme moves during the course of its production may be the two distinct constraints suffered by each of the systems. In ETV we suffer from an economic constraint, which means that we cannot spend money on details, and it is often the details that make the programme

stimulating. Broadcasting does not have this problem as its constraint is time, so long explanation is not possible—ETV does not have this problem. Thus, combined with the ideologies of the respective organizations and these constraints it is fairly clear why ETV is so distinctly different from broadcasting.

How then in ETV can we change this situation if, in fact, we wish to—because if left unchanged ETV is effectively producing programmes that are low on the arousal dimension. Will it be cost-effective to change this situation? I should like to argue that to be educationally effective we should aim for a higher arousal level in ETV.

To see how we can achieve this we must examine the broadcast model and examine the packaging aspects of the model.

Packaging
Under this heading I include the following aspects:

1 Attention to detail ● opening and closing film, background music.

2 Set design ● a programme can be given a specific identity by the settings used. These can provide subconscious cues to the viewer which can shape his attitudes to the programme.

3 Scriptwriting ● broadcast television usually employs professional scriptwriters who are practised in the art of writing a 'spoken word" script.

162

4 Skills performer ● broadcast television usually uses a broadcasting voice to present information — ETV uses the available 'talent'.

Conclusion

If it can be accepted that ETV programmes, because of the cost-effective policy, are low on the arousal dimension, we can justify the measures that need to be taken to change the situation—measures such as stimulating opening film sequences, expensive settings, and a professional presenter. I have suggested that to be educationally effective a programme does need to be moderately high on the arousal scale, but in the present economic situation it may not be politically wise to apply the expensive solutions that I have suggested to the ETV programme.

PAPER NO 17: EVALUATION AND RESEARCH AT THE CENTRE FOR DISTANCE TEACHING, CATHOLIC UNIVERSITY OF PERU (CETUC)

Estela B. de Garland, Director, CETUC, Lima.

1 Introduction

Peru may be considered a young state, not only because a large part of its population is under 15 years old, but because it has only 150 years of independent life from Spain. Until the present time its autonomous development had been slowed down due to many factors common to developing nations, plus the complexity of its population distribution and characteristics.

Geographic characteristics add more problems to the communications system. Even though a number of laws have been passed and large investments made to implement the communication's network, there are a number of difficulties in the area of educational communication. However there is a formal decision to use mass media to support and extend the educational system.

2 Cetuc's project. Basic information.

Realizing the importance of mass media within the social and educational development process of the country, the Catholic University of Peru presented a project (CETUC) to work in the area of educational communication through media, and requested financial support from MISEREOR and the Konrad Adenauer Foundation's Institute for International Solidarity.

The Centro de Teleducation de la Pontificia Universidad Catolica Del Peru (CETUC) was designed as an academic service unit. It started to work in November 1972 and in October 1974 opened on campus a two-storey building with a fully equipped colour TV studio and control room, a radio studio and its control room (both with tape units, radio and TV, to broadcasting standard) and film equipment for 16mm and super 8mm productions (excluding laboratory facilities).

CETUC's basic services are:

● Training personnel for educational radio, TV and film: producers, researchers and users.
● Production of prototype materials to be evaluated: radio and TV programs and film documentaries.
● Research and evaluation.

CETUC's organization includes a University Advisory Committee, the Director, the Administrative Unit, the Production Unit, the Research and Evaluation (R & E) Unit, the Technical Unit, and the Training Unit.

3 Research and evaluation at CETUC

(a) *Role of R & E at CETUC*

From the very first stage of CETUC's planning, research and evaluation of educational and instructional broadcasting was given a prime role. Due to the very diverse nature of Peru's population, local research is a basic need, and was assigned first priority within CETUC. Many research studies done elsewhere actually represent working hypotheses for our specific situation, since the way society is organized influences every other process and especially the educational process. Therefore at CETUC it was decided to establish two main areas of research:

(i) *Research on general aspects of educational media, not necessarily related to CETUC's productions.* Studies designed to build up a better panorama of media situations in Peru, of media impact on specific groups, of methodological and technical variables of programs produced outside CETUC.

(ii) *Research related to CETUC's productions* either to determine new programming lines or structures, or to provide guidance for scripting, or to evaluate our own 'products'. Within these studies could be surveys on needs, interests and characteristics of target audience, evaluation of reaction to specific programs and tests on learning outcomes in relation to expressed objectives.

To implement this plan of research, several managerial decisions were needed at CETUC.

● personnel to be used: researchers, assistants, and clerical support.
● equipment: office space and equipment, and access to computers.
● prototype materials (productions) to experiment with appropriation of funds.

(b) *CETUC's management decisions to implement R & E services*
To provide the requested resources and implement the R & E service already approved, the following decisions were made:

Personnel To establish a Research Unit with a full-time staff of two professionals: the head of the unit and his assistant. Given that two persons were not going to be enough to provide the whole service needed to carry out the different studies, the Research Unit was able to contract other researchers (psychologists, anthropologists, educators) and university students as temporary assistants. All clerical support was to be provided by CETUC's Administrative Unit.

Equipment Office space and equipment to be assigned within CETUC's building by the Adminis-

trative Unit. Computer service (when required) to be contracted at the University's Computer Center. However, manual procedures were suggested when computing simple data, as in the evaluation of learning outcomes (comparison of results from pre- and post-tests) especially when working with small student numbers.

Prototype materials When special productions are needed to experiment with, CETUC's Production Unit would assume the whole production process.

Funds To assign a specific budget for R & E activities within CETUC's budget.

(c) *Research and evaluation done at CETUC*
CETUC's R & E activities may be described as:

(i) *Studies at CETUC's initiative*
Studies done by CETUC's personnel or by other university researchers under CETUC's contract on topics selected by the center. Among these are:

● *Surveys at an exploratory level*
Examples. Movie theatre opinion poll with regard to locally produced short films presented as a package with another movie (in process of data analysis). Surveys on specific audience groups' characteristics, e.g. a research study on levels of identification, audience-message and film language comprehension at a marginal suburban community (Pueblo Joven) (already finished). A sex, violence and ideological impact's study of the Barnaby Jones and Kung Fu series on youngsters 6 to 8 years old (in process of data gathering).
● *Surveys to support new program series* e.g. a survey on parents of children up to six years old to collect knowledge and interests of children and their psychology (at idea's discussion stage).

● *Content research studies for script writing* e.g. an anthropological study on the migrant women problem, for a 16mm black and white documentary. This film will be used for experimental purposes (a second study on audience-message identification and film language comprehension).

● *Evaluation of CETUC's experimental products* Almost every one of CETUC's productions is subject to evaluation. The most frequent type of evaluation done is comparison of learning outcomes (pre- and post-test) based on the program's content.

Another way being used is attitudinal reactions to programs, either by questionnaires to measure level of program's acceptance, or by simply observation of audience reactions while presenting the program. This last method is specially used with children or youngsters. These evaluation results are used to modify the programs, either to revise the content, the treatment, or the presentation techniques. Special instructional programs are usually produced at least in two versions. Alternatively, these results are used as guidelines for future productions.

(ii) *University Students' Initiative* These are mainly university student's dissertations. CETUC participates at the students' or departments' request. In these cases CETUC's role varies. Sometimes, it is a simple source of information, or it may help with problem definition, or it may provide a specialized bibliographic support, or provide systematic advice during the research study. It even offers CETUC's production of specific programs for testing, if necessary. The criteria we use to decide on CETUC's role in these cases are a combination of students' interest

and qualifications to do the study, and CETUC's own interest in the topic.

(iii) *Third Person's Initiative* Institutions interested in specific local studies who request CETUC's R & E services through a contract, grant or other type of agreement.

(d) *Structure of research and evaluation work at CETUC*
When the R & E work is done at CETUC's initiative and financed by CETUC's budget, it goes through the following process:

(i) *Subject area selection* Any member of CETUC's staff or member of another University Department may suggest an interesting area for research purposes. The tentative proposal is discussed with the Research Unit. Criteria for the first stage of approval is based on the topic's relevance and CETUC's priority policy. If approved:

(ii) *Researcher's selection* CETUC's Research Unit decides if they will assume the study or if other professionals are going to be contracted. Criteria for deciding on this item includes consideration of the type of specialists required and the amount of work already assumed by the R & E Unit at that moment. When contracting researchers, preference is given to our own University Department's professors.

(iii) *Research proposal* Those who assume the responsibility of the research study prepare a final proposal including: Problem definition, methodology to be used, approximate timetable, resources needed other than money, and budget requested.
This proposal is submitted to the head of the Research Unit and discussed with him. When the proposal comes from the same Research Unit it is discussed with CETUC's Director and any other of CETUC's staff members concerned with the study; frequently the Production Unit's staff participate in these discussions.

165

When the final proposal is approved CETUC's Administrative Unit takes care of budget expenditures, contracts, clerical support, etc.

(iv) *Research development* From that moment on, the researcher is almost free to develop the study. He selects his student assistants. He reports to the Research Unit at each stage of the study and when any problems may arise. Strict control is focussed on budget expenditures, and secondly on the research schedule.

(v) *Research report* The first report is presented to the Research Unit who may comment on it prior to the presentation of the final document. Copies of the final report are circulated among CETUC Units' and members of the Advisory Committee.

According to the purpose of the study it may be forwarded for typing or duplicated and distributed either in full or as a summary.

When the research study is requested and financed by a third agency, the process is slightly different since it has to go through the regular university procedure for contracted research studies.

4   Conclusion

Up to the present, CETUC's Research and Evaluation activities have been very valuable. They represent an effort to respond to the need for local studies in the area of educational media. The limitations faced are directly related to the limitations of social science, and the newness of the development of educational media studies in Peru. However we consider there are several advantages from these R & E activities.

First we are using available human resources at different university departments and at the same time we are promoting interest in the area of educational media. Secondly, we have started to produce programs based on facts supported by previous research studies. Thirdly, we have begun to make experimental productions, that is to say, more systematic materials

with better chances of controlling the variables. And lastly, we expect to make a contribution from our findings eventually to other societies similar to ours, especially in the Andean countries.

PAPER NO 47: ON RESEARCH AND EVALUATION OF TV AND RADIO PROGRAMMES AT THE FREE UNIVERSITY OF IRAN

Hamid Naficy, Director, Broadcasting and Media Centre, Free University of Iran.

The Free University of Iran (FUI) was established in late 1973 and is to receive its first intake of students in early 1977. The FUI constitutes an effort to introduce and institutionalize in Iran very different and innovative concepts of education. The innovations which the FUI hopes to introduce and implement, and which make the differences between it and other institutions of higher education in Iran, consist of its goals and objectives, educational programs, teaching system, the nature of its student body and mode of operation.

1   Goals and objectives

Briefly, the goals and objectives of the Free University of Iran are: training of needed specialists, expansion of higher education opportunities, up-grading of the quality of higher education, provision of life-long education, and up-grading of the public's general knowledge.

2 The University programs

In line with the goals and objectives of the University and based on studies carried out by a number of organizations as well as that of the University Educational Planning staff, it has been decided that in the first five years of its existence the FUI would offer four educational programs, i.e. Teacher Education, Paramedical Training, Rural Development and General Education.

3   Teaching system

In order to realize the goals, the objectives and the educational programs mentioned above, the FUI will develop a unique teaching system. Unlike conventional universities, the FUI will have no residential students, no dormitories, nor many of the other structures commonly associated with traditional higher education systems. Instead the FUI will teach its students at a distance. It will develop a learning environment to which its students will have access from their places of residence and/or work. The actual delivery system is comprised of a number of different and highly integrated elements. These are: a network of regional and local study centers scattered across the country, printed course materials, television, radio and radio-vision programs, audio visual and scientific kits, and self-assessment materials. Each study center will provide library services, computer terminals, video and audio playback and micro-teaching facilities, science and language labs, tuition, counselling and cultural activities.

4 Course design and production

The design and preparation of the course material are carried out by course teams, which in general consist of subject matter specialists, educational technologists and curriculum developers, television and radio producer-directors, and editorial assistants.

With help from media production and publishing staff the course team will create integrated multi-media packages for students' use. These packages will consist of texts and printed materials, television, radio and radio-vision programs and science and audio-visual kits. The media-mix is determined in such a way that the lion's share of material to be taught is carried via text.

The radio and television programs are to be produced and transmitted by National Iranian Radio and Television. In the first year of operation, the transmission load of the university's programs will be around $1\frac{1}{2}$ hours per day six days per week, for each medium. This figure is expected to grow to 10 to 14 hours per day six days per week for each medium. Each radio and television program will be transmitted twice, and reference copies of these programs will be available at the local centers. In addition, media notes, which are sent to students on a regular basis, inform them of the content of broadcast programs and

help them view those programs in the context of the course.

5 Research and evaluation

Research and evaluation is an integral and permanent feature of the FUI's teaching system, in that it will yield continuous information regarding the quality of course material, course team performance, student performance and students' use of materials. This kind of research, evaluation and assessment aims to identify weak spots in the university teaching system and to propose alternative plans for improving the quality of the education provided.

In this sense, therefore, research and evaluation at the FUI will be used as tools for making and improving decisions. When extended, this concept of research and evaluation will encompass prospective planning.[1] A modified Policy-Delphi was run during the early phases of the effort to design the teacher-preparation program of the FUI, stressing competency of performance – based learning.[2]

The Delphi method in broadcasting has been used for the first time in Iran by the Prospective Planning Project of NIRT.[3]

On a more immediate level, a quick survey of published research results indicate that little practical help can be obtained from the broadcast media research carried out so far. There are several reasons which account for this, some of which are:

First, almost all available media research has been carried out outside of Iran, in different social contexts, thus making their applicability to the FUI and the Iranian situation somewhat dubious.

Second, the research methodologies used have often been fraught with major weaknesses, including the use of incorrect or insufficient evaluation techniques, an over-reliance on comparative studies of teaching by one medium—of the same material—with that of another medium, attempts to try and isolate the impact of one medium from all the other media and influences, failure to come up with practical solutions and guidelines for the producers and teachers who use media as part of their teaching system.[4]

Third, not enough is known about the effects of broadcast media and how they should be integrated with other media used by a multi-media teaching system.

167

Fourth, no substantive agreement exists regarding the kind of (if any) learning that takes place using media.[5]

(a) *Media Research and Evaluation at FUI* For the above reasons it was considered immature to rely solely on the existing research findings as tools for decision making regarding the use of media at the FUI. In a multi-media distance-teaching system, university planners, managers, course designers and producers are separated by vast distances, both temporal and spatial, from their students and therefore cannot easily determine the result of their decisions. If this situation is allowed to continue it will eventually result in the failure to improve the quality of teaching provided.

It is precisely to avoid such a situation that institutional research, and media evaluation in particular, are deemed a necessary part of the FUI teaching system. Media evaluation at FUI refers to the collection, organization, analysis and interpretation of appropriate data for decision making regarding the use of media.

(b) *Main Features of Media Research and Evaluation* If media research and evaluation is to be categorized it can be divided into the following categories:

(i) Library Research. This activity forms a very important part of the pre-production stage of FUI's radio and television programs. Although there is a vast and diversified reservoir of excellent audio-visual resources material available elsewhere in the world, there is a dearth of such valuable material in Iran. Because of this, identification, selection, purchase, review and evaluation of these materials is very important and must be an on-going process at FUI. This activity is carried out by the producer-directors, course unit authors and the staff of the university library.

(ii) Pre-transmission (formative) evaluation. This activity involves the production of pilot television and radio programs which can then be tested on an FUI student body sample group. This kind of evaluation might attempt to ascertain student's reactions to the various program components and formats. The information derived from these tests can then be incorporated into FUI's broadcast programs.

(iii) Evaluation of the effects of media (summative). The aims of this kind of evaluation, which will be carried out by FUI's staff on a regular basis after the television and radio programs are broadcast, are to determine the reactions of students to various program components and formats, to reveal value, attitudinal and behavioral changes in students as a result of using media, and to determine the effectiveness of television and radio programs as integrated components of the FUI educational package.

(iv) Audience Research. This type of research could yield detailed information regarding composition, size, and interest of FUI students as well as those of the general public who might view and listen to FUI Public Educational Programs. Because of the dual nature of the audiences, this kind of research could be carried out by both FUI and NIRT, which has a large Audience Research Department.

(c) *Conditions for Media Evaluation* There are several conditions under which effective media evaluation can be carried out.

(i) Research and evaluation infrastructure. Effective research and evaluation can occur in an environment where favorable attitudes towards it already exist and where research skills and resources are available. Generally speaking, it can be stated that research and evaluation is a very recent enterprise in Iran, especially the kind of on-going and rapid feedback system that is envisaged for FUI. Planners are not used to forecasting and basing their decisions on research results. Also course designers, teachers, and producers of radio and television programs are not used to designing quick and systematic feedback systems and might even fear such an immediate and direct response to their performance.

In addition to a non-committal attitude to research and evaluation, there exists a dearth of institutions of higher learning which offer a substantial number of courses in research and evaluation design and methodology. Further, there are few institutions which regularly conduct and support any kind of regular and systematic research and evaluation, especially those that concentrate on determining the effects of media. For example, so far as is known only the following organizations have conducted media research on a regular basis in Iran: Audience Research Department (NIRT), National Institute of Psychology, Institute of Sociological Studies and Research (Tehran University).

What is more, both the quantity and quality of research and evaluation which has been generated so far leaves much to be desired, and the applicability of these efforts seems limited. In addition, the dissemination of research and evaluation results has been mostly restricted to internal users of the research organization.

(ii) Felt Need. The above factors have not helped to stimulate and sustain the kind of environment which is conducive to the implementation of research and evaluation systems as tools for decision-making. When the need for carrying out research and evaluation is not clearly felt, then no substantial commitment can be made in terms of manpower and funds.

(iii) Research and evaluation personnel. The lack of qualified and competent personnel to design and carry out research and evaluation can be explained from the above statements. It can also be seen that FUI cannot expect to rely on a strong research and evaluation infra-structure for the design and implementation of its feedback and evaluation system.

In the first two years of FUI's operation a good number of competent people have joined the University. These people have the necessary educational and professional experience and interest to work on the design of an institutional research and media evaluation system for FUI. Since, however, the FUI is a newly formed organization, it has found it necessary, initially, to devote whatever high level manpower and skills it could muster, to the development of efficient planning and management capabilities rather than concentrating them on the design of a research and evaluation system.

Notwithstanding the above considerations, during the same period, arrangements have been made to recruit and train in the US a number of future staff in the area of media evaluation. Also, assistance has been sought from external organizations (such as Audience Research Department of NIRT, Institute of Educational Technology (The Open University), on determining the framework and parameters of a media evaluation system.

(iv) Budget. When the appropriate environment and skills for research and evaluation are lacking, and when the need for such endeavours is not immediately felt, no major financial commitment to research and evaluation can be expected to be made. The main stumbling block at FUI, however, has not been the lack of funds for research and evaluation; rather the scarcity of competent and qualified personnel has presented itself as the major constraint.

(v) Linkage of evaluation to planning, management and program production. It is evident that media research and evaluation constitutes an integrated part of the FUI's teaching and decision-making. Considering the importance of research and evaluation, and in view of its potential but precarious capability for objectivity, ways must be sought whereby research and evaluation becomes closely related to planning and production policies and procedures.

6 Decisions regarding media evaluation at FUI

There are a number of decisions that must be made in order to ensure a steady and reliable flow of feedback information regarding the use and effectiveness of media. The decisions that have so far been made are enumerated below. The University has made the following decisions:

(a) To relate media research and evaluation groups to the highest level of university planning and course design.

(b) To establish a procedure whereby information regarding the results of internal and external research is disseminated and made available to all those in the university who might benefit from it.[6]

(c) To coordinate closely the planning and implementation of the research and evaluation system with that of course design and program production. This is evident in the 'life time' of a course (6 years) and by the percentage of yearly revisions (10 per cent) in television and radio program content that is deemed necessary. These program revisions and remakes are made possible through the use of a regular media evaluation effort.

Moreover, it is believed that continuous evaluation of the FUI's television and radio programs will lead to new information which will contribute to the development of new message and program designs, reflecting the unique demands of the Iranian audiences.

(d) Evaluation of media at FUI will not be limited to assessing the broadcast components of the course package. It will encompass the evaluation of the pattern of use and the effectiveness of other ancillary audio-visual materials which will be used by the students at the local centers.

In addition to the above, the university must make the following decisions before effective and continuous media evaluation can be carried out at FUI.[7]

(i) Clearly define evaluation and the various forms it might take (e.g. evaluation of media, students, tutors, text, pre-transmission, post-transmission evaluation).

(ii) Set objectives and determine criteria for evaluating media.

(iii) Establish priorities for the media evaluation effort.

(iv) Determine activities and data which involve evaluation (e.g. admissions, computer-marked assignments, examination, monitoring by tutors).

(v) Determine the number of personnel needed to carry out media evaluation (e.g. educational technologists, unit authors, tutors, broadcasters).

(vi) Ways must be explored to determine the best methods by which the results of evaluations are interpreted and fed back to planners, course designers and media producers.

(vii) Allocate a percentage of FUI annual recurrent budget to media evaluation.

Once the above decisions are made the university can launch its media and broadcast evaluation system. There are a large number of topics that await evaluation, some of which are enumerated below without regard to their priority:

1 The role and function of individual media.

2 The best methods by which broadcast media can be integrated with the other learning materials, such as texts, to form a multi-media package.

3 The program format and filmic lan-

170

guage most suitable to the Iranian audience and the subject matter areas.

4 The most suitable length for radio and television programs for different subject matter areas and presentation formats.

5 Effects of broadcast media in facilitating learning and increasing student motivation.

6 The criteria needed for allocating media to a course as a whole (especially when funds are limited and demand for use of media is large) and to the content of courses.

7 The effects of utilizing bi-media as opposed to mono-media producers.

8 The comparative effects of using producer-directors with strong academic background vs producer-directors who are professional media producers and who lack the necessary academic experience.

9 The optimum number of high quality television and radio programs a producer-director can be expected to produce.

10 The most suitable procedure(s) and organizational arrangement for producing broadcast programs within the existing time, budget and manpower limitations.

11 The effects of using non-indigenous programs and films on Iranian audiences (their attitudes, learning and motivation).

12 The most suitable times for both the original and repeat transmissions of radio and television programs.

13 The pattern of use of media available at local centers (e.g. audio-video cassettes and films, micro-teaching facilities).

14 Students' response to discussion and interactive broadcast programs.

15 The possibility of using low-cost and/or non-broadcast media as alternatives or supplements to broadcasting (e.g. filmstrips, electronic black boards, ceefax, two-way radio via satellite, computer-managed instruction).

7 Summary

In addition to lack of existing usable data, the university has faced a traditionally lackadaisical attitude towards on-going research and a severe shortage of qualified manpower. None the less FUI hopes to establish an evaluation system for media, on whose results will be based the yearly revisions of television and radio programs and the life-time of each course.

This paper is not intended to offer definite solutions on media evaluation questions. Instead it is designed to stimulate discussion and seek guidelines from practitioners (media evaluators and broadcast producers) who are present at this conference.

References

1 For a detailed discussion of prospective planning techniques, see: *Prospective Planning Project, Purpose, design, methodology, timetable*, Prospective Planning Project, National Iranian Radio and Television, Tehran, 1975.

2 *A Report: The Planning Framework for the Teacher Preparation Program*, The Free University of Iran: Tehran, 1975.

3 *World Wide Trends in the Future of Broadcasting, a Delphi Study of Issues and Capabilities*, Prospective Planning Project, National Iranian Radio and Television, Tehran, 1975.

4 BATES, A. W. *Research into O.U. Broadcasting:* 1971–1972, Milton Keynes, The Open University, 1973.

5 JAMISON, D., SUPPES, P., and WELLS, P. *The Effectiveness of Alternative Instruction Media:* A Survey, Washington, D.C., Academy for Educational Technology, 1973.

6 *A Report From the Free University of Iran to the Eight Ramsar Education Conference*, The Free University of Iran, 1975, p. 57.

7 In the compilation of this list Dr. Tony Bates' Paper, *A proposed program of evaluation*, Institute of Educational Technology, The Open University, 1975, has been of great help.

PAPER NO 16: PROGRAMME EVALUATION METHODS AT THE OPEN UNIVERSITY

Margaret Gallagher, Research Officer, Institute of Educational Technology, The Open University, UK.

The need for programme evaluation

Distance-teaching situations in general present difficulties for both teachers and learners in that the normal direct feedback loop, often taken for granted in face-to-face teaching, cannot be established. Consequently, the usual mechanisms through which teachers learn of the necessity for adjustments to content or presentation of their materials, in response to the demands of particular learners, must be substituted by other, more indirect, ways of discovering how individuals are approaching, reacting to and using these materials. In the Open University, where a highly heterogeneous mass of students receives a roughly similar teaching package of printed correspondence texts, television and radio programmes, and tests or assignments, this problem is particularly acute in the area of broadcasting. Whereas authors of the printed texts can obtain, via students' assignment answers, a broad indication of particular problems posed by any or all of the written teaching material, producers of the television and radio programmes generally receive no such minimal guidance, since the broadcast component of courses is not normally assessed.

With the presentation of its first courses in 1971, the University did, in fact, establish a system which allowed students to report and comment on the teaching materials provided to them.[1] Pre-coded questionnaires elicited student feedback on the various course components, including broadcasts, on a weekly or fortnightly basis. Another system, established in 1973, was designed to obtain similar information from course tutors.[2] Although neither of these systems was designed to provide detailed evaluative information on broadcasts, it is not surprising that, in the absence of anything else, producers at the University looked at this aggregate and mainly quantitative data in the hope of finding answers to their very immediate and specific preoccupations regarding student use of television and radio.[3] Naturally, they were disappointed. This standardized information told producers nothing about *why* particular programmes had succeeded or failed: it was consequently of little use in assisting decision-making about *future* programmes. It was with these problems in mind that the University's audio-visual media research group evolved its policy towards programme research.[4] In order to attempt to answer producers' demands for detailed feedback on broadcasts, and at the same time to test a number of more general research hypotheses about students' use of television and radio, it was decided to investigate the following areas:

1 The relative success of typical or potential uses of broadcasting within each of the University's six faculties.
2 Problems experienced by students in:
(a) learning from television and radio in general,
(b) responding to particular uses of broadcasting i.e. specific formats or teaching methods.
(c) relating the broadcast element to other course components.
3 Individual student differences in attitude, reaction to, and use of the broadcast media.

Methods and techniques

The method adopted to tackle these areas of investigation has been suggested as much by the practical, operational constraints on the research group itself as by the particular demands of the research problems. The University now spends £3½ million each year on the production of 300 new television programmes and a similar number of new radio programmes. These, together with programmes produced in previous years, are transmitted to over 50,000 students for over 30 hours a week, in 36 weeks of the year. Faced with such vast numbers of both programmes and students, the research group, whose total annual budget (including salaries) is less than £20,000, has had to evolve new solutions appropriate to its own particular situation.[5]

A possible solution: developmental testing

One possibility might have been to pre-test or pilot programme material, along the lines developed by the Children's Television Workshop (CTW) researchers for

Sesame Street and *The Electric Company*. However, the resource implications of this type of trial and experimentation are enormous: the CTW's £9 million annual budget,[6] of which a notably high proportion is allocated to research (for an output of 260 programmes) contrasts not only with the Open University's lower actual overall broadcasting budget, but with a more general University principle which pushes for the production of an impressively large number of courses within an equally impressively short period of time. All resources are consequently under operational strain, in the effort to meet the production goal which the University has set itself. The BBC (which is contracted to produce the University's broadcasts) turns out about 300 television programmes a year from one main studio; producers are fully occupied; there is little or no slack at present for pretesting of broadcasts.

Something of a start has, however, recently begun in this area within the context of a larger University project which aims to pre-test an entire course before its first presentation to students. But the principles involved here are quite different from those behind the CTW work, where an extremely protracted production phase allowed for experimentation at every stage of production. In the present Open University project, testing of more-or-less finalized material is fitted in to the standard production cycle. It is still doubtful that testing of broadcast material can be accommodated within this model: even if it is, given existing and foreseeable budgetary constraints, it will be fulfilling a very different function from that of the CTW experiments.

Other possibilities: existing methodologies
Apart from the purely practical constraints posed by budgetary and manning levels, the group tackled a number of conceptual issues in its attempt to derive a method or approach which would allow for both rigour and flexibility. In so doing, we were forced to reject some of the more traditional research methodologies. Conventional approaches to educational media research have on the whole followed the experimental and psychometric traditions: their general aim has been to employ controlled and objective methods, which re-

duce to a manageable number the variables under examination. Emphasis on control and objectivity has led to a proliferation of artificial and restricted studies which have been intrinsically incapable of getting to grips with the considerable complexity of the problems which they purport to tackle. In the search for respectable *statistical* significance, media researchers have tended to ignore the inevitable human dimension in any educational situation: in so doing, they have lost sight of the reality of educational intercourse, in which—to an interested teacher/producer—*significance* may have little to do with chi-squared differences between 'high' and 'low' performers on a test, but a lot to do with the mental pictures or associations triggered by a particular piece of teaching.

Concentration on the collection of 'hard' quantitative data obtained by objective measurement has led to two severe limitations in terms of the extent to which such data can actually be used. In the first place, information of a more subjective, anecdotal or impressionistic nature has tended to be disregarded on the grounds that it is difficult to measure or compare. Now, although some researchers would have us believe that the data speaks for itself, I have personally never experienced statistical revelation: no 'average' has ever intoned a recommendation for action to me, no standard deviation has even whispered an explanation of its nature. But if evaluation is to be usable, it surely must attempt to explain its findings, weight their importance and place them in context. To do so, it is almost inevitably forced to wrestle with the difficulty of making sense of whatever 'soft' qualitative and subjective information is available. The second limitation imposed by the search for statistical generalization is that evaluation of this kind is generally insensitive to unusual effects or atypical results. Often these may be fundamental to a complete interpretation of findings, or to the identification of particular problem areas. They rarely come to light for discussion, lying buried beneath the more solid means and medians of the final tabulations.

Besides the crippling limitations imposed on controlled, objective evaluation by its very design, it is in practice weakened by a further, less tangible factor. This is the element of human complexity. Educational situations can rarely be subjected to the sorts of control which would be necessary to ensure that all relevant parameters had indeed been accounted for. Further, the very idea of experimental control implies the highly questionable assumption that it is possible to anticipate all relevant parameters. Take, as an example, those many studies which have attempted to answer that question by now calculated to turn any researcher's hair grey: Will they learn more from a video-tape than they would from a slide-tape presentation? When this question has been investigated in experimentally controlled situations, the various unique advantages of each medium have been systematically and artificially levelled out, in the decision to present exactly the same information through each medium in exactly the same way: in reality, such a decision would never be made. More seriously, such studies assume that meaning can be held constant while media are varied. McLuhan's old adage has been shown valid, however, by work which suggests that supposedly equivalent meanings are significantly changed simply through presentation via different media.[7]

Quite apart from these intrinsic weaknesses in the experimental research paradigm, we judged it to be immensely difficult to apply to the Open University's use of broadcasting because of the overwhelming number of variables presented by independent home-based learning. Nor, for similar reasons, was it possible for us to rely on evidence from performance testing. The University's teaching rests on the principle of an integrated multi-media system: it is consequently seldom possible to deduce just what a student has learnt from *which* medium. Moreover, performance testing often fails to acknowledge the very diffuse nature of the aims or objectives of instructional broadcast material. Many Open University programmes, as well as having some precisely stated and measurable instructional objective, are intended to do something else, such as to convey a certain experience, provide a particular awareness, or promote a sense of involvement: these complex, diffuse aims do not readily lend themselves to established measuring techniques.

The shortcomings we found in traditional media research methods did not, however, lead us to reject the importance of collecting objective, reliable and representative information. The problem was to find a method which, in addition to gathering data which met such standards, would allow us to investigate, as fully as possible, the complexity of students' use of broadcasting in the Open University. For our review of established methodologies had led us to other, seemingly minor, conclusions: for instance, that at the receiving end of the broadcast message, evaluation has tended to overlook the unique interactions of circumstances, pressures, expectations, opinions, work styles, which lead to considerable differences in individual reactions to broadcast material. But consideration of factors of this sort, we felt, was essential if we were to begin to understand *why*, for example, six per cent of Open University students never watch television, or *why* a minority of students find a particular programme a waste of time when the majority find it helpful. At the beginning of 1974, however, there were already almost 2,000 television and radio programmes in existence: there were two full-time researchers.

Our solution: contextual evaluation

We settled for a method which, although involving concentrated and detailed investigation, is designed to provide data applicable to a wide range of programmes and students. This involves focussing on a small number of programmes which are believed to be typical or potential uses of broadcasting within the various University faculties, and following a *contextual* and *illuminative* model of evaluation in which the individual programme is examined within the contexts of both the total work unit and the course as a whole. These contexts throw light on certain aspects of student response to the programme, while others are illuminated by in-depth analysis of students' *overall* reaction to the broadcast. The general aim has been to discover which programmes, or parts of programmes, either cause problems to, or are readily assimilable by, which groups of students, and why. The emphasis has been on the improvement of broadcasting as a teaching device: we have been concerned with learning how to make future programmes more helpful for students rather than with passing summary judgements on individual programmes.

Our method has been, firstly, to read all course material related to the programme under evaluation: the course guide, broadcast notes, related correspondence text and any preceding texts which may have a direct bearing on the programme. We then view or listen to the programme before discussing it with the producer and academic responsible. These, separate, discussions are deliberately unstructured but cover such ground as: what it was intended to convey to students in terms of both concepts and experiences; why the programme was made in that particular way; any specific problems which students might have on viewing or listening to the programme; the relationship of the programme to other course components. The idea behind this method has been to get, as far as possible, an understanding of the total context of the programme, as well as of its content.

To guide us in our collection of data three main criteria were applied to the programmes:

1 Was the programme made with a clear *educational* intent, in the sense of providing students with knowledge or experience relevant to the course as a whole? and were students able to grasp this purpose or to use the material constructively in relation to their study of the course?
2 Was the programme able to provide students with *knowledge or experience which it would be difficult to provide as cheaply or conveniently in any other way* in the Open University teaching system?
3 What was the *intended relationship between the programme and other components of the course?* to what extent was this relationship achieved? and were students able to integrate the broadcasts with the rest of their learning activities?

Contextual evaluation techniques

A variety of techniques has been used, including postal questionnaires aimed to combine a certain amount of quantifiable information with as much free, spontaneous comment as is possible, telephone interviewing, group discussion, content analysis—both of programmes and of relevant documents and texts. An important aspect of the approach has been the involvement of programme producers and text authors in the planning, administrations and analysis of each study. This has given both researchers and producers of teaching materials enlarged perspectives on the questions which need to be asked, how best to ask them, and ways of interpreting the answers. Thus drafts of questionnaires or interview schedules have been amended or approved by the producer and academic; in some cases the latter have helped with telephone interviews or attended group discussions (this has been done incognito to avoid disturbance effects); and draft reports have been discussed in detail with producer and academic before finalization.

No individual evaluation has drawn simply on one information source: all have used at least two, although each study has used a basic questionnaire sent to a sample of about 200 students (this has normally been approximately equivalent to a 25 per cent sample, sometimes more). Using a system of reminder letters, we have obtained high response rates—averaging about 75 per cent across all our studies—and thus are confident about the validity of the data. Our analyses have aimed to treat each questionnaire as a whole, rather than to break it down into responses to particular questions. Thus we attempt to analyse and assess each individual's overall response to the programme under evaluation by looking at the totality of his answers, and by comparing his response to one specific question with his answers to all the others. This allows us to build up a picture of the sorts of factors which seem to be important both to individual students and to the general success or failure of the programme. Clearly, data which is treated in this way cannot be pre-coded or computer-analysed, but must be sifted manually. This is at once a subjective and a time-consuming business. However, the use of a variety of techniques which provide a number of different information sources has helped to underline, explain or give weight to findings which might perhaps be questionable if based simply on a single set of data.

Based on this method of analysis, draft reports are prepared for discussion with

M

producer and academic. These reports are lengthy (anything up to 100 pages), containing a complete interpretation of the data, conclusions including any implications for the University's wider use of broadcasting, and a set of recommendations. Circulation of the final full-length reports is made to the course team members on the course to which the programme under evaluation belongs, and to senior production staff. Summary reports (three or four pages in length) are distributed to all producers, educational technologists, faculty members and some regional staff.

Findings from the studies*

The work has provided important insights into the frames of reference with which students approach particular teaching materials and into their attitudes to and expectations of certain media. It has provided information as to *why* students respond to particular programme contents and formats in particular ways, and has indicated that individual affective preferences may sometimes be as important as specific cognitive difficulties in determining the extent to which a programme achieves its intended purpose. This latter relationship has been observed to work in a number of conflicting ways: while we have found[8] that students antipathetic to a particular programme format, for example dramatic presentation, have mentally 'switched off' and missed the entire educational message of the programme, we have also found[9] that some students who are particularly attracted to specific formats, such as 'actuality' recordings of real events, may be so seduced by the format that they, too, miss the point of the programme. Moreover, while programme formats have been used with complete success to 'anchor' specific ideas or concepts in students' minds,[8,10] we have found problems caused by the actual intrusion of a specific production technique—for instance, a highly successful and interesting demonstration of a mechanical model[11]—on students' understanding of the overall purpose of the programme.

Reactions to particular programmes have been found to be deeply influenced by the type of assessment procedures used in the course and the relationship of these to broadcasts: for instance, students were found[10] in general to ignore the work related to a pair of programmes in a science course and to undervalue the programmes themselves until they discovered later in the course that they would be required to complete an assignment based on the programmes. The constraints of a study schedule can radically affect students' ability to make the most of broadcast material: for example, when students pace their work to meet assignment deadlines and when these assignments are unrelated to broadcasts, students have been found to be inadequately prepared for programmes or to skip them altogether.[9,12] Other important constraints on the value obtained from specific broadcasts are posed by the work-load and difficulty of a course as a whole,[9,10,12] as well as of the particular units to which any one programme is related.[8]

Within this general framework, a wide range of individual differences, in terms of student response to specific programmes, has been identified.[8,10,13] While some students have difficulty with particular *media*, for example radio,[9,10] others encounter problems within the media with particular *formats* or *teaching styles*.[8,9,13]

Conclusions

Subsequent to every one of our studies completed so far, changes have been made to the programmes, related broadcast notes, or study schedules. More importantly, the results have influenced programme policy on new but similar courses at the planning or preparation stage. We have also been able to draw on data derived from these specific studies to help us advise course teams in more general areas, such as the use of broadcast notes and the amount and nature of guidance needed by students in using particular sorts of broadcast material.

Although time-consuming—each study takes at least two man-months to carry through—the work has produced findings of a highly generalizable nature and has won wide support within the Open University system.[14] Perhaps the most important aspects of the studies in this respect has been the deliberate involvement of producers and academics in their design and analysis. For although every pro-

---

* It is impossible in this paper to do more than broadly indicate the range of our findings.

gramme is indeed unique, it is likely to be underpinned by a number of general principles and to be set within an overall educational framework; once aware of these, programme-makers can carry their implications over into new situations. Data obtained from particular evaluation studies will not provide anyone with direct and unequivocal answers to questions thrown up in specific new situations; however, the process of contextual evaluation does provide a real learning experience which should allow those who have been involved to bring widened frames of reference—influenced by contact with researchers, producers, academics, students and tutors —to bear on the solution of future educational media problems.

References

1   McINTOSH, N. Research for a new institution—the Open University, in FLOOD-PAGE, C. and GREEN-AWAY, H. (eds.), *Innovation in Higher Education*, London, Society for Research in Higher Education, 1972.

2   BATES, A. W. The role of the tutor in evaluating distance-teaching, *Teaching at a Distance*, Vol. 1, No. 1, Milton Keynes, The Open University, 1974.

3   GALLAGHER, M. *An Evaluation of the CT4 Scheme*, Milton Keynes, The Open University, 1973 (unpublished paper).

4   BATES, A. W. *The British Open University: Decision-oriented Research in Broadcasting*. (Paper presented at the National Association of Educational Broadcasters' Convention, Washington, D.C.), 1975.

5   BATES, A. W. and GALLAGHER, M. The development of research into broadcasting at the Open University, *British Journal of Educational Technology*, Vol. 7, No. 1, 1976.

6   MIELKE, K. W., JOHNSON, R. C. and COLE, B. G. *The Federal Role in Funding Children's Television Programming*. Bloomington, Indiana, Institute for Communication Research, 1975.

7   HEIDT, E. V. Research in media and the learning process: the relation of internal learner operation and functional media attributes, CEREB Conference Paper No. 22, 1976.

8   GALLAGHER, M. Broadcast Evaluation Report No. 8: *E221: Radio Plays*, Milton Keynes, The Open University, 1975.

9   GALLAGHER, M. Broadcast Evaluation Report No. 2: *E221: Cumbria Case Study*, Milton Keynes, The Open University, 1975.

10   GALLAGHER, M. Broadcast Evaluation Report No. 4: *S24–: Industrial Chemistry Component*, Milton Keynes, The Open University, 1975.

11   BATES, A. W. Broadcast Evaluation Report No. 3: *T291: Instrumentation*, Milton Keynes, The Open University, 1975.

12   AHRENS, S., BURT, G., and GALLAGHER, M. Broadcast Evaluation Report No. 1: *M231: Analysis*, Milton Keynes, The Open University, 1975.

13   KOUMI, J. Broadcast Evaluation Report No. 19: *A302: Studying the Novel*, Milton Keynes, The Open University, 1976.

14   BATES, A. W. Towards a Policy for Broadcast Evaluation. CEREB Conference Paper No. 7, 1976.

STUDIES OF PARTICULAR PROJECTS

PAPER NO 44: EVALUATION OF ECONOMICS TEACHING BY TELEVISION

Robin Moss, Deputy Director (Productions), University Television Service, University of Leeds, UK.
Neil Costello, Lecturer, Economics, University of Leeds, UK.

1 The context of the study

At the University of Leeds in 1972 the second year Economic Theory course on Welfare Economics and General Equilibrium was not entirely popular. The lecturer (Neil Costello) had found by questionnaires and interview that there was fairly widespread dissatisfaction with the lectures, which were described by some students as 'boring' or 'irrelevant'. This experience is apparently neither new nor rare. For example, work at the University of Sussex has reported similar frustration and boredom among students studying economic theory at about the same period (terms 3 and 4) of their academic career.[1]

In February, 1973, two short video-tapes on *The Welfare Optima* were produced by Neil Costello, working with A. B. Haigh of the University of Leeds Television Service. The first video-tape (*Production*) consisted of a series of complex animated diagrams, with commentary over, and lasted 4 minutes 50 seconds. The other (*Exchange*) ran for 5 minutes 10 seconds, and was similar in design. The two video-tapes were shown at a conference at the University of Sussex on 'Problems of Economic Teaching At University', where they were well received later in 1973.

The two video-tapes were assessed by a simple Course Evaluation questionnaire in scale form, issued to and returned by 72 (55 per cent) of the 131 second year students following the 1973 Welfare Economics and General Equilibrium theory course.[2] The relative simplicity of their design from the point of view of the lecturer, and the enthusiasm displayed by the students for the experience, encouraged a similar approach to the production of the two new video-tapes in the summer of 1974, for use with the two original video-tapes in the second year Microeconomics course. The new video-tapes were to be shown early in that course in the autumn of 1974, and would cover revision of relatively elementary (but for some, conceptually difficult) first year work on cost curves and returns to scale and the concept of the production function in general. These short video-tapes were to be seen as lecture 'inserts' at appropriate points in the course, about half-way through each 50-minute lecture. Later in the term the 1973 recordings on the Welfare Optima were to be shown. Thus the sequence of showing of the four video-tapes in the autumn term of the academic year 1974–5 was as follows:

1 Production Function, Total Cost and Return to Scale (10 minutes).
2 Short Run and Long Run Average Costs (7 minutes 50 seconds).
3 The Welfare Optima—Production (4 minutes 50 seconds).
4 The Welfare Optima—Exchange (5 minutes 10 seconds).

The first two were shown in the second and third weeks of the Michaelmas term in lectures beginning at 9 am on a Tuesday morning. The second two were shown a fortnight and three weeks later, respectively. The first pair, which covered topics familiar to most students, were supported by handouts. Each video-tape was also copied into video-cassette format and stored in the University library for students to study in their own time for revision purposes, as had been requested by a large majority of responses to the pilot questionnaire.

2 Purpose of the study

We agreed to devise jointly and administer a series of questionnaires (see below, Section 3) to test both the success of students in terms of immediate recall of factual information, and their attitudes to the experience of using the video-tape inserts. It was hoped to compare these two major sets of results to see if there was any further support for the evidence earlier reported (in the context of a first year Computer Science course) that the expressed attitude of students to teaching by video-tape was a poor index of their actual achievement in immediate recall.[3] More generally, it was hoped that student comments on the experience would be of value in increasing our understanding both of educational television production in this field and of student attitudes to some aspects of economics teaching.

3 Design of the study

At the end of each of the four lecture occasions on which one of the video-tape inserts had been shown, the students were requested to complete a duplicated questionnaire. Questionnaire 1 was headed with this rubric:

Please answer the following questions carefully.

Your answers will help us to assess the effectiveness of the video-tape you have just watched, and improve future recordings.

Four questions to test the student's understanding of the lecture followed: the first two were multiple-choice questions referring to the general content, questions 3 and 4 were 'visual', in that they required students to reproduce the shape and location of a curve or curves described in the video-tape. Question 5 was intended to test the student attitudes to the video-tape; its wording is set out in full below.

Finally, students were invited to make any other comments they might have.

The other three questionnaires were similar in design, although the number of questions testing understanding of academic content was reduced to three for the second lecture, and only two for the remaining two; the 'self-created' scales for rating attitudes to the experience were increased to two in later questionnaires, allowing students more opportunity to frame their own modes of reacting to the experience.

Questionnaire 4 concluded by inviting students to comment on the use of television in general, to assist in the teaching of economics.

The completed responses to the questionnaires were subjected to a computer analysis

---

Q.5 *Please rate the video-tape you have just seen, at a point on each of the three scales shown below. The last one is for you to set up. In other words, what, in your view, is an important factor in assessing the success of the video-tape, and how do you rate it on your scale?*

The pace of the presentation was far too *fast*.

The pace of the presentation was far too *slow*.

The topic was explained very *clearly*.

The explanation of the topic was very *confusing*.

....

....

1   2   3   4   5

---

by D. L. Harkess, Research Officer in the School of Economic Studies; attitude scales were also analysed, having been coded for relative strength of approval (or hostility) vis-a-vis the video-tape. Both the comments and the self-created scales were also categorized by topic and tested for possible relationships with, for example, academic success in the first year examination and/or success in answering the content questions concerning the lecture.

The cost of the enquiry has not been calculated since it was undertaken by us and our colleagues in the course of our regular duties and/or in spare time.

4 Results of the study

There were 67 students taking the course, with between 8 and 11 absentees on each occasion. The mean scores on each of the four questionnaires are tabulated below (Table 1).

The initial impression (from column 3) was that students had generally answered the questions very successfully, which implies either that the teaching was effective or that the questions were set at too low a level to discriminate satisfactorily between those who had learned effectively and those who had not, or some combination of the two. A classic control group design for the project would of course have allowed us to test these hypotheses, but this opportunity had been ruled out from the start.

As Table I shows, differences between responses to 'visual' and 'non-visual' questions were measured. These differences were not significant for questionnaires 1 and 3, but highly significant (by zM Test, at less than the 0.2 per cent and 1 per cent level respectively) for questionnaires 2 and 4. No generalizable conclusion can be drawn from this, but the measurements (in favour of the 'visual' questions on questionnaire 4, but against them on questionnaire 2) have encouraged us to review the visual content of programme 2 for future usage.

Students were grouped by their overall performance on the 4 tests, and these results were compared with their performance on the first-year examination (Table 2).

No correlation between the mean examination marks of the groups and their test scores could be found, but Group A tended to perform somewhat more successfully on the four tests than Group B, as would be

Table 1   Scores on 'academic content' questions

	1 Mean	2 s.d.	3 % of max
Questionnaire 1 (n 58)			
2 'non-visual' questions (max score 4)	3.59	0.795	89.75
2 'visual' questions (max score 4)	3.41	1.077	85.25
All four questions (max score 8)	7.00	0.936	88.00
Questionnaire 2 (n 59)			
1 'non-visual' question (max score 3)	2.90	0.305	96.67
2 'visual' questions (max score 3)	2.47	0.751	82.33
All three questions (max score 6)	5.37	0.528	89.50
Questionnaire 3 (n 56)			
1 'non-visual' question (max score 1)	0.86	0.353	86.00
1 'visual' question (max score 1)	0.91	0.288	91.00
Both questions (max score 2)	1.77	0.321	88.50
Questionnaire 4 (n 57)			
1 'non-visual' question (max score 1)	0.35	0.481	35.00
1 'visual' question (max score 1)	0.68	0.469	68.00
Both questions (max score 2)	1.03	0.475	51.50

Table 2 *Student test scores summed and expressed as a percentage, and first year examination scores*

	Group A (n 28)	Group B (n 39)
	%	%
Range of test scores	93–100	20–90
Mean examination mark	57.04	51.64

expected. On each of the four tests, students were also divided into two groups on the basis of the attitudes expressed in self-created scales and comments, classified as favourable or unfavourable to the television component in the lectures (Table 3). Of course, not all students' responses could be so classified.

There was no significant difference between the scores of students who professed a favourable attitude to television and the scores of those who did not. This would accord with previously published evidence that individual student attitudes in this context are not an accurate guide to their performance.[3] On the other hand, it is noteworthy that questionnaires 1 and 2 attracted a less favourable set of expressed attitudes than the other two, and that relative group performance on visual questions shifted in step with each shift in attitudes almost exactly (compare column 3 of Table 1). In our view these two findings may be seen as consistent, since individual attitudes and performance need not match, even when an overall broad matching of group attitude and performance can be observed. The development of an increasingly favourable attitude to television is also noteworthy, perhaps implying the same 'training' element in the use of a novel medium over several weeks that had been

observed in the earlier study. Since videotapes 3 and 4 were made before tapes 1 and 2 it is not the case that the former were markedly superior in style of production.

None of the results so far reported were of startling interest to us, and at this stage we were somewhat disappointed. It is perhaps worth commenting that these results were almost entirely drawn from the figures delivered to us by the computer, on the basis of questions we had wrongly expected to be fruitful. Perseverance, as will be seen, did produce some more interesting information and in this hazardous area of examining human behaviour is perhaps more to be recommended than designing questions that are analysable by computer.

Student comments and self-created scales for each questionnaire were now grouped into what emerged as six categories of response, and also divided into the two groups described in Table 2 (relative success on tests). The categories of response were:

1 Self-access (i.e. references to speed of presentation, length of presentation, usefulness of video-tape for revision, need to take notes, etc.). (Note that *Speed* of presentation was an imposed scale for questionnaire 1.)

2 Clarity (i.e. references to the video-tapes being relatively 'understandable', 'lucid', 'hard', 'intelligible', etc.).

Table 3 *Attitudes to television component, expressed in self-created scales and/or comments*

	Favourable to TV		Unfavourable to TV	
	n	(% of total)	n	(% of total)
Questionnaire 1 (N 51)	20	(39)	31	(61)
Questionnaire 2 (N 46)	11	(24)	35	(75)
Questionnaire 3 (N 38)	21	(55)	17	(45)
Questionnaire 4 (N 44)	29	(66)	15	(34)

Table 4   Number of comments and self-created scales completed by questionnaire

	Number of responses		
	Group A	Group B	Total
Questionnaire 1	23	23	46
Questionnaire 2	18	22	40
Questionnaire 3	33	33	66
Questionnaire 4	33	30	63

3 Comparison with other media (i.e. references such as 'better than lecture/book', or specific comments on visual quality of video-tape, on use of animated diagrams, etc.).

4 Interest ('interesting', 'boring', 'dull', 'exciting', etc.).

5 Content (i.e. criticisms of teaching content).

6 Production (i.e. criticisms of production).

It should be stressed that these categories of response grouped together favourable as well as unfavourable judgements and that there was a certain amount of overlap between categories (e.g. 3 and 6). The nature of the imposed scale (e.g. for questionnaire 1, concerning speed of presentation) may also have framed student selection of the category of response to some extent. There was no overall difference in the number of responses made by Group A (successful) students and by Group B students (107 and 108 responses, respectively, for the four questionnaires, and a similar division for each questionnaire). The first two questionnaires attracted far fewer responses than the last two, further confirming the relatively greater interest and approval the latter attracted. Indeed Table 4 shows an interesting parallelism with Table 3.

It may be that a group's willingness to comment on a video-tape offers a rough indication of its relative teaching success; it would be interesting to know if this possibility has been examined by the Open University Institute of Educational Technology.

In the earlier study it was tentatively suggested that students who were relatively high achievers were more likely than others to be critical of a video-tape, and that the less successful tended to stress the relative helpfulness or interest of a video-tape more than their high-achieving peers. This was not supported in the present study so far as an examination of categories 5 and 6 (content and production) were concerned, but there was clear evidence that Group A were more interested in the material being available to them in self-access form than were Group B, who stressed clarity and interest more frequently (Tables 5 and 6).

5 Implications of the study

The most important single factor about the holding of this conference, in our view, is that it should be held at all. The idea that evaluation and research into teaching and learning might fruitfully affect decision-making in institutions of higher education is so alien to traditions in this country that its exploration is in itself exciting. We should like to comment further on this in these final paragraphs.

Seven conclusions may be drawn from our study:

(i) the technique of creating short video-tape inserts and related handouts to support a lecture course in micro-economics theory offers satisfactory results on immediate recall tests;

(ii) able students are particularly interested in the presentation of such short video-tape recordings in self-access form;

(iii) less able students tend to lay particular emphasis on the importance of clarity and interest in the teaching material;

(iv) the range and variety of student attitudes to such an experience is very considerable, but they have been satisfactorily grouped in six categories (referred to above);

(v) individually expressed attitudes of

Table 5   Relative achievement and references to own control of teaching material and to intelligibility

	'A' Group Students	'B' Group Students
'SELF-ACCESS' REFERENCES (speed of presentation, its length, the usefulness of the tape for revision, the need to take notes)	33	23
'CLARITY' REFERENCES ('understandable', 'lucid', 'hard', 'intelligible', 'hard to grasp', etc.)	22	31

$X^2 = 2.66$ (Yates' X^2 Test) significant at the 0.1 level

Table 6   Relative achievement and references to own control of teaching material and to interest

	'A' Group Students	'B' Group Students
'SELF-ACCESS' REFERENCES	33	23
'INTEREST' REFERENCES	2	10

$X^2 = 6.84$ (Yates' X^2 Test)
$P = 0.01$

enthusiasm or the reverse for a video-tape do not correlate with relative success or failure in learning from it;

(vi) students tended to respond more favourably to later inserts in the series, and to learn more effectively from them (i.e. an element of self-training in the use of an unfamiliar medium may be observable);

(vii) the self-created scale is a useful device for encouraging students to consider carefully their attitude to an experience, and to express it in quantifiable terms.

Since these inserts were used in the 1974–5 second year Microeconomics course, Neil Costello has resigned from the School of Economic Studies at the University of Leeds, to take up an appointment with the Open University. It is significant that although the four video-tape inserts are available in video-cartridge format in the University library, no member of the department has made use of the material in the equivalent 1975–6 course. We do not believe that this is a criticism of the quality of the material in itself, nor indeed of the academic staff. It is an inherent problem for the effective use of educational technology by and in institutions of higher education, and is clearly described in the recent report of the Nuffield Foundation's Group for Research and Innovation in Higher Education:[4]

It is scarcely surprising to find a battery of defences raised against change, some representing genuine doubts based on experience, others ingenious rationalizations.

There follow a list of seven familiar arguments. The last is perhaps the most important of all, namely that each lecturer teaches in his own private, indeed secret, way, so that attempts to create generally valuable learning materials are doomed to failure.

In December 1975, a senior member of

the Economics Department staff viewed one of the four inserts at the invitation of the Television Service. His comment was that the ingenuity and accuracy of the work was excellent, but that he 'would not have taught the topic in that way'. While a carefully prepared item of this nature, tested in use, tends to attract this type of lukewarm response, scores of lectures, presumably less carefully prepared and certainly rarely tested, are delivered each term without colleagues evincing any interest in content or style.

Fortunately there are signs of a change of atmosphere. *Supporting Teaching For A Change*[4] offers a number of valuable suggestions for the more effective use of support services in universities. Meanwhile it is to be hoped that such services will persevere in their attempts to examine the complex nature of teaching and learning and to stimulate changes where appropriate.

In this context, the recent article on economics teaching published by members of the University of Sussex Centre for Educational Technology deserves attention.[1] This comes to radical conclusions about what it calls the 'myth' of educational development. The authors urge instead consideration of courses in which students themselves discuss and develop teaching programmes, acquiring in the process a deeper mastery of the subject and its concepts. Certainly such a democratic approach to learning is of interest, but it is utopian to believe that such an approach is generally practicable at present. Indeed, a radical approach of this sort is so far removed from methods in general use that it is reasonable to ask if educational development really has been given a fair test. For example, it is reported by the Sussex group that introductory 'learning packages' devised there proved unsuccessful, even after revision, in terms of student learning gains and student attitudes. On the basis of this statement, and without describing in any detail the nature of these packages, the authors wish to recommend abandoning the whole idea of educational development (which, incidentally, two of them have done much to propagate). The simpler explanation of the reported results is that the packages deserved further modification or replacement. Our own evidence on the complexity of the learning experience supports this judge-

ment, which Ockham himself would have approved.

References

1 ERAUT, M., MACKENZIE, N., PAPPS, I. The Mythology of Educational Development: Reflections on a Three-Year Study of Economics Teaching, *British Journal of Educational Technology*, No. 3, Vol. 6, 1975.

2 COSTELLO, N. and MOSS, J. R. (forthcoming) Economics Teaching—a use for television, *Economics*. Enquiries to publishers.

3 MOSS, J. R. Assessing The Learning Experience: University Students Evaluate Video-tapes, *Programmed Learning*, May 1973.

4 NUFFIELD FOUNDATION (Group for Research and Innovation in Higher Education), *Supporting Teaching For A Change*, 1975.

PAPER NO 6: GUIDELINES IN ETV PRODUCTION: SIX EXPERIMENTS

John P. Baggaley, Lecturer in Communication, University of Liverpool.
Stephen Duck, Lecturer in Psychology, University of Lancaster.

Summary

In a discussion of the research strategies likely to aid the design of effective ETV production techniques, it was emphasized that investigators should accumulate insights into television's impact in specific educational situations,

> rather than waiting for a single 'learning' theory to cope with them all. Practical solutions within any educational situation—from the process of teacher training onwards—are reached as guidelines for the acquisition of teaching and learning skills are defined and ratified.[1]

Subsequently, six experiments have been conducted, in each of which the effects of a particular television production technique were examined. The practical implications of this research for the educational producer are discussed in a series of research notes recently published in *Educational Broadcasting International*.[2]

The articles indicate that a number of basic production procedures influence the psychological impact of ETV material powerfully and quite unwittingly. Particular effects are noted on the performer's perceived credibility. It appears that the viewers of educational material use certain information suggested to them by incidental variations in presentation, in the basic decision: 'Is the performer worth listening to?'; and only then—if they decide that he is—may they give closer attention to what he is actually saying. Each of the articles offers specific guidelines for the more deliberate control by television producers of such effects in future.

The specific results are as follows:

1   The edited insertion of varying audience reaction shots significantly affected the performer's perceived popularity and interest value, expertise and intelligibility.

2   The electronic insertion of a picture background significantly increased the performer's perceived credibility—more honest, profound, reliable and fair.

3   The re-recording and edited insertion of the interviewer's role in a discussion significantly increased his perceived sincerity, tension and intelligibility.

4   The re-recording and edited insertion of the interviewer's role in a discussion favourably increased the impact of the interview also.

5   When a performer was framed so that his notes were visible he was rated less fair and more confusing than when the notes were not visible.

6   When seen to address the camera directly a performer was considered significantly less reliable and expert than when seen in profile.

Collectively, the results suggest that the major emphasis of previous media research on factors of programme content (i.e. subject matter) has been misguided, since the audience's interpretation of content may itself be affected by the presentation strategies mediating it. Certainly, the role of production factors has been overlooked, and is to form the central theme of an SSRC research project at Liverpool under the direction of Dr J. P. Baggaley (1976–7).

The further implications of the present work are discussed by Baggaley and Duck.[3]

References

1   BAGGALEY, J. P. Developing an effective educational medium. *Programmed Learning and Educational Technology*, 10, 1973.

2   BAGGALEY, J. P. and DUCK, S. W. Research notes: Experiments in ETV. *Educational Broadcasting International* 7 & 8 (series of six articles), 1974–5.

3   BAGGALEY, J. P. and DUCK, S. W. *The Dynamics of Television*, London, Saxon House, 1976.

> The six experiments are described in detail in the September 1974, and January 1975 editions of *Educational Broadcasting International*. We reproduce here, in full, with kind permission of the publishers, the first of these six experiments.

Experiment 1   ETV production methods versus educational intention—some unintended biasses

Recent discussion in this journal has drawn attention to the need for examination of the effects on an audience of ETV production methods traditionally employed. It has been suggested, for instance, that the effectiveness of ETV presentation may be improved by the adoption of a 'textbook' approach involving a long process of checking and re-checking at both the molecular level (proof reading) and the molar level (reviewing by consultants) before the final product is released. Notwithstanding the logistic problems of any lengthy process, such arguments will bear extension. Indeed it sometimes occurs that co-operation between academic disciplines of diverse style but similar interests can create awareness of the ways in which the impact of ETV can be improved. While the subject specialist may advise on details of content, and the audio-visualist on aspects of presentation and production, the psychologist can play a part by alerting both parties to unintended behavioural consequences of their techniques.

For some time psychologists have been studying aspects of communication ranging from the transmission of errors by morse-key operators to the effects on social communication of gesture, posture and 'behavioural' signals. In the middle ground (and perhaps more germane to ETV) lie studies of context and its influence on perception. For example, Levy[1] placed single photographic portraits of 'neutral' faces in arrays of other photographs where the faces looked 'tense'. Instead of seeing the neutral portraits as neutral, observers saw them (in the context of the 'tense' photographs) as 'extremely relaxed'. By this and other tests, Levy was able to show that the context sharply interfered with normal perception of the photographs.

In ETV production similar types of context effect occur, perhaps due to the conflicting interests of the production team and the educators, and sometimes to the detriment of a presentation's educational value. The possibility that production techniques in regular usage may reduce a programme's educational impact certainly deserves scrutiny. How unfortunate it would be for a technically perfect presentation with intrinsic educational merit to be undermined by the unforseen psychological effects of production technique alone.

In the standard presentation of a recorded lecture, for instance, a fairly basic tenet of the producer is that unrelieved 'straight' shots of the speaker can be tedious. While the focus or position of one camera is altered, shots of the audience are sometimes inserted; camera angles are varied; close-up shots are employed along with long shots, and so on. Though standard practice, the educational value of such manipulations is as yet untried: in the light of Levy's findings, what effect do they have on a lecture's recorded impact? Do shots of an audience, for example, indeed help to retain the viewer's interest, or might they have entirely unintended effects?

Bias in audience reaction

To permit an experimental test of these questions, two video-tapes were prepared, each showing the same sequence from a lecture on welfare economics. The sequence lasted $3\frac{1}{2}$ minutes and was made with a single camera at a fixed distance from the lecturer. At the same points in each recording, shots of an audience were inserted, prepared independently with the help of a group of student actors and edited into the

lecture to give the illusion that audience and lecturer had been together at the time of recording. On one tape, members of the audience were shown looking interested, attentive, stimulated and impressed ('positive'), and on the other tape they appeared bored, inattentive, stultified and unimpressed ('negative'). Care was taken in editing to ensure that the amounts of time devoted to lecturer and audience shots were identical in both tapes. And the prediction that judgements of the lecturer would be influenced by the types of audience activity shown was then tested on two groups of students, each of which saw one of the tapes.

On the assessment of the viewers' responses by psychological rating scale techniques, it was found that this prediction had been convincingly upheld. In the 'negative' condition the lecturer herself was seen as significantly more uninteresting and unpopular—results which validate the credibility of the editing process, and show that the two tapes really did present a 'positive' audience on the one hand and a 'negative' one on the other. But by far the most interesting and significant findings were that in the negative tape the lecturer was seen as more confusing, more shallow and more inexpert. It is important to remember here that the presentation of the lecture and its content were absolutely identical in the two tapes and these effects cannot, therefore, be due to any activity on the lecturer's part. They are due solely to the inclusion of the audience shots in the final production, indicating that production techniques and educational intentions may indeed come into sharp conflict due to effects on the viewers which such production methods can create at a psychological level. In itself this indicates that technical presentation methods may need somewhat closer scrutiny if ETV is to achieve its maximal educational impact.

But there is another side to the coin. In the positive tape the lecturer was seen as more straightforward, more profound, more interesting, more popular and more expert. Whilst one would be loath to argue that inherently boring lecturers should be cushioned from their just deserts by production techniques such as the insertion of positive audience shots, these results do suggest that intrinsically difficult subjects could be enlivened somewhat for the viewers by shots of an audience reacting positively and being seen as interested and involved. While such consideration will serve greatly to enhance the educational value of ETV techniques *ipso facto*, it should also encourage greater co-operation between production teams and the educational expositor. Eventually, the final product of their collaboration must become more clearly the sole province of neither and serve the credit of both.

The authors are grateful to Miss Sheila Smith for allowing her recorded lecture to be used in the experiment, and to Mr S. McHale for his technical assistance.

Reference
1 LEVY, L. H. Context effects in social perception, *J. abnorm. soc. Psychol*, 61, 1969.

PAPER NO 51: EDUCATIONAL TELEVISION TO DIFFUSE A TEACHER-TRAINING SYSTEM (With the use of Mediated Cueing)

Pierre Pérusse, Director, Section de Technologie Educationelle, Université de Montreal, Canada.

Statement of the problem
Teachers, scattered over wide areas, have to be reached for in-service training purposes. This problem is emphasized by the lack of available experienced supervisory personnel and the time they can devote to come to training centers. The above is also applicable to teacher trainees sent for internship at various locations.

One way of solving the above problem could be by diffusing, with television, supervisors and innovative systems and suggested learning situations, transmitting also teachers' skills to be learned, repolished or readapted to a new environment. It could even be hypothesized that the students of those in-service or in-training teachers could also be trained or influenced by a similar approach. The solution to solve the present problem has to be based on feedback possibilities and must guarantee learning and positive changes.

The experimental design tested hypotheses made about an effective training system being diffused. In doing so, the basic assumption underlying all the hypotheses was that the rate and level of learning a complex teaching skill (probing) varies as a function of the mode of discriminatory cueing. This was tested with a teacher-model tape presented differentially to four experimental groups. Also, various feedback arrangements were made for discrimination on trainees' taped lessons. It was predicted that the optimal treatment would consist of a mediated supervisor (televised), using symbolic cueing in presentation and feedback. This treatment would be more efficient than a live supervisor not using symbolic cues, in increasing response frequencies of probing.

Procedures
Fifty-one in-service experienced French-speaking college teachers were randomly assigned to four experimental groups:

1 *Self-feedback*, in which the subjects self-discriminated the teacher-model tape and the replay of their prior taped lesson.
2 *Live-immediate feedback*, a live supervisor gave discrimination to a trainee in presenting the model tape and on the trainee's tape in feedback.
3 *Live-delayed feedback*, as per group 2, but with a two-day interval between the trainee's lesson and feedback.
4 *Mediated-delayed feedback*, where a supervisor was mediated through television carrying the same task as in 2 and 3, but using mediated cueing in presenting the model tape and in giving feedback. In order to add mediated cueing in the televised feedback production, a two-day interval was necessary. It was introduced in group 3 as well, for comparison purposes. Shifts in response strengths on the dependent variable were determined by counting the frequency of desired responses in each of the subjects' video-tapes lessons.

Results
A one-way analysis of variance was used to confirm the predictions. A covariance, a repeated measures, and a nonparametric analyses were also conducted. It was found that no significant differences existed be-

tween groups from pre-test to post-test. However, learning on the skill increased significantly for all supervised groups (2, 3 and 4) (p. <.001).

Throughout training, the mediated-delayed feedback group (group 4) was superior to all other treatments in the study. It differed significantly from all other groups on trial four (p. <.05).

Conclusion
The data provided some support for the optimal hypothesis. The mediated-delayed feedback group, in presenting the teacher-model tape and feedback with symbolic cueing, did lead however to greater gains in response frequencies of probing within groups. The differences tend to be obscured in presentation and feedback because all treatment conditions were powerful.

Implementation with the use of educational television
Presentation of various demonstration tapes (models) including different types of teachers and learning environment can be diffused. Tapes of teachers in real situations can also be used and evaluated on a discrimination basis with well defined criterion. In feedback sessions, mediated cueing can be incorporated easily. Even more so, peer supervision can be taught and a better use of educational television emphasized. Microteaching to macro-teaching (real class situation and normal group of students) can be better implemented. Training students in the same manner may lead to significant change in learning.

PAPER NO 70: THE EVALUATION OF A MEDIA RESOURCE-BASED LEARNING PROJECT AND ITS MODIFICATION OF TRADITIONAL CLASSROOM PROCEDURES

G. A. B. Moore, Director, Audio-visual Services, University of Guelph.

Introduction and overview
The improvement of learning opportunities is becoming a major thrust within the Canadian University community and considerable interest is to be found in innovative approaches to university education.

The experience reported in this paper covers an instructional development project in the teaching of introductory French at Sir George Williams University, Montreal, commencing in 1970. The project involved the collaborative work of the Department of French and the Centre for Instructional Technology in the University. An instructional strategy was developed in which the traditional pattern of three lecture periods plus laboratory per week was replaced by student work with specially designed and constructed learning resources. The course format allowed for increased flexibility in student attendance and attempted to improve the opportunities for study and practice.

The evaluative approach taken in this review has attempted to follow that which has been identified as illuminative evaluation. This approach as described by Parlett and Hamilton seeks to look at the program as a whole and provide elucidation of 'its rationale and evolution, its operations, achievements and difficulties'.[1]

The problem and the project strategy
1 Problem
The problem addressed by this project was located in the introductory credit course, French 201, and had four components—three pedagogic and one administrative. The first pedagogic aspect was faced by Gilbert Taggart, Associate Professor of French, as he sought to secure appropriate instructional resources for students beginning the study of a foreign language. Beginning in 1962 Taggart had developed a series of visual illustrations which through classroom testing had become a highly structured system of abstract symbols to clarify ambiguous aural cues such as number and gender and complex space, time and conditional relationships. While he had elaborated on the theory and application of visual cues and stimuli in his doctoral dissertation[2] the then current style of offering the introductory course did not allow for the opportunity to build these findings systematically into the course of instruction.

The second aspect of the problem was that faced by the Department of French in achieving reliability in its introductory course offering since the course was given in multiple sections using temporary part-time instructors.

A further consideration was the desire of Taggart and the department to transfer the instructional emphasis from the traditional reliance on translation methods to the more current audio-lingual approach. Class groups of thirty students presented serious limitations to the development of this method in the course as it was then offered.

The fourth aspect of the problem emerged in the budgetary planning process for the academic year 1970-1. The existing enrolment of 180 students necessitated the appointment of six instructors for each section of French 201. A general reduction in the university of part-time appointments had resulted in the availability of only four appointments in the academic year 1970-1 with a corresponding limit in enrolment to 120 students in this course. Evidence existed that the demand for the course was increasing but instructional resources were not available on the scale required.

2 *Proposed solution*

In consultation between the Center for Instructional Technology and the Department of French, a program plan was developed whereby specially designed and constructed learning resources would be presented to students in a learning laboratory context. This presentation was designed to reduce dependence upon the relatively low faculty-student ratio which then pertained in the traditional approach. The resources, it was proposed, would include video tapes and audio tapes to be used in existing laboratory facilities on an individual study access basis. A specially prepared workbook and self-correctional marking key would complement the oral work with written grammatical exercises. The proposed resources were intended to meet two basic objectives. The first was to create materials which would stand on their own in presenting language structures, vocabulary and pronunciation with the emphasis on aural-oral skills. The second objective was to systematically develop an application of television to university instruction as opposed to a prevailing tendency, in some quarters, to rely on the televising of traditional lecturers.

Students would be required to view the video tapes, practise the oral exercises in the laboratory, complete written assignments and sit both oral and written midterm and final examinations. The achievement of students would be assessed in the four basic skills of language acquisition, i.e. aural comprehension, oral expression, written comprehension and written expression.

The project proposal was presented to the vice principal-academic jointly by the Department of French and the Center for Instructional Technology with a request for special project funding of $8,000 to cover the incremental costs of producing the learning resources. The request was granted in May 1970 and plans formulated to have the resources available for the full term.

Reporting on the experience with the project
1 *Implementation*

The instructional materials (learning resources) were produced using university staff and facilities during the summer of 1970 with Taggart as the principal academic. A series of 52 half-hour video taped lessons with corresponding eight minute audio tapes containing stimulus-response exercises for each lesson were produced. A workbook with written exercises following the structures presented in the video tapes was produced along with a separately bound self-correctional marking key. The resulting package of instructional materials was identified as 'Cours audio visuel de francais, langue seconde'. A course text 'L'Echelle' by Politzer et al was selected to accompany the 'Cours audio visuel' materials as a reference grammar.

The video tape programs were designed to include opportunities for student response to provide reinforcement for the material presented. The structure of the video tape programs and their relationship to the other resources is illustrated in Figure 1.

In the fall registration 126 students enrolled in French 201 and these were assigned into four sections of nominally 30 students each to be taught in the traditional classroom manner. An additional 75 students enrolled in a supplementary section identified as 'section X' and were scheduled to receive instruction via the 'Cours audio visuel' resource materials.

189

Figure 1   Structure of learning resources in 'Cours audio visuel de francais, langue seconde'

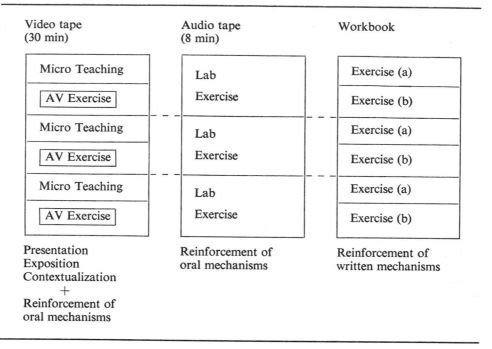

Video tape (30 min)	Audio tape (8 min)	Workbook
Micro Teaching	Lab	Exercise (a)
AV Exercise	Exercise	Exercise (b)
Micro Teaching	Lab	Exercise (a)
AV Exercise	Exercise	Exercise (b)
Micro Teaching	Lab	Exercise (a)
AV Exercise	Exercise	Exercise (b)

Presentation
Exposition
Contextualization
+
Reinforcement of
oral mechanisms

Reinforcement of
oral mechanisms

Reinforcement of
written mechanisms

Figure 2   Instructional format for three treatment groups in introductory French on a weekly basis

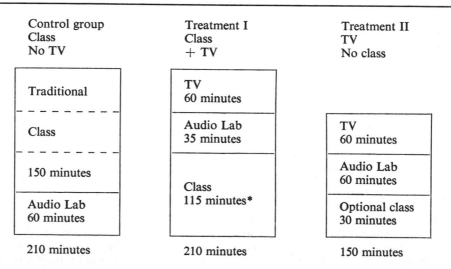

Control group Class No TV	Treatment I Class + TV	Treatment II TV No class
Traditional	TV 60 minutes	
Class	Audio Lab 35 minutes	TV 60 minutes
150 minutes	Class 115 minutes*	Audio Lab 60 minutes
Audio Lab 60 minutes		Optional class 30 minutes
210 minutes	210 minutes	150 minutes

*This group of students was enrolled in the regular Evening Division program which allowed one 115-minute period per week as the equivalent to three 50-minute periods in the Day Division.

The four instructor-taught sections were divided into a control group receiving traditional instruction with laboratory and treatment group I receiving classroom instruction as in the control group but with an expanded laboratory which included the 'Cours audio visuel' resources. Section X was treatment group II receiving all instruction via the 'Cours audio visuel' resources in the laboratory but with no formal classes. The organization of the three groups is shown in Figure 2.

2 Student acceptance and performance

In the first trial year, 1970–1, an extremely high attraction rate of 40 students or 53.3 per cent was observed in treatment group II with an overall attrition rate of 27.8 per cent for the entire class of 201 students. In the year immediately preceding the attrition rate had been 8.3 per cent in a population of 180 students. However, when performance was examined in the three treatment groups it was found that the control group (class alone, no TV) and treatment group II (TV, no class) both scored group averages of 75 points on written and oral tests whereas treatment group I (class with TV) scored a group average of 85 points on the same tests.

Despite the troublesome attrition rate initially experienced the satisfactory academic results in student performance along with the continuing shortage of staff led the department to continue the trial into the second year. In the second year the traditional format of three weekly class meetings was discontinued and the format of treatment group II was used with the addition of regular but optional conversational class meetings, in small groups, which were made available to all students.

In the second year, 1971–2, student acceptance improved as inferred from a reduced dropout or attrition rate of 18.6 per cent in an enrolment of 215 students. The modified format adopted in the second trial has continued to be employed in successive years. Enrolment increased to 241 in 1972–3 and 245 in 1973–4 with attrition rates of 12.4 and 8.1 per cent respectively.

3 Resource management

In the year I offering of 'Cours audio visuel' the available instructional staff was committed to the four class meeting sections. This left the TV section of students somewhat orphaned and in a totally self-study, self-motivating mode. Taggart provided several conversational class meetings for the TV section. These were voluntary on his part and optional for the students. However, these meetings did not commence until well into the second month of the term and were held at infrequent intervals of one to two months. The students dropping out of the course appeared to do so before the commencement of these optional meetings.

In the year II offering of the course the part-time instructional staff was reduced to one person with the equivalent part-time assignment of two courses. This person became responsible for meeting the students, assisting with problems and conducting weekly conversation meetings.

In year I and year II of the project the video tape and audio tape resources were available in the Language Laboratory in carrels used by other students in such a way as to suggest very little spatial autonomy for the course. In year III of the project, with a renovation of facilities, a smaller laboratory room was equipped for this course and a specific area designated in the laboratory complex for the French 201 conversational group meetings. This change has increased the visibility of the French 201 study area and may have improved the students' perception of it as belonging to them.

4 Cost analysis

A precise cost analysis is difficult to construct due to the manner in which universities handle their internal accounting. The analysis does not attempt to compute a full market value for the course but rather to compare the course against itself in the two format modes of traditional instruction and resource-based instruction.

(i) TRADITIONAL

In computing the cost of the traditional format allowance has been made for not more than thirty students per course section. The actual enrolments served by the course have been used in the calculation and since it is planned to use the resource-based approach in the current year, 1975–6, a time frame of six academic

Table 1   Annual and cumulative instructional costs of French 201 (traditional)

Year	Student enrolment	Number of instructors	Total cost of instruction	Cost per student
			$	$
1970–1	201	7	8,400	41.79
1971–2	215	8	10,560	49.12
1972–3	241	8	11,600	48,13
1973–4	245	9	14,400	58.78
1974–5	300	10	17,600	58.67
Total	1,202	42	62,560	52.04

years has been used. In a longitudinal review inflationary increases make comparisons difficult so that in this analysis the salary costs* of base year I, 1970–1, have been used with an annual upward adjustment of ten per cent on the previous year's rate.

The annual and cumulative instructional costs of offering French 201 in the traditional context with the above assumptions are outlined in Table 1.

(ii)   RESOURCE-BASED

In arriving at an annual instructional cost for the resource-based format it was necessary first to compute the original production cost and then to prorate this over the active life of the project. Since the resources have been used in other applications, e.g. workshops, staff non-credit courses, etc, an allowance of ten per cent per year has been made for this supplementary use. The instructional cost of offering the resource-based course will include the annual recurring costs plus the cost of producing the learning resources written off over the six years in which they will have been used.

The development and production costs are as follows:

Direct Fixed Costs (1970–1 dollars)

Existing academic, professional and technical staff	11,950	
Existing equipment and facilities	12,000	
		23,950
New direct costs		12,240
Total Direct Costs		$36,190
Proportion charged to this project @ 90%		$32,580

A pro rata distribution of these production costs over six years yields an annual cost of $5,430 after the ten per cent allowance for supplementary use. The annual and cumulative instructional costs for the resource-base approach are shown in Table 2.

(iii)   COMPARISON

An examination of the costs for these two instructional modes reveals that the costs of the resource-based approach required a term of four years for the developmental and operating costs to come into line with the cost of the traditional approach. In the fifth and subsequent years the savings became significant. By 1974–5 the cumulative costs of the traditional format had exceeded the similar costs for the resource-based format by $18,350 or by 29.3 per cent. It will be noted that in the resource-based context inflationary costs are marginal since the investment in the resource package is resistant to pressures of

---

* All instructional positions are at part-time lecturer stipends. It should be noted that substantially higher costs (or cost reductions) would result if full-time salaries were used in the calculation.

Table 2   Annual and cumulative instructional costs of French 201 (resource-based)

Year	Student enrolment	Number of instructors	Cost of instructors	Cost of resources	Total cost of instruction $	Cost per student $
1970–1	201	4	4,800	5,430	10,230	50.89
1971–2	215	2	2,640	5,430	8,070	37.53
1972–3	241	2	2,900	5,430	8,330	34.56
1973–4	245	2	3,200	5,430	8,630	35.22
1974–5	300	2	3,520	5,430	8,950	29.83
	1,202	12	17,060	27,150*	44,210	36.78

*The use of these materials in 1975–6 as scheduled will complete the write-off of $32,580.

inflation whereas in the traditional context these forces apply fully.

The above analysis has not contained provision for the language laboratory annual operating costs. Such costs would be incurred in either approach and the objective here has not been to show the complete cost of teaching a second language but rather the comparative costs for those aspects of the two formats which differ.

The analysis has assumed a constant class size of thirty students per section in the traditional format. However, Taggart reports that in 1974–5 only a smaller class section size approaching twenty students each could be envisaged. On this basis the instructional staff required would be fifteen appointments at an annual cost of $26,400 as compared with the demonstrated cost of $8,950 for the resource-based approach. Thus the advantage to the department in resource allocation is more striking in actuality than that shown in the analysis.

5   *Student evaluation*

The resource-based approach continued to be offered each year through 1975–6 and during a special summer school offering of the course in the summer of 1975 the students were invited to respond to this instructional approach. Thirty students completed the six-week offering of the course and during week four they completed a thirteen item evaluative inventory. Ninety per cent of student responses indicated a positive attitude to the course.

Student attitudes to the media resources were surveyed with respect to the television, workbook and audio exercises. Seventy-seven per cent of the group indicated 'somewhat' to 'extremely favourable' attitudes to the televised resources and sixty-three per cent registered similar attitudes to the workbook. Specifically unfavourable attitudes were indicated respectively to these resources by ten and thirteen per cent of the students. Attitudes to the audio exercises were indeterminate.

From the response of the students surveyed it may be inferred that this resource-based approach has met with general acceptance and no evidence was found of overall rejection although areas were identified for improvement.

Discussion and Conclusion

In assessing the experience of this instructional development project several points are suggested from the data.

1 A specific and significant instructional problem was identified within an academic department.

2 Interaction between the department and an instructional support agency facilitated the formulation of a plan of action.

3 The resulting plan built upon an already well developed interest in

instructional modification with the department.

4 Supplementary funding was available as required from central university resources to actualize the plan.

5 In-process evaluation and project modification were carried out to meet a serious student rejection phenomenon as inferred from the initially high attrition rate.

6 The project was given adequate run-in time to overcome its problems.

7 The project has demonstrated that cost benefits are achievable in a sustained resource-based learning application.

8 Cost benefits are functions of size of the target population, duration of the format application and role distribution between human and material resources.

9 In this application a complete removal of teacher-student interaction in favour of a total mediated format was not accepted.

10 The project has benefited the department by providing for extended deployment of teaching staff into higher level courses. The current offering of the department could not be sustained in the absence of this resource-based approach.

11 A resource-based learning strategy is relatively flexible in terms of student enrolment.

12 The existing materials are now rapidly aging and a new educational management problem has emerged. What are the department's instructional plans as the present resources approach terminal utility?

In summary it may be stated that from the study of this project a resource-based approach to learning can be expected to provide a viable alternative to traditional labour intensive approaches. Cost benefits may be attributed in a specific application but the major advantages appear to be in improved human instructional resource allocation and in the flexibility afforded to students enrolled and in the number of students admitted for study. It should be noted that in this project a mix of live teacher contact and learning resources was required to achieve these results.

References

1 PARLETT, M., and HAMILTON, D., *Evaluation as Illumination: A New Approach to the Study of Innovatory Programs.* Occasional Paper 9, Centre for Research in the Educational Sciences, University of Edinburgh, 1972.

2 TAGGART, G. *Etude Experimentale de Certains stimulus auditifs et visuels dans l'acquisition d'une langue seconde,* L'Université de Montreal, 1969. (Unpublished doctoral dissertation.)

PAPER NO 43: THROUGH A GLASS DARKLY

Frank Morgan, Senior Lecturer in Educational Media, Canberra College of Advanced Education, Australia.

Introduction

The truth is, I suspect, that we refer to research principally to support or justify the decisions we would prefer to make, or to clarify and elucidate those we have made already. Either way, the decision is made first, more or less tentatively, and only later subjected to the light of research.

Several modern philosophers have paid attention to the idea of agency, that is, of beings taking initiating or planning action involving bodily behaviour, meanwhile knowing what they are intending and doing. Andersen stresses the importance to education of seeing human beings as agents. Yet Popper reminds us, that whilst through seeking we may know things better, we cannot know the final truth,

'For all is but a woven web of guesses.'

This is a salutory reminder for the scientist (natural, behavioural, or social) struggling to formulate a problem, studying the literature, scanning his own experience (and that of others), or awaiting an inventive leap of the mind. It is even more salutory for the technologist. Baker surveyed the literature on the technology of instructional design, examining first the linear models which propose:

(i) that technology is the derivative, or application, of an underlying science,

(ii) that research is the free pursuit of understandings of phenomena,

(iii) that development is the design and refinement of processes and products, on the basis of such understandings, and,

(iv) that, both logically and operationally, research must precede development.

Her conclusion, however, was that research is more a case of deliberate enquiry than of free pursuit, and that frequently it is stimulated by prior developmental problems. Development is more intricate, tortuous, and often discontinuous, a process more complex than is suggested by the neat linear and cyclical paths of classical systems theory. This would seem particularly to be so in the case of educational technology, with its relationships to the physical, behavioural and social sciences (not to mention the arts).

The experience to be reported here supports the conclusion that pragmatic considerations take precedence over the theoretical in determining the production and use of educational media, due largely to the failure of media research to generate sufficiently compelling prescriptions for producers, managers and teachers. It also supports the view that decision-makers draw eclectically upon research, as grist for their mills, and retrospectively to elucidate the decisions they make. The paper is admittedly subjective, yet thereby consistent with the phenomenological view of Greenfield that social reality is the perception by individuals of what they can, should, or must do in dealing with others.

Finally, it suggests that future research and theory will need to accommodate this wider range of variables.

The Context

Colleges of advanced education, together with universities and teachers colleges, are part of the national system of higher education in Australia. The Martin Report, commissioned by the Australian government in 1961 and presented in 1964, recommended greater diversity in the universities, and the establishment of a new system of tertiary colleges, different from but equal to the universities.

The new colleges would draw their students from a wider range of the socio-economic spectrum, and (compared with the universities) they would have a greater technological emphasis, pay less attention to postgraduate training, and place primary emphasis on teaching rather than research.

In 1967, a diverse collection of existing colleges of technology, music, agriculture, and so on, was recognized by the Commonwealth as the initial group of colleges of advanced education. Also, some new institutions were established, among them the Canberra College of Advanced Education.

By 1975, the Canberra College had grown to have an enrolment of 4659 (1969 full-time; 2690 part-time) and a teaching staff of 261. Its academic programs were closely similar to those of most universities in North America, many in Europe and several of the newer ones in Australia. It had six schools (of Administrative Studies, Applied Science, Environmental Design, Information Sciences, Liberal Studies and Teacher Education), offering both sub-graduate and graduate diplomas, bachelors degrees and (in education) a masters degree. Various short-courses were offered, but, despite the majority of part-time students, no extra-mural program.

The project

The Instructional Media Centre of the Canberra College of Advanced Education was proposed in the College's submission for funds for the triennium 1973–5. The proposal was in two parts. The School of Teacher Education proposed the Centre

> to assist staff in defining appropriate courses, in developing suitable methods using the range of available media and equipment, and in utilizing reliable and valuable means of assessment.

and echoed the Martin Report in pointing out the College's commitment to a high quality of teaching. This proposal was linked (*inter alia*) with one to establish a course, eventually to become a masters degree in education, with a specialization in educational media.

Elsewhere in the submission, the College Administration argued the urgent need for a central facility for audio visual work on the grounds of possible economies of expenditure. The models implicit in the two parts of this proposal could both be called technical, but are quite disparate. By tech-

195

nical, one meant the techniques of teaching and curriculum development, and the other the management and operation of equipment and materials. These disparate emphases indicate the disparate perceptions and personal preferences of their different authors.

The disparity is clarified by Merritt (1971) in an analogy with biological systems. Merritt proposed that they have six levels of subsystem, related hierarchically in descending order:

(06) Evaluative systems e.g. those which relate to preferences and priorities,
(05) Epistemic systems e.g. those which facilitate the acquisition and organiza- of knowledge,
(04) Co-operant systems e.g. those which affect social relationships,
(03) Operant systems e.g. the ambulatory and manipulative systems,
(02) Responding systems e.g. the sensory nervous system.
(01) Maintenance system e.g. the respiratory and circulatory systems.

The old visual aids view of the media in the curriculum was that they were simply devices for the delivery of alternative sensory stimuli. Little or no attention was paid to their implications for the social organization of learning, to their capacity to modify meanings, or to their power to affect values. Thus, they were related only to the lower three levels of a learning system, seen in terms of this model. At the 01 level they involved considerations of power supply, blackout blinds, and equipment availability, at the 02 level the choice of sense modality, and at the 03 level the manipulation of materials and equipment. The curriculum development view extends consideration to the 04 level with questions of social organization such as whether to individualize instruction, to broadcast to remote students, to provide flexible timetables, or to build open classrooms; to the 05 level with questions of the cognitive learning outcomes from various media; and to the 06 level with questions of affective outcomes.

At the beginning of 1972, a senior lecturer in educational media was appointed (*inter alia*) 'to assist the Principal, through the Head of School of Teacher Education ... in the detailed planning of the proposed Instructional Media Centre'. In fact, this appointment constituted the establishment of the Centre. A separate budget was provided, and the immediate demand for services precluded any passive planning stage. Theoretically, it may be possible to distinguish between plan and action, and to divide plans into logically sequential components of gathering data, defining objectives, implementation and evaluation. Practically, in this case at least, the components were telescoped in time, and action was based more often on intuition and 'experience' than on hard data. And, to the complex of perceptions and preferences mentioned above, were added those of the people employed to implement the project.

The original staff of the Centre was a senior lecturer and a technical officer. The staff proposed for 1975 in the original triennial plan was 1 principal lecturer, 2 lecturers, 4 technicians and a clerical assistant. In the event, the staff in 1975 comprised 1 senior lecturer, 1 lecturer, 1 electronics technician, 2 photographers, 2 graphic artists, 2 clerical assistants, (the equivalent of) 6 operators and a library assistant (supplied by the library).

The two academics, as members of the School of Teacher Education, taught media courses to students both undergraduate and postgraduate. They worked in staff development programs, and assisted teaching staff with the design, production and evaluation of media materials. They administered the media production and delivery services for the college. Both were experienced teachers and media producers. One had worked in broadcasting, the other in the film industry.

Routine production and delivery services were established to provide teaching staff with maximal access to support staff and technical facilities, and students with media materials and activities both in class and as a directly accessible resource.

During the period 1972–5, the Instructional Media Centre operated in temporary accommodation in the College Library. In July 1973, a brief was prepared by the staff, for a building to house the Centre permanently. After some skirmishing, the funds and final documentation were approved at the end of 1974. The building is due for completion in April 1976, at a cost of $A1.3 million.

Television has been developed as part of an integrated media system, rather than separately. It has been used in three major ways: to produce teaching material, to provide simulation experiences, and to enable students to learn to produce their own programs.

Teaching material has been produced in two ways: by video-taping broadcasts and by shooting and editing original material. The most extensive use of off-air material has been for the teaching of education, sociology, law, politics, history, biology, drama, English (as a second language) and professional writing. On average, each hour of recorded material has been replayed for about 70 student-hours. The largest amount of original material produced has been for the School of Teacher Education, most of it observations of classroom practices and interactions. Such material has been produced fairly widely elsewhere using studio cameras connected to a mobile van or other outside-broadcast-type facility. This technique required lights, microphones and large crews. Its obtrusion on the situation under observation frequently interfered with the value and validity of the material recorded. A less obtrusive technique has been developed, therefore, using tape recorders (Sony, model AV-3420 CE), remote directional microphones, available light, and crews as small as three for a two-camera operation.

Finished tapes are catalogued in the central Library index, lodged in the audio-visual collection in the Media Centre, and then are available for use by staff and students as required throughout the 75 hours in which the Centre is open each week. A member of staff wishing to show a video-tape to a class can book its replay in a lecture theatre or a small tutorial room and in either case can have hands-on control of the video-tape recorder. Alternatively students can be referred to the tape individually. Individuals can see tapes on a monitor in a carrell or can use a small viewing room. Students often use video-tapes to augment the papers they present to seminars. Video-tapes are used as components of live teaching situations, or as reference material, rather than as substitutes for lectures.

Video-tape has been used extensively in the college for simulation activities, and in particular microteaching in the School of Teacher Education. Elsewhere in the college similar activities have been used with encounter groups by the student counsellor, for training systems analysts and public administrators.

Student teachers, librarians, journalists, scientists and drama students have been given courses in television production appropriate to their needs and interests.

The cost of the television service is almost impossible to isolate, because of its integration with the other media services. Still photographers are used as television cameramen, cine projectionists as video-tape operators and the carrel supervisor manages slides, audio-tapes and so on as well. Together, the Media Centre and Television Service costs in 1974–5 were approximately \$A160,000—or an average cost of \$A34.50 per student.

There were 17,500 student hours of viewing in the year, making a cost of \$A1.22 per student-hour of replay-time. This does not account for the time spent by students in simulation gaming, or in producing their own program material for course projects.

Insights from research

Insight, psychologically, describes both a type of problem-solving (the Ah so! type) and the understanding of one's own behaviour. The experience reported above has drawn insight from a number of research areas.

The overall state of media research has been seen to give teachers a sound theoretical reason to stretch other pragmatic constraints to the limit to exercise their personal preferences in the selection of educational media. The plethora of available cross-media studies shows that television and other media can teach most things to most people about as well as a traditional instructor. A need remains for more attention to the attributes of particular media and it seems plausible that such attention to television would result in more findings of significant differences between television and alternative instructional treatments. Yet, it has been suggested that attention should be diverted away from particular media to mixes of media, and the results attributable to them. Taken together with work on the significance of teachers' attitudes and the social organization of learning situations upon students' learning, this diversion may lead back to no significant differences, due to generally improved effectiveness. Cost-effectiveness considerations seem sometimes to have led to inhibited or inappropriate developments in television. The criteria for determining cost-effectiveness, however, seemed to need further clarification.

Procedures for analyzing and formulating program content and desired outcomes have been accessible through the available taxonomies of educational objectives, the application of learning theory to instructional design, and communication theory.

Algorithms for the design of programs have not been accessible, but this is not surprising in the light of research into the relationship between language development and learning, particularly given that a language is a set of symbols which people use to create meanings for themselves, and to convey them to others, and the absence of any universal rules for contextual determination or production. Some attempts have been made to consider film as a language object, yet here it seems that educational technology needs to recall the artistry of science, and to recognize the scientific respectability of the creative leaps made occasionally by the best media producers. Too often the results of a mechanical approach have been media materials which fail either to delight or to instruct. It may be even that all teaching behaviour is akin to a language object. It has been suggested that teacher education would be improved by drawing on Stanislavsky's method approach to acting. Perhaps a similar approach, focussing on the best artistic developments in cinema and broadcasting, would enrich the repertoires of teachers, managers and media producers.

Perhaps my most striking personal insight into the relationship between research and development in educational television came in a conversation, several years ago, with Ed Palmer, the research director of the Children's Television Workshop. Upon which learning theory, I asked, had *Sesame Street* been modelled? Was it Dienes' of multiple embodiment of concepts? Or Ausubel's of organizers? No, he said, it was inspired by the variety show *Laugh In*. Ah so! And *Laugh In* was inspired by *The Goon Show*. And so, folks, perhaps Ned Seegoon was right, and it is all in the mind.

Summary

The paper is a case study of the development of educational television in a college of advanced education in Australia. It describes significant decisions made in the process of that development and their relation to a number of determinants, including both theoretical and pragmatic factors.

The pragmatic factors to which particular attention is paid are the skills and preferences of the people involved in the project, the financial and material resources available, the time-scale of the project, and the educational context within which it has been set.

The more political of these pragmatic factors is given a theoretical framework by the phenomenological view of organizations. The other theoretical factors considered are derived from learning theory, from cross-media comparisons of instructional effectiveness, from communication theory and from the sociology of learning situations. Account is also taken of work on language acquisition and the analytical study of the cinema and television.

Underlying the discussion are questions of the relationships between science and technology, and research and development. Reference is made to a review of the literature on instructional design, which concluded that research is a process heavily dependent, both in itself and in its application, upon inventive leaps of the mind. The experience reported supports the view that research relates to development primarily in a retrospective fashion, to clarify the significance and meaning o events or to justify certain preferred events. Prospective decision-making seems to be determined much more by pragmatic factors than by theory. To the extent that theory does influence decision-making it seems to be through the creation of general sets of attitudes rather than through specific prescriptions to be implemented mechanically.

Another underlying question discussed is whether it is possible for people to know absolutely what they are doing and planning, or whether they can only guess at the reality of their experience.

The frequently reported findings of no significant differences between traditional instructional and alternative media treatments are taken as theoretical justification for teachers to exercise their personal preferences and skills in the selection and use of educational media. The evidence from studies of the power of students' and teachers' attitudes to determine learning outcomes is seen as another reason for people to exercise their personal judgement. Further evidence relating to the social organization of learning situations is seen similarly. A remaining constraint is consideration of cost-effectiveness. Yet the experience reported, and the literature cited, suggest that existing measures of effectiveness need refinement. The project reported has cost less than one per cent per annum of the recurrent cost of the college in which it was placed, and it is considered doubtful that effectiveness could be measured meaningfully to that accuracy.

The study supports the view that pragmatic factors take precedence over theory in such an exercise. However, it also strongly supports the view that traditional mechanistic views of the place of media (such as television) in the curriculum are much less adequate than a view which sees them significantly affecting the social organization, and the epistemic and evaluative outcomes, of learning. The media, as extensions of man, are seen as extensions not just of the nervous system, or the body, but also of the mind.

In this connection, the paper recalls the creative aspects of science, the scientific respectability of inventive leaps of the mind, and suggests the need for educational technology, with its relationships to the physical, behavioural, and social sciences, to take greater account of the arts also.

PAPER NO 18: MORE THAN MEETS THE EYE: DISCREPANCIES IN COGNITIVE AND AFFECTIVE ADULT STUDENTS' RESPONSES TO LIVE TELEVISION PRODUCTION STYLES

David Giltrow, Dean of Media Research and Production, City Colleges of Chicago, USA.

Introduction

In the light of the Children's Television Workshop research-guided productions of *Sesame Street* and *The Electric Company*, relatively inexpensive production styles such as camera in the back of a classroom and the simple studio set with the camera on the teacher have drawn harsh criticism. A theoretical basis for this criticism has been that the available audio-visual message capacity is not being used to its full potential, particularly the visual portion, in the simpler, teacher-centered styles.

Arguments in favor of the faster paced, more visually complex commercial style for instructional television go against the small body of media research which indicates that unnecessary embellishments do not add to cognitive gain for the viewer and, in fact, can detract from overall cognitive performance. The unanswered question arising from the Children's Television Workshop research and use of commercial production styles is: can the techniques which apply to appropriate use of the media for under-privileged preschoolers and 4th/5th graders in teaching basic alpha-numeric literacy be used with the same success for adults enrolled in college courses?

Recent programing by TV College of the City Colleges of Chicago presented an opportunity to conduct an evaluation of two distinctly different instructional television production styles for adult open-learning students. In this research a Miami-Dade (Florida) Community College documentary film program which was part of the 30-program series *Man and Environment* (M & E) was compared with a program locally produced by TV College (TVC) which was broadcast back-to-back with the M & E program. This programing was part of the Miami-Dade instructional design for the television course in *Environmental Science*.

The M & E program, *Individual Maladjustment*, contains a wide variety of filmed sequences—dramatic sequences, animated filmographs combining old photographs and newsreels, and man-in-the-street interviews—including specially filmed as well as stock footage from a variety of locations in the United States and the rest of the world. The voice-over narration was professionally done and designed to integrate with the accompanying textbook. Some

199

sequences contained synchronized sound. Music and sound effects combined with the picture to form a high quality documentary format program. The cost was estimated at $1,000 per minute.

The complementary Chicago TV College production, *The Individual in an Urban Environment*, featured the course instructor, Professor Roger Podewell, as host for a talk show format. His guest was an expert from a well known local arboretum who spoke of his concern for the role of plants and gardens interacting with people's lives in the urban setting. The discussion included 35 mm color slides from New York, Philadelphia and Chicago which had been taken by the guest in the course of his work. No film footage was included and the audio was limited to the two gentlemen speaking in a limbo setting in a television studio. The cost of the program was approximately $100 per minute.

Purpose
The purpose of the study was to determine which of the two production formats was more successful in meeting the needs of our students in terms of both their learning, and their satisfaction with the program formats. We were particularly interested in the following questions:

1 Which of the two programs provides more cognitive gain?
2 Which production format is more attractive to the students?
3 Which of the two program styles has had more impact on their attitudes toward environmental issues?
4 Which format would the students prefer to have as their television style?

Notice that while the first of these questions deals with the cognitive gain, or *learning* of the students, each of the last three questions is concerned in some way with how the students *feel* about the different formats. Thus our investigation followed in large part the distinction traditionally made in the psychological literature between *cognition* (learning, knowing, etc.) and *affect* (feeling, attitude, etc.).

Procedure
A decision was made to conduct telephone interviews rather than rely upon paper and pencil questionnaires. This decision was independently reinforced by researchers from SUN (State University of Nebraska) who felt that personal interviews enriched their understanding of the data. Since we were interested in developing insights into what people recalled from the programs and what they felt about the programs, the interview approach provided an optimum vehicle for the student to express impressions and knowledge without being limited to forced choices. The interviewing period began shortly after the programs were shown and was completed within 72 hours after the broadcasts. Students were informed by letter that they would be interviewed.

Out of a pool of 361 students enrolled for credit in the Environmental Studies 102 course, 60 were randomly selected and each researcher was assigned 20 students to interview. There were 24 people who either were not reached or had not seen the programs. Out of the 60 initially selected, 36 completed the interview.

The sample selected from the course roster was found to be typical of current TVC students with regard to characteristics such as sex (53 per cent females), age (average 31 years), and number of credits accumulated (average 30 semester hours, or one year's previous college work).

Selection of the programs for comparison was based primarily upon their being broadcast prior to the first of three examinations but after the students had already viewed five sets of the film-simple production combinations.

Results
The questions in the telephone interview were designed to yield information about:

1 Students' viewing habits.
2 Their cognitive ability to recall and interpret visual and spoken material from the two programs under study.
3 Their affective responses to the two production styles along a number of dimensions.

The telephone interviews were tape recorded with the students' permission and then content analyzed later. This permitted greater accuracy and reliability.

At least two interesting pieces of information emerged from the questions regarding viewing habits:

1 While only 46 per cent of the respondents indicated that they read the text prior to watching the lesson, 84 per cent indicated that they read the locally produced study guide prior to viewing.

2 Only 59 per cent of the respondents indicated that they take notes during the telecast, but a surprising 51 per cent tape record the shows. The reason for such a high incidence of recorders, inferred from student interview comments, is the feeling that it is too difficult to watch and write at the same time, particularly during the M & E series programs.

In order to obtain a rough measure of relative cognitive gain, two interview questions were put to the students for each of the programs under consideration. The students were asked to name images or sequences of images which stood out in their minds from the program, and then to state any ideas or meanings that they associated with those images. While this question asked for recall and interpretation moving from the specific recalled image to an abstracted idea, the second question for each program was designed to reverse the order. That is, the subjects were asked to state their impression of the main idea of each of the programs and then to support that impression with any relevant images or spoken lines from the programs. Our working hypothesis was that students would be able to recall more images from the M & E program, since there were many more images in that program, but that there would be a greater accuracy and consistency in the stating of main ideas and associated meanings for the TVC production.

In abstracting main ideas, 58 per cent of the respondents correctly stated the important theme of the TVC program, 16 per cent stated a relevant but not a central idea of the program, and 26 per cent did not state any relevant ideas. Although roughly the same percentage of respondents for the M & E program as for the TVC production did not state any relevant ideas, there were no students who stated the principal theme of the M & E program. The specific phrase 'individual maladjustment', the official title and theme of the M & E show, was not mentioned by any respondent during the interview, in contrast to multiple student references to the phrase 'people-plant interaction', the theme of the TVC program.

More spoken lines and images were recalled from the M & E program than from the TVC program (3 to 2 ratio). This difference may be due to a less visual viewing style employed by the students for the more static TVC production, or simply to a more limited selection of images from which to recall.

On the other hand, no spoken lines at all were recalled from the M & E program as opposed to 10 specific recollections of lines (or paraphrasings of lines) from the TVC program. This difference might be attributable to a more aural than visual type of attention for the TVC program, or to the closer connection of spoken lines to main theme in the TVC program.

The interview was concluded with a series of affective questions, designed to gauge the students' cumulative feeling toward the two program styles after their having seen at least six programs of each style. The questions in this series asked the students:

1 Which style he finds more interesting?
2 What style of narration he prefers?
3 Which style he thinks he learns more from?
4 Which style he thinks has made a greater impact on his attitude toward environmental issues?

Thus in asking a student these questions, we do not expect that he/she will *know* the answer so much as that he/she will *feel* the answers and express an *opinion*.

The results indicate that a consistent majority (65 per cent) of respondents favor the M & E production style for each of the four questions enumerated above. A fifth question offered three choices to the students: to vote for the M & E style, the TVC style, or the alternating pattern to which they had been exposed in the course. Surprisingly, a solid majority (67 per cent) of the respondents chose the last category, indicating a clear preference for some combination of production styles.

Conclusions and implications
It should be noted before stating our conclusions that we would, of course, like to

have employed a true experimental design in this comparative study of ITV presentation styles. In our situation, however, the demands of such a design were prohibitive. Some of our procedures illustrate our desire for a design which was as rigorous as possible, given our limitations: the choosing of two programs with at least complementary content (adaptation to an urban environment), the constructing of a questionnaire which we thought was not biased toward either presentation style, and the random selection of the study sample.

The basic conclusion to be reached from our results concerns the discrepancies between the cognitive and affective measures. If we were to look only at the results of the questions designed to elicit *affective* responses, we would conclude that the documentary film style (M & E) is clearly the expressed favorite. If we look, however, at the responses to the 'cognitive' questions, in which the student is asked to demonstrate his *learning*, we find that students are much better able to recall the main ideas together with related images and lines from the TVC program than from the M & E program.

There seems to be a need, at least among credit students, for some kind of combination of the two styles of presentation. This notion is reinforced by the fact that two-thirds of our respondents would vote for an alternating pattern of the two formats.

It should be remembered that the M & E producers intended that the filmed program be followed either immediately or later in the week by the locally oriented and produced television show. The present study seems to support that pattern where interest is aroused and stimulated and the local teacher takes advantage of the interest to develop an idea in greater depth.

This study also suggests a production design for *single* programs consisting of an alternating or checker-board pattern of:

1 Polished dramatic and documentary-type location sequences.
2 Instructor-directed discussions preceding or following them.

Such a format would integrate the affective pulling power of the M & E style with the less information dense, central figure style of TVC productions. This is a common sense approach but one which can get aborted by the sincere but misguided desire to be 'creative' at the expense of solid instruction.

We would remind producers of the 10 to 1 cost factor between the two styles and the clearly better cognitive learning results from the more direct style.

The study's limitations are readily apparent (order effects, single treatment, limited sample, no control or delayed vs immediate recall effects, etc). However, we would note the consistency with other, more elaborate studies. As evaluators involved with providing administrative and production personnel with clearly understandable and operational suggestions, we are the college's only unbiased interface with our open learning students. By combining telephone contact together with traditional paper and pencil evaluations, we feel our work takes on more meaning and has greater validity.

PAPER NO 29: THE TELEVISION AGRICULTURAL SECONDARY SCHOOL IN POLAND

Richard Janucik, Researcher, The Main Centre of Improvement of Cadres and Popularization of Progress in Agriculture, Poland.

Origins, aims and tasks
The idea of the creation of an educational television system for agriculture in Poland was put forward six years ago to get more skilled cadres for the Polish farms. The initiative met the objective needs of peasants and especially young people in rural areas. The organizers' main target was to extend extra-mural non-residential agricultural education at the secondary level and to connect it with modern farming. They wanted to give more effective help to students directly in their homes.

The existing number of schools and teachers made it impossible to enable all those wishing to acquire qualifications in farming to attend residential schools. The newly created TV educational system has provided possibilities to increase substantially the number of extra-mural students.

The social and educational tasks which the TV Agricultural Secondary School (ASS) set itself are as follows:

1 To create possibilities of further education to all those who for various reasons could not continue studies at residential or non-residential agricultural secondary schools.
2 To create an efficient form of assistance in self-education to agricultural workers studying at evening secondary schools and extra-mural courses.
3 To popularize the best didactic experience in agricultural education by means of television.
4 To create possibilities to enhance farming skills and general education in an informal way for people working in agriculture and interested in an improvement of their vocational qualifications.

The main aim of the TV Agricultural Secondary School is to train cadres for individual and socialized farms at the secondary educational level.

The introduction of the TV ASS courses was preceded by one year's preparatory work on the organizational conception of the scheme, the programme and the curricula of studies, the textbooks, and training headmasters and teachers of extra-mural educational centres. This short period of preparatory work showed the need to base the TV courses on the existing curricula of studies of residential agricultural schools and their textbooks.

Study materials
Apart from that, special methodological materials were designed (study guides, which were used also as exercise books and intended for learning individual subjects) with the aim of helping students in their self-education through appropriate instruction, and in the combining of knowledge acquired from textbooks with the knowledge supplied by the TV lessons. An original and innovative form of assistance in studies is also provided to the TV ASS students by the weekly 'Mlody Rolnik' ('Young Farmer') which brings information on the organization of the school, methodological instructions and specially prepared materials corresponding to some of the subjects or lessons.

The TV ASS lessons are broadcast by local and central TV stations on Channel 1 to all students of the School all over Poland. The TV lessons embrace all the subjects of the curricula of studies for the first two years of a typical residential agricultural secondary school.

The series of lessons is composed of 440 programmes, each 30 minutes long. The lessons are broadcast during the week in such a way that every particular subject is transmitted on the same day and hour of the week, between 12.45 and 3.45 pm. All the lessons are repeated in the same way on the following day between 6.30 and 8.30.

The programme of teaching embraces 7 terms, i.e. 3.5 years. For several reasons, and especially because of the limited broadcasting facilities of Polish Television, the TV ASS broadcasts only the lessons for the first four terms, i.e. the first two years of studies. The remaining three terms, that is 1.5 year of studies, can be completed by the TV ASS students at the traditional extra-mural agricultural secondary schools. After the completion of two years of studies the TV ASS students receive certificates enabling them to study for the third year within the traditional educational system, that is without the aid of TV. After the completion of the whole 3.5 year programme of studies, the students take their final examinations (corresponding to the British 'A' level).

Student requirements
All those who want to study at the TV ASS must meet the following requirements:

1 To work directly in socialized or private farms.
2 To complete a basic agricultural school or an agricultural training school, or to take three degrees in agricultural training, to have a certificate of a qualified worker or a diploma of a master in farming.

Candidates for TV ASS are admitted without entrance examinations. However, some must complete a special initial term preparing them to start studies at the TV ASS, according to their previous education or farming experience.

The students of the TV ASS are expected to watch the TV lesson, carry out systematically all the recommendations and exercises contained in the study guides, send their homework to the technical schools in which they are registered and receive tutorials, and pass the examinations at the end of every successive term of studies and the final examinations for the TV ASS diploma.

The whole of the work of the TV ASS students is coordinated by the schools in which they are registered during periodical didactical meetings. Such meetings of the TV ASS students are held at the beginning and the end of each term. The first of them has an organizational and didactical character, while the second one is devoted to revision of the whole of the material and examinations. Apart from that, individual and group tutorials are provided by every school in accordance to the needs of students and the facilities available at any given school.

TV ASS in the light of the present research
Along with the inauguration of the activities of the TV ASS, scientific research has been carried out on all the problems connected with this form of education. Research work has been conducted by the Higher School of Agriculture, the Institute of the Development of the Countryside and Agriculture, the Centre of Research on Public Opinion and Programme Studies, and many other centres.

The results of research in this field obtained by the above mentioned centres were identical or similar. This applies both to the research conducted during the initial period of the activities of the TV ASS and the recent ones. This paper is based above all on the research of the Centre of Research on Public Opinion and Programme Studies.

Great attention was devoted to the socio-economic characteristics of the TV ASS students. The analysis of the data concerning the period up to June 1975 proved that the socio-vocational structure of the people attending the first term of studies was as follows:

individual farmers	70%
members of farming co-operatives and workers of state farms	4%
vocations connected with agriculture	9%
not connected with agriculture	11%
non-working people	6%

The above data shows that those connected with agriculture in one form or another constituted the decisive majority.

Of those students of TV ASS who were working, 81 per cent were under 29 years of age. People over 50 accounted for only 1 per cent. The proportions of female and male students were roughly equal.

An essential question for the researchers was the period of time which had elapsed since the students left school of lower level. The most numerous group (63 per cent) were students who had left school no more than 5 years before they started studies at the TV ASS. 12 per cent had discontinued education more than 10 years previously.

Thus the average student of the first term of the TV ASS was a young man or woman, most often an individual farmer or working directly in agriculture or a similar vocation, who had completed education at the primary school level relatively not long before he (or she) joined the TV ASS.

A total of 18,400 people applied for the admission to the TV ASS which inaugurated its first term in February 1973. 4,200 students attended semestral meetings. Out of the total number of candidates, 87 per cent attended organizational meetings and the first tests were sent in by 50–70 per cent of students. After the first term 4,356 passed examinations; this accounted for 35 per cent of those who attended organizational meetings, plus another 5 per cent of those who joined the correspondence-and-meeting system (a traditional system without the aid of television).

Motivation to start
The completion of the TV ASS could be interpreted either as a road to the countryside and agriculture or as a way of escape from the countryside through the acquisition of secondary education. However, the research indicates a commitment to agriculture. 67 per cent of individual farmers are of the opinion that the completion of the studies at the TV ASS will help them to run their farms better and in a more modern way, 44 per cent hope that it will help them enhance the profitability of their farms owing to the knowledge acquired at the TV ASS, and 38 per cent of individual farmers started the studies because, as they say, they were always interested in agricultural studies. The same three motives were

given as reasons to continue studies in the second term.

Out of the total number of working students, 36 per cent want to earn more in future, 31 per cent want to continue studies at schools of higher learning, 30 per cent want to complete the studies at the TV ASS in order to implement their work better. The opinion prevails that a man with secondary education enjoys greater respect in his community. An insignificant percentage of people covered by the research treated their studies at the TV ASS as a way of escape from the countryside. As many as 71 per cent of young individual farmers studying at the first term stated that they intended to continue to work in agriculture. About 20 per cent of the young student farmers planned to take over or lease a farm.

The analysis presented above suggests that farmers have begun to regard work in agriculture as a vocation requiring expert training and education. The research shows that the importance of having agricultural knowledge has been increasing, as in many other fields.

The students of the TV ASS are people seeking agricultural knowledge in various sources. The research showed that 89 per cent of them avail themselves of the TV lectures on agriculture. Yet the fact that the youngest students show the lowest interest in taking advantage of previously existing forms of agricultural education is alarming. According to the answers concerning the motives of choice of this system of education, TV lectures are regarded by students as an attractive form of study, especially as a 'school at home'.

As many as 72 per cent justified convincingly their choice by stating that they 'can learn without having to leave home'. They also expect the TV system to provide a high standard of teaching using attractive and efficient didactic methods. The consequences of this opinion should be regarded as satisfactory. This is proved by the fact that 46 per cent of students of the first term continued studies in the second term lasting from September 1973 to February 1974. It should be added that the social structure of students in the second term did not change significantly in spite of the nearly 50 per cent decrease in the number of students.

The percentage of female and male students (48 per cent and 52 per cent respectively during the first term) did not change in the second term. Compared with the average decrease in number of students of extramural schools, which amounts to around 75 per cent, the figure of 54 per cent reduction after the first term of the TV ASS may be regarded as supporting the continued development of this form of school. It proves that the television system of agricultural education is successful.

The evaluation of TV lectures

The research showed that in spite of the distance between the broadcaster and the receiver, 66 per cent of those covered by the research said that they had sometimes or almost always an impression of a direct contact with lecturers; 25 per cent of them had such an impression almost all the time. According to the results of the research, TV lectures provide a real assistance. In general, except for objectively difficult subjects such as mathematics, chemistry and mechanization of agriculture, 87–93 per cent of students stated that TV lectures during the first term were satisfactorily easy and interesting.

Questions about the day, hour and frequency of broadcasting the TV lectures show that the majority (94 per cent) of students found them convenient. The remaining 6 per cent suggested changes, as, for example, broadcasting the lectures also on Sundays. As regards the frequency of broadcasting, the difference in opinion was almost identical. The present frequency was accepted by 85 per cent, the remaining 15 per cent suggested various solutions, as, for instance, more lectures on subjects considered as particularly difficult. The greatest number of reservations was aroused by the time of broadcasting the lectures and their repeats. 85 per cent accepted the hour of broadcasting; the majority of those suggesting changes would like to watch TV lessons a little later in the day, preferably after 4 pm. These were people working in socialized enterprises. A very low percentage suggested earlier hours. Most of the reservations concerned the hours of the repeats which were found inconvenient by 67 per cent, but no clear preference for alternative times emerged.

Tutorials

The research proved that tutorials are an indispensable link between the broadcaster and the receiver. 83 per cent of students made use of tutorials which were held once a month on the average. The tutorials were usually organized institutionally by the management of respective extra-mural secondary technical schools and not at the request of students. 61 per cent of the students questioned stated that the consulting teachers were not able to devote them as much time as they needed. 25 per cent of the students suggested that consultations should be organized according to needs, especially as regards subjects considered as difficult.

It appears then that in the opinion of students the frequency of consultations—once a month—is insufficient. Some students (20 per cent) also suggested that during the consultations stress should be laid on practical training, independent of the subject.

The researchers also studied the problem of efficient forms of didactic work. The results confirmed the pedagogical principle that a lecture conducted in a consultative form, arousing cognitive interest among students, is more effective than the traditional type of a lecture conveying ready knowledge. Nearly 50 per cent of students were against the traditional lessons conducted during tutorials.

Textbooks

Three of the textbooks, i.e. those for mathematics, chemistry and mechanization of agriculture, were recognized as 'not good' by 31 per cent, 13 per cent and 6 per cent students respectively. The same persons often evaluated the textbooks for other subjects as 'good'. The textbooks for more difficult subjects were less often appraised as 'good' by 27 per cent of students, for chemistry by 43 per cent and for mechanization of agriculture by 63 per cent.

Study guide

The opinions on this form of assistance were similar to those concerning textbooks. The researchers noticed that the feeling of the usefulness of these books was higher at the end of the term than at the beginning. This form of assistance was accepted by the students.

Causes of discouragement to continue studies

One of the main factors discouraging students from continuing the studies of various subjects was a too high level of lectures in relation to the academic level of students. This applies above all to mathematics, chemistry and mechanization of agriculture. Another reason discouraging students is a feeling of uselessness of certain subjects or parts of them, as, for example, technical drawing. According to the research, 89 per cent of students found mathematics too difficult. This is due above all to a break of several years in education.

The reception of the TV lessons in the Polish language and literature

The typical TV lesson was an innovative, experimental form of a lesson conducted by a well-known actor Wojciech Siemion. 58 per cent of students questioned at the beginning of the term and 67 per cent questioned at the end of the term were in favour of maintaining the existing proportions between the basic lecture and the illustrative section of the lessons. At the same time, 25 per cent of students questioned at the beginning of the term and 20 per cent of students questioned at the end of the term suggested that the lectures should be longer than the illustrative sections. In both cases talks by lecturers were accepted by 50 per cent. The research showed that 75 per cent of students learned the most important things while watching TV lessons; 6 per cent that after listening to TV lectures they did not have to use textbooks. In general, it may be said that the lectures met the expectations of students.

90 per cent of students said that films screened during lectures explained problems discussed in a sufficiently clear way. 81 per cent were in favour of using illustrations to explain foreign terms in the first survey and 73 per cent in the second survey. At the end of the term the order of preference changed. Films on ancient times were placed first, next came parts of theatrical productions, presentations of historical monuments, while grammar was put in fourth place. The research proved that lessons in the Polish language and literature should be diversified and contain many important elements, with the application of many didactic means.

As regards the assessment of persons conducting lectures, the students laid stress on the clarity, comprehension and easiness to follow the lectures. These features were recognized as the most important.

Conclusions

The research on the first term of the TV ASS shows that the broadcasts gained the approval of students in general, although mathematics and chemistry appeared to be too difficult (this state of affairs has changed in the next terms). Students found this form of studying attractive. Despite many difficulties students worked efficiently. Minor modifications in the TV programmes were introduced, especially after the first term. Essential changes were made with regard to content and the way of conducting lessons in mathematics and physics. In both subjects revision of material at the primary school level was introduced. The programme of studies in mechanization of agriculture was simplified and technical drawing was replaced by the subject 'motorization' which helps students obtain driving licences. Textbooks for mathematics, physics and chemistry were modified and so was, partially, the system of tutorials. Improvements were introduced in teaching some vocational subjects and also in the guiding exercise books. The research also showed a lack of an effective, close contact between the students and the teachers.

The TV ASS has been developing its activities for over two years now. During this time the organizers of the School have gained a lot of valuable experience which enabled them to draw conclusions indispensable for introducing certain changes both as regards the organization and the curricula of studies. The basic assumption that the TV ASS should be integrated and co-operate with a school in a given region proved correct in practice, and so was the importance of TV lessons in guiding the students in their self-education, and the role played by special methodological materials (study guides). They will be maintained in future in an improved form.

The experience gained so far also proved that the candidates to the School should be properly prepared to start studies at the TV ASS. In this connection a preparatory term was introduced for the first time as from 3 February 1975 with the view to enable students to refresh and supplement the knowledge gained at the previous stage of education, and to acquaint them with a new system of learning which they did not know before.

After the introduction of many changes the first term of the TV ASS began its activities in its new edition in September 1975. One of the major innovations of the first term in its new edition is a series of TV lessons for teachers and, separately, for students. The aim of this undertaking is to provide them an indispensable range of knowledge necessary for the organization and conduct of lessons with the aid of television.

The audio-visual means of teaching are more and more appreciated in pedagogical circles. Poland can boast considerable achievements in this field. The Polish TV Polytechnics have attracted international attention and a scientific symposium devoted to their activities was held by UNESCO in Warsaw in 1971. At present intensive preparations are being made for a successive symposium to be held in Warsaw in June 1976 and devoted to the Television Agricultural Secondary School as an improved form of education.

Practical activities and the general trends of the development of contemporary didactics confirm the conviction that in future television will constitute one of the main pillars of didactic process.

PAPER NO 77: RADIO-TELEVISION UNIVERSITY FOR TEACHERS IN POLAND

Stanislaw Krawcewicz

Original aims and tasks of the radio-television university for teachers (RTUT)

In 1973, the Parliament of the Polish People's Republic adopted the resolution to reform the national education system. The aim of this reform is to extend general secondary education by setting up for everyone a homogenous ten-year school, followed by a specialized school system preparing pupils for professional work and university studies. The current modernization is aimed at forming closer ties between educational activity and present and future social needs.

The teacher, his professional qualifications, and personal values, will determine whether the modernized school system is effective. This modernization is now one of the basic conditions of the successful realization of the planned social and economic development of our country. Therefore, the successful completion of university level education is considered a necessity in order to be an efficient teacher in the new school system, and permanent contacts with current events and the widening of knowledge must accompany the professional work of the teacher.

The present multi-level system of teachers' education actually results in a majority of teachers who have completed secondary education, but who have not obtained any university degree.

As a result, a new system of education and professional improvement of in-service teachers was created. Universities have been included and they organize correspondence and evening courses for working teachers and their staff in as much as their scientific background makes it possible. Each year the educational authorities send about 20,000 teachers for professional training and provide them with different forms of scientific assistance before and during their studies. Including the mass media into the system of complementary education and professionally-active teachers' improvement has immensely enlarged the system's potential.

In January 1974, the Radio-Television University for Teachers (RTUT) began its activity. In the first period of its existence, its tasks are the propagation and popularization of current tendencies in such disciplines as pedagogy, psychology, philosophy and political science. RTUT is therefore involved in the process of completing the education of in-service teachers (program conducted by the universities) and, at the same time, involved in the general professional improvement of teachers and in the raising of their pedagogic qualifications. The year after the beginning of its activities, RTUT's tasks were extended to preparing teachers to assume the realization of a new program in mathematics from grades 1 to 3.

For much of the school staff, including teachers, school directors and pedagogic supervisors, listening to the RTUT lectures is an important method of education and professional improvement. Furthermore, the parents and the employees in different educational posts also benefit from RTUT since, besides its participation in the complementary education and improvement of teachers, it is also concerned with the education of the whole society leading to a greater understanding of the educational duties of family, school, youth associations and non-school educational institutions.

RTUT is a didactic part of the Institute of Teachers' Education (ITE), which is responsible for its program, selection of lecturers, and preparing, together with the Polish Radio and Television, the organizational and pedagogic base of the teachers' education and improvement. The Institute also organizes research work on the effectiveness of this form of raising the qualifications of the educational staff.

The RTUT programs of individual disciplines are prepared by the units formed of highly specialized scholars who cooperate steadily with ITE, didactic workers of ITE, and the representatives of the Ministry of Education. The lectures are run by the specialists in particular subjects from the scientific centers all over the country.

The RTUT program includes psychological, pedagogical, social and political sciences, because complementary education and improvement in these disciplines correspond with the needs of all our teachers and educators, however different their educational level, specialization and type of vocational employment may be. The programs of these subjects are presented in a cycle of lectures during one school year (i.e. nine months) and repeated with any necessary modifications in the following years.

The following features of the above mentioned program were considered as essential: the introduction of modern knowledge faithfully presenting the state of research work in a given discipline, and, at the same time, the most useful means of educational and pedagogical practice.

The latter point implies that the RTUT program in individual disciplines should not strictly reflect their structure but should also present their choice of certain problems and so enrich the professional practice of the teachers.

During the 1975–6 school year, 62 units on the first program of Polish Radio and 93 units on the first channel of Polish Television were transmitted for RTUT.

In the beginning of 1975, a new subject was included in the RTUT program; an elementary teaching of mathematics. This began the campaign of improving the competence of mathematics teachers in the first three grades of the future ten year school. The necessity of improving the great quantity of mathematicians who teach in primary grades was created by the present situation in schools. In 1975–6, the new program of teaching mathematics in the first grade was introduced. In the following years, second and third grades will also be included in the new program. This program cannot be accomplished efficiently without an important advancement in teachers' qualifications (the majority of them have graduated only from secondary pedagogic schools or sub-university level colleges for teachers), and in their familiarization in theory and in practice with the great progress which has taken place during the last few years in the field of mathematics elementary teaching all over the world.

On the other hand, many specialists are needed to properly train around 30,000 teachers, and there is only a small number of them at our disposal. In such a situation the traditional methods of education cannot be applied. The desirable effects may be attained only with an integral system of broadcast lectures, along with some complementary activities (control works, exams, printed aids). In this manner, the teachers fully benefit from the small group of scholars specializing in elementary teaching of mathematics.

The RTUT school year starts in October and ends in June of the following calendar year.

The basic group of teachers educated within the RTUT system consists of professionally active teachers who improve their competence by correspondence courses or evening courses at the universities. They are required to listen to the RTUT lectures. This relieves the schools of educating these teachers in the subjects encompassed by the RTUT lectures and also limits their duties to conducting com-

plementary studies (tutorials, exercises, seminars) and organizing credit-giving exams.

The RTUT program is also used according to the above rules by the schools of university level in training postgraduate teachers and in educating new teachers.

The basic structure of RTUT's required education is also interesting because it is financially advantageous. Let us consider: each year about 20,000 teachers are able to start correspondence or evening university level studies and about 20,000 other teachers are able to improve their professional competence in other ways; this means that RTUT acquits the university level schools and ITE and its branches from conducting the lectures in four subjects for 40,000 persons a year. The number of teachers required to listen to the Study of Elementary Mathematics Teaching, which should be estimated separately on the ground of its three year-duration, is estimated now to be more than 60,000.

As of yet, we have no definite cost estimation of the education within the framework of RTUT. However, we may state that it is almost certainly less expensive than the traditional forms of education and improvement of such a large group of persons.

The method and means used within the RTUT system of education

The creation of proper conditions in order to fully benefit from this form of vocational training and improvement required the following:

● lectures broadcast on radio and television in an appropriate form,
● instructional aids integrating the radio and television capacity in transmitting the knowledge; audio-visual apparatus and other methods were also used in the organization of education within the radio-television system,
● proper ways to control the mastering of knowledge through radio and television.

The RTUT audience listens every week to the four lectures (2 on the radio and 2 on television) in pedagogic and social-political subjects. For the Study of Elementary Mathematics Teaching listeners, there is a lecture once a week on television and once a month on the radio. The radio program is twenty minutes long and the television program lasts thirty minutes. All the RTUT programs are repeated.

The lectures on the radio are often presented as a discussion between a lecturer and an announcer, or between a lecturer and other specialists in the same field invited to the studio. Sometimes the lecturer discusses the questions and remarks made by the teachers invited to the studio. All this is done in order to make it easier to understand the contents, to underline the most important problems and to avoid monotony.

As to the lectures on television, the form of discussion between two or more persons is also sometimes used. Moreover, the lecture's contents is illustrated by educational films, fragments or documentary inserts sometimes especially made for the needs of RTUT (for example, the course of experiments carried in the educational branches), interviews, setting etc. . . . The problems are explained with the help of such instructional aids as drawings, tables, diagrams and charts.

The texts of all the radio and television lectures are published in a fortnightly publication, *Education*, printed in more than 90,000 copies. Together with the contents of the lectures in mathematics, the sets of control problems to be done at home are printed. Every RTUT listener may subscribe to it or buy it at a bookstand.

The contents of printed lectures generally cover more material than the broadcast programs; sometimes the broadcast serves only as a preparatory and illustrating introduction to the further explication of the problems in print. The published texts are supplied with the sets of control questions. This makes it possible for the listener to test if he has mastered the lecture contents and to which degree it develops his independent thinking ability to draw conclusions. The published lectures are also supplied with the lists of basic auxiliary readings, which introduce different degrees of difficulties so that teachers of an unequal level of training (but possessing the elementary set of concepts and information in RTUT's disciplines) can find the appropriate material to correct the deficiency of their knowledge.

Every RTUT listener may ask the counsellors' assistance in the subjects discussed in the programs; he may also listen again to the tape-recorded ones. Such tutorials are run for the professionally active correspondence course students and the students attending evening courses at the universities. Furthermore, the proper recording apparatus is gathered there. For the teachers taking postgraduate education, participating in the one year studies in subject and method or special courses, the tutorials are conducted by the teachers' improvement centers, the ITE branches and the professional improvement field branches. Finally, for other teachers listening to the RTUT lectures, the counsel is run by ITE branches in special meeting centers. Lately such centers are also organized at schools.

Additional didactic works in RTUT subjects such as exercises or seminars are conducted by the schools of university standing and within the framework of all types of improvement studies. They are aimed at explaining problems discussed in the RTUT lectures and covering those subjects in particular disciplines that are not part of the RTUT program.

The necessary auxiliary readings and the printed contents of the RTUT lectures are to be easily found in pedagogic libraries which are included in the general system of assistance for the RTUT listeners.

The examinations, conducted for different groups of teachers, are not only a way of controlling the acquired knowledge level and, eventually, a way of becoming aware of the actual deficiencies, but they also serve to find out how effective these methods and means of education are.

The exams in mathematics, which are distinct from the oral examinations in pedagogic, social and political subjects, are written examinations. Similar to the control homework, they lie in solving definite sets of problems. On the basis of their results the student's capacity to listen to next year's program can be determined (as stated before, the elementary teaching of the mathematics program takes three years).

RTUT in the opinion of the listeners

In order to acquire the necessary information to properly direct the further improvement of the new form of complementary education and improvement of teachers' training in RTUT, in 1974 ITE started research work on the perception of information broadcast on its programs, and also on the usefulness of this acquired knowledge in the teacher's work and the degree of interest it adds to the educational environment. Research is conducted through interviews with the assistance of the press, radio, television, inquiries, questionnaires and pedagogic information tests. All this work is generally done by the sociologists, psychologists and pedagogues employed by ITE and its branches.

Certain general conclusions can be drawn on the basis of the results of the above mentioned inquiries connected with the first period of RTUT's activity. The majority of respondents (92 per cent) found RTUT's lectures very useful due to the immediate assistance in coping with current behaviour disorders and due to the actual improvement observed in teachers' professional competence. It should be mentioned that the programs in pedagogic and psychological subjects (which are also the most often and regularly listened to) rated the best comments. We can hereby perceive a definite connection: regular listening to the broadcast lectures is accompanied by understanding its practical usefulness.

The above opinions are the most characteristic for the groups of questioned teachers with secondary or college sub-university level (vocational) education (i.e., for those who have accomplished the pedagogic secondary schools or colleges). The following conclusion can be drawn: the higher the level of the professional competence of teachers, the more useful they find the lectures to be. The lectures were considered less useful by the groups of teachers with an accomplished higher education and MD and by the groups with the lowest education level.

Several other relationships can also be noted on the basis of the described research work. For example:

● the usefulness of the RTUT lectures depends on where the teacher resides: the smaller the town or the village, the more useful the lectures are considered to be. This can easily be explained: the listeners from villages and small towns have less opportunity to deepen their interests and to improve their competence than the listeners in larger cities,

● the relationship between the listening regularity of the lectures and the professional position of a teacher and his active professional experience. The largest percentage of the regular listeners, considering both listening to the complete cycle of lectures and the particular lectures in particular disciplines, was observed in the directors' group. No clear relationship between the education level and listening regularity was found. This indicates that the greater experience and professional responsibility of a listener, the more regularly the lectures are listened to,

● the relationship between the regularity of listening to the lectures and the opinions on the point of particular elements in the lectures (language, tempo of speech, number of examples, etc. . . .). The regular listeners have fewer points against the elements in the lectures than the irregular listeners.

In the opinion of all the groups of listeners questioned (i.e., the pedagogic supervisors, school directors and teachers) of every educational level, radio and television are generally an effective means of communicating knowledge, with priority to television. This can be explained by the greater technical possibilities of television.

Pertaining to the listeners' demands concerning the contents of the RTUT lectures, the following requests were made:

1 Inform listeners of the recent achievements in particular branches of knowledge

2 Present new methods in didactic and educational practice

3 Increase the number of examples drawn from a concrete school practice

(the two latter demands pertained to the lectures in pedagogy and psychology). The above suggestions were formulated in the first place by school directors and by the staff of the education sector's administration. The teachers were mainly concerned only with the formal aspect of the programs. The lecturers were asked to give definitions and the other important parts of the lectures more slowly and distinctly and to present tables, diagrams and charts longer on the screen.

As the research work indicated, the teachers do not complain of getting (within RTUT's framework) the information as prepared for the very different groups of pedagogues, but they complain of the fact that the programs are not adequate to the practical needs of school (didactic and educational). Simultaneously, the lectures on the elementary teaching of mathematics arouse an enormous interest among the teachers. The reason for this enthusiasm is their high scientific level and their practical utility. Not only did the numerous and disparate groups of teachers who were registered take advantage of the lectures, but also other groups of teachers and even other professional and social groups found listening to the RTUT programs beneficial. This was confirmed by soundings with the help of the radio, television and the press, because answers came not only from teachers but also from other educational representatives (for example, the workers of the re-education branches of the justice sector, health service, army educational posts, parents, etc . . . and even of other professions not connected with educational problems, such as farmers). As can be seen, the investigation showed a significant enlargement of RTUT's social range, which is one of RTUT's main purposes.

Some conclusions and after thoughts

It became a tradition in Poland to use the mass media to improve the teachers' professional competence. In 1935, Polish radio started to broadcast once a week the cycle of programs called 'We discuss'.

At the end of 1948, the Radio University was organized. By the end of this year, 4,800 listeners were registered, 70 per cent of them were teachers. Inclusion of radio in the spreading of knowledge permitted rational usage of a rather small (at that time) staff of scientists for influencing wide collective bodies of teachers.

During the period just before the creation of RTUT, only two institutions used radio and television to educate adults (the TV Polytechnics and the TV Agricultural Secondary School).

But the educational potential of radio and television was reconsidered in 1973 when the school system reform had been drawn. The urgent necessity appeared to be to find a system which could secure a significant improvement in teachers' competence on a mass scale. It was decided at this time to use radio and television to educate and improve the teachers' competence, but at the beginning only in the disciplines which are of a prime concern to all teachers. However, we realize that such a situation cannot be permanent. We shall surely have to return to the concept of specialized improvement in the future. Then the permanent relation to current interests of the specialized knowledge will be the most important task, so the permanent education system for educational staff will have to be established.

Recapitulation: the analysis of the activity of RTUT makes it possible to formulate several significant conclusions concerning the organization of a permanent self-educational system.

1   It is necessary in the first place to define precisely the purpose of the education and professional improvement of teachers, taking into consideration both the real needs of the school system and the differential needs of listeners themselves. The result will be a closer connection between the teachers' educational process on one hand, and the real problems of didactic and educational work and the needs of the personality development of a teacher on the other hand. This will imply the activization of that process.

2   Radio and television programs cannot perform all the tasks of education and professional improvement. Therefore a selection and proper combining of all the elements to be used in this process are necessary. At the same time, it is essential to avoid an excess of didactic help, in order not to overweigh the listener with too many obligations and too much work and overlook the main idea of audio-visual education.

3   In radio and television education and professional improvement, the program structure should be elastic in order to permit the listener to choose the contents, rhythm, and ways of realizing self-education. It is important because it is well known that an adult person prefers to think rather than to memorize.

Therefore, if radio and television is used in the educational process, it is necessary to work out the most efficient, specific forms of presenting the contents of the program.

The listeners should be properly prepared

to receive the broadcast, thereby assuring that they will not receive it passively; they should be capable of further developing their activity by discussions and eventually depending on their scientific discipline, during other activities, such as laboratory exercises, etc.

The integrated educational system will imply certain changes in the listeners' personality. Essentially it will change his attitude towards education. And this is the very idea of the whole basic strategy of continuous education.

PAPER NO 34: CATERING FOR INDIVIDUAL DIFFERENCES AMONG OPEN UNIVERSITY STUDENTS

Jack Koumi, Production Director, BBC (OU Productions), London, UK.

1 Introduction

This paper summarizes the conclusions of an evaluation of an Open University radio programme (Radio 6: *Studying the Novel: A Discussion*) of the third level Arts course, A302: *The Nineteenth Century Novel and Its Legacy*.[1]

The main preoccupation of the paper is with the effects of differences in A302 students' personal circumstances, intellectual abilities and 'learning styles', on their likelihood of listening to the broadcast, and on the extent to which the programme achieved its purposes, and discusses possible ways in which educational programme-makers might use information about individual differences to produce 'multi-level' programmes—i.e. programmes which would be apprehended at different levels by different types of student, thus benefitting and appealing to a wide variety of students, in parallel.

The effects of individual differences among A302 students are reported within a discursive account of the overall conclusions and recommendations of the Radio 6 evaluation, composed in a form similar to that which was communicated to the A302 course team. (This sets the results in the context for which they have been used within the Open University.)

2 The programme in context

The basis of the A302 course is the study of a representative selection of (twelve) nineteenth-century novels. The first five TV programmes and the first five radio programmes were each presented by 'experts' in their subject matter. However, unlike these preceding programmes, Radio 6 was a discussion between A302 students, mainly on the first three novels, chaired by Graham Martin, a member of the course team.

It was intended that the broadcast should take the form of a largely undirected discussion on the problems of studying the novel, between students of average ability, who were at the same point in their studies as the listening students. As far as the producer, Nuala O'Faolain, was able to judge, this intended format was finally realized in the third (1975) version of the programme, through the strategies adopted for the choice of students, the date of recording, the style of Graham Martin's chairmanship and the editing. (Graham Martin's contribution to the discussions in the two previous versions, recorded in 1973 and 1974, had been judged to be too 'dominant'.)

The rationale for the 1975 format can be discerned in the list of purposes for the programme (in order of priority):

(a) *Motivational* To encourage self-reliance and to reinforce self-confidence in the listeners' own views by demonstrating a profitable student-discussion on 'Studying the novel' (thereby suggesting that the student's views can be as valid as the expert's and that there is no single 'correct'/'expert' way to study the novel).

(b) *Affective* To provide reassurance and alleviate feelings of isolation by exposing the listener to the (similar) views of other students.

(c) *Cognitive* To develop listeners' views through their reactions to and their assimilation of a variety of student-level views.

3 Method

(a) A questionnaire was sent to a random sample of 290 of the 1170 students who were registered for the course in March 1975. (The broadcast was in April 1975.) The questionnaire was returned by 258 students, 3 of whom had withdrawn from the course, leaving 255 questionnaires from the 287 'live' students (89 per cent response).

(b) A letter was sent to the 63 current A302 tutors, asking for their reactions to the 1974 and 1975 versions and for the reactions of their students to the 1975 version. Eleven tutors replied with such reactions.

(c) A (recorded) discussion was held with a group of 13 students from 2 London area tutorial groups after playing them recordings of the 1974 and 1975 versions.

(d) Eight students were interviewed by telephone.

4 Results, Conclusions and Recommendations

(a) Listening Figures

The proportion of respondents to the questionnaire who heard Radio 6 was 50 per cent, but this reduced to 47 per cent for the whole sample, when an estimate is calculated for non-respondents. (This gives an estimate for all A302 students of between 42 per cent and 52 per cent—95 per cent confidence interval.) However, since a quarter of the students gave 'unavoidable' reasons for not listening (rather than 'discretional' reasons), we can deduce that, of those for whom listening was physically possible, 63 per cent did listen to Radio 6.*

The (unadjusted) 50 per cent listening figure and the 'listening twice' figure of 2 per cent compare badly with the A302 average in 1974: 61 per cent and 14 per cent respectively. This probably reflects a generally lower listening figure for A302 radio in 1975, probably due to the inconvenience of the early morning repeat transmission time.**

There were far more non-listeners than listeners below the median age of respondents' age distribution, whereas the reverse was true above median age. Consequently, non-listeners were significantly younger

---

* Another estimate, derived from classifying the reasons given for not listening into 'enduring' vs 'transitory' reasons, was that 25 per cent to 32 per cent of the students would listen very infrequently to A302 radio programmes in 1975 (between 0 and about 4 programmes of the 16).

** One-fifth of the non-listeners complained about transmission-times.

than listeners (38.5 and 42.3 years respectively).

The reason for the relative youth of non-listeners appeared to be that more students in the younger age-group had enduring 'discretional' reasons for not listening: mainly conflicting domestic commitments.

Unlike previous findings for other programmes, non-listeners of Radio 6 were not significantly further behind in their studies than listeners. However, several other results supported previous findings in suggesting that non-listeners 'skimped' in their studies and in their tutorials, as well as in their listening behaviour. Firstly, their grades for the first three tutor-marked assignments (TMAs), i.e. the TMAs submitted prior to Radio 6, were significantly lower than those of listeners, being an average of one grade down on listeners for one of the three TMAs. Secondly, non-listeners submitted significantly fewer TMAs than listeners. Thirdly, although listeners who were further ahead in their studies had obtained significantly higher TMA grades than other listeners, this was not true for non-listeners; in fact, those non-listeners who were well ahead in their studies had obtained significantly lower grades than other non-listeners. Finally, on tutorial attendance, non-listeners were significantly worse than listeners, and this was true even when other forms of student/tutor contact were taken into account.

All the significant differences above, except the one involving the relationship between novel being read and TMA grades, were greater when 'circumstantial' non-listeners (the 'atypical' non-listeners with 'transitory, unavoidable' reasons) were omitted from the analysis.

(b) Proportion of 'isolated' students listening to Radio 6—and their reactions

The listening figure for 'isolated' students (those with little or no contact with tutors or fellow students) was even lower—36 per cent (adjusted for non-respondents)—than that for students as a whole, thereby diminishing the hope that the programme would help 'isolated' students in particular (purpose 2). This hope was then dealt a further blow by the result that the 'isolated' students who did hear the programme found it slightly less enjoyable and useful than other listeners.

(c)   Reactions of listeners as a whole
In fact, a very low proportion of all listeners liked the programme. For example, only six per cent (8 listeners) found it 'very useful' (and only 24 per cent found it 'fairly useful'), compared to 33 per cent in 1974 finding A302 radio programmes 'very helpful', (and 48 per cent finding them 'fairly helpful'). Another comparison, with A302 programmes in 1975, is available from the distribution of 'further comments' made by students at the end of the questionnaire: there were far more adverse than favourable comments about Radio 6 (a ratio of eleven to one), whereas the reverse was true about previous A302 radio and TV programmes (in a ratio of one to two).

One redeeming feature was that 7 of the 8 'very useful' raters got an improved grade for the TMAs which came after the programme, compared to the three TMAs before it. This was a significantly greater incidence of improvement than among other listeners (55 improved, out of 117).

As to the proportion who liked the programme to any degree, only one-third of the listeners found the programme 'useful' or more than minimally enjoyable. In fact, if we consider this question in more detail, we find that the programme was an unqualified success in one or other of its purposes for only one-quarter of the students. Indeed, even if all favourable reactions are taken into account, it can only be argued that half the students derived some benefit from it.

But perhaps the most serious indictment is that the programme appears to have been *counter-productive*, for nearly half the students, with respect to its prime purpose of encouraging self-reliance—it seems to have reinforced or engendered the conviction, in these students, that there *are* 'expert/correct' ways to study the novel or that the student's approach is far inferior to the expert's.

(d)   Individual differences in reactions to the programme: implications for A302 broadcasting
Seven-tenths of the reasons given by those who disliked the programme censured the

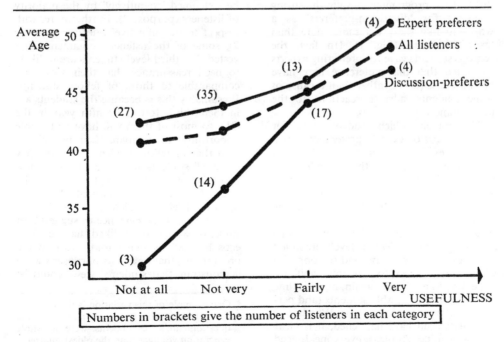

Figure 1   Ages of listeners giving different 'usefulness' ratings among 'discussion-preferers' and 'expert-preferers'

lack of originality and the low intellectual level of the views expressed in the programme (although about one-seventh of the 'dislikers' were more frustrated at not being able to participate in the discussion). In fact, the students who did find the programme useful (30 per cent) had significantly lower grades than the others, for the three TMAs prior to the programme (an average of one grade lower for one of the three TMAs). So, as expected, the low intellectual level of the programme appealed mainly to the less able/successful listeners. Also as expected, there was a significant trend for those who found the programme less useful to be younger (Fig. 1).

There was some evidence to support the (a priori) hypothesis that this was because younger students are more arrogant and thus place less value on the views of fellow students.

This evidence consisted of the finding that the above effects of age and prior TMA grades were much more attributable to listeners who preferred the alternative of taking part in student-discussions than to those who preferred listening to experts (Fig. 1).

Thus, the younger, more successful 'discussion-preferers' were the group who most disliked the programme, despite the strong tendency for 'discussion-preferers' as a whole to like the programme more than 'expert-preferers' (Fig. 1). (In fact, the reasons students gave for preferring experts suggested that this preference may have been a consequence rather than a cause of some students' adverse reactions to the programme.)

The reasons which students gave for their 'discussion/expert' preferences, also provided evidence which suggested that at least three-quarters of them would have preferred the usual type of programme: an expert-talk. This was even true for almost half of those who found the programme 'useful'.

One could conjecture that a programme at a very high intellectual level, presented by an expert, would have had the opposite effect with respect to students' abilities, appealing to a minority again, but this time mainly to the more able students (and perhaps to the younger students). Whether or not this would have happened, it is clear that one can't easily please everyone. Indeed

the range of personalities and intellectual levels revealed by the questionnaire is quite intimidating—it presents an almost insuperable obstacle to the task of providing a programme which would please the majority.*

However, this obstacle has to be overcome somehow. It is just not feasible, in the foreseeable future, to provide a large variety of different programmes on each topic to suit the large variety of different types of learner. The discussion below investigates the feasibility of providing a single programme to suit the majority. Consideration is restricted to programmes of the same general type as Radio 6—'pastoral/feedback/tutorial' programmes—because the evaluation of Radio 6 cannot be applied easily to programmes of an entirely different nature.

(e) *The potential efficacy of alternative types of 'pastoral/feedback/tutorial' programmes*

Firstly, concerning programmes like Radio 6, in which students express their view, and for which the purposes are those of Radio 6 (see section 2), it seems very unlikely (from the discussion above) that one could find a group of students whose views would be welcomed 'cognitively' by the majority of listeners (purpose 3). Furthermore, with respect to the 'affective' purpose (purpose 2), some of the listeners' comments suggested that third level students are unlikely to need reassurance that their views are comparable to those of fellow students. Presumably this is because the students are in their third, fourth or fifth year in the OU, so most of them will have had ample opportunity to compare their proficiency with that of fellow students; and the few 'isolated' students liked Radio 6 even less than the others because, they essentially claimed, it merely confirmed their low opinion of fellow students.

There was some evidence to suggest that students would have liked having their egos boosted by being told, prior to the programme, that one of its purposes was to demonstrate that students' views could be

---

* One example of this variation is the distribution of ages: the youngest quarter of the questionnaire's respondents were a whole generation younger than the oldest quarter.

'as valid as those of experts': those who ascribed purpose 1 to the programme liked it more than those ascribing purpose 2 or 3 to it. While it is unlikely, for other reasons, that this would have increased the programme's success to any great extent, the idea of an 'ego boost' in some other form has some intuitive merit.

On the other hand, one could criticize the related 'motivational' purpose of disabusing students of the notion that there is a 'correct'/'expert' way to study the novel, which they should 'regurgitate'. If the course as a whole had consistently given this impression,* then a single radio programme so late in the course is unlikely to have much effect.

Secondly, if a programme were to be devoted to students' problems rather than their views, then it would be necessary to conduct a comprehensive prior survey to determine the most frequent problems encountered. Otherwise, one would be defeated by the enormous range of personal circumstances, personalities, intellectual levels and 'learning styles', which were so dramatically exemplified by the range of questionnaire responses. Indeed, this range was so striking that even a comprehensive survey is unlikely to unearth even a single major problem which would be shared by the majority of listeners.

Finally, in the discussion with the group of London students, two suggestions arose (which they were encouraged to elaborate on) which appear to have more promise than the two above.

One was the suggestion that there should be a programme in which two experts, with differing views, discussed some topic. This desire for more exposure to disparate viewpoints was also expressed by some of the questionnaire respondents in their comments about the course in general. Such a programme would not be of the 'pastoral/ tutorial' type under discussion, but it is mentioned here because the idea of presenting 'expert protagonists' can be realized in the second type of programme discussed by the London students (which drew almost unanimous approval).

This second suggestion was for a (pastoral-type) programme in which tutors discussed their different criteria for evaluating and grading essays. (The objection that this would unleash cries of 'non-egalitarian treatments of students' is discussed below.) Such a programme is likely to appeal to OU students in most subject areas due to their vested interest in assessment criteria. But for an Arts course like A302, it would be possible to incorporate 'disparate' views on the novel, taking care, of course, to avoid the impression that tutors' grading is actually determined by their differing viewpoints: that is, emphasizing that it is the excellence of the argument which counts. (In other words, the tutors could be seen to arrive, eventually, at agreement in their evaluation criteria, thus alleviating students' suspicions in this respect.) Moreover, it may be possible to incorporate one or two of the most predominant of students' problems. Furthermore, it would even be possible to boost students' egos: for example, the tutors could agree that even those students to whom they give bad grades have something valuable to say (but that they are not yet saying it very adroitly). And finally, such a programme might appeal to both 'discussion-preferers' and 'expert-preferers', and to a wide range of intellectual abilities. (It would be appropriate for the programme to be at a relatively low intellectual level, since much of it would concern students' work. This would presumably suit low-ability students; for high-ability students, the possible unsuitability of the intellectual level would hopefully be swamped by their vested interest on the subject of tutors' assessment criteria.)*

---

* The distribution of reasons given for 'discussion/expert' preferences did suggest that as many as two-fifths of the students prefer to assimilate experts' ideas passively rather than to participate in generating ideas— although the evidence was rather questionable and it is impossible to judge the degree of 'passivity' involved.

---

* Radio 6 is being remade, not on the lines recommended above, but as an 'expert talk' about Turgenev, the author of the fifth novel: *On the Eve* (on grounds that there is no broadcast devoted to Turgenev).

5 Issues for educational programmes in general, in relation to differences between students

The previous section discussed the relevance to 'pastoral/feedback/tutorial' radio programmes of the wide range of individual characteristics revealed by the questionnaire.

However, for any type of educational programme, it is obviously essential to 'know your audience' as intimately as possible. And this includes a thorough appraisal of the extent to which individual members of the audience differ. It is clearly inadvisable to try to tailor a programme precisely to fit a single hypothetical 'average' student. And yet, even though educational programme-makers are aware that there is a wide range of individuals in their audiences, it is impossible to know how to cater for this variation when the extent and the nature of individual differences is unknown.

Hence more research into the effects of individual learner-differences, particularly in 'learning styles', is similarly likely to be fruitful in pointing the way towards the production of successful 'multi-level' programmes.

Reference

KOUMI, J. Broadcast Evaluation Report No 19: *A302: Studying the Novel*, Milton Keynes, Open University, 1975.

PAPER NO 40: THE USE OF RADIO IN THE OPEN UNIVERSITY'S MULTI-MEDIA EDUCATIONAL SYSTEM

John R. Meed, Research Consultant, Institute of Educational Technology, The Open University, UK.

In 1975 the Open University transmitted a total of more than 1,000 television and 1,000 radio programmes. These programmes accompanied courses on a wide range of subjects, divided into six faculty areas: Arts, Education, Social Science, Maths, Science and Technology. They covered music, architecture, ecology, chemistry, psychology, atomic theory, and a host of other disciplines. Within such a range of subject matter individual programmes were likely to vary greatly, but this was documented only to the extent of a list of titles and a series of brief synopses. True, individuals involved in the production process, or connected in other ways with broadcasting, all had varying degrees of knowledge of the sorts of programmes being transmitted to students. However, this knowledge was limited, and provided a series of viewpoints of the subject rather than an overall perspective. A newcomer to the University, a visitor, or even one of the established members of staff would have needed either to watch or listen to the programmes themselves, or else consult half a dozen different people, if he were to acquaint himself with the broadcasting output. Either exercise would have proved exceedingly time-consuming.

For a number of reasons, this could be seen as a problem. The University's Audio-visual Media Research Group receives many requests for a general account of OU broadcasting, both from within the University and from outside. In addition, the research group felt the need for an overall picture to balance its evaluation of individual programmes[1]; both for the selection of programmes for evaluation, as a means of assuring a wide-ranging and representative choice, and for the generalization of results, as a means for placing individual evaluations in context. I have looked at radio only, because we considered that a study of this medium would present fewer problems, but would prove a useful groundwork for a similar future study of television. The results are available in report form.[2] In this paper, I intend to draw out some of the themes of this report. Although the study was based on an examination of OU programmes, many of the problems encountered, especially those of devising an appropriate framework of programme categorization, will be common to other studies of this kind, while others carried even wider implications for educational broadcasting in general.

Background to radio at the Open University

What place does radio occupy in the Open University teaching system? To answer that question, let us look at a week in the student's life. Theoretically, he is expected to undertake ten hours' work, though in practice this may be nearer fifteen. Of this time, a radio broadcast will take up twenty minutes; activities associated with the broadcasts, usually answering questions on the broadcast, might add more to this; anything up to half an hour. On average, however, the radio programme is likely to occupy five per cent of the student's work time. The bulk of his work will go into reading the correspondence text and set books. In addition to this, he will be faced with tutorial sessions, television programmes, home experiments, summer school (in session) and so on.

Who decides what is to go into radio programmes?

Policy for radio on each course lies, theoretically, with the *course team;* the group of academics and producers working on the course. This team is responsible for the integration of the various components of the course, and one might expect this to be the source of a role or roles for radio. In practice, however, it is often left to individual producers and academics to come up with programme ideas. The way they use radio is affected by the University's assessment policy. Owing to the fact that some students may be unable to receive the relevant television or radio channels, it has been ruled that no broadcast can be the sole basis for assessment; alternative questions, on the written material, must be set.

Are students advised on how to use the programmes?

Advice to students about the broadcasts, and any associated activities, are contained within *broadcast notes*. These are rarely contained within the correspondence text, but are usually mailed to students as supplementary material. Responsibility for writing them lies with the programme-makers and text writers; again the practice is often different from the theory, with notes sometimes being left in the hands of the course assistants (the administrative co-ordinator of the course team, who may not have been involved in production).

Finally, the transmission. At the moment, most programmes are broadcast twice. Generally, one of these transmissions occupies a time when most students could listen, such as Saturday morning, or an early weekend evening; the other frequently falls at a more obscure hour, such as 6.40 am. The development of further courses will lead to increasing pressure on transmission times, and repeats are likely to become a rare occurrence.

Method: sampling and interviewing

My study began at the end of 1974, and I was therefore able to draw only on programmes transmitted during the University's first three years of existence. Even this constituted a total of over 800 programmes, so I decided to draw a 22.5 per cent random sample. This left me with a total of 191 programmes. Of these, 49 were from Arts or arts-based courses, 53 Social Science, 25 Education, 25 Maths, 23 Science and 17 Technology.

To discover the characteristics of these programmes, I drew on a number of sources of information. Firstly, I interviewed wherever possible the producer of each programme. I aimed to solicit information concerning the intention that lay behind the programme, by asking how the broadcast functioned in relation to the rest of the course, and how it was intended that students should use the broadcast. To balance the information gained this way, and to gain a more intimate knowledge of the programmes themselves, I listened to tapes or read scripts of the broadcasts, and consulted the broadcast notes and other associated printed materials. Finally, I drew upon the experience of colleagues in the research group, and in the Institute of Educational Technology as a whole.

During the study, I was conscious of a difference of attitude between people working in production and those in educational technology, and this is likely to have parallels elsewhere. The producer is involved with the programme from beginning to end: he deals with a whole crop of problems rarely seen by the educational technologist. He is concerned to maintain not only the educational aspects of broadcasting, but also the high technical standards of the BBC. The educational technologist, however, deals mainly with the outcome of production, and is concerned solely with the educational attributes of the broadcast. I found that moving between these viewpoints posed a number of problems, especially as both are, within their frames of reference, equally valid. The most marked problem for this study came when I asked producers about the *use* students might be expected to make of the programmes. This aspect of programmes seemed to have occupied many of them less than other aspects that I questioned them about, possibly because it implied a more 'directed' approach to teaching, one that removed an element of choice from the learning process.

Designing the descriptive framework

When I began the study, I was unsure which form of classification or description would prove most appropriate. I could find little literature concerning taxonomies of educational broadcasting that was applicable to the Open University, and so the initial design of a system was based upon the experience of members of the research group. At first, I had hoped to define broadcasts in straightforward terms such as 'talk', 'interview', 'discussion', and so forth. However, it became apparent that this would be inadequate, because it would not bring out the most unique features of radio broadcasting. Furthermore, it became apparent that any study would have to take account of the function of the broadcasts in the overall context of the courses to which they belonged. The reasons for this stemmed from the multi-media nature of the OU's teaching system. The situation in a multi-media system is considerably different from a single-medium set up, particularly when one is looking at a relatively minor component, as is radio at the Open University. The medium is not called upon to provide all the information; instead it can be used for purposes to which it is more suited. For the researcher, this means that he cannot describe programmes in isolation, or just in relation to other broadcasts. For example, a large number of Open University radio broadcasts take the form of straight talks; however, amongst these, one may consist of a personal account designed to increase students' awareness of the practical side of a subject; another may be a direct piece of instruction, designed purely to reinforce another part of the course; yet another may advise students on how to go about an exam. In other words, the researcher must consider the overall context of a broadcast, and its relationship

to other components, before he can discuss what its use will be to students.

The method I adopted, then, concentrated on a consideration of the radio programmes along three main dimensions:

(i)   the *component(s)* to which they related
(ii) the *closeness* of this relationship
(iii) the *manner* of this relationship i.e. the role they played in the context of the rest of the student's study at the time of transmission.

I did not go on from here to attempt to devise a rigorous classification system. There were a number of reasons for this. It would have proved very time-consuming, and I doubt whether it would have produced a better overall view than the method I eventually adopted. More importantly, I wished to take account of the intentions and views of the people involved in production. As these are necessarily subjective matters, they are not particularly amenable to classification. However, they are particularly important in the OU context, where attitudes to radio have undergone, and are still undergoing, considerable scrutiny and change. I wished to bring out these views, and thereby impart more of the 'flavour' of radio production at the OU.

I eventually divided programmes into a number of *types*. These were, as far as possible, based on existing similarities between radio programmes. They were not exclusive, being based frequently on points of a continuum where a larger number of programmes congregated.

Main type of radio programmes

I began by considering where such programmes stood in relation to other components. This was generally straightforward. The majority of programmes were linked primarily to the concurrent written unit (71 per cent out of the sample of 191). A further 11 per cent was closely connected with one or two other broadcasts as well as the text. This occurred most regularly in the Educational Studies Faculty, where it was a point of policy that broadcasting should be closely integrated with the written material. Elsewhere this happened less frequently.

Within these programmes a number of dominant types could be identified. This is summarized in Fig. 1.

Figure 1   The relationship of radio to other components of the course

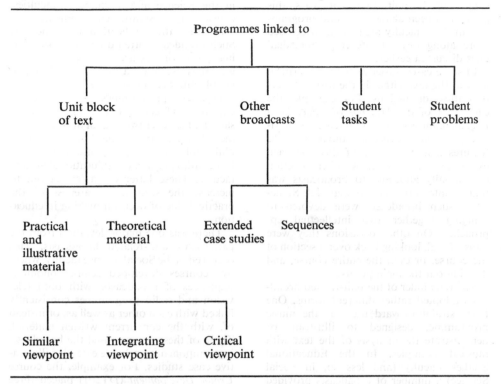

A particular aspect would be chosen for consideration; the reason for choice and the treatment dealt out would vary. Two-thirds of these programmes provided material of a theoretical nature; in other words talks or (less frequently) interviews that formed extensions of the approach found in the text. Furthermore, most of the programmes (and these accounted for nearly half the total sample) were of a similar viewpoint to that of the text. However, the exact function they fulfilled, and their centrality to the student's work varied. In some cases they were designed to reinforce what had gone before. This was particularly true of some maths, and (to a lesser extent) science broadcasts, which picked up a section of the unit which was likely by virtue of its abstract or theoretical notion to have caused students difficulty, and went over it more slowly.

Other broadcasts developed an aspect of the text. In some cases the programme was very closely related to the text: for example, a broadcast from the *Age of Revolutions*

course (A202 Radio 6) associated with the Industrial Revolution used John Wilkinson as an example both of entrepreneurship and of the work then being carried out in the iron industry. It formed a major source of information for both subjects with self-assessment questions being set in the text on the programme. Most programmes occupied a less central position, dealing with subjects of varying relevance to students. This relevance often depended upon the individual student's interest in the particular subject, but programmes were designed to throw light generally on the unit. At the other extreme, there were broadcasts of little direct relevance to students, designed to enrich his study. These were found generally in the maths, science and technology faculties, and were the result of an early policy for radio. It was decided to use the programmes to provide interesting background information—historical, social and biographical—to the course. For example, a broadcast from the *Maths Foundation Course* (M100 Radio 22) considered the origins and history of linear algebra, the subject of the unit. In recent years, this policy has been abandoned, and programmes in these faculty areas tend to be used more along other reinforcing, 'remedial' lines discussed earlier.

In some cases, broadcasts took a critical look at the text, either in the form of talks or critical discussions. For example, the early part of the *Methods of Educational Enquiry* course (E341) adopted an empiricist approach. The second radio programme features a leading critic of this approach expounding his views. Another function occasionally allocated to broadcasts was that of integrating course material. Sometimes such broadcasts were devoted to bringing together two intellectual approaches. On other occasions they were more global, looking back over a section of the course, or even the entire course, and drawing out the main points.

The remainder of the unit-related broadcasts adopted rather different forms. One fairly straightforward use was the music programme, designed to illustrate or demonstrate the analysis of the text with musical examples. In the Educational Studies Faculty (and less so, in Social Science) a number of broadcasts provided 'source material' for analysis by students. This generally took the form of interviews with, or recordings of pupils, teachers and other people in their situations. For example, the fourth programme from the *Personality, Growth and Learning* course (E281) presented a number of excerpts of children reading poems and describing uses of artifacts, which students were required to analyse in terms of the factors of creativity outlined in the text. This type of programme differed quite radically from most, in that it requires considerable active participation on the part of the student, both during and after listening.

Practical material was also used in another way, to provide case studies illustrative of the text. These varied according to the subject area. One of the programmes from the *Decision-Making in Britain* course (D203 Radio 21) followed the course of a scandal in a mental hospital to illustrate one of the ways reform in the National Health Service may be inaugurated. The programme drew on newspaper reports, political speeches and other information from the time. Case studies were used also in the Science and Technology faculties, considering systems, environments and sometimes the application of principles. Such broadcasts often drew upon an existing piece of research. Frequently, programmes were used to present eminent people and decision-makers.

Dramatic programmes were a rare occurrence: in fact only two cropped up in my sample. However two uses of drama deserve mention. The first is the dramatization of philosophical dialogues, and the second is the radio plays of the Educational Studies faculty. These latter examples set out to increase the student's awareness of the practical side of decision-making in education.

There was one major deviation from the pattern of unit-related broadcasts. This occurred in the Social Science faculty, where five courses developed semi-autonomous sequences of broadcasts, with both television and radio programmes consistently linked with each other as well as, or instead of, with the concurrent written material. Three of these courses used the broadcasting component to provide extended illustrative case studies. For example, the course *Urban Development* (DT201) placed three case studies of cities on the broadcast media; one from the West (Chicago), one from the Third World (Ibadan, in Nigeria) and one from an Eastern European country (Warsaw). Each case study received on average five programmes on both radio and television, and considerable amounts of accompanying background information in written form. The case studies were not linked directly to the correspondence texts, but students were expected to draw upon them for assessment purposes. The broadcasts concentrated on various aspects of the city under discussion, using both source material and expert comment.

The other two Social Science courses used broadcasting not for case studies but as the primary source of instruction for one of the course subjects. The *Comparative Government and Politics* course (D231) used the broadcast media to teach the 'inequality and politics' section of the course, because the course team believed it was a subject suited both to radio (because its contentious nature was suited to discussion) and to television (because visual aspects of inequality could be displayed). Again the broadcast received support from supplementary written material; furthermore attempts were made to link each broadcast with the concurrent unit. An optional question in both the exam and a continuous-assessment paper was set on this section of the course.

These five courses provided 6 per cent of the programmes in my sample. When added to the unit-linked broadcasts, this still leaves 13 per cent of the broadcasts unconsidered: these were rather different. A number (8 per cent of the total sample) were devoted to assisting students with tasks, such as projects, home experiments, exams and assignments. They tended to take two forms. Sometimes this was an expert giving advice on how to go about the various skills that were necessary (for

Table 1   Quantification of the types of broadcast

I	Programmes linked primarily to textual unit or blocks*		
	(a) Theoretical material	No	%
1	Remedial' direct teaching' programmes	17	(9%)
2	Developing an aspect of text	43	(22%)
3	Enrichment programmes	23	(12%)
4	Integratory programmes	12	(6%)
5	Presenting a critical or alternative viewpoint	17	(9%)
	Total	112	(58%)
	(b) Practical and illustrative material		
6	Primary source material for analysis by students	11	(6%)
7	Case studies and practical examples designed to illustrate text	16	(7%)
8	Presentation of decision-makers, eminent people	3	(2%)
9	Demonstrating applications	5	(3%)
10	Aural illustrations of the text	8	(4%)
11	Dramatic programmes	1	(1%)
	Total	44	(23%)
II	Extended broadcast case studies and sequences		
12	Extended case studies	7	(4%)
13	Sequences	3	(2%)
	Total	10	(6%)
III	Task-assisting programmes	15	(8%)
IV	Feedback programmes	10	(5%)
	TOTAL	191	(100%)

*I have included in these categories those programmes which link simultaneously to other broadcasts, but remain related to the units rather than parts of the more ambitious broadcast sequences. These totalled 7 per cent of the sampled programmes.

example, students might be called upon to use certain interviewing techniques for a project; they might have to learn certain statistical calculations; or they might have to learn how to carry out an experimental technique). On other occasions the programmes advised by example, perhaps by demonstrating an interviewer or by proceeding through an exam question to give students an idea of how best to go about it themselves.

The remaining 5 per cent of the programmes in my sample utilized radio's capacity for late-production. Generally this consisted of answering students' problems concerning both the content and the practical side of the course. On one or two occasions the OU experimented with 'phone-ins', with students putting questions direct to a panel of course team members. These feedback-based broadcasts were used regularly in the Maths faculty, at four- or five-programme intervals, and occasionally elsewhere. A number of times, programme 'slots' were left open for the purpose of updating course material.

To summarize the preceding section I have included Table 1, which gives the frequency of occurrence of the various types of broadcast in my sample.

Summary

By way of summary, I would like to point to any implications that might arise from the study. Obviously, there are direct implications for the OU; the study revealed considerable uniformity among programmes; two-thirds of the programmes took the form of talks or interviews, and only 5 per cent provided a critical or alternative viewpoint. More importantly, perhaps, are the planning problems for radio; it has not been the rule for course teams to develop overall roles for radio, nor for programmes to be planned as parts of the written units. Often it has been left to individual producers and academics to come up with programme ideas, and this largely accounts for the fact that a considerable number of programmes are appendages of units, rather than integrated parts of them. Furthermore, the majority of programmes required little activity from students other than that of listening. The education programmes requiring analysis of source material provided guidelines for this analysis in the broadcast notes, and the mathematics and science programmes often provided diagrams and working, also in the notes. Elsewhere, broadcast notes were generally restricted to providing summaries or synopses, and background material. At the same time, there have been many developments in attitudes to radio at the OU; particularly in the increasing use of radiovision (the use of printed and visual material that students are expected to co-ordinate with listening). This has been developed considerably in the Maths, Science and Technology areas, where diagrams and equations, etc, accompany the programme. More recently, the architecture course has used radio programmes to go over the plans of buildings, again using extensive printed and diagrammatic material. In addition, the recent development of comprehensive course policies in the Social Sciences faculty reflects an increased awareness of the problems of radio in a multi-media teaching system, and a desire to do something about them.

There are implications arising also from the method that I have developed. The difference in attitude between producers and educational technologists is something that might well have gone unnoticed if the study had concentrated solely on the programmes themselves. I believe, also, that the study has provided a good general picture of the situation while preserving the individuality of programmes. There are drawbacks. The sampling technique resulted in my cutting through courses. In those cases where a coherent policy had been adopted, this meant that I had a less clear idea of what this policy was. Though I tried to allow for this by questioning producers about the overall role of radio on each course, I fear this did not compensate sufficiently. In addition, I realize that, while the study has gone some way towards throwing up a system for describing broadcasts in a multi-media teaching system, it would require considerable additional work to produce a rigorous classification. These drawbacks remembered, I hope that this description of the method, and the brief account of OU radio has proved illuminative.

References

1 BATES, A. W. *Summary of the Activities of the Audio-Visual Media Research*

Group, 1975, IET Paper on Broadcasting No 56, Milton Keynes: The Open University, 1976.

2 MEED, J. R. *The Use of Radio in Open* *University Course Design 1971–4*, IET Paper on Broadcasting No 54, Milton Keynes, The Open University, 1976.

SECTION D
THE CONTEXT OF EVALUATION

INTRODUCTION

We were anticipating that this section would be an odd assortment of those papers which did not fall into our simple categorization of target audiences, a categorization which we felt to be important for understanding the context of the papers. These papers though do seem to have a common thread running between them, in that they are nearly all concerned with the broader context, the environment, in which evaluation and decision-making take place. Taken together, these papers highlight the fact that evaluation and decision-making are not merely a set of mechanical procedures which can be used deterministically, but are bound up in very complex processes, involving value judgements, professional expertize, ideologies, organizational structures, and plain political manoeuvring.

We have therefore arranged the papers in this section into three sub-categories:

1 Those papers concerned with the broader *political* framework within which decisions about educational television and radio are made. This can be seen most clearly in the Glikman and Corduant paper, which reveals how differences in the relationship between governments and broadcasting organizations lead to radical differences in programming, in what are basically very similar areas of educational television and radio. The quality of educational programmes can also be radically affected by Federal or State financing policy, as can be seen from the paper by Mielke and his colleagues. The Federal/State relationship is also an influencing factor in the papers by Lamy and Daniel, on Radio Québec, and by Oliveira, on ETV-Maranhão. Cowlan and Foote's paper on the American ATS-6 satellite experiments on the other hand indicates that the justification for the use of television in education does not always reflect clear user needs. The technology itself provides a strong motivational thrust in decision-making. As they succinctly put it:

> 'This ATS-6 demonstration was a technological solution looking for a social problem.'

2 Those papers concerned with the *organizational* framework in which evaluation is carried out—how researchers need to relate to decision-makers (and vice-versa), the kinds of decisions made in organizations using television and radio for educational purposes, and the role, range and limits of the work of professional evaluators. These issues for instance were clearly of central concern to Bates and McAnany in particular.

3 Those papers concerned with the *professional* context of evaluation: the problems chosen for study, and the theories, methodologies and ideologies underlying evaluation and its procedures. For instance, Van der Voort's paper describes the areas in which researchers in the past have been interested, papers by Baggaley, Heidt and Jacquinot are concerned with more theoretical aspects, particularly with the psychological processes which operate when people watch or listen to educational programmes, and papers by Klasek, McIntosh, Seibert and Chiam Tah Wen look at the procedures and methods of evaluation. This group of papers then provides insight into the intellectual framework underlying the process of research and evaluation.

Although the papers in this section deal with more general issues, reference can be found to the following projects:

Project	Country
ETV—Maranhão	Brazil
Radio-Québec	Canada
RTS/Promotion—BBC Further Education	France/United Kingdom
Film and Television Training School, Poona	India
Satellite Instructional Television Experiment	India
ETV for schools	Malaysia
Open University	United Kingdom
ATS-6 satellite experiment	USA
Children's television programming	USA

THE POLITICAL CONTEXT

PAPER NO 11: THE ATS-6—AMERI-
CAN CASE STUDIES*

Bert Cowlan, Consultant, New York,
Dennis Foote, Institute for Communi-
cation Research, Stanford University,
USA.

1 The ATS-6

The essential difference between the ATS-6
and previous satellites in this NASA series
is its capacity to broadcast to small, relatively low-cost ground antennae and receivers. This offers the potential for radical
changes in the way communications satellites may be employed in health care,
education or other social services, or for
personal communications.

Each of the two video transponders on
the satellite can transmit a video image plus
four simultaneous audio channels. Receivers must be equipped with a switch
allowing them to select a particular audio
channel; once this is done, the viewers
of a particular programme may choose
among, for example, four different languages which might accompany the video
picture.

There are three categories of remote
stations. The *receive-only terminal* (ROT) is
the basic unit; it can receive color video
signals and associated audio channels, but
it cannot transmit. The second level of
installation is the *intensive terminal* (IT)
which can transmit an audio signal as well
as receive video and audio. *Comprehensive
terminals* (CTs) can both receive and transmit audio and video.

---

* Reproduced in part from December 1975
issue of *Educational Broadcasting International* by kind permission of its publishers.

2 The health, education and telecom-
munications (HET) programmes

A broad range of education and health-
related activities was tried out on ATS-6
during its year of availability in the United
States (1974–5). ATS-6 is now, of course,
employed in the SITE project. These were
undertaken in three main regions—in the
Rocky Mountain area, in the Appalachian
States and in Alaska.

Within each region, a number of different programmes was conducted, usually by
more than one organization. Six organizations were chiefly responsible for the satellite demonstration projects, half of which
were agencies of the federal or state government. The remaining three were non-
governmental regional organizations. The
projects operated quite independently of
each other, except in the case of hardware
procurement.

The HET demonstrations were a late
addition to the ATS-6 and formed only a
small part of the entire programme. The
shortage of planning time was a source of
problems for the projects. The regions were
chosen because they represented a mix of
isolated rural areas, deficient (by US
standards) in educational and social services and communications facilities. There
was throughout these areas, however, a
high level of familiarity with technology
and ability to maintain it.

(a) Rocky Mountain Educational Project
The Federation of Rocky Mountain States
(FRMS) project was the Satellite Technology Demonstration (STD). It consisted
of several components, implemented by a
core staff in Denver, Colorado and by field
staff at each site, with an intermediate staff
level in each state.

The target audience varied for each

series, but all employed the same reception equipment. A total of 68 receiving stations was established, 56 of which were in rural schools. Of the school-based terminals, 24 (three in each state) had two-way audio communication capabilities, in contrast to the other 'receive-only' terminals. The remaining 12 terminals were installed at public television stations so that the STD programmes could be rebroadcast to a much wider audience viewing on conventional receivers in private homes and schools.

(i) *Time Out* was a one-semester career education course for junior high school students in the seventh to ninth grades (12–14 year olds). The broadcasts were daily, 29 minutes in length and were followed by six minutes of live 'interaction' for the intensive sites, three of which were chosen each day. The local teacher usually selected a volunteer from the class to ask a question over satellite radio. There was no opportunity for the class to discuss programme content or pool their questions; the interaction followed immediately after the taped portion. Each Friday's broadcast was devoted solely to interaction and review of the previous four days' programmes. Most of the sites had the opportunity to interact if they wished during the Friday sessions.

(ii) *Careers in the Classroom* was an in-service training series aimed at classroom teachers and school administrators. It was broadcast every other week; 16 programmes were spread out over 32 weeks. The format was a live lecture from an authority in the field for 20 to 30 minutes, followed by approximately a half-hour of interaction with the teachers at the intensive sites. One programme was devoted entirely to interaction.

(iii) *Commercial education films* on a wide variety of topics were distributed via the satellite for video-taping and later use by the schools.

(iv) *Footprints* was an evening series concerned with topics of interest to the adult rural communities, such as mail fraud, strip mining, and agri-business. There were ten 50-minute programmes in the series; eight of them presented information on the evening's topic, and were followed by interaction. One of the programmes was entirely interactive and the remaining programme had no interaction at all.

(b) *Appalachian Education Satellite Project*

This was run by the Appalachian Regional Commission (ARC) through existing Regional Education Service Agencies (RESAs) at the local level. There were fifteen sites participating in the AESP, arranged in five clusters of three sites each. Each cluster fell under the jurisdiction of one RESA. All three sites in each cluster could receive the satellite broadcasts; only one of them, however, could transmit. The two receiver-only sites interacted directly with the instructor on television through the third site, to which they were connected by telephone. The transmitting site could transmit voice and teletype (not video) to the main studio.

The AESP offered courses in in-service training for teachers on basic elementary reading instruction and on career education instruction. Interaction here was accomplished, for the most part, through a hybrid teletype system. Receive-only sites sent their questions over teletype via lines to the transmitting site in their cluster. Nonredundant questions were sent from that site to the broadcasting studio as teletype messages over the AST-3 satellite, either before or during the programme. A person in the studio received all the sites' questions, filtered out duplicate questions, arranged them roughly by order of importance and gave them to the television instructor to answer.

Following most of the television lessons, there was a 15-minute pre-programmed audio review that made unique use of the four audio channels that accompanied the video picture. The participants each had a four button 'response pad' that actually selected the audio channel that they heard on a set of earphones. All the channels carried the same review material and multiple-choice questions. The students heard identical material until they pushed the button corresponding to their choice of answer to a multiple-choice question. They then heard, on the selected audio track, a description of the factors they should have considered in making their choice. Each answer choice had a different description that was appropriate to that particular answer. The students heard the one most appropriate to his choice and then the common text resumed.

(c) *Appalachian Region Veterans' Administration Hospital Project*

Video seminars constituted the bulk of this experiment. The audiences were physicians, nurses or other health professionals. Approximately 20–30 minutes of each programme were devoted to a pre-taped presentation on the issue of the day, following which the lecturer answered questions from the audience for half an hour.

(d) *Alaska Education Project*

The largest of the projects in Alaska was run by the Governor's Office of Telecommunication (GOT). Primarily an educational project, with programmes for primary school children and in-service training for teachers, it also produced other programmes, including a topical evening show for adults. This, and the two primary school programmes, were designed with the help of 'consumer committees' composed of parents, native leaders, teachers and administrators.

Seventeen sites participated in the demonstration. Each village could receive a video signal and could transmit an audio signal back via ATS-1. A part-time 'utilization aide', recruited locally, was present at each site, to make sure that things ran smoothly, to turn the set on and off, align the antenna where necessary, collect data, distribute project information and supplies to participants, and publicize coming events.

(i) *Primary school programmes* A language development programme, called BOLD (Basic Oral Language Development) was directed at five, six and seven-year-olds. It attempted to increase proficiency in spoken English through the use of repetition drills directed by the studio teacher. The teacher interacted on camera with a robot and then two 'space creature' puppets, trying to teach them English. She also directly prompted the students watching on television to vocalize responses. A set of simple materials for use in the drill exercises was provided to the teacher at the remote schools, together with a lesson guide.

Each programme lasted twenty minutes and was followed by a ten-minute interaction period. The main programme was pre-taped and transmitted from Fairbanks, but the live interaction portion used a different teacher and was transmitted from Juneau. The interaction was used to conduct a roll call of the sites for comments and questions, and to rehearse the drills.

The other primary school programme, *Right On*, was a course for eight, nine-and ten-year olds on health education. It was transmitted immediately before the language development course. Thirty-two programmes were produced in this series.

(ii) *In service training* One programme for local community library personnel employed a correspondence course, plus interaction between the remote students and the studio teacher. The course could be taken for three units of college credit. The students also completed written assignments, participated in televized interaction sessions and attended workshops.

The second teacher in-service training programme offered a package series on motivating students and responded to specific educational needs of the remote teachers.

(iii) *Public programmes* Alaska Native Magazine was a series of 32 evening programmes for adults, presented by an Eskimo. The format included extensive use of film clips, mini-documentaries and news features from the participating sites. Two of the ATS-6's audio channels were used for simultaneous translation of some of the programme content into two native languages. Viewers at a particular site could choose which language they wanted to listen to, but everyone at the site had to listen to the same language, because the sound was played through the speaker on the television monitor.

Interaction was possible at any time during the broadcast, but most occurred when the host solicited reactions from the remote sites. Each week, the programme was broadcast for an hour, about half of which was expected to be devoted to interaction.

(e) *Medical education*

The Washington-Alaska-Montana-Idaho Regional Medical School (WAMI) was an experimental programme in medical education, with headquarters at the University of Washington in Seattle, the only medical school in the region. In one of its experiments, students at the University of Alaska, Fairbanks, received part of their instruction from Seattle via the ATS-6 satellite. These classes were the only ATS-6 educational transmissions able to make use of full duplex video, that is, a professor in Seattle saw the students in Fairbanks at the same time as the students saw him.

An important use of the satellite link was for administration. It was also being used for computer-aided evaluation, medical consultations and for monitoring the progress of students during their clinical period.

(f) Alaska Indian Health Service Project

The Indian Health Service (IHS) project in Alaska was the only one to focus exclusively on health care by satellite. Because the task differed from the educational projects, the organization and procedures followed were somewhat different.

Two of the larger villages have community clinics which became the focal point of a new tele-medicine experiment. Both were equipped with television cameras and transmitters, and consultations could be carried out on live video with the doctors at the Tanana Service Unit's field hospital and specialists at the Anchorage Native Medical Center. The field hospital is about 250 miles from Anchorage and can be reached only by air or river boat. Both clinics are well over 100 miles from the field hospital, and are equally hard to reach.

The nurse or health aide in the remote clinic presented a patient to the field hospital doctor on the video; sometimes the remote doctors presented patients to the specialists in Anchorage.

When necessary, the consultants could transmit video to the remote site. However, only one site could transmit at a time; when the doctor could see the patient, the patient could not see the doctor, and vice-versa. The privacy of medical encounters could be protected with a system of scramblers and descramblers.

3 Observations

In many ways, this ATS-6 demonstration was a technological solution looking for a social problem. This is not necessarily a bad thing, if a country can afford either the costs or the errors that may result. In very large programmes, the risks are proportionately large and planners will probably want to use all available information to minimize the risks. Hopefully, the lessons learned from the US experiences will benefit others who are considering satellites.

Formal evaluations and policy studies of the ATS-6 projects will be forthcoming in 1976 from a variety of sources. Meanwhile, this section reports some observations which we feel may be of interest to planners. We shall not present detailed descriptions of problems and successes of the projects, but try to present findings that have valuable generality.

(a) Some reservations

There is a number of ways in which these projects are not representative of operational projects or the kinds of projects that might be undertaken in less-developed countries. Their lifespan was very short. The knowledge that they would cease to exist after ten months of operation probably affected the planning of the projects and the amount of co-operation they were able to enlist. It certainly had an effect on available man-power resources. In some cases, it meant that staff time and energy was devoted to trying to find some means of continuing the programmes past the termination date of the satellite.

It is doubtful whether the cost data so far available would be meaningful to planners of operational systems (especially those designed from the start for the delivery of educational and social services) or to planners in other countries. The scale of the demonstration project was much smaller than would be reasonable for an operational venture. Thus, while the unit costs for the hardware were higher than might be expected if large quantities were to be manufactured, the total costs of a large system would be higher. The same is true of costs for developing software or programmes; although these were high in per-student or per-hour terms, the total cost of software would be higher for the number of programmes required for any large-scale system. Further, costs quoted at this stage do not include such elements as long-term maintenance and repairs. It must also be noted (and this is one reason why actual costs are difficult to derive) that there are seventeen experiments over and above the HET ones on board the ATS-6; costing out HET's proportion alone would be an extremely complex, if not impossible, procedure. The ATS-6 satellite is heavy and bulky, and requires a larger and more costly launch vehicle than might be needed for a non-experimental satellite. In short, these costs do not reflect what it would cost to build a satellite that would satisfy the needs of an operational system doing similar tasks to those attempted by the ATS demonstration.

One advantage of a satellite is that it is easier, within certain limits, to add additional channels than is the case with a ground-based system, but the ATS-6 project did not explore the advantages of multi-channel capability.

Costs of the ground equipment are unrepresentative, for it was essentially hand-made in small quantities by manufacturers willing to risk venture capital in the hope that the demonstration would create a potential market. Costs now being quoted for similar equipment for planned future systems are higher than were costs for this project. At least part of this problem is due to inflationary trends.

There were many hidden costs in these projects. Facilities, such as roads, school houses, telephones and power supplies already existed. In some cases equipment, such as video-tape recorders and television sets, was purchased by the remote sites. Personnel and assistance were sometimes donated by other organizations. Retraining teachers was not the major cost factor that it has been in some less developed countries.

(b) Hardware

In the ATS-6 projects, system design was determined by technological considerations rather than health or education needs. For example, the two-way capability was available technologically, but the planning was not concerned with *whether* to incorporate it into an educational system, but with *how* to incorporate it.

Here also, no attempt was made to seek out alternative technologies that might have served the same educational/developmental needs as well, better, or more cheaply. The satellite was 'there' and had to be used by a certain date. An operational system would undoubtedly wish to take advantage of an existing communications network, not only because it may have already been fully paid for, but also because it is one which people are accustomed to using and maintaining.

Very specific details of the user's en-

vironment must be taken into account at the design level. For example, one school house was so small that it was impossible to separate the children by appropriate age groups to view the programmes. The net result was that all of the children (ranging from five to twelve years of age) watched the programmes intended for five- to seven-year olds and eight- to ten-year olds. This caused discipline and attention problems.

Equipment will not always be used by engineers and engineers may not be readily available when needed. Often instructions were not suitably worded for non-technician users and there were no labels affixed to the myriad of wires and switches. A good policy for repairs might be to furnish a checklist of things for local staff to do, so as to try to isolate the source of the problem, and then trade the inoperative part for a working one by mail. Alternatively, there should be some spares on-site.

Even for an experimental project in a country with good communications which is able to manufacture its own equipment, it is essential to allow plenty of time for installing hardware, to train people in its use and to maintain a generous stock of spare parts. Centralized purchasing would probably provide technical compatibility, would make for easier repairs, and certainly should offer economies of scale.

(c) Field support

Trained field support is essential for any educational broadcasting project. Regardless of the availability or interaction, the need for having a local expert is greater when the audience at the site is larger, when the goals of the programme are more explicitly educational, when the audience is less motivated, when the subject matter is more general, when the educational level is lower, and when the audience is younger.

It is doubtful whether any single individual, in a remote site, would have sufficient training and the necessary qualifications to be able to cope with several streams and levels of in-school instruction and with several streams of content directed to adults and dealing with development information. As the least well trained teachers are usually found in the most isolated areas, this question needs to be seriously addressed. In the IHS programme in Alaska, for example, the limiting factor was still the level of skill available in the field, rather than some characteristic of the medium.

The level of training required will, of course, vary with the nature of the course, but the use of highly-trained persons may not be necessary if proper support is provided by the project headquarters. The issue of communication between the project management and the project users is one that produces a great deal of emotion, and one that has a direct effect on the users' attitudes and participation. The existence of a communication channel and a person to contact at project headquarters can make a positive contribution to overcoming the problems resulting from inadequate information.

(d) Management

A clear definition of project objectives is a critical necessity from the outset and there is a need for clear, simple lines of responsibility within a project. In one ATS-6 project, curriculum design and scripting were done in one city, production and broadcasting in another, and the interaction was transmitted from still a third city. Not enough provision was made, either in the budget or in the diffuse way management authoriy was exercized, to see to it that these three elements met often or meshed.

A method of creating interdisciplinary cooperation must be devised and implemented from the beginning. One of the major problems of an enterprise such as the ATS-6 project is that those who come from different academic and professional disciplines must be forged into a smoothly working team. This is perhaps the hardest task of all.

Externally, relations with sponsoring agencies must be clearly understood, goals must be clear at all levels and the project should develop good relations with existing institutions. Innovative projects must have consistent high-level support. For some of the ATS-6 projects, its absence created tensions, uncertainty, delays in procurement and problems with staff recruitment. What is at issue here is not only money, although consistency of funding is a major factor.

(e) Software

The users of a programme must be brought into the design at the earliest stages. In some cases where planners conducted 'needs assessments', they seemed to be conducting a 'market survey' instead. A needs assessment ought to start out with as few preconceptions as possible about what it is that the project ought to deliver. A market survey seeks to find out whether people will accept what planners have already decided to do. It is not surprising to find this pattern. Since most projects will be initiated by an entity that already has a plan, there is a tendency to focus on a market approach.

Planners consistently seem to underestimate the importance of supplementary activities and materials in their concentration on the technological aspects of the education system. In one project, a second programme began immediately after the first, which precluded any review of the first or preparation for the second. The rigid schedule imposed by the satellite made it impossible to interrupt a broadcast to seize an opportunity to develop a class's interest or to clarify a confusing point.

Teachers would praise the intent of the programme guides, but noted that because the course designers often seemed not to have been aware of the local constraints, they often had no opportunity to implement the suggestions in their case.

The production of video software, whether for transmission by satellite or not, requires more time and effort than many planners expect. The scripting and production effort must involve people from all relevant disciplines, possibly using 'course teams' from the beginning. It is sometimes forgotten that student time has a dollar value. The cost and effort required to produce educationally effective programming is high, but it is spread over a very large number of students. Programme designers and producers must be certain that a programme actually works before it is distributed. The ATS-6 projects were unable to do this: they had to produce programmes in a context where speed and quantity was more important than quality. In many cases their funding was too limited.

Software may have to be adapted to accommodate local and cultural differences, but unfortunately the ATS-6 projects in the United States did not shed much light on the extent to which it may be necessary. Alaska Native Magazine was the only

235

example of multiple language programming and there were several factors which made it difficult to draw any firm conclusion from this experience. To begin with, everyone at a site had to listen to the same language. Almost all of the audience spoke English and many did not speak the indigenous languages. Secondly, the presence of whites who spoke only English might have inhibited requests to listen to indigenous language versions. Finally, the programme topics were of strong interest to all Alaskans, whatever their place of origin, and to people of many different socioeconomic groups.

An example of localization by turning the control of programme choice and scheduling over to the sites was found in the Rocky Mountains Materials Distribution Service. This was very well received; perhaps because it was addressed to fairly limited goals. It might be difficult to administer in another larger application.

Interaction

Interpretation of the wide variety of evidence on interaction is difficult, because of the technical problems encountered. But the important issues for planners of other systems are conceptual ones, concerned with whether the application of a particular type of interaction in a given situation is likely to succeed.

For large audiences of young students, two-way interaction with a studio teacher does not seem to contribute to educational goals. For adults however, interaction for educational, medical or administrative purposes can be valuable if it is properly structured. They are much better able to cope with the procedures involved.

Unfortunately, there seems to be no way of replicating the successful two-way video interaction of the WAMI experiment in a mass system, although a possible solution to the problem of how to structure 'mass' interaction so that it is valuable was tried in one of the AESP teacher training projects. Several projects tried unsuccessfully to incorporate sessions that relied exclusively on interaction.

As interaction can have good and bad effects on student motivation and acceptance, we should like to see more research on the use of the mails or of occasional interpersonal contacts, for they may provide some of the positive aspects of interaction more cheaply, or more effectively, or both. The provision of an audio channel for administrative communication, however, is essential for the smooth functioning of a satellite system, especially in areas that are not well served by more conventional communication channels.

Wider perspectives

A less developed country planning a satellite system would have a distinct advantage over the ATS-6 projects because it would have time to conduct a comprehensive needs assessment beforehand, and could base its planning on the findings of the research. However, one problem for such a country could be that it may not be economically, or even technologically, feasible, to provide services to the entire population. Serious consideration needs to be given to what the political implications of such a decision will be.

Some of the planning required is very long term. For example, there is a danger that the frequencies that would be the most desirable for an operational satellite broadcast system may be allocated to other uses by the time the demand exists. A parallel problem is that a shortage of geostationary orbit parking spaces for satellites may develop.

Finally, the cost data from the ATS-6 projects are difficult to apply elsewhere. However, it seems likely that the total cost of the education system will be higher, if it is partially based on educational satellite systems. In this sense, technologies such as this represent an addition to educational costs. The value of such an addition must be judged by the value of the increased benefits it supplies.

PAPER NO 19: RTS/PROMOTION AND BBC FURTHER EDUCATION: A COMPARISON BETWEEN TWO ADULT EDUCATION TELEVISION ORGANIZATIONS*

Viviane Glikman, Chef de la Division des Evaluations, Department des Actions Educatives, OFRATEME, Paris, France *Jean-Pierre Corduant*, Department of Educational Activities, OFRATEME, Paris, France.

Two television organizations concerned with adult education appear to be quite similar at first sight, both in their aims and the type of media that they use. These are RTS/Promotion in France and BBC Further Education in Great Britain.

RTS/promotion

RTS/Promotion (Radio-Television Scolaire Pour Adultes) is part of the French office of Modern Educational Techniques (OFRATEME). It is a public institution under the control of the Ministry of Education. The programmes produced by RTS/Promotion are transmitted by the French television organizations (ORTF) on the basis of agreements signed with ORTF. RTS/Promotion's first programmes were produced in 1963–4. The aim of RTS/Promotion's programmes was, from the beginning, to raise the level of basic knowledge, which appeared to be inadequate for many young people, in order to encourage the growth and effectiveness of professional development. The programmes therefore were intended for the broad public of less well-educated adults. Since 1968, the development of RTS/Promotion has been closely linked with the laws which regulate continuous professional education in France, as well as with the bodies responsible for the application of these laws. RTS/Promotion therefore has had to develop broadly and to diversify its televized programmes.

BBC Further Education

BBC Further Education is a part of the

---

* Translated from an original French article, published in *Pour* 43–4, October 1975. We are grateful to the publishers for permission to translate the article.

BBC. The BBC was founded in 1922 and became a public service in 1927, with a Royal Charter which granted it complete independence. Since 1924 the BBC has produced and transmitted educational radio programmes aimed at school children and adults. The extension of this audience to television and an increase in the number of hours of transmission time available made it possible to develop educational television programmes for adults, in close conjunction with organizations responsible for adult education in Great Britain, and so in 1963–4 the radio and television departments of BBC Further Education were set up. From the start, the educational aims and the target audience were broadly defined—'those who cannot be reached by other institutions'—aiming to provide an equal opportunity to all groups of adults. A more detailed description of BBC Further Education and the activities of RTS/Promotion in their use of television, and a comparison between the two organizations, both created at about the same time, provides evidence of a number of points in common, but also evidence of some significant differences.

The media

BBC Further Education and RTS/Promotion organize their multi-media educational activities around a transmission of programmes of 25 or 30 minutes each, arranged in a series of at least 10 programmes on the same theme (economics, science and technology, foreign languages, etc), and for the most part transmitted in the morning and during the weekend—as well as in the early evening (about 7.00 pm.) by BBC Further Education.

Altogether, BBC Further Education television programmes take up nearly 300 hours a year, or about 10 hours a week for 30 weeks, on BBC 1 and BBC 2. RTS/Promotion's programmes cover in all, 125 hours in 1974–5, or five to five-and-a-half hours a week for 20 weeks on FT 1 and Antenne 2, plus 24 hours on a regional network. Many of the BBC Further Education programmes are transmitted twice a week, while only one of RTS/Promotion's series were transmitted twice in 1974–5. BBC Further Education also transmits radio programmes for adults, in the region of 350 hours a year, on Radio 3 and Radio 4.

OFRATEME uses radio for programmes aimed at schools only.

The series of programmes are almost always accompanied by written materials, and, sometimes, other various educational materials: slides, discs, sound cassettes, etc. All the publications of BBC Further Education, most of which are more like books, and are often attractive, are advertized and sold in book shops, at a price which varies between 50 pence and £5. The RTS/Promotion material, the paperback books, are only sold by subscription at 10 francs (£1) per series. A newsletter (Télé-Formation) is sent periodically to all subscribers.

The programmes of both organizations can be followed at home, by individuals, or in further educational centres, through classes run by tutors. For these groups, some of the items are available in advance: printed guidelines for tutors (free from BBC Further Education, 20 francs (£2) per series from RTS/Promotion) and film copies of programmes are hired or sold.

The educational aims

For both RTS/Promotion and BBC Further Education, the aim of their educational activities is more to provide information, an awareness and an introduction than to provide a complete training in a given area of study. It is left to each individual to decide on how much time he will give to studying the materials which accompany the programmes: it could be nothing or it could be several hours a week; there are no controls over this work. Although several series could help in the preparation for examinations, taken together the series do not correspond to any academic course, nor does either of the two organizations give any certificate or qualifications (in contrast with the Open University in Great Britain or Telekolleg in Germany). Besides, neither BBC Further Education nor RTS/Promotion has at its disposal a network of associated centres. It is up to the organizations already involved with continuing education to organize and run classes for the television courses.

Contrary to other French educational television organizations which are concerned with very specific audiences (pupils enrolled with CNAM, agricultural workers) RTS/Promotion aims theoretically at a very broad public. Overall, these are less well educated adults, wishing to improve their general development or to adapt themselves to the development of knowledge, technology and society. At the moment, following the publication in 1974 of the Russell Report, BBC Further Education's attention has also been directed to the 'less fortunate in society' whose initial education has been inadequate. But up to now the range of series offered by BBC Further Education has been drawn up to 'satisfy all types of public' and has tried on the whole to respond to professional educational needs, as well as other needs.

The programmes

BBC Further Education produces series related to problems of the contemporary world and to professional life, but it also devotes a large part of its work to cultural and leisure pursuits. The themes of the 33 radio series and the 54 television series transmitted in 1974–5 were:

- political, economic and social life (race relations, delinquency, adolescence, mass communications, etc),
- professional life (Trade Unions, business, careers, management, teachers' problems, etc),
- modern languages (French, German, Russian, Spanish) and foreign civilizations,
- family life and leisure pursuits (parent-child relationships, rugby, flower arranging, travel, contemporary music, etc),
- arts and sciences (poetry, prehistory, Victorian civilizations, etc).

Some of these series are more specifically aimed at Colleges of Further Education, which cater for a large proportion of adults in training and education in Great Britain. These series then are often transmitted in the day-time, during the week.

Ten of the twelve televized series on offer from RTS/Promotion were concerned with more academic matters:

- economic and social life (economics, social work),
- modern languages (Russian and English),
- oral and written expression and communication (modern French language, human relations),
- mathematics and technology (maths for everyone, mechanics, electronics, computer sciences).

totally responsible both for the expenditure he makes and for the content of the programme. If a problem comes up which might require consultation with more competent authorities, he must decide for himself whether or not to refer the matter to his superiors; it is called the 'referral system'.

The producers are employed by BBC Further Education on a full-time basis in most cases, although some are contracted on a short-term basis. They belong to the television or radio department of BBC Further Education, but can request changes of placement within the BBC. They come from varied backgrounds, and only some of them are university graduates. In summary, they are generally audio-visual specialists, trained within BBC Further Education, other sections of the BBC, the Open University or other organizations. The salaries depend on the work they do, and not on paper qualifications. They are then above all producers of the same status as producers in other sections of the BBC. For this reason, the style of their programmes resembles much more that of other BBC programmes than RTS/Promotion programmes resemble programmes produced by the French national television companies.

Information about the programmes

The brand image This similarity between BBC Further Education programmes and general BBC programmes is reinforced by the fact that educational programmes are not presented as a separate category, but as all other programmes, under the sign of the BBC. Furthermore, BBC Further Education programmes are advertized in daily and weekly publications (in particular in the *Radio Times*, the BBC's weekly magazine about programmes), amongst the other television programmes and are given in as much detail as other programmes.

As far as RTS/Promotion's programmes are concerned, there is a great confusion in the mind of the public, which, when it knows about them, believes that the programmes are ORTF's, but of a lower grade, transmitted at difficult times. The programmes are usually preceded by a rather inexplicit description: 'Ministry of Education/OFRATEME'. They are always introduced very quickly by the television announcers as 'academic' television. This gives them a marginal position, which is hardly appealing, and this is not made any better by the very limited space given to them in papers, compared with other programme details.

In fact, information on programmes is generally more developed in BBC Further Education than in RTS/Promotion. With its own team responsible for publicity, BBC Further Education brings out twice a year a supplement in the *Radio Times*, 'Look, Listen, Learn' which provides a list and a brief description of the term's programmes. This supplement is also sent for distribution to libraries and further education centres. The BBC's General Publicity Department is responsible for liaison with the national, regional and specialized press, and for making use of traditional publicity means. Finally, BBC Further Education publications are directly available to the public through being on sale in bookshops and this also is a form of publicity for the programmes.

Despite the existence, in RTS/Promotion, of an information service, and within OFRATEME, of a Publicity and Sales Department (responsible for publicizing OFRATEME's products, but above all a sales office), no actual publicity has been carried out (up to now) aimed at those individuals likely to follow RTS/Promotion's programmes, apart from some printed publicity articles. Only those who have subscribed, in the past, for the accompanying printed materials are sometimes sent information from one year to another, but these materials themselves, for which it is necessary to subscribe, are not a supplementary outlet of information on RTS/Promotion. In fact, almost all information concerning RTS/Promotion must go through other channels: further education organizations, businesses, regional institutions, education offices, etc. This consists essentially of posters, leaflets and programme lists sent each year, at a time near the start of transmission. Sometimes days for passing on information or studying the material aimed at these organizations are organized regionally. Approached for the most part only after the series have been produced and not at the time when the series are being prepared, the organizations are often not very much interested in

241

passing on the information and are poorly organized to do it. They operate then at a low level of efficiency: 90 per cent of French viewers are unaware of the existence of RTS/Promotion and most of those who do know about it found out by chance.

The audiences

Most of the information that BBC Further Education has on the particular audience following its programmes is provided by the Audience Research Department, which covers all BBC production. The information is of two types: quantitative (number and characteristics of the viewers), and qualitative (opinions on programmes obtained by questions completed by panels), but less detailed all the same than at RTS/Promotion, where evaluation is carried out by a specific team.

The audience for one of BBC Further Education's programmes can vary, at least from 0.1 per cent to 2 per cent (between 50,000 and one million people), depending on the timing and the subject, but there is little information available on those who follow programmes on a regular basis. The number of accompanying booklets sold is between 2,000 to 70,000, according to the series. It is particularly high for foreign language and leisure series. There is also little information about those who buy these materials, if they are not registered with one of the teaching institutions.

At RTS/Promotion, the subscribers are surveyed and enquiries can be made about them. They are well-known, regarding both their characteristics and their reactions to the programmes. But there are relatively few of them: about 5,000 subscribers per year, in total, and at least 15,000 accompanying booklets. It is difficult to compare the audiences of RTS/Promotion and BBC Further Education. In effect, evaluated by the agency of Centre of Opinion Research, responsible for audience measurement for all televised programmes, RTS/Promotion's audience is not calculated by the programme, but by the series and by the whole of the programming. In 1973–4, each series had been followed regularly or occasionally by between 100,000 to 500,000 people; taking all its programmes together, RTS/Promotion acquired a regular public of about 600,000 people (2 per cent of viewers) and reached altogether about 1.8

million people (6 per cent of viewers). In both cases, the times of transmission are not helpful for the public at large, although the more numerous times for BBC Further Education are relatively less restrictive. It is one of the factors which, among many others of a more sociological and economic nature, affects the public reached by these organizations.

Whether it's a question of purchasers of accompanying booklets or the total number of viewers, the public is made up, both for BBC Further Education and RTS/Promotion, above all of people belonging to the 'middle class', and of a medium level of education (8 to 10 years of study), motivated by an intellectual curiosity and a wish for general culture rather than by precise professional necessity.

The publics reached by BBC Further Education and RTS/Promotion are very similar. RTS/Promotion though, which must justify the use of its budget by its success in achieving the objectives laid down for it, measures its success by the extent and the characteristics of the public on which it has an impact. BBC Further Education, on the other hand, attaches importance above all to the quality of its programmes, which are generally very favourably received. This has implications for the situation and actual prospects of each of the organizations.

Prospects

The two organizations are facing problems of an important and different nature. BBC Further Education is to redirect its activities towards the 'disadvantaged', following the conclusions of the Russell Report. It sees this new orientation of its programmes being directed towards the deaf, the elderly, and most of all, towards a series of television and radio programmes aimed at adult illiterates. The television programmes, lasting 10 minutes each, will be transmitted at a peak time, throughout the year, for three years. In another direction, BBC Further Education, in collaboration with the Trades Union Congress, is preparing a series, also for three years, aimed at trade unionists. Finally, its development will be at least partly influenced by the conclusions of the royal commission (Annan Committee on the Future of Broadcasting) which is looking at future prospects in broadcasting, particularly the possibility of a fourth television network.

As for RTS/Promotion, after seeing a very rapid growth between 1968 and 1973, it is now forced to reduce the number of hours per week of transmission: 8 hours in 1973–4, 5 hours in 1975–6, and 3 to $3\frac{1}{2}$ hours is anticipated for 1976–7. The reason for this is first and foremost financial (the increase in tariffs). But it is especially criticized for reaching a smaller public with its televised programmes, particularly with regard to subscribers, and this does not correspond with its initial objectives. To remedy this situation RTS/Promotion is tending to develop multi-media educational productions which are not destined for television transmission. Besides giving up the development of a new series, it will limit its transmission firstly to programmes covering training activities or aimed at adults in training, and secondly to stimulating programmes aimed at encouraging a public with little previous formal education, through changing their attitude to continuing education and training, although even this project is running into difficulties.

From this short description, two principal factors seem to explain the differences we have described between the two organizations:

- the place they occupy in relation to the television system and the adult education system,
- the different structures of these two systems in France and Great Britain.

The lack of integration of RTS/Promotion with the television set-up is an essential cause of the limit on the volume of production and hours of transmission; this influences the content and style of the programmes and clearly reduces the potential audience and the public actually reached. This handicap is not helped by being a part of the Ministry of Education's educational set-up for adults, for this is strongly centralized, recently restructured, and has a minor role in the public and private network of continuing education. Hence it does not offer sufficient support.

BBC Further Education, which is an integrated part of a highly independent television organization, but which also works in liaison with a decentralized education system, has a number of advantages, among which is the prestige of the BBC. Furthermore, there are also political reasons why BBC Further Education looks to its future without great anxiety, and plans for its future development, while RTS/Promotion's television activities are set back each year, and therefore must constantly fight for its very existence.

In France, the most transmitted television programmes are those which have the best chance of being watched by the largest audience, and these programmes are those aimed at pleasure and entertainment. Although some cultural programmes are produced by the television networks, despite low audience figures, the principal criterion for judging the educational programmes produced by development and training organizations—and by RTS/Promotion in particular—is that of rapid success in achieving the objectives assigned to them. If these objectives are not achieved, the reaction is to reduce or even to stop televised productions, instead of doing something about the factors which are known to be the cause of the relative failure of the production (such as publicity, transmission times, budget, the programmes themselves, etc).

While aiming at a large audience and although aware of the fact that education through television, without any final qualifications, cannot attract spontaneously those who have not received a certain initial level of education, the management of the BBC does not seek to offer to viewers just the entertainment programmes that they expect. They believe that by concerning themselves with the daily problems and difficulties of ordinary people, and by providing the necessary facilities of time and resources, they will succeed in reaching more of the disadvantaged. They judge that it is worth the effort, and they are trying to improve their activities in this way. To transmit good educational television programmes is considered then by the BBC as a duty that it must carry out as a public service, even if these programmes do not correspond to the explicit expectations of the general public and even if the relationship between cost and audience is high, for it reckons that in the long term the programme can contribute to changing the attitude of this public, by bringing to it a certain level of awareness and by helping it to 'live in a better way'. If this optimism and practical educational determination are possible in the British social framework, they are hardly imaginable in the French political and institutional context.

PAPER NO 35: THE POLITICAL EVALUATION OF EDUCATIONAL BROADCASTING: A CANADIAN CASE STUDY

Thérèse Lamy, Educational Technologist, Télé-Université, Québec, Canada, *John Daniel*, Director, Educational Technology and Production, Télé-Université, Canada.

Radio-Québec and the Canadian broadcasting scene

Much of the interest of Canadian politics lies in the continual tug of war between the federal and provincial governments in the many grey areas where jurisdiction has never been established to everyone's satisfaction. In recent years communications, and particularly television, has been the most sensitive of these areas. Many colourful confrontations have punctuated the ongoing quarrel over who should control the delivery of television to the Canadian public and in 1975 the Mounties and the provincial police almost came to blows with each other in trying to carry out the orders of their respective masters concerning a cable TV station in Rimouski, Québec.

The British North America Act, Canada's constitution, gives the federal government jurisdiction over communications facilities which cross provincial boundaries. In the 1860s when the act was written, communications meant principally railways and the development of Canadian communications law can be summarized as the application to each new medium (telephones, radio, television) of the legal framework designed for the railways. Naturally this creeping extension of jurisdiction has not gone unchallenged. Several legal battles took place before the federal

jurisdiction over open air TV broadcasting was confirmed and an even longer series of court cases is still continuing over the question of who controls cable television.

It was in October 1969, as a result of frustrations engendered by the seemingly endless appropriation by the federal government of the tools required to maintain cultural identity in the modern world, that the Québec government passed a law creating the Office de Radio-télédiffusion du Québec (ORTQ). This body, known, somewhat confusingly since it is almost exclusively a TV operation, as Radio-Québec, had a mandate to produce educational radio, TV and audio-visual productions and to co-ordinate audio-visual services within the Québec government.

However, frustration seemed to breed frustration, and for the first five years of its existence Radio-Québec seemed like a solution in search of a problem. The role of co-ordination of governmental audio-visual services passed to the newly created Ministry of Communications in December 1969 and from then until 1974 Radio-Québec's production consisted mainly of school TV programmes for the Ministry of Education. These were either broadcast by the Canadian Broadcasting Corporation's French language network or carried on private cable stations.

In 1967 the federal government had legislated that throughout Canada the UHF broadcast band should be reserved for educational programming and that all TV receivers sold after 31 May 1969 should be able to pick up such transmissions. In spring 1974, after another flare-up in the Québec-Ottawa quarrel, Radio-Québec decided to take advantage of this provision and applied to set up a UHF TV network. Since the decision-making structure of Radio-Québec was such as to satisfy the (federal) broadcast licensing authority of its political independence, the appropriate permits were obtained and broadcasting began in Montreal and Québec City in January 1975. The network is planned to cover almost all the populated area of this vast province by 1980.

Not surprisingly the combination of Radio-Québec's independence with its increasingly heavy demands on public funds created some tensions within the Québec government and it was felt appropriate, before giving the go-ahead for the extension of the network to other regions, to hold public hearings so that the inhabitants of all regions could make their views known. In submitting memoranda and in raising points at the public hearings, individuals and groups were asked to address the following issues:

1 the type of TV programming Radio-Québec should carry in your region;
2 the setting up of a Radio-Québec UHF transmitter in your region;
3 the possibility of regional productions;
4 air time for regional programming;
5 two-way traffic between your region and the Radio-Québec network.

The hearings: what was heard

The hearings lasted six months, visiting in that period all the major cities and regions of the province and receiving some 150 memoranda from school boards, credit unions, trade union groups, universities, associations, government departments, and others, both institutions and individuals. Amongst all that was written and said two things stood out: firstly the virulence of the criticisms directed at Radio-Québec, and secondly the similarity between the alternatives proposed by different critics.

The virulence of the criticisms, which surprised and shocked Radio-Québec, was all the more remarkable in that when the hearings started Radio-Québec had been on the air for less than a month—and that only in two cities. Admittedly many people had had a chance to see Radio-Québec's cable offerings in the previous years, but it is an open question whether criticisms arose in all cases from an analysis of the programming rather than from an aversion to Radio-Québec's publicity campaign in favour of the new 'third network', or from purely philosophical considerations.

The criticisms centred round four points.

● It was generally felt that Radio-Québec should abandon the 'third network' approach—since this obliges it to ape the two others—and become instead a real tool for social development by allowing the people to determine the content.
● Radio-Québec does not reflect the regional realities of Québec since it is essentially a metropolitan, Montreal-based operation. (Montreal contains nearly half of the population of the province.) Production should be decentralized so that regional groups can produce to their own needs.
● Radio-Québec has fallen for the élitist, technical mystique associated with professional, broadcast type equipment. Instead it should make greater use of light, inexpensive $\frac{1}{2}''$ and $\frac{3}{4}''$ equipment which would also facilitate production in the regions.
● Radio-Québec should cease to be a production centre pushing out to the people pseudo-educational programming designed by a minority 'cultural establishment'. It should become instead a central nervous system allowing exchanges between communicators and groups around the province to whom Radio-Québec technical assistance would be made available.

These criticisms were combined in an especially cogent fashion in the memorandum submitted by the Institut Canadien d'Education des Adultes which stated:

Radio-Québec has reached an *impasse*. Either it remains television by an élite for an élite or it becomes an instrument for the development of the masses and therefore controlled by them.

University attitudes

Only four of the memoranda submitted presented the institutional positions of institutions of higher education and, significantly, these were from the three most remote campuses in the University of Québec network and the University of Sherbrooke, which is the smallest of the French language universities in the province.* Each of these campuses has given itself a strong regional vocation, claims to understand local needs, and has partly decentralized its own services in an attempt to reach students scattered over wide areas. The University of Québec campuses attach particular importance to the development of media permitting two-way communication between students and instructors. In

---

* Memoranda from the urban universities appeared when this paper was in the press. However, these memoranda echoed the views of those mentioned here and contributed little to the debate.

their memoranda these campuses expressed the wish that Radio-Québec promote this development.

Not surprisingly they also endorsed the criticisms already enumerated. The University of Québec at Rimouski, for example, inveighed against, 'the domination of the metropolis, the dependency of the peripheral regions and the disequilibrium in the exchanges between centre and periphery'. The same memorandum complains that these peripheral regions suffer from unilateral decisions made in Montreal not only about the programming they are to receive but about the development of their own communications infrastructure. It also denounces the pseudo-educational character of Radio-Québec's programming which promotes culture of an individualist type rather than strengthening collective cultural phenomena.

Although these universities would like to see Radio-Québec become a repository for instructional materials and collaborate with them in the production and broadcasting of strictly instructional (course-based) television, they place even more emphasis on influencing the general educational programming in their areas and on the development of interactive systems.

What of the silent majority?

There is obviously a temptation for Radio-Québec to suggest that since malcontents tend to shout loudest the memoranda submitted at the hearings were unrepresentative. This is obviously partly true, for the university submissions were all from numerically marginal outlying institutions rather than from the large urban campuses in Montreal and Québec City. However it seems unlikely that throughout the six months of hearings the grinding of partisan axes could have drowned out a popular groundswell in favour of Radio-Québec's present programming.

We are led to the conclusion that there is little enthusiasm in Québec either for the cultural type of educational broadcasting currently being provided by Radio-Québec or for a more directly institutional type of approach. The authors' own institution, a distant study university serving students province-wide, would probably have proposed, had it submitted a memorandum at the hearings, an OU-BBC type arrangement

between the university and Radio-Québec. However there was little in the memoranda actually submitted suggesting a public demand for this type of 'open university' TV.

The feasibility of the alternatives

The objections raised at the Radio-Québec hearings are really objections to the whole notion of using broadcasting for popular education, and the alternatives proposed are based on a common carrier approach. Broadcasting is by definition a centre-to-periphery operation and, as Radio-Québec's president asked somewhat plaintively after the hearings, where does regionalization stop? Small towns can resent the hegemony of regional capitals just as much as the regional capitals resent that of the metropolis. International comparisons, of course, tend to make talk of the regionalization of programming in Québec seem excessive, for there can be few places where a population only 6 million strong already generates so much of its own television. However, the argument that the whole population of Québec would fit into Paris ignores the physical reality of the vast distances between regions. The regional capitals of Rouyn and Rimouski are some 1300 km apart and local differences cannot be denied.

More radical than regionalization is the concept of a two-way television service on common carrier lines. The regional universities seem to be asking for a video version of an educational telephone network such as that in use in the state of Wisconsin. Since it is only in the last few years that technology has advanced sufficiently to make such audio networks successful a multi-point interactive video network seems years away, not to mention the much greater costs inherent in the extra bandwidth requirements. Fortunately Québec is an active experimenter in the use of satellites in interactive education and hopefully such experiments will enable universities to identify more clearly the role of real-time interaction between teacher and distant student. Such studies may show that multi-point interactive video systems are, like the simpler video telephone, a nice expensive technology which no one really needs! Inherent in all the objections to Radio-Québec's present offerings was the idea that the selection of programming should be done 'by the people and for the people'. Laudable though this aim certainly is we are unsure how it can be achieved or even how to measure the extent to which it is achieved.

Conclusion
The public hearings into Radio-Québec have raised more questions than they have settled, showing that the political evaluation of educational broadcasting is a complex process.

Since there are few scientifically-based conclusions about the instructional, educational and cultural capabilities of broadcast television, people inevitably bring to any political evaluation a host of unproven assumptions and muddled hypotheses. Hopefully this situation will improve as the corpus of knowledge on the evaluation of broadcasting expands, and it is in such a way that this conference can facilitate future political decisions.

PAPER NO 42: THE FEDERAL ROLE IN FUNDING CHILDREN'S TELEVISION PROGRAMMING

Keith Mielke, Rolland C. Johnson and Barry G. Cole, Institute for Communication Research, Indiana University, USA.

Scope and methodology of the study
United States Office of Education's (USOE) Office of Planning, Budgeting and Evaluations contracted this policy investigation to the Institute for Communication Research, Indiana University, and specified its scope, which focuses ultimately on USOE policy in funding national purposive television programming for children. Information and policy recommendations were gathered from existing sources in the general literature, USOE file materials, ten single-topic commissioned papers, a ten-member advisory board, a Federal advisory group, and interviews. Over ninety interviews were conducted in six locations, including Washington, DC, with personnel directly involved in or knowledgeable about the dispensing and/or utilization of Federal

dollars in support of children's television programming. Children's programmes examined primarily from a funding viewpoint included *Big Blue Marble, Carrascoledas, Inside/out, Sesame Street, The Electric Company, Villa Alegre,* and *Zoom.*

The Final Report[1] provides a descriptive map of the various components essential to an integrated system of broadcasting; gives a side-by-side comparison of USOE's two major investments, totalling over $50 million, in children's programming (Children's Television Workshop and series and spot announcements funded under the Emergency School Aid Act); and summarizes major policy issues, alternatives, and recommendations.

Compatibility with requirements of broadcasting
A fundamental decision for USOE is whether or not it wants to participate in purposive national television programming in the first place. Television operates as an enormously complex system, and cannot be dealt with simplistically by the government or any other institution with expectation of success. Purposive programming, aimed at in-home use and in competition with commercial programming, must first succeed in television terms before it can succeed in other terms. The risks of failure are high; but the potential pay-off is also high.

The need for Federal support
Another fundamental decision is whether to launch projects which must then in some way become self-sustaining or supported by other funds, or whether to provide a long-term service through sustained funding for programmes for which consumer loyalty and demand can be demonstrated. For five reasons (given in the main paper), the report suggests that the options and probabilities for maintaining successful series without Federal support are unpromising.

Sustaining successful programme series
In USOE policy, there is no apparent answer to the question of what should be done in case an experimental series succeeds; policy orientations and expectations seem more geared to failure than to success. A policy is sorely needed to determine the means by which 'survivors' of fair market trials can be funded for the duration of

demonstrable consumer demand for a children's series. In the final report, three alternatives are presented as suggestions (these are listed in the main paper).

Policy and administrative needs

There was a generally recognized and urgent need for an improved administrative structure that could generate, co-ordinate, and administer short-term and long-term policy in the area of television. Personnel qualified with the necessary dual expertise in broadcasting and areas of programme content are in very short supply in USOE. More direct lines of communication between project officers and policy co-ordinators were also necessary. Three alternatives for reorganization are presented in the main paper.

Federal control of television programming

There is a trend within USOE toward greater control and in-process monitoring of television projects involving USOE funding. Few USOE persons advocated greater delegation of flexibility and responsibility to the contractee/grantee. Professional broadcasters opposed this trend, and their reasoning and experiences were persuasive. The record to date suggests that the more freedom and responsibility given to a production agency after the basic commitment has been made, the greater the likelihood of a successful programme, and hence the better the Federal investment. Producers resented the presumed adversary relationship invoked by some Federal project officers and its implication that responsible production agencies were somehow trying to cheat the government. Federal monitoring has now extended into areas that intrude upon the aesthetic and management decisions of the producer, such as casting and shooting locations, and in some cases, prior script approvals by Federal personnel were required. There is both a legal and a philosophical commitment that public broadcasting should not become, and may not be perceived as becoming, a government information distribution agency. The need is great for policy that is more knowledgeable about and sensitive to the requirements of broadcasting.

CTW and ESAA-TV

The success of the two CTW programmes (*Sesame St* and *The Electric Company*) is now a matter of record. The record of ESAA-TV projects is still being written, but its early history has been plagued with many problems. While CTW has operated under discretionary funding in an environment of minimal interference with USOE, the ESAA-TV projects were funded under legislation with rather specific language and administered in a far more restrictive manner. Given past efforts and continued determination within USOE to discontinue funding for both CTW and ESAA-TV, the policy importance of what *is* desired for future funding increases.

Evaluation

Evaluation is important in program development and production, where pretesting can provide corrective feedback to the production staff before the product is finalized. This function is best carried out by in-house evaluation staff communicating directly with in-house producers. Dysfunctional pressures are brought to bear on the formative evaluation process when in-house formative data are utilized by out-of-house decision-makers for summative-type decisions, such as in the review of pilot-testing data for go/no-go decisions on an entire series.

The in-school audience

Current funding for learning resources at the state and local level will permit co-operative production (whether through AIT or another consortium) of only one major series per year. The theoretical maximum for the system as a whole is seven series. The limiting factor is funding at the state level, and this is where the Federal dollar can play a constructive role.

Reference

1 MIELKE, K., JOHNSON, R. C. and COLE, B. G. *The Federal Role in Funding Children's Television Programming*, Bloomington, Institute for Communication Research, Indiana University, 1976.

PAPER NO 50: ETV—MARANHÃO: AN EFFECTIVE CASE OF ENDO-GENOUS GROWTH

João B. A. Oliveira, Federal University, Rio de Janeiro, Brazil.

1 Objectives

The purpose of the present paper is three-fold:

(a) a description of Educational Tele-vision—Maranhão (ETV) since its formation up to the present stage;

(b) an analysis and evaluation of the educational results and the process of institution building which accom-panied the introduction of this particular innovation;

(c) the discussion of institutional changes required for the expansion of the system.

2 Background

The State of Maranhão with an area of 328,663 Km², is situated between the Ama-zon forest and the north east of Brazil. It is one of the poorest areas in South America, with a GNP per capita under US$500. Its population rose from 1,500,000 inhabitants in 1950 to about 3,000,000 in 1970. Most of its inhabitants (75 per cent) live in rural areas. The State Capital is São Luis, with a population of 324,650 inhabitants in 1970. Tropical rains fall about six months per year, as in the Amazon. Industries are very few and small and the most important product is 'babacu' oil extracted from the native coconut.

(a) Educational situation

The sixties were a phase of great educational expansion. By the end of 1968 only 34 per cent of the school-age population (7–11) were enrolled in the primary school, mostly concentrated in São Luis. There was a growing demand from an extremely wide-spread population, in areas where teaching conditions and the availability of primary schools were very limited. The few existing secondary schools were private-owned, leaving no chance of schooling for a signifi-cant part of the population.

(b) Planned strategy

While substantial improvements were plan-ned for the primary level in the whole

state, a major effort had to be made in the four upper grades (5th to 8th), in order to create better opportunities for the adoles-cents and meet social and labor-market demands. As a part of the overall state-government plan, it was then decided that public schooling should be extended from 5th to 8th grade, starting in São Luis, where the calculated demand was in the range of 6,000 openings by 1968.

(c) Educational needs

Teaching conditions and the availability of primary schools (60 per cent in rural areas) were very limited and the rural population was very widespread. This situation was even worse at the secondary level.

(d) ETV—the experiment

ETV—Maranhão was conceived by a team of educators led by Mr Macedo-Costa, the founder and director of a 10-year experi-ment of a community-based school in the small village of Colinas (4,000 inhabitants). As Mr Macedo-Costa described it at the time, the main consideration evolved around the need to understand the target population—adolescents living in slums in a rapidly changing São Luis.

The main philosophical and pedagogic objectives were detailed in a document approved by the State Governor. Most of these principles can still be detected in the operations of ETV, though their enunci-ation is not fully operational and unam-biguous. However, when compared with the objectives and educational practices used in the north east at that time, they certainly reflected and still reflect a major departure from tradition. These main ob-jectives are:

● the school should be community-ori-ented, taking into account the realities of the environment. The curricula must consider the changes that local society is under-going from the perspective of the student's chances of participation;

● the school is not merely to instruct, but to educate. Intellectual skills will by no means prevail over socio-emotional and psychomotor educational goals, and that must be reflected in curricula and evalu-ation plans;

● the adolescent should be an active ele-ment in the school operation, and not a passive recipient. The organization of

TV-classes must be his responsibility as much as ETV's responsibility;

● the basic unit of the school's organization is the small-group; group-dynamics, group-centred learning and teaching, peer-tutoring are key elements, with 'monitors' playing an important animating role;

● TV and printed materials should provide 'support to learning';

● there will be remedial instruction;

● students as well as the monitors and the overall system have to be constantly evaluated.

The educational process was conceived as a *four-phase learning-cycle:* a *stimulus* or challenging situation presented after each televized lesson: *reflection*, which is individual and collective, to develop the function of criticism; the third phase is *individual* and *group response* to the stimulus, carried out in a number of ways, and intended to foster assimilation; finally there is *group evaluation synthesis.*

The plan also anticipated difficulties such as equipment, lack of trained personnel for TV, shortage of money, reaction from the traditional educators. These were considered a part of the reality to be changed.

(e) The operation
FMTVE (Fundação Maranhense de TV Educativa) was created in 1969. The first year consisted of an experimental phase on closed-circuit, followed by open broadcasting in 1970. Though following the general educational laws, it was left with a broad margin of autonomy.

FMTVE's President is the State Secretary of Education. It is managed by an Executive Director and three Directors of Operations: Pedagogic, Production and Administrative Services. There is a 5–7 member staff reporting to the Executive Director, in charge of co-ordination and training.

(f) Production and broadcasting
Special teams of specialists from education and production prepare TV-classes and printed materials for students and teachers. The degree and form of relationships between the specialists varied in time, although education has always somehow prevailed. Production goes from curriculum development to summative evaluation of materials. There are several formal and informal checkpoints and feedback mechanisms.

The two studios have always been under-equipped while operating. The average daily production is 4 tapes of 20 minutes per studio. Televised lectures with increasing usage of films and illustrations are the predominant approach. Each program is planned in terms of specific objectives and integrated with other subject-matters and printed materials. Classes are re-taped every year, due to a chronic shortage of tapes. Though raising the amount of work, it allows for revisions.

The schedule allows for four emissions per class per day, each emission being typically followed by 30–40 minute in-class activities following the basic pattern of the small-group-based learning cycle. A class consists of 6 to 7 groups of 7 students. Formerly, the organized TV-class was the responsibility of the local community and students. The growth of the system led to increased centralization and standardization, though most of the responsibility for the operation of the classes and common facilities are still left to students and monitors. There are active student councils, teachers' meetings and several committees to run the 'school' and the in-class and extra-curricular activities, which take 5 hours a day.

Evaluation is a major concern. There are weekly TV-tests, teacher-made tests and several in-class, club and homework assignments. There are individual, small-group and monitor-led evaluations, involving intellectual and social skills with monthly grades and evaluative remarks. Monitors, TV classes, extra-curricular activities and several other aspects are constantly monitored and evaluated, and feedback is communicated by means of meetings, reports or organizational decisions. Passing criteria are criterion-based, evaluated at a high performance level (70 per cent) in a regular and innovative way.

The main departures from 'traditional' schools are: community-orientated curricular content, active participation of individual students and small-groups in all aspects of school life, evaluation philosophy and practices, career-development for teachers, no principals in schools. And, of course, TV.

3 Educational results

Passing rates are never below 90 per cent of students still enrolled by the end of the period. Enrolment has stabilized at about 12,000 students, which can be entirely explained by the full satisfaction of the current demand.

With regard to the absolute and relative number of ETV alumni who passed the upper-secondary school entrance exams in São Luis, the figures tend to favour ETV students as compared with all other students from private schools: 43 per cent of those passing come from ETV, and this represents a passing rate of 60 per cent of ETV candidates. Though 57 per cent of the total students passing come from other schools, they represent only 35 per cent of candidates from these schools.

Passing rates are extremely high, considering that it is by grades and not automatic. This could be partially due to the fact that most tests are group based. An additional confounding factor may be the inclusion of socio-emotional and psychomotor performance data in the passing criteria, although available data considering cognitive aspects alone would not indicate differences below 90 per cent for final passing.

Attendance rates are considerably above average figures for São Luis and for Brazil, although there are no special incentives such as free lunch. In fact freedom to come or leave school is greater than in other schools, although group effects on attendance rates are striking. The results could possibly be explained in terms of group-pressure.

FMTVE students come from the lowest socio-economic status groups in, as indicated, São Luis, by lower family income, the localization of TV-classes close to slum areas (no bussing) and the fact that the private schools are fee-paying and the TV-school is free. In consequence the results in terms of grade passes appear remarkable, since it indicates a clear superiority of lower-class ETV students in the entrance exams, which do not favor ETV students on curriculum content grounds.

The program strengthens social mobility considerably by providing eighth-grade diplomas to lower-status students. In addition it tends to encourage emigration to more developed areas. Leadership and social abilities of ETV alumni are apparently extremely and positively differentiated from the other students, even at the 2nd grades of upper-secondary school. However, existing evidence to date is only anecdotal.

When the national educational reform law started to be implemented in São Luis in 1972, ETV had already anticipated not only virtually all the innovation adopted by the law but still could be considered ahead in many points. It is also notable that these results were achieved despite the doubling of student population of 6,000 in 1969 to 12,000 in 1972–3.

4 The process of institution building

Some of the major factors in the institutional development of ETV are analysed in the remainder of the paper.

(a) Institutional doctrine

A clear body of doctrine was embodied in the experiment, as described in section 2. It reflects Piagetian psychology mostly in the presentation of group-dynamics, functioning characteristics and objectives. The instrumental plan anticipated in Brazil most of the now commonly used terms and operations familiar to educational technologists, such as operational objectives, formative evaluation, learning feedback and remedial instruction. The principal key to success was the appropriateness of the small group approach and the secondary though vital helping role of TV. The actual operation of classes and the annual teacher-training programs reinforce these doctrines.

(b) Leadership

Political support from Governor Sarney and State Secretary of Education, Dr Cabral, were vital to the first two years of the project. The whole doctrine and implementation characteristics can be attributed to Mr Macedo Costa and his brother, Mr A. Macedo, who succeeded as Executive Director up to 1972. They developed a very powerful, dedicated and technically competent staff group, most of whose members still remain at FMTVE and can be regarded as the key elements of the system. Since its creation FMTVE has had 5 Presidents and 4 Executive Directors, each of whom left important contributions to the project.

This high turn-over of top management may be regarded as symptoms of major institutional crises, particularly from 1972–4. Under these circumstances, the endurance of the philosophy, doctrine and the system's basic characteristics can be attributed to the staff. Some members of the staff, all of whom remained with FMTVE since the beginning until 1974 are starting to leave the system, attracted by job offerings in the south. It may be asked what would have happened if the Macedo brothers were still there. It must also be pointed out that the technical directors never exerted a prominent leadership position, certainly due to the behavior of staff members.

(c) *Personnel*
Table 1 shows the present distribution of personnel:

Table 1   Personnel at FMTVE March 1975

Monitors	359
Supervisors	29
Producers	47
Pedagogists	56
Technicians	53
Administrative Staff	168
Managers	20
Total	732

It is interesting to note that monitors have been very influential not only in the classes but in the whole system, since the career plan allows them to become producers, technicians or managers; that is also the case of supervisors. The actual production of TV-classes is performed by producers, curriculum and communication specialists, and the training is almost always on-the-job. The internal relationships of those groups reflect management changes over the period, and the present trend is toward integration in all phases of production, as originally.

The salaries are generally low, even compared to the labor market in São Luis, although labor opportunities are restricted. The monthly payroll amounts to about US$75,000 with an average of US$100 a month per person. Political influence from the State Secretary of Education still helps to complicate admission and firing procedures thereby lowering productivity.

(d) *Organization*
It is noteworthy that the chronic problems of FMTVE, such as lack of tapes, equipment maintenance, physical facilities, labor disputes, evaluation procedures, training and funding, despite being well known, have never been solved simultaneously, due either to lack of money, personnel, expertise or political support.

As one problem was solved, others remained, precluding stabilization of a phase and the development of another. Problems became more critical as the system grew older, staff became worn out and political pressure for the expansion of the system to the whole state grew increasingly stronger.

(e) *Resources and costs*
In 1975, FMTVE's annual budget was equivalent to approximately US$1.65 million, (84 million cruzeiros), of which nearly 95 per cent came from the State budget. FMTVE's expenditure in 1975 was just over 16 per cent of the total State educational budget (including Federal funds). In relative terms it represents a major effort in education and tele-education. In absolute terms it also illustrates the extremely poor situation of the State, the educational sector and ETV. The spasmodic nature of outside financing, which took four years to become reality represents a strong help, though it could be considered small when compared to the Federal resources allocated to other tele-education projects. A cost analysis of ETV is the theme of further studies tentatively planned for 1976.

(f) *Enabling linkages*
State Secretariat of Education, as previously shown, has always been responsible for major financial effort to support the project. Operational independence from the Secretariat may be one of the key reasons leading to the feasibility and success of the project. However this may also explain most of the difficulties, particularly related to its expansion towards students of other socioeconomic groups and to the diffusion of innovative values into the Secretariat.

Financial help was not accompanied by other types of political and technical support, mostly in regard of federal agencies like PRONTEL—the National Tele-Education Agency. The development of a national policy of tele-education, anxiously expected since 1969, has never become a reality.

(g) Functional linkages

There is an evident disfunctional link between the tele-education project and regular schooling, even in São Luis. The project is still generally regarded by the establishment as a compromise solution, not suitable for middle and upper classes. This is also true for the rest of Brazil, where tele-education is commonly understood as a second opportunity for adult education. Being almost unanimously recognized as a successful project by leading specialists in the field, (which is not true of most of the other projects in the country) this seems to raise opposition at those places where school-TV is not regarded as a priority for educational TV. The expected help in terms of training, technical support and programs from other centers was never possible, due to the lack of a national policy and co-ordination.

Rather than discussing compatibility of the institution's values with custom, mores and law, it would be more appropriate to consider *tolerance* of the official educational doctrine with the project, which is typical in most innovations. The resources and support can be explained in great part due to the lack of conditions to afford the 'regular schooling system' and the inertia that organizations typically acquire. The fact that Maranhão was until recently the only tele-education project in formal education, and is still the biggest, may explain the uncertainty of federal authorities to recognize its merits and endorse its operations.

Conclusions

FMTVE still faces the fact that several problems need to be solved more or less simultaneously: political influences on personnel; very low salaries; lack of local people to guarantee a good performance and maintenance of the new equipment; need of renewal and upgrading of the staff's level; and the need of internal reorganization.

An evaluation of the institutional perspective should be based on the future, rather than in the present or contemporary adequacy to ongoing tasks, objectives or needs.

ETV as an innovation failed to apply itself to other educational problems in São Luis. It did not innovate outside ETV-classes. It is not accepted as an alternative for students from higher socio-economic groups. As time passes, ETV's values become more and more differentiated from and less integrated with the 'official' thought at the State Secretariat of Education. A linking between the two value systems is badly needed, although there are no signs of ongoing actions in this direction. FMTVE keeps worried about its own problems and the expansion, while the Secretariat thinking does not go beyond funding problems. Initial independence, essential in the beginning, may now appear as a major threat to the application and diffusion of an innovation which seemed well on the road to success.

As far as the national co-ordination agency is concerned, which could officially amplify the merits and adequacy of ETV—Maranhão, it is not possible to foresee any major technical or political backing due to the very low-key position in which PRONTEL has placed itself. It is an important linkage that must be maintained but not a very promising one.

Finally there is the pressure to expand the ETV system for the whole state, and the fact must be understood not only from the point of view of the demand for schools as well as from the fact that 1976 is an election year for most of the mayors of the main cities and villages. Federal money from a special developing fund—POLOAMA-ZONIA—has already been allocated to FMTVE's expansion and represents about $2.5 million dollars for a two-year period.

It is a natural outlook to expect major changes in ETV—Maranhão in the coming years. Personnel may get tired of working so hard for such low pay, after 5 to 6 years. The philosophical principles may start to fade, when new leadership has not the same charisma as the founders, and when old leaders have been fired for defending so strongly their independence and the innovative features of the system which they deemed essential. Idealism may start fading, mostly when the financial difficulties are not solved, and when it is so hard to attract other equally able idealistic people to come

253

to work on the project. Time itself contributes to strengthen and fix the various behavior patterns which may hinder the adoption of new behaviors and new innovations, so badly needed for the revitalization and expansion of the system.

The reasons which probably led to the success of the experiment, like a strong philosophy, leadership, direct political backing from a dynamic governor and state secretary, gradual growth from within, educational innovation, community-centred activities, idealism allied to a certain margin may not be there in the future. The most important question which FMTVE should bear in mind as a permanent effort of institutionalization would be: will FMTVE be able to keep from exporting to the villages a city-made model? In other words, will FMTVE consider itself as a packaged solution, forgetting its own origin, where educational innovation was based on content and relevance, and not on the media or the system they now may simply 'apply'?

It is hoped that the present study helped FMTVE and those interested in it to clarify the main institutional issues concerned with the adoption of innovations in tele-education in Brazil.

PAPER NO 73: EXCUSE ME—IS ANYBODY THERE?*

Piers Pendred, Educational Technology Training Officer, Media Department, British Council, UK.

How many of the schools with sets watch the programmes?
All of them.
All the schools watch all of the programmes?
Yes.
But what about problems of maintenance? There must be some schools with sets which are out of order.
Yes.

---

* Reproduced with kind permission of the publishers from *Educational Broadcasting International*, March 1976.

So—er—not all the schools watch?
All the schools with sets which are working watch the programmes.
How many schools have broken sets?
Oh, a few.
How many would that be?
Not many.
How do you find out that the schools use the programmes?
We have an evaluation section.
How do they collect the information?
The teachers send in cards.
Do the evaluation officers visit the schools?
Yes.
Often?
Well, occasionally. There is a problem with transport.
So they rely on the teachers returning the cards?
Yes.
How many of these cards say that teachers are not using programmes?
None.
None of them?
Yes, none.
Did you get cards back from all the schools?
Most of them.
And every one said they were using the programmes?
Yes.
And did you—er—believe this information?
Yes, of course, Why not?

There's no such thing as educational broadcasting in this country.
What do you mean?
Oh, programmes are transmitted, but the schools don't use them.
How did you find this out?
We visit the schools. Some students of mine wanted to do some research into the use of educational broadcasting. Of 50 schools that we visited, we only found one that had watched any programmes at all in the previous month.

I recently visited a number of countries in Africa and Asia to look at problems of educational broadcasting. These are two conversations I had in the same country; the first with an educational broadcaster and the second with a teacher trainer. I had similarly contrasting conversations in many of the countries that I visited. In most cases, official information on viewing and listening figures supplied by the broadcasting authorities was collected by means of questionnaires filled in by teachers. Unofficial information, which was not published, was gathered by inspectors, and advisers visiting schools unannounced during transmission periods. I was left in no doubt about one thing. Official statistics on utilization should be treated with some scepticism. But what's it all in aid of? Who is supposed to be taken in by these figures? And what are the figures trying to prove?

Lies, damned lies and statistics

I did not, of course, expect educational broadcasters to bare their souls to me—to tell me that teachers couldn't fit the transmissions into their crowded teaching periods, that sets didn't work, that the notes didn't reach the schools in time, that timetables couldn't be altered to fit transmission times, that sets had to be kept under lock and key, either in the headmasters' houses or in cupboards guarded by reluctant and seldom available storekeepers, or that power failures were so frequent as to make viewing an agonizing suspense. I didn't expect to be told of any of these things, although some of them affect every country to some degree or another. But on the other hand, I didn't expect to find statistics which were at best distortions of data and at worst just lies. The disturbing thing is to analyse the motives of those who produce such seemingly miraculous figures.

For a start it is worth considering the teacher's view when faced with a questionnaire. A card arrives asking him to state whether he watched a certain programme. The easiest thing for him to put is 'Yes' whether he used the programme or not. He knows that 'Yes' is the answer educational broadcasters want to hear. He feels some slight obligation to use the programmes. He knows that by putting 'Yes' the matter will end there. But if he puts 'No' he could land himself with all sorts of trouble. Someone may want to know why. He could be variously accused of ratting on the headmaster, who's got it in his house, of criticizing the deputy headmaster for not fitting his class to the transmission times when he made up the timetable, of complaining that the storekeeper wouldn't release the set, and a possible host of other crimes. 'Yes' is easy, final and comforting. And by no means is it the teacher's fault. He's got enough problems without bringing more on himself.

So why do the evaluation staff in the broadcasting service believe the information on the cards? Many of them have been teachers themselves and know full well that much of the information must be untrue. But if they choose not to believe it, then they have to prove it. And this means visiting schools involving transport and permission, finding out why programmes are not watched and feeding all this information back to the relevant people— those who mend the sets, those who distribute the notes, those who transmit programmes and those who make programmes. How much better to take 'Yes' as an answer —for it's what everyone wants to hear. And so the information reaches the desk of the head of the educational broadcasting service. His job, more often than not, is to produce a service that is well used, not one that solves or helps to solve educational problems. A minister is breathing down his neck wanting figures. And up they go. The minister is delighted. The service is used and is therefore a success. Money is voted for more programmes. Everything can settle down again to another harmonious year of producers making programmes and teachers not using them.

If this seems harsh, it's meant to be. For distortion of utilization figures can only mean one thing—that some people really don't care whether educational broadcasting is effective or not. This is a tragedy. Broadcasting is a scarce and expensive resource which no country can afford to waste. The effort involved in making programmes, particularly for television, is considerable. I met many capable, concerned and hardworking people involved in production and many of them were worried about the use that was being made of their programmes. They were becoming disillusioned. Why spend so much effort making programmes which are not used? To them the problem was not only one of utilization; it concerned the whole rationale for educational broadcasting. As one asked, 'What is the purpose of the service for which I work, and how do my programmes relate to this purpose?'

In search of a cause

This leads me to another conversation with

R

someone working in an educational broad-casting service.

What's the purpose of your service?
Ah, well, there are two kinds of educational television; direct teaching and enrichment. Our programmes are intended as enrichment.
What is it that you're trying to enrich?
Classroom teaching.
Why does the classroom teaching need enriching?
It's very boring.
Surely that depends on the imagination of the teachers and the demands of the curriculum?
To a certain extent, but students find lessons boring.
And television can make them less boring?
Yes.
So enrichment means relieving boredom?
That's one of the things it means, yes. If the students are bored, they won't learn anything.
How do you decide whether your programmes are boring or not?
How do you mean?
Well, presumably the producers are told to make programmes which are not boring. So how do you decide, once they have been made, whether they meet your criteria of unboringness?
The problem doesn't arise.
Why not?
The students find all our programmes interesting. Television can't be boring.
Can't be boring?
Yes, of course, Don't you agree?

I didn't but I left it at that. What emerged as interesting about this conversation was that it was only the educational broadcasters who had identified the boredom problem as important. The teacher trainers and curriculum people seemed concerned with other things. I was left with the impression that the boredom issue had been developed by the broadcasters to suit their own cause. It may well be that boredom is a major problem, but one can hardly be asked to believe that one television programme per week could relieve about twenty hours of classroom monotony. If boredom were a serious problem, then the money might have been better spent on in-service teacher training courses or more classroom resources. The real problem seemed to be

one of educational broadcasting services in search of realistic causes.

What can such services achieve? Are utilization figures affected by the purpose of the services? Can achievement in educational broadcasting be measured? Should it be measured? To what extent is the fact of having such a service more important than its actually achieving anything?

To deal with the last point first—there does seem to be a ray of hope. Educational broadcasting is no longer seen as the panacea of all ills. No longer do many people seriously believe that educational broadcasting is a 'good thing' which is bound to 'enrich' educational systems. As equipment gets older and more commonplace, fewer dignatories are shown round studios to marvel at the wonders of live electronic pictures. More educationists are saying that broadcasting is a resource that must be selectively used as a part of a package of resources. More administrators in search of cash are asking what they get for their programme investment. Fewer articles are appearing in periodicals extolling the miraculous educational achievements of this medium.

Rethinking the role of educational broadcasting
In many places educational broadcasting is becoming a conventional resource, and stripped of a rather glorified position, it must compete with other resources—books, buildings, transport, paper, furniture and people—for money. To do this it has to make a case for itself, not based entirely on utilization figures, but based on its educational purpose. But what is, or what should be, the purpose of educational broadcasting?

It's obviously impossible to say, 'This is what educational broadcasting is for'. It depends on the country, on the problems, on the facilities and the purpose of the educational system. But one common denominator has emerged; that is that no educational broadcasting service has managed to achieve anything by acting independently from other agents of change in education, particularly teacher training and curriculum development. This may seem like common sense, but in a number of countries I found situations in which curriculum developers and educational broadcasters steadfastly refused to talk to each other. In one instance a producer told me that he had been severely admonished for discussing a script with someone working on curriculum reform. Many curriculum people regard broadcasting as an expensive and fringe resource. Conversely, educational broadcasters have done little or nothing to convince their curriculum counterparts that they have a role to play in educational change. But that too seems to be changing.

Many countries are entering or have entered a second decade of educational broadcasting. The excitement has worn off and the hopes sometimes have worn thin. The questioning has to begin. First a purpose has to evolve for these services; a purpose more profound than the relief of boredom and better described than just 'enrichment'. Direct teaching and enrichment are clichés of educational broadcasting which have lost any value that they might once have had. In any case they never described purpose, merely a method of making television programmes, characterized in the direct teaching sense by someone performing as a teacher, talking directly to the students from the television set. Purpose now must be both problem-based and linked to general effort for change, which necessarily involves other elements in the educational system, particularly curriculum developers, teacher trainers and the teachers themselves.

Given a realistic role and the resources to achieve it, educational broadcasting might be resuscitated in a lot of places. This in turn would lead to demand for accurate utilization figures, for the curriculum developers and teacher trainers would want reassuring that the programmes were being used and playing their part. And the teachers would be more likely to use programmes that they could see a need for and which they had been consulted about. Will it happen? I think it might, but very gradually. In some places the debate has already started.

We've suspended our broadcasts for the moment.

Why is that?

We were concerned about the role the broadcasts were playing in the education system as a whole. The television programmes were only reaching a small urban population and the radio programmes were not relevant to our national needs.

What are those?

Developing the rural potential of the country.

How are you planning to use broadcasting now?

Our ideas are only at a formative stage. We may well move the production centre out of the capital and into the country. We have organized groups of producers to work alongside other ministries involved in rural development. Out of these discussions, a role for radio will emerge.

What about television?

Television is a problem. We either have to find ways of getting the service into the rural areas or use it for a different purpose.

Such as?

Well, we could make the whole of our existing television system mobile and use it for selected purposes, such as teacher training schemes.

So you might not transmit programmes at all?

It's quite possible. After all, this equipment is only a resource. We have to use it to some effect. Broadcasting is one of the things it can be used for, but its closed-circuit potential might be more appropriate at the moment. We want to get away from the tyranny of transmission schedules, with producers making programmes at the last minute. We want to try to use all this hardware to solve problems. Maybe it will work, maybe it won't. But we intend to try.

THE ORGANIZATIONAL CONTEXT

PAPER NO 1: A STUDY IN FRUSTRA-
TION

Gale Adkins, Director of Broadcasting Research, Indiana State University, USA.

Instructional radio and television on trial

Education does not stop at the borders of
the campus, and television offers another
way to reach out into homes and serve
people where they live.[1]

In this statement made 25 years ago, the
president of Ohio State University was saying about television the same thing that
had been said about radio 25 years earlier.
Today in the most educationally advanced
countries in the world, instructional radio
and television are still on trial. Neither professional educators nor the public know
quite what to think of instructional broadcasting. Fundamental practical questions in
vast numbers remain unanswered. We
admit to great uncertainty as to how to
achieve specific results precisely and efficiently through use of the electronic media.
Research has been brought to bear on
educational broadcasting since the early
days of radio, but the results have never
satisfied the needs. We continue to look to
research to provide answers through the
application of scientific procedures. So
many questions in educational broadcasting are still awaiting that research.
Our feet remain near the bottom of the
ladder.

Levels of decision-making appropriate for research

But whatever the flaws and shortcomings of
research methodology, the contributions of
research to the development of educational
radio and television have been limited fully
as much by administrative and utilization
problems. These relate more to organizational processes and to the potential users of
research than to the researcher himself. To
assess the problems and difficulties involved
in using research as an aid to wise decision-
making we should begin by recognizing the
levels and stages at which research-assisted
decision-making should occur.

Managers, producers, directors, writers
and others who determine whether or not
activities are undertaken or who determine
the nature, content and use of materials are
all in their turn decision-makers. These are
the people who could use research results as
a guide in making the decisions they must
make. The levels or stages of decision-
making activity that invite research assistance are:

1 *Involvement decision* This is the point
at which a policy decision is made to begin
or not to begin using instructional television
or radio. There is a great likelihood that
research may not be used to best advantage
in decision-making at this point. Awareness
and access to a body of appropriate research experience is least likely to exist when
prior involvement has been lacking. The
decision as to whether or not to undertake
major use of electronic media will probably
involve only a few people, and rationalizations that lead to predisposed conclusions
can more easily prevail than when the
decision-making base is broader.

2 *Project initiation* Assignment of key
personnel; formulation of broad concepts;
reference to related projects conducted elsewhere; definition of project objectives;
selection of program format; layout of
budget items; construction of grant applications.

258

3 *Program planning and preparation* Definition of individual program objectives; conclusions as to student interests, needs and abilities; selection of nature and quantity of content; plans as to nature and schedule of efforts to measure effects; selection of on-camera personnel; selection of production techniques; selection of visuals; staging decisions.

4 *Feedback during production* Adjustments concerning idea density, existing information level, pacing, vocabulary, student interest, retention aids, production and performance techniques, supplementary materials.

5 *Utilization of program materials* Setting up educational objectives; choice of utilization strategies; selection and use of supplementary materials; selection of preparatory activities; selection of follow-up activities.

6 *Appraisal of results from television or radio programs* Measuring, evaluating or accounting for change or lack of change in overt behaviour, psycho-motor skills, cognitive behaviour, affective behaviour, involvement and motivation. Evaluation of utilization procedures.

7 *Evaluation of the total product* Evaluation of project planning and execution in all its aspects; budget, personnel, program planning procedures, use of formative research, television and radio programs used; feedback procedures; measurement of results, use of research information, publicity and promotion activities, program utilization practices.

8 *Application of research knowledge to new plans* Making the best use of all research-based information and insights when planning new projects.

Many of us feel that in actual practice research and evaluation are by no means employed to the extent that they are needed to guide decisions in these diverse areas.

Obstacles to the effective use of research
Why does this gap between research needs and research service continue to exist, and what can be done about it? One very im-
portant step toward the more effective use of research in decision-making would be recognition of the reasons that research does not serve better now. What are the causes of our frustrations?

1 Too often there is a tendency to make decisions prompted by emotion, predisposition, or egocentric motivations. Persistent rationalization may occur. Selective exposure or selective perception may operate to reinforce a belief that a favored position is indeed correct. No real desire may exist for objective data or analysis of experience. There may be opposition to a search for existing data or to local research for fear evidence will be produced which would run counter to personal preferences or convictions.

2 Well intentioned decisions may be made without an awareness of the valuable assistance that could come from knowledgeable recourse to research. Data bearing on the situation at hand may already exist. Efforts to consult the existing research may even be made, but unfamiliarity with the field may result in reliance on data that is undependable, inappropriate, or atypical. Research techniques may be available and practical for local use in ways that would provide a better basis for decisions. Management should come to regard exploration of what research can contribute to decision-making as a vital and normal step. A qualified research consultant should be available when needed to identify and assemble relevant data or conduct local research.

3 There may be a feeling that research relating to the problem at hand has been conducted elsewhere, but knowledge as to how to locate and obtain the appropriate data may be lacking. Unfortunately, research results are not always released outside an organization and if they are the news of availability may not be widely known. Those who may need to seek guidance from the accumulated body of research would be greatly aided by better systems of research reporting and indexing, dissemination of information and information retrieval. In the United States, the Educational Resources Information Centres (ERIC) are a useful step in that direction.

4 It is a regrettable fact that some decision-makers are simply too hasty and impatient

to look or wait for helpful research information. The delay and complication caused by a systematic search for information is to them less tolerable than is the risk of a bad judgement. Such inclinations might be restrained if there were a better realization of the nature and relevance of the research experience. Decision-makers should know more about the research services available to them and should be provided with more encouraging precedents of expeditious and usable research assistance.

5 Decision-makers may fail to recognize conditions under which locally conducted research may serve better than would data from similar studies conducted elsewhere. Applying to one's own situation research findings that were based on populations and conditions in another place must be approached with great caution. Variables affecting the outside study and variables that may operate locally must all be carefully identified and their influences considered. Injudicious dependence on research from another place or another time must be regarded as one of the classic traps for the unwary. Local research can involve persons who may be skeptical of studies reported from other communities, but they may find their interest captured and their questions answered through their own participation. Such demonstration research may not be expected to produce new information, but simply to test the applicability of known research findings to the local situation.

6 Needed research may not be conducted because of budgetary limitations. When a project budget is initially constructed funding needed for research may be seriously underestimated or even sacrificed to accommodate line items thought to be more nearly essential. It is all too common for research and evaluation to be regarded as among the foremost of the activities that could be minimized or eliminated with least damage to the total project. Such a point of view fails to recognize the contributions that research can make to the preparation of effective materials and to utilization. It fails to appreciate the potential of research for revealing the less desirable ways of doing things, thus making possible greater benefits to be realized from funds and efforts expended in the future.

7 Research and evaluation may fall short of maximum contributions to a project because the planning and procedures were not begun early enough. Ideally research and evaluation strategy should begin evolving during the earliest stages of project planning and budget construction. The fullest understanding of project purposes, educational objectives, operational problems, and utilization difficulties is necessary if research and evaluation are not to work under a handicap. Great damage has often been done to the image of research because researchers were called in too late to organize possible services or to begin the most meaningful evaluation. These instances could be avoided if research consultants were part of the team involved in initial project planning.

8 Research and evaluation activities fail to provide the greatest possible assistance to radio and television instruction because research reports do not achieve useful communication with many who could profit from the information. It is too often the case in academic environments that research reports seem to be written to convey an impression of the greatest possible sophistication of research expertize. It is a rare instance when a researcher seeks to express his complete findings and deepest insights in the least complicated and most understandable terms. Teachers, producers and managers are not research experts and cannot be reached through the language with which a researcher may strive to impress his colleagues. And it is likely to be the teacher, producer or manager who most needs to understand and use the answers the researcher has obtained.

9 The state of the art in the methodology of research into human behaviour accounts for much of the failure to provide needed answers. It is little consolation to know that this limited capacity also frustrates the experts in education, social work, advertising, law enforcement, politics, and countless other spheres in which the influencing of human behaviour is important. The fact is that after fifty years of increasingly intimate cohabitation with the broadcast media we are still unable to satisfactorily identify and measure the effects of radio and television.

Douglas Cater cites an impressive example of the problem:

Consider . . . Surgeon-General's inquiry into the effect of televised violence on the behavior of children. Conducted over a period of three years, at a cost of $1.8 million, and based on 23 separate laboratory and field studies, this probe was the most far-reaching to date into the social consequences of television. In its final report, the Surgeon-General's committee could acknowledge only 'preliminary and tentative' evidence of a causal relationship between TV violence and aggression in children . . . These studies, mostly gauging immediate response to brief exposure, could not adequately measure the impact of the total phenomenon.[2]

To further compound the frustration, the honesty and professional integrity of the researcher is often turned against him by those who lose interest and lose faith in research because they cannot find conclusions that profess certainty beyond doubt. Obviously the tools of the behavioral scientist need to be multiplied and more finely honed. Because such development tends at best to be slow, there should be a re-ordering of priorities to turn the best minds to work on questions of communication theory and research methodology. The communication-related problems of society in our time demand it.

10 Decision-making is not guided by research as much as it should be because the supply and availability of suitably qualified researchers is inadequate. Well-informed research counsel should be conveniently available to decision-makers on all levels of educational television and radio operations.

The need for mutual understanding

Our compleat researcher may need to exercise the proficiencies of a promoter, a manager, an educator, a behavioral scientist, and a popular writer. This may seem to be expecting too much. That leaders in media research throughout the years have been unable or unwilling to successfully wear these several hats may explain in large part why research has failed to develop to meet its challenge. We cannot expect research personnel to quickly multiply themselves and display new competencies, but there are practical possibilities. Consortium-based research teams composed of specialists assembled from several co-

operating institutions might be one solution. With each team member supplying some special competency needed in the total research effort, the possibility of weak links in research planning, execution and reporting would be reduced. Costs, resources, and ideas could be shared, and the service enjoyed by each cooperating agency might be substantially improved.

Decision-makers point to researchers and say, 'Why don't you provide definitive answers? Why must uncertainty about fundamental choices continue so long?' Researchers point to decision-makers and say, 'Why don't you utilize our findings and avail yourselves of our services?' Some of the most troublesome reasons for these dissatisfactions and frustrations have just been reviewed. The road to improvement of the research-decision-making relationship must be paved with mutual understanding of barriers, limitations, needs and possibilities. Instructional television and radio are being called upon to perform increasingly critical tasks in the effort to inform and educate populations for greater self-fulfillment and more importantly for survival. Our use of the electronic media for educational purposes must become less tentative, more precise and more efficient. Better planned, better executed, and better reported research can increase the likelihood that decision-makers will advance the quality and quantity of electronic materials of instruction and take steps to improve their use. If the importance of research service can be recognized and if the problems in the research-decision-making relationship can be understood, great doorways will have been opened to a more productive interaction between research and decision-making in educational television and radio.

References

1 The Future of ETV, *The Newsletter*, Columbus, Ohio State University, February 1951.
2 CATER, DOUGLAS, The Intellectual in Video Land, *Saturday Review*, 31 May 1975.

PAPER NO 7: TOWARDS A POLICY FOR BROADCAST EVALUATION

Tony Bates, Head, Audio-Visual Media Research Unit, The Open University, UK.

The purpose of the paper

It is natural that researchers should take it for granted that evaluation and research are highly necessary activities for organizations using or designing educational television and radio. There are many producers and managers though who are by no means convinced of the value or practicality of systematic and objective evaluation and research, so it may be worthwhile briefly looking at why such activities are necessary.[1]

Perhaps more worrying for those who advocate the cause of evaluation and research is the singular lack of success it has had so far in bringing about a continuing and lasting improvement in the way television and radio are used in education. To advocate the need for increasing research at a time of economic crisis may seem to many organizations like throwing a drowning man both ends of a rope. It may then be worth looking at why evaluation and research have had such little impact, and what might be done to improve their effectiveness and usefulness.

Evaluation and decision-making

Evaluation is an activity that goes on all the time in any organization; and this applies just as much to educational television and radio. Judgements are made at all levels of activity, from deciding in the control room whether to mix or cut between shots, to deciding in the President's office whether or not to invest in a satellite. Evaluation is an attempt to assess the merits of various decisions, and is therefore an important part of the decision-making process, and is certainly not the exclusive domain of 'professional' researchers or evaluators.

One of the most important aspects of decision-making is determining goals and priorities, choosing from a wide range of possible action those objectives which are most desirable within the limited resources of an organization. The choice of such objectives will to some extent reflect the values of those responsible for making decisions. In educational television and radio, the problem is further complicated by the wide variety of people with a direct interest in such decisions: broadcasters, teachers, sponsors (who may be tax-payers, licence-holders, advertisers, or philanthropic funding agencies), and frequently politicians as well. The merit of various decisions will depend on how such interests are brought together or represented during the decision-making process, and by the extent to which the goals set actually meet the needs of users of educational television and radio. The measurement of such outcomes again depends on the values held by people regarding goals and priorities—success to some may well mean failure to others.

The suitability of any given decision then will depend to a large extent on the ability of decision-makers to predict accurately the likely consequences or outcomes of possible decisions, and also on the ability of the organization to implement decisions within cost, time and administrative limitations. Such abilities require a knowledge and experience of the result of previous, relevant decisions, and skill in applying to new situations such knowledge or experience in an appropriate way. Intelligent guesswork —fundamental to any 'good' decisions— depends very much on previous learning.

Information about programme users

Now a feature of educational television and radio is that they both neatly separate those responsible for investment, policy and production decisions from those who actually use the 'product'—the students. This has a number of important consequences for the decision-making process. The decision-maker is often acting on behalf of the potential users (who may in fact be a very mixed assortment of people, even in a limited educational framework). It therefore becomes essential that decision-makers have accurate information about the users of educational television and radio—who they are, what they want or need, and how previous programmes have been used.

Information about users has been collected by organizations designing educational television and radio in a number of ways. Producers may draw on their knowledge of themselves and their families, friends, close acquaintances or colleagues, and use these as 'models' of their audience. If they were previously teachers, producers may draw on their knowledge of the children with whom they worked. Producers may have more recent and direct contact with users, through visits to classes using their programmes, or through letters from users. There may be advisory bodies (such as the BBC's Further Education Advisory Council), consisting of representatives of various sectors of education. Other members of a broadcasting organization in closer contact with users (e.g. education officers) may relay information back to the centre. Finally, surveys may be made to find out which programmes are used, and under what circumstances.

Information not only must be received, it must also be interpreted, particularly since information from different sources can be conflicting. This process of interpretation is crucial to evaluation and decision-making. Information from sources close or personal to the decision-makers is more likely to be influential than information from sources which appear to be more distant or less relevant. For instance, comments from colleagues within the same production department about one's own programmes are likely to be more influential than education officers' comments about another series. Furthermore, qualitative information—i.e. comments expressing personal opinions in a personal style of language—is more likely to be influential than quantitative information—i.e. statistical data about viewing figures, written in a neutral style. And of course, when information from different sources conflicts, it is natural that information reinforcing the decision-makers' prior views is more likely to be influential than information challenging such views, other things being equal.

The kind of information usually available to decision-makers in educational television and radio has a number of drawbacks. Apart from measurements of viewing and listening figures (which themselves are of limited value, as I shall argue later), most information available to producers about users' reactions is unrepresentative of the majority of programme users. It is often unreliable (in that if a producer, for instance, went to a different source, he would get a different response). It is often not properly evaluated, in that the criteria for judging the comparative merit of different sources of information are not clearly

thought out. Finally, the information available often lacks penetration, in that it rarely tells the producer something new, or suggests what action might be taken in the future.

This situation has meant that judgements in educational television and radio tend to be dominated by production values (since other producers tend to be the most immediate and informed source of criticism and feedback) and by political and cost factors (using 'political' in the broad sense of the word, meaning factors related to the overall policies and values of the organization producing programmes). These influences can be counterbalanced to some extent in a 'team' situation, where teachers (used in a broad sense) and producers are jointly responsible for production decisions. However, it must be recognized that there will always be a tension in such a situation.

Wrong kinds of research

Producers and managers of course are well aware of the need to know more about the effects of the programmes on their audiences, and have looked to researchers to provide this information. Unfortunately, though, organizations which have tried to evaluate their programmes systematically have often found the exercise a total waste of time. 'What have you told me that I didn't know already?' 'OK, so the students didn't watch (like) my programme, but *why* not? What should I do about it?' All too often evaluation exercises have not been able to answer these questions.

One obvious reason is that the amount of money made available for evaluation, compared with production, is derisory. The Open University, which is currently transmitting more educational programmes than any other sector in Britain, spends less than £20,000 per annum on research and evaluation into all forms of audio-visual media. This is less than 0.5 per cent of the £3½ million spent by the OU on broadcasting. A reduction of less than 2 per cent in the number of OU television programmes produced each year (270 instead of 275, and an overall reduction of 0.2 per cent in actual spending) would release enough money to double the evaluation output. It would be interesting to obtain similar figures from other organizations. I suspect that the OU would be no worse, and probably better, than most. As the saying goes, 'If you pay peanuts, you get monkeys'.

Unfortunately, though, when evaluation is properly mounted and funded, too often the least useful kinds of studies are carried out. It has already been pointed out that the decision-making process is complex, and therefore it is disappointing that most public broadcasting organizations have concentrated on collecting the most superficial information about users of educational programmes. Target audience research is of course a natural development from general broadcasting. Obviously, an organization wants to know whether its programmes are being used. Unfortunately, that is just about all that such studies indicate. Sometimes judgements can be made about which areas are more popular, but to extrapolate from this that high viewing or listening figures indicate a successful use of the medium is extremely dangerous. We have evidence from other kinds of study at the Open University[2] that viewing and listening figures are significantly affected by a variety of factors, some totally unconnected with the value of the broadcasts themselves. Cooper[3] and McIntosh[4] have both pointed out that adult education programmes have a wide variety of subgroups in their audiences, some of which might be considered much more important than others. High numbers—or even high percentages—are not of themselves sufficient criteria for judging the value of educational programmes, and there is a danger that such figures are used as a justification for future programme policy. It may for instance be more desirable to teach 1,000 adult illiterates to read, with the help of television, than to reach an audience of 500,000 with language programmes, if the level of involvement of such an audience is very low. One thing target audience research will not indicate is whether television was largely instrumental in getting people to read, or to learn Italian.

The second major area of research is located not in broadcasting organizations but in universities. 'Classical' experimental research into media, often comparing the effectiveness of different media under controlled conditions, and usually heavily dependent on learning gains as measures of success, has been frequently criticized,[2] primarily because such research fails to take account of the reality of the production process. It is also probably more than just coincidence that the methodology of both target audience research and classical experimental studies are derived from mainline academic disciplines, and that both methodologies can be applied without any necessary knowledge of the production process.

Evaluation priorities

I am not arguing that such research areas have no value, but that other kinds of research, more relevant to the decision-making process, are more urgently needed. These can be classified roughly into three main types, related to the levels at which decision-making takes place. These are:

(a) research aimed at the design of individual programmes;

(b) research aimed at the determination of broadcast policy;

(c) research aimed at the design and implementation of new systems using television and/or radio for teaching.

I want to show, by drawing mainly on Open University experience, that more broadly based research can have a major impact on decision-making.

Programme research

Research on general television and radio has shown that broadcasting does not exist in a vacuum, but is used by viewers and listeners in response to their wider needs and expectations.[5] This finding is even more appropriate to a teaching situation. Television or radio are hardly ever the only media of instruction available to the student. This has important consequences for the evaluation of individual programmes, because research must take account of a wider context than just the programmes themselves, and this leads to a rather different set of questions from those often asked by researchers. For instance:

(a) What are appropriate *functions* for television and radio in specific curricular areas, when television and radio are only two of a range of instructional media available to students?

(b) What *difficulties* are encountered by students in learning from television and radio?

(c) What *differences* are there in the way students use television and radio?

(d) Do students need to be *trained* in their use of educational television and radio? If so; how?

The answer to such questions will vary according to the conditions under which students are using educational television and radio. The answers are therefore likely to be specific to the organizations designing educational television and radio programmes. Consequently, these organizations should themselves find the answers to such questions, if they wish to improve their use of educational television and radio. Furthermore, the answers to such questions are most likely to come from a careful study of individual programmes, within the context of the students' total learning situation. Questions of appropriate production techniques, the level of difficulty and the pace of the programme, would be answered again within the general context of the programme, rather than as absolute statements. Finally, the aim of such research would be more concerned with providing information to help future policy decisions rather than with remaking programmes. The research therefore would be aimed at deriving general principles (but within the conditions of study specific to an organization) which can be applied in new situations.

There must therefore be some means by which to describe programmes reliably and accurately, so that when general principles are derived from the research, it is clear to what range of programmes these principles apply. That is why we have developed a system for describing Open University radio programmes.[6] We have been carrying out this kind of research into individual programmes at the Open University since 1974. This research is reported more fully in other papers.[2,7] It is clear though from these studies that the success or failure of a programme may have nothing to do with the quality of the programme itself. Students may be overloaded with reading, may have dropped behind in their schedules, and may therefore not be sufficiently prepared to be able to understand the programme when transmitted. It may be necessary to correct these faults, rather than alter the programme itself. Alternatively, the programmes may succeed for some students, and not for others. It may be necessary to assist weaker students in the comprehension of programmes through broadcast notes, which explain the purpose of the programmes, and provide follow-up activities for such students during or after the programme. It is clear though from this research that it has enabled producers and academics involved in the evaluations to learn about the consequences of certain decisions, and to carry over this learning into the design of new courses.

Policy research

This aspect of broadcasting has been grossly neglected by researchers. Managers and policy makers within educational broadcasting systems are faced with a range of problems which could be tackled more effectively with the help of relevant research. I would select four areas in particular where I believe research could provide a useful service to managers:

(a) the identification of priority target audiences and programming policy,

(b) the allocation of television and radio resources to different curricular areas,

(c) the choice of appropriate transmission times,

(d) the implications of new technologies (cassettes, discs, CEEFAX, etc) for course design, operation, management, utilization and expenditure.

There are various ways in which priorities in programming are decided. Some organizations (such as the BBC) have advisory bodies made up of representatives from various sectors of government, industry and education. In a number of countries, where educational television and radio are State-controlled, priorities may be determined by inter-ministerial committees. Both these mechanisms might be described as advice from above. Researchers could usefully service such committees by providing, at the committee's request, statistical and analytic evidence about possible target audiences, which may assist such committees to come to more objective judgements about priorities. When global or overall audience priorities have been agreed, some organizations have used researchers to identify more precisely the interests and needs of these audiences, with a view to providing producers with information about the kind of programmes which might be successful. Some developments in community media, such as in Quebec, have used low-cost video technology to enable communities to develop their own programme ideas. As well as directly servicing such means of identifying audience priorities, researchers can be used (and some would say have a responsibility) to record and analyse critically the advantages and disadvantages of these different methods. Comparisons between different methods of reaching some policy decisions can be very enlightening.[8]

One particular aspect of determining priorities in programming is the allocation of television and radio resources to different curricular areas. In the Open University, we have a committee which decides how many programmes (television and radio) each course will have. Now how do you decide how many programmes to give for instance to a biology course, or to a geography course? Should they have the same number of programmes? Or are the needs of one greater than another? To be able to answer such questions, one must have criteria for deciding between competing bids. We have tried to use two main criteria:

(i) would it be possible to put on this course in the Open University context, and gain academic credibility outside the University, without an extensive use of broadcasting?

(ii) would it be possible to achieve the objectives laid down for broadcasting as cheaply or as conveniently in any other way in the Open University situation?

By applying these criteria to the reasons put forward by course teams for the use of broadcasting over the period from 1971 to the present (involving over 1,000 television and 1,000 radio programmes), and also by applying these criteria to Meed's study of different uses of radio,[6] we have been able to identify a list of functions appropriate for television and radio within the Open University context.[9] (The evaluation of individual programmes provides an opportunity to examine the extent to which the stated functions are actually achieved.) As well as being used for determining allocation policy, the functions derived can

be used as a guide to course design. Indeed, we have now produced a compilation package, consisting of taped examples of these functions, for training and consultancy purposes.[10]

At the Open University, just as great a problem as the allocation of production resources is the allocation of suitable transmission times. We do not have enough transmission time for all the programmes we want to produce, and we are also in a situation of rapid growth in the number of courses available each year. This raises questions as to which times we should use, which of these times are better than others, which courses should get repeat transmissions, which courses should get poorer times, what will happen when courses do not get repeat transmissions, how many programmes should be produced and transmitted each year, and a host of other such questions. So, to provide information to help the University examine these issues, we carried out at the end of 1974 a postal survey of over 12,000 students across all courses (58 at the time), obtaining an 82 per cent response rate.[11] We found that virtually all students had access to both the television and the radio programmes (98 per cent had BBC 2 sets, 93 per cent VHF radio sets). Secondly, we were already using virtually all the time suitable to most students that the BBC were likely to make available. The third and most crucial finding was that without a repeat facility, the maximum potential audience for any single programme was 80 per cent (because there were always students who were unable to be home at any one specific time), but that the combination of two times meant that nearly all students could watch at least once.

The report in fact raised fundamental issues about the role of broadcasting, because it became apparent from the figures collected about viewing and listening on each course that although television in particular was heavily used, its use—and value to students—was found to be much greater when it was linked to student assessment. However, if programmes were not to be repeated, it would be difficult to examine students on programme material, because many would not be able to watch the broadcasts. This will fundamentally affect the way new courses will be designed, since many course teams would like to integrate fully the broadcasts, but will be reluctant to do so unless ways are found to ensure that all students can watch and listen if they want to.

Anticipating the problem likely to be caused by lack of repeat transmissions, we carried out in 1974 and 1975 (in 10 of the 270 local study centres) a pilot investigation into the feasibility of providing video-replay facilities for students in all local study centres.[12] We experimented not only with different kinds of machines, but with different ways of organizing a cassette or cartridge system. The experiment resulted in recommendations to the University on the need for and feasibility of both a video-cartridge and audio-cassette replay facility, recommendations on the most appropriate equipment, on the method of copying, distribution, and organization in the study centre, and maintenance arrangements. The study also provided detailed costings. New developments in technology, such as video-cassettes and discs, clearly have major implications for organizations using tele-vision and radio for education. Careful piloting and experiment are therefore crucial before major investment decisions are made, and that demands skilled research and evaluation.

Research into the design and implementation of new systems

I have been arguing so far for an increased range of research areas for organizations already established in their use of educational television and radio. It will be seen that most of this research is not so much summative, in the sense of determining whether or not television and radio are worthwhile investments, as formative, in that it is concerned with improving the use and effectiveness of television and radio in an on-going situation. In a sense, this is using research and evaluation to correct weaknesses in the system. Many weaknesses however tend to be structural, in that they stem from the basic premises or assumptions which underly the setting up of a system using educational television and radio. If the original assumptions were wrong, no amount of tinkering will remedy the situation to any great extent.

There is curiously little research into the most appropriate ways of designing such systems. Indeed, there is a danger that other organizations will too slavishly copy the designs of the more successful, established systems, when the conditions for which the new system is being designed are quite different from those for the master model. Research therefore is urgently needed in the following areas:

(a) the identification of factors to be taken into consideration when deciding how to select and use media, including television and radio,

(b) the development of decision-models for determining the choice and mix of media,

(c) the relationship between the potential of different media in specific geographical contexts and national or regional educational objectives,

(d) alternative methods of control over educational television and radio,

(e) the social and economic side-effects of the introduction of educational television and radio, particularly in developing countries,

(f) the development of relevant national styles of programme making.

Partly through our consultancy work overseas, we have been forced to consider a number of issues. It seems clear that the choice and design of multi-media teaching systems are influenced by factors other than purely educational ones. Factors such as the need to maximize fully existing resources, the degree of flexibility of existing institutions (not least government departments), methods of financing and financial control, pressure from vested interest groups, such as existing broadcasting organizations, manufacturers, and educational lobbyists, and most important of all, high-level political and governmental motives, can all combine to swamp consideration of other basic issues, such as educational priorities and the needs of potential students. It is therefore the instructional designers' job to be aware of such pressures, and where possible to counterbalance them. This means knowing how such decisions are made and implemented, and knowing the range of decisions and the order in which they must be made.[13]

More is required than a bland publicists' account of how a particular established system works. Accurate reporting and evaluation of how decisions came to be made, the important influences on such decisions, and their outcomes, are required. Decision-making models need to be developed and tested in new situations. More study is required of the potential of different media to meet differing educational priorities. Alternative methods of control over educational television and radio, and in particular the way in which the content of programmes is decided, need to be described and analysed. At the Open University, we have a team system which involves joint responsibility between academic and producer. Such an arrangement depends on equal status for producer and academic, and a willingness to work together and compromise. In different cultural situations, such a relationship may not be possible, and alternative models may be required. The introduction of educational television and radio can—and usually does—mean major disruptions and changes in organization and attitudes within a country. These may turn out to be culturally and socially alien. The system of financing such developments in developing countries usually entails considerable assistance with capital expenditure from international agencies, but this can mean saddling the developing country with crippling recurrent expenditure, in some cases annually in excess of the original capital loan or grant. Finally, methods of programme making may be imported either directly or via training in other countries, which do not reflect the style or character of the country concerned. It may be necessary to develop ethnic styles of programme making, with the general public and local people participating heavily in programme design and piloting.

Managers, politicians, producers and other key decision-makers tend to be too involved and too busy themselves to monitor, record and analyse such activities. Even if they want to, it is often difficult for them to find penetrating and revealing accounts of other systems' difficulties. I would argue that all major innovations in the use of educational media should be serviced by an evaluation and research group (not necessarily large), with a responsibility not only for assisting the organization itself, but also for providing an open forum on the lessons learned. For this to happen, though, a major shift in attitude towards evaluation is necessary.

Requirements for effective evaluation

I hope I have been able to show that research and evaluation does have the potential to help organizations in their use of television and radio. If this potential is to be realized though, some fundamental changes are required.

The point has already been made that too little in the way of resources are allocated to evaluation and research. This is not just a question of attitude, but of the way organizations are funded. I would argue that money for evaluation needs to be kept independent of money for programme or course design and production, and should be earmarked by the funding organization. Evaluation and research will in most cases be a relatively small component of total expenditure, and as a power group within a democratic organization competing for scarce resources, researchers will always be weak because of their relatively small numbers. A 'downward spiral' situation is easily created. Too little money is initially allocated, the impact of research is small, and consequently even less money is allocated in the future, until the whole research effort is seen as being futile. To prevent such a situation, research and evaluation investment should be geared to the level of production. I would argue the need for a fixed ratio between production and evaluation expenditure, at least in the 1–2 per cent range, possibly more.

Funding of research also needs to be on the same time-scale as the funding of the organization itself. Too often research is seen as a 'once-only' activity, aimed at supporting or condemning the original investment decision. Not only has research and evaluation a continuing role to play within an organization, researchers require time to acquire knowledge of the system itself, an understanding of the production and management methods and problems and an expertise in specialized media research techniques. Continuity of funding for research allows identification and anticipation of problems, and the development of a coherent research programme.

Much more attention needs to be given also to the recruitment and career prospects of media evaluators. I would argue strongly that media researchers require not only a good research background in the social sciences, but also a thorough understanding of the production and management process, and that the latter is best achieved 'on-the-job'. Media researchers in organizations using broadcasting should have the same status and conditions of service as production or academic staff. Usually they do not.

Finally, if media researchers are to be sensitive to the issues and problems facing decision-makers, they themselves must be part of the decision-making process, at all levels. This is a fundamental point. Many decision-makers are happy to limit the role of researchers to mere providers of data, and believe that the interpretation of data and consequent follow-up action is the sole prerogative of the decision-makers. Data though needs to be interpreted, and for this to be done meaningfully requires not only an understanding of the broader issues, but also of the limitations of the data collected. This is not to argue that researchers should have a special position or even equal weight in the decision-making process, but they do have a real contribution to make on the interpretation and application of their findings. The possible loss of objectivity in a commitment to a preferred line of action not only is more than compensated by the depth of analysis and understanding of the issues involved gained by the researcher but is also helpful in forcing other decision-makers to think through the issues more deeply themselves.

At the same time, it is equally important that managers and producers themselves are heavily involved in the research process both in the identification and commissioning of projects, and in the actual collection and interpretation of data. Just as it is becoming increasingly accepted that teachers and producers must work as a team, so I believe it to be true that researchers and decision-makers should work in the same way. Such teamwork will be necessary, if only to diminish the increasing scepticism of researchers that decision-makers don't really want to learn from evaluation and research, they only want it to show how right they are.

References

1 SCRIVEN, M. The methodology of evaluation, in *AERA monograph series on curriculum evaluation, Book 1*, Chicago, Rand McNally & Co., 1967. (This provides a clear and comprehensive introduction to the concept and process of evaluation.)

2 GALLAGHER, M. The evaluation of programmes at the Open University, *CEREB Conference paper no 16*, Milton Keynes, The Open University, 1976.

3 COOPER, A. The instructional use and evaluation of a BBC multi-media German course for adult beginners: Kontakte, *CEREB Conference paper no 10*, Milton Keynes, The Open University, 1976.

4 McINTOSH, N. E. Evaluation of multi-media educational systems— some problems, *British Journal of Educational Technology*, Vol. 5, No 3, 1974 (also *CEREB Conference paper no 37*).

5 McQUAIL, D., BLUMLER, J., and BROWN, J. R. The television audience: a revised perspective, in McQUAIL, D. (ed.), *Sociology of Mass Communications*, London, Penguin, 1972.

6 MEED, J. *The use of radio in Open University course design 1971–4*. Milton Keynes, The Open University, 1976 (also summarized in *CEREB Conference paper no 40*).

7 BATES, A. W., and GALLAGHER, M. The development of research into broadcasting at the Open University, *British Journal of Educational Technology*, Vol. 7 No. 1. 1976.

8 GLIKMAN, V. and CORDUANT, J. P. Comparaison entre RTS Promotion et BBC Further Education, *Pour 43–44*, 1975 (also *CEREB Conference paper no 19*—in English).

9 THE OPEN UNIVERSITY. *Second submission of evidence to the Annan Committee on the Future of Broadcasting*, Milton Keynes, The Open University, 1976.

10 BATES, A. W., DUNKLEY, P. and MEED, J. *Uses of television and radio in Open University courses: a compilation package*, Milton Keynes, The Open University/BBC, 1976. (This consists of five video-cassettes, two radio tapes, and supporting printed handbooks.)

11 BATES, A. W. *Student Use of Open*

University Broadcasting, Milton Keynes, The Open University, 1975.

12 GALLAGHER, M., and MARSHALL, J. Broadcasting and the need for replay facilities at the Open University, *British Journal of Educational Technology*, Vol. 6, No 3, 1975.

13 BATES, A. W. *Educational and cost comparisons between open-network, cable, and cassette systems of multimedia teaching*, Belgian Ministry of Employment and Labour, 1973 (mimeo).

PAPER NO 36: STANDING ON THE SHOULDERS OF GIANTS—OR DO WE LEARN FROM THE PAST (OR PRESENT) IN ETV EVALUATION?

Emile McAnany, Institute for Communication Research, Stanford University, USA.

Introduction

It is the premise of this paper that evaluation research on educational television (ETV), and especially that done in and for developing countries, is not utilized, not because it is not well done technically (though this may be the case at times) but because it remains unadapted to the needs and interests of the decision-makers and the context of the decision to be made. In other words, evaluations about ETV are conceived of in a vacuum and remain an accumulation of facts or knowledge, as I shall use it here, and do not become wisdom or knowledge adapted to action for a specific decision-maker. As a consequence evaluations most often fail to serve the needs of the immediate potential user and later do not serve to guide newly conceived projects because the evaluator-advisor does not adapt the knowledge to the new planning context. The consequence is that we do not learn from past history by standing on the shoulders of giants, or even ordinary-sized people and projects, but ignore a great deal of what has been learned about the outcomes of ETV projects.

1 Historical perspective of educational television: giants of the past or forgotten ancestors?

There has certainly been an accelerated growth in the use of educational media and especially educational television in the developing countries over the past fifteen years. With the accession of satellites, the size and cost have multiplied and the need for evaluations has consequently increased in the minds of national planners. The need, too, of taking advantage of what is already known from past evaluations also becomes more urgent. In this brief section, we simply wish to remind the readers of some of the milestones of the past and the documentation available on them. Table 1 provides a selected list of ETV projects in their historical order, and their general purposes and any widely circulated evaluation on them.

One can conclude from this list that a significant number of projects, a wide variety of settings and a spread of educational purposes, have been initiated. Schramm,[10] has admirably summarized much of this history and the evaluation findings, including what is known of costs. There are two questions to be asked and hopefully answered in this paper: have these evaluations been used either in their own project contexts or later? And, if not, why, and how can this be remedied?

2 Problems of utilizing evaluations: why we don't stand on the shoulders of giants

As evaluations have historically been on the increase, there is a corresponding concern that they be used. There is a growing consensus however, that evaluations have not been very useful and, indeed, have largely not been used in decision-making. Evaluators often blame the decision-makers for ignoring their research findings for political reasons, while decision-makers dismiss evaluators and their work as either taking too long and costing too much or simply being irrelevant to their real needs.

Smith,[11] in a recent review of the literature on the utility and utilization of evaluative information concludes that *utility* or usefulness of the evaluation is much more under the control of the evaluator but the *utilization*, or whether the decision-maker actually uses the evaluation for a decision, was 'associated with the decision-maker's value judgements and choices and is almost entirely out of the control of the evaluator'. After briefly reviewing Smith's findings, I would like to suggest a way in which the evaluator can enhance not only the intrinsic

270

Table 1   Educational television: projects and research

Projects		Purpose	Research/Evaluation*
1962	Cuba	Formal instruction for adults/ youth	Jimenez[1] Wertheim[2]
1964	Samoa	Formal: primary/secondary	Schramm[3]
1964	Niger	Out-of-school to 1971. Formal school from 1971	AUDECAM[4]
1964	Colombia	Formal: primary	Maccoby and Comstock[5]
1966	Mexico	Extension of secondary junior high school 7–9	Mayo, McAnany, Klees[6]
1968	El Salvador	Formal junior high school grades 7–9; later 4–6	Mayo, Hornik, McAnany[7]
1969	Sesame Street (USA)	Nonformal: preschool	Ball, Bogatz[8] Cook et. al.[9]
1970	British Open University	Out-of-School: University	Various internal and external studies
1971	Ivory Coast	Formal: primary Out-of-school: from 1974	(in progress)
1973	Plaza Sesamo Spanish Latin America	Nonformal: preschool	(in progress)
1974	Korea	Formal: junior high school grades 7–9	(in progress)
1975	India (SITE)	Nonformal: adults	(in progress)
** 1976	Indonesia	??	(in planning)
1977	Iran	Out-of-school: High School	(in planning)

* Not all research and evaluation studies are cited.
** Satellite television projects.

usefulness of the research he is doing but also, and here is where I would disagree with Smith, its likelihood of actually being used.

Briefly, the primary features of evaluations that lack usefulness, according to Smith, are the following:

1 there is a lack of an identifiable, interested audience;
2 the evaluation was perceived by the decision-maker as not relevant, not timely and not credible;
3 the information was not communicated in a way to evoke a response in the decision-maker.

The first and third of the above points have to do with the evaluator in his often overlooked role as advisor-communicator to the decision-maker. Unless the evaluator can create some dialogue with the decision-maker to discover his information needs and potential decision areas, then the work he can do, though technically competent, cannot help to influence a decision.

The relevancy aspect of the second point also has to do with the evaluator's role as advisor. If the evaluator conceives of his work as relevant but the decision-maker does not, then since the evaluator is not in a position to make the decision himself the work will actually be irrelevant (but not, perhaps, in other contexts later on). Smith seems to argue that whether the evaluation is technically competent or not may have a great deal less to do with the use that is made of the evaluation than whether the

271

decision-maker thinks that the evaluation is really responding to his needs.

Finally, timeliness is the constraint most often cited for the non-use of evaluations by decision-makers. There is the dilemma of trying to answer the question posed by the decision-maker in a way that is reliable and still gets the answer to him when he needs it (usually the need is immediate and the time frame is 'as soon as possible'). Often by the time an evaluator has gotten an answer, the decision has already been taken. The evaluation, then, simply corroborates what the decision-maker has already done or goes against the decision and is correspondingly suppressed.

Taking Smith's argument one step further, I would propose that the evaluator should not only enhance the potential use of the research by means of genuine dialogue with the decision-maker in determining his needs, but increase the probability of utilization, as Smith defines it, by taking what I would call a 'strategic' approach to the decision context. By this I mean that to enhance the chances of the research to be used, the evaluator needs to understand the constraints on the action of the decision-maker, the bureaucratic and political circumstances not only of the evaluation itself but of the decision toward which the evaluation is geared. In a sense, this approach goes against the objective and often distant stance of 'scientific' evaluation and makes the evaluator an actor in the scene much more than he has been taught to be by the classical value-free approach of social/behavioural science.

But if evaluation is partially a descendant of the scientific method in its design and methodology; it is also a descendant of the art of politics, where action and application are the primary criteria of value. Some may think that such a strategic approach goes beyond the interests of evaluation as an intellectual endeavour. If so, then such evaluators should define their work as social/behavioural research and not pretend that what they do has relevance to the area of decision-making. But then they should also not expect society to continue to fund them in the belief that what they do will be directly useful. The dilemma of evaluation is especially acute, but it is becoming so in a society where 'big science', whether social or natural, demands big budgets and where society may demand a greater demonstration of usefulness.

What are some of the characteristics of 'strategic' evaluation in educational television? Let us start with an example. In Mexico in 1971, an ETV project, the Telesecundaria, was in its fifth year of operation and was reaching about 30,000 junior high school students, mainly in rural areas, with televised lessons. A primary teacher monitored the classes. What was important strategically was the particular political setting. Mexico had a new president and a new administration including the director of Telesecundaria. It was an appropriate time to evaluate the project in a summative sense, not only because it had been going for five years and probably had passed the 'Hawthorne' stage, but because it was time for Mexico to make some decisions as to the future growth and structure of the Telesecundaria, and, most importantly, because a new administration was more likely to listen to evaluation results and act to change (or even to suppress) the project, since they had not started it and would have the burden of defending it. Moreover, Mexico was seeking to expand the education opportunities of rural students, especially in post-primary schooling, and might be interested in expanding and changing an already existing project rather than creating another one from scratch. The evaluation was undertaken at that time and completed in two years[6] and a number of decisions for change were taken subsequently.

A careful estimation of the constraints on the decision is then a primary concern of a 'strategic' approach to evaluation. Other characteristics would follow from this basic approach. First, the evaluator, in this approach, is an advocate of change. He does not simply do the evaluation as an academic exercise but sees it as a means for introducing change into a situation. In other words, his evaluation begins with a premise that a decision is to be made. He estimates the likelihood of such a decision being made, and then gears his evaluation to that decision. In Mexico, there was an opportunity for an innovation to be tested. If, in comparison with regular secondary schooling, ETV or the Telesecundaria did not offer Mexico a way for tackling a basic problem, then the evaluation might act as the excuse for eliminating an expensive

272

experiment and getting on to something more positive. If, on the other hand it proved to be a promising path to a solution, then the evaluation might stimulate an adaptation and expansion of the innovation on a national level. In either case, the evaluation was a means for introducing a decision and therefore change into a situation that allowed it.

Second, the evaluator must attempt to understand the historical circumstances in which the project is situated. Each setting has peculiar constraints and a 'strategic' evaluation must attempt to adapt its research to the constraints both of the decision-maker (the limitations he has in the surrounding bureaucracy and political environment) but also of the project (the culture, politics, competing bureaucracies, socio-economic conditions of the populations to be served, etc). This task is often impossible for an outside evaluator and therefore demands the collaboration of the decision-maker (thus the absolute need for dialogue) but also with other local persons who understand the 'reality' of the situation. The evaluator must recognize and balance the often short-term political needs of the decision-maker for research on a certain problem and the longer term, historically more important needs of the project and its target populations. He must balance off these needs and not sacrifice the short for the longer-term needs. Thus, for example, although the decision-maker may not be able to do anything about structural constraints and therefore might be less interested in that aspect of rural education, the evaluator sees this as a critical factor in understanding to what extent ETV may be better or worse than traditional education for rural areas.

Third, the evaluator does not present the decision-maker with mere information (and there I would disagree with those who see the evaluator's role as a mere gatherer of information), but directs his research toward the solution of a problem. He thus presents his findings in the form of various alternatives to answering the decision-maker's need to act on the problem. This assumes, of course, that as Smith suggests, the evaluator has defined with the decision-maker a problem or a decision to be taken. Thus the evaluation is not just a 'research' finding but a set of alternative answers to a

problem and the contribution from research to a decision.

Finally, the 'strategic' evaluator must take a stand, according to a defined value position that is clear to the decision-maker on which of the alternatives he feels is best and why. Thus, the evaluation is not only a list of alternatives but a set of concrete recommendations. True, the decision-maker does not have to follow the recommendations, but his failure to follow a certain alternative does not mean that he will not use the evaluation, for he may decide to follow a different alternative for reasons that lie outside of the scope of the evaluation. This point makes it clear that the evaluator, even one who is 'strategic' in his approach, does not confuse himself with the decision-maker. He may recommend but he does not make the decision himself.

I would suggest that making evaluations useful and actually used in the context of ETV projects might benefit from following the suggestions made above.

3 Has wisdom accumulated in ETV evaluation: or are there any shoulders of giants to stand on?

We have another outstanding problem concerning evaluations of television and their usefulness. The question is a simple one: have we learned anything from the past with regard to planning the educational use of television (and other media), and specifically, have we learned anything from the evaluations that have been done on these projects? There are several answers to the question. The idealist may say that we have learned from the past (and, therefore, we can); the pessimist that we have not (and, therefore, we can't); and the realist that we have not (but that perhaps we may). Having been involved in a number of these past evaluations and being certain that they have not been widely used, I suppose I had better adopt a realist approach.

Failure to use past evaluations in planning new systems is, as I see it, a variation of the problem of use and usefulness discussed above. If evaluations have historically not served planners, we may be able to say why and how they might better serve that purpose in the future.

(a) Failures and their causes
In the planning context, we will use the

273

words evaluator and decision-maker, re-membering that the expert or advisor to a decision-maker need not be an evaluator himself. But we would maintain that he must at least understand what the evaluations have to say if they are to be of use. Some of the reasons why past evaluations have not entered sufficiently into the planning of new systems are suggested below; some though not all may be remediable.

(i) *Failure of the decision-maker* Although no thorough review has been made of how decisions to use educational television in Third World countries has actually been made, one has the suspicion that the majority of decisions to use ETV have been made for personal or political reasons and that planning is subsequent to the fact. At best, decision-makers are not asking planners whether ETV is the most cost-effective alternative to an educational problem but only how best to use it.[12] Even further specifications about the ETV system may have been decided upon before planning is introduced, and this reduces the possibility that previous knowledge about ETV can enter into the decision-making process. This is to say that, for whatever motives (political pressure, ignorance, a selling job from equipment manufacturers, etc), the decision-maker has made it difficult for the evaluator-advisor to make any contribution at all. In this case, there is simply no identifiable audience for the wisdom from past evaluations to enter in. But this is not the only failure, and the decision-maker may be open to doing things differently if the evaluator-advisor can play a different role.

(ii) *Failures of the evaluator-advisor* The expert advisor can play a critical role provided certain assumptions are met. First, the advisor may not have real knowledge of the research results of past ETV projects and therefore cannot render it as a useful part of the planning decision. Second, even if the advisor comprehends the results, he would need to follow much the same 'strategic' approach as was outlined above, making sure in a dialogue with the decision-maker that the necessary steps are taken to define objectives and constraints of both the decision and the potential project. In other words, even if the advisor brings a wealth of knowledge about ETV and its results in other projects, he must adapt that general knowledge to the action framework of the particular setting at hand.

(iii) *Failures of the evaluations* If there have been failures in using past evaluations, we simply cannot blame the political nature of the decision-maker's situation nor the ignorance of the advisor. It is rather likely that much of the failure stems from the nature of the evaluations themselves. Some of the problems are as follows:

● the quality of the evaluations themselves has often been lacking. Evaluation research is the application of social/behavioural research in an applied setting. Its real world setting makes the demands greater, not less, than in a laboratory setting (since there is an expectation that the results will be put into practice and affect people's lives). The evaluator must not only understand evaluation methodology but how he can compromise in the real setting without invalidating his results. This is not to say that any evaluation is ever perfect; faults are always possible to find, but hopefully one does not undermine all of the conclusions. Even expensive and well publicized evaluations can be faulted for technical failures, as Cook and colleagues[9] have recently demonstrated about the positive conclusions on *Sesame Street*.[8]

● some other faults of evaluation that make them less than useful for planning decisions later on are related to the frameworks in which they are carried out. Many evaluations are mere descriptions of what happened, or at most measures of pedagogical effectiveness. Often results do not answer the comparative question: educational television is more effective or more cost effective than—what? Chu and Schramm[13] years ago quite convincingly presented a summary of evidence that television could teach and perhaps teach as effectively as traditional methods; but evaluations done in the field as opposed to the laboratory and in Third World settings at that must demonstrate something about relative costs and effectiveness of several feasible alternatives, if they are to provide answers that most planners need. Until now, there have been relatively few evaluations that have tried to accomplish comparative studies, and fewer that have considered costs seriously. This latter problem has been due partly to lack of proper methodology of cost studies, a problem that is being worked on by some economists.[14] No evaluations have tackled the problems of benefits since the time span has not allowed sufficient accumulation of data on ETV projects. Nevertheless, country planners are demanding what the relative benefits of a major investment in communication technology might be for the economy as a whole (a first attempt at setting up a paradigm for answering such a question in more detail has been undertaken by Gandy[15]).

(b) Making evaluations more useful to planning decision-makers

It would be nice and certainly more satisfying to be able at this point to suggest a 'model' for making evaluations more useful to communications planners. The following suggestions unfortunately are just a list. But hopefully they may themselves be useful to evaluators, advisors and decision-makers who are concerned with the educational use of the media. You will notice that the list contains primarily a series of human actions and interactions and not the wider distribution of printed knowledge. It is not that printed evaluations are not useful but that, as I have argued in this paper, their usefulness for decisions often is dependent on whether advisors can translate them into meaningful form for decision-makers. For the following actions to be implemented change in the behaviours of evaluators and decision-makers is called for. Some suggestions for changing these two actors are made in the third section of recommendations.

(i) *Actions for decision-makers/planners* Rather than simply assume that the decision-maker is uninterested in evaluation results, we begin rather with the assumption that he often does not know how to get an evaluator-advisor to be responsive to his own set of needs. If previous evaluations are relevant to those needs, the decision-maker should expect the advisor to render the results useful in the concrete setting and not be expected to read the evaluations himself:

- the decision-maker or planner does not choose an ETV or other media system without defining his educational and development objectives and asking for the evidence for television (radio) and the alternatives, with costs estimates as well;
- the decision-maker should define the questions he expects the evaluator-advisor to answer;
- the decision-maker helps to define the major constraints under which a decision for television would have to be made;
- the decision-maker will allow several times for interaction with the evaluator over the period in which information is being prepared for a decision.

(ii) *Actions for the evaluator-advisor* The context of planning new projects will not ordinarily generate new data gathering but rather depend heavily on past studies. The role of the evaluator-advisor is paramount in making the best possible use of this knowledge.

- the evaluator-advisor helps the decision-maker to specify the precise decision to be made; often that decision will be for or against using television; however where a satellite system is justified on other grounds the advisor may be asked for the best way of using television.
- the evaluator-advisor helps the decision-maker to specify the constraints to a decision involving television, constraints that include the political, the bureaucratic, the economic, the cultural, etc.
- the evaluator-advisor presents the results of his study in the form of alternatives, but makes a choice among them in terms of concrete recommendations for action (and their justification);
- the evaluator-advisor includes among his considerations for recommending an action the constraints to making a decision and a strategy for the implementation of the recommendations;
- the evaluator-advisor communicates his final recommendations in a dialogue form with the decision-maker, through a face-to-face meeting, or at least in the form of a personal letter, least of all in report form, even if brief, and never in a long technical report.

(iii) *Other actions for improving usefulness*
Although personal interaction between decision-maker and advisor is probably the best way of translating evaluations into planning decisions, other actions are needed to reinforce this central activity:

● synthetic summaries of research in straight-forward language are helpful to both advisors and even, at times, to decision-makers;[10,13]
● better training for Third World decision-makers and planners can help a great deal, both in longer-term degree programmes or in shorter-term workshops or conferences; this training should stress comparative planning so that media are not presented as the only option for educational problems;
● a better network of institutions and of written information in summary form could help decision-makers find information more readily; among written sources and institutions are the French publication, *Direct*, the *Instructional Technology Report* of the Information Center on Instructional Technology and Stanford's retrieval system (SPIRES) for research on media projects.*

Conclusion
The accumulation of knowledge in itself does not guarantee that it will usefully serve the needs of present or future audiences. Evaluations can be made more useful to the immediate decisions that they are to serve and have an opportunity of serving planning needs at a later time provided care is taken to make them correspond to the concrete contexts of the decision-makers. This concern is part of the 'strategic' approach to evaluation that will help to make evaluations both more useful and more used.

References
1 JIMENEZ, G. J., *Television Educativa para America Latina*. Mexico, D. F., Porrua, S. America, 1970.
2 WERTHEIM, J. *Educational Television and the Use of Mass Media for Education in Cuba*. Mimeo, Stanford University, November, 1975.

* See also section on continuing links in this publication.

3 SCHRAMM, W. *ITV in American Samoa After 9 Years*, Washington, USAID, Academy for Educational Development, 1973.
4 AUDECAM (TeleNiger Evaluation, in French, 1975).
5 MACCOBY, N. and COMSTOCK, G. *The Peace Corps ETV Project in Colombia: Two Years of Research*, Stanford, Institute for Communication Research, 1967.
6 MAYO, J., McANANY, E. and KLEES, S. 'The Mexican Telesecundaria: A Cost-Effectiveness Analysis', *Instructional Science*, 4 (1975, special issue on evaluations of instructional technology).
7 MAYO, J. K., HORNIK, R., McANANY, E. *Educational Reform with Television: The El Salvador Experience*, Stanford, Stanford University Press, (in press).
8 BALL, S. and BOGATZ, G. A. *The First Year of Sesame Street: An Evaluation*, Princeton, Educational Testing Service: 1970.
9 COOK, T. et. al. *Sesame Street Revisited: A Case Study in Evaluative Research*, New York, Russell Sage, 1975.
10 SCHRAMM, W. *Big Media, Little Media*, Washington, USAID, Academy for Educational Development, 1973.
11 SMITH, S. *The Utility and Utilization of Evaluative Information: A Review and Analysis of Influential Factors*, Washington, A Report to the National Institute of Education, 1975.
12 CARNOY, M., 'The Economic Costs and Returns to Educational Television', *Economic Development and Cultural Change*, 1975.
13 CHU, G. and SCHRAMM, W. *Learning from Television. What the Research Says*, Washington, National Association of Educational Broadcasters, 1967.
14 JAMISON, D. T. and KLEES, S. 'The Cost of Instructional Radio and Television for Developing Countries', *Instructional Science*, 4 (1975).
15 GANDY, O. *What alternatives are there for using mass media in Tanzania? Towards a broader perspective on choice*. Paper read for African Studies

Association Conference, San Francisco, October 1975 (mimeo, Inst. Comm. Res., Stanford).

PAPER NO 45: DECISION-MAKING: A COMMUNICATION STRATEGY IN TV PROGRAMME BUILDING

S. K. Mullick, Dean (Television), Film and Television Institute of India, Poona.

Management of communication institutions is a challenging business. There are no easy answers to problems of management, or how to be a success in management. As a matter of fact many theories and techniques of management are available—some appear to work for one manager, some do not; some managers may find a completely different approach which works for them. But there are unlimited ideas available to an inquisitive manager, who is keen on effective management and is always exploring modern ideas to suit his particular area of work.

The concept of management in media has changed over the years. The managers have to deal with human beings and the tools they use for effective management have to keep pace with the developments around them. Researchers say that man's knowledge is doubling at a very fast rate. The net speed of technological developments thus have tremendous impact on jobs and skills.

Thinking ahead

In most areas—as in the field of television—the facilities and services that we now enjoy, quickly become obsolete as better and more sophisticated ones are invented. It is quite clear that most of us have to add to our basic jobs and skills several times before we retire. In order to achieve maximum results and better output in terms of quality, the practitioners of media skills have to adapt themselves to new situations and keep abreast of innovations. The researcher, the programmer, the manager—all have constantly to think how best and how effectively to direct and develop the organization's human resources to achieve optimum results.

How do we harness the technology in maximizing our utilization of new knowledge to the interest of an organization's objectives, in harmony with the needs of the individual, the environment and society?

Communication policy goals determination should always follow need-assessment of the audience so that goals are based on priority of needs and programme proposals are evolved, based upon clearly identified goals. An information goal will be based on its impact on the audience.

In India where television is geared to developmental purposes and social change, there is a major constraint with regard to the use of modern media. In this backdrop, the researcher/practitioner who is learning to master the techniques of Western oriented mass media, has almost become stranger at home. Our own attitudes have been found irrelevant when communicating with rural people. It is very necessary to get familiar with other development communication agencies, their structures and methods of operation and thus develop an integrated approach to communication strategies.

Participant management

Development research for meaningful and effective programmes, if it is to be successful in our context, needs a different approach to research methodology and programme building activity. The researcher-producer collaboration involves a participant style of decision-making, where discussion is marked by a give-and-take approach crystallizing through consensus.

This skill of the management of research is an integral part of the research process. Both practitioners and researchers need to be associated in agreement over the basic principles of research and its uses. The gap between the researcher and the producer should be bridged as far as possible. In the Indian situation we must make a shift in the *concept of communication in general, to the more specific and functional approach to communication, i.e. development*. It also should be our aim to find out whether the systems of analysis followed in the west are applicable in the countryside here. If not, what are the modifications that need to be done before any strategy is developed? In other words, methodology will have to be adapted to the unique socio-economic, linguistic and cultural background. New conceptual models would have to be devised. The practitioner needs to cull out the material from the researcher in a joint effort right from the beginning of programme building.

Selling social change

It is well-known that media expertise relies heavily on marketing techniques. But there is a difference between selling goods and selling ideas for social change. Much more is required for the success in the field of developmental programmes in the form of training and retraining, feedback and evaluation, which has to be a continuous process. But the media man and the researcher must possess a mastery of the local language and the principal dialects, a good grounding of the peculiar sense of humour and a general psychological feel of the target audiences.

Equally vital is a good sense of what will amuse or fail to amuse or possibly annoy. This capacity has to be cultivated along with the ability to adapt and use new hardware. Knowledge of hardware infinitely extends one's mastery over software.

One has to always remind oneself that it is not enough to be convinced oneself. The real test is to convince the other. If the other fails to be convinced, something may be wrong or wanting in one's own conviction.

With my limited experience, I am inclined to infer that the researcher and the producer need to be researching themselves all the time to imbibe that kind of *attitude which will fit into particular situations or projects.* If I may use a figure of speech: the researcher provides the raw material, the producer is a middle man and the consumer of the product is the audience for whom the researcher is researching and the producer is programming. Thus, the production staff must be motivated to make use of research results. They must be able to understand the research findings and the researcher must address his research for the benefit of the producer. The producer, on the other hand, must use his skill, which the consumer i.e. the viewer will be willing to accept. If the producer fails, *the whole edifice of communication process tumbles. So action-oriented researching combined with consumer-oriented production, to my mind, is the key to meaningful, effective programming.*

Research-based production

In media strategy and creative management, scope has to be allowed for innovative behaviour and unusual insight of the media personnel. A built-in system of flexibility which is geared to accountability, creativity, co-ordinative capacity and social relevance has to be evolved. Above all, intellectual ability should be blended with the capacity to evolve practical solutions for media problems within the external constraints of the organization.

There is no shortage of research material available all over the world and also in our own country. A number of papers have been written on the Delhi Television, especially on the agricultural programmes. But unfortunately, they have always remained on the academic plane, more to be added to the shelves of the library than for the use of the practitioner. Recently in a lecture Mr Henry Geddes of the British Film Institute said,

> There is a plethora of research papers written on various subjects. Seminars galore are being held all over the world. But when it comes to culling out any concrete policy or for that matter programme strategy, one looks at the masses of the written material and the words of wisdom resound in one's ear without ever coming to the screen in any form of real good programme.

This in short we should try to avoid in our work. Yet another crucial variable in media decision-making in developing countries is that in media planning one has to avoid contradiction between the expectations raised and the facilities and reliability of the environment of the audience. Here again, it is on-the-spot field-worker whose grasp of local environment that is to be taken into account.

Television often descends to sheer entertainment. In communication the target audience has to be constantly borne in mind—its social, economic, and cultural profile—so that decision-making for media programmes is relevant to the consumers. After all TV is show-business and its prime aim is to hold the interest of the audience, to make the audience believe that it is getting its money's worth. The switch-off knob is a nightmare to those who are in the entertainment trade. That's why content becomes secondary. What we have to do is face this great challenge of subtly combining entertainment with content, if we want to bring in social change—which is the major objective of TV in India. As Professor Yashpal of ISRO rightly said recently:

> We experts have to occasionally de-expertise ourselves and go down to the grass roots and reinforce our knowledge by constant contact with the audiences we seek to serve.

And this can only be done by keeping our batteries charged with new knowledge and not letting ourselves become victims of our own expertise by talking to the audience from our ivory towers.

TV research and prototype production project

The setting up of the Television Research and Prototype Production Unit at the Television Training Wing of the Film and Television Institute of India will try to get over a *recognized area of weakness* in the TV system in India.

If Indian TV is to meet its well-defined objectives in the field of education, family planning, health and agriculture it will need the backing of a strong and comprehensive programme of research into programme content and forms and their suitability to the Indian situation. There is also the need to develop a feed-back and evaluation system designed to ensure continuing effectiveness.

The TV Research and Prototype Project which became operational in July 1975, was set up in collaboration with UNESCO through funds provided by the Ford Foundation. The collaboration period is two and a half years, after which the unit will be a permanent part of the training component at the Institute.

The unit has the main objectives of developing through research and experimentation television programme forms most suitable for India's social change in education, health, family planning and agriculture, and developing for the broadcasting authority a suitable system of continuing feedback and evaluation. The Prototype Unit is given to developing research techniques and programme formats

suitable for communicating particular categories of messages in specific geographical and cultural contexts to rural audiences, without of course the exclusion of urban audiences. It will also develop from research findings and from the testing of Prototype Production full-scale professional programme formats with social relevance for use in Indian TV. The Unit will identify qualities and backgrounds required for staff and talents for the most effective TV broadcasting in the Indian situation.

No universal models could apply in media decisions because the response of audience, local cultural conditions and the available infrastructure have to be reckoned with in devising or adapting prototype models that could be replicated under normal broadcasting conditions and with the existing hardware facilities in other parts of India.

Priority has been assigned to research into children's needs of TV programmes and the appropriate formats suitable for them.

A seminar was held in Poona in October 1975 attended by over sixty participants from different parts of the country belonging to various media organizations and communication disciplines engaged in children's welfare and developmental activities. The workshop was assisted by the resource personnel of Children's Television Workshop of New York, which produces the successful pre-school and children's reading TV programmes *Sesame Street*, and *The Electric Company*.

Among the significant conclusions arrived at was that children's programmes to be produced by the Research and Prototype Production Unit at Poona should be devoted to experimenting with traditional formats, including the use of realistic documentary, animation, puppetry, fantasy, etc geared to the problem of developing self-awareness among children, with the longer-term aim of developing models of programmes founded in indigenous conditions. It was agreed that television-viewing children will develop through vicarious experiences the necessary positive and co-operative character traits helpful to meet the rural needs.

Conclusion

I have given the background of the

Research and Prototype Unit in the Film and Television Institute of India simply to illustrate the fact that isolated work in various parts of the country is being done—but no co-ordinated effort is in sight. This unit thus serves as a catalytic agent for the only broadcasting authority in India (All-India Radio)—since this Institute trains the staff of AIR (TV). It also now has its own professional research and production staff for building research-based programmes to be tried out first on a limited scale and then given to AIR for evaluation on a larger scale in actual broadcast situations. These are decisions that had to be taken before we set about identifying the strategy of work in Film and TV Institute of India.

Our decisions and prototype research programme activity are conditioned by the need of the broadcasting authority. The needs assessment, goal selection, formative research, production, evaluation—all have a definite set of objectives.

In research as well as in production, the Prototype Unit keeps pre-testing as an important phase of work to guide production and to test the effectiveness of research tools and production formats. This is where decision in research and programme-building activity has to be laid down clearly and watched for implementation.

PAPER NO 58: EVALUATION AND DECISION-MAKING IN THE MANAGEMENT OF EDUCATIONAL BROADCASTING*

Richard Sherrington, Head, Courses Unit, Media Department, British Council, UK.

From north-east Brazil to Addis Ababa, from Ankara to Singapore, educational broadcasting organizations maintain groups of people entirely devoted to evaluating the processes and products of their working life. Sometimes these Units or Sections are described in terms of 'Research and Evaluation'. Sometimes they are linked

---

* Reproduced with kind permission of the publishers from *Educational Broadcasting International*, March 1976.

to a 'Utilization and Liaison' function. Sometimes—as in the Ivory Coast—they are simply called 'Information Processing'. All of them work at producing a great deal of information about the system. The nature of this information and the methods by which it is obtained form the basis for a wide and varied literature. It is rather the purpose of this paper to look at these people as an element in an organizational structure. Just as the administrative necessities and constraints of a large school affect the teaching-learning situation, so it may be that the organizational setting of an Evaluation Unit affects its efficiency and effectiveness.

Why are such units established? It is rare for a school or college textbook unit or teacher-training establishment to set up a working group entirely devoted to assessing its activities. Yet the media in education have adopted the educational technology model as a matter of course. A learner with feedback does better than the learner without:

The chief function of evaluation is to improve the effectiveness of our teaching.[1]

Intellectually, evaluation and decision-making go hand in hand. It is also currently fashionable to be able to point to some evidence of evaluative activity. And, of course, it is useful for a broadcasting organization to have evidence of reception figures, viewers' attitudes and so on. Indeed, in some schools' broadcasting systems, such units are mainly justified in terms of the psychological effect on the teachers questioned or surveyed; they feel in this way that they are participating in the broadcasting decision; it is a substitute for access.

Separation

Whatever the reasoning behind the decision, a Unit or Section or Institute is established as one branch of the organizational tree, responsible for some kind of evaluative job. The function might even be placed with an independent body outside the main organization, such as a University or a separate Ministry Department. In either case, the functional Unit is set apart from the main line of organizational authority and decision-making.

For the workers in this Unit, this separation is welcomed. They are free of departmental barriers, their specialized work can be properly planned and carried out in their own way. Standing to one side, they have an overview of the system as a whole. As their own masters, they can decide upon their approach: a standard form of all materials for computer analysis; a more detailed depth investigation of a few key areas, perhaps. In the educational technology model, the Evaluation Unit would be the co-ordinating heart of the system, and the educational technologist himself the benign genius who gives order and sense to planning, budgeting, teacher education, textbook production and educational broadcasting.

In practice, however, the separation of the functional role leads to problems. The Evaluation Unit suffers as do other functional units—personnel, for example, or organization and methods. Who does it work to within the organization? Does it have executive authority over other parts of the system? Does its existence constitute a constant criticism of management and production decisions, which causes resentment and ostracism? The Unit produces different types of information: it might concern a temporary fault on a receiver in one school; it might concern the unacceptability of vernacular language programmes. At which point in the managerial hierarchy is this information registered and authorization for action given? Does the final responsibility lie with the staff of the Evaluation Unit, who have personal contact with the source of complaint, or with the main line of decision-makers? Furthermore placing the specialist unit at one remove from the main administrative structure means extra effort in consultation, minuting, presentation of information, in easily digestible form, dissemination of information and so on. No wonder that it often means a considerable slowing down of administrative action.

Sadly, it is often managerial problems of this nature which bedevil Evaluation Units within broadcasting organizations and which have led to the view that:

in retrospect, there have been few users of the evaluations that have been done, and the information gathered in even the best formative and summative studies has rarely affected decisions in an important way.[2]

It is not enough to exhort evaluators to work more closely to the needs of decision-makers, or to hammer at producers and managers for not making more use of the results from the Evaluation Unit. Very often, it is simply a feature of the organizational structure and management that information remains unused and unloved. Evaluation Units will worry about their methods and the communication of their results in vain, if the bureaucratic structure is against them. The answer to the problem will not be found in techniques of educational measurement, but in an analysis of how managerial decisions are made.

Bases for decision

It seems that decision-makers in an organization do not rely upon information—such as that by an Evaluation Unit—as the basis for their decisions. This does not mean that it is the wrong information, simply that decisions are rarely made on the basis of facts presented for one alternative rather than another. American studies suggest that the internal politics of the organization and the subjective desires of the decision-maker are more instrumental in deciding his course of action.

> Executives who make effective decisions know that one does not start with facts. One starts with opinions . . . the understanding that underlies the right decision grows out of the clash and conflict of divergent opinion and out of the serious consideration of competing alternatives.[3]

The crux of a decision is not the choice between alternatives but the identification of the costly, invisible consequences of such a choice and the fabrication of a choice which tip-toes its way through them without setting any of them off.[4] To make a decision is to deal in uncertainties. Evaluation results, presented as information for decisions, are hedged about with qualifications, with statistical generalizations and variable interpretations. The decision-maker has to make up his mind about them and in addition decide upon their relevance to the decision in hand. There is always an element of uncertainty; never an objective fact. Hence the decision-maker will compromise in favour of a decision which he feels will achieve his desired result; one that he can justify; one that he feels happiest in being made accountable for.

It is hard to know what influences that final choice of action. The 'costly invisible consequences' may well be relationships within the organization or the ministry, or the image which the decision-maker feels the organization should project. Weighted against factors such as these, evaluation returns to the choice of a presenter for a television programme, or the acceptability of a particular series—even viewing figures —may have little power to persuade.

The time factor in decision-making is also important, in relation to the level in the administrative hierarchy at which the decision is made. Decisions affecting the immediate future tend to be made at lower levels. The further into the future the results of a decision are felt, the higher up the hierarchy it will be made.[5] Thus evaluation returns concerning picture quality, programme enjoyment or learning achieved, details of production techniques, script balance, and so on, may involve decisions by practitioners at middle and lower levels for whom these are daily preoccupations. Information about areas for development, programme language policy, cost-effectiveness, the integration of broadcasts with the work of other departments and agencies may involve higher level decisions, evolving over a number of months or years. It is important that the information goes to the appropriate level of decision-maker and that it involves decisions within the time-scale of his normal decision-making behaviour. For example, a producer may be used to making clear-cut, rapid decisions for the immediate purposes of the programme in hand; if the evaluation data he receives can be perceived in terms of instant and obvious changes, he is likely to use it. He may be less happy with broad, indeterminate data for which he personally can see no immediate use, though for senior management it would fit into the framework of ongoing policy meetings.

A lot of evaluative information is simply 'interesting'. If it is not used in decision-making, that is not a criticism of its interest or its influence in forming ideas in those who read it; it may be simply unusable in terms of the type of decisions which a particular person has to make in his job. Much evaluation is retrospective, some-times many weeks or months after the time at which decisions might fruitfully have been made: much evaluation is irrelevant at one time and has been forgotten when it becomes relevant; and much evaluation is presented in an inappropriate way to particular types of decision-makers.

These problems are features of the administrative system which sets up an Evaluation Unit as a service to the main line decision-making hierarchy, and then leaves it to get on by itself. The Unit's job is to produce information and it does so, assuming that those who set it up will know what to do with its results. It is important to recognize that the failure of this process is frequently not a failure of goodwill or interest. It is an administrative problem and requires an administrative solution.

Alternative organization patterns

There are various possible alternatives[6] which can be applied to Evaluation Units:

1 At the most frugal level, the Evaluation Unit could be discontinued as a permanent entity, endlessly producing information which might or might not be useful, simply because it exists. Management might employ specialists for a specific evaluative project—rather as management consultants operate—with clearly defined objectives for specific decision-making requirements. The danger is, of course, that management would not use this facility for anything but the most vital issues; that many unforseen problems would go unrecognized. It might, however, lead to more fruitful use of results than the present situation.

2 The staff of the managerial departments and the specialist department might rotate every so often; thus, producers/writers will expect to spend part of their career in the Evaluation Unit and vice versa. There will always be arguments against this alternative: that each side demands a highly professional standard incompatible with a sudden change in roles. This is truer in some broadcasting establishments than others. It would certainly help to upgrade the influence of evaluation on the individual decision-maker at the point of decision.

3 Part of the problem may be the status of the Evaluation Unit in the overall

organization. If the director of the Unit is recruited into middle management level, the Unit will obviously have little weight in getting its views heard. One solution would be to ensure that the head of the Unit at least is part of the top management structure, reporting direct to the Director-General or Managing Director. In this way the influence of the Unit would move upward to the top of the decision-making pyramid and thence downward through the various levels of decision-making in other departments. The status which this solution provides requires ancillary networks of communication to ensure the right information gets to the right managerial decision-maker. But it would make for a more welcome reception for the results of evaluation.

4 Another alternative is not to create a separate Unit of specialists in evaluation, but to incorporate them at various levels throughout the entire organization so that they are part of the managerial staff of different departments, with special responsibility for evaluation. They would meet with their co-specialists regularly but informally. Each evaluator would then be a colleague of the decision-makers he is serving; would know their problems at first-hand; could serve their immediate decision-making needs. His career prospects, status, job orientation would be identical with those he serves and the specialist/manager devision would not interfere with the evaluation/decision-making process.

Tactics

In addition to these broader issues of organizational structure there are common-sense tactical steps which need to be taken by evaluators within any organization. They should not undertake research projects and produce results which will cause problems to other parts of the organization. This is a sure way to have information ignored. It is better to begin with projects with limited objectives, where there is a guarantee of success, in which information leads to clear-cut action and improved performance. Certain areas will exist where simple problems can be easily solved, given certain evaluative data; the task of the Unit should be to identify these areas, offer assistance and make sure improvement takes place. On the basis of success in small matters it will be possible to move on to more controversial areas, making sure all the time that the right information gets to the right decision-making level at the right time.

It is interesting to note how discussions in educational circles concerning objectives, systems design and evaluation are paralleled in discussions concerning Scientific Management and Management by Objectives. Conceptually, a teaching-learning system and an administrative system conform to the same model in which evaluation of outcomes has an immediate implication for decisions about inputs. In practice, both systems concern frail humanity. To some evaluators, it is necessary to assume a 'rational consumer' for their information; a decision-maker who operates only in terms of the conceptual model, basing his choice only on evidence provided. 'Without him evaluation can only be regarded as a costly waste of time'.[7] On the other hand, such an assumption denies the value of evaluation in the real world where there are irrational decision-makers. Management studies are concerned with the behaviour of people in decision-making situations in the real world. There is no reason why an Evaluation Unit should only see itself in terms of a model and should not come to terms with the administrative reality within which it hopes to operate. A first task for such a Unit might be to study the structure of decision-making inside its organization and plan its future activities according to the results of the study. Where better to link evaluation to decision-making than in the Evaluation Unit itself?

References

1 ROWNTREE, D., *Educational Technology in Curriculum Development*, London, Harper & Row, 1974.

2 McANANY, E. G., *Study Instructional Television: What should be Evaluated?* Stanford University, 1973.

3 DRUCKER, P. F., *The Effective Executive*, London, Heinemann, 1967.

4 GORE, W. J., in STEWART, R., (ed.) *The Reality of Management*, London, Pan, 1967.

5 BROWN, W. and JAQUES, E., *Time-Span Handbook*, Heinemann, 1964.

6 McGREGOR, D., *The Human Side of Enterprise*, New York, McGraw-Hill, 1960.

7 ERAUT, M., GOAD, and SMITH, *The Analysis of Curriculum Materials*, Brighton, University of Sussex, 1975.

THE PROFESSIONAL CONTEXT

PAPER NO 78: MEDIA RESEARCH AND ANTHROPOLOGY: SOME OB-SERVATIONS ON SITE

Binod C. Agrawal, Research and Evaluation Cell, Space Applications Centre, Ahmedabad, India.

Introduction

The Satellite Instructional Television Experiment (SITE) is a multi-disciplinary project. One of the aims of this project is to bring about desired social change in rural areas with the help of a mass medium—TV. This one year project, we hope, will help develop a better national system of TV communication covering the remotest parts of the country.

Anthropologists, sociologists, psychologists, political scientists and media researchers are involved in measuring the social impact of SITE in terms of generating positive attitudes towards new innovations, thereby leading to integrated rural development. Essentially, the social research for this purpose has been conceived as inter- and multi-disciplinary, in which a variety of theoretical concepts and adequate methodological tools are being used to collect comprehensive data for assessment and understanding of the impact of TV communication.

One of the social evaluation methods we have followed is strengthened by the anthropological approach and is known as 'Holistic Study'. In this paper, an attempt has been made to delineate the usefulness and strength of holistic study in assessing the impact of television and its role in integrated rural development. The paper is based on preliminary data being collected from nine villages in seven States of India. Television programmes on agricultural, health, hygiene, family planning, nutrition and national integration are shown in these villages to adult audience, whereas in the morning, school children between the age of 5–12 are exposed to enrichment-oriented television programmes.

Anthropologists, contrary to other social scientists, are interested in understanding all the manifestations of human beings and of human activity in an unified way, conceiving it as a whole.

Secondly, Man must be studied in his totality. It is at this juncture that anthropology comes closer to the concept of integrated rural development, where attempts are being made to develop the various facets (parts) of rural life as a whole. Having this assumption in mind, we decided to study the process of communication using anthropological methods and techniques. This decision was based on our experiences which show that detailed indepth analysis of Indian rural life would allow for a better understanding and grasp of rural reality. This study emphasizes the understanding of the process of existing rural communication, the role of TV as a new medium of communication for integrated rural development, and the process of change brought about by Satellite TV in the rural social structure at micro-level.

For this purpose we have planned a comparative study of seven States (for our purpose we have referred to them as SITE Clusters), which are—Andhra Pradesh, Bihar, Gujarat, Karnataka, Madhya Pradesh, Orissa and Rajasthan. We have evolved a common design not only in terms of objectives but also in terms of uniform data collection. In each of the above States, we have selected at least one village among those villages having a TV set installed under SITE. About three months before the experiment started we placed nine anthropologists, after intensive training, in the nine selected villages. They will continue to live there until three months after SITE is over. They are observing as far as possible the whole village and the various aspects of routine village life, including patterns of agriculture, social and economic organization. In addition, they are closely observing the TV audience and their behaviour after viewing developmental TV programmes. Further, they are investigating who uses what kind of communication channels for what purpose; what channels are thought to be most credible in the village; what are the consulting patterns regarding problem areas of family planning, agriculture, health and hygiene and education. We have already collected detailed demographic and economic data from these villages.

Based on the weekly reports received from the field and personal observations, in the next few paragraphs an attempt has been made to present some of the preliminary observations.

Preliminary observations

Agriculture

In all cluster villages under this study, we have observed that audiences are highly appreciative of mythological programmes. However, if these programmes are used for conveying developmental messages, even if these programmes are enjoyed, the message is lost. For this reason, it seems the farmers of Bhutera (Rajasthan) village found the programme on 'How to grow potatoes' having a direct message valuable. Similarly, the programme on use of fertilizer and bumper crops of wheat were also appreciated by them. Some farmers have shown an inclination towards using fertilizers for *Bajra* crop in Baraser (Bihar). They have recently approached the village level worker for getting new varieties of wheat seeds after viewing the TV programmes. Also, the *Madigas* (Harijans) of Kawadpalley (Andhra Pradesh) want more programmes on agriculture instead of music and songs. Repeated exposure of agricultural programmes, it seems, has led to better understanding of modern agricultural technology in Ismailpur (Bihar).

Some of the agricultural programmes, in which recommendations for fertilizers and other inputs were made, have not provoked positive interest in Ismailpur (Bihar) due to lack of financial resources. In Ghenupally (Orissa) use of a thresher was not found practical as viewers thought that it could not be operated by a single person continuously. Bhutera (Rajasthan) audience was observed to be showing disinterest during programmes of vegetable growing. It seems that the farmers do not like to grow vegetables as they do not eat them in this area. The programme on dwarf varieties of paddy shown to Ghenupally (Orissa) audience was not effective. One of the main reasons was that the viewers thought that such dwarf varieties of paddy would lead to the production of a lesser quantity of straw required for hut building and animal fodder.

Family planning

In general, the audiences in villages under study show a high level of awareness regarding family planning campaigns and are able to recognize the family planning worker and various contraceptive methods, due to the repeated exposure of the family planning programmes through TV, but these programmes have not generated any further interest. Instead, the audience seems indifferent towards family planning programmes. Again, it seems that the direct approach for tackling the family planning problem may yield better results. The major portion of our audience is still not women, but they do constitute a substantial proportion of the audience viewing TV programmes. Changes in their viewing behaviour and adoption of some recommendations have been observed in the villages under study.

Culinary programmes for female audiences have evoked a variety of reactions. For example, Baraser women appreciated these programmes and took keen interest in experimenting with new dishes shown on TV. On the other hand women of Ismailpur could not comprehend the culinary programme due to language difficulties. Ghenupally women showed apathy towards the culinary programmes, and this was the case too, with women of Kawadpalley.

Observation shows that school and non-school children are the most sincere viewers in the village under study. They seem to be quite influenced by the visuals they see and have tried to utilize the TV programmes for crafts and have learnt pretty well. One observes paper toys displayed in the schools made by children. However, programmes seem to be comprehended and enjoyed only by students of higher grades. This is more true in Bihar, Rajasthan and Karnatake villages under study.

Attendance

Anthropologists in their villages have kept a daily record of the viewers in terms of sex, age-grades and *jati* population categories. There has been a fall in audience size in all the villages under study between August and October 1975. This may be because of (a) the novelty effect wearing off (b) increased agricultural activities (beginning of *Kharif* harvesting and sowing of *Rabi*), (c) intense cold, and (d) a change in the TV transmission timings. Based on our data, it is safe to predict that attendance of the viewers will increase after the sowing period is over and until *Rabi* harvesting starts.

Change

One of the most frequent questions asked is whether the presence of a television in the village has helped in breaking the *jati* (caste) barriers. Our observations show that TV is not contributing towards breaking the barrier, but TV has brought children of all *jatis* and religious groups together for viewing TV. They have been observed sitting together in front of the TV without showing any sign of *jati* differences.

Among adult viewers the ecological TV setting of the religious *jati* composition, neighbourhood and kinship relationships within the village seems to be influencing the sitting pattern of the viewer's. For example, in Kawadpalley (Andhra Pradesh) and Dadusar (Gujarat) villages, the television is located at the junction of two distinct religious and *jati* neighbourhoods. Therefore, each group uses its own passage and sit near the passage while viewing the TV programmes.

An outside observer, not knowing the spatial distribution of religious/*jati* groups in the village, may get the impression that there are strong *jati* barriers in these villages. While in Ismailpur (Bihar) more than sixty per cent of the population belong to a single *jati*, one observes no such barrier. Visitors from other villages have been observed sitting separately. Again, this is not any reflection of *jati* barrier. Rather, the ecological setting and demographic factors have contributed towards a particular kind of sitting behaviour. We hope to study this phenomenon in further detail after collecting diachronic data for a year from all these villages through daily TV observation sheets.

PAPER NO 5: DEVELOPING AN EFFECTIVE EDUCATIONAL MEDIUM

John P. Baggaley, Centre for Communication Studies, University of Liverpool, UK.

Note This is a summary of a paper published in full in *Programmed Learning and Educational Technology*, Vol. 10, No 3, 1973.

The media will contribute few solutions to the main educational problems until techniques and criteria for their effective use have been developed. In a discussion of the present and future demand for instructional technology, emphasis is given to the potential teaching functions of television. Areas for essential research in media effectiveness are discussed, and an initial theoretical orientation to the problems of media development is provided.

The main sections of the paper may be summarized as follows:

1 *Introduction* General uses of the media in British education are represented by an analysis of the television work at Liverpool University's AVA unit during a sample two-term period. The analysis gives percentage uses of the medium:

- (a) to provide information usually inaccessible,
- (b) to provide magnification of material,
- (c) to enable subsequent re-analysis,
- (d) for collation of disparate material,
- (e) for formal production purposes,
- (f) for instantaneous relay,
- (g) for off-air recording.

Since the paper's initial publication in 1973 the proportional usage of TV at the university for each purpose has fluctuated, though the basic classification of functions continues to represent the demands on the facilities by university staff.

Yet, the paper argues, while technical resources multiply, the methods for using them remain capricious and arbitrary; and the greater role within our institutions that educational technologists foresaw for themselves has failed to develop. It is still 'a technology without techniques'. Accordingly, the more general problems of the educational system are defined, and the potential of educational technology to solve them is examined.

2 *Problems in Media Research* Future development of educational technology will, it is indicated, depend on effective research strategies. Current approaches to media research are discussed, and also the methodological drawbacks which prevent them from providing information useful in the development of media effectiveness. The problems of individual difference in human performance are discussed, with reference to sensory and personality factors. The benefits of applying existing theoretical knowledge of skill and communication processes are indicated.

3 *An Heuristic Approach to Media Development* A more objective and heuristic strategy to research in the educational media is now suggested. On the basis of evidence for individual learner needs (derived from perceptual and judgemental psychology) objective criteria for educational effectiveness may be established and specific principles for the effective educational use of a medium may be tested. The prime commitment of educational research to the development of self-instruction and individual access techniques is questioned, and a basis is offered for the necessary research into group instructional methods. A means of guaranteeing the objectivity of research in educational media is recommended in Kelly's 'role construct repertory grid test'.

4 *Educational Technology in a Practical Perspective* The most valuable role for educational technologists in the future will be to prescribe the media production techniques appropriate to specific problems and to specific situations.

It is emphasized that research should aim at the constant accumulation and modification of teaching principles on a pragmatic basis, rather than waiting for a single learning theory to cope with all problems at a single stroke.

PAPER NO 64: EVALUATION OF ETV PROGRAMMES IN DEVELOPING COUNTRIES

Chiam Tah Wen, Evaluation Officer, Ministry of Education, Malaysia.

The concept of evaluation

Evaluation forms an integral part of a comparatively recent approach to problem-solving—the Systems Approach. This approach, in essence, is a method for developing a framework which can be used to design, implement and evaluate the components which need to be assembled to reach a desired goal. The approach identifies and defines the requirements which must be met for an overall objective to be achieved, specifies the characteristics of resources which must be assembled to fulfil these requirements, and provides a developmental plan which permits the resulting product to be evaluated, revised and updated with minimum waste.

The schematic outline of the systems approach cycle is defined in the diagram (see opposite page).

Recognition that education is a system, and that the interactions among its constituent parts more frequently than not determine how faithfully its goals will be achieved, has been one of the outstanding contributions of educational technology.

A crucial element in the systems approach is, as stated, evaluation. This is an important process in the whole concept of educational technology, which may be defined as the design, development, dissemination, implementation and evaluation of instructional materials, used for enhancing the quality of educational outcomes. The five process words used in the

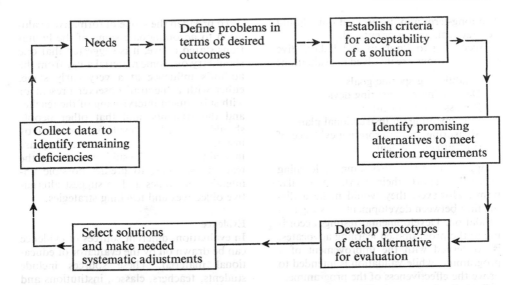

above definition are of great significance because they have not usually been given the same emphasis. Materials have been designed and disseminated, but very few have been *developed*—a process which implies considerable attention to testing and revision i.e. to formative evaluation. Moreover there has been little systematic study of problems of implementation and very little evaluation. What is evaluation then? What basic operations does evaluation consist of? To draw attention to its full range of functions, one may define 'evaluation' broadly as the collection and use of information to make decisions about an educational programme.

The fundamental purpose of evaluation is to produce information which can be used in educational decision-making. Thus evaluation is not only concerned with measurement or assessment, in terms of students' achievements—scores, but also with value judgements for decision-making. The decisions may be concerned with the continuation, termination or modification of an existing programme, or with the development or adoption of a new programme. In this context, we have two types of evaluation, the 'formative' evaluation and the 'summative' evaluation. 'Formative' evaluation is conducted in conjunction with the development of new educational programmes, and 'summative' evaluation is used to assess the effectiveness of existing programmes. In 'formative'

evaluation, we are concerned with assessing the pupil's learning needs, his readiness for learning and problems he encounters while learning. Its purpose is to assist the teachers and pupils to reprogramme the teaching and learning programmes, not just at the end of the school year or even at the end of school term, but preferably at the end of each lesson or unit of instruction. As far as 'summative' evaluation is concerned, we note that it is used to ascertain, measure or assess how far the existing programme has been effective in the context of teaching and learning. It is conducted at the end of a course of programme and its main purpose is to assist in certification or validation and in future selection. Both these types of evaluation will help in educational decision-making, which is the main goal of evaluation in general.

In teaching-learning situations, then, many types of decisions are to be made, and many varieties of information are useful. It becomes apparent that evaluation is a diversified activity, and that no one set of principles will suffice for all situations. This is particularly true in the use of media. As Richard Hooper stated at the end of the 1972 NECCTA Conference, one has to bear in mind:

the very fluid dynamic situation of learning, where there is an enormous number of variables, and all sorts of things are happening at once.[1]

The long-term aim, as pointed out, should be practical, action-orientated.

According to Popham and Baker,[2] five basic operations are involved in evaluation:

1 Establishing specific goals
2 Developing a measuring device
3 Pre-assessing students
4 Implementing an instructional plan
5 Measuring and interpreting evidence of student achievement.

People involved in programmed learning generally report their work in similar terms. However, they would make a distinction between developmental testing and validation. Developmental testing, according to the programmed learning advocates, is concerned with the improvement of a programme, while validation is intended to prove the effectiveness of the programme.

Both these terms, developmental testing and validation, have however in the past generally referred to only one kind of evidence, the gain in performance by students on tests which are derived from the programmers' statement of objectives.

Eraut feels that this view of evaluation is 'deceptively simple, dangerously simple', as developmental testing and validation refer to only the formative and summative aspects of evaluation, and that other aspects concerning attitudes, motivation and long-range effects of programmes should also be considered. Developmental testing, according to Eraut, has some severe limitations. It is a closed system approach to formative evaluation which tends to reveal mistakes in the fine structure of programmes but to ignore their more fundamental messages. 'When results are disastrous, some radical rethinking may occur, but developmental testing will not of itself suggest alternatives, either more desirable alternatives with more valued objectives or even more effective alternatives which achieve the same objectives more efficiently by adopting different teaching strategies.'

Secondly, Eraut feels that developmental testing gives little information about outcomes not anticipated in the statement of objectives and that in this sort of testing, there is such a strong interaction between the tester and the student that major difficulties in student motivation (i.e. in an 'untested' or 'normal' situation) may remain undetected.

To broaden the scope of formative evaluation to accommodate some of the limitations stated above, it is suggested that one should try out some material away from the author's influence at a very early stage, either with a 'neutral' observer present or with subsequent interviewing of the teacher and the students, and that other people should be used to 'evaluate' material by inspection at a very early stage. They are invited to criticize the subject matter or the teaching strategy, to predict possible unintended outcomes and to suggest alternative objectives and teaching strategies.

Evidence

In evaluation, different sources of evidence can be drawn on by the evaluator of educational material. These sources include students, teachers, classes, institutions and experts. All five would probably be used in any evaluation study though in varying proportions. Based on these five sources, eleven models are envisaged by Eraut.

1 *Evidence from students*
   (a) *The Tutorial or Clinical Model* The intensive study of a few individual students as they interact with the materials.
   (b) *The Agricultural-Botany Model* The study of a large number of students, usually through batteries of tests and questionnaires.

2 *Evidence from teachers*
   (c) *The anthology model* A collection of all the best 'Little Johnny' stories. Useful in indicating the kind of effect materials can have, it is however unreliable and not generalizable.
   (d) *The teacher opinion model* Involves the trial of materials in a large number of schools and the collection of teachers' opinions by questionnaires or feedback meetings.

3 *Evidence from classes*
   (e) *The interaction model* Based on direct observation of interaction in the classroom, avoiding danger of bias and of retrospective rationalization.
   (f) *The environmental model* Uses direct evidence from visits about the

classroom environment, keeping an eye on the integration of materials with the other aspects of the student's curriculum.

4 *Evidence from Institutions*
(g) *The cost-benefit model* Who adopts the materials and why? Does adoption enhance the teacher's prospects for promotion or the Head's image?
(i) *The anthropologists model* The 'neutral' observer assesses how innovation changes the structure and value systems of the institution.

5 *Evidence from experts*
(j) *Desirability model* Are the likely outcomes desirable and of sufficient priority?
(k) *Feasibility model* This is concerned with the achievement of intended outcomes through suggested teaching strategy and consideration of alternative strategies.

In so far as educational television is concerned, the various feedback or evaluation methods, according to Schramm,[4] are:

1 Pretesting programmes
2 Teaching to pupils in the studio
3 Immediate electronic feedback from the classroom
4 Testing at frequent intervals on learning of programme content
5 Obtaining regular comments from classroom teachers
6 Making regular observation of classroom activity
7 Obtaining regular reports on attitudes of pupils and teachers
8 Obtaining reports 'on specific problems'
9 Expert reviews of programmes and materials.

There probably is no such thing as an 'ideal' programme for obtaining information since information from the different channels overlaps. One has also to decide what combination of methods—within the capabilities of the system, including cost and technical expertise—will most efficiently give the amount of feedback needed. Thus, the preferred strategy is to select some combination of feedback methods to serve local needs and fit local capabilities.

The Malaysian experience

Having made a general (and brief) review of the state of the art, let us now consider the Malaysian experience.

An in-depth, carefully structured programme of evaluation was initiated to coincide with the beginning of ETV's first full year of broadcasting in 1973. Initial efforts focussed on formative evaluation: teachers were asked to react to a series of questions about the television programmes they utilized. The questions drew teachers' attention to the following salient points:

Instructional Value of the Programme The programme content must be factually accurate and the pacing correct. A programme will serve no purpose if it does not instruct or if the student does not follow the programme. Besides, each programme is directed to a particular grade or age-group; as such, the question of appropriateness of production approaches or choice of vocabulary must be carefully considered.

Instructional Design In viewing an ETV programme, the student is expected to learn certain concepts. To facilitate this learning process, the programme must be so designed that concepts are built in a sequential way into an unit or series on a particular subject area. The development of the programme should be clear, concise, precise and logical.

Presentation Technique This is concerned with the way the television presenter performs his or her on-camera work. One looks for the poise, confidence, clarity of pronunciation, and facility with the language of the presenter. The ability of the presenter to identify with students is also an asset.

Teacher's Notes The teacher's notes play an important role in the effective utilization of the programme in the classroom. The teacher should look for the quality of each of the following:

(a) objectives of the lesson;
(b) vocabulary introduced in connection with the programme;
(c) pre-telecast activities;
(d) the programme content;
(e) post-telecast activities;
(f) references and other bibliographical listings;

291

(g) suggestions for extension of learning through related media.

Production Technique In this area, one should comment on whether the technique used in the telecast helps or hinders the instructional process, and suggest alternatives. Creative production includes the effective use of delivery and theatrics concerning appearances and voices of the presenter; it also involves the integration of music, action, animation, visuals, graphics, clowns, humour, lighting and background setting with the content of the programme. The production should evoke and sustain interest; it should provide intellectual stimulation, motivation and impact.

Effect on the Student The students are our target audience. The foregoing criteria should combine to bring about learning gains for the students. A well-produced and well-utilized ETV programme can motivate, stimulate and involve students in the instructional process.

Research experience has shown that for programmes to be effective, the medium should be well utilized. To facilitate this, schools are requested to go through a checklist concerning the physical environment, and motivation, involvement and reinforcement aspects of the telecast lesson.

For formative evaluation, teachers are requested to fill in a pre-addressed computerized form. Their reactions are compiled and given to the producers who use the information to alter, improve and redesign new programmes to more closely meet the needs of the schools. This evaluation follows a systematic procedure. Each State EMS Officer selects on a random sampling basis 50 different teachers each school term and requests their assistance in completing and returning the forms for compilation by the EMS staff. These forms have undergone three revisions and it is hoped that with computerization, a greater variety of information is made available to producers and other interested officials at a faster rate. In addition to this, each year a quantitative survey is conducted by the EMS staff in order to determine the size of the ETV viewing audience and the distribution of that audience over the various subjects that are broadcast. Significantly, the quantitative survey indicates that the Malaysian ETV is following the same viewing pattern as that experienced by most nations. The highest percentage of viewing is at the primary school level. That is probably due to the fact that it is easier for the primary school to incorporate ETV into their timetables than it is for the secondary school.

In April this year, a pilot series of summative evaluation to determine the immediate effect of television programmes on the learning of the student was initiated. Evaluation was conducted in a Standard Five English programme and a Form II Mathematics programme in both English and Malay language. The results reveal that television does make a significant contribution to the immediate learning of the student.

For the pilot summative evaluation scheme, tests consisting of both Multiple Choice Questions (MCQ) and the Open-ended questions were administered to children in different types of schools, i.e. rural and urban schools using different media of instruction.

With regard to the Standard 5 English Programme, the pre-test-post-test (the post-test was administered immediately following the telecast) analysis indicates that, of the four schools where tests were conducted, three schools showed significant gain. Investigation reveals that the majority of the pupils in the non-significant school came from a rural, low socio-economic background. They had received only two years of instruction in English since they started to learn English only at the Primary three level. Added to the fact that the majority of the pupils had difficulty in comprehension and mastery of concepts, utilization of the programme left much to be desired. The evaluation team was told that the regular ETV teacher was on leave and the person who stood in had no prior utilization training whatsoever. The motivation aspect was clearly missing.

Generally speaking, before an ETV lesson is broadcast, a preview of the programme is carried out by producers, subject specialists, curriculum developers, utilization and evaluation officers, teachers and other interested outside bodies. Reactions are noted by producers for reprogramming. To test the reaction to the Standard Five English programme by a more diversified group, this programme was shown to participants of the ETV utilization and evaluation courses held in Sabah and Sarawak recently. The participants included Senior Education officers, inspectorate of schools, training college lecturers and EMS officers. Three quarters of the 30 participants in Sabah and two-thirds of the 19 participants in Sarawak returned favourable comments as a whole, at the same time giving critical analysis of certain segments of the programme.

For the Form II Mathematics Programme, it is significant to note that, though the Malay version is identical to the English version, the pre-test and post-test means of the Malay-medium school were much lower. The difference in performance of the pupils could be due to a variety of factors which the MCQ—orientated test found it very difficult to unravel. Some of these factors might be ethnicity, place of residence, motivation of pupils and the attitude of the parents.

Discussion

The need for a more analytical approach involving the use of other techniques such as observation, interview and background probing in the context of the learning milieu is evident from the Malaysian experience. Studies indicate that the MCQ responses offer little or no detailed information about the student's reactions to the learning experience. Research studies on the effects of learning through the evaluation of video-tapes indicate that imposed scales may give a false impression of reactions to the learning experience, though admittedly the imposed scales were more sensitive measures than MCQ's. It has been demonstrated that some students using self-created scales (without having to confine themselves to given reference points) developed a considerable ability to criticize the method of instruction more constructively.[5]

ETV as an innovation is vulnerable to manifold extraneous influences and one has to be constantly aware of its significant characteristics and recurring concomitants. Experience in El Salvador indicates that for ETV to be successful, other elements in the package for educational reform, including curricula renewal, teacher-training, and production, technical operation, programming and utilization aspects of the programmes, need to be closely examined. Research studies on ETV in developing countries including Columbia, Samoa, Niger and El Salvador highlight the fact that for ETV to be an effective instrument in the complex learning process, the educational programme should be utilized in the way it was designed to be used. Further the attitude of the teachers, parents and community at large to the medium and the motivation of students and other socio-psychological dimensions have to be given due consideration. In such a context, learning experience is involved with many factors and evaluation of ETV programmes is necessarily complex. A combination of evaluation techniques is called for to illuminate the complexity of the learning experience. The need for an exploratory, descriptive and interpretative approach in addition to the statistical experimental approach cannot be over-emphasized. This balanced, cross-check approach needs to be borne in mind when the whole Malaysian ETV project, launched in 1972, comes up for a major review in 1976. The evaluation team's scope of activities includes investigation into such areas as needs assessment for future programming, cognitive achievement, affective achievement, utilization techniques and long-range effects. A massive effort is required for this undertaking. It is hoped, however, that the findings would help to identify the common elements necessary for the successful evaluation of technological effects in emerging nations.

References

1 HOOPER, R., *Speech* at NECCTA Conference, University of Leeds, unpublished photocopy, 1972.

2 POPHAM, W. J. and BAKER, E. L., *Systematic Instruction*, Prentice-Hall, 1970.

3 ERAUT, M., Strategies for the Evaluation of Curriculum Materials (see page 313).

4 SCHRAMM, W., *Feedback for Instructional Television*, AED., Washington D.C., 1969.

5 MOSS, J. R., *Assessing the Learning Experience: University Students Evaluate Videotapes*, University of Bradford, England.

PAPER NO 22: RESEARCH IN MEDIA
AND THE LEARNING PROCESS: THE
RELATION OF INTERNAL LEARNER
OPERATIONS AND FUNCTIONAL
MEDIA ATTRIBUTES

Erhard V. Heidt, Head of Audio-Visual
Centre, Pädagogische Hochschule, Bielefeld, W. Germany.

Introduction

During my search for a basis on which to
found a classification of instructional media
I turned to the relevant research reports
and reviews, only to recognize a desolate
situation. There were research studies and
reports in abundance but next to none
generally accepted or even acceptable results with respect to the instructional
effectiveness of different media. As one of
the main reasons for this unsatisfactory
situation several reviewers—I only name
Campeau[1] and Levie/Dickie[2]—state the
lack of a theoretical framework, which
leads to poorly conceptualized research
studies.

As I agree with them, this paper will be
an effort in this direction, that is, an effort
to define a theoretically valid frame of
reference which can serve as a basis for
experimental studies as well as for guidelines for the design of instructional media.

One conclusion, however, can be drawn
from the otherwise inconsistent results of
media research: most objectives can be
achieved with different media. This observation at least partly qualifies the present
approach to media in instruction, which
often gives the impression that the achievement of a certain objective would depend
upon the use of a certain medium or that
the use of the one appropriate medium
could guarantee a positive learning outcome. The experiences, however, of the
preceding centuries have shown that a
literate public can be taught almost all
subjects with written and pictorial materials. There are, of course, differences
between different types of media, but these
are only gradual differences of effectiveness.

Content versus process

The fact that it has not been possible to
discover significant differences or generalizable results does not necessarily mean that
they do not exist. It could well be that it

has not been possible to discover them with
the methods and research designs employed.
A chief cause for the disappointing results
is that most studies begin with the premise
that it is possible to vary only the factor
'medium', while all other variables of the
instructional system can be kept constant.
This constancy is especially claimed for
the factor 'content'. Consequently, one
finds that those studies regard above all
'knowledge of content' and 'retention of
content' as criteria of effectiveness. This is
a symptom of a general over-emphasis of
the 'knowledge' component as against the
'skill or ability' component. This leads in
the majority of studies to a confinement to
the verbal substance of the content; the
medium is only regarded as a vehicle for
the 'invariable meaning' of the information.

Even if one tries to guarantee by very
thorough pretests that the meaning of
statements in pictorial as well as in written
and spoken form are equivalent, there can
be shown important differences depending
upon the channel of communication even
for very simple concepts. J. A. Anderson,
who conducted a study to find out if
statements which were thought to have the
same content really meant the same when
presented through various media, summarizes as his results:

> The results presented demonstrate that
> statements equated in content and com-
> plexity but presented in different media
> evoke different connotative meanings.
> Further, the specific form of these differ-
> ences varies substantially with the subject
> matter of the statements. No patterns of
> differences among media were found to
> be consistent across concept types.[3]

The printed word 'cow', for example, is
only identical on a conceptual level with
the information which a photograph of
the same animal conveys. Learning does,
after all, not only mean the acquisition of
actual information, but always at the same
time the experience of the process of acquisition itself. Bruner/Olson, who emphasize
this role of process rather than that of
content, distinguish two facets which are
involved in any acquisition of knowledge,
that is 'information about the *world* and
information about the *activity* used in gaining knowledge.'[4]

Aspects from a theory of cognition

I can only very briefly refer to the basic philosophical problems implied here. It is above all the question of the fundamental mediation of all human knowledge. This topic is often dealt with only under the aspect of the mediating quality of language. Plessner, however, discusses it[5] with special reference to the non-verbal domain. He emphasizes the importance of the different human senses for the cognition of the world around us, the experience of reality. He starts from the consideration that each sense represents a form of access, an aperture to the outside world which has the often neglected function to supply a specific substratum for thinking. Plessner does not maintain that knowledge is completely determined by sensual perception. He contends on the contrary, that it is a specific human characteristic that the different forms of sensual perception can act as a substitute for one another with reference to the conceptual content. He considers, however, all knowledge of reality as fundamentally mediated by the senses and therefore closely linked to the respective form of perception. The mode of sensual access coins in a specific manner the cognition of each object in such a manner that it cannot be seen independently of the respective mode of its perception. Such a view is in contradiction to the widely held opinion that information reception can be neatly distinguished from the subsequent information processing and that therefore perception is of lesser value than thinking.

The consideration that even the supposed most direct experience of reality is fundamentally mediated is especially important with reference to the different sensory modalities. It is, however, not restricted to differences in sensory access but applies also to differences and variations within one and the same sensory modality. A proof for this from the domain of media research is the fact that often differences within the same medium, for example between motion pictures of similar content, were more important with respect to learning results than the use of different media, for example motion picture vs textbook.

Kaiser who takes a look at the relations between methods in instruction and theoretical aspects of cognition,[6] tries to remove the conventional reduction of method to the function of just conveying a certain content, a specific knowledge. If conceptual content or knowledge does not exist independently, detached from the method or mode of its acquisition, that means that both facets can be separated only from a heuristic point of view and that the method, the mode of acquisition influences and even generates the object of cognition; that is knowledge or content. A similar consideration led McLuhan to his one time provoking statement: 'The medium is the message'.

Operational ability as a fundamental objective

The process of the acquisition of knowledge is not only of interest for a researcher with a theoretical bias. It rather bears considerable implications for the reality of learning and teaching: the kind of learning process —and that is the meaning of 'acquisition of knowledge'—will not only influence the time required but also the degree of later availability of the acquired knowledge. Bruner/Olsen[4] report a number of experiments which show that the context in and the purpose for which a specific kind of knowledge was acquired influences and often restricts the recall and application of that piece of information.

In many instructional situations the objective is not only that the student should acquire factual information, but also that he should come to know the appropriate learning strategy for a whole class of similar informations. This ability of transfer depends not mainly on the conceptual content of the information but upon the manner of its encoding and presentation, in short its structure, which—as was shown above—is of great importance for the manner of internal processing and storage by the learner. These considerations led Stolurow[7] to the conjecture that the informational content of instructional media consists in the information processing activities which are released in the learner. This then suggests— when one is talking about instructional media—that a special emphasis should be put on the intellectual skills and operations which are connected with the acquisition of specific kinds of knowledge. Such a view is in accordance with a more general trend in instructional thinking, which holds that the learning *process* (seen as the internal operations of the learner) is of greater

U

importance than the possession of factual information.

If the emphasis changes from a similarity of content to a similarity of operation, of internal process, as the most sensible starting point, then comparative studies of media effectiveness should not proceed from the assumption of the constancy of factual information but from a similarity of internal operations, while the factual information can vary to a certain extent. To give a rather simplified illustration: on the basis of internal operations, that is necessary intellectual abilities, which are supposed to be similar, one could treat the following contents as similar even if they look very different at first sight:

- read a survey map of your home town/ read the ground plan of a gothic cathedral—the same internal operation would be: cognition of visual units and transformations from a figural to a symbolic dimension;
- solve a problem in formal logic/solve a similar (the similarity has to be specified) problem in mathematics/detect logical fallacies in political propaganda—the same internal operation would be: convergent thinking in the domain of symbolic and semantic systems.

This suggestion towards a stronger consideration of the internal operations of information processing must not be interpreted as if now the facet of the meaning of information, of content could be completely neglected. This change in emphasis is rather to make clear that instruction has of course to pay regard to the logical structure of the subject matter, that this, however, is but one component which is to be supplemented by the cognitive organization of the respective learner, to whom 'something' is to be imparted. The consideration of both facets, that is the aspect of meaning as well as the aspect of information *processing*, is also postulated by Stolurow, who states that it is necessary to plan and develop instructional materials with the same or even more care in regard to that what the students ought to do while they are learning with regard to the accuracy and completeness of content.[7] Hence the structure of the learning material, of the information— or more generally, the structuring of the learning situation—is of crucial importance.

The presentation of an item or a problem (for example in mathematics) can be without fault from a subject matter point of view (here, for example, with respect to arithmetical facts). The presentation may, however, be structually disadvantageous, that is with respect to certain operations of problem solving or transfer expected to take place within the learner. Ausubel refers to the same fact when he distinguishes between the logical and psychological structure of knowledge, between potential or logical meaning, or between phenomenological or psychological meaning in verbal learning; the second term in each comparison signifies an individual component in each information, which depends upon the cognitive structure of the respective single learner.[8]

If media are thus considered, not as more or less neutral carriers or vehicles of information, but as objects which, because of their structural quality, control or at least fundamentally influence the learning process, then as a consequence media must be distinguished and differentiated on the basis of their function for releasing, influencing, and controlling different kinds of learning processes. What we need in instruction is discrimination based on the psychological effects of media and not their technological features.

The problem now is, how to convert this theoretical suggestion, that is to put a special emphasis on the internal information processing of the learner, into actual research studies, or rather, how to find or define a frame of reference which can comprise the considerations elaborated above.

The interaction of learner characteristics and media variables

To answer these questions I suggest we should look to the domain of differential psychology, known under the label of 'aptitude-treatment-interaction', or 'trait-treatment-interaction research'. The general hypothesis behind this approach is that the learning result depends not on isolated factors but upon the interaction of personality variables on the one hand and on variables of the instructional situation— especially media—on the other.

The present state of TTI research can be summarized in the following way.

Only very few significant interactions

These considerations entail a number of results for actual TTI research projects which pay special attention to the problem of instructional media:

- learner characteristics must be classified in a system of internal operations or operational abilities.
- learning tasks must be specified with reference to the internal operations of the learner which they require.
- media must be described with respect to the supplantation they can provide for these operations in various ways because of their different specific structural attributes.

In my following suggestions of how to fill this framework just outlined. I shall focus on the special intellectual abilities or cognitive skills of the learner.

A classification system of cognitive skills

Considering the purpose of this article it is essential to find a system that comprises in great detail the cognitive skills or intelligence factors required to cope with a specific learning task. In my view Guilford's structure of intellect model meets this requirement to a high degree.[11] He used a three-dimensional model to organize these factors into a system. The three dimensions are the kind of *content* of information, the supposed kind of mental *operation* involved, and the kind of *product*, that is the form in which the information occurs. Guilford's system is particularly suited for the purpose of this article, since it comprises not only the different mental operations in great detail, but with its content and product categories refers to stimulus characteristics which are in any case of great relevance when dealing with instructional media.

The identification of functional and structural media attributes

On the basis of the approach suggested in this article, the categories for the specification of media attributes must be directly related to the categories of cognitive skills. To be more specific: they must take up the definitions of the internal operations of the learner and furthermore give information about which kind of internal operation can be supplanted to what degree by a specific medium. While the *nature* of the

learner activity to be supplanted is largely defined by the learning task at hand, the *amount* of supplantation necessary depends on the degree of the availability of the respective operational schemata by the learner, upon his repertory of information processing abilities.

In the content of this paper, I can only very roughly outline the basic method of how to identify the functional media attributes with regard to a specific learning task and a specific learner. The following steps are required:

- in the light of the learning task at hand, the intended learning process is described with categories of the required intellectual abilities (with reference to Guilford's S-I model). Thus the *nature* of the learning process to be supplanted is determined.
- the appropriate *amount* of supplantation is decided depending upon the degree to which the learner has at his command the required operational abilities.
- on the basis of these informations, the necessary *functional* media attributes are specified. These do not yet refer to the medium as a software/hardware configuration; they are rather described with categories corresponding to those of Guilford's model and refer to sensory modalities, to the encoding form and the duration dimension of the stimuli required.
- now those *structural* attributes of media must be determined which can be used in the sense of the functional attributes defined before. The structural attributes include the whole scope of design techniques and can already be regarded as the features of specific software/hardware combinations. In most cases there will be several alternatives, several structural attributes which can be employed in the sense of a specific functional attribute.
- finally, it must be decided which kind of *technical equipment* meets the structural specifications best.

Theory into practice

In the original paper a detailed example is given of how the theory could be turned into practice in the design of instructional material.

I must admit that the translation of these TTI based considerations into instructional development is not an easy task. There are a number of difficult problems involved already in the decision on the relevant personality traits (other than the usual demographic data about age, sex, and so on) and even more in the coordination of the appropriate treatments. There do exist, however, several model projects which do not comply in all details with the theoretical framework outlined here, but which can be seen as an outflow of similar considerations about the connection of learner traits and an appropriate design of instructional programs.

One such attempt is reported in detail by Mendelsohn.[12] He describes the primary social research and evaluation that was developed in connection with 'Canzion de la Raza', a public television program of 65 instalments especially designed as socially ameliorative educational programs for the socially neglected minority of the Mexican-American sub-population in the area of Los Angeles. From the point of view of this paper, one feature deserves special interest:

> From the start it was decided that all major decisions regarding audience targeting and thematic development and implementation would be based to a significant degree upon primary, objectively-derived, empirical social science data.[11]

This orientation, which led to a permanent participation of mass communications and social research staff in the planning and development of the program, resulted in the effort to describe the precise target audience not only on the basis of raw demographic characteristics like social status, etc, but rather in psychological terms. The following categories were used:

- the level of satisfaction and dissatisfaction with social conditions,
- the general morale-optimism level,
- the degree of anomie, that is, the sense of individual powerlessness in coping with external conditions, and
- the predominant personal life-goal values.

It proved extremely difficult to consider these research data in the actual decision process of program development and to draw the appropriate consequences (which meant here, above all, special thematic orientations). Mendelsohn's report, however, about the subsequent evaluation of 'Canzion de la Raza' indicates that the approach chosen here to a high degree brought about the intended positive reaction in the audience and thus can be regarded as a successful way to tackle the problem of developing appropriate programs for specific learner groups. This and other examples which I do not have space for here make me rather optimistic that the model outlined in this paper is not only theoretically attractive but is also a feasible approach for future media research and evaluation projects.

References

1. CAMPEAU, P., *Selective Review of the Results of Research on the use of Audio Visual Media to Teach Adults*, Council of Europe, CCC/TE (72) 5, Strasbourg.

2. LEVIE, W. H./DICKIE, K. E., The Analysis and Application of Media. In: TRAVERS, R. M. (Ed.), *Second Handbook of Research on Teaching*, Chicago, 1973.

3. ANDERSON, J. A., Equivalence of Meaning Among Statements presented Through Various Media. *AV Comm. Rev.*, 1966.

4. BRUNER, J. S.,/OLSON, D. R., Learning through experience and learning through media. In: *Prospects*, 1, 1973.

5. PLESSNER, H., Anthropologie der Sinne. In: PLESSNER, H., *Philosophische Anthropologie*, Frankfurt, 1970, 189–251.

6. KAISER, H. J., Erkenntnistheoretische Grundlagen pädagogischer Methodenbegriffe. In: MENCK, P./THOMA, G., *Unterrichtsmethode*, München, 1972.

7. STOLUROW, L. M., Learning Environments. In: *How Teachers Make a Difference*, U.S. Dept. of Health, Education and Welfare: Office of Education, Washington, 1971.

8. AUSUBEL, D. P., A Cognitive-Structure Theory of School Learning. In: SIEGEL, L. (Ed.), *Instruction. Some Contemporary Viewpoints*, Scranton, 1967.

9 SALOMON, G., Heuristic Models for the Generation of Aptitude-Treatment Interaction Hypotheses. In: *Review of Educational Research*, 3, 1972.

10 SALOMON, G./SNOW, R. E., The Specification of Film Attributes for Psychological and Educational Research Purposes. In: *AV Comm. Rev.*, 3, 1968.

11 GUILFORD, J. P., *The Nature of Human Intelligence*, McGraw-Hill, New York, 1967.

12 MENDELSOHN, H., 'Canzion de la Raza' Evaluated. In: *Educational Broadcasting Review*, 5, 1971.

PAPER NO 25: SPECIFIC STRUCTURE OF THE DIDACTIC AUDIO-VISUAL MESSAGE*

Geneviève Jacquinot, Department of Educational Technology, University of Paris VIII, France.

Our research, which is linked with the systematic analysis (both textual and classificatory) of a selection of school television programmes and of educationally oriented film, has led us to adopt the following positions:

1 Communication through educational film is a communication specific to film

(a) From the study of educational audio-visual material, two kinds of problems have emerged:

- those which relate to the educational nature of the material,
- those which relate to their semiological nature.

Put another way, the educational film 'is not only a species of cinema, but also a species of education'. What interests us is the interface, where the teaching aims (in the shape of the content) combine with a method of expression through film (the substance and manner of expression).

---

* Translated from the original French.

(b) By applying to this area the most productive analytical techniques of classical semiology, we have shown how instructional aims involve particularly meaningful configurations which create from the educational film communication a communication specific to film, clearly different from the narrative film communication and which is defined by:

- a teaching immediacy in three directions (for the general public, for the specialist, for the class),
- a sequential ordering linking intellectual operations,
- a type of film grammar based on breaks in sound and the use of 'clean cutting' as a 'rough link',
- the presence of emphasized meaning embedded in verbal statements (code of implication),
- the restraining function of the commentary which ensures a perfect control over the picture.

2 What characterizes the classical teaching film is the absence of a genuine film style

(a) Most existing materials more or less structure their message by more or less implicit reference to the linguistic mode of expression which is the basis for the whole tradition of teaching communication. It is only very rarely that one finds a genuine style of film-making (defined as 'an activity integrating diverse cinématographic and non-cinématographic principles').

(b) This is due to:

- the circumstances of production (the priority of the teacher's contribution over that of the producer, who merely 'translates' into pictures in the customary manner);
- the under-use of the picture, which is used in education only as analogy (the educational image 'overwhelms' everything else);
- the significance of the narrative model. One is used to looking at a film and understanding it through the story it tells and the words that it contains, not through the

script. The instructional film, always a little anxious about not being 'genuine cinema', either tries to resemble a film of fiction in order not to be boring, and accepts that it isn't instructional or turns its back on the cinema of fiction and accepts that, although it will be boring it will be instructional: in both cases there is a lack of research into the exploitation of the specific properties of the medium in which the meaning is embedded (film)* when it serves an instructional aim.

(c) There is a dimension in this form of film production which we propose to call the 'degree of performativity'** of instructional film, that is, its capacity to achieve the instructional aims through the way the medium itself carries the meaning (an analogy would be with what in linguistics one would call operational statements, which result in what they mean). This allows us to sketch out a classification of instructional film materials according to the extent to which they are in a genuine film style.

3 **The absence of a film style seems to correlate closely with the continuance of a traditional instructional model**
(a) There exists a critical relationship between, on the one hand, the contents and the manner of expression, and on the other between the instructional model and the film script. The lack of a film style testifies to the persistence of an instructional model which makes the instructional act an act of transmitting a body of knowledge (the message) from someone who knows (the sender) to someone who does not know (the receiver), according to a narrowly marked-out route.

(b) Now it could be done in another way. Since the word is not so im-

mediately 'rich'* as the picture, this leaves more freedom for the 'interpretation' and it could thereby allow this difference to be usefully exploited, by means of a method of teaching which would put more emphasis on the process than on the product, less on the acquisition of knowledge than on teaching ways in which the operative constructivism** is understood.

(c) Instruction is defined in this new perspective less as a kind of material as a sort of treatment of information and a new educational relationship, a new relationship to knowledge.

4 **From the semiology of the instructional film to the semiotic of instruction***
The study of a selection of school television programmes has therefore led us to research into the specific nature of instructional film and in so doing, to examine the instructional model underlying film material; the semiology or the semiotic of instruction, which would allow us to analyse instructional communication as a meaningful practice independently of the framework which carries it, remains to be worked out.

Our hypothesis is that it would be possible to progress from instructional aims merely expressed through film to an instructional act brought about by a genuine film style. This would be done by modifying the learning process from that which merely teaches through film. Instead of making a product, one would find a way of production which does justice to the specific nature of the meaningfulness of the medium. It would then remain to put this hypothesis, which is theoretically based, to proof by experiment.

But classical semiology, with its essentially linguistic origin carefully spelling out meaning at the level of secondary processes, and which does not concern itself with the forces which produce the structures which it transgresses, cannot do justice on its own to this vast field of investigation. The

---

* 'de la specificité de la matière significante'.
** 'degré de performativité'.

* 'choix'.
** 'constructivisme opératoire'.
*** 'didaxie'.

semiotic, defined as a theory of social consciousness as it is manifested by historically determined structures, must enlighten some other day the teaching act when studied as an act of communication.

So a methodological approach is defined in an area peculiar to the Science of Education, and derived from a new science which could contribute to increasing knowledge of the educational process.

PAPER NO 33: A PARADIGM FOR THE DETERMINATION OF THE COST-EFFECTIVENESS OF INSTRUCTIONAL TELEVISION IN DEVELOPING NATIONS

Charles Klasek, College of Education, Southern Illinois University, USA.

The problem

I had only been on the job as Unesco Expert in Utilization and Evaluation of Instructional Television and Radio less than a week when the Head of the Division with whom I was working for the next year burst breathlessly into my office. He was obviously flustered. He had just returned from a meeting called by the Director-General of Education where he had been asked a question which he had no idea how to begin to answer. Representatives of a large American philanthropical foundation had asked him matter-of-factly, 'Is Malaysian instructional television cost-effective?'

My Malaysian counterpart, whose astuteness and intellect I highly respect and admire, looked at me and said 'You are the Expert; what is the answer to that question?' Now it was my turn to be flustered. Twelve years of experience in the ghettos of US instructional television had not prepared me to even begin to answer the question. I promised him I would try to find a response that would satisfy the questioners; yet, today, I am still in search of that satisfactory response. The foundation representatives, I am sure, have forgotten their question, my counterpart has moved on to higher levels of responsibility but I am bridled with a conscience that demands that I seek an answer and offer a solution to those individuals, agencies, ministries, and governments who are increasingly demanding a hard-data which would reveal a dollar's worth of learning for a dollar's worth of expenditure.

It is the purpose of this paper to review the literature which approaches the question of ITV cost-effectiveness, survey a selected number of international ITV efforts to determine if they have considered the question at all, and to propose a paradigm by which a developing nation may determine if the use of ITV in its educational effort will be or has been cost-effective.

Survey of cost-effectiveness studies in developing countries

Wilbur Schramm posed the problem for developing nations in a paper delivered at the first assembly of the Asian Mass Communication Information and Research Center in Singapore in 1971 when he raised the question of cost-effectiveness of ITV for developing nations. He asked these nations, 'How much can ITV improve the quality of learning and can it make the money available go any further?' But he only asks the question and then concludes, '. . . but many more questions should be asked than have been asked about whether its contribution to learning is worth the cost.'[1]

For Schramm to ask these questions in 1971 was not unusual, because in 1970 public sentiment in the United States held that the public schools should be held more accountable for the progress of the students. Landers[2] points out that the Coleman Report placed emphasis upon educational output rather than input; the minority groups were demanding a corresponding rise in educational expectations; and the taxpayers were questioning the rapidly rising costs of education without a corresponding rise in student achievement.

Accountability had arrived on the educational scene—the year 1970 had given birth to an educational trauma whose side-effects were vouchering, performance contracting, new budgeting procedures, and above all, cost-effectiveness. It was very simple for travelling consultants, familiar with the new phraseology, to flippantly inquire, 'Is your educational effort cost-effective?' When the word accountability did not appear in periodical indexes until June 1970, it seems hardly possible for anyone in a developed or developing nation to have created and put into effect the models of determining accountability and cost-effectiveness of any educational effort, let alone instructional television. The educational community was just not prepared for this turn of events.

Jamison and colleagues[3] summarize the turn of events so well when they indicated that financial pressure in the schools emanates not from a lack of resources but from a continued dilution of what administrators can buy with a fixed amount of resource availability. The prices of inputs, particularly teachers, have been rising in real terms, but there has been no comparable rise in productivity. In fact several British and American studies have indicated a decrease in this learning output.

A study by Layard and Oatey[4] reviews the benefits of technology and shows that media can be indeed economic if used on a wide enough scale. They then raise the final organizational question of how this broad utilization scale can be reached.

Instructional television, in its more than twenty years of existence, concentrated its research on production techniques and on various experiments with student achievement. ITV projects in the USA or emerging nations were not concerned with cost-effectiveness or cost-benefits. On the contrary they were interested in student achievement or cost per student per program broadcast or numbers of students served. Only rarely did an ITV project address itself to the question of cost-benefits. One school district in California, the Anaheim Elementary School District, conducted a formal evaluation of its project between the years 1959–63. Anaheim was one of the systems involved in the national ITV experiment called the National Program in the Use of Television in the Public Schools, underwritten by the Ford Foundation.[5] The Anaheim experience revealed that savings due to increased efficiency in the use of personnel and resources under the ITV systems were estimated at approximately $152,000 per year. Therefore, the District's investment in its ITV system became self-liquidating in about 7 years. Other cost-benefits studies revealed that the ITV system handled approximately 12 per cent of the curriculum at less than 3 per cent of the instructional dollar. Anaheim

claimed one other cost-saving figure of $500,000 in physical plant investment. But it must also be remembered that Anaheim pursued a modified Stoddard-plan school organization involving large group-televised instruction—a device that has almost entirely disappeared from the US-ITV scene.[6] Cost-effectiveness in Anaheim was achieved through a student achievement mean increase level of 4 months in ITV classrooms.

The Anaheim findings should have caused a major tremor of excitement in US education circles, but instead cost-effectiveness was rarely reported but the results of achievement tests were widely publicized. Aside from the unpublished report cited earlier, no correlation was drawn by Anaheim school officials or the Ford Foundation staff between cost savings and student achievement—simply because no one demanded such an accounting.

It is interesting to review recent UNESCO publications which summarize ITV activities in a number of developing nations. Martin[7] in his description of ETV in Iraq reviews organization, structure, deficiencies, subjective feedback, programme schedules, but omits references both to costs and effect on learners.

Bretz and Shinar[8] reviewed the ETV situation in Brazil from the standpoint of production personnel training requirements. They made few comments about budgets and effect on student learning. However, one program was described which could offer interesting insight into the broad discrepancy between ITV's potential audiences and actual audience. Bretz and Shinar made reference to a new series being produced by Fundaçao Centre Brasilerio de TV Educativa which has a slated target audience of 20,000,000. Yet the total number of people that were being instructed at the time of the writing of the report in organized centers of TV reception in Brazil was less than 20,000.

A similar situation was cited by Martin[9] in Jamaica where the government had elected to use television in its literacy project. The problem was formidable. Estimates indicated that a figure of between 400,000 and 500,000 Jamaicans were functionally illiterate. The Literacy Section of the Social Development Commission was making 4,000 to 5,000 people literate annually. But, the number of illiterates in Jamaica increases by 20,000 each year. The losing battle was taken to television and at last count surveys revealed that about 9,000 persons were following the TV literacy programs at home. An ideal project for cost analysis and cost-benefit figures, but the report fails to even mention funding.

Even Schramm in his research summary, *Learning From Television*,[10] limits his discussion to per pupil costs of television and the methods of determining cost alternatives of various types of media. He does not refer to one research effort which ties costs of ITV with pupil achievement to provide a cost-effective determinant.

In October 1972, a summary report was released by the Academy for Educational Development[11] whose title caused hopes for some insights into ITV costs, benefits, and pay-offs in El Salvador, but instead the report concluded with the comment:

A preliminary estimate, based on incomplete data, is that the ITV program in junior high school raises costs per student by 15 per cent. Further expansion of ITV should reduce the cost per student. So far, however, the research has not shown any large-scale improvements in student learning based on television alone. Thus the results of the ITV program point to the need to link ITV with changes in the input mix to education to raise cost-effectiveness. It may be useful to consider an increase in the student-teacher ratio, which is the costliest input to education. So far this has not occurred in El Salvador.

Accepting the fact that the data was not yet all in, I waited patiently for the final report from El Salvador. When I read it, I must admit I was not disappointed but I was most frustrated. The chapter written principally by Dr Dean T. Jamison on 'Efficiency and Costs of ITV and the Reform,' discussed in detail all of the costing categories such as costs of education reform, comparative ITV and total educational costs, per pupil costs, cost-benefit alternatives. Further, it discussed pupil achievement in a number of categories. Although the preliminary reports promised an association between additional ITV costs and improvement in student learning,

the final report stopped short of providing this cost-effectiveness analysis and therefore fell short of providing us with sorely needed models, data, and procedures for planning, developing, instituting, and computing cost-benefit studies for ITV in developing nations.[12]

Finally, a study commissioned by UNESCO in 1973[13] performed by the Institute for Communication Research, Stanford University outlines the parameters of ITV evaluation and suggests what should be evaluated. The report outlines what has become fairly standard fare in ITV evaluation, suggests no new or insightful evaluation techniques and makes this one comment about cost analysis:

Cost Analysis ... is another area that has been sorely neglected in most ITV evaluations. Budgets constrain all ITV projects, but few planners or administrators are provided with the kind of information needed to make better budgetary decisions. Problems of estimating true costs, of describing cost functions and then properties, and of introducing methods for coping with temporal structure of ITV finance are just beginning to interest economists and such topics will undoubtedly become more important in future ITV evaluations.

UNESCO could do well to push forward with great effort to pursue its study into developing instruments for media evaluation with greatest concern for the development of instruments which will provide data for cost analysis, cost-benefits, and cost-effectiveness.

Guidelines for cost-effective studies

Am I being Quixotic? Am I chasing cost-effectiveness windmills? Or can we find and/or develop models, matrices, paradigms, instruments which will ferret out data correlating dollar input with learning output? Are the factors affecting the data within our control? Is it not the time now for the Specialized Agencies of the United Nations, (UNESCO particularly), the World Bank, The Columbo Plan, and yes, even national governments themselves to question the efficacy of the spending of the education dollar? It is my contention that it is both timely and necessary to do so and that ITV is one place where we can begin.

Forbes[14] provides us with guidelines for a cost-effective analysis of educational programs which might accept modification for instructional television purposes. He indicates cost-effectiveness analysis provides decision-makers with information related to:

1 the cost of achieving program objectives
2 overall effectiveness of a program in achieving its objectives
3 program effectiveness with sub-groups of students.

He suggests that the four elements of such an analysis would include program descriptions, student characteristics, effectiveness measures, and costs.

Wilkinson[15] concludes that cost-analysis studies could be undertaken to describe actual, on-going or completed programs; other techniques could provide data for predictive studies which would establish the cost of proposed systems; and still other studies could compare alternatives in a systematic manner. His cost-effectiveness process is:

1 determination of objectives
2 determination of viable alternatives
3 determination of relevant costs
4 presentation and interpretation of results.

With Forbes and Wilkinson providing a broad framework for a cost-effectiveness paradigm, Abt[16] provides the suggestion of four areas which could be used to determine typical measures of effectiveness of a learning system. They include change in student achievement, dropout rate, number of graduates, and attitude/effort. Pino[17] specifically identifies measurement instruments which could be used to provide external measurement data for later correlation with cost data. He recommends the Iowa Test of Basic Skills for the Cognitive domain; the Cooper/Smith Inventory of Self-Esteem for the Affective Domain. The data required for dropout rates and numbers of graduates is merely a task of data collection.

Is it possible then to take techniques which have been developed to determine cost-effectiveness of educational programs in general and adapt them to the specific task of determining the cost-benefits of instructional television? I feel it is not only possible but also mandatory to do so in this current era of cost sensitivity. It requires a two-fold approach—first a systematic approach to a general evaluation effort and second, the application of cost-analysis techniques which would result in cost-effectiveness information.

A systematic approach to ITV cost-effectiveness

1 *Establishment of broad educational goals* —such goals may already be in existence, contained in a nations' five-year plan or outlined by an external agency which had been contracted to assist a government in ascertaining these goals. Should none exist, then a needs assessment should be conducted which would establish the major problematic areas in the nation's educational system.

2 *Identification of broad curricular areas*, for the assessment and preparation of specific objectives for achievement in those curricular areas.

3 *Investigation of alternative instructional strategies*—such strategies would include curricular approaches, print materials, delivery systems (i.e. television, radio); human systems; and supplementary materials. The task here is to determine if one or a combination of strategies will be required to create the learning environment.

4 *Determine the design for the evaluation strategy*, which will provide all data required for effective cost-analysis and cost benefit determination:

(a) Measurement of cognitive learning
(b) Measurement of affective learning
(c) Cost data for:
  (i) teachers
  (ii) ancillary personnel
  (iii) learning space
  (iv) materials
  (v) delivery systems (media)
  (vi) capital outlay amortization
(d) Statistical data for:
  (i) teacher-pupil ratio
  (ii) dropout rate
  (iii) number of graduates
(e) Research data for:
  (i) pre-assessment cognitive achievement
  (ii) pre-assessment affective measurement (if available)

	DESCRIPTIVE	PREDICTIVE	COMPARATIVE	Study / Item	
Budget report cost accounting	×		×		
Budget forecasting or cost allocation	×		×		
Teachers	×	×	×		COST DATA
Ancillary personnel	×	×	×		COST DATA
Learning space	×	×	×		COST DATA
Learning materials	×	×	×		COST DATA
Media systems operational costs	×	×	×		COST DATA
Amortization costs, capital	×	×	×		COST DATA
Teacher pupil ratio	×	×	×		STATISTICAL DATA
Drop-out rate	×		×		STATISTICAL DATA
Graduates	×		×		STATISTICAL DATA
Cognitive testing	×		×		MEASURE-MENT DATA
Affective testing	×		×		MEASURE-MENT DATA
Cost data			×		RESEARCH DATA
Statistical data			×		RESEARCH DATA
Cognitive data			×		RESEARCH DATA
Affective measurement			×		RESEARCH DATA

Figure 1   Cost-effectiveness matrix for decision-making

(iii) pre-assessment cost data (in categories previously indicated)

(iv) pre-assessment statistical data for teacher-pupil ratio; drop-out rates; and number of graduates.

5 *Implement the educational program*, and the attendant evaluation design.

6 *Collect, evaluate, and summarize the data*—it is possible to summarize the cost-effectiveness procedure in a matrix which could be used for decision-making and eventually for determination of final cost-effectiveness data (see Fig. 1).

To pursue a study of descriptive nature, one seeks to acquire information about actual, on-going, or completed projects. Such studies will provide information relative to the economic viability of instructional technology. Combining the information gleaned from a descriptive study, with certain estimated costs, it is possible to predict the cost of a proposed system. Cost-estimating involves the application of statistical techniques to descriptive data to predict a range of costs and effectiveness for a given strategy. While all comparative studies compare alternatives in a systematic manner we have the choice of either determining the effectiveness of alternative strategies in achieving certain objectives or determining the benefit of the strategies by comparing the level of achievement of an objective.

In the matrix, the column headed 'media systems operational costs' and the column next to it headed 'amoritization costs, capital' can be used to indicate data for ITV or can be sub-divided to accommodate a number of alternative media strategies. Data can be deleted or inserted as the various comparative analyses are made. When the data is collected, the evaluation entity should then be able to make such statements as:

(a) Having tested a variety of strategies, it has been determined that strategy A, involving the use of television, at a cost of 250 dollars per student resulted in a y mean increase in achievement; while strategy B, omitting the use of ITV, cost 247 dollars per student but resulted in a y–z mean increase in achievement. Therefore, through the expenditure of $3.00 more per student per year we can predict or guarantee a significant increase in cognitive achievement.

(b) Since the introduction of ITV into the educational system, the dropout rate has decreased by 7 per cent.

(c) Since the introduction of ITV into the educational system, the number of graduates from the secondary schools has increased by 5 per cent.

We possess all of the instruments to measure student achievement; we have all of the data available to provide us with the various costs involved in an educational program; and more often than not, we have statistical data to give us a picture of the past with which we can compare. It is now mandatory that we take that one additional step which results in an integrated evaluation system providing the educator and the ITV administrator with the information necessary to answer that traumatic question, 'Is your ITV system cost-effective?'

References

1 SCHRAMM, W., *Television Reconsidered*, Singapore, Asian Mass Communication Information and Research Centre, 1971 (paper delivered orally).

2 LANDERS, J., Accountability and progress by nomenclature: old ideas in new bottles, *Phi Delta Kappa*, 54, 8, April 1973.

3 JAMISON, D., SUPPES, P., and WELLS, S., The effectiveness of alternative instructional media: a survey, *Review of Educational Research*, 44, 1, 1974.

4 LAYARD, R. and OATEY, M., The cost-effectiveness of the new media in higher education, *British Journal of Educational Technology*, 4, 3, 1973.

5 FORD FOUNDATION, *Teaching by Television*, New York, Ford Foundation, 1961.

6 ANAHEIM CITY SCHOOL DISTRICT, *Summary of Instructional Television Evaluation*, Anaheim, City School District (no date—mimeographed).

7 MARTIN, D. P., *Iraq—Educational Television*, Paris, UNESCO, 1972.

8 BRETZ, R., and SHINAR, D., *Brazil —Educational Television*, Paris, UnESCO, 1972.

9 MARTIN, D. P., *Jamaica—Educational Broadcasting*, Paris, UNESCO, 1972.

10 CHU, G. C., and SCHRAMM, W., *Learning from Television—What the Research Says*, Washington, D. C., National Association of Educational Broadcasters, 1974.

11 SPEAGLE, R. E., *Educational Reform and Instructional Television in El Salvador: Costs, Benefits, and Payoffs*, Washington, D.C., Academy for Educational Development, 1972.

12 HORNIK, R. C. et al., *Television and Educational Reform in El Salvador: Final Report*, Stanford; Institute for Communication Research, 1973.

13 McANANY, E., HORNIK, R., and MAYO, J., *Studying Instructional Television: What Should be Evaluated*, Stanford, Institute for Communication Research, 1973.

14 FORBES, R. H., Cost-effectiveness analysis: primer and guidelines, *Educational Technology*, 14, 3, 1974.

15 WILKINSON, G. L., Cost evaluation of instructional strategies, *AV Communication Review*, 21, 1, 1973.

16 ABT, C. C., Forecasting cost-effectiveness of educational incentives, *Educational Technology*, 14, 3, 1974.

PAPER NO 37: THE EVALUATION OF MULTI-MEDIA EDUCATION SYSTEMS—SOME PROBLEMS*

Naomi McIntosh, Reader in Survey Research Methods, and Pro-Vice Chancellor, Student Affairs, The Open University, UK.

Appropriate research models for evaluation
Traditionally, educational evaluation has been identified with curriculum evaluation. And within the field of curriculum evalu-

* This is an extensively abbreviated version of an article in *British Journal of Educational Technology*, Vol. 5, No 3, 1974, reproduced by kind permission of the publishers.

ation, the 'test and measurement' model of evaluation has been dominant. However, Eraut[1] lists as many as eleven alternative evaluative models, all of which have at some time been applied to curriculum evaluation. Parlett and Hamilton[2] in their discussion of one of these alternatives comment on the dominance in conventional approaches of the experimental and psychometric traditions in educational research. They introduce 'illuminative evaluation' based on anthropological research as an alternative research paradigm, and emphasize the study of a programme as a whole. Increasingly the traditional 'test and measurement' approach is found to be inadequate as evaluators are confronted by innovatory educational programmes. The evaluation of multi-media systems cannot even confine itself to curriculum evaluation and certainly cannot confine itself to the 'test and measurement' model. One important characteristic is shared by both the new 'social anthropology' paradigm and the traditional 'agricultural—botany' paradigm —the dominance in their development, of one research technique. But in both cases, the technique has dominated the development of the paradigm and not the nature of the programme or the purpose of the evaluation.

The paper does not attempt a comprehensive discussion of educational evaluation, and concentrates on the special problems involved in evaluating multi-media post-school educational systems, particularly as they affect researchers. It works to the broad definition of a programme given by Astin and Panos[3] of any 'on-going educational activity which is designed to produce specified changes in the behaviour of the individuals who are exposed to it'.

It argues that the view that evaluation should produce information for educational decision-making is particularly applicable to the evaluation of multi-media systems, since the financial and educational penalties for bad decisions are so great. Many multi-media programmes are innovatory in nature, but it is the fact that they are multi-media which dominates the research problem. The innovatory nature of many of the programmes merely makes the adoption of any one technique-dominated paradigm more questionable. To accept as dominant any one technique may be to be pre-judge or prejudice the outcome of the evaluation. Ideally a researcher should select from a total armoury of techniques those that are suitable for that particular research problem within that particular research environment.

Evaluators in this field have traditionally concentrated on courses which use the *media* for education.[4]

Increasingly, a course is using some sort of *media* for *mass* education, or alternatively using the *mass-media* for mass education. The 'tidy' test-and-measurement model may be adequate for evaluation which is confined inside an institution. Mass multimedia systems are unlikely to be so confined. They are likely to have social, economic and political implications which evaluators cannot ignore. The development of satellites is an example of this. Research, it is argued, has an important role to play in the overall set-up, design and evaluation of multi-media courses. [Points at which research can make a contribution are categorized, the nature of the objectives of multi-media systems are discussed, and the limitations of the 'objectives' approach commented on fully in the main paper. Sets of people with differing objectives are also noted.]

Categories of multi-media systems

McIntosh and Bates[5] distinguished between 'open' and 'closed' student groups. Do the producers of the course know exactly at whom they are aiming the course? If so, are they able to locate them? The course may be aimed at an 'open' group who may choose to follow the course, but do not have to formally enrol or register in any way, and are therefore not necessarily known. Any course using open network broadcasts, either of radio or television, is likely to have an audience of this kind. Alternatively, the course may be aimed at a 'closed' group who are known, or at least can be located, since they have to formally register and perhaps pay a fee for the course, Irrespective of which of these types of groups the course is designed for the evaluator needs basic information about the characteristics of the students. For 'closed' groups, this and subsequent information is relatively easy to obtain, provided the energy and resources are forthcoming.

For the 'open' category this background information, and indeed any other information, is very difficult to obtain, if only for the reason that there is no infallible means of locating the students or even knowing how many of them exist. The problem is exacerbated for the 'open' group by the fact that the student may not have the motivation to co-operate that those in a 'closed' group have. By actually joining a 'closed' group the student has committed himself either financially, personally or socially to such a course. This distinction between an 'open' and 'closed' group has implications both for the designer and the evaluator.

Of course there may also be eavesdropper 'open' audiences for courses designed for 'closed' groups. The desirability and/or difficulty or evaluating these is a separate issue. The second fundamental distinction between multi-media courses and more conventional courses which needs to be made, is one that affects both the designer and the evaluator of such courses. In conventional courses, the course designer, lecturer or writer, is usually in direct contact with the student, i.e. the user.

This direct contact has the strength of adaptability and allows an immediate response to the student. The course can, in effect, be individualized. Design problems are less acute, since mistakes can be remedied individually on the spot. Design is therefore less expensive, and time scales for production shorter. On the other hand, the course is more expensive to run and less easily transferable to other students and other institutions.

From the point of view of the researcher, however, it is more difficult to evaluate. It is true that 'inputs' and 'outputs'[3] may be easier to measure, but 'operations'—the means to the achievement of the educational ends—will be more difficult. The course could be viewed as, in effect, a purpose-built product for each individual student. No two products will be the same, since the interaction of the tutor and student will always differ, and attempts to measure the 'operations', even if the same measuring devices are used, will inevitably be affected by the differing nature of the 'operations'.

In a multi-media course, in order to utilize the media to full advantage, one seeks and requires economies of scale. These economies may have to be gained at the expense of flexibility. To this extent, evaluation taken on its own, might be made easier. This will be the case when large numbers of students are studying the course 'directly'.

Frequently, however, it is not as simple as this. The other way to achieve economy of scale is by several institutions adopting the same course, which may or may not originally have been designed for this purpose. The institution in this way acts as a type of agent or 'intermediary' in the educational process. Yet another 'intermediary' may intervene in the form of a tutor, and more complicated still, the course may be utilized in different ways by different tutors in the same institution. This provides a welcome opportunity to mediate between the, of necessity, undifferentiated educational message and the needs of the individual student in order to individualize the learning system. But although the middle-man or intermediary may introduce flexibility into the educational system, he may alternatively if he is not adequately familiar with the design and objectives of the course actually impede the learning process. His intervention, and/or the institution's intervention will certainly make the process of evaluation more difficult, since their goals may not be the same as those of the course designers, and in fact they may not be interested in evaluating the course at all.

The very nature of multi-media courses for mass education is likely to imply a heterogeneous student population. If the course is 'open', this heterogeneity may not be known. If the course is 'closed', it may be known or partly known, but this is not, on its own, enough. To recognize a problem is not to solve it. The evaluator will at minimum be able to determine some of the more obtrusive characteristics of the student population and may be able to predict with some accuracy which groups of students should be able to benefit from any particular course pitched at any particular level. If courses are likely to be remade, then formative evaluation may be able to make a contribution to this remaking. If the course is not to be remade, then prior research is even more necessary to attempt to diagnose which students would prove to be unable to benefit. Pre-

ferably even before then, the potential student audience should be researched to help determine the level at which the course should be pitched. The more clearly defined the target groups, the easier all these problems are.

It may be helpful to characterize multi-media courses in terms of their key features in an attempt to build up a framework for their evaluation. The following set of features, though not exhaustive and not mutually exclusive provide a basis for further discussion.

1   Is the course aimed at an 'open' or 'closed' student population or both?
2   Is the learning system 'direct' or via an intermediary?
3   Is the course to be repeated, or is it to be run once only?
4   What is the relationship of the cost of the course to the cost of possible evaluation procedures?
5   Does the course have an 'assumed entry behaviour' or not? If yes, then is it known, and if so, by whom?
6   If the course has an 'assumed entry behaviour' is it desirable to measure it or not?
7   Is the performance of the student to be assessed or not?
8   What combinations of media are to be used, and in what ways?
9   Is the course to be evaluated unit-by-unit (week by week) or as a whole or both?

Taking the first two sets of features as basic provides a matrix which enables us to characterize the four main types of courses which are likely to confront the evaluator (see Fig. 1).

These categories of courses are not mutually exclusive, and some courses may be designed for both types of audience and/or for both types of teaching system. The Satellite Technology Demonstration (STD) in the Rocky Mountain States is an example of a programme which is designed to come into all these categories. The STD's matrix for research is based on a distinction between 'closed' sites—delivery to school/community sites by satellite through a terminal—and 'open' sites—delivery through PBS or cable television. They have built in varying degrees of interaction, and varying sorts of course provision. Addition-

Figure 1 *Types of audience*

Audience

		Closed	Open
Teaching system	Direct	1 Closed and direct	3 Open and direct
	Via an 'inter-mediary'	2 Closed and mediated	4 Open and mediated

ally they will vary the amount and quality of student and teacher support materials.

Some courses may be designed for one type of audience, but also be used by chance or as a bonus by the other type. The 'eavesdropper' audience of academic and other interested persons who watch Open University programmes, but are not registered students, is an example of this. This distinction between 'open' and 'closed' audiences and 'direct' and 'indirect' teaching systems provides a framework for discussion of problems facing both course-designers and researchers.

Problems of level, integration and controlled experimentation

Multi-media programmes require to be evaluated at different levels. [These are discussed in full in the main paper.] For a whole course to be optimally effective, it is desirable for each component to be individually effective. But the sum of the whole may be different from the sum of the individual parts. And integration, a desirable end, increases the probability of this.

[The difficulties of controlled experimentation in multi-media systems is also discussed, particularly in 'open' systems or when 'intermediaries' are involved. It is pointed out that Campeau's study[4] concentrates almost entirely on projects which fall into categories 1 and 2 in Figure 1, since controlled experimentation is extremely difficult, if not impossible, for categories 3 and 4.]

The cost and value of evaluative research

It is particularly necessary with multi-media courses to consider the notion of the 'cost' and 'value' of evaluative research. Costs involved in the actual setting-up of multi-media courses have three main components.

● the investment in the development of the course itself,
● the basic cost of running the course each time it is put on,
● the variable cost associated with the number of students taking the course. The variable cost will depend not only on the number of students studying each time the course is run, but also on the amount of personal contact with academics that is built into the course. At the one extreme, it may be nil in an 'open' course, or it may include only postage. At the other extreme it may include regular personal contact, and therefore be quite great.

The cost of evaluative research needs to be looked at differently in relation to the three different costs listed. Inevitably, different media have widely differing development costs. The more expensive the medium, the more it is necessary to know how the medium works and how effective it is. Heavy development costs of particular media can only be justified either if the educational gain is overwhelmingly greater than an alternative method, or if the course is likely to reach such a large audience or be repeated so often that the set-up cost is spread over such large numbers over time as to be justified. Exceptions to this statement have been argued on the grounds, for example, of the motivation provided by television. This is not yet proven. A more difficult argument is the quasi-prestige one, that a course looks like a poor relation unless it contains television. If a course is to be run once only, then the development cost will be great in relation to its other

v

Figure 2   Variable costs and degree of personal support

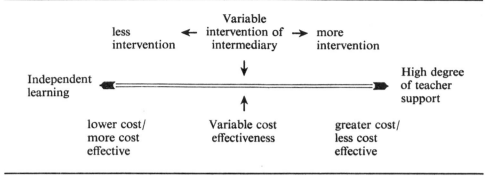

costs. Theoretically it would make sense to research into it at this stage. On the other hand, if the course is not to be re-run, then no *action* is likely to take place as a result of the evaluation and there is therefore no point in carrying it out. Additionally, heavy set-up costs may not be justified for subject matter which is likely to become out-of-date soon.

The second cost, that of running the course, will be a recurring cost and money spent on researching the operation of the cost to reduce this recurring cost may well be cost-effective, particularly if the course is flexible enough to allow amendments to be made before it is re-run.

The variable cost associated with the amount of personal support is more complex. It is helpful to look at the variable cost associated with the amount of personal support along a continuum with the en-

tirely independent-learner at one end to the teacher-supported at the other. Putting on one side the educational implications, the more an intermediary intervenes, the more expensive the course is likely to be. This can be seen from Figure 2.

The amount that is worth spending on evaluation of this area of cost is likely to depend on the *proportion* of the cost of the course that is 'variable' cost, i.e. the more personal support that is provided, the more this cost is likely to be. At the same time the research will become more difficult and more expensive.

It is possible to look at the continuum in relation to research in the same way (see Fig. 3).

The variable cost associated with the number of students is another matter. When one course can meet the needs of large numbers of students without too great a degree of

Figure 3   Research costs and degree of personal support

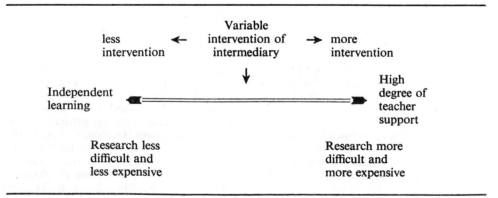

intervention, then the economies of scale are likely to be sufficient to outweigh the increased set-up costs. But as evaluative research does its job better, and more is known about the target audience, so the defined group is likely to become smaller, more specific and less replicable. As this happens, the relative advantage of the media, and of multi-media systems, that of communicating economically to large numbers of students in different places and at different times, becomes less marked in comparison to conventional systems. This is particularly likely to be true as the courses get more advanced and more dependent on previous subject matter. It will be ironic but very useful if our increasing efficiency in evaluative research proves that many multi-media courses are not effective either at a particular educational level, or at the available cost level for the size of the audience. It will, however, be in the best tradition of applied research if we can so specify our objectives and analyse the components of our problem that we are able to decide *in advance* when it is or is not appropriate to devise multi-media courses for specified groups or on specified subjects. Evaluation is conventionally retrospective. Its scope should be extended, since it will ultimately only justify itself if it is able to build up predictors of success or failure and thus avoid investment in poor or not-needed courses.

References

1 ERAUT, M., Strategies for the evaluation of curriculum materials, in AUSTWICK, K. and HARRIS, N. D. C. (eds.), *Aspects of Educational Technology*, London, Pitman, 1972.
2 PARLETT, M. and HAMILTON, D. *Evaluation as Illumination*, Edinburgh, Centre for Research in the Educational Sciences, University of Edinburgh, 1972.
3 ASTIN, A. W. and PANOS, R. J. The evaluation of educational programmes, in THORNDIKE, R. L. (ed.), *Educational Measurement*, Washington, American Council of Education, 1971.
4 CAMPEAU, P. L., *Selective review of the results of research on the use of audio-visual media to teach adults*. Strasbourg, Council of Europe, 1972.
5 McINTOSH, N. and BATES, A. W.

Mass-media courses for adults, *Programmed Learning*, July, 1972.

PAPER NO 57: THREE METHODOLOGIES FOR EVALUATION AND RESEARCH IN EDUCATIONAL BROADCASTING

Warren F. Seibert, Director, Office of Instructional Services, Purdue University, USA.

Introduction

While the contents of this paper are of three distinct kinds and in other circumstances could serve as subjects for three separate papers, each pursuing its subject at some depth, they are combined here to make a single, larger point. Depth may suffer, but we trust not too seriously, and the larger purpose is, we trust, worth that risk. That purpose is to suggest and encourage an ingenuity in evaluation and in research that are more consistent with the ingenuity that the best of educational radio and television represent. In educational radio and television evaluations, and quite generally in educational evaluation endeavors, we suffer still from what may be called a 'mentality problem'. We have, it seems, been brought up to believe certain things and to follow certain prescribed procedures and we continue to rely too greatly on these. And if this is so, we not only miss opportunities that could be within reach, but we also harness novel, even ingenious uses of broadcasting to anachronistic evaluation methods taken from a much more traditional and a less flexible era in education and research.

The three topics considered here are referred to as tailored evaluation, broadcast media as psychometric media, and correlational-Brunswikian approaches to evaluation and research. In discussing each one, we will first describe and give some background for the methods they suggest, then we will sketch some examples of their use or possible use. Beyond this, limited time and space as well as the stated interest in fostering ingenuity recommend, if not require, that imaginations should play freely with the essential ideas and in that way seek further implications and applications of the ideas. Each method represents a potentially large family or cluster of applications, none of which has yet been exploited or adequately explored.

Tailored evaluations

The first of the methods, tailored evaluations, is one that computers now make possible. In our experience with it, a flexible, computer-based system of course-and-instructor evaluation was devised and has now found wide acceptance with faculty on forty or fifty campuses, including our own. This evaluation system, which we call CAFETERIA,[1] permits an instructor to select instructional rating items from a large pool of (currently 200) items. Selected items then appear in tailored rating forms, together with a standard set of five items that are automatically included or imposed on each computer-printed form. After ratings are made by students, responses are computer analyzed to create diagnostic instructional reports and these are returned to instructors. The report summarizes the demographic composition of the student group and it lists every rating item. Then, for every item, the distribution of students' responses is recorded, together with the calculated median of the response distribution and the percentile equivalent of that median. This percentile is taken from accumulating norm file and is based on medians achieved during past uses of each item.

We suggest that a similar need for instructional diagnosis frequently exists in settings where radio and television are used educationally. Examples of this might be applied at the level of individual lessons, units or sections within a course, and/or whole courses, as is presently the case. We envisage, first, a counterpart of the five imposed rating items, but probably a larger number and certainly with different contents than the five now in use. The questions or items might well include examples addressing the clarity of instructional goals, pacing of the instruction, adequacy of instructional sequencing and organization, technical quality of production, quality of reception conditions, emphasis given to specific educational content as contrasted with conceptual

understanding of content, maintenance of learner interest, extent of learner difficulty or learning 'burden', and perhaps some general or global evaluation(s) of instructional quality. These item ideas are only suggestive, not ideal for all circumstances nor exhaustive. But in any case, such items should seek to represent a set of evaluative dimensions which are commonly important in understanding students' judgements of individual programs, of course units, and/or of whole courses.

Also, as in present applications of CAFETERIA, a catalog or 'menu' of more specialized items would be prepared for selective use, when and as appropriate. These items should be developed to encompass the range and variety of courses, instructional goals, and educational strategies. It seems clear that this variety is usually underestimated and that its breadth can barely be suggested here; however, let us try. Consider for example, the variety of learning goals that instruction may pursue. These can include factual or informational learning, attitude development or attitude change, conceptual understanding and applications of concept or principles in problem solving, psychomotor or manipulative skills learning, and improved personal awareness or self-understanding, as well as other varieties. But since not all lessons, units, or courses include goals of each kind, evaluation concerning specific types of learning need to be employed selectively. Similarly, instructional strategies can vary from the most didactic expositions of content to the most hypothetical, process-oriented modes of teaching, with by-paths and special methods branching in many directions from these. In radio and television education it is especially common to employ techniques unknown in more traditional settings: documentaries, drama, staged or simulated events, and a variety of production devices not available to most educators. When these are employed, it is often desirable to have feedback concerning them and so, again, the catalog or 'menu' of the range of strategies that lessons, units, or courses might employ. Further sets of questions in the catalog seem desirable, for example, to assess methods employed to adapt instruction to individual learner differences, to assess perceived importance

314

have been experimentally proved thus far. Results were not only often contradictory, but even the positive studies, that is those that detect a TTI effect, are so inconsistent that they resist any generalizing summary. Nearly all researchers and reviewers attribute the absence of conclusive evidence for TTI effects above all to the haphazardness in the selection and combination of treatment and personality variables. As another reason they state that only very few studies were planned from the beginning as investigations of trait-treatment-relations. These shortcomings, however, do not lead to a rejection of the basic approach but to a call for increased efforts to formulate a theory about *how* personality and treatment variables interact in an instructional situation.

One of the best known and most convincing attempts to identify a theoretical model about possible interactions was put forward by Salomon.[9] He bases his considerations on the observation that the stimuli presented by the teacher or by different media explain—if taken in isolation—only part of the reaction of the learner or the learning result. Different learners often respond to the 'same' information in quite different ways; that is, they perceive the 'same' stimulus in various ways, encode and process it in different manners. This leads to the assumption that the crucial point in the reaction of a learner is not the overt and observable behavior but the internal operations in processing the stimulus. Salomon therefore adds a new component to the conventional stimulus-response-model and changes it to a three stage S-r-R model. The new component, 'r', signifies the internal operations of information processing, which are released by the stimulus 'S' and lead to the overt behavior 'R'. The initial tentative hypothesis about the relations between the media and the learner was stated in a rather general form: different qualities or attributes of media affect or stimulate different internal operations of the learner.

In a later article, in which he labels his view as a cognitive-functionalistic one, he claims that the most important function that media can fulfil with regard to internal learner operations is the function of *supplantation*, that is the external simulation of internal operations:

. . . supplantation is the function accomplished by an explicit presentation of what would otherwise have to be done covertly by the learner himself, such that a certain learning objective will be attained . . .

This means that learning will be most effective when the teaching process or the presentation of the knowledge to be acquired is precisely adjusted to the internal operations the learner has to carry out. With a reference to Piaget the hypothesis can be defined even more precisely: if an information is presented in such a manner that a specific internal operation, a mental process is simulated or supplanted, then the learner will internalize the process observed by imitation and incorporate it into his repertory of actual available schemata.

Supplantation, however, is not an all or none function. There are rather a number of possible gradations and variations with regard to the *nature* of the process supplanted and with regard to the *amount* of supplantation provided. Media now differ with respect to these two dimensions: while some media can show steady transformations without a break, others can only present situations or steps of a transformation. Some media can present only information of an oral kind, while others have the potential for visual and iconic information.

The specification of this sort of *structural* media attribute is only a first step. It is then necessary to construct 'a functional list which contains only those attributes having a unique psychological effect on the viewer'.[10] While the structural attributes of a medium can be compiled in a single list, the functional list, which is a subset of the former, is a flexibile one. As the function of a structural attribute depends upon the intended learning process, that is the task at hand, each change in the learning task causes—at least potentially—a change in the functional valence of the structural attributes. Thus the same attribute can—for different learning tasks or in different instructional situations—become functional, neutral, or even disfunctional. It is evident from this point of view statements about instructional media are meaningful only when they include a specification of the learning task or the specific learning situation.

is also able to serve both as the test itself, presenting the items or other test contents to examinees, and as a thoroughly standardized test administrator or examiner. Thus, unlike traditional situations in which a well informed and possibly professionally trained examiner is required to establish and maintain effective testing conditions and controls, these functions can often be accomplished by television itself; this could prove especially important where teaching is done at a distance.

Television also provides opportunities to test while at the same time minimizing dependence or reliance on the printed word; this can be contrasted with the vast majority of customary tests which rely both on printed language and on the language abilities of examinees. In many circumstances, this dependence may be no more than an inconvenience; however, in certain circumstances—for example, in examining very young students, in examining those with language handicaps or the culturally deprived, as well as in situations where the abilities to be tested are essentially nonverbal—it seems desirable to minimize the role of language in order to heighten test fairness and validity.

Finally, we can mention precision in the control of testing which television (or film) can afford. We are all accustomed to tests that control the duration of total testing time, but that provide no precise control over events within these relatively large time spans. We have found, however, that sequencing and precise timing of tests events is not only possible, but can at times be quite important in determining the nature of the abilities that examinees employ.[7] Especially in circumstances where memory span or short-term memory abilities are of interest, this capability of television should prove valuable.

Correlational—Brunswikian approaches

The third and last of the suggested 'mentality problems' is entitled correlational and Brunswikian approaches. It seems likely that these approaches are both the most promising and the most challenging to comprehend. They are promising because of their great efficiency, relative to customary experimental designs for research and evaluation, challenging because they appear to imply no difference between correlation and causation, a difference which investigators are trained to emphasize and to discriminate carefully. But at least for many evaluation purposes, if not also for other kinds of research, the value of correlational evidence has, we believe, been seriously underrated.

Consider as examples the question of the influence of documentary methods on students' reported interest in lesson presentation or perhaps their interest in the subject under study. For such questions and for countless others, we can conceive of having, or readily obtaining, information which distinguishes between instances of documentary methods' use and non-use, and at the same time provides student interest data. The question is, then, whether a correlation exists between use/non-use (or the extent of use) of documentary methods and students' reported interest. Such analysis provides an efficient way to scan many questions or hypotheses and to identify those which appear the most promising for further work and, while the correlational evidence is not conclusive, neither is it costly (see Campbell and Stanley[8] for a fuller discussion of this point).

In our own early work with such correlational designs[9] we were also reminded of similarities to work on readability (see e.g., Klare[10]), similarities in both the nature of the problems and the methods. Clearly, some prose materials are easier to comprehend and recall than others, much as some television or radio lessons communicate more effectively than others; both also are enormously varied in their permissible arrangements and in the sequences they employ. But in written materials as in radio or television materials the opportunities to experiment realistically and to manipulate suspected variables are limited, even though these same variables can be observed to vary naturally. Thus, the strategy of most readability research has proved and may yet prove useful. In its customary outlines, a sample of written materials is first gathered and the comprehensibility of each selection is measured, usually by means of tests or quizzes based on each selection. Thus, selections are ordered on a continuum of comprehensibility, from high to low. Then, each selection is analyzed to create statistics such as the average number of words per sentence, the average number of syllables per word, the number of prepositions in each 100 word sample, and so on. Using these variables as predictors, multiple regression analysis is applied and typically shows that the comprehensibility (readability) of selections can be reasonably well predicted on the basis of only a few variables. For example, one of the more widely used indexes for English prose materials, the Flesch reading ease index, considers only average words-per-sentence and average number of syllables-per-100 words. After more than a generation of such research, no one can yet say with certainty what the processes are that underly the general success of readability indexes, yet the indexes are frequently used, frequently helpful—especially to educators, and analogous we believe to methods and indexes which also could serve educational broadcasting.

The probabilistic functionalism of Brunswik provides tools that are available and, we submit, highly serviceable in educational broadcasting research and evaluation. We find two main reasons for offering this encouragement, the first suggested in the parallel already drawn between the problems of prose comprehensibility/readability and our own problems in achieving more effective forms of educational radio and television. The other is that we regard evaluation in educational broadcasting, if not also its research, as essentially pragmatic and as flexible enough to employ any ethical means that can help to achieve its purposes. This being so, the principle objections that have been raised against Brunswik's views, objections based in epistemology, are of little importance. We are hopeful that Brunswik's conceptions and his proposed methods can prove helpful and we can leave the epistemological duels to others. In addition, it seems inconceivable that the myriad variables that can be hypothesized to influence educational results can, in less than infinite time, be systematically manipulated and studied, then understood to be of greater or less significance. Furthermore, as with prose, there are serious limits upon our ability to manipulate suspected variables independently of others. Thus, to some extent, traditional experiments involving certain variables will remain confounded or, if you

prefer, untidy, but in any case not clearly interpretable.

As indicated, the second reason derives from the feeling that a pressing need in our field is for evaluation methodologies. If so, the epistemological objections raised against Brunswik are hardly important. What is important instead is to acquire practical means for developing improved instruction. During Brunswik's life, detractors concentrated on his probabilistic views, regarding them not as a reasonable alternative to the dominant, deterministic views but as a retreat or resignation from the search for uniform laws. Nevertheless, Brunswik seems especially convincing when he argues that no single cue is normally sufficient to indicate accurately the condition of the environment with which organisms interact.

Similarly, he argues, courses of action are probabilistically related to their results. Thus, means to achieve goals are seen as selected for their likelihood not their certainty of success. In dealing with human behavior, man is seen, then, as an 'intuitive statistician'. By now, the term 'probabilistic functionalism' should be reasonably clear as meaning a psychological theory in which causes are seen as imperfectly related to their effects and in which a functional or organism-serving view of behavior prevails. Brunswik argued forcibly that psychological research must preserve nature's relationship among variables; he regarded traditional experimental designs, those that often force nature's related variables to be orthogonal, i.e., uncorrelated, as indefensible and as hopeless—or nearly so—in their generalizability.[11] Let us consider for example one possible application of Brunswikian thinking to educational media. Among the goals and variables of interest to educational broadcasters is the development and maintenance of students' interest in lesson materials. Assume, then, that measures of such interest have been taken for each of, say, fifty or sixty television lessons in a science series. We can reasonably assume that these lessons will employ many strategies, forms, and methods to teach their subject and at the same time to maintain students' interest. That they employ varied and selected means can be considered an 'implicit theory' held by the series' producers. Now, when the

317

individual programs of the series are analyzed, we can expect that the programs will show much variability in the 'Brunswikian cues' they provide. For example, they will very probably differ in the number and duration of episodes or scenes within each lesson, in the estimated or judged difficulty of each lesson's goals, in their use of this or that device for securing student participation, in the clarity with which they state lesson purposes, and so on. At a minimum, such data can be used as Campbell and Stanley suggest, to expose hypothesized causal relationships to the chance of disconfirmation; is there, for example, a positive correlation between the number of episodes or scenes in lessons and students' expressed interest in these lessons? Beyond this minimum, one can always hope to 'capture the students' policy' and thus to account for much of the variability of interest by means of a weighted combination of several cue variables. (The principal difficulty here, in our experience, is that one too rarely has a suitable ratio of programs or program sequences to promising cue variables; there is normally a shortage of the former and a surplus of the latter. This constitutes poor conditions for reliably capturing policies, since correlations and their weights are subject to chance errors.)

There is no conclusion to be reached here concerning any of the three suggested evaluation methodologies. But it can be said that each is feasible, each has found some limited use in the past, and each suggests possibilities that evaluators of educational broadcasting may want to examine further. We hope others will find them interesting, as we have, and rich with constructive possibilities.

References

1 SEIBERT, W. F., *Faculty Evaluation.* Paper presented at the 83rd Annual Convention of the American Psychological Association, Chicago, September, 1975.

2 SEIBERT, W. F. and SNOW, R. E. Cine-psychometry. *AV Communication Review*, 13, 1965.

3 LEIDY, T. R., REMMERS, H. H., STARRY, A. R., ALPER, S. W. and SHUMAN, D. L., *The influence of network television on the knowledge and expressed attitudes of public high school students: An analysis of the CBS–TV National Citizenship Test.* (Report of Poll No. 76) West Lafayette, Indiana, Measurement and Research Center, Purdue University, November, 1965.

4 GIBSON, J. J. (Ed), *Motion picture testing and research.* Report No. 7, Army Air Forces Aviation Psychology Research Reports Washington, US Government Printing Office, 1947.

5 CARPENTER, C. R., GREENHILL, L. P., HITTINGER, W. F., McCOY, E. P., McINTYRE, C. J., MURNIN, J. A. and WATKINS, R. W. The development of a sound motion picture proficiency test, *Personnel Psychology*, 7, 1954.

6 SEIBERT, W. F. and SNOW, R. E., *Studies in cine-psychometry I: Preliminary factor analysis of visual cognition and memory*, West Lafayette, Indiana, Audio Visual Center, Purdue University, July 1965.

7 SEIBERT, W. F., REID, J. C. and SNOW, R. E., *Studies in cine-psychometry II: Continued factoring of audio and visual cognition and memory*, West Lafayette, Indiana, Audio Visual Center, Purdue University, December, 1967.

8 SEIBERT, W. F. *A compilation of existing motion picture tests* (unpublished mimeo), Ann Arbor, Michigan, University of Michigan, 1971.

9 SEIBERT, W. F. and SNOW, R. E., OASIS: A methodology for instructional and communications research, In *Proceedings of the 73rd Annual convention of the American Psychological Association.* Washington, American Psychological Association, 1965.

10 KLARE, G. R. *The Measurement of readability*, Ames, Iowa. Iowa State University Press, 1963.

11 BRUNSWIK, E. *Perception and the representative design of psychological experiments*, Berkeley, University of California Press, 1956.

PAPER NO 62: EDUCATIONAL TELE-
VISION RESEARCH—A BRIEF RE-
VIEW

Tom H. A. Van der Voort, Leyden State
University, Holland.

The paper presents the main results of a
collated research study[1] based on the television research literature up to 1974. Its
purpose is to provide an overview of the
current status of research-based knowledge
of educational television (ETV). Not all
potential functions of ETV are covered
equally: the use of television for the presentation of (parts of) courses is emphasized.
The paper discusses the results of television
research under eight headings. This short
summary does not mention these results;
it cannot do more than make brief reference
to the topics considered.

1 The relative effectiveness of educational television

Consideration is given to the comparative
studies in which the effectiveness of ETV is
evaluated by comparing the performance of
students instructed by television with the
performance of students instructed face-to-
face by a classroom teacher. The design,
results and implications of these comparative studies are discussed. A distinction is
made between 'interpretable' comparative
studies, which allow conclusions about the
relative effectiveness of ETV as such, and
'non-interpretable' comparative studies,
which allow conclusions about the relative
effectiveness of ETV as used. Three factors
possibly interacting with the relative
effectiveness of ETV are discussed: school
level, subject taught and student ability.
Finally, the results of studies comparing
ETV with educational radio and radio-
vision are briefly noted.

2 The attitude of pupils and students towards educational television

The attitudes towards ETV of learners at
different school levels are considered. Then
the determinants of these attitudes are
discussed. Four classes of determinants are
noticed:

● 'Object variables' (characteristics of ETV
as such),
● 'context variables' (characteristics of the

television lessons experienced by the
student),
● 'subject variables' (characteristics of the
student),
● 'situational variables' (characteristics of
the student's environment).

Finally, attention is paid to the relationship between students' attitudes towards
ETV and their achievement.

3 The attitude of teachers towards educational television

The attitudes towards ETV of teachers at
different school levels are discussed. A
distinction is made between the attitude of
teachers using ETV and those not using
ETV. Several sources of teacher resistance
of ETV are discussed. Next, several factors
increasing teacher acceptance of ETV are
considered. Consideration is given of the
ways in which teacher attitudes are
influenced by utilization patterns of
ETV.

4 The interaction between television teacher and pupils

A distinction is made between 'one-way'
and 'two-way' educational television. In
one-way television the pupils are unable to
interact with the television teacher. The
effectiveness of four measures to meet the
absence of feedback in one-way television
is discussed:

(a) the use of experienced teachers as
television teachers,
(b) the use of a studio-classroom,
(c) alternating television lessons and
discussion sessions,
(d) empirical try-out and revision of
television lessons.

In two-way television, which is confined to
live closed-circuit television, electronic
means are applied to restore the communication between television teacher and
pupils. The effectiveness of several
systems, permitting either learner or
teacher initiated interactions or both, is
discussed.

5 Motivation, interest and attention during television instruction

Several motivational factors which may
influence learning from ETV are mentioned. Attention is paid to the part the
classroom teacher may play in motivating

319

students to learn from ETV. Next, the relationship between the student's interest in (the content of) a television lesson and his achievement is analyzed. Finally, the attention of learners of different age-groups is compared. The effectiveness of both relevant and irrelevant attention-directing devices, which may be used in television, is discussed. The question of how long ETV can hold the learner's attention is examined.

6 Visualization of television instruction

Three different approaches to the research into the visual aspects of ETV are distinguished. A first approach consists in an experimental study of isolated visual factors. The following visual factors are considered.

(a) extent of visualization
(b) realistic versus schematic visualization
(c) the effectiveness of ETV production techniques
(d) colour versus black-and-white ETV.

In a second approach visual perception (eye movements) during television viewing is studied. Among others, the relationships between types of eye movements as well as the parts of the screen being focussed with intelligence and learning have been investigated. A third approach consists in the study of the effectiveness of the simultaneous use of visualizations, printed texts and spoken commentary in a television lesson. In this connection two theoretical positions have been defended: the cue summation and the selectivity theory. The implications of these two theoretical positions are briefly noted.

7 Improving and programming television instruction

Two encouraging developments in television research, both giving directions for improving the quality of television instruction, are discussed. The first trend is 'empirical course development'. In this approach television lessons or courses are developed on the basis of measurements of the extent to which the program (or its parts) is able to create changes in pupil behaviour in the desired direction. The phases of the process of empirical course development are described. A second trend is the incorporation of programmed learning into ETV. In 'programmed television instruction' the subject matter is fractionated into frames. At the end of each (or most) frames a question is presented on the television screen. The pupils answer these questions and are given knowledge of the correct answer. The consequences of the absence of self-pacing in programmed ETV are discussed. Finally, the effects of inserting participation questions into a television lesson are considered.

8 The context of television instruction

The need of research on the ways in which educational television can be integrated into classroom learning is stressed. The effectiveness of combining television instruction with additional student activities is considered. Finally, attention is paid to the ways in which the classroom teacher can contribute to the effectiveness of television instruction.

Reference

1 VAN DER VOORT, T. H. A., *A survey of educational television researches*, The Hague; Stichting NOT, 1975.

PART 2: THE CONFERENCE PROCEEDINGS

Professor Asa Briggs, Vice-Chancellor of the University of Sussex, was the speaker at the conference dinner.

OPENING ADDRESS

Guest speaker   Mr Donald Grattan, Controller, Educational Broadcasting, British Broad-
                 casting Corporation, London, UK.

Chairman   Professor Russell Stannard, Pro-Vice Chancellor, Planning, Open University,
                 Milton Keynes, UK.

DONALD GRATTAN

Introduction

Actually we are an interesting combination on this platform. The three of us represent, I suppose one might say, the tripod of an Open University course team. Russ might in fact be described as a University academic. I have to tell you now he is actually a bureaucrat, because he is concerned with planning and so on. On my left, Tony Bates could be described as an evaluator and researcher, though I suspect he's a bit of a bureaucrat now. And I could, I suppose, be described as a broadcasting or media specialist. Of one thing I am absolutely sure. I am now *certainly* a bureaucrat! So we have three of us, each of whom at one stage or another in our careers has at least done something in the field, even if force of circumstances has taken us a little bit out of it.

I do confess to being exceedingly apprehensive about addressing you tonight. There are a number of reasons for that, some of which will become increasingly obvious. The final blow to my confidence was struck when I read research paper no 6* of your Conference deliberations: 'Is the performer worth listening to?' in which I found:

> When a performer was framed so that his notes were visible he was rated less fair and more confusing than when the notes were not visible.

However, I have found a compensatory factor to this, for the paper no 6 also lists a research finding:

> When seen to address the camera directly, a performer was considered significantly less reliable an expert than when seen in profile.

However, all joking apart, my nervousness arises from the fact that I have flown by the seat of my pants for nearly 30 years of educational experience, teaching, lecturing, administration, management—a lot of it in the classroom, much of it in television production, and I seem to have come to no harm. Perhaps the more important question, however is: what harm have I inadvertently done to others? And then how much less might I have done had I had the advantage of being at the receiving end of informed field enquiries on research of all sorts? Well, that could well be so, and as the Italian literacy programme told us almost 20 years ago, 'It's never too late'.

---

* Paper nos. refer to papers submitted to the Conference. These are listed in no. order on pp. 1–5, which also indicates where edited versions of each paper can be found in these proceedings.

So, with that thought in mind, I think there is still some hope for me in bringing myself up-to-date on all these research findings.

I had hoped that Wilbur Schramm might have been here to open your Conference. Indeed I am sure he would if he could, but what would he have said? He might very well have brought us down to earth with a bump. The Schramm Commission in its feasibility study for Everyman's University in Israel[1] a year or two ago on the subject of the educational role of television said:

> We think that the general rule for Everyman's University should be that television should be used where only absolutely necessary.

and went on to say:

> More television, more radio and more films, more instructional talk of any kind have never solved basic educational problems anywhere in the world. Solutions lie not in the media but in the instruction for which they are used and the instructional systems of which they are a part.

Well, that is stirring stuff, but it is probably not quite as provocative as it sounds. You can have as much paraphernalia as you like, with sophisticated methods of distribution, but if you have nothing to say worth saying and you have not assisted your students to be in a learning situation, then you have wasted your time and money, to say nothing of the students' time and commitment. Still, Wilbur Scramm's observation gets us off to a good fighting start and might prevent the media people from getting too big headed or too obsessed with their television and media production.

This is, I believe, the first world conference to be devoted entirely to research into educational television and radio. It is a considerable achievement to bring into the same forum educational producers and broadcasting managers, field-survey specialists, behavioural psychologists, and not forgetting good old-fashioned teachers—though not, I suspect, many good old-fashioned students.

We have tried to bring about such a gathering in the European Broadcasting Union, but without success. We have such difficulty in appreciating other people's crafts. Very few of us are qualified in all the various forms of production of radio, television and radiovision, in the management and planning of resources, except on a mini-scale. We touch our hats respectfully to other professionals, but on the whole we are simply curious, so long as our vital interests are not threatened. It is more like the exploratory preliminaries of a flirtation, than the mutually beneficial contacts of a marriage.

The other problems we find are due to the enormous variety in the circumstances of our respective countries. Let me give you an example. Here in the UK we are at the present moment considering what contribution open-learning systems could make to the developing field of continuing education for mature people. This becomes a very complex question because there are so many potential providers also in the field and it is very difficult to determine national and individual needs. The Council for Educational Technology in Britain called a Conference and while we knew by and large what we meant by 'Open Learning' systems, we could find no instrument capable of determining priorities or needs, except hunch. On the subject of hunch, let me read from a paper given at a recent Conference on Open Learning Systems:

> A need can exist even when there is no pressing evidence of it—the Open University is the classic example. The OU was not created because the streets were full of demonstrating would-be graduates. It came about *despite* a failure to demonstrate the need for it.*

But by comparison, the situation might be very simple elsewhere where the economic and social needs can be more readily agreed. What seems to be the relevant and vital solution for one system of learning in one particular country may be quite academically irrelevant in another. So my feeling is that there is a risk that we might simply experience each other's presence, rather than get to grips with the intellectual problems that we jointly face.

---

* Richard Freeman, National Extension College, UK.

The conference themes

Well, how are we to interact in the next few days? Your Steering Committee is to be congratulated on at least giving us the chance to move between a number of themes and to give these doubting Tom's, like myself, something to think about. The three themes you have chosen seem to me to be the vital ones, in as much as they have a good practical feel about them:

First   What can we learn from research already done in the field?
Second   What has been learned about the choice of most effective research methods?
Third   How can we improve the dialogue between researchers and decision-takers?

Well, they are good practical questions and themes. The themes are not, of course, consecutive. In practice they are, or should be, interwoven at each stage of development. So I am sure that the Conference will find that while it is most important and useful to devote a day to each theme, it is, in fact, important to bear them all in mind throughout the discussions. Certainly, reading the summaries of the Conference papers suggests that many of them could have appeared under any of the themes, or perhaps under all three.

Research and decision-taking

So, if I may be allowed a few thoughts on the Conference themes, I should be so perverse to take them for my purpose in the reverse order. First, then, the interaction between research and decision-taking. Clearly it is important to see decision-taking as an outcome of research activity, but we can also see it as a starting point for such activity. In these terms, it seems useful to see it as one of a number of important influences which together make up our attempt in broadcasting to achieve public accountability in our educational broadcasting provision. Other influences are, of course, educational advice and consultation; the professional experience of educational broadcasting staff; the collection of evidence other than by research; and perhaps various forms of official pressure or persuasion.

The relative effect of these different influences varies a great deal from one area of output to another—very often in the same organization. Take the question of educational advice, for example. In some countries, including Britain, school broadcasting is provided by the broadcasting organizations, but under direct sponsorship of representative councils or committees through which the schools make their needs and wishes known. In other countries, it is the responsibility of a service working direct to the Ministry of Education. In all these cases, educational advice—perhaps prescription—is of primary importance. In adult education broadcasting, such advice is still important, but its exercise is generally less direct because the provision is not institutionally directed. In other cases, such as adult courses for credit, the advice will come precisely from the institution awarding the credit. There is a fascinating paper, no 19, presented by Viviane Glikman and her colleague from OFRATEME, which provides a comparative study of decision-taking in two central organizations—the RTS and BBC Further Education, both organizations working in the continuing education field. I am, therefore, talking about the politics of policy making.

Of course, none of these situations influencing the taking of policy decisions makes research any the less necessary. Indeed, the existence of sponsoring and advisory bodies may help to clarify research objectives and make it easier to commission research projects. But the different situations must affect the precise functions of the research and how its results can be assimilated.

Just as there is an interaction between research and decision-taking, so there is similar interaction between research and professional broadcasting experience. Such experience has been built up over many years and has been shaped by successive impressions of audience response. The broadcasters should be keen to study the findings of audience research, but they will need some persuading to change their style in any radical way. If the research carries conviction, then the practice should certainly respond, but all too often the research is non-committal; or it does not exist in sufficient depth to be convincing.

I was reading this afternoon some evidence the BBC submitted to the Annan Commission on the future of broadcasting. Let me quote one paragraph. It's from an advisory group on the social effects of media and television:

> Although its terms of reference invite the Group to put forward to the BBC its recommendations for new areas of research, it has not yet in fact done so. It has evaluated a number of research strategies, and has, for example, discussed their long-term projects with a number of longitudinal researchers . . .

—that's an interesting phrase!

> . . . It has encouraged the BBC to add questions to a research project on child physical and mental development, but it has not yet gone further. This admission is an acknowledgement of the difficulty of finding the right areas for research.

Now that summary, which is just one paragraph from that report, and another one which I could quote about research which may or may not be done by Professor Katz, whose research work you may know, indicates the problem for the broadcaster of seeming to have to wait very often for a number of years before research can be carried out into a project to which broadcasters can respond. Though research methods may require you to do so, it is one of the frustrations with research that a producer-person finds.

So, too often the research results seem non-committal, or do not appear in sufficient depth to be convincing. In that case, the broadcaster must depend on his own experience—his own intuitive evaluation. This point is expressed in splendid academic prose in Chapter 6 of the recent UNESCO report on Open Learning Systems in Post-secondary Education. The authors suggest that:

> such evaluation may entail intuitional and professional judgement not to be under-valued because they are not susceptible of quantitative verification.

In other words, the best decisions are sometimes made by sheer creative hunch.

The authors of that report, having studied some 16 international case studies, have chosen to say on the subject of Theme 3, the international relationship between research and decision-making:

> Just as the educational potential of broadcasting is best realized when it is integrated into an educational entity, so the potential of research and evaluation is best recognized in a system where it is both the servant and guide of the course makers and the representative of the interpreter and consumer. The story of the use of modern media over the last 30 years is littered with the disappointments and misunderstandings attributable to this organizational failure.[2]

So that is telling us once again.

The point remains that I am glad, for example, that no one said to the producer of that famous Italian adult literacy programme some 20 years ago, 'You musn't use that music as a background because the use of such emotive music has not been validated by research'. And we would not say anything similar to the producer of our present adult literacy programmes in Britain. But, of course, we know that he has read a vast amount of what has been written on the subject and we were delighted when he planned to make two stages of pilot programmes to pre-test with sample groups.

So, we like to think that planning and evaluation are both co-operative activities. Certainly, the professional researcher has an important part to play; but wherever possible as a member of a team in which many talents and many areas of experience are represented. Again, the way that this can be done must depend largely on local circumstances—particularly on how large, how complex, and how new the broadcasting operation is. Also on how fully integrated it is with other learning media. If the whole service has been established for many years it will have developed its own experience but may find it difficult for that reason to make any changes. A new system in the process of formation may well be more susceptible to new ideas, but it may lack confidence in its own experience. Only by genuine co-operation of functions can either the long-established system or the brand new project make any real progress. It is also the kind of co-operation which could lead to the application of the most successful research methods.

Research methods

Regarding the second theme of your conference, it is easy for a non-researcher to be rude about some research methodology. Some of it, not represented here, I am sure, does seem to merit occasionally the description of 'a long-winded and expensive way of providing evidence that was obvious to commonsense already'. Or another kind of research is summed up as 'to copy from one person is called cheating; to copy from two or more is called research'. But I know, as you know, that it is not so easy at all to tackle the real problems of research. What perhaps a decision-maker and a producer can say about methodology is that the most useful kind is the sort which produces evidence that is both precise and yet reasonably transferable. That is normally preferable to the kind that produces evidence so general and so qualified that it leads in no precise directions.

What then is it that producers want from evaluators? I hesitate to answer that question because if you are a researcher you may feel that question displays qualities of arrogance. Never mind. The facts of life are that a great majority of producers will not take much notice of research unless it gives them specific answers to specific questions. Take say a programme in the field of educational studies. You can ask this sort of question:

> This programme showed aspects of the curriculum at a training college. What lesson could be learnt and applied to a school curriculum?

or,

> This outside broadcast explored the limits to the autonomy of a College Principal and showed his relationship with his staff and pupils and with external agencies. How does his relationship with the Vice-Chancellor of the University differ from that with other personalities in the programme?

The producer will say that these questions, which are by the way genuine questions, are bound to illicit hopelessly inadequate information. Or rather information which is of no help whatsoever to the producer.

Almost without exception producers are pragmatic people. They seek mainly for two things. The first, for information which helps them to increase their awareness of how students (whether children or adults) make use of broadcasts. The second is for particular answers to particular questions about programme design, such as:

> 'Was the pace too fast or too slow?'
> 'Was the programme overloaded with information, or was not enough provided to enable you to come to a critical judgement of the programme material?'
> 'Could the viewer follow the narrative, argument, or experiment, clearly?'
> 'Was the viewer/student stimulated to further reading or viewing?'
> 'Could the student relate what he watched or heard to his own experience or knowledge?'
> 'Was the use of drama helpful and legitimate?'
> 'Was the use of music instructive and helpful?'
> 'Was the use of foreign material instructive for comparative purposes, or was it too remote?'

All these types of questions, which may strike you as being rather fiddly and trivial, may get different answers when applied to different programmes, but producers need this kind of evidence to guide them when producing their next programme. All sorts of factors govern the production of television programmes, but in the absence of good and reliable feedback evidence, the producer is always driven back to his hunch based on his experience. So that from the producers viewpoint, evaluation can only be respected and considered helpful when evaluators start asking the appropriate questions from the producers' point of view. However, producers often feel that evaluators seem to them to ask questions that only interest them as academic researchers and while their conclusions may, therefore, be interesting, they can often be totally unhelpful to the producer.

So this type of earthy criteria provides a useful lead to your first theme and the last of mine.

The most useful findings of research

Here again there is a terrible temptation to be somewhat rude about some research findings. Some of them do seem to be like the churchgoer who was asked what the parson had preached about at the morning service and replied that he had preached on the subject of Sin. When asked what the parson had said about Sin, the churchgoer replied, 'Well, I think that on the whole he was against it'.

So to the producer some research seems to tell us hardly more than that. But then, of course, I know that that is unfair. The fact is that many of us working in management or production have not made nearly enough effort to find out what research findings can tell us. The English poet Wordsworth wrote in a reflective mood—'The world is too much with us'. He went on: 'Getting and spending we lay waste our powers'. It is, perhaps, inappropriate for me to judge, but it is certainly true that in my line of business immediate pressures occupy most of my attention so there seems no more time to sit and read than there is to stand and stare. When we do read, there seems to be so much to read that research reports tend to get put aside. If this is true of me, then I think it is true of many.

Certainly time is a continuing problem and it is going to be a problem at this Conference —no doubt of that. So I will not occupy any more of it. I will just wish the Conference every success and hope that it does achieve the kind of dialogue that will make you feel that it has been worthwhile coming the 50 miles from London, the 500 miles from Stockholm, or the 5,000 miles from Bangkok, that you may have come for this purpose, and I am sure that most of you will want to keep this dialogue going across the five continents and across the years.

References

1 SCHRAMM, W., HAWKRIDGE, D., and HOWE, H., *An 'Everyman's University' for Israel*, Jerusalem, Rothschild Foundation, 1972.
2 McKENZIE, N., POSTGATE, R., and SCUPHAM, J., *Open Learning Systems in Post-Secondary Education*, Paris, UNESCO, 1976.

ANIMATEURS

Theme 1 Research Findings—Animation

Animateur   Dr Edward Palmer, Vice-President, Research, Children's Television Workshop, New York, USA.

Chairman   Mr Peter Dannheisser, Senior Research Officer, Independent Broadcasting Authority, London, UK.

DR PALMER

Serendipity

One of the funniest experiences that ever happened to me in this business was on a radio talk show, in New York City. I was appearing with three other people in the business of educational television. I was the fourth in the row, and everybody ahead of me had five minutes to talk on whatever they would like to talk about on the state of the art of children's television programming in the United States. Everybody had talked for five minutes, and I had just assumed my five minutes as of right. So I cleared my throat and I began. I really wanted to say some things about how we sometimes have unintended effects, and we have to take care that when we are doing one thing we don't do something else inadvertently at the same time that may be harmful (of course unintended effects can be serendipitous and useful also). But I didn't mention anything about unintended effects. I launched right into having read in *Match* magazine a couple of weeks earlier about a couple of experiments with male birth control pills. The upshot of these studies is that as far as the scientists can determine the pills were perfectly effective, except for one little problem. They had an unintended and unexpected side-effect of creating red eyes. Now at that point, having just said that and expecting to have five minutes to talk, the announcer cleared his throat and said: 'Well, Dr Palmer, that's very interesting and now a word from our sponsor.'

I recall that it was one of my more fumbling times coming back on the air, as I tried to explain what it was I had in mind!

Well, one of the unintended side-effects that we sometimes have as television researchers is, I believe, to appear somewhat self-serving. I think so because, to the people who are on the outside, we often-times seem to be focussing on our *own* selection of problems, and not on the selection of problems that best serve the television producer, the television industry, the television audience. Sometimes we tend a little too much to use our own jargon. We write our research reports obviously in so many cases for the researchers and not really for lay readership. We write for our colleagues and not necessarily for decision-makers.

Another point about unintended side effects is that I think we need to do more research that sets the stage for serendipity. Serendipity is the unexpected. It's usually defined as the uncovering of good and useful things. But there is such a thing as serendipity management, I believe. And when I go out into the field to study children, I'm very, very conscious of the fact that in addition to learning what I set out to learn, I'm going to learn a few other things on

328

the side as well. In training researchers in our organization from time to time, one of the problems I have is to convince them that they *can* say things that were not necessarily part of the questionnaire, that they *can* report their impressions, and they can report their own experiences.

So I hope that the experience of this conference will be one of serendipity. I hope that as we all come together and discuss these many topics this morning, we'll try to see to some serendipity management, we'll try to share not only what we have written in our reports, but what we have learned the hard way through experience in the field.

Historically, I think it's true that never before have we taken on ourselves more of the burden of responsibility for the learners' learning. There was a time in the past when learning was considered entirely a rote process. And the organ of learning was memory, and memory was seen in those times like a muscle. If one exercises it, it becomes more and more powerful. And if the learner fell short, the solution was that the learner should better apply himself, and if the learner fell short his failure was laid to sloth and indolence. Those were the old fashioned terms. Sloth and indolence and day dreaming were the problems that were most often ascribed to learners that fell short. Today, on the other hand, if the learner falls short, we revise his structural material, and we take the responsibility upon ourselves, and we beat our breasts, and say 'mea culpa'.

The new view puts a very considerable amount of responsibility for the learners' progress in our hands. This grows out of the discovery of individual differences, and no one was more involved in bringing to our attention the importance of individual differences than Alfred Binet, back around the turn of the century. Binet's commission was to find out what it was that was responsible for the fact that some students were consistently performing poorly, and some rather steadily were performing well. And his answer was intelligence: that individuals differ in their innate ability.

Now intelligence does not provide us, as we now know, with perfect predictions of achievement performance. We do know that achievement as well as being influenced by intelligence, is also largely influenced by motivation.

So we have another variable in individual differences, called motivation. Binet, in his discussions on intelligence, draws our attention to our genetic side. Like Mendel's peas, which may be giants or dwarfs, in intelligence we are one or the other or in-between. Motivation on the other hand is like our phenotype side. It's concerned not with the gena type or with genetic endowment, but with the environment side. It's concerned with cultivation. It's concerned with seeing that the proper nutrients are available, including sun and water.

I think we are now ready to take up our first question, which has to do with motivation, and the first question I would like to pose, for our beginning session, is this one:

Q. 1 *What do we know from our results today about the uses and limitations of television to motivate learning?*

I'd like to suggest some sub-topics:

1 What do we know about motivating learning from within the televised presentation itself?

2 What do we know about the use of television to motivate learning which takes place outside the viewing-listening context? (When I say television, take it that I also mean radio.)

3 When should the television portion of a multi-media presentation be mandatory and when should it be optional, and how does that relate to the question of motivation?

4 When does the students' own responsibility for motivation to learn begin? Does this vary according to the age of the learner; the social-economic status of the learner; the learning level, or the learning status of the learner?

My second question also relates to the topic of discussion earlier, the topic of individual differences:

Q. 2   *What do we know about how to design and utilize programmes in the light of individual or inter-group differences among viewers?*

---

or

1   What do we have to do to take into account differences in intelligence or in specific or general motivation?
2   What do we have to do to take into account differences in the viewers' purpose; for example, whether he is there viewing for the purpose of acquiring vocationally orientated skills or for general self improvement, or for entertainment?
3   What do we have to do to take into account differences in viewers' and listeners' expectations? Viewers come to television, I'm sure, with different expectations, to be entertained or to be taught, and I think they are either satisfied or disappointed according to the expectations that they bring to the situation. I think they expect to receive either a more dense concentration of instruction and information, or a more sparse kind of spreading out of instruction per unit of viewing time. And what do we know of individual differences in expectations about density of the learning materials?

The next question has to do with what we know of a production that may be responsible for its success (success *or* failure, I suppose). I'm reminded of Skinner working with pigeons in pigeon boxes. The pigeons have to peck a certain little lever, and then they are given a piece of grain as a reinforcement, and they go back to peck the lever again and they get more grain. But one of the things that happen early on in that kind of learning experiment is that the pigeon does a little dance, flaps his wings, pecks the lever, scratches his ear and it notices that it gets some grain. And it doesn't know if it got the grain because it did a little dance, ruffled its feathers, pecked the lever or scratched its ear, so it does the whole routine all over again, and only very, very slowly do these non-functional behaviours drop out. Skinner has a very apt term for this phenomenon of performing behaviours that you think are effective, but in fact aren't. He calls them *superstitious* behaviour. I think we may indulge in an inordinate amount of superstitious behaviour. We put together the entire combination of things that we think worked well on a earlier occasion, and we hope they'll work well on new occasions. So I think that's a suitable background of understanding for this next set of issues.

Now here's the question:

Q. 3   *What do we know from our research and evaluation results about elements responsible for successful educational applications of the media?*

For example:

1   What do we know about the effects of needs assessment on the ultimate success?
2   What do we know about the effect of adequate definition of educational goals?
3   What do we know about the selection of a proper medium or mix of media?
4   What do we know about staffing and organization, that affects the outcome?
5   What do we know about the allocation of resources, about the importance of adequate funds, adequate talent—adequate to prepare a programme?
6   What do we know about programme message design? For instance what do we know about the performer coming on in profile—like our speaker last night? (And in fact that comment came from a research paper which itself is part of a considerable tradition of researching in which some of you are more involved than others.) What do we know about the juxtaposition of elements in the presentation? What do we know about the use of certain kinds of visual aids in order to enhance learning?
6   What do we know about the importance of formative evaluation, and empirical testing and revision as a part of programme development?

7   And a question related to this overall set, and flowing out of them, how can the separate contributions of each of the above elements be isolated and evaluated? How would we go about doing that? Has anybody here done it?

The next question:

Q. 4   *How can we best ensure the productive and efficient accumulation of knowledge from our research on educational television and radio?*

What is the potential contribution of the following for this accumulation of knowledge?

1   Specialized courses of training in educational television and radio research to provide better systems for describing treatments. I'd like to elaborate on that part of the question, because some of you may wish to discuss that. It seems to me that we often fall very, very short in describing the treatment. By treatment, I mean whatever it is that is presented by television, by radio, or in a multi-media package, which in experimental viewing groups you might look at, but in a controlled group you might not look at, so that you could do some testing for loss or relative gain over a period of time between those groups. When we look at research results from an experiment of the kind that I have just described, we are very frequently left wondering: 'Just what *was* the televised presentation about?' When we describe treatments we need to describe them with reference to the elements that were effective in bringing about the results. We don't know very much about doing that or doing it well. It is cumbersome to send everybody who receives a research report a copy of the television series to go with it. One could do that, but of course it's also difficult to put into a verbal or graphic description a sufficient account of what was done, so that we can accumulate knowledge. Our problem here is that unless we know exactly what it was that led to changes, it's not going to be accumulating knowledge. We are only going to be working on vague impressions of what happened. So we need better ways of identifying what I call *presentational* attitudes—the attitudes of the presentation: what is most and least effective in producing its appeal; most or least effective for its comprehension; the attributes of presentation most or least responsible for the active involvement of the viewer?

2   Another question relates to the accumulation of knowledge. Do we need more recourse to theory? Do we need more efforts at theory building? And if so, what avenues of theory should we try, what is fruitful? What is happening now that yields results? And we need better methods for dissemination of research results. Do we need a more elaborate system of research exchange?

I did not read all the papers from all the groups. I read all from the first group, and selected ones from the other groups. I stand to be corrected, but I did not find a single paper whatsoever that highlighted the patterns of relationship among different media used in multi-media presentations. When people talk about a multi-media presentation, we say, yes, there was a book, yes, there was a television component, and so on. But this precise relationship between the media is often left unstated and unclear, and the precise relationship probably is very significant, as a factor contributing to whatever research results we get when we test multi-media presentations. So, my next question is:

Q. 5   *What do we know, and what do we need to know, about how to tie different media into one another, for maximizing their combined educational effectiveness?*

And I have some subsidiary questions to go with that one.

1   Can we make any use of classical 'transfer of training' paradigms and look for savings in learning from one medium as a result of prior exposure to another? In other words, if we expose a learner to a television or radio presentation, and then consequently to a textbook or classroom or workbook lesson, do we find greater learning progress than if the learner had not been previously exposed to television and radio? That's one way we can look at the relationship between different media. Now of course we don't always use the media in that precise sequential fashion. If we were to use the media in that fashion, if we were to think of it in that fashion, what would we do differently in planning for a production than we do now?

2   How important is it to use common elements in the different media in a multi-media presentation? How important is it to use the same charts, how important is it to use the same formats, the same sequence of questions and answers, or the same sequence of topics and subjects with the same outline? How important is it to use the same characters, within various different components of multi-media presentation?

The next question is a very general one:

> Q. 6 *Is it possible that we are regularly underestimating in our evaluation work the effectiveness of educational television and radio?*

For example, are any of the following factors, or perhaps are many of the following factors, too frequently operating:

1   Are we too frequently measuring less than the full range of effects that might be produced by our programmes or a multi-media presentation? This can happen by simple omission, it can happen by virtue of limitations in the state of the art of measurement, it can happen because individual researchers lack the training or expertise to do the kind of measures needed. Do we too frequently measure short-term, but overlook long-term effects? Do we frequently measure portions of presentation, or separable components of presentation, but not the entire presentation? (I've seen this done many times.)

2   Is funding for evaluation typically, unrealistically low? (Of course, we know the answer to that!)

3   Are we too frequently washing out differences because of experimental design problems? I think almost all of us have encountered the situation where subjects assigned as non-viewers have viewed, and subjects assigned as viewers have failed to view, and as a result any differences between viewing and non-viewing groups are attenuated. There are many ways in which we are underestimating the effectiveness of television and radio, and this subject is worth considering, worth exploring.

Next question:

> Q. 7 *What do the results tell us about the kinds of outcome the media can bring about? In what ways and for what sorts of application have they proved most effective?*

Another question:

> Q. 8 *Can we now begin to develop some decision rules about such things as when and when not to use television or radio?*

For example:

1 When or when not should we use television instead of some other medium or some other kind of delivery system?
2 When should we and when should we not use television in the light of the amount of funding available, or in the light of the types of students (e.g. their motivational status, for example)?
3 When should we or should we not use television in terms of the different types of objectives involved?

One more question:

> Q. 9 *What role can television, and other media used in association with it, play in bringing about educational reforms?*

Here we are talking about large-scale reforms, of the types you've read about in the various developing countries, and in particular, about specific curriculum reforms in classrooms as sections of national curriculum are changed, or as entire national curriculum changes are developed and ready to be put into effect. So what role can television and other media used in association with television play in bringing about educational reform, in terms of cost effectiveness, (i.e. cost effectiveness relative to other ways of trying to bring about the same reforms). How effective can it be, for example in bypassing costly teacher training? What role can it play in introducing new curricular reforms, or, if not reforms, new educational practices?

Last but one question:

> Q. 10 *What are the cost-benefit advantages of educational television and radio?*

To what relative extent do rational versus irrational considerations enter into decisions to use or not to use educational television or radio? What are the implications for production and research groups? What research approaches best lend themselves to cost-benefits analysis? The reason for asking that question is that we can often position the cost-benefits analysis well by providing them with certain kinds of information when we do our evaluation reports. We can often serve them poorly, and serve decision-makers poorly, if we do not collect just the right kind of information.

The next question is the last:

> Q. 11 *What criteria should we use to judge the value of research in educational television and radio? How valuable has research been up till now?* (That's a big one.)

Now, I would like to make a couple of closing observations. The questions here grew mostly out of the papers I read. But I've not endeavoured to remain particularly close to the basic topics. I think you will find an opportunity to discuss all of the different papers within the said topics, but don't hesitate at all to add your own questions and new topics. This is not meant to be restrictive. The whole idea is to be provocative, and not at all to be limiting, and so please feel free within the separate groups to add any questions that allow you to explore further topics that you have a special interest in that I may have not treated here.

Theme 2   Methodology—Animation

Animateur   Mr Richard Hooper, Director, National Development Programme in Computer Assisted Learning, London, UK.

Chairman   M. Etienne Brunswic, UNESCO, Paris, France.

RICHARD HOOPER

> This day is called the feast of Methodology,
> He that outlives this day, and comes safe home,
> Will stand a-tiptoe when this day is named,
> And rouse him at the name of Methodology.
> He that shall live this day, and see old age,
> Will yearly on the vigil feast his neighbours,
> And say, 'Tomorrow is Saint Methodology'.
> Then will he strip his sleeve and show his scars,
> And say, 'These wounds I had from Methodology'.*

All of you should have a hymn sheet for this occasion with seven questions. I specifically kept them short. There's a large gap at the bottom of the page to add your own questions, because you will almost certainly not want to discuss mine, if yesterday is anything to go by. I'd like to talk my way through these seven questions, suggesting some possible answers. For the difficult questions, obviously I haven't any answers, so I'll leave them to the working groups (that was a technique Edward Palmer used very successfully yesterday!).

Q. 1   *What is the distinction (if any) between evaluation and research—and does it matter?*

The first question is about the words 'evaluation' and 'research'. Tony Bates cheated in the title of this conference. He called it *both* evaluation *and* research.

The papers are littered with different uses of these terms, and there is no very clear distinction between them. I think that some of the confusions in this area are due to confusions about terminology.

In trying to distinguish between evaluation and research, the first thing to do would be to look at some of the languages we have represented at this conference, to see whether they throw light on this question. For example, in Mexican Spanish, evaluation is 'Evaluación', and research is 'Investigación', so that's not very much help. In French, 'Evaluation' and 'Recherche', and again I don't think it's very helpful. German: 'Evaluation' and 'Forschung' —again not very helpful. American: 'Evaluation' and '*Re*-search'.

Mr Foote, from Stanford, California, in the coffee break yesterday—coffee breaks are a major source of information in conferences—suggested a very nice distinction between evaluation and research: 'Evaluation was answering someone else's question, and research was answering your own'. I think there is a lot of good sense in this definition. Evaluation is very much linked with helping decision-makers. On the other hand, research tends to be purer, further away from decision-making, often based in a University or independent research unit. Research is more interested in extending knowledge, pushing back the frontiers. Evaluation has a more practical and developmental aim, research a more theoretical aim. Evaluation is more short-term, I would argue, and research more long-term. I think on the whole, evaluation tends to be cheaper than research.

---

* With apologies to W. Shakespeare, *Henry V*, Act 4, Scene 3.

Evaluation leads to less in the way of generalizations. Dr Mielke from Indiana, in our working group yesterday, was suggesting that one cannot expect to get very many generalizations out of evaluation. Research, however, is in the business of producing generalizations. The question that Professor Sparkes asked at the plenary session yesterday morning, highlights this—'What hypotheses are you trying to test?'. Now that tends to be a research question. In evaluation I think we all have hypotheses, but we don't usually use that sort of grand name. They are less explicit.

Taking this rough definition of the two, I would think that something like 95 per cent of the papers at this conference are about evaluation. For example, Noguez from Mexico on Telesecundaria (paper no 47) and the Stanford studies of Telesecundaria (paper no 69), are, in my terminology, evaluation papers. There are very few research papers. One of them is the Baggaley paper (no 5), which has been referred to at each major session, so I had better refer to it. Mlle Jacquinot from Paris, I would describe her paper as research (no 25), and Erhard Heidt from Bielefeld, his paper I would also describe as research (no 22). But they are very much in the minority. The majority of papers are about evaluation.

Robinson and Barnes in their paper (no 52) have a very interesting distinction between evaluation and research, which I don't think I can accept, but it certainly has some support. They said: 'Evaluation is a purpose, and research is a method'.

Faced with this problem of definition, we can always go for a British compromise, and Naomi McIntosh has provided one in her paper (no 37) and called it *Evaluative Research.*

> Q. 2 (*first half*) What is the range of methodologies we have available . . .

The major distinction I would make straight away is between survey methods of evaluation, and experimental methods. In sociological and psychological research, there is a similar distinction, between *survey* and *experiment*.

Survey research is essentially finding out who has done what with a particular television programme, who has watched it, what socio-economic class they were, whether they watched the following programme. It does not intervene very much in what is going on. The paper from Gerry Mullins of the University of Adelaide, Department of Adult Education (paper no 46), reports a survey of students following a particular adult education radio programme. This is a typical example, to my way of thinking, of survey evaluation: fairly straight-forward questions, questionnaires, response rates and so on.

The survey area can be divided into two: head-counting and measurement of attitudes. 'Head-counting' is the classical audience research method, and is used a lot in the Open University. For example, finding out how many OU students watch a particular television programme yields very useful information. But it is of course open to an enormous amount of interpretation, which is one of the problems of head-counting. In this area we've got a paper from Poland, the Agricultural Secondary School, Janucik's paper (no 29). He uses head-counting as a way of finding out who is actually involved in the course, and what sort of characteristics they have.

The second sort of survey (usually most survey evaluations mix the two) looks at attitudes. For example, Warren Seibert's paper from Purdue (no 57) talks about the Cafeteria system, getting students to rate the course, or rate the particular instructional event. This is also very prominent in the IBA (Dannheisser and Haldane) paper (no 12) where they're trying to assess adult education needs in broadcasting. They have done an attitudinal survey, in which adults respond to particular questions about what they want to see provided in adult education broadcasting.

There are problems with attitudinal surveys. If somebody says that they like something, does that necessarily mean that they are actually learning from it? If, for example in the Open University, 83 per cent of the students are saying that they find science television programmes very worthwhile, does that in fact tell us that they are learning something? That is a non-trivial question, I would argue.

335

The late Richard Spencer of Illinois worked on a course evaluation questionnaire, which was an attitudinal survey instrument, but which had a relatively good correlation with learning gain. That is to say, if the students liked the course, the correlation with whether they actually learned something was getting rather good. Unfortunately, he died young, and didn't complete this work. But I think those sort of ideas are very useful.

Turning away from survey techniques of evaluation, experimental work is the one which tends to get all the academic glory, or has in the past got all the glory. I think Edward Palmer's evaluation comes under the category of experimental. His use of the distractor in the Children's Television Workshop, to my mind, is an example of the experimental approach, intruding somewhat into the event. He puts a distractor away to one side when children are watching the box, seeing how often they turn to it, and at what point they lose attention.

The paper by Robert Hornik (no 24) is very interesting, because he takes the control group/experimental model of evaluation and applies it to developing countries, introducing the nice idea of 'natural' control groups. He points out in the paper that there is an ethical problem in control groups, giving one treatment to one set of people, and another treatment to another. Hornik suggests some nice ways around this, pointing out, for example, that mountains have a habit of getting in the way of broadcasting signals. Now that is very helpful for the evaluator. If mountains are in the way then you may have a village on the other side, which has a similar composition to the village that is actually getting the broadcast. You can do some natural control group experiments without interfering very much. In the literature this has often been called a 'blind' control group, which I think is an unfortunate choice of words.

So, in experimental work as compared with survey evaluation, we are intervening a bit more, we are doing pre- and post-tests, and we are often doing control group experiments. I think it would be true to say that this area is under some attack, and has been under some attack for some years, as we are not quite sure what evidence it has produced of value.

You can split the experimental type of evaluation into two—attitudinal and achievement. Again, a lot of the experiments fall into both categories. For example, in the Finland paper, by Karvonen and Nöjd (no 30), they look at a particular way of developing an in-service course for teachers. Their main comparison point is teacher attitudes; how do teacher attitudes change, given varying treatments of a particular course?

On the achievement side, the Americans have dominated the field, and the papers at this conference show it. For example, the Stanford work on the Mexican Telesecundaria has a strong element of learning-gain measurement, and control groups. It shows, in the case of the Mexican Television Secondary School, that the television approach is certainly no worse than the traditional approach—in other words, the classical 'no significant difference' findings. This may again be difficult to interpret. Some people would say that the measurement instruments are so blunt, that we are not picking up the significant differences. Some would say that the control-group experiment tends to forget about, or not be able to accommodate, the differences amongst students, so that a particular treatment may in fact be successful for part of the class and unsuccessful for another part. Yet the control group experiment may hide that.

So, we've got these two main areas of evaluation, surveys and experiments, and both of them are well established. The survey area, I suspect, is more useful at the present time from the broadcaster's or practitioner's point of view. He's much more willing to listen to survey data, telling him how many people watched the programme, how many thought it was worthwhile, and how many came back tomorrow. This is 'voting with your feet'. If students come back and use the material, if teachers use the material and go on using it, this may be as good an evaluation as we can get, particularly if you set up the programmes in a reasonably democratic way. Clearly, if the students *have* to watch them, then that method is more doubtful!

Illuminative evaluation

In recent years, and this comes through very well in the papers, we have seen the arrival of a new animal on the evaluation scene, called 'illuminative evaluation'. This is referred to by Chiam Tah Wen from Malaysia (paper no 64), and the method is central to Margaret Gallagher's and Tony Bates' work at the Open University. Naomi McIntosh also talks about it in her paper (no 27). This approach really stems from dissatisfaction with the experimental and survey methods of evaluation, a feeling that not enough is being picked up by them.

I think one has to be a bit wary of illuminative evaluators. They are the new breed, very fashionable. Some rather preposterous claims are being made (I hasten to add not in the papers of the conference). There is plenty of feeling that this is the greatest thing in evaluation since sliced bread.

The important point about illuminative evaluation is that it examines the *context* of what is being evaluated. The experimental approach does not get into what Donald Grattan on Friday night called 'the politics of policy making'. I believe that educational innovations are political processes, severely political, having to deal with particular personalities at particular times, doing things and exerting pressure in certain ways. Now, surveys and experiments don't tend to pick up this particular aspect.

Let me give you an example from my own experience. Why is it in the Open University that radio consistently comes off worse than television; for example, in terms of the size of student audience? Now if one just looks at the message of the radio programme, I suspect we're not going to find out why. The reason is that in the BBC/Open University, there are significant cultural contextual reasons why radio is to a large extent a second class medium. It is not, if you are a BBC producer, the main medium through which you will make your career, and you will not, if you are an academic, be seen by granny at home. So there is a tendency to underrate the value of radio, and go to television.

I think that unless we look at the political and cultural context, then we are going to miss out on a great deal of information.

Formative and summative

There is another way of carving up the evaluation methodology pie and this is noted in a number of papers. Saul Rockman from AIT (no 53), Keith Miekle from Indiana (no 41) and Naomi McIntosh (no 37) all draw attention to *formative* and *summative* evaluation. Again, there can be a confusion when some people are talking about formative evaluation, and others are talking about summative evaluation, and the distinction between the two is not sufficiently realized.

In formative evaluation, we are essentially doing a sort of developmental product-testing. We have an idea for a programme, we try it out on a few people, perhaps carefully selected, we feed back those results very quickly into the design, and come up with the finished product. Summative evaluation on the other hand is more involved with the finished product and the evaluation of the whole system.

I think a lot of us here are actually in the business of formative evaluation. Our attempts at summative evaluation tend to run into problems. If you are trying to help practitioners, decision-makers, television producers (who are an extremely difficult breed to deal with), formative evaluation will get to them far more quickly than summative evaluation. In my experience, it seems to be immediately relevant to their needs, and you are actually feeding them with useful information.

Financial evaluation

There are other sorts of evaluation which we should not forget about. We've largely been talking about educational evaluation. Financial evaluation though shouldn't be forgotten. Jamison, and Yoon Tai Kim from Korea, have a paper (no 27) on the costing of educational broadcasting, and Jamison clearly has a monopoly on costing since all the papers in this area seem to have his name on them! This is something that in the USA has been taken very seriously, and which I suspect a lot of us tend to underrate.

In many ways it poses just as many methodological problems as educational evaluation. There is a temptation to say that costing something in education is simple, but I would argue that methodological problems abound. For example, what do you do about the costing of educational space? This lecture hall is very expensive, how do you cost it? How do you write off development costs? Do you write them off in five years, seven years or in one year? Very, very difficult. If you go to the Ministry of Education and ask them what is the cost of one hour's teaching at school, they would almost certainly not have an answer for you. There are very few decent costings of conventional education, and those that do exist lead to academic controversies. People say that, depending on what assumptions you make, it will come out at £5 a student hour, £10 a student hour, £15, £20. You get an enormous variation. These methodological problems will not go away easily.

Other evaluation types

There are two other sorts of evaluation which concern me. One of them is *technical evaluation*, which among television and radio people is very important. In other words technical quality, technical standards and so on. I think it's actually an easier problem, but it is still something we shouldn't forget. If an educational evaluator really wants to get in with the practitioner, then he's got to get into technical areas to a certain extent. If he just keeps to the educational dimension he may lose some friends.

Another area of evaluation is *management evaluation*. It may sound rather a peculiar one, and may indeed come under illuminative evaluation for some people. Certainly in my own work (running the National Development Programme in Computer Assisted Learning), one of the major evaluation problems is: how good is the management of the project? Let's suppose we are setting up a project in a particular country or institution, and the result is that it fails. One has got to be very careful before one says it's *instructional television* that's failed. Failure may be due to the way the whole project was set up in the first place—nothing to do with the medium at all, just the way that the people interacted. What if the person who ran the project was politically uninfluential in his institution, in fact was on a nose-dive towards demotion? Or if that person was very isolated in his teaching department, and was considered a nut-case? So management evaluation I think is quite important.

Q. 2 *(second half)*: *How do we begin to choose between this range of techniques, and the other techniques that we have?*

Most of the conference papers do not get into the question of *how* one chooses the appropriate methodology from the range available. Perhaps this is significant. Often the approach is: here is a problem and here is our methodology. We might on occasions think slightly *more* about our choice of methodology before we go into it.

I don't think there is any very easy answer to this question. There is certainly no definitive answer that I have come across. I suggest that the answer will be very pragmatic, and will depend on your circumstances. I would like to suggest four things that might influence choice of methodology.

The first thing I would look for is the *audiences* for the evaluation. I say audience*s* not audience, because I think there are many audiences for evaluation. One of the problems we have in evaluation is people not recognizing the existence of multiple audiences. For example, in the research mode, a major audience for the researcher is his academic colleagues, his academic peers, and in many cases they may be his only audience. He wishes to get more publications, so that he will get a promotion. That is an important factor determining the way he will work. If you then hand that report to a television producer, he says: 'What? I don't understand it', but it wasn't aimed at him in the first place. There may be many different audiences: research audiences and academic peer audiences, the decision-maker, the teacher/administrator, the producer. Even the students themselves might be considered by some to be an appropriate audience for evaluation—evaluation is there to help the students, not just to provide ammunition to the teacher or administrator.

Decision-making is the main subject for tomorrow's debate, and I don't want to go into this in any great detail. But the *model of decision-making* you believe in will affect the methodology you adopt. I happen to believe in a somewhat irrational view of decision-making. I would like to believe that decisions are made on the basis of cost-benefit analysis. I suspect they are not on the whole. They're made by a rather disparate collection of factors and choices and judgements—some rational, some not. The University of East Anglia team doing the educational evaluation of the National Programme have written:

> . . . the citadel of established practice will seldom fall to the polite knock of a good idea. It may, however, yield to a long siege, a pre-emptive strike, a wooden horse or a cunning alliance.[1]

If you ask a decision-maker why he did something, it often reminds me of my favourite joke from *The Magnificent Seven*. In that film you will remember there is a guy who jumps into a gorse bush, and when asked why he did it, he replied, 'I thought it was a good idea at the time'.

A second factor to look at in the choice of evaluation methodology is the problem itself, the purpose of the evaluation, the hypotheses that you're testing. That is an obvious point. What is perhaps less obvious is the interaction between form and content, between the methodology you choose and the aim of the evaluation. Dr Heidt in his paper (no 29) refutes the idea that the medium is neutral.

One of the difficulties in evaluation is that we often set ourselves purposes that are too ambitious. The mark of a good scientist is that he attacks soluble problems. The winners of Nobel Prizes are, as I understand it, the people who go for soluble problems. Choosing soluble problems is important.

The third factor, and a very significant one, is how much money you've got, and how much time you've got. This may enormously constrain your choice of methodology.

The fourth factor is the state of the evaluation art. There are atmospheric movements of evaluation. It is useful to be *au courant* with the state of the art in your choice of methodology.

I think those are four possible ways of choosing an appropriate methodology. All I'm really saying is that perhaps we should think for five more minutes before we go immediately to a particular methodology.

> Q. 3 *Should/can the evaluator be independent? Does this influence his methodology?*

The third question, on the hymn sheet, has to do with the independence of the evaluator. A number of papers raised this issue. Christer Frey, from Sweden talks about it (paper no 14). Alain Flageul, from Paris, talks about it (paper no 13). Again it's a major subject for tomorrow's debate, and I want to comment just briefly. The reason for worrying about the notion of independence, I believe, is credibility. The problem that we all face at this conference is credibility. Even if we produce lovely research or evaluation results, there may be a sneaking suspicion that really they are rather self-serving. Our evaluation studies are proving something is good because it's to our career advantage to prove it, especially if we're paid by the person we are evaluating. It is very difficult for the evaluator to be as open as he wants to be, if he is paid by the organization he is evaluating, especially if he is living with them. Here is a real issue.

This notion of independence does perhaps affect methodological considerations—for example as regards intrusiveness. The problem with evaluation is that it may be intrusive. A reaction against control group experiments is that they are too intrusive, that they are too removed from the way people normally act. People resent the evaluator coming in and disturbing the events that he is evaluating. I think that if you are an independent evaluator, you have got to be very careful about your choice of methodology, and make sure it is not too intrusive. For one thing if you're intrusive, you make a lot of claims upon people's resources of time and money, and you may have to be very wary about that. I think the independence of evaluators is a very important thing to concern ourselves with, because of the problems of credibility, and I suspect it does influence certain choices of methodology.

339

> Q. 4 *Can we relate costs to benefits in evaluation—if so, how?*

The fourth question brings us back to financial evaluation. The only person who talks about this in any detail is Charles Klasek from Southern Illinois (paper no 33). He makes an impassioned plea in his paper for costs to be related to benefits, and vice-versa, and I think it is one we should take very seriously. We are able to establish to a certain extent the costs, and we can sometimes establish the benefits. But how do we actually put one alongside the other? How do we make some sort of ratio? I don't think that he is saying he has the final answer, but rather he is suggesting a methodological approach.

Here, we are facing a difficulty which Edward Palmer raised yesterday. One of the questions that he posed for the working groups was: 'How do you decide which element in a particular presentation causes what effect?' This is, in a sense, a cost-benefit question: 'How do you relate which input to which output?' We are experiencing great difficulty relating outputs to inputs, on a one-to-one relationship. I personally feel, I'm sure people will disagree, that this is actually impossible at the present time. It's impossible because we are going towards more and more integrated multi-media systems. The more integrated our system becomes, the more difficult it is to identify one-to-one relationships. I think we should try and relate cost to benefit, but I am somewhat doubtful that we will achieve it. A more sober objective would be to get some clear ideas of costs and benefits, in two columns, on the left-hand side of the paper, and on the right-hand side of the paper, without making many claims about causal links one to the other.

> Q. 5 *Should the evaluator give a value judgement on the programme being evaluated? Does this affect methodological considerations?*

The next question comes out of the paper by McAnany (no 36). He suggests that an evaluator should actually recommend a course of action to the decision-maker—it's not enough to show the alternatives.*

I think that this is a very open question, well worth debating. Again, this relates to tomorrow's theme on decision-making, but it does affect methodological considerations. The moment the evaluator gets into a position of displaying value, I think in a sense he is becoming a decision-taker. The moment he starts setting priorities he is becoming a decision-taker. I personally favour the evaluator staying with his job, rather than doing the decision-maker's job. I recognize that there are a lot of decision-takers who may want easy answers from the evaluator. They want to be told what to do next. I wonder whether evaluators should follow these requests, rather than say 'It's not my task to tell you what decisions to take, but I will provide you with a lot of information, and a lot of alternative courses of action, a lot of alternative value judgements, and leave you to choose between them'.

I also think that there is a philosophical problem here. Once you are in the game of value judgements, you are right out of any scientific area. Science is not about value, but about proof. To start saying what ought to be is not a scientific statement. Once you start saying what ought to be, then you may be out of your main area of expertise, and one should perhaps be careful about that.

One of the main points about the illuminative approach to evaluation is that it tries to identify a range of value judgements. One of the difficulties with attitudinal testing is that the television producers who produced the television programme are likely to think that it was a

---

* In the discussion following the paper, McAnany felt that he had been misrepresented a little. He felt it was the responsibility of the evaluator to present a range of alternative courses of action to the decision-maker.

great programme, and the academic staff working on it are also likely to think that it was a great programme, generally speaking. What you've got to do is try and get value judgements from a much wider range, including possible dissident voices in the system, students, people unfamiliar with it. Then those value judgements will begin to cohere with the value judgements of the insiders.

Sir Toby Weaver, recently appointed at the Open University as Professor of Educational Management, and formerly a senior official in the Department of Education and Science, has said: 'Is there no way to give the community some confidence that the vast sums they are being asked to pay for education are being well spent? My answer is that they must be willing to rely less on measurement and more on human judgement'.[2] I think there is a tendency at a conference like this to be a little cynical about the notion of human judgement, and to say 'Yes, but that just becomes self-serving, people judging their own work as great'. I think in fact there is a way that a good evaluator can pick up this notion of human or professional judgement, and use it to his advantage, by showing the *range* of judgements, not just one judgement. Gradually the audience will pick up some flavour of what's going on. Let's face it, teachers use things in education, I think in all countries of the world, on the basis of subjective, professional judgement, which evaluation and research can feed. We may need to think a little more about how we could build evaluation on professional judgement.

Q. 6   *"Sed quis custodiet ipsos custodes?"*

I've chosen Latin on the assumption that there will be no problems of translation at this international conference. This quote comes from Juvenal—I think it has to do with locking up a married woman, certainly with locking up a woman. So the problem is who is going to guard the guards? Who is actually evaluating what the evaluators are doing? How can we evaluate evaluation studies? Emile McAnany in his paper has suggested some useful ways of looking at this question.

One of the criteria to help in evaluating evaluation, is *value for money*. There's an enormous amount of duplication in the evaluation of educational broadcasting, and decision-makers are saying: 'You know this has already been done four hundred times, why should we spend more money on it?

I think *brevity* is important, especially for decision-makers. They do not have time to read fifty page reports. We all like to write fifty page reports, but it's got to have a two page summary on the front and forty-eight pages in the appendix if we are going to deal with decision-makers. But here we have a conflict of audiences. To the academic audience, the two page summary is unacademic, because it's a simplification. Yet the decision-maker wants to have it fairly simplified and will glance at the appendix only if he needs to.

Comprehensibility is something to look at, the jargon, the technical language. I think people often are very unfair about jargon. Jargon is somebody else's technical language. But often there is a problem of technical language and we cannot avoid the issue.

Utility is an important idea. How useful is the evaluation. Will it actually be used? And then a notion from Donald Grattan on Friday night, he talked about the need for *preciseness*. There is a temptation for evaluation to answer very general questions, rather than answer the precise questions that the practitioner is looking for.

Lastly, a fairly obvious criterion for evaluating evaluation would be the sort of *rigour* with which the evaluation is being done. In one of Wilbur Schramm's compilations of instructional television research, he makes the point that something like 80 per cent of the experimental research designs were suspect. If somebody can drive a coach and horses through the methodology, then nobody is going to take seriously the results, whatever they are.

Evaluation is a political business. There is a case for saying that a lot of people use evaluation to protect themselves from taking decisions. If you have an innovation coming into sight, the quickest thing to do is to take it away and evaluate it, because that means you don't have to take a decision for three or four years: death by evaluation.

> Q. 7 *What is a good television programme?*

I've put this final question in because, if you are working with broadcasters you will hear a lot of talk about 'good television programmes', 'bad television programmes', 'good radio programmes' or 'bad radio programmes'. I think it might be worth spending a bit of time in the working groups thinking what people actually mean by this. In the BBC, television and radio producers have definite notions of 'good' and 'bad' programmes. What do they mean by it? *Who* is saying what is good? Good *for* whom, good *to* whom?

Conclusion

So those are the seven questions. I hope you will find them useful. They are the ones that intrigue me, and they are the ones that seem to come out of an analysis of all the papers. I thought I would like to end on just the last bit of that speech from Henry V.

> Old men forget; yet all shall be forgot,
> But he'll remember, with advantages
> What feats we did today. Then shall our names,
> Familiar in their mouths as household words
> Bates the King*, Palmer and Allebeck,
> McAnany and McIntosh, Jamison, Yoon Tai Kim
> Be in their flowing cups freshly remembered.

References

1 CENTRE FOR APPLIED RESEARCH IN EDUCATION, *The Programme at Two*, Norwich, University of East Anglia, 1975.
2 WEAVER, Sir T., *Education*, 16 January, 1976.

Theme 3   Decision-making and Research—Animation

Animateur   Mr Sten Sture Allebeck, Assistant Head Educational Broadcasting, Sveriges Radio, Stockholm, Sweden.

Chairman   Dr Robin Moss, Deputy Director, Television Service, University of Leeds, UK.

STEN STURE ALLEBECK

Once upon a time there lived in Scandinavia a young prince. He was handsome and rich and the whole world seemed to be smiling on him. But he had one great problem. He could not make decisions. Thus you could find him in the middle of the night in the most unexpected places talking to himself:

---

* Editor's note: There is a Bates in Henry V, but he was only a common soldier (see Act 4 Scene 1)!

> To be, or not to be—that is the question;
> Whether 'tis nobler in the mind to suffer
> The slings and arrows of production problems,
> Or to take arms against the wrong decisions,
> And by opposing end them?
> To die, to sleep, no more . . .
>
> And thus the native hue of resolution
> Is sicklied o'er with research results;
> And enterprises of great pitch and moment,
> With this regard, their process turn awry,
> And lose the name of action.*

I would like to start by attempting to define what is meant, or rather what the authors of papers mean, by research and evaluation. Then I will go on to look at the concept 'decision-making'—how should it be interpreted, and who is involved?

1 Definition of research and evaluation in terms that are meaningful to educational broadcasting

Robinson and Barnes (paper no 52) declare that:

> The process of research may be taken to include all systematic collection of evidence, designed to test a hypothesis or to answer specific questions, which evidence can be used in the making of future decisions.

The educational broadcaster would also be wise to take a stand from the very beginning on the classical issue of basic versus applied research. So, my first question is:

Q. 1 *Should research within a broadcasting organization be basic or applied?*

Much discussion could be avoided if there is an early agreement on what the role of research and evaluation should be for our organizations.

Here is a policy recommendation by Keith Mielke for the Agency for Instructional Television, USA (paper no 41): that the agency . . .

> commit its research and evaluation resources exclusively to decision-oriented and product-specific research, thus not engaging at all in in-house research designed to test general theories or hypotheses. This places top priority on meeting the specific decision-making needs of the organization and excludes from the research mission the objective of making a contribution to new generalizable knowledges . . . This should not be interpreted as a lack of interest in theoretical developments . . . It is, however, a proper allocation of resources for an organization whose mission is not academic or even scholarly, but mission-oriented and action-oriented.

When attempting to define what is *relevant* research, several papers have made classifications into types related to the levels at which decision-making takes place. For example, Tony Bates (paper no 7):

(a) research aimed at the design of individual programmes;
(b) research aimed at the determination of broadcast policy;
(c) research aimed at the design and implementation of new systems using television and/or radio for teaching.

Keith Mielke (paper no 41) offers a different classification, following a chronological order, and leading to the following scheme:

---

* With apologies (again) to W. Shakespeare, *Hamlet*, Act 3, Scene 1.

1　Background research (preproduction)
2　Formative research (done during the production period)
3　Summative research ⎫
4　Policy research　　　⎭ (conducted after production has ended)

These categories should be subject to the criterion of utility. When they are not appropriate for an occasion, they should be modified—or abandoned.

Category 1　Background research

The generic mission here is to reduce uncertainty in the planning process. It seems appropriate to include within the category of background research at least such activities as the assessment of needs that can be addressed properly via television, the assessment of a host of audience or student variables, the assessment of the physical system for production, distribution, and reception, and feasibility studies for tentative program ideas. These are all proper subjects for research contributions that are not tied to any particular program or product. (The many similarities to the processes of marketing research should not go unrecognized.)

Category 2　Formative research

Formative research is typically defined in comparison with summative research, as research or evaluation administered during the formative stages of a product (a television program in this case) that provides feedback to the production staff, enabling them to modify and improve the product before the final production decisions have been made. Formative research is pretesting programs early enough in the process to take corrective action.

Category 3　Summative research

Summative research assesses the extent to which a program (or series) has reached its objectives. Summative research probably resembles the most common expectation of what research and evaluation is about. It is conducted because decision-makers need overall performance data. Did I spend my money wisely? Does this program merit additional funds for revision? Should this program be scheduled for next year? These are decisions that need the summative research output.

Category 4　Policy research

The machinery required for background research would also be ideal for serving policy-making needs of an organization. As in background research, the data could lay the groundwork for intelligent planning of specific broadcasting materials, by providing a basis for the sustained review, modification and creation of general policy. This brings me to my second question:

> Q. 2　*Can you place these four categories of research into order of relevance for your own organization?*

If we now have a broad idea what research should be about according to papers submitted to the Conference I should like to have a look at 'decision-making'. What do you mean by it? Who is involved?

2　Who is the decision-maker?

In any organization, decision-making is a difficult activity but, to quote Tony Bates (paper no 7):

> . . . in educational television and radio, the problem is further complicated by the wide variety of people with a direct interest in such decisions: broadcasters, teachers, sponsors

(who may be tax payers, licence-holders, advertisers, or philanthropic funding agencies), and frequently politicians as well. The merit of various decisions will depend to some extent on how such interests are brought together or represented during the decision-making process.

Much emphasis is put on the need for wide participation in the decision-making as well as evaluation processes. They are activities that go on all the time in broadcasting organizations (Tony Bates again):

> Judgements are made at all levels of activity, from deciding in the control room whether to mix or cut between shots, to deciding in the President's office whether or not to invest in a satellite.

Many organizations have advisory bodies made up of representatives from various sectors of government, industry and education. Such mechanisms might be described as conventional and as advice from above. In a paper from India the need for new attitudes to management and decision-making is expressed. Mr Mullick (paper no 45) underlines the importance of relating the organization's objectives to the needs of the individual and to the environment and the society of India.

> The Researcher/Practitioner, who is learning to master the techniques of Western oriented mass media, has almost become a stranger at home. Our own attitudes have been found irrelevant when communicating with rural people. It is very necessary to get familiar with other development communication agencies, their structures and methods of operation and thus develop an integrated approach to communication strategies.

The strategy even includes a mastery of the local language and a general psychological feel of the target audience. Against this background it might be a good question to put to participants of an international conference:

> Q. 3 *What ideas presented here are 'exportable' from one culture to another? Are there factors that are true whatever the content or the subject or the target audience? What can be transferred from industrialized Europe to the village population of India or Iran? Strategies? Research and evaluation techniques? Programme formats?*

I shall now go on to a discussion of to what extent research results have had implications for organizations in various parts of the world.

3 Implications of research results. Some examples

I would like to begin by putting my fourth question for discussion, and then putting my own views, with which I am sure many will disagree:

> Q. 4 *Broadcasting organizations and universities are blamed for having carried out wrong kinds of research in the past. Is this true, if it ever was?*

Looking back over the early years of educational broadcasting, research on the media cannot claim to have made any glorious contributions. The promoters of educational media and television would have needed its support but either they did not ask for it or did not know what to ask for. Or if they knew and asked for it, they did not get it. On one report it is broadcasting managers that are to blame:

> It is disappointing that most public broadcasting organizations have concentrated on collecting the most superficial information about users of educational programmes, as their main or even sole contribution to evaluation . . .
> Obviously, an organization wants to know whether its programmes are being used. Unfortunately, that is just about all that such studies indicate, and nothing more.
>
> Tony Bates (paper no 7)

In another area of research the universities are held responsible for a number of useless results (Tony Bates again):

> Classical experimental research into media, often comparing the effectiveness of different media under controlled conditions, and usually heavily dependent on learning gains as measures of success, has been frequently criticised, primarily because such research fails to take account of the reality of the production process. It is also probably more than just coincidence that the methodology of both target audience research and classical experimental studies are derived from main-line academic disciplines.

To take a more positive view, it is quite clear from the papers submitted to the Conference that the area of research which has been really useful is what we have categorized as formative research. The discussions on 'Findings' and 'Methodology' will already have provided you with many examples. Here is just one, from Granada Television, UK.

> The series *Our Neighbours* produced by Granada Television for 10–13 year old pupils was the choice for one investigation . . . First, research had a potential bearing on the company's judgement as to the value of this kind of programme series, and the complexities involved in achieving its desired ends, and thus on general policy in opting for such a series. Second, it offered pointers for some improvements in production (a revision of the series was envisaged). Third, a striking diversity of reaction which was found between different types of schools, but also among pupils within each school emphasized the delicate role of the teacher, required to build on broadcasts likely to stir up complex thoughts and feelings in children. Such insights could be built into teachers' notes to help them plan follow-up discussions.   Graeme Kemelfield (paper no 31)

There *are* then effective methods for seeking out advice and monitoring series. This has brought about media products which even in details bear sign of high quality as we all know.

> Even such common sounds as a Land Rover engine can often not be identified by children, particularly in poor reception conditions, unless the test makes it quite clear that a Land Rover is involved. This research had led to very controlled use of effects in Schools Broadcasting programmes and identifying text being incorporated.
>
> Roy Thompson (paper no 61)

But at the same time the BBC feels that its research, which is primarily formative and partly summative, needs to move into new areas:

> However, what have been lacking in the past are independent surveys, by qualified educational research teams, into the effects of broadcasts on learners or teachers. Research of this nature could provide evidence in five major areas. The research in this field would indicate the pupils' gains in distinctive cognitive areas, or examine changes in attitudes and interests related to broadcasts, or examine particular techniques of presentation.   Alan Jamieson and Carol Stannard (paper no 26)

(What the five areas are can be seen in Jamieson's and Stannard's full paper.)

What though can be reported on the role of research in the area of policy-making? This is, I believe, one of the most important questions to be discussed today. There is very little evidence that research has had implications on higher level decisions. By 'high level' I mean decisions on priorities, such as whether one should set up a multi-media learning system demanding heavy new investments, or rather build teacher training colleges for instance; or— having doubts about the potential of traditional education for development within a reasonable time—prefer to use the money to build roads or hospitals. Decision-makers in industrialized countries are faced with similar problems—although not as dramatic. Can research findings tell us how the media should be used over the next fifteen years or help us prove that a new educational radio/TV organization and an efficient distribution and reception network is worth its price? How can we, or could we, justify the establishment of a Telescuola or an Open University system? It is now perhaps timely to put a provocative question:

> Q. 5   *Has the impact of research on high-level policy-making been over-rated? Do you know of any cases where research results have influenced high-level decisions, such as the introduction of a new multi-media based school system?*

Let me give you some quotes:

> Whilst through seeking we may know things better, we cannot find the final truth.

> For all is but a woven web of guesses.

> Decisions are rarely made on the basis of facts for one alternative rather than another. American studies suggest that the internal politics of the organization and the subjective desires of the decision-makers are more instrumental in deciding his course of action. *Executives who make effective decisions know that one does not start with facts. One starts with opinions.*   Richard Sherrington (paper no 58)

4   Credibility

My sixth question is concerned with the credibility of research results.

> Q. 6   *What factors may influence the credibility of research results of educational broadcasting?*

An element of uncertainty is a beautiful understatement if we consider the cautious attitude to research expressed in several papers:

> ... most information available to producers about users' reactions is unrepresentative of the majority of programme users. It is often unreliable (in that if a producer, for instance, went to a different source, he would get a different response). It is often not properly evaluated, in that the criteria for judging the comparative merit of different sources of information is not clearly thought out. Finally, the information available often lacks penetration.   Tony Bates (paper no 7)

The data lack definitive qualities:

> The following data should be used extremely carefully. The reader should not extrapolate the findings of this study to any other setting, at any other time, or any other way. These data are based on a limited sample, possibly not representing the total population involved.   Anon!

There is also a break away from the mechanistic approach to learning of the sixties.

> Much of instructional development remains art, not science. In some respects, development viewed as art represents a barrier to the use of *research and evaluation data* ... The creative activity of making a programme will not necessarily be a direct consequence of applied research findings, but rather an intuitive response expressed in words, music, drama and other artistic ingredients.   Dennis Gooler (paper no 20)

347

The importance of the television programme

The central role of the radio and TV production seems to be generally recognized by the participants of the Conference. This is noteworthy as in learning systems the broadcasts constitute only one of many ingredients:

> Already implied is the centrality of the television production process and the television product itself (i.e. the program). This is done in full recognition that the terminal objective is not to produce programs, but to effect learning and behaviour change. In that small sector of the total milieu scrutinized here, the television program, the stimulus is the basic point of reference. The chains of decisions around which the various types of research and evaluation will be developed are related directly to the planning, production, validation and utilization of television programs. The center of this small universe is television production.
>
> Keith W. Meilke (paper no 41)

So let me put my next question, or rather statement, for discussion:

> **Q. 7** *No matter how many different components there may be in an extensive learning system, the television programme, the stimulus, is the basic point of reference. The chains of decisions are related directly to the planning, production, validation, and utilization of television programmes.*

The time element has also to be taken into account if policy research is planned as an instrument for decisions on important government involvement. I wish to refer to the report on The Federal Role in Funding Children's Television Programming. I cannot go into details, only make a quote of what time it takes to find out how a federal investment of $500 million in children's programming should be spent:

> It can be very wasteful to pay the tremendous start-up costs of a high-quality purposive television series for a single broadcast season, and then withdraw support to go on to other projects. A fair market trial can take four to five years. Experience at the Children's Television Workshop (CTW) indicates that it takes one to two years just to prepare a major purposive series for national distribution, and then it takes two to three years of promotion and remake to determine how well it can do in the market place.
>
> Keith Mielke (paper no 42)

But the wide range of ordinary programme-making in school broadcasting organizations in Europe and elsewhere allows little time for the organization of an experiment involving piloting, teaching, transmission, testing, evaluating, reporting and decision-making. So:

> **Q. 8** *How then would this process be compatible with the contemporaneity of the programme, which is one of broadcasting advantages?*

I shall conclude this chapter on the usefulness of research in decision-making by offering for your discussion some quotes of a more positive and constructive nature:

> With some notable exceptions, the primary impact of research and evaluation data on the decision-making process in UMA will come in a wholistic form. That is, it will be difficult to trace a one-to-one relationship between a specific bit of evaluation data, and a specific impact on a specific decision. Rather, decisions in UMA will be impacted as a result of the wisdom that accrues from aggregate data and experience, developed over time.
>
> Dennis Gooler (paper no 20)

The Purpose of Evaluation
is not to Prove
But to Improve

Phi Delta Kappa

Have we had too high expectations about research? In a meeting in EBU last summer the usefulness and credibility of research was discussed. A representative of a member state who was involved in some important policy discussions on the potential of educational broadcasting in his home country was sceptical about the value of research work. It seemed to him that there were too many different and opposing methods to measure results. Even the most advanced uses of computers and training courses could not provide precise answers to decision-makers for optimal planning of broadcasting. The conclusion drawn by the group was that what we really mean when we talk about research in this context is probably something like 'development work'. The value of the research would then not be the result but the process itself. That is, 'not to prove but to improve'.

5 Structures and management: towards a better utilization of evaluation research

Concern is often expressed that research on educational television is not utilized, not because it is not well done technically, but because it is unadapted to the needs of the decision-makers. Evaluations about ERTV are conceived of in a vacuum and remain an accumulation of facts or knowledge and do not become wisdom for a specific decision-maker. How they might better serve its purpose will be discussed here.

One view is that evaluation may be a value-free social behaviour science,—but could it also be a descendent of the art of politics? I quote from Emile McAnany's paper (no 36):

> I would propose that the evaluator should not only enhance the potential use of the research by means of genuine dialogue with the decision-maker in determining his needs but increase the probability of utilization, by taking what I would call a 'strategic' approach to the decision context. By this I mean that to enhance the chances of the research to be used, the evaluator needs to understand the constraints on the action of the decision-maker, the bureaucratic and political circumstances not only of the evaluation itself but of the decision towards which the evaluation is geared. In a sense, this approach goes against the objective and often distant stance of 'scientific' evaluation and makes the evaluator an actor in the scene much more than he has been taught to be by the classical value-free approach of social/behavioural science.

If the evaluator is accepted as an 'actor on the scene' the following actions are proposed by Mr McAnany for the decision-maker and for the evaluator:

(a) *Actions for decision-makers/planners*
  (i)   the decision-maker or planner does not choose an ETV or other media system without defining his educational and development objectives and asking for the evidence for television (radio) and the alternatives, with cost estimates as well;
  (ii) the decision-maker should define the questions he expects the evaluator-advisor to answer;
  (iii) the decision-maker helps to define the major constraints under which a decision for television would have to be made;
  (iv) the decision-maker will allow several times for interaction with the evaluator over the period in which information is being prepared for a decision.

(b) *Actions for the evaluator-advisor* The context of planning new projects will not ordinarily generate new data gathering but rather depend heavily on past studies. The role of the evaluator-advisor is paramount in making the best possible use of this knowledge.
  (i) the evaluator-advisor helps the decision-maker to specify the precise decision to be made; often that decision will be for or against using television; however, where a satellite system is justified on other grounds, the advisor may be asked for the best way of using television;
  (ii) the evaluator-advisor helps the decision-maker to specify the constraints to a decision involving television, constraints that include the political, the bureaucratic, the economic, the cultural etc;

(iii) the evaluator-advisor presents the results of his study in the form of alternatives, but makes a choice among them in terms of concrete recommendations for action (and their justification);

(iv) the evaluator-advisor includes among his considerations for recommending an action the constraints to making a decision and a strategy for the implementation of the recommendations;

(v) the evaluator-advisor communicates his final recommendations in a dialogue form with the decision-maker, through a face-to-face meeting, or at least in the form of a personal letter, least of all in report form, even if brief, and never in a long technical report.

I think these issues are well worth discussing, so I give you my next two tasks:

Q. 9   *Discuss 'actions for decision-makers'.*

Q. 10   *Discuss 'actions for the evaluator/advisor'.*

In several papers it is argued that evaluation should be an on-going activity. It would then make no sense to make short-term contract appointments for research staff. By the time a person has gained sufficient experience, the contract has expired. An Open University paper (no 7) reckons that it takes at least three years of postgraduate work before a researcher can be independently useful.

The research function might be placed with an independent body outside the main organization, such as a University or a Ministry department, or form an in-house body. There are advantages and disadvantages: separation means independence but also creates problems of consultation and dissemination of information.

It is also argued that background research and formative research should be done by in-house personnel, while summative research should be done by outside, independent organizations. One reason for this is of course that a higher degree of objectivity—and credibility—might follow from a position of cool detachment. A paper from Kenya (no 61) reports that it would be wrong to expect the Service itself to set money aside from its own budget for independent research. Paying the piper might affect the tune. This leads to a discussion of principles of funding, but also leads me to my next question:

Q. 11   *Should evaluation be an on-going in-house activity or executed by various external bodies recruited on a short-term basis?*

To start this last session on a pessimistic note:

It is all too common for research and evaluation to be regarded as among the foremost of the activities that could be minimized or eliminated with least damage to the total project.
Gale Adkins (paper no 1)

The money available for evaluation, compared with production, is derisory, says Tony Bates (paper no 7):

The Open University spends less than £20,000 per annum on research and evaluation into all forms of audio-visual media. This is less than 0.5 per cent of the £3½ million spent by the OU on broadcasting.

The fact that the budgets are limited need not only be a question of attitude on the part of the funders (Tony Bates, again):

The point has already been made that too little in the way of resources are allocated to evaluation and research. This is not just a question of attitude, but of the way organizations are funded. I would argue that money for evaluation needs to be kept independent of money for programme or course design and production, and should be earmarked by the funding organization. Evaluation and research will in most cases be a relatively small component of total expenditure, and as a power group within a democratic organization competing for scarce resources, researchers will always be weak because of their relatively small numbers.

It seems obvious that funding is a more serious problem to the research unit than to any other essential function in the organization. Some talk about a 'downward spiral': too little money initially, the impact of research is small; consequently even less money is allocated in the future. And this trend may affect the whole organization.

No paper has a ready solution to propose. Should we argue for a fixed ratio between production and evaluation expenditures? And insist that funding of research should take place at the same time as the funding of the organization itself? I suggest that the working groups should make sure that sufficient time can be devoted to the exchange of experience in this area, so my last question is:

Q. 12   *How high a percentage of the budget of your organization goes (should go) to evaluation and research?*

---

of presented content, to assess adequacy and fairness of examining and grading procedures, to assess the value of assigned readings or other learning assignments, and so on.

In summary, then, in more than three years of experience with tailored evaluation, we have found it to be a flexible, efficient, and useful tool which because of existing computer technology can be employed on a large scale without becoming burdensome. It provides faculty with rapid access to evaluative information on questions that are stable and recurrent, but it preserves flexibility to obtain specialized information where special conditions are present. And while the rationale for employing tailored evaluation is somewhat different in traditional and in non-traditional educational settings, we suggest that the benefits can be great within both.

Broadcast media as psychometric media

The second 'mentality problem', hopefully one that afflicts educational radio and television specialists less than most colleagues, can be introduced with a quotation from the philosopher-mathematician, Alfred North Whitehead, who wrote that 'The success of language in conveying information is vastly overrated, especially in learned circles'. It seems fair to say that educational radio and television, certainly the best of it, strives to reflect this view, but are there further uses of these media that have been overlooked? Might we not consider radio and television, especially television, not only as media for educating, but as media also for testing or assessing what students have learned?

There are a number of reasons for exploring this, at least one of which has roots in the earliest days of ability testing. Then, Alfred Binet, father of intelligence testing, proposed that intelligence be measured in terms of the accuracy of an individual's report of a witnessed event, i.e., by using the 'fidelity of report' method. It then developed that to standardize events for such testing the motion picture was a useful medium.[2] As testing media, both film and television remain under-developed, however. There are nevertheless several persuasive demonstrations of film and television employed as psychometric media. For television, the examples best known to

the writer are those of the Columbia Broadcasting System (CBS) during the mid-1960s, when televised programs entitled 'National Drivers' Test', 'National Citizenship Test',[3] and 'National Health Test', were presented.

For film the pioneering work is that of Gibson and his associates.[4] Further work has been done by Carpenter, et al[5] and by the writer and his colleagues.[6,7] For those who are interested, the writer has also prepared a mimeographed, non-exhaustive compilation of about 50 film and audio tests,[8] produced in the course of the studies cited above. A brief annotation accompanies each listed test and these can give some understanding and appreciation of the potential that film, television, and other non-print media have as vehicles for psychological testing.

A variety of reasons may be given for considering the use of television, especially, as a testing medium. First and most generally, its devices, means, and forms are more varied than those of printed and largely verbal tests, much as educational television offers more variety of means and forms than the printed test; television is a highly versatile medium. Its ability to simulate real decision situations is great and in some circumstances has potential to provide advantages and validities greater than those of customary printed tests. In discussing psychometric values of the motion pictures, Gibson wrote[4] that it has the characteristics of:

> . . . motion, sequence, pacing, and realism. These characteristics presumably have their psychological counterparts. Human behavior, and the capacities latent in it, also involves motion, order, tempo, and the experience of reality. It is reasonable to suppose, therefore, that the motion picture makes available to the test designer not only a special method of measuring known factors of human ability but also gives him access to new and unnamed functions not accessible to conventional methods of test construction.

Clearly, Gibson's analysis applies equally to television and to its simulation capabilities, capabilities that were used to especially good advantage in the CBS 'National Driver's Test', mentioned above. Television

RAPPORTEURS

Theme 1   Research Findings—Report

Rapporteur   Mlle Viviane Glikman, Chef de la Division des Evaluations, Department des Actions Educatives, OFRATEME, Paris, France.

Chairman   Dr Tony Bates, Head of Audio-Visual Media Research Unit, Open University, Milton Keynes, UK.

VIVIANE GLIKMAN

First of all, I want to thank all the rapporteurs. You have given me very good reports, and they have been very helpful to me. I would also like to thank all of you for working so hard for these three days. I'll try to sum up what you said over the first day on Theme 1 (Research Findings), but it is a hard job. So many of you have said such brilliant things on so many subjects, that I am not sure that I am going to speak so much about the research findings. I'll try to do my best, and I ask in advance those of you who do not recognize what they have said, to forgive me. I also ask all of you to forgive me because of my broken English. Please, if you don't understand somewhere, don't hesitate to stop me. Something I should say is that I hope I won't be boring, but I have no quotations of Shakespeare, and I have no jokes—sorry!

The problem of generalization

The first point which appears to me to have been treated in every group is the problem of generalizing and transferring the results of one piece of research to another situation or another context. Most of the groups arrived at the conclusion that to do this was very difficult, because the results of the research are dependent on certain points, such as the educational objectives, the target groups, the learning situation of the students, all of which may be completely different in another context. For instance, you may have students in a classroom, or children in a classroom, or students alone at home, but working to get a degree or some kind of exam, or you may have what is called informal education, which I understand as adults learning merely in order to improve their general knowledge. All those situations make a very great difference to the way the educational message or information is received.

There are also some other important differences. One is the type of system which is set up by the institution. I mean, there may be 'open' or 'closed' systems, and that would lead to many differences—in the use of media, in the learning process, and so on. The type of instructional system seems to be an important variable in analysing the transferability of results. (Maybe I should define what I mean by 'closed' and 'open'. I mean by 'closed' a system whereby students are registered and easily identifiable. They have to look at television as part of the educational process, which they have entered by deliberately registering. The other situation is open education given over the air, for instance, and anyone can listen to or look at it without having to identify themselves, in any way.)

352

There are also other variables which are important in the analysis of results, such as the means available to produce and transmit the product. Of course, it is also very important to take into account all the environmental factors, whether they be social, economic, cultural, educational, or political.

Even given all those different variables, it should still be possible to generalize some results, at least. Why is it so difficult? Some groups gave the answer that it was because of the lack of theory behind the interpretation of results. The research studies were sometimes too immediately applied, but there were also other reasons. Television and radio are nearly always used inside a multi-media system, and it is often very difficult to isolate the influence of each of the elements of the system. We can say, for instance, that teachers are part of that system, and we can say that the type of organization which makes the product is a part of the system too. That makes a lot of variables, which really means you cannot find the same situation in two places.

But I think there is another point which is important when we try to understand why generalization is not more possible. It's that to make, let's say, a television programme, is in a way for a producer an act of creation. It's maybe one of the most difficult because at the same time as he has to create he also has to respond to certain objectives, so he cannot be free, and say, as an artist would say, 'Well, I used my sensitivity, and those with the same sensitivity will like it'. That's not at all the purpose of an educational programme. But as it is, in some degree, a creative act, it is very difficult to say that it can be made twice in the same way. So even when people have tried to use some methods where the results of research showed that the use of television has been good—for instance, the use of the puppets from *Sesame Street*— sometimes it didn't work in the new situation. But nothing is the same when you do something like that. You cannot say, 'I did exactly the same thing and it didn't work,' because it was different. The programme was not the same, and if it was the same programme, the previous reasons I gave—the variation in the students, the way they are expected to learn, etc—apply.

It seems though that the results of research *may* be used as *hypotheses* for new projects, but not as certitude, and it seems very important to check these hypotheses before starting a new project or a new television programme. This is not so redundant as it may appear. If the results are the same as previously, then the hypothesis is reinforced, which is valuable in that it proves the hypothesis to have been a good one.

Motivation and needs

What we can say is that we already know a lot of things about the first question that our animateur gave us. This was about the motivation of the student. With regard to the motivation of the student, the distinction I made between 'open' and 'closed' systems seems to be very important, because in an open system the first act has to be to get the student to look at the programme, and maybe *then* he will get involved in the learning process. In a closed system, you begin with people who want to get a degree, or an exam, or any kind of certification. They come into an educational system, about which they may have heard through TV or some other medium, and *then* you suggest to them that they should look at television, as part of the learning process. Then the important thing is to keep them in front of the television and make them look at it more than once. But in the open system, the first thing is to get people to turn on their TV sets at least once without their knowing what will be in the programme except by the title or rather short summary of the contents, even when, as often happens, the time at which it is broadcast is not very convenient.

So the motivation of the students is at the same time more important to take into account and more difficult to get in an open system. In this situation evaluation and research have to work to provide information about students' interests and their listening habits, and there are studies which have to be made before the planning of the broadcasting, to identify the needs and the expectations of the students.

This kind of study may be dealing with the widest audience, or with specific target groups. It is of course much more difficult to deal with the widest audience when you want to identify their needs. The analysis of needs is very difficult. There have been many studies made about that, but we cannot really say that the problem has been solved, because we need to make a distinction between explicit and implicit needs. People can express some needs, but there are other needs that they cannot express, sometimes because they are not aware of those needs, and sometimes also because they are people who are not used to speak in terms of educational needs. They don't know their needs as far as education is concerned, so we have to *interpret* results in order to be able to make assumptions. Another problem as far as needs are concerned is that in the minds of broadcasters, there are already assumptions about the needs of the audience, and sometimes we find a gap between those assumptions and the results of the research. Extensive research into needs may even be carried out deliberately to mask some obvious needs which for some reason the organization prefers not to meet. Indeed, it's sometimes some political motive which will win, and it may well be a decision already taken before the research began. It is not so obvious then that things go as they should go, which should be: analysis of the needs, then a decision about the subject, and then analysis of what should be the content of the subject, and so on. But I think we will be talking about that later on in Theme 3.

Specificity of the media

I would now like to tell you about another aspect of the research which has been talked about on the first day. This was the specific characteristics of the media. Many groups have thought about the problem of the motivating power of television, and that's a question which doesn't seem to have been solved in fact. There might be a motivating power of television, but is that power orientated towards education? It could also be said that this motivating power of television is a very short-term power, and then afterwards it needs something else, and very quickly.

On another side, it is very difficult to speak only about the specificity of the media, because you cannot really choose a medium because of its specificity. Any kind of research about media choice must take into account many other variables, such as the means students have at their disposal, because maybe in some situations television would be the best medium to transmit a certain type of message, but if students haven't got television, the problem is completely different. Then it seems to be very important regarding the problem of media choice, to take into account not only the specificity and the utility of the medium by itself, but also the whole situation—the learning process, the means the students have got, and also the objectives of the educational project.

By the way, there have been some groups who had some discussion about what was the difference between an 'educative' and an 'educational' programme. The answer which every-one seemed to agree on was that in an educational programme there is a progression, there are professionals consulted, and there are also most of the time printed materials accompany-ing the television or radio media.

Another problem which arose is the problem of the neutrality of the media. Is a medium neutral or not? There doesn't seem to have been much disagreement about that within the different groups; it seems clear that media, and especially mass-media, are not neutral, because someone or some groups have power over them. For instance, television can be under the power either of the government, or of private companies, and those power groups would use the media to transmit to people a certain kind of information, and not other kinds of informa-tion, and so on. Also, for people living under that power, the media have an image which is not neutral.

Of course, with the wide spread of people reached by the mass-media, they have always appeared to almost all societies as a marvellous way of helping educational disparities to be reduced, but in fact one of the results of the different researches is that it is more or less only a *potential* power. There is much more to do in research and in projects to make these mass-media really a tool to reduce educational disparities, because till now those who profit from education given through mass-media are *not* those who are the most deprived, except very occasionally.

Finally, with regard to the specificity of the media, I would just give you a checklist of the advantages and disadvantages of television, because really this problem has been discussed in every group almost, even though it did not always appear as a crucial one.

Advantages of television

The advantages I found for television through the reports I got are the following:

- To be able to get in touch with a very large number of people very geographically spread out, and also, as I said previously, potentially deprived people, too.
- Television can show to students things that you cannot show them in their homes or in their classrooms in other ways (except of course sometimes in classrooms by film).
- With regard to classrooms, it appears too that television has been a very important means of raising again the question about the relationship between the teacher and the children. Television then seems to have an important part to play in the classroom or universities.
- Also, at the level of presenting things in an educational way, it seems that television is very useful, because it allows information to be restructured by successive images or by the use of special means, which is one of the elements of education—the structuring of information, or the restructuring of information after it has been presented. Television allows for both, which is not the case for all media.

Disadvantages of television

But there are also, of course, going with those advantages, a list of inconveniences which are attributed to television, and mainly to educational television.

- As I said before, it may get in touch with a big lot of people, but then it is a very heterogeneous audience, and you have to give to that very heterogeneous audience a very unique message. A teacher in his classroom can more or less adapt the message to the different learners. When you teach by distance through television, it is much more difficult, if not impossible, to adapt it.
- Secondly, there is the problem of the relation of television to education, because television is mainly considered in our society as a leisure tool, and suddenly we require it to play another part, and it's not so easy to get people used to that.
- Also, while I talked about television production helping to restructure information, television is usually used to present information as a whole, so there is a kind of contradiction between the general use of television, which is to present information as a whole, and the specific use of educational television, which is to restructure information.
- We also said that television can have a good motivating force, but we can also say that afterwards people think that education is not so easy as television showed them at the beginning, so there may be more dropouts than with another kind of education.
- Lastly, there is another problem, which is that the students (less for the more deprived students than for the others) are used to working with paper media, but they are not at all used to working with mass-media. A very important point is therefore the necessity of teaching students and teachers who are going to use television programmes *how* to use them, and how to profit from them, because if we don't do that and we just put over the air an educational programme, it might do more harm than good.

What should be evaluated?

The problem is now to know out of all these things, what evaluation can do. Perhaps I've been talking more about the *problems* associated with evaluation findings, than about the findings themselves, but it seems in each group that this was the main pre-occupation.

The task of evaluation is very difficult. There is a sentence which says:

If you cannot count it, it doesn't count—and if you can count it, it's not it.

That's very often a problem for evaluators. Moreover, what they can evaluate does not always interest those who ask for evaluation, and those who ask for evaluation often ask for things that the evaluator has the biggest difficulty to evaluate.

We can say though, as we said previously, that there must be *a priori* evaluation before production, which should be taken into account when decisions are taken to carry out certain projects. We also said during the groups that the producers were mainly interested in the problems of formative evaluation because, of course, it's more directly related to their job. They would like to know what is best to put in a film, if they want to put over to the student a certain idea, or a certain piece of information, or a certain impression. Is it better to put a landscape or a talking face?

Well, there have been a lot of discussions, almost arguments, like that in the groups, and for sure evaluators and researchers have to take into account those demands. But we have also to take into account the research about other parts of the system. That means evaluators should also concentrate on the *global process* and the *global meaning* of a system, instead of trying to help the system to retain its students from one programme to another. That means too that evaluators have to take part in collecting information relevant to the global decisions which have to be taken, and not just concentrate afterwards on how to help implement things which it has been decided in another way to put on television or radio. It means also that evaluation must not try just to analyse the pedagogical or financial effectiveness of an educational system, but also deal with the social, political and economic implications of that system—which the researchers are very seldom asked to do.

The need for publication

The last point which appeared, and with which I quite agree, was that it's very important for evaluators to have a way of publishing and getting their work read. On the other hand we have been speaking about the need to give the results of research by means of discussion with the producers or with the decision-makers; but it's also very important that the results are published somewhere, so that they can help other people to get the information to consider it, and eventually to use it for testing hypotheses, even if the variables they deal with are partly different. The last point is that maybe the evaluator should care not only about the research made in one organization or the same type of organization, but also be interested in the research made in other fields, such as, for instance, sociology, psychology, or other human sciences, and other kinds of fields, which can also sometimes be very relevant to the problems of educational television or radio.

Well, that's all I have to say. Thank you for listening.

Theme 2   Methodology—Report

Rapporteur   Professor Emile McAnany, Stanford Institute for Communication Research, Stanford University, California, USA.

Chairman   Dr Tony Bates

PROFESSOR McANANY

I'd like to do three things today:

(a) I'd like to review with you what the group said on the seven questions we had to discuss on methodology,
(b) I would like to make a few comments summarizing a little bit the current situation,
(c) Finally, if I might take the privilege, I'd like to use this time to talk about what I think are some trends for the future. The last part is mostly my own, but it stems from the papers and the summaries that I read.

Evaluation vs research

The first question that was set was the distinction between evaluation and research. I think that there is a large agreement among people about the difference. People seem to pretty well agree on this, and most give them different kinds of names.

So *research* is referred to as fundamental, long term, *a priori*, generalizable, university-based, conclusion-oriented, academic in depth, searching for knowledge, based on a very strict scientific method for collecting evidence, etc etc.

Evaluation is applied, action-oriented, short-term, programme-specific, project-based, decision-oriented, assesses the known (whatever that means), quick and dirty, and a few other epithets.

One person though sums it up very well. Perhaps this is not a humorous summary, but I think it's one distinction that we would agree with as a summary phrase:

Not all research is evaluation, but all evaluation is research.

I think that's important, because it seems to me there is a general opinion shared by most people here, whether they are researchers or not, that evaluation should use the tools of research, but in the different setting of decision-making and in practical projects. Most people did not think that there was a great deal of importance in sticking to this sort of distinction as if it made a lot of difference, but to understand it and to accept it; I think that is accurately reflecting the feelings of the groups.

The range of methods

The second question was about the range of methods that was suggested, and again let me just create a list. To the list that was suggested the day before yesterday, I came up with about ten or twelve so-called methods, and I think this presents a problem. Among other things that were discussed I mention:

the anthropological method, the case-study method, the survey method, the experimental method, the illuminative-evaluation method, cost effectiveness and cost-benefit methods, marketing research method, systems analysis method, the historical method, the critical path method, the test and measurement model or method, operations research method, and then (really all under one title) the formative evaluation method.

Now all these seem to be methods, and the problem I think is precisely there. The problem was put by Henri Dieuzeide when he asked the question yesterday about what method does evaluation use. The difficulty we have had in discussing methodology indicates the problem of evaluation. In addition to listing a number of these methods, a lot of people said that *all* the methods should be used, that evaluation should really have many methods, it should be multi-method. But the difficulty then becomes that we haven't come to grips, in the papers I read, with what you mean by methodology, other than just a passing reference to it. Some people talked a little bit about making sure it is reliable or it is valid. But that is actually talking about instruments.

Let me see if I can add a brief phrase that might help. It seems to me that when we talk about method, it can be any of the methods mentioned above. Method can be a tool for gathering evidence, or it can be a tool for analysing data, because there can be research analysis methods or data analysis methods. Now in any case, it is a tool for gathering and presenting evidence. So, indeed, the historical method is quite appropriate, the anthropological method is quite appropriate—but appropriate to what?

I think what we need to do is ask ourselves to define the research question, and indeed the research audience, before we can come to a conclusion as to what method is appropriate for that particular question. One of the drawbacks or difficulties then that faces evaluation is that we don't know what question we want to answer. When we go to decision-makers, often times they don't know what question they want to ask. So, as long as the research question is left very vague or general, the methods remain totally open. That's a point I think that didn't quite come out in the summaries, but I think was implicit and I would like to make it explicit.

The definition of the research problem is primary. When one has done that then the method can be chosen as appropriate or inappropriate.

Another point on methodology that was discussed but only briefly, and I will come back to this later, is the whole question of the appropriateness cross-culturally of different methods. One person was pointing out that in India, (it may have been in another country) many of the methodologies that have been introduced do not seem culturally appropriate. My interpretation of what that means is that because methodologies are available, either students from India go to the United States or to Europe to study and take these methodologies back with them, and apply them as they have been taught or foreigners come to India or to another country and apply their methodologies.

I think the question of cross-cultural appropriateness may have to be refined—at least this is what I do with my own students who come from foreign countries. I cannot as an American define a research problem for you. I can help you once you have defined your research problem, and so seek a method that is appropriate for answering that question. But it seems to me what is confused very often is that we accept methodologies as convenient instruments, and with the acceptance of the instruments, we accept the research question that instrument is supposed to answer. In other words we give other people hammers and they have got to go around looking for nails to pound, even though what they are really interested in doing is designing a house.

So it seems to me the danger here in methodology is not so much that a methodology is culturally inappropriate, it's that the research question that lies behind the methodology may be inappropriate. I don't say that all methodologies are culture-bound. In some sense I believe that methodologies can be adapted to other cultures, if the other cultures really want to answer the question that lies behind the methodology.

The independence of the evaluator

The third question I put together with the fifth question. The third question, if you remember, was on how independent the evaluator can be. The fifth question, suggested partly by my own paper, is whether the evaluator does have value judgements, and how these should be handled in doing evaluation.

There were fewer people who dealt with these two questions, but there seemed to be again a general consensus, although there were dissenting judgements. People said that you had to trade off between being independent and being involved and really understanding the project. The more outside, the more independent you were, the less you really understood, the less you were accepted by the project, and perhaps the less good job you could do in terms of really evaluating it. On the other hand, they said, the closer you were tied to a project, maybe the better you understand it, but also the more tied down you are to fulfilling the precise goals that the director of the project may have for you. So, there was a trade-off between independence and involvement.

I think most people came down on the side of involvement. They said it is better to be within a project or at least to know it well and take the risk perhaps of being under some sort of bureaucratic constraint, rather than just coming in from the outside, totally without knowing what the project is all about, analysing superficially and making a judgement for which you have no responsibility, and then going off. I would say most people felt that responsibility and involvement were better than was total independence from the project. Most people pointed out that an evaluator is never independent because he is always paid by someone, presumably, and even if it is by another agency he is dependent on that agency.

The question of independence was, I think, put in a fairly qualified way. One group reported that a goal for the evaluator was to be totally objective and cautious to give only what the data show. I want to mention that, because that certainly goes against the idea that the evaluator has value-judgements which enter into his evaluation. Again that's a trade-off and I think we could argue a lot about that, and I think you did in your groups.

My own position is that research especially is value-laden, at least in the sense that people or institutions choose what will be researched, what will be evaluated. If you choose to do a certain thing, you choose not to do a whole series of other things, so that the evaluation at least is directed in one direction. We'll come back to that later, because I think that has a lot to do with some of the fashions and trends in evaluation today.

Let me add one other thing, as I think it is an important point which I believe Ed Palmer or somebody in his group made. Formative evaluation and pretesting probably should always be *within* the group, always be inside the project, but summative evaluation should probably be done from outside a project. That's a simple distinction, but it does make sense to me, it rings true.

Cost-benefit analysis

The fourth question is on cost-benefit analysis, what people thought of it, and what their response was to it. Apparently their response was very small. Only two groups discussed it, and these came to very general conclusions, and I ask myself why.

It seems to me that the reason is basically that most people here are not economists. This meeting has two economists who are interested in this question. This area is new for economists. Although Dean Jamison has been in the business a long time, he has only been working and writing about this for maybe the last seven years, so it is a new field, a new area for technology and radio and television to be thinking about. That is reflected in the lack of discussion on the question of costs and benefits.

I would just make one observation here, since it is going to come up in what I'm going to talk about later, but it seems to me that in the push towards creating big systems we necessarily get to considerations of cost effectiveness, of management, of cost benefit, of investment, and all of these questions which planners, who have to make big investments of millions of dollars for a country, have to be concerned about. So economists are being pushed into the area of school system management and analysis.

I just wish to quote a manager who said, 'I wish that my school system could be run like General Motors'. From his point of view he felt that General Motors was a big, well-run, efficient, corporation. From his point of view as a manager he saw the school system as a very big corporation that spends millions of dollars, and he needed to make it an efficient system.

The difficulty with that is that the school system, first of all, is not General Motors, and does not try to achieve the same thing as General Motors. Right there, the systems people get into a certain amount of difficulty in applying a systems approach, and a management approach, from business to school. Now I think there is an overlap, there is indeed a point in which school systems should be run much more efficiently, but one has to remember that the product is not a car, but rather a process of education. Although we do produce graduates, that is not the only way of looking at the school system.

I don't think there is going to be a simple solution to the school management problem, but I do think there is a confrontation shaping up between managers that are concerned with cost efficiency and people who run school systems who have a totally different point of view. I think most of you share this latter view, and just don't understand what the manager is talking about when he talks about efficiency or effectiveness or cost-benefit analysis. But I do see this as coming into play much more, and I see it as a problem for people who are working in television and radio and school systems, to begin to understand that language and to begin to deal with it.

It seems to me that it has to be a compromise. School-systems do cost more and more money, and you've got to have a more rational way of spending it. But on the other hand we can't let systems analysts run the school system like General Motors, because we are going to end up with chaos. So there has to be a meeting of minds here which I think is only just beginning. Perhaps with François Orivelle and a few others we can begin to understand better the economic implications, the cost implications of educational technology and why those are important, and how best to deal with them.

Evaluating evaluation

The sixth question can be dealt with very briefly. It says, 'how do you evaluate evaluation?'

Most peoples' response to that was a sort of little jingle. You know, a good evaluation is . . . and then you fill in the blanks. And these are the blanks that they filled in:

> long term
> decision oriented
> credible
> persuasive
> in touch with areas for potential change

and finally, last, but not least,

> well funded.

I think you can all agree with the last point at least! To summarize the discussions, in order to judge how good evaluations were, the evaluations had to fulfil some criteria, and those criteria were relevancy and competency. I would say they fell into these two categories. Good evaluation is relevant for a decision maker. And secondly a good evaluation is well done scientifically, so that it can be persuasive.

What is 'good' television?

The seventh question was on what was good television, and again we can turn this into a 'fill in the blanks' exercise. Good television is . . . and then there was no agreement, so I can't fill in the blanks!

However, I have three blanks that I did fill in, from out of the maze of the disagreements. People basically said that good television is technically well-produced television. However, that doesn't necessarily mean it's good. It is good television if it's technically well produced and achieves its educational objectives. But then they said that that's not quite it either, so they said that good television is technically good, *and* achieves its objectives, *and* is also entertaining and attention-getting. In general terms, that is what I got from the seventh question.

The historical perspective

Let me take a few minutes to go in a slightly different direction and give you again some thoughts that I think come out of the notes, but also partly come from my own experience. I'd like at least to share it with you and get your comments, feedback and disagreements perhaps. It seems to me that in order to understand what's going on in evaluation or in communications, I come back again and again to a better understanding not of quantitative methods—although I think they are important—but a better understanding of history.

I say that because I am not an historian, but I really believe that if we look in perspective at evaluation and research and communication and educational technology, if we even look at the words and how they develop, we'll begin to understand that we are living in a historical period, which like everything else, is full of trends and of fashion, intellectual fashion, of cultural fashion, of research fashion. I think if you are from a discipline, if you are from psychology, or if you are from one of the other disciplines, if you have a grasp of how your discipline develops, you will realize that we are only at a point in the development of a certain kind of intellectual history, and also a technological history.

I have been struck by this at this Conference more than ever before, because in this Conference I have found a large number of people, from a great number of disciplines. And yet you're all here and seemingly very interested in the question of evaluation, and I say to myself that this couldn't have happened ten years ago.

Ten years ago the word evaluation had hardly even been put into print. In fact one of the first people who wrote about it, Michael Scriven at Berkeley, wrote his essay on the roles and goals of evaluation, and it was published in 1967 and everybody quotes that as a classic or *locus classicus* (if I can use Latin). In 1966 many of us outside of educational psychology really did not know what evaluation was about, or at least we didn't talk about it in these terms.

I think that if we understand that we're in this process, then we will get a better grasp of some of the problems and see them in perspective. Instead of jumping on to what I would call fashion, which I think is short sighted and ahistorical, I think we will look at trends which I would define as more long term and grounded in historical developments. Then we can grasp what the problems are, as opposed to what somebody else is doing in another country.

Cultural influences

In particular I feel that there is a tremendous kind of influence, and not always a good influence, from the US on other countries. As Americans, if I might make a statement for the rest of us—or I'll make it for myself anyhow—we often fail in understanding our own cultural and historical situation. We are raised in a kind of a method, and we believe that is *the* method. It is historically true that we in the United States have been raised in quantitative research terms, and it is difficult for us to get outside that. But I think that unless we do, we fail to grasp some of the larger problems, and also fail to communicate with other people who have been raised in quite different kinds of evaluation methods.

For other people coming into contact with the intellectual culture of the US, it's as important for them to understand what those historical developments have meant and to be able to take what is good and useful for themselves, without being simply overwhelmed by the belief in a single methodology that can turn science into scientism. So my feeling would be that it is important to distinguish between fashion and the whole idea of different cultural traditions.

Let me see if I can just give you an example of what I mean, and again I'm making some big generalizations which I'm sure some of you will disagree with. I think it is very clear, when I do research, the way I do it stems from the kind of intellectual training I've had, and so I come in and use the method that I know how to use. It is very clear if you read the research that I and perhaps other Americans have done in common, we are generally quite quantitatively orientated.

Take another example, which is perhaps the most clear cut example, the French tradition. It is a totally different tradition. I don't think that necessarily the two are incompatible, but they are different. So for instance in reviewing the methodology papers. I was very much struck by the difference between Mlle Jacquinot's paper and some of the American papers. There is a very, very different perspective. There are a different set of research questions, and there is clearly a different set of methodologies to answer those research questions.

So my earlier distinction between the research question and the methodology comes back and is important, because it isn't a question just of handing on a methodology. It's a question of what sort of answers you are looking for. Now the kind of answers Mlle Jacquinot is looking for in her research is something that is extremely rare in the United States. What she is looking for is a very careful and critical analysis of the structure of educational films. It's extremely sophisticated, it's looking at a series of I think quite important variables, which could make a difference once a method is worked out. I think it could make a difference in the production of good educational films. That is not something by and large which Americans do. It is a different cultural and methodological approach to the problem of educational technology.

Fashions and fads

So I do think there are different cultural approaches. But what would I call fashion? A fashion is something that is intellectually stimulating, but perhaps has no relevance to the particular environment in which it is found. I can't think of a good example, and if I took an example I would probably step on someone's toes, because there is no one in this room that perhaps doesn't have his or her particular intellectual fashion at this time.

So let me step on my own toes. Let me tell you what I'm interested in. I don't know whether it is a fashion, but let me say what some of my interests have been directed at now. Some of you share this and some of you probably do not. My own feeling regarding working in third world countries is that it is terribly important to understand the historical perspective, how technology gets transferred from one place to another. When I talk about technology I'm not just talking about the hardware, but the whole way of working with that hardware,

361

the whole approach to the hardware, how it's used, how it's organized, how people are organized around it. And it seems to me that it is important that we have that perspective in mind, so we can better understand, and perhaps predict, what the result of a decision to buy, for example, a satellite for a particular country would be.

This in a sense relates to a theory which has been developed in Latin America. It's called dependency theory, and it is a view of how different kinds of social and economic structures are developed in a country, and the economic and the socio-cultural dependence of one country on another. Now this is certainly a fashion. It has a certain amount of evidence for it. It has a certain amount of predictive power. Very little empirical work has been done in this area, although some is being done, especially by economists in Latin America. But still it could be identified as a fashion, because people can say, 'Well, right now, that is very in. What is it going to be in five years from now?' Maybe we will have another word, we will have another interest. It seems to me we will have to be careful that we just don't grab on to a fashionable research idea or a theory that right now is being talked about a lot.

That is why I think evaluation and its relation to decision-makers is very important for researchers to be concerned with because decision-makers are not interested in intellectual fashion. They are interested in running a project, and they bring us back to earth, and say, 'OK, you're interested in dependency theory, or you are interested in some other kind of theory. What's that got to do with my project?' And in this I think that perhaps the interface of the researcher with the decision-maker, which is what evaluation is all about, is a very healthy one, because it puts certain theories to the test. We have intellectual theories that appeal to us, and the evaluation process tests these theories against the reality of running a project, of making something happen, of teaching people, or changing rural areas. We test the theory against the very, very hard evidence of what happens when we use television or radio for very grand schemes.

We have to be careful that we just don't grab on to a fashionable idea, or even a fashionable method. Now, with the influence of American-type research, everyone wants to use the computer for multiple regressions or critical path analysis. Well, why? Well, because some people seem to believe that if it comes out on computer print-out, then it must be true. It really is a belief, instead of being a tool which has limits to its usefulness. Many times we simply say, 'It's great! Look at all these numbers!' We really have to be careful that we don't get drawn into that, and use it simply because it looks good or is fashionable, or we believe it's modern, or it's going to answer questions. I think we have to be very, very careful to see how it helps to answer the research questions in evaluation.

Long-term trends

OK, what about the trends? I believe there are trends that are important and will continue, and are not just fashions.

I believe the trend towards the involvement of more economists in evaluating educational technology is not just a fashion. I think it is an important trend and for one very simple reason, that we are getting to the point of creating larger and larger systems. Technology is costly. Even though the unit costs are going down, educational technology is a very expensive undertaking. We know countries are reaching their limit on what they can spend on education, and they are searching for alternatives to just having more schools and more teachers, and here is where technology is appealing. But it can only prove useful, it seems to me, if we really know how much it is going to cost, and if we have some inkling as to what kind of benefits we can expect from it. That is why I think economists have been involved at all even though that involvement is relatively recent. It seems to me that they will probably be involved for many years to come—and more closely involved from the planning stages of projects.

So that the one economist who is sitting in the room doesn't get the idea that he is going to be the only important one, I would point out that economists in this field more and more have to collaborate with other people, like sociologists, like psychologists, like anthropologists, so that the kind of data that they generate to make judgements in evaluation is not strictly cost data, or even only quantitative data. So I think the economist, in working with other people on the economics of education and technology, necessarily modifies some of his approach to collaborate with people who bring another perspective and perhaps another methodology.

A second trend that I think is important was mentioned very little here. If evaluation is to continue and not be a fad or a fashion, if it is to be a genuine trend, and really become a useful tool, it is going to be absolutely necessary that evaluators learn to talk to and relate to those people who are looking for the evaluation to be useful. I think there has to be a growing participation of the users, of the decision-makers, in the evaluations. The record to date is very dismal, and I think it will continue to be so unless more users participate. Otherwise I think that evaluation will simply disappear. As long as we keep doing evaluations that simply sit on shelves and are not integrated into decisions and actions, then I think evaluation will have degenerated into a fashion. So, in order not to do that, which I think would be too bad, we need to integrate the decision-makers, to let them participate in the definition of the research questions, to participate even in the ongoing evaluation, and certainly to participate, in some sort of dialogue form, in the results and their application to problem areas of projects.

The third trend I see developing, and I think again it is extremely important, and again for a kind of macro-level of evaluation, is historical and comparative studies. Someone said (and I can't remember who it was) that we cannot judge the outcomes of an educational system for at least five or ten or even twenty years. Now how can we do that kind of evaluation? We are just not going to be funded for twenty years. No agency is rich, or perhaps crazy enough to do that, not even the United States Government. I think we are going to have to go back to case studies. We're going to have to go back to all of the cases where television was used, ten and fifteen years ago, and start looking at what happened there, to find out what happens over the long haul.

I'll mention here one thing that was brought up in our group. It seems to me that if television, if technology is to be useful as an introduction to an innovation, it probably is useful for only a short historical period. That technology may then have to be diverted to other uses, totally different from the original one, in order to keep the innovativeness alive. This though is very rare. If you look at the case studies, you will find that television or radio once it gets put into a school system, often becomes a static or bureaucratic element, and that it doesn't change. So I think that by looking back at historical cases, and comparing those cases, looking at some of the major organizational factors, we find that television has a built-in difficulty of becoming rigidified. Now it seems to me that one job for evaluation is to help plan better our technology systems so that they don't fall into that sort of historical pattern.

The fourth point is once again reflected in the discussions, but again I think it is a point that relates to the historical study of cases. What we find if we look at historical cases is that the big problem is not television as such, the big problem is the management of a system, and that is why I talked about the necessity of having better management. So if evaluation is to respond to a genuine need, and I think it should and will, there will have to be developed better methods for studying the organization and management of educational technology. How can we study historically what the management problems have been, and how can we take the knowledge and put it into some sort of methodology? How can we study management in a way that will be useful to projects as they begin, right from the beginning? I think that is an important and hopefully an historical trend.

Finally something again that reflects at least part of the thinking of this group. Many people have talked about the evaluations taking into account the social and political setting of a particular project. I think that is absolutely crucial. I think that historically there is a trend towards the macro-problems of technology systems, one of which is the political setting. To put it concretely, are we going to be able to develop methods, a methodology, that can genuinely take into account the political factors or the political constraints on the creation of a technology system? Are we going to have methods that will be able to study the social structures into which a technology system is placed? Unless we have that, it seems to me that we are going to founder, or if the project doesn't founder, at least the evaluation of the project will, because the evaluation then will be irrelevant to a lot of the basic problems that a decision-maker faces, which are social problems and political constraints.

So I would suggest that evaluation of educational technology has been influenced both by fashions and by trends, and hopefully the trends will continue long after fashions have fallen by the wayside. Methodology will hopefully grow in relation to need and in accordance with the research problems that each project defines for itself. That in a sense is what I wanted to say about methodology, and I hope that these ideas do not betray the sense of the groups, which I trust I reflected in my summary.

I thought I should end by quoting something, not from Shakespeare, but about the International Development Jet Set, of which I am fortunately or unfortunately a member. I read this for myself:

> Excuse me friends, I must catch my jet.
> I am off to join the development set.
> My bags are packed and I've had all my shots.
> I have travellers' cheques and pills for the trots.
> The development set is bright and noble,
> Our thoughts are deep and our vision global;
> Although we move with the better classes,
> Our thoughts are always with the masses.
> In Sheraton hotels, in scattered nations,
> We damn multi-national corporations.
> Injustice seems easy to protest,
> In such seething hot-beds of social rest.
> We discuss malnutrition over steaks,
> And plan hunger talks during coffee breaks.
> Whether Asian floods or African droughts
> We face each issue with open mouths.

Thank you. Now I must leave to catch my plane.

Theme 3   Decision-making—Report

Rapporteur: Mr Brian Groombridge, Head of Educational Programme Services, Independent Broadcasting Authority.

Chairman: Dr Tony Bates

BRIAN GROOMBRIDGE

The decision-maker's dilemma

It's been the kind of morning that makes me feel not only that I don't know very much about the subject of the conference, but, in a terrifying kind of way, that I don't actually know anything about anything! I hope there might be waves of empathy coming up from the producers, executives, and bureaucrats present, to sustain me through the rest of this session. In fact, while on this bid for sympathy, let me put it to you this way: if you didn't know already, would you suppose this Conference was organized by a researcher or by a decision-maker?

Consider this morning's sequence, for example. We started with Viviane Glikman, researcher. Time allowed to prepare her statement—two days. We then moved on to Emile McAnany, academic. Time allowed to prepare his statement—one day. We then moved to the final session of the morning, Brian Groombridge, decision maker. Time allowed to prepare his statement—well, really, no time at all! I was given eight rich papers at five o'clock last night and the final paper this morning at breakfast time, so it is very typical I think of the situation we've been discussing these last three days. Here am I the decision maker, constrained as ever by lack of time for deliberation, having done nothing more than skim-read these excellent documents. So Tony gave this final session to somebody used to hasty, ill-considered judgements, which he is then subsequently too insensitive to regret.

I suppose that the decision-makers among us therefore are as vulnerable as I now am to what I'm going to call 'Sherrington's Disease'. I'm adopting here the convention as in medicine. I don't mean that Richard Sherrington, of the British Council, suffers from this. I mean he discovered it, or at any rate he wrote about it, and in the summary to his paper (no 58) he says:

> How are managerial decisions made? American studies indicate that information and research rarely provide the basis for decision. Managers do not operate on rational grounds but are more influenced by their subjective desires and their personal needs to justify and account for their decisions.

So this is Sherrington's Disease, and I suppose, shorn of my research, I am about to plunge into my subjective reactions to, and no doubt capricious distillations from, the nine available reports.

The pattern of the discussions

With that disease as a starting point, it seems to me that in the course of the group discussions, we've undertaken a kind of group therapy. One of the consequences of that group therapy is that we have at least purged ourselves of several unhelpful 'either/ors'. We've already met

> 'Either decision-makers use research *or* they are irrational',

and allowed that one to pass without making too much of it. But there were four others we could do without.

> 'Either research is academic, abstract, theoretical, *or* inhouse, operational, mission-oriented, topic-specific.'

Emile dealt with that issue, but I don't feel he quite got at the rather nasty either/or feel about it. Another one:

> 'Either you are a teacher *or* you are taught',

an incredibly dated antithesis, one would have thought. Here's another:

> 'Either there is research *or* there is ignorance'.

Not very much allowance made, it seemed to me, in that particular antithesis, for experience (dare I use such a quaint phrase), or for knowledge that was once researched. And finally,

> 'Either one is a decision-maker *or* one is a researcher'.

Now you will know that in English we have the expression 'sitting on the fence', which is a distinctly uncomfortable posture, signifying uncertainty more befitting the scrupulousness of a researcher than the uncouth directness of a decision-maker. But there is in fact one thing that is more unpleasant even than sitting on the fence, and that is being straddled on a matrix.

It seems to me that considering we have been straddled on a matrix for three days, it's amazing that our discussions were as good as they were. But there is a tendency when you are in this very uncomfortable position to find that you are over-simplifying everything. You tend to pretend that there is something called 'television', or that there is something called 'education', or that there is something called 'research', or that there is something known as 'decision-making'. And we all know that this is not quite the case, that we are all importing different models simultaneously as we use those phrases. But it has been quite a matrix. We have been talking about levels of decision-making, types of evaluation and research, and also types of educational broadcasting—as Viviane was saying, the open kinds and the closed kinds—*and* about different perspectives of decision-making.

I hope that Tony and the managers of the Conference will actually consider reproducing the reports that were given to me last night, because they are lucidity itself, and I hope I can emulate them to a degree, by abstracting a few points under these headings:

1 levels of decisions
2 categories of research
3 factors affecting relationships between the two
4 the changing context and meaning of educational broadcasting.

Levels of decision

A number of people have pointed out that really one needs to start right at the top, at the level of government or at the level of society as a whole. And although you find this in Sten Sture's excellent paper, I felt personally that it was somewhat muted. There is something about the way the theme was conceived and presented to us that made it look as though the highest order with which we were concerned in some way was the broadcasting organization. But in the discussions people pressed on to a higher level—to government or to society as a whole, and they were considering such questions as whether you need or should have research to make policy judgements—such as whether you need an Open University, as was decided in Britain, or whether you don't need one, as was decided in Australia, or whether you need a satellite or not; or whatever.

Perhaps it's worth observing that there's another matrix in the wings, as it were. First of all there is the dimension: autocratic—democratic. Then there is the dimension: with research —without research, and then there is the dimension: right—wrong. And just to show how tricky that is when actually applied, it's worth observing that the decision to have an Open University was an autocratic decision taken without benefit of research, which turned out to be splendidly right, and I find that rather chastening as a democrat and a sort of believer in research.

Countries need, do they not, instruments for such research and it's not clear to me from the reports whether we gave really quite enough consideration to this, something which Ignacy Waniewicz and I were discussing in 1967 or thereabouts. Then we came to the feeling that there needed to be in each country something that you might call The Council for Educational Technology or some fairly high order piece of machinery through which decisions of this sort could be discussed and through which decisions of this kind might be researched. It is I think the kind of thing that Kaarle Nordenstreng was trying to do with Finnish Broadcasting. It is the kind of thing that is beginning to happen now, through the Council for Educational Technology in Britain, which is just on the verge of deciding that it ought to be looking at the whole question of open learning systems; and perhaps to mount some experimental pilot projects, to see what kinds of analogue of the Open University might be needed at other academic levels.

There is a good deal of talk, as some of you know in Britain, about the possible need for some kind of Institute for Broadcasting, something which is capable of developmental thinking, and if need be, developmental research of a kind that perhaps the broadcasting organizations are not themselves best equipped to undertake. I'll go on a little bit about that because I felt, on reading these reports, that although people had spoken about that level, we've not perhaps been sufficiently concrete, in terms of how you actually administer it. What kind of machinery do you need? And I suppose that if I'm to be sitting here as a bureaucrat, I have to ask bureaucratic questions like that.

Just below that level, though, we are talking about the summits of the educational and broadcasting systems. These need to be using research to inform policy. Below that again, middle management, below that again if this is the right way of describing the pyramid, production.

Producers or production teams don't always need research. I sometimes got the feeling that some of my research colleagues felt that in an ideal world there would actually be enough money and enough researchers to make sure that nobody ever made a programme or sent anything by mass medium without properly pre-testing and evaluating. A very strange, imperialist ambition that, because surely one needs to be thinking in terms of a fine tennis player. If you take a tennis player, then he doesn't need to be coached for every stroke of every game. But it is good that he has recourse to the judgements of the coach, and it is even better that he has a video facility to enable him to see from time to time an action replay. Now the relationship I would have thought between a researcher and an evaluator on the one hand, and a production person on the other is rather like that. From time to time you need to be knowing what you are doing. You need to be coming much more aware of the purposes you are serving.

This idea was very nicely put, the members of one group thought, at the end of Graeme Kemelfield's paper (no 31):

> Research and evaluation can in a sense tie both producers and teachers to the range of children's reactions to programmes, and the variables which influence them, and must provide greater awareness and knowledge of the complexities of the communications process. What research and evaluation is unlikely to be able to achieve is scientific formulae for production, which will enable producers to adopt precise presentation techniques, in order to obtain predictable results and reactions on the parts of their audiences. The research described here would seem to indicate conclusively that the network of interacting variables—producers' style, the experience and preconceptions which children bring to a programme, classroom mood, and the influence of the classroom teacher—are not amenable to strict control, nor does such an aim appear to be attractive to schools' broadcasters at least in the context of British broadcasting—and nor, one would have hoped, anywhere else in the world.

Of course this collaboration surely is meant simply to make us as producers more discriminating, more aware of what we are doing, like my saying to my friend Claire Chovil at the back of the room from time to time, 'Can I be heard?' I don't want Claire Chovil nodding throughout this talk that I can be heard, but I do need from time to time to check on the technique. This surely is the relationship. Perhaps one of the reasons why people are hoping for more than that, is because, as Frank Morgan's group reports:

> Research is seen everywhere as magic. Research is reification, research is seen as an artifact, which is valued for its believed reliability, objectivity and intrinsic authority. However, it is used fairly subjectively and politically and at least in part its political power and utility lies in our belief in it.

So we owe to Frank and his group a notion that a lot of the prestige of research and evaluation stems from our superstitious awe of them.

Categories of research

I don't know whether that applies to all categories of research, but there are obviously several of these, and just as Emile was warning us of certain fashions in global labelling I suspect that there has been a touch of fashion about some of these specific labels that we have been given, as though they were some platonic entities known as 'background', 'formative', 'summative', and so on.

Not all of the groups have been equally passive, in the face of these taxonomies. Summative research was felt to be useful, by some, and by others thought to be only applicable in a very narrow range of situations—an insufficiently dialectical concept, not particularly useful. People then did seem to have very different concepts of what summative research meant and very different judgements on whether it is valuable or not. But were there not, some of us have asked, types of research not represented? In the end it was all based on agricultural or medical or social science survey models. 'What about history?' was a question being very forcefully put.

Then—I suppose this is partly my own view rather than anything that has come right out of the research reports—I'm interested in the kind of research that stems from a different perspective altogether. What about research that stems from social critique if one could call it that? Tony, in introducing me, talked about a study I did some years ago on the London Libraries. It certainly had the goodwill of the Library Association, but it was not sponsored by them and it was not the kind of research that ever would have been sponsored by them; and are we not interested in research that does not stem, if we are broadcasters, from within the broadcasting organization?

Just to give one instance of this, there's some research going on at the University of Glasgow at the moment. This is not into educational broadcasting, but never mind. Nor am I concerned here with whether this is particularly good research or not, and I know that a lot of broadcasters are unhappy about it. But in principle it seems to be extremely valuable that the University of Glasgow has a unit which is studying the way in which industrial relations are presented in television news, and analysing television news in order to identify the pre-dispositions of television news makers. How do they treat subjects in this kind of field? It is very important that there is some kind of outside critical body based in a University, since they are much more likely to undertake this kind of research than a broadcasting organization. The broadcasting organizations are already showing a certain defensiveness in the face of that research.

It also seemed to me that the way the papers were structured, there was almost a tendency to think that research had to stem from inside the organization, which might from time to time look outside for allies. But surely we should be accepting that there are decision-makers outside the media, and outside the educational establishment who need research, who might need their own kind of investigation.

Put it another way—and this did come straight off two or three of the reports—the audience itself is a decision-maker as well. Now that is, if you like, a very over-simplified way of putting it, but it is surely an extremely important dimension, because there has been a tendency for us somehow to have been so concerned with the efficiency of our own system, that we have not been sufficiently concerned with the accountability of that system, and the relevance of research to that accountability.

A question in my own mind was: 'Do various kinds of background research really "represent" consumers or the audience?' It's like saying: 'Is market research democratic or manipulative?' and one isn't going to stay and answer that question right now. There were other categories again from Frank Morgan's group: 'seductive', 'sedative', 'latent', 'blatant'. And perhaps when Naomi McIntosh comes back in ten years time to discuss these things with us we will be into seductive research in a big way.

Factors affecting relationships between research and decision-making

I start with, if Peter Dannheisser and Ian Haldane will forgive me, a candid reference to their paper (no 12), which refers to an extremely useful, valuable, well-conceived piece of research undertaken by them for the Independent Broadcasting Authority. It would not be true to say that no notice whatsoever was taken of it, but it would be true to say that very little notice was taken of it, and that of a purely superstitious and political kind. It contains a great many insights into the interests of the audience, and anybody who was so minded (though nobody was) could use the information that it contains to work out very valuable teaching strategies.

I suspect there were two reasons for it not being so used. One was that it came from a remote body, the Independent Broadcasting Authority, full of grey men who don't actually make programmes, and therefore not likely to be taken seriously by the alive and virile men in the companies who do actually make programmes. The second reason was I suppose that they (the young men, the virile men, I mean) were not actually involved in the process of designing it and deciding what it was all about.

So it may be relevant to this business of relationships that people should, for many purposes, share a common institutional framework. This is beautifully exemplified, if you like, in the Open University, and in Children's Television Workshop. There are other models appearing also (remembering though as I have said just now, that for *some* categories of research I think it is important that they should *not* share the same framework. The researchers need sometimes to be accountable elsewhere than to the broadcasting or the educational institution).

Producers and other decision-makers should understand about research. Many people have said this and it does seem a fairly basic sentiment that we are uttering in this final session. That means understanding what it is for, what it is reasonable to expect of research. It often seems to me that researchers can't win, because either they are told that they are only producing information which is already in the hands of the decision-makers (the 'I know that already' response), or they are accused of being obscure and irrelevant. It's sometimes exceedingly difficult for them to communicate, not because they are obscure of utterance (although they are) but because there are unreasonable expectations of them in the minds of the decision-makers.

Researchers conversely need to understand about production and other forms of decision-making. The constraints that are imposed upon decision-makers, such that they ignore the findings of research, is not as I was hinting earlier always irrational. Researchers need to understand the strictly backroom position of research. They are not driving, they are providing the headlights.

The whole question of demeanour between these two categories is very important indeed. A good example of how demeanour can be improved is the suggestion that dialogue rather than the exchange of turgid memoranda might sometimes be adopted between these two consenting parties. It has implications, all of this, for the education and training of personnel. The producer, as manager of a team, needs to learn how to include a researcher in that team, the producer needs to be literate enough, to know about, and to read research, or at any rate to have heard of sources.

Somebody this morning was talking about Wilbur Schramm's *Big media, Little media*.[1] Somebody in one of the groups was talking about Joe Trenaman's book *Communication and Comprehension*,[2] which is now ten years old, and certainly contains a lot of answers to the questions that were put, as though they were new questions, in the course of these three days. This kind of reference has come out of several of the groups, that decision-makers need an appropriate kind of training and education. Conversely researchers need to be educated as diplomats, knowing where power really lies, and then there is the whole difficult business of the researcher writing limpid and lucid prose.

This takes us to the possibility of decision-makers themselves taking part in the research, thereby being committed to it, thereby understanding it, helping to initiate it, helping to design the question, helping to design the research. For a good exposition of this see the paper by Margaret Gallagher (no 16). This does not necessarily mean that research somehow insists on the insertion of element X, because X can be tested, or that research suffocates creativity with all its beautiful human risks and uncertainty.

Researchers will also understand that decision-makers often want results quickly, like yesterday, and they want it quick and dirty. And paradoxically we can often get quick and dirty pretesting facilities, in some countries at any rate, by collaboration between closed circuit people in institutions of higher education and open circuit people. Not enough perhaps is made of some of those opportunities there. But generally speaking, surely there is a greater need for more interplay between broadcasting researchers and academic research centres, much more interplay, much more dialectic between theory and practice.

More generally still it was felt that we should be concentrating emphatically on the learner as the nub of the learning system. It was interesting to see the different results of the different groups to that question: 'Is it the case that television or the TV system is at the centre of the whole decision-making nexus?' One group said: 'We rejected that unanimously', which was a little suspect in a way. There were other groups that said: 'Well . . . '. They made a very clear distinction in other words between 'ought' and 'is'. There was a grudging recognition that really television was quite fun, and furthermore if you were in the distant learning business, then the learners *were* distant, weren't they, and the thing that you were very concerned with were cameras and scripts and so on. So there was a feeling in several of the groups that television did tend to be or the decisions about broadcasting did very much seem to be at the centre of concern, while believing that maybe it ought not to be like that. There were some tributes to the Open University as one of the systems now operating that is making itself increasingly conscious of the learner out there—bringing the learner out there into here.

I suppose it would help too, to bring these parties together, if we build increasingly on the growing amount of familiarity that there is with team work, with collaborative work of all kinds. Emile was talking about the progress in ten years on his side of the house, but on the active side of the house, on the decision-making side of the house, the changes have been quite extraordinary. We are now seeing partnerships developing—not without difficulty, not without tension—between some of the most individualistic people in the world, broadcasters on the one hand, academics on the other, yet learning how to make something by collaboration which is not just demonstrative nonsense. I would have thought that out of that experience of collaboration, it will become much more apparent that the researcher or the evaluator needs, from time to time, and for those special purposes, to be part of the team.

Changes in educational broadcasting

Although we were very conscious of change and changing relationships I sometimes wonder whether we were perhaps aware enough about the way in which educational broadcasting is itself changing. The old stimulus-response model of educational broadcasting seems to be giving way to a much more open and collaborative model. More broadcasters, in all sorts of fields, not just education, are developing a feel for what I believe in Germany is called transparency. That kind of mood of openness and responsiveness in broadcasters is colouring the whole business of educational broadcasting. I think there is much more talk now about open learning systems, or partnerships, and much less talk about multi-media systems, which has an altogether more rigid, more systems-engineering, feel to it. One sees this happening in the developing countries, one sees this happening in the Netherlands, and so on.

Second, we are still talking as though research is either gathering up bits and pieces within a broadcasting organization or it was something which happened here in a university. I would have thought that if the whole business of education and message-dissemination was going to be collaborative, then surely the whole business of evaluation might be as well; that research needs now to be jointly funded, not just because it has got so expensive, which I think explains why a lot of research is now jointly funded, but because people share interests in that research.

We often need, not research, but information retrieval. There is a great deal of knowledge about, which we don't always apply, don't always use. An example is the University of Texas research on adult performance levels. What do adults need to know in order to survive in contemporary America? This is obviously a very much more penetrating question than: 'Do they know how to read or write?' That research, or similar research at the University of Saskatchewan, is surely of interest to anybody concerned with the education of adults, whether in broadcasting or not.

If that is so one can envisage major research undertakings of that kind being jointly organized jointly funded and a sense of joint responsibility in implementing and making use of it. Just a final remark, if I may, deriving loosely from the whole business, which wasn't discussed very well, the whole business of whether you can transplant cultural experience of this sort from one place to another. I think that we all realize that we have a vested interest in the answer: 'yes'. We are prone to believe that not all consultancy from persons in one country visiting another is in the realm of the fraudulent con, but that some of it does actually make sense, some of it actually is a valuable transfer of experience. Certainly speaking not only of myself, but for us all, we must be grateful to the Open University and to Tony Bates for giving us this cross-cultural opportunity to have some peer-group learning.

References

1 SCHRAMM, W. *Big Media, Little Media*, Washington, Agency for International Development, 1973.
2 TRENAMAN, J. *Communication and Comprehension*, London, Longmans, 1967.

CLOSING ADDRESS

Guest speaker   M Henri Dieuzeide, Director-General, Division of Methods, Materials and Techniques, UNESCO, Paris, France.

Chairman   Ms Jane Steedman, IBA Research Fellow, Centre for Television Research, Leeds University, UK.

HENRI DIEUZEIDE

Input

A little bit of quantitative evaluation first, before we come to a more qualitative and perhaps more clinical approach. I asked Tony how many people had come to the conference, and he said, 'Of the data available, the best is from the money collected, as usual'.* So there are 180 participants, out of which 65 are British. To these 65 British we have to add another 50 people coming from the Open University and the BBC. Apparently in Tony's classification they are neither foreign nor British. I'm not clear whether this is a sign of intellectual elitism, or whether they are transcendental to the meeting, or if this is another anthropological trait of Great Britain or the British culture, or whether they belong to what Ghandi called the Harayan, the children of God, which I think in English is translated as the untouchables. So if we add all these, we come up with a total of 230 participants. If we add to the 65 the 50 untouchables I have 115 British, which means they are almost in a minority. They then managed to force the majority of foreigners to speak English—even the Americans. This is very nice, a very smooth UNESCO job. The non-British, the 115, come from 29 different countries, 11 countries which are classified as developed, and from 18 developing countries.

Now what categories are participants? My evaluation becomes a little more difficult, more fuzzy, because there is no clear quantification yet. The declared evaluators and researchers appeared to be a minority, a vocal one, but a minority. Producers are said to be a vast majority, because of this block of the untouchables, and an interesting trait is that managers and decision-makers are mostly from developing countries. There will be more data in the final report I hope.**

I have calculated that, in view of the fact that there are 230 participants, there has been a total of about 4,500 man hours of common work. These 4,500 hours of contribution to this common task have been preceded by the submission of 350,000 words in the working papers and the reports which have been distributed to you. This will represent more than a 1,000

---

* The figures given in this report are the correct figures. The differences between these and those given originally are not large, and do not significantly affect what M Dieuzeide said.

** Of the 180 full participants:
   47 (26 per cent) were policy-makers/managers
   32 (18 per cent) were media producers
   85 (47 per cent) were researchers/evaluators
   16 (9 per cent) were users.

printed pages, which means that the conference has produced probably between 300,000 to 400,000 printed sheets of paper. (How many trees, Tony?) This represents a considerable investment by the Open University and by yourselves in terms of mobilization of human resources, in the preparation and the running of this conference, in time and effort, which in my mind should represent a critical mass.

Output

To try and evaluate the output of course we have to beware of two contradictory feelings which we all face at the end of an international gathering. The first one is *euphoria*. We have discovered some kind of community of interest, some solidarity has developed. At the same time, *frustration*, because we feel we have achieved very little, and we have discovered from experience that international inter-cultural exchange is a very slow process.

But if I come to some of the things that have struck me as being original contributions from this meeting, first of course is the exchange of information. We have learned a lot of facts and experiences. According to many participants a common language has developed. We know more about the global implications of research, about the needs, explicit versus implicit, the distinction between evaluation and research, and so on and so forth. Therefore we have tried to find a common language to cover a very vast field.

The paradox is of course that this conference is organized by the Open University, where broadcasting takes only a small part of the general teaching and learning activity. The other paradox is that we have talked supposedly about media, but in fact we've talked mostly about broadcasting, and in fact we've talked practically only about television, which has been in the centre of our thoughts, almost all the time. And this to me is a very interesting and striking fact and I'm not going to analyse it any further, but this raises problems for people from developing countries.

The second thing that I see emerging from the conference is a new awareness of the research and evaluation problems, as they have been very clearly evinced by the reports this morning. There is, from all I have heard, a lot of individual interiorization of the need for more research, and new angles for approaching the problems of research have also been identified. I have noted by going from group to group that there is also a lot of realism developing as regards evaluation—and also perhaps a certain amount of cynicism as regards the problem of decision-making. I don't think we should expand too much on the cynicism, but it was there.

A third aspect I find interesting is that we gathered a lot of material which is already formalized, and which probably will lend itself, with some amendment, for publication. What I would like also to see, together with this material, is probably more recognition of the problems in the existing national and international journals. I think to put pressure on such organs would probably be a better strategy than to develop a specialized publication, because the more papers there are, the less they are read, of course.

Another indication of output is follow-up, national and international. You're going, some or most of you, I hope, to get together to discuss continuing links, which shows that a gathering of this type is *not an end but a start* of better co-operation.

Another interesting output of this conference that I noticed was a new method of working during the conference itself, which I think will prove valuable for other conferences of this kind. The methods which have been used are not without risk. The technique which has been used is not exactly the one of the academic tradition. It more resembles what I would call group therapy, by putting together people coming from various fields, organizing mixes, and seeing how they work. Apparently the mixes among professional responsibilities were rather satisfactory. The national mixes were also it seems satisfactory, (but there were complaints, I understand, that sex was not used as a variable in organizing these mixes!) I would also suggest perhaps that to progress beyond the cynical attitude which developed in relations between researchers and decision-makers, that another meeting dealing with similar problems could use more advanced techniques, like perhaps *role-playing*, but this is for the organizing committee to brood over.

The final outcome for a conference, of course, is that each of us has been alerted to some critical issue and each of us is bringing back to his own work some more worries, and some more uncertainties, and I would like to add my own contribution. Of course, these thoughts were evoked by listening to you, especially this morning. As a reference base, I'll use the three basic themes of the conference: the findings of research, the methods, and the relations between researcher and decision-making, and I will conclude on some international implications.

The need for a philosophy of educational communication

I was quite interested, not disappointed, but interested to see that the findings seem to be *more media-centred than system-centred*, and they were more product-oriented than process-oriented. I won't dwell on this point because this was dealt with at length this morning. This showed that there is still a certain type of attitude to the use of media in education, which perhaps is not the most advanced one. Why?

I think that the discussions have shown the need for a better theoretical framework for reference and orientation. I liked the participant who reminded us that there is nothing as practical as a good theory. This is very true when one looks at the reports which we have gathered for the conference. Reading through the juxtaposed findings, even through the impressive batch of research which has been developed by the Open University, a foreign expert has some difficulty in orientating himself and seeing what is the underlying rationale. There was also some apprehension expressed by some participants in face of an implicit ideology based on pragmatic values. There is some risk in offering instrumentalist thinking as a universally accepted theory.

I would like to go a little further into this, in the form of a question. Isn't there a need at an international level for a better consciousness of the implicit ideologies which are underlying the application of communication to education? I'd like to put to you: what makes the educational communicators tick? Skinner? MacLuhan? Paulo Freire and his Utopia of Conscientization? Theories of autodidactism? Probably not Illich, to the extent that these educational communicators belong to institutions. What kind of pattern do they want to develop? The ecologist approach to the learning environment? The programme-cybernetic approach based on algorithms of learning? I think there is quite some indecision on what finally we are talking about and what we are trying to be part of. How long can this kind of soft-belly situation stand up to the challenge of hard, economic systems for some kind of educational solution? To what extent can this last much longer in the face of new, political, social, economic options and projects in society, in the face of new socio-economic orders being discussed in such instances as the United Nations? This is my question: is there room for a universally significant theory of educational communication which would help research and evaluation to define its own place and its own value? These are questions. I only have questions—I am sorry!

The future

Another question I have is: what about the future? I have been rightly or wrongly under the impression that little was said of the future, except by people who stuck their neck out like Brian Groombridge this morning. Have we not the tendency to act as if we were to last forever in the same pattern, as if educational broadcasting was a kind of given, a fact of God? We were told by several people, and especially I think by Richmond Postgate, that educational broadcasting has changed enormously in the past 25 years. To what extent can we try to orient our research towards the future?

Secondly, what is the future of research? We have very few findings about the ways and means to protect flexibility in systems. There were interesting indications about some institutions that have managed to find through research more flexibility—the case of the Japan Secondary School System was given, the case of Telekolleg also. Both went from formal secondary education to some kind of adult education. There were examples given also of non-survival because of lack of adaptability. The best case in point I think is Telescuola, which didn't foresee the fact that one day it wouldn't be useful any more as it stood, because the kind of schools that it was supposed to replace were being built very quickly. To what extent will there be a revolution in the demand, in the needs, in terms of process and not of product, of production by the learner of his own knowledge? What evolution of the structure of media, towards new access, towards new approaches, like the uses of portable video will there be? There were not very many indications, and should not research try and be involved, so that not only decision-makers but also researchers, be not taken by surprise? The sad story of cable television shows that perhaps if research had warned about the limitation of the needs—assessment that had been conducted, if there had been a better evaluation of its cost-effectiveness and of the possibility of investment in cable television, the clock would not have been set back ten years.

So there are some remarks I had about the problem of the shape of the future. We are not enough *future-oriented*, and this is a general problem of education, of course. I've been studying the problem of training of teacher trainers. I discovered to my surprise, with a very simple kind of calculation, that the influence that we are exerting through the training of teacher trainers is more than we expect, and that it extends beyond the century. If we train today a teacher trainer, this teacher trainer will train teachers, who will teach children, who will be active citizens by the year 2,100. This is frightening. Our present attitude has some kind of effect through a chain of events we can't control, but has or should have immediate effects more than a hundred years ahead. This is frightening, but this is also reassuring, because we are the product of this kind of situation. We ourselves are obviously a product of the values of the year 1850. This has a lot of meaning I think for us.

So the need for *more flexibility* in systems, in institutions, is absolutely necessary. And the study of the new configurations which are coming and which go beyond the truck driver's weather communiqué which we talked about last night, and to which Brian alluded this morning, namely the development of the two-way flow of communication and the new forms of participative learning, all this is research helping us in understanding what it means and how it could shape the future of education.

Appropriate methodologies

I have more questions now about methods. And the first one was taken up by Emile McAnany this morning, and deals with the problem of culture-free methods. I wonder to what extent most of the measurement techniques that I see tried in various countries are really culture-free. I even wonder to what extent evaluation itself is not part and parcel at present of the ideology of the western world, to the extent that they are based on the ideas of productivity, effectiveness, individual competition, analysis, engineering, more than on the values of ecological balance, group elaboration, collective development, that may well be the raison d'être of other cultures. So this to me is a very important problem.

I was absolutely fascinated by discussions we had in our group on the problem of techniques based on opinion surveys used in developing countries, and which break against rural cultures of silence and acceptance. Should we go to people who do not articulate their needs, and their desires, who may have no explicit desire, with these kinds of technique, which represent an entirely different set of values? Can we try and develop for developing countries, within developing countries, with the specialists that we are training for these countries, new methodologies that are relevant to their culture?

This leads me to a question which is very near this one, and which is the need for simplified low-cost evaluation techniques. The need for the international community at large, and the need for developing countries, and certainly the ultimate aim of measurement, after all, is not quantity, but quality. Therefore can we develop quick and dirty techniques? We had there again very fascinating examples coming from India and Botswana, testing scripts and elements of a programme, rather than the whole of a programme. Can we try and standardize such techniques? Can we give them universal circulation? We are trying in UNESCO to gather evaluation techniques for our own projects, and we would like to have as much support as possible for the development of these soft, appropriate technologies of evaluation. There is international value at large in this effort, and I think those who are developing them should be proud of them.

I was quite displeased by the reaction of one of our most effective participants at this conference, who said about some of these techniques, 'I wouldn't imagine one minute having them published in a professional paper'. What are these professional papers that don't accept that kind of effort? Shouldn't we change the criteria of professionality, if they are such? I think we should develop the circulation of these new attitudes. I think these quick and dirty methods, or instruments rather, are especially valid for the improvement of the product, for formative evaluation, where you have to fight against time and lack of resources more than anywhere else.

Decision-making and research

In decision-making, a lot of issues were raised. Obviously this was a powder casket. The problem of legitimate power has been lurking in the background of the discussion all the time. I think that any study of the decision-making process should take into account more clearly the problem of the infra-structure, the hierarchy, and the mechanisms of decision-making. The whole bureaucratic culture should be studied more carefully. There are internal tensions, interactions, that have to be identified, if the researcher wants his product to be of some use. Of course, there was the famous McKinsey study of the BBC, but I know of few recent studies on the sociology of institutions of communication, with reference to the decision-making process, even less of course of educational institutions. So this research, if it were undertaken, would not be marginal. It's central to the kind of ontology we have been trying to develop, especially this morning. We could be led to abandon the linear approach we have been developing here, and replace that with a multi-dimensional matrix, (even if Brian Groombridge finds that uncomfortable to lie on!).

Someone said, 'Let's train no more naïve evaluators'. This idea I like. I think we have to improve our knowledge of how our decision-makers think, under which constraints, along which patterns. This is important if, after having discovered that evaluation tends to reinforce solutions that have already been opted for by decision-makers, we want to alter this fact.

I have tried in this respect to identify summative evaluations which have been used to bring a project to an end. I was indicated one, only one, but someone else very aptly remarked that if there is a case of sudden death for a project, the formative evaluation becomes *de facto* summative.

To sum up my first impressions of the discussions, I found, to use a saying we probably all treasure, that decision-makers are using research as drunkards use lamp posts, not to look around but to lean upon.

The second point I noted in this problem of decision-making in relation to research was the role of the affective element. I noted a lot of beautiful qualifications. 'Evaluation has to be swept under the carpet'. Emotional involvement is a dominant factor in research, and this has been one of the fascinating experiences in listening to you, because I have tried to connect that to the larger credo I have that the whole of the education system is in some way a deeply irrational process. Any educational planner, any economist will tell you that the demand for education is absolutely irrational. We all know that the teaching relation is irrational. We know that motivation is more essential than cognitive aptitude, and so on and so forth.

Therefore what is the function of research? Can we say that researchers have to reduce the irrational elements in the educational system? I would say, yes, but what is the degree of irrationality that can be compressed by research? This to me is a very important point which we could think about.

Now a lot has been said about the real functions of research, of course. I like the idea that the content of research, however important, may be less important than the new attitudes that research can generate within an institution, that it has a double function of conscience, reminding one of existing objectives and to what extent they have been reached, and also pointing to the existence of new objectives.

This has to be done of course within the development of inter-disciplinary attitudes, and I could also sense this in relation to my first point, the lack of a theoretical framework or a fundamental rationale for research. There is more sensitivity than in the past for inter-disciplinary work, and many people are on the lookout for contributions from other sciences. This I think should become systematic, because, after all, educational research is *not a science of its own,* but lies at the margins of various other human sciences. This approach to research taken in this meeting seemed to me extremely fertile.

This kind of research will help those that are responsible for communication less to decide than to implement. The big, basic, ultimate decisions are likely to be outside the power of evaluators and researchers. Especially in developing countries, problems such as the appalling quality of the educational system, or the need for strengthening national unity, for developing a new alternative configuration, for serving many local strategies, all these big ultimate decisions, because of the political aspects of such decisions, are outside the scope of evaluation. But evaluation is there to help *implement* the big decisions, to help make the subsequent sub-decisions, to serve the application. Another phrase I heard that I liked, 'Evaluation is less there to prove than to improve'. This means nevertheless that work has to be done on alternatives. I found surprisingly little assistance to be passed on to countries that are faced with priorities. Multi-media approach or one medium? Choice between media? Media or no media? For instance, teacher training *or* television? On this definitely more data are needed.

Now the technique of dialogue in decision-making was another point which interested me very much. It was obvious that the conference started talking about the relation between producer and researcher, but that little by little this grew bigger—so far as to embrace the idea of a general dialogue of researchers with all the components. As Sten Sture Allebeck has said, there is not only a Director-General who takes decisions. Everybody in the system is responsible at one level or the other.

The question is immediately posed: should roles therefore be better defined within the system, or should we adopt or recommend more flexible attitudes? On this I have mixed feelings. I wonder to what extent what a researcher writes is always research, and I wonder if all research is always written by researchers. (I'm not going to develop this because this touches on corporative problems.) But I would recommend that the suggestions about team work as opposed to separate functions be pursued, the idea of joint responsibility, of *common accountability*, is, I think, one of the new important ideas which are developing at present, thanks to this conference.

Perhaps also this flexibility could be combined with more mobility. Is there any possibility of swopping roles within an institution of education or communication? To what extent could an evaluator become a decision-maker? To what extent could a producer become an evaluator? Very few instances of this were given during the conference. But this is very important, because probably this attitude of evaluation, if generalized, could be the training school for everybody involved in the process. I could develop this point but we all sense that these kinds of discussion are very fundamental, that they raise far-reaching questions on the global problem, of the role of the researcher in human groups. It ties in with the function of the researcher, his status, his effective power, in a modern society, and also his involvement and commitment to the progress of human society.

International implications

I would like to conclude on the problem of international implications. The first problem I would like to raise has been on my mind from the beginning. It is the problem of *intellectual dependence.* I have to explain what I mean. There's been some talk about technological dependence during this conference. Taking the responsibility to develop some sophisticated system in developing countries creates some kind of special relation of dependence between these countries and the donor advanced, sophisticated countries. Now I think that this development of technological dependence which very often results from educational technology developments, also applies to the problem of research and the results of research.

I'm struck by the fact that we are so often prisoners of preconceptions, images, myths, and how little informed we are very often of the reality of research on education. There are hidden opinion leaders, who peddle myths. And we are dependent on insufficient networks of information. I would like some research to be done some day on how myths on educational communication can develop, how images of success or failure develop within an international community. This is not necessarily linked with scientific evidence. There are the mystics of innovation, there are the myths of technical development, the prestige of delivery systems.

I'll take only one example. My contemporaries may remember that ten years ago the Samoan experiment was presented as the most successful in reaching its objectives through the use of television, and what is the image of the Samoan experiment today? Here's a myth which has completely vanished, so I would like us later perhaps to talk some other year, in some other instances, about this very basic problem.

Of course things can be done immediately to improve the quality of this international exchange. And of course there have been proposals already that UNESCO should do something about it, about improving the circulation of information, assisting people in the transfer of technology. As you know there is a UNESCO programme about this. I am not going to describe it; this is not the time for any publicity. But are we certain that we are at present making the best of all resources that already exist in the field of international communication, in terms of publication, networks, professional non-governmental organizations and so on? Should there be an attempt somewhere at an evaluation leading to optimizing these resources at the national level?

UNESCO has just published for instance the report on Open Learning.[1] We are planning in June a report on cost-effectiveness, which has been reached from an analysis of 200 studies, and which will help set up a network of institutions involved in cost-effectiveness study. We are helping some who have started this work about two years ago, trying to answer the need that was expressed today. UNESCO did give support to quite a few institutions in the field of educational technology, the International Council for Educational Media, with which we are developing this cost-effectiveness study, with the assistance of the International Council for Film and Television, with the National Broadcasting Institute, etc. So I would recommend that in each country we look better at the *existing resources* before asking for more. Let's look first at making full use of these existing resources.

Conclusion

Now I would like to have dealt more with the problem of transfer of techniques, the 'adapt, not adopt' approach, the development of appropriate methods for research, the development of a joint approach for quick and dirty methods, the need for comparative studies, but I think enough has been said this morning on this.

But I cannot however avoid making some reference to the book that some of you know probably well. It's called, *The Report of the Third International Conference on Educational Radio and Television*,[2] which was organized in Paris in March 1967. Part of the book is entitled 'Evaluation'. I'm not going to read that part of the book, although you should, and I advise you to do so. These were the topics which are described:

> needs and users of research and broadcasting;
> ways to make research usable to broadcasters;
> present findings that might be applied;
> working groups reporting on the requirements for exchanging and disseminating research results;
> problems of co-operative research between countries;
> and problems of terminology which make it difficult to share research results between researchers of different countries, and between researchers and broadcasters.

This makes excellent reading. At the same time, this is a very sad mention. Why is it that so little is followed-up? This was ten years ago. Where do we stand now? What can be done about it? Here is something that can be discussed in the continuing links session.

I have only one request to the organizers for future common research. Perhaps the subject 'try and identify significant differences between the educational effectiveness of organizations with an evaluation service, and organizations which have not an evaluation service', would be a worthwhile kind of research. I've tried to follow the instructions that decision-makers always give to researchers: 'do not confuse me with facts.' I've done my best, and to the managers in this room I would remind you of what Chesterton used to say of virtue, and which I think applies very well to evaluation: 'It is not that it was tried and found difficult—it is that it was found difficult and therefore not tried.'

References

1 McKENZIE, N., POSTGATE, R. and SCUPHAM, J. *Open Learning Systems in Post-Secondary Education*, Paris, UNESCO, 1976.
2 EUROPEAN BROADCASTING UNION, *Third EBU International Conference on Educational Radio and Television*, Paris, ORTF, 1967.

GROUP DISCUSSIONS: ADDITIONAL POINTS

Because of the pressure of time, both in preparation and presentation, all three main rapporteurs wanted us to include in the proceedings those main points raised in the discussions that the main rapporteurs did not have space to include, although we doubt that this will be as useful as the 'quick and dirty' reports that they prepared.

THEME 1: RESEARCH FINDINGS

Of the three themes discussed, Theme 1 was by far the most difficult to summarize. The discussions on this theme took place on the first full working day of the Conference, and consequently each participant had to get to know the other members of his or her group. Inevitably, there was a good deal of delicate probing and establishing of roles in the groups on the first day. Also, as Viviane Glikman reported, there was genuine doubt in many of the groups about the transferability of research results and a concern about the lack of any strong or explicit theoretical framework for the use of educational media. Another reason was more mundane, but still important. Many of the participants had clearly not been able to find time to read through all the 60-odd papers that had been distributed in advance, and consequently were unaware of some of the relevant studies. Add to these reasons tiredness from long-distance travelling, and a different cultural environment for many, and it is not surprising that the discussions on this theme lacked the clarity of those on the following two days.

> **Q. 1** *Use of television to motivate learning*

Five groups discussed this question to some length. A distinction was made by two groups between using television or radio to get people interested in learning in the first place ('open' systems), and using television or radio to motivate students already enrolled in a multi-media course ('closed' systems). This distinction was important, because of the differing expectations about programmes of the two kinds of audience. Research showed that programmes for 'open' target audiences had to be entertaining and attractive, but for students enrolled in 'closed' systems, relevance and helpfulness in learning were more crucial than entertainment.

One group also pointed out that where courses lead to professional or recognized academic qualifications, it is the qualification rather than the media which is the main motivator. Indeed, motivation may work the other way round, in that if the programmes are directly related to assessment or the examination, then this will motivate students to watch or listen to the programmes.

> **Q. 2** *The implications of individual differences in learners*

One group reported that students on the same course will vary in their reactions to different components of a multi-media course, and that therefore the *variety* provided by different media helped to some extent to allow for different learning styles. For instance, it was suggested that loosely structured television programmes were more likely to be suited to associative thinkers, while print material would be more suited to linear thinkers.

Several groups drew attention to the need for training students in how to use television for study purposes, and agreed that in general the more able students or children benefited more from television, because they had better general learning skills. If television was aimed at the more deprived, a specific style of programming appropriate to such audiences must be developed, requiring formative research based on the reactions of the specific target audience being aimed at (e.g. *Sesame Street* and the Indian Pre-production Research Unit). There was some doubt expressed in one or two groups about the value of the teacher in helping to cope with different responses to the same programme, since teachers themselves were often unskilled in using media.

It was generally agreed that not enough attention is being paid to individual differences, either by researchers or producers.

> **Q. 3** *Elements responsible for successful applications of media*

There was considerable overlap in the discussion of this question with the discussions of Questions 5, 7 and 8. Several groups discussed at length the need to ensure that media met the real needs of the people, although one group believed that an overemphasis on needs assessment research can reflect a *lack* of clear goals. Rather than spend time on needs assessment, this group thought systems should attempt to serve reasonably clear pre-existing needs. Some research had indicated the need to look beyond the programmes themselves, to the social and political factors which lead to success or failure in using educational media.

One or two groups discussed particular programme policies which had been researched. For instance, the SITE studies in India found that animation did not generally work with rural adults or children, and that programmes which initially relied on the teacher as an intermediary did not work as well as self-sufficient programmes, because teachers were not able to intervene in the special circumstances in which programmes are viewed in rural villages in India.

Several groups commented on research showing that more effort was necessary to communicate with and train teachers in the use of media.

> **Q. 4** *Accumulating and disseminating a body of knowledge*

Most groups discussed this question. There was a very strong emphasis on the need for team work, with researchers and producers working closely together. One group felt that producers should have some research training, and researchers should have some production training. Another group pointed to the need for research to concentrate on areas where the educational broadcaster has a continuous, long-term commitment to specific educational goals. *Ad hoc* projects, with the illusive hope of rapid solution to complex problems, can hardly be helped by research. Another group felt that theory and practice in educational broadcasting were too far divorced from one another, and that the research, planning, production, and evaluation process should be on-going, in which educational theories and media use were combined to test explicit hypotheses, so that a body of knowledge could be built up.

Q. 5 *Integrating different media in multi-media presentations*

Q. 7 *The outcomes that media can bring about*

Q. 8 *When and where not to use television and radio*

These three questions were usually dealt with together in most groups, and a major part of Viviane Glikman's presentation was concerned with these issues (what she called the 'specificity of media'). One group argued that decisions about 'which' media to use require carefully thought out criteria for selection, but another group stated that at present decisions are based on intuitive hypotheses, not on a systematic analysis of the learning process and the characteristics of media as educational tools.

Two groups independently emphasized the need for a better understanding of the learning process, of *how* students learn from television, before better criteria can be provided for the selection of different media. One group pointed out that there was too much emphasis on what producers and planners wanted to know immediately. In the long run, answers to such questions depended on a better understanding of learning processes, but this kind of research was all too often seen as academic and not dealing with real issues.

Another group saw a conflict between the academic approach, which very much uses analytic methods, and television's capacity to provide a 'holistic' approach to the presentation of knowledge. This was reflected in the dilemma of whether to present unstructured or loosely structured material in television programmes, thereby allowing students to interpret and use the material in a variety of ways to suit their own purpose (another way of dealing with the problem of individual differences), or whether to present carefully structured material, which demands less in the way of learning skills, but which often proves to be boring and unimaginative.

Q. 6 *Do we underestimate the effectiveness of educational television?*

Few groups reported on this. The problem of using paper and pencil techniques to test what is primarily a visual medium was mentioned—it may well be that certain kinds of learning take place which are never adequately tested. The need for researchers to have a clear idea of *producers'* objectives was also stressed by one group, otherwise the researchers may be missing important outcomes. One group felt that the unintended side-effects of educational broadcasting had been ignored and required serious attention, but another group pointed out that research and evaluation were usually concerned with short-term effects, and in any case were not funded sufficiently to discover long-term effects.

Q. 9 *Role of media in bringing about educational reforms*

One group pointed out the importance of television as a catalyst for change—prompting or setting into operation new social organizations, such as the adult literacy project with which the BBC is associated, or curriculum reform, as in El Salvador. In-service teacher training in particular was seen as an important and useful role for television and radio in many countries.

On the other hand, one or two groups were less confident on this subject. The use of *broadcast* media for some types of education appeared to be limited. For example, much of education is concerned with 'animation' of sections of the community. This concerns groups which do not identify with traditional learning structures, who have informational needs, but have not expressed them, and may not even be aware of them. For these groups, work at the person-to-person level using media such as portable video as a catalyst, was needed before such people were likely to identify with formal courses. Also, one group noted that the hardware was usually manufactured by profit-making corporations, or by organizations trying to 'sell' a certain ideology as well, and consequently the introduction of television need not always result in 'reforms'.

Q. 10 *Cost-benefit advantages of educational television and radio*

The first day was obviously too soon for most to tackle this difficult question. Virtually nothing was reported on this question, except for one group that felt that the terms 'cost-effective' and 'cost-benefit' are at the present time meaningless.

Q. 11 *Judging the value of research*

There was considerable criticism in several groups of research reports being unreadable or written merely for other researchers. Good research should sensitize producers to the questions they should ask about their own programmes—and provide suggestions as to what would constitute a good answer. More information on research from different countries was desirable, since relatively generalizable results can help producers just as much as researchers. Very often, though, research findings were not easily available to others, and a list of information centres with a note on their functions and publications is needed.

THEME 2: METHODOLOGY

Q. 1 *Distinctions between evaluation and research*

Groups 3, 4, 5, 6, 7, 8 and 9 tackled this question; and their reports showed a fair degree of consensus. Drawing on their own words, this consensus could be expressed in the following table:

Evaluation	Research
More specific in purpose.	More general in purpose.
Concerned with practical and immediate application.	Concerned with building up a sound body of theory.
More short-term.	More long-term.
Directed towards decisions.	Directed towards conclusions.

Most of the groups thought these were useful distinctions, but there was a danger of over-stressing them. The most important qualities were clarity of purpose and definition of objectives.

Q. 2 *The range and choice of methodologies*

All the groups spent some time on this and generally accepted the alternatives posed by Richard Hooper. In addition the following distinctions were made:

Formative studies (with all the problems of time pressure) and summative studies (the problem of too long and too late).

'Quick and dirty' (useful for broad-sweep decisions) and elaborate (necessary for long-term effects).

Survey research and experimental research (each determined by the objectives).

Evaluation of 'policy' decisions, 'production' decisions and 'use' decisions (each demanding its own methodology).

Evaluation in closed systems (audience already identified) and in open systems (audience to be discovered).

Large-scale evaluation and individual ('do it yourself') evaluation.

The anthropological approach of illuminative research compared with highly statistical research.

Research based on cognitive and affective criteria (demanding separate methodologies).

Research into needs and research into effects (again demanding separate methodologies).

Short-term research and cumulative research.

Most of the groups stressed that choice of methodology must depend on a careful assessment of the purpose of the evaluation. It should be the purpose that decided the choice, not the predisposed interests of the researcher.

Two groups also made a strong recommendation that the study of methodology should apply to the reporting and dissemination of the research findings as well as to the research itself. Too much research effort became wasted effort in poor reporting. It was essential that researchers should study the most effective way to make known their results—whenever possible in consultation with the potential users of the results.

In most cases this led naturally to:

Q. 3 *The independence or otherwise of the evaluator*

Groups 1, 3, 4, 6, 7 and 9 all reported on this question. Some doubts needed to be resolved about whether 'independent' meant 'objective in approach' or 'working outside the production department or organization'. It was generally taken to mean 'independent of the production discipline'.

Within these terms, four groups made the point that it is almost always better to have formative evaluation conducted within the production team or with close collaboration between the researcher and the producer. Summative evaluation may often be more effective if conducted by an external evaluator. In all cases it was hoped that the results would be openly reported. One group reported that a range of evaluators had proved to be the best solution, with varying degrees of proximity to the production operation.

Q. 4 *Relation of costs to benefits in evaluation*

Only Groups 5, 6 and 7 tackled this question. Their reports agreed that such a relation was only possible in very broad terms—and these terms should be social and political rather than strictly financial. Any attempt to draw a precise financial relationship would inevitably produce a distorted picture of the situation, which should be seen in educational and social terms. There were many examples of clear social benefits of research which could be assessed financially only in the very broadest way.

It was further reported that no uniform criterion of benefit should be applied to the wide variety of research projects. At the same time a measure of cost-benefit analysis should be attempted for every project, on the lines outlined above.

Q. 5   *Value judgements and methodological considerations*

All groups commented briefly on this question and all accepted that individual evaluators must *have* value judgements about the project they are evaluating. Whether they should *give* such judgements, and if so when, was a more sensitive question. It was generally felt that the most effective way of avoiding such judgements having undue influence on methodology was by ensuring that decisions on objectives and methodology were taken jointly by policy-makers, producers and evaluators.

Phrases such as 'common understanding', 'mutual acceptance of each other's values' and 'close working relationships' occurred repeatedly through the reports.

Q. 6   *Evaluating the evaluation*

No report attempted to identify *who* should evaluate the evaluation; but Groups 5, 6, 7 and 9 all suggested that it would in fact be assessed in practice by the extent to which its findings were adopted within the project organization and influenced future production. Some reports also suggested the additional criteria of generality and long-term value.

Q. 7   *A good television programme*

Groups 1, 4, 5 and 7 all reported briefly on this question; and all revealed something of the dichotomy between 'production' judgements and 'evaluative' judgements. The former tended to stress qualities of motivation, attention-holding and clarity of message; the latter emphasized the meeting of learning objectives, as evaluated. All would probably agree that both groups of qualities come together in the good educational programme. Some reports also drew attention to the relationship of the broadcast component to the other parts of the learning system and made the point that an effective system relationship was another essential to a good programme.

Additional points made by the groups

Group 1 made the point that some researchers' training, with emphasis on the behaviourist approach, might not prepare them suitably for research in educational broadcasting. They might well have to adapt to more flexible methods, with each method designed for the objective in view. It was also Group 1 that attached particular importance to the effective dissemination of research findings.

Group 2 suggested that media research was too much influenced by the 'audience research' tradition; it was perhaps too inclined to supply confirmatory data, rather than to explore new objectives. It was important that evaluation priorities should be decided by policy-makers in consultation with producers and evaluators.

Group 3 argued that evaluation should generally be directed towards areas that are still 'changeable'; it should be diagnostic rather than retrospective. It should also take the whole learning system into account and not be limited to isolated parts.

Group 4 suggested that 'methodology' needed more precise definition. It could be taken to include the whole research design or the deployment of research staff or just the detailed techniques employed. This group also stressed the importance of reporting—saying that weaknesses as well as strengths of the study should be included.

Group 5 paid particular attention to the ways in which choice of methodologies must inevitably be limited by the circumstances of the project: e.g. closed or open systems, time and resources available, degree of flexibility in the system, etc. They would also like to see all research data used, whether predicted or not.

Group 6 discussed the question of whether research methodology was essentially 'culture-bound' or could be 'culture-free'. The evidence suggested that it was generally the former and was not easy to transfer intact from one country to another. Certainly there was no universal methodology; but there were lessons to be learned from one country to another.

Group 7 was much concerned with the context factor in all evaluative projects, which meant that every project had circumstances that were specific to itself and other circumstances that were common to other projects. This meant that each project required a dynamic 'servo-regulative' system, by which initial decisions could be modified in the light of experience and lead to results that had both specific and general value.

Group 8 agreed that each methodology should depend on the nature of the questions to be answered and accepted the difficulty of transfer of findings from one set of circumstances to another; but the group believed that a major aim of all evaluation was to produce answers that could be both validated and where appropriate replicated. In this way a cumulative body of research could be created. The group believed that interpretation of findings, like the setting up of projects, should be a management team activity.

Group 9 attached considerable importance to the distinction between short-term, middle-term and long-term research. The whole methodology of a particular research project would depend to a great extent upon its time-scale; and that would depend on the scope of its objective.

THEME 3: RESEARCH AND DECISION-MAKING

Q. 1 *Basic versus Applied Research*

Five of the groups discussed this question. There was broad agreement on the value of both kinds of research, but with a discernible preference for applied research, with its more specific, decision-orientated approach. Two groups considered that the choice between the two would in any case usually depend on the funding available and that this would generally steer it in the 'applied' direction. Such a movement would be further encouraged by the clear current trend away from summative research projects toward more formative research.

One group made the interesting distinction that applied research was more appropriate for evaluating a particular component in a learning system, while basic research would be better devoted to evaluating the whole system.

Groups 1 and 5 both made the point that applied research should have a sound theoretical basis and should call on the lessons learnt from basic research. As Group 1 said, 'Applied research is aimed at answering specific questions; basic research helps to formulate the questions to be asked'.

385

> **Q. 2** *Four categories of research in relation to decision-making*

Seven of the groups spent a fair amount of time on the four categories of *background, formative, summative* and *policy research*. Most of them felt some unease at the inclusion of *policy research* in an apparently chronological order of categories. The first three categories seemed usefully distinguishable; but the last seemed to several groups to be of a different order of logic. Some thought it essentially a composite of the others.

Most groups were also reluctant to attempt any order of priority. Each category fed into the others and made them more useful. And one category could become another with time. Group 8 made the point, for example, that summative research on the early stages of a project could become formative in the later stages. This group developed the idea of 'cumulative' research.

Three groups also noted that choice of evaluation methods depended largely on the history and the organizational structure of the production. Group 5, however, saw a definite current shift towards more formative evaluation.

> **Q. 3** *Has the wrong research been done in the past?*

Again seven of the groups commented on this question—conveying a general feeling that too much inappropriate research had in fact been allowed to go on. Sometimes this had been of the head-counting kind, though one group at least thought this to be a necessary and useful part of a many-sided research strategy. Others thought head-counting methods were of strictly limited value, because they answered no 'why' questions. Other research thought inappropriate was the isolated small-scale study which took no account of wider policy issues.

Nearly all groups commented that behind these weaknesses lay the major shortcoming: poor communication between broadcasting-based staff and education-based staff. No great improvement could be expected without a major improvement in that situation.

> **Q. 4** *Influence of research on high-level decisions*

Seven groups reported; but the only examples they could find of research having a direct and immediate influence on a high-level decision to launch a major project were the systematic researches into learning needs conducted in Mexico for Telesecundaria and in the Netherlands in preparation for the Open School.

However, all the groups suggested that research provided a broad basis of information on which high-level decisions could be made with greater conviction. This was well summarized by Group 7 when they suggested that 'research has (variously) informed the key players in the game of decision-making'.

> **Q. 5** *Is long-term research compatible with programme contemporaneity?*

Seven groups reported and there was general agreement that the implied conflict was a false contradiction. Several groups said that there was a great deal of difference between the time scale of launching a major new project and the making of individual programmes. The time-scale must depend on the needs of the system. One group put their view rather more strongly: 'Contemporaneity is a red herring'.

Q. 6 *Television as the basic point of reference in any extensive learning system*

All groups disagreed firmly with the statement. Some said that the basic point must depend on the particular design of the system; some said that no one component should be basic to the system in the way suggested; two said that only the learner should be the basic point of reference. At the same time it was suggested in some reports that there was a danger of television, because of its particular appeal, being treated as the basic point of reference.

Q. 7 and 8 *Actions for decision-makers and evaluators*

All groups discussed these questions in association and all related them to the important need for decision-makers and evaluators to work more closely together and to have a better understanding of each others' purposes, functions, and problems. Group 6 felt very strongly 'that the emphasis should not be on *action*, but on *interaction*'. Group 2 also felt strongly on this and thought that each group should receive some basic training in the nature of the other's work.

Q. 9 *Transfer of experience from one country to another*

Five groups reported and four agreed that programme formats were the least readily transferable. It was almost certain that cultural differences would demand major modifications in programme styles, at least. Strategies also required considerable modification. Basic research techniques, and training in those techniques, were likely to prove the most usefully transferable; but again differences should not be underestimated. It was important that learning from failures as well as successes should be passed on.

Q. 10 *In-house or external evaluation*

This was similar to a question discussed under Theme 2 and the five groups that reported gave similar views. There was general agreement that formative evaluation should be increasingly seen as an in-house commitment. Summative studies might well be carried out by external bodies on an agreed basis; but they might also be an internal activity.

Q. 11 *The credibility of research results*

Three groups reported and between them they produced three main criteria: effective dialogue with producers and decision-makers; imaginative and efficient research design; and well-considered presentation of results.

> Q. 12 *Percentage of budget on evaluation and research*

Five groups had a shot at this and their estimates of present average research percentage varied between 1 per cent and 5 per cent of total costs. This was generally thought too low, but no group seemed confident in estimating what it should be. It was thought to be dependent on too many factors.

Additional points

Groups 1, 7 and 8 all placed particular emphasis on the organizational structure within the producing body, whether broadcasting organization or academic institution. Without an understanding of the management structure, the kind of functional co-operation advocated by this Conference might never be achieved. Group 2 attached particular importance to training and believed that broader-based training courses, involving several functions, might lead to better co-operation.

Group 3 drew attention to the different levels of decision-making and the different forms of evaluation that were needed to influence these levels. No one approach to evaluation was useful for all purposes. Group 4 also stressed the need for a battery of evaluation techniques. Group 5 drew attention to the quite different frames of reference in which university research and broadcasting research have traditionally been conducted. This was a further strong reason for better communication.

Group 6 pointed to the value of the same researchers being involved in both pre-production and post-production evaluation. Again it was important to use a variety of approaches to meet the needs at each stage. Group 8 stressed the function of the evaluator in representing the interests of the users, rather than merely serving the producers.

Group 9 considered the value of calling in research techniques at a point of time and in areas where genuine choices had to be made. Such techniques could be used either to help such choices, if time allowed, or to evaluate the effects of a choice that had been made.

CONTINUING LINKS

JOHN ROBINSON — Member of the Conference Steering and Management Committees

The Steering Committee foresaw that, if the Conference proved to be both enjoyable and successful, many of its participants would hope to see opportunities explored for keeping them in touch with one another, beyond those made on a personal and informal basis. It was agreed, therefore, that an optional session should be provided after the Conference, at which those who wished to discuss such continuing links could get together for that purpose. Their suggestions could be referred to the Steering Committee, who would leave appropriate recommendations for future action.

The clear need for adequate time for the main reports and final summary meant that the Conference was scheduled to end at 4 pm on the fifth day, which just allowed time for most conference members to reach their next staging post that evening. It was not surprising, therefore, that there was a general exodus at 4 pm. However, some thirty members, including the majority of the Steering Committee, stayed on for an informal discussion at 5 pm.

The discussion after the conference

The discussion lasted about an hour and raised four important topics:

1 The possibility of a further conference, perhaps after two or three years, perhaps in either North America or a developing country, at which ideas exchanged at the present conference could be further explored and examined on an intercontinental basis.
2 Possibilities for other forms of communication and co-operation in the field of evaluation of educational television and radio, through the networks provided by international organizations in education, in broadcasting and in research. (There was general agreement against setting up yet another international body.)
3 The specific idea of a list of national and international journals which might be expected to carry regular articles and papers in this field of education (which we have drawn up in Appendix 5).
4 The possibility of increasing the volume of international funds available to finance such evaluation and of channelling such funds to the areas of greatest need.

It was finally agreed that a brief questionnaire should be sent to all 180 full conference members, inviting their comments on specific aspects of these four topics, with space for their further comments.

The questionnaire and the response

The questionnaire was prepared and sent out with the minimum delay; and returns were requested by 31 May, in time for the meeting of the Steering Committee on 11 June.

68 completed questionnaires were in fact returned by the date of the meeting—almost 38 per cent of those sent out. This return was felt by the Steering Committee to give at least a fair indication of continuing interest. There was obviously no time for any reminder; and it was appreciated that a number of participants were still away from their regular base and that most would have returned to a large backlog of work.

Before seeking to interpret the majority views of the respondents, it is interesting to note their distribution, both geographically and according to their function, compared with the total of full conference members. These distributions should certainly be considered in assessing the weight of their replies. The comparison can be seen in the following tables:

Table 1   Geographical distribution of participants

	Respondents		All conference members	
Geographical distribution	No	%	No	%
Europe	47	69	125	70
North America	11	16	21	12
Central and South America	3	5	11	6
Africa	2	3	6	3
Asia	4	6	15	8
Australasia	1	1	2	1
Total	68	100	180	100

Table 2   Distribution of participants by function

	Respondents		All conference members	
Distribution by function	No	%	No	%
Policy-makers and managers	17	25	47	26
Media producers	14	21	33	18
Researchers and evaluators	32	47	85	47
Users	5	7	15	9
Total	68	100	180	100

A further world conference

Of the 68 replies, 64 were in favour in principle, two were unsure, and two were against having another conference. With regard to the timing 53 thought 1979 and 23 thought 1978 would be the best time. There was less agreement about where it should take place though. European venues were suggested by 23 respondents, 19 suggested a Third World country, other than Central or South America, which were suggested by another 14 respondents, while the USA was suggested by 15 respondents. The only other areas mentioned (and by no more than three respondents) were Canada, Japan and Australia.

Whether organizational help could be enlisted by respondents

Possible to encourage	30
Not possible to encourage	31

17 organizations were mentioned by the 'Yes' respondents; with two or more mentions each for Council for Educational Technology (UK) National Educational Closed Circuit TV Association (UK), The Open University, the BBC and the National Association of Educational Broadcasters (US).

Quite a number of additional comments were made on this question (including reasons for time and place suggested). From these comments it would be fair to draw the following recommendations:

(a) That a future conference should not be limited to educational television and radio as such, which tends to make it 'product-based', but to learning systems which use these media, thus enabling it to be more 'process-based'. This should clearly be a consideration for any future conference planning committee; and it suggests that the fourth category of members (called 'users' in this conference) might be termed 'learning supervisors', or just simply teachers. These could be either class teachers or group tutors with wide experience of using these media, or they might be distance learning tutors or counsellors or members of course teams as academic staff or educational technologists. They were hardly provided for in the categories of this year's conference.

(b) That at the same time the theme of any future conference should assume an acquaintance with the general questions discussed this year, should seek to build on that acquaintance and be more specific in its terms of reference and objectives. It might also be advisable to limit the levels of complexity of the systems it included, so that the range was not too wide for effective discussion.

(c) That in view of the frequent reference to organizational problems, resources and communication, a possible theme for a future conference might well be 'to examine the organizational problems and resources involved in creating a media system that encourages working relationships among policy-makers, learning supervisors, media producers and evaluators that are likely to lead to the most successful results'.

(d) That the planning of any future conference must take careful account, in date, place and theme, of other international conferences being planned on themes at all closely related.

Activities by existing international organizations

The two networks most frequently mentioned were UNESCO (17 mentions) and the internationally linked broadcast unions: EBU, ABU, NAEB (13 mentions). Other bodies mentioned once or twice were British Council, International Council for Correspondence Education (ICCE), International Broadcasting Institute (IBI) and United Nations Development Project (UNDP).

Ideas mentioned by several respondents included:

(a) Closer and more continuous links between UNESCO and the Broadcasting Unions.
(b) Regular reports by UNESCO of educational media research, both in existing publications and in special reports.
(c) The setting up of international regional workshops, to bring researchers producers and managers together more often on an inter-country basis.
(d) Reporting the discussions held at the CEREB Conference to other conferences or existing organizations.

National and international journals

54 journals were mentioned by respondents, including 31 in English, 5 in French, 5 in German, 2 in Spanish, 1 in Portuguese, 6 in English *and* French, 1 in English, French *and* Spanish, and 1 in English, French, Russian and Spanish.

A complete list is attached as Appendix 5.

Journals mentioned several times included Educational Broadcasting International (15 mentions), Audiovisual Communications Review (14), British Journal of Educational Technology (5), the Journal of Communication (4), and the EBU Review (4).

International funds for evaluation and research

The only idea mentioned with any frequency was the international distribution, perhaps by UNESCO, of a list of bodies which have funded or assisted educational broadcasting research and the kind of criteria that they use in their choice. This idea was mentioned in one form or another by 10 respondents.

Final considerations by the 1976 Steering Committee

At this meeting on 11 June 1976, the Steering Committee for the 1976 conference gave careful consideration to the points raised at the discussion held during the conference, to the question-naire responses, and to letters received subsequently from Etienne Brunswic, UNESCO, Leslie Gilbert, Council for Educational Technology, UK, Frank Morgan, of Canberra College of Advanced Education, Australia, and Warren Seibert, of Purdue University, USA.

Arising from these discussions, a number of decisions were made:

1 To ask the Chairman of the Steering Committee to prepare a brief report on the conference, for sponsoring bodies and participants. (This has subsequently been written and circulated.)
2 To ask the British National Commission to bring to the attention of UNESCO Council the need for continuing support and links in this area, by means of the conference report, and to ask participants from other countries to act similarly regarding their own delega-tions (at the time of writing, we are waiting for a response).
3 To ask Warren Seibert to pursue any initiative which he believed to be appropriate for preparing for a future large-scale conference, in consultation with named representatives in other continents and UNESCO.

We also hope that readers will make use of these proceedings for developing personal contacts with people in other countries working on similar problems, and that individual organizations will take the initiative in organizing smaller, more frequent, international workshops and seminars within their own regions (e.g. NW Europe), bringing together researchers and producers, educationalists and broadcasters, for an exchange of experiences and for the strengthening of evaluation practices in each organization using television and radio for educational purposes.

APPENDICES

APPENDIX 1: NAMES AND ADDRESSES OF PARTICIPANTS

* = author of conference paper   † = group chairman or rapporteur
‡ = member of management/steering committee

Name	*Address*
Prof. G. R. Adkins*†	Director of Broadcasting Research, Indiana State University, Terre Haute, Indiana 47809, USA
Dr B. C. Agrawal*†	Space Applications Centre, Ahmedabad 380 015, INDIA
Mr P. H. Alegria*	CEMPAE, Av Insurgentes for 1480–14 Piso, MEXICO 12 D.F
M S. S. Allebeck*	Assistant Head. Educational Broadcasting, Sveriges Radio, 105–10 Stockholm, SWEDEN
Dr M. Al-Mazyed	College of Education, University of Riyadh, SAUDI ARABIA
Mr Lars E. Amling*†	TRU, Fack, S-128 71 Stocksund, SWEDEN
Mr D. Anderson	Open University, 60 Melville Street, EDINBURGH, EH3 7HF
Dr M. Arbadzadeh-Tehrani	NIRT, PO Box 33-200, Tadjrish, Pahlavi Road, Jamajam Ave, Tehran, IRAN
Dr J. Baggaley*†	Centre for Communication Studies, Liverpool University, Chatham Street, LIVERPOOL, L69 3BX
Ms A. Barkatolah	C/o Mlle G. Jacquinot, Université Paris VIII, Route de la Tourelle, 75012 Paris, FRANCE
Mr N. Barnes*†	BBC (FE), The Langham, Portland Place, LONDON, W1A 1AA
Dr J. Bartels	Fernuniversität, 58 Hagen, Postfach 940, WEST GERMANY
Dr A. W. Bates*‡	IET, Open University, Walton Hall, MILTON KEYNES, MK7 6AA
M. G. Berger	Section Audio Visuelle, Université de Paris VIII, Route de la Tourelle, 75012 Paris, FRANCE
Ms F. Berrigan†	IET, Open University, Walton Hall, MILTON KEYNES, MK7 6AA
Dr J. Blumler†	Research Director, Centre for Television Research, The University of Leeds, LEEDS, LS2 9JT
Dr J. P. Boorsma*	C/o Pedagogic Didactic Inst, University of Amsterdam, Prinsengraat 225–227, Amsterdam, HOLLAND
M. E. Brunswic†‡	Division of Methods, Materials and Techniques, UNESCO, 7 Place de Fontenoy, 75700 Paris, FRANCE
Dr H. R. Cathcart	New University of Ulster, Londonderry, NORTHERN IRELAND, BT48 7JL

Name	Address
Lic F. Chacon	Centro de Television Educativa, Universidad del Zulia, Maracaibo, VENEZUELA
Mr B. A. Chaplin‡	Dept of Education and Science, 86 Northgate Street, CHESTER, CH1 2HT
Chiam Tah Wen*	Ministry of Education, Jalan Ampang, Kuala Lumpur, 04–05, MALAYSIA
Ms C. Chovil	School Broadcasting, BBC Villiers House, Haven Green, LONDON, W5 2PA
Ms M. Christopher	Radio Telefis Eireann, Donnybrook, DUBLIN, Ireland
Mr J. R. Clapperton	Dunfermline College of Physical Education, Cramond, EDINBURGH, EH4 6JD
Dr G. Goldevin*†	Concordia University, Sir George Williams Campus, Montreal, CANADA
Mr A. Cooper*	Dept of Communication and European Studies, Brighton Polytechnic, Moulsecoomb, BRIGHTON, BN2 4CJ
Mr R. Cosford	Open University, Aristotle Lane, OXFORD, OX2 6UB
Ms M. Cran	Centre for Communication Studies, The University, LIVERPOOL, L69 3BX
Dr J. S. Daniel*†	Université du Québec, 2875 boulevard Laurier, Saint-Foy, Québec, CANADA
Mr P. Dannheisser*‡	IBA, 70 Brompton Road, LONDON, SW3 1EY
Mr P. Delahunty	10 Sunny Way, Pinelands, Cape Province, SOUTH AFRICA
Miss M. Delort	Room 4018, 17 Rue de l'arrivée, 75015 Paris, FRANCE
M. H. Dieuzeide*	UNESCO, 7 Place de Fontenoy, 75700 Paris, FRANCE
Prof G. Dohmen†	Director of DIFF, Wöhrdstrasse 8, 7400 Tübingen, FEDERAL REPUBLIC OF GERMANY
Mr B. Durkin	Scottish Council for Educational Technology, Rose Street, Glasgow, SCOTLAND
Mr R. Dyke	Audio-Visual Centre, University of Warwick COVENTRY, CV4 7AL
Dr K. E. Eapen	Bangalore University, 125 UVCE, K. R. Circle, Bangalore 560 001, INDIA
Mr S. Edington†‡	Director of Consultancies, British Council, Tavistock House, LONDON, WC1
Mr M. Edmundson	Dept of Education and Science, 60a High Street, Harpenden, HERTS, AL5 2TS
Mr A. Etherington	Botswana Extension College, Private Bag 43, Gaborone, BOTSWANA
Dr C. Faber†	Free University, De Boelelaan 1105, Amsterdam, HOLLAND
Mr D. Fagnon	Radio-Québec, 1000 Fullum, Montreal, Quebec H.2K, CANADA.
Mr I. Falus	C/o M. E. Brunswic, Division of Methods, Materials and Techniques, UNESCO, 7 Place de Fontenoy, 75700 Paris, FRANCE
M. A. Flageul*	GREP, 13–15 rue de petites Ecuries, Paris 72010, FRANCE
Mr D. Foote*	Institute for Communication Research, Stanford University, Stanford, California 94305, USA
Mr M. Freegard	Audio-Visual Centre, University of East Anglia, NORWICH, NR4 7TJ
Mr C. Frey*†	Head of Educational Research Group, Sveriges Radio 105–10 Stockholm, SWEDEN

Name	Address
Dr H. Fritsch	Fernuniversität, 58 Hagen, Pstfach 940, WEST GERMANY
Miss M. Gallagher*†	IET, Open University Walton Hall, MILTON KEYNES, MK7 6AA
Dr E. B. de Garland*†	CETUC, PO Box 1761, Lima, PERU
M. R. Garnier	OFRATEME, 29 Rue D'Ulm, 75-Paris 5, FRANCE
Miss S. Gasser*	Dept of Communication and European Studies, Brighton Polytechnic, Moulsecoomb, BRIGHTON, BN2 4GJ
Mr L. Gilbert‡	CET, 3 Devonshire Street, LONDON, W1N 2BA
Dr D. Giltrow*†	City Colleges of Chicago, 6210 N. Francisco, CHICAGO, Illinois 60659, USA
Mlle V. Glikman*	OFRATEME, 31 rue de la Vanne, 92120 Montrouge, Paris, FRANCE
Dr D. Gooler*†	University of Mid-America, PO Box 82006, Lincoln, Nebraska 68501, USA
S. Govedic Esq*	RTV Zagreb, JRT, Subiceva 20, 1000 Zagreb, YUGOSLAVIA
C. Griffaton	OFRATEME, Division Evaluation, 31 rue de la Vanne, 92120 Montrouge, FRANCE
Dr P. Griffin	Middlesex Polytechnic, Ivy House, North End Road, LONDON, NW11
Mr B. Groombridge*	Dept of Extra-Mural Studies, University of London, LONDON, WC1
Mr I. Hakim	Audio-Visual Center, Riyadh University, Riyadh, SAUDI ARABIA.
Dr I. Haldane*	IBA, 70 Brompton Road, LONDON, SW3 1EY
Miss S. Hammond	University College, 22 Gordon Street, LONDON, WC1
Dr K. Hanak*	Magyar Radio es Televizio, BUDAPEST 197, v111 Brody Sardor utca 7, HUNGARY
Mr R. Harrison	IET, Open University, Walton Hall, MILTON KEYNES, MK7 6AA
Mr B. Hartmann	Memorial University, St. John's, Newfoundland, CANADA
Mr D. Hartt	2 Rue Cesar Franck, 78100 st. Germain-en-Laye, FRANCE
Ms C. Haslam†	BBC (OU) Alexandra Palace, Wood Green, LONDON, N22 4AZ
Prof D. G. Hawkridge†	Director, IET, Open University, Walton Hall, MILTON KEYNES, MK7 6AA
Dr E. U. Heidt*†	Pedagogische Hochschule Bielefeld, 48 Bielefeld 1, Lampingstrabe 3, WEST GERMANY
Mr R. Hooper*	Director, National Development Programme in Computer-Assisted Learning, 37–41 Mortimer Street, LONDON, W1N 7RJ
Mr P. Hurst	22 Spencers Field, Lewes, East Sussex, BN7 2HH
Mlle G. Jacquinot*	Université Paris VIII, Route de la Tourelle, 75012 Paris, FRANCE
Mr A. Jamieson*	The School Broadcasting Council, The Langham, Portland Place, LONDON, W1A 1AA
Mr D. T. Jamison*†	Educational Testing Service, Princeton, New Jersey 08540, USA
Mr R. Janucik*	226 Barry Road, LONDON, SE22
Mr T. Kaye†	Consultancy Service, Open University, Walton Hall, MILTON KEYNES, MK7 6AA

Name	Address
Mr L. Kern	IET, Open University, Walton Hall, MILTON KEYNES, MK7 6AA
Dr C. Klasek*†	College of Education, Southern Illinois University, Carbondale, ILLINOIS 62901, USA
M. K. Kouadio	Service d'Evaluation, SEEPTE, BP v. 40, Abidjan, IVORY COAST
Mr J. Koumi*	BBC (OU) Alexandra Palace, Wood Green, LONDON, N22 4AZ
Dr J. Kraft†	Nat Endow for the Humanities, 806–15th Street, NW, Washington DC 20506, USA
Dr S. Krawcewicz*	Inst Krtatcenia Naucsycieli, Warsaw, ul Mokotowska 16/20, POLAND
Mlle O. Lausecker	C/o LACTAMME, 46 rue Barrault, 75634 Paris Cedex 13, FRANCE
Mr L. J. Lawler	The University of Manchester, Oxford Road, MANCHESTER, M13 9PL
Dr R. Lee	PO Box 11350, Johannesburg, SOUTH AFRICA
Dr R. Lefranc*‡	Ecole Normale Supérieure, 2 Avenue du Palais, 92210 Saint Cloud, FRANCE
Mr P. Loehr	IZJB, Rundfunkplatz 1, D-6000, Munchen 2, WEST GERMANY
Prof E. McAnany*	Institute for Communication Research, Stanford University, Stanford, California 94305, USA
Mr J. McCormick	School Broadcasting Council for Scotland, 5 Queen Street, EDINBURGH, EH2 1JF
Mrs N. McIntosh*	Survey Research Department, Open University, Walton Hall, MILTON KEYNES, MK7 6AA
Mr R. McLean†	University of Glasgow, Television Centre, Southpark House, The University, GLASGOW, G12 8LB
Mr C. McNamara†	Memorial University, St. John's, Newfoundland, CANADA
Mr S. Matias	Inst Kntatcenia Naucsycieli, ul Mokotowska 16/20, Warsaw, POLAND
Ms C. Mares	Faculty of Arts and Design, Brighton Polytechnic, Grant Parade, BRIGHTON, BN2 2JY
Khunying Amphorn Meesook†	Ministry of Education, Bangkok, THAILAND
Prof K. Mielke*†	Indiana University, Bloomington, INDIANA, USA
Mr J. Miller†	BBC (OU) Alexandra Palace, Wood Green, LONDON, N22 4AZ
Dr L. Miller	Head of Research & Planning, OECA, 2180 Yonge Street, Toronto, Ontario, CANADA
Ms B. Mody†	Space Applications Centre, Ahmedabad 380 015, INDIA
Mr F. Morgan*†	Canberra College of Ad Ed, PO Box 381, Canberra City, ACT 2601, AUSTRALIA
Dr R. Moss*†‡	The University of Leeds, Television Service, The Television Centre, LEEDS, LS2 9JT
Dr G. Mullins	University of Adelaide, BOX 491, Adelaide, AUSTRALIA 5001
Mrs P. Nabili	NIRT (ETV), Educational Television, PO BOX 44 1294, Tehran, IRAN
Mr H. Naficy*†	The Free University of Iran, 101 Kakh Street, Shahreza Avenue, Tehran, IRAN
Mr C. Neads*	Centre for Communication Studies, The University of Liverpool, Chatham Street, LIVERPOOL, L69 3BX

Name	Address
Prof A. Noguez*	Calz Circunvalecion Tabegueras, MEXICO 2, D. E. MEXICO
Mr O. Nöjd*	University of Jyväskylä, 40100 Jyväskylä, FINLAND
Ms M. Ochoa	Apartado Aereo 4976, Bogota DE1, Colombia, SOUTH AMERICA
Dr J. B. Oliveira*†	Rue Alverto de Campos 101/602, Ipanema, Rio de Janeiro, BRAZIL
Mr S. Onofrietti	CEMPAE, Av, Insurgentes Sur 1480–14, Piso, MEXICO 12 DF
Mr F. Orivel	Chercheur, Iredu, Faculté des Sciences Mirande, 21000 Dijon, FRANCE
Mr D. Owens	The Communications Centre, Booterstown Avenue, Blackrock, CO DUBLIN
Mr M. L. Pacheco	XHFN-TV Channel 8, 8 CEMPAE, Ave, Insurgentes Sur 1480–14, Piso, MEXICO 12 DF
Dr C. Palmer†	Audio-Visual Centre, University of East Anglia, NORWICH, NR4 7TJ
Dr E. Palmer*	Children's TV Workshop, 1 Lincoln Plaza, New York 10023, USA
Dr G. Pask*	2 Richmond Road, Richmond Hill, Richmond, SURREY
Ms S. Pearl	Inst Planned Parenthood Federation, Dorland House, 18–20 Lower Regent Street, LONDON, SW1
Dr L. Pena-Borrero	Open University Project, Universidad Javeriana, Apartado Aéreo 034194, Bogotá, Colombia, SOUTH AMERICA
Mr P. Pendred*	The British Council, Tavistock House, Tavistock Square, LONDON, WC1
Mr H. Perraton†	International Extension College, 131 Hills Road, CAMBRIDGE, CB2 1P
Mr M. Philps†	BBC (OU) Alexandra Palace, Wood Green, LONDON, N22 4AZ
Mr M. Pilsworth	Dept of Adult Education, The University, MANCHESTER, M13 9PL
Mr R. Postgate	40 Clarendon Road, LONDON, W11 3AD
Mr J. Radcliffe†	BBC (Further Education), Villiers House, Ealing Broadway, LONDON, W5
Miss M. Read	Guildown Road, Guildford, SURREY, GU2 5ER
Dr K. Rebel†	DIFF, 7400 Tübingen, Wöhrdstrasse 8, FEDERAL REPUBLIC OF GERMANY
Mr J. Reid	Chief Assistant, BBC Schools Radio Dept, I Portland Place, LONDON, W1
Prof J. G. Remy	Directeur du LACTAMME, 46 rue Barrault, 75634 Paris, Cedex 13, FRANCE
Mr J. Robinson*‡	Chief Assistant to Controller, Educational Broadcasting, British Broadcasting Corp, Broadcasting House, LONDON, W1A 1AA
Mr S. Rockman*†	Agency for Instructional TV, Box A, Bloomington, INDIANA 4701, USA
Ms S. Rodwell	NCAVAE, 254 Belsize Road, LONDON, W6
Mr R. Rowland†‡	British Broadcasting Corp, Alexandra Palace, Wood Green, LONDON, N22 4AZ
Ms B. Salinas	Av Revolucion 1291, San Angel, MEXICO 20 DF
Mr G. Samnegard	TRU, Fack S-182 71, Stocksund, SWEDEN.
Mr H. Schalkwijk	Stichting Teleac, Jaarbeursplein 15, Utrecht, HOLLAND
Mr P. Scroggs†	Yorkshire TV, The Television Centre, LEEDS, LS3 1JS

Name	Address
Dr J. Scupham	26 Crabtree Lane, Harpenden, HERTS
Mrs A. Searle*†	Plymouth Polytechnic, Tavistock Road, PLYMOUTH, PL4 8AA
Dr B. Searle*	Stanford University, Stanford, CALIFORNIA 94305, USA
Dr W. F. Seibert*†	Purdue University, West Lafayette, INDIANA 47907, USA
Mr Seoud	Instructional Media Center, King Abdul Aziz University, Jeddah, SAUDI ARABIA
Mr T. Sevenheck	TELEAC, Jarrbeursplein 15, Utrecht, HOLLAND
Mr R. Sherrington*†	The British Council, Tavistock House, Tavistock Square, LONDON, WC1
Dr Shukla	NCERT, Sri Aurobindo Ashram, Sri Aurobindo Marg, New Delhi 110016, INDIA
Miss R. Simon	PO Box 31793, Braamfontein, Transvaal 2017, SOUTH AFRICA
Dr G. Smol	Technology Faculty, Open University, Walton Hall, MILTON KEYNES, MK7 6AA
Mr C. Sonnemans*	TELEAC Foundations, Postbus 2414, Jaarbeursplein 15, Utrecht, HOLLAND
Prof J. J. Sparkes	Technology Faculty, Open University, Walton Hall, MILTON KEYNES, MK7 6AA
Ms C. Stannard*†	Schools Broadcasting Council, The Langham, Portland Place, LONDON, W1A 1AA
Ms J. Steedman†‡	IBA Research Fellow, Centre for Television Research, University of Leeds, LEEDS, LS2 9JT
Mr A. Sterman	Manager of Stitching Teleac, Jaarbeursplein 15, Utrecht, HOLLAND
Mr R. Stinga	AVRO Radio and TV, 3 Hoge Naarderweg, Hilversum, HOLLAND
Dr F. R. Stuke	Fernuniversität, 58 Hagen, Postfach 940, WEST GERMANY
Mr H. Suer	PO Box 10, Hilversum, HOLLAND
Mr R. Svensson*	Educational Broadcasting, Sveriges Radio, 105–10 Stockholm, SWEDEN
Mr A. Taraldsen	Schools Television, Norwegian Broadcasting Co, Oslo, NORWAY
Mr A. M. Taysseer	UNESCO Expert, Riyadh University, Riyadh, SAUDI ARABIA
Mr J. Thomas	324 The Langham, BBC, Portland Place, LONDON, W1A 1AA
Mme J. Thoveron†	Radio TV Belge, Boulevard Auguste Reyeres 52, B-1040, Brussels, BELGIUM
Prof G. Tulodziecki	D-4790 Paderborn 1, Kircherweg 5, Postfack 1576, WEST GERMANY
Dr Van der Haak	Postbus 10, Hilversum, HOLLAND
Dr Van der Voort	State University of Leyden, Stationsplein 10, Leiden, HOLLAND
Dr A. Van Zon	Stichting Nederlaose, Onderwijs Televisie, Riouwstraat 163, Den Haag, HOLLAND
Mr J. W. Varossieau	Director, Educational Media, State University of Utrecht, HOLLAND
Dr M. Veenendaal	NCRV, Schuttersweg 8, Hilversum, HOLLAND
Dr H. Verduin-Muller	State University of Utrecht, Heidelberglaan 2, Utrecht, HOLLAND

Name	Address
Mr P. W. Verhagen	Onderwys Research Centrum, Katholieke Hogeschool, Tilburg, Hogeschoollaan 225, Tilburg, HOLLAND
Mr I Waniewicz*†	The Ontario Ed Comm Authority, 2810 Yonge Street, Toronto, CANADA
Dr F. E. Wermer†	Teleac, Post Bus 2414, Jaarbeursplein 15, Utrecht, HOLLAND
Mr P. Whittaker‡	Director, TV Service, Birmingham University, BIRMINGHAM, B15 2TT
Rev P. Wigfield	Churches TV and Radio Centre, Merry Hill Road, Bushey, WATFORD, WD2 1DR
Dr L. Wüst	Director, KRO, Hilversum, HOLLAND
Mr S. Young-Harry	Nigerian Broadcasting Corp, Broadcasting House, IKOYI, Lagos, NIGERIA

APPENDIX 2: MEMBERSHIP OF THE STEERING AND MANAGEMENT COMMITTEES

Steering Committee

Dr A. W. Bates (Chairman)	Head of Audio-Visual Media Research Unit, The Open University
Ms L. Taylor (Secretary)	Administrative Assistant, The Open University
Mr R. Rowland	Head of Open University Productions, BBC
Mr S. Edington/Mr G. Grimmett	Head, Consultancies and Information Unit, Media Department, British Council
Mr A. Clarke	Secretary-General, Commonwealth Broadcasting Association
Mr L. Gilbert	Council for Educational Technology
Mr R. McPherson	Controller, Educational Programmes, Scottish Television Ltd
Mr B. A. Chaplin	HM Inspector of Schools, Department of Education, and Science
Mr E. Brunswic	Division of Methods, Materials and Techniques, UNESCO
Dr K. D. Stephen	Chairman, National Educational Closed-Circuit Television Association
Mr P. Dannheisser	Senior Research Officer, Independent Broadcasting Authority
Dr I. Griffiths	Educational Advisor, Ministry of Overseas Development
Mr M. Roebuck	HM Inspector of Schools, Scottish Education Department
Dr J. R. Moss	Deputy Director (Productions), University of Leeds
Ms J. Steedman	IBA Research Fellow, University of Leeds
Mr J. Robinson	Chief Assistant to Controller, Educational Broadcasting, BBC
Mr R. Cosford	Regional Director, The Open University
Ms F. Marriott	British Council
Dr P. Whitaker	Director TV, Birmingham University

Management Committee

Dr A. W. Bates (Chairman)
Mr S. Edington/Mr G. Grimmett/Ms F. Marriott
Mr P. Dannheisser
Ms J. Steedman
Mr J. Robinson
Dr J. R. Moss
Ms L. Taylor

APPENDIX 3: CONFERENCE PROGRAMME

Friday, 9 April

Opening of conference

14.30   Programme at Open University: display of Open University materials; films and discussion of Open University activities.
18.30   Sherry reception.
20.30   Official opening of conference: F. R. Stannard, Pro-Vice-Chancellor, Planning, Open University, introduced *Donald Grattan*, Controller, Educational Broadcasting, BBC.
21.30   Meeting of rapporteurs and chairmen.

Saturday, 10 April

Theme 1: The main findings of evaluation and research in educational television and radio

09.30   Introduction by the Animateur, *Edward Palmer*, Children's Television Workshop, New York.
11.00   Working Groups, various seminar rooms: session 1.
14.00   Working Groups, various seminar rooms: session 2.
16.00   Working Groups, various seminar rooms: session 3.
16.30   Theatre or other activities in London; or BBC Studios, Pebble Mill, Birmingham.

Sunday, 11 April

Theme 2: The most appropriate methods of research and evaluation for educational television and radio

09.30   Introduction by the Animateur, *Richard Hooper*, Chairman, National Development Programme in Computer Assisted Learning, UK.
11.00   Working Groups, various seminar rooms: session 1.
14.00   Working Groups, various seminar rooms: session 2.
16.00   Working Groups, various seminar rooms: session 3.
20.00   Opportunity to show/view participants' programmes or presentations; group rapporteurs for Themes 1 and 2 met with main rapporteurs.

Monday, 12 April

Theme 3: The relationship between decision-making and evaluation and research in educational television and radio

09.30   Introduction by the Animateur, *Sten Sture Allebeck*, Assistant Head, Educational Broadcasting, Sveriges Radio, Sweden.

11.00	Working Groups, various seminar rooms: session 1.
14.00	Working Groups, various seminar rooms: session 2.
16.00	Working Groups, various seminar rooms: session 3.
17.00	Group rapporteurs for Theme 3 met with main rapporteur.
20.00	Sherry reception.
20.30	Conference Dinner: guest speaker, *Asa Briggs*, Vice-Chancellor, University of Sussex.

Tuesday, 13 April

Conclusions and Reports

09.30	Rapporteur: Theme 1: *Viviane Glikman*, OFRATEME, Paris.
11.00	Rapporteur: Theme 2: *Emile McAnany*, Stanford University, California.
12.00	Rapporteur: Theme 3: *Brian Groombridge*, IBA London.
14.30	Official Closure: *Henri Dieuzeide*, UNESCO, Paris.
16.00	Meeting: continuing links.

APPENDIX 4: PAPERS SUBMITTED BUT NOT INCLUDED IN PROCEEDINGS

There was a small number of papers submitted which for various reasons we have not been able to include in these published proceedings. Readers who would like copies of the papers should write directly to the authors concerned (full names and addresses are given in Appendix 1).

Paper No	Author	Title
65	J. DANIEL M. UMBRIACO	*Distance study in French Canada: the Télé-Université*
67	C. FREY	*Why we need educational research and evaluation*
69	J. K. MAYO E. McANANY S. J. KLEES	*The Mexican Telesecundaria: a cost-effectiveness analysis* (available from: Information Centre on Instructional Technology, Academy for Educational Development, 1424 Sixteenth St NW, Washington DC 20036, USA)
71	H. NAFICY	*The Free University of Iran: the broadcasting perspective*
72	G. PASK	*An outline theory of media: education is entertainment* (available from: Systems Research Ltd., 4 Richmond Hill, Richmond, Surrey, UK)
74	S. GOVEDIC	*The thematic and organizational conception of the educational programme of Zagreb television* (JRT)
75	CENTRE AUDIO-VISUAL ST CLOUD	*Cost-efficiency research on university distance studies in France* (NB in French—available from: M. R. Lefranc, Ecole Normale Supérieure, 2 Avenue du Palais, 92210 St Cloud, France)

APPENDIX 5: INTERNATIONAL LIST OF JOURNALS WHERE RESEARCH/EVALUATION STUDIES ARE PUBLISHED

Name	Address (where known)	Languages
Asian Broadcasting Union		English
Adult Education	NIAE, 35 Queen Anne Street, London, W1M 0BL, England	English
Adult Education and Development	5300 Bonn, Bad Godersberg, Heerstrasse 100, W Germany	English, German, French, Spanish
American Educational Research Journal	AERA, 1126 Sixteenth Street, NW, Washington DC 20036, USA	English
A/V Communication Review	Association for Educational Communication and Technology, 1201 Sixteenth Street, NW, Washington DC 20036, USA	English
Audiovisual Instruction	Association for Educational Communication and Technology, 1201 Sixteenth Street, NW, Washington DC 20036, USA	English
AVCD	29 rue de la Grange-aux Belles, 75010, Paris, France	French
Bulletin de Technologia Educativa de la OEA		Spanish, English, Portuguese
British Journal of Educational Psychology	Councils and Educational Press Ltd, 10 Queen Anne Street, London, W1M 9LD, England	English
Bulletin of Paedagogical Research	Paedagogical Research Association, c/o Ministry of Education, Nicosia, Cyprus	English
Canadian Journal of Higher Education	Canadian Society for the Study of Higher Education, Suite 300, 102 Bloor Street, W, Toronto 181, Canada	French, English
Canadian Journal of Psychology	University of Toronto Press, 390 Sherbrooke Street, W, Montreal 109, Quebec, Canada	French, English
Combroad	c/o Broadcasting House, London, England	English
Communications	Paris, France	French
Communication et langage	Paris, France	French
Communication Research and International Quarterly	Sage Publications, Inc, 275 South Beverly Drive, Beverly Hills, California 90212, USA *Editorial:* F. G. Kline, Dept of Journalism, Room 2040, LS + A Building, University of Michigan, Ann Arbor, Michigan 48104, USA	English

Name	Address (where known)	Languages
Communicator	Indian Institute of Mass Communication, New Delhi, India 110049	English
Convergence	PO Box 250, Stn F, Toronto 5, M4Y 2L5, Canada	English, French, Russian, Spanish
Direct	Agence de Coopération Culturelle et Technique, 21 rue de Constantine, 75007, Paris, France	French
Dossiers Pédagogiques	AUDECAM, 100 rue de la Université 75007, Paris, France	French
Education and Culture	Director of Education, Council of Europe, 67006 Strasbourg, Cedex, France	English, French
Education	13 rue du Four, 75270, Paris, France	French
Education 2000	Centre d'Information sur les Techniques d'Enseignement, 5 Quai aux Fleurs, 75004, Paris, France	French
Education Canada	Canadian Education Association, 151 Bloor Street, W, Toronto 5, Canada	
Education and Psychology Review	Maharaja Sayajiroa University of Baroda, Lokmanya Tilak Road, Baroda 2, India	English
Education et Developpement	11 rue de Clichy, 75009 Paris, France	French
Education Quarterly	Ministry of Education, Civil Lines, Delhi 6, India	English
Educational Broadcasting International	British Council, Tavistock House South, Tavistock Square, London, WC1H 9LL, England	English
Educational Media International	International Council for Educational Media, 33 Queen Anne Street, London, W1M 0AL, England	English
Educational Technology	140 Sylvan Avenue, Englewood Cliffs, New Jersey 07632, USA	English
Erziehung und Unterricht	Schwarzenbergstrasse 5, Vienna 1, Austria	German
ETV Singapura	ETV Service, Ministry of Education, Singapore	English
European Broadcasting Review	1 rue de Varembé, Ch-1211, Geneva 20, Switzerland	English, French
Fernsehen und Bildung	Internationales Zentralinstitut fur das Jugend und Bildungsfern-sehen, München, W Germany	German
Ghana Journal of Education	Ministry of Education, Box M45, Accra, Ghana	English

Name	Address (where known)	Languages
Instructional Science	Box 211, Amsterdam, Netherlands	English, French, German, Dutch
Interchange	The Ontario Institute for Studies in Education, 252 Bloor Street, W, Toronto, Ontario, M52 1V6, Canada	English, French
Journal of Communication	International Communication Association, PO Box 13358, Philadelphia, Pa 19101, USA	English
Journal of Educational Television	Centre of Communication Studies, University of Liverpool, PO Box 147, Liverpool, L69 3BX, England	English
Jugendfilm und TV	W Germany	German
Magyar Pedagogia	Box 502, H1363, Budapest, Hungary	
Media	29 rue d'Ulm, 75230, Paris, France	French
Malaysian Journal of Education	Box 53, Petaling Jaya, Selangar Kuala Lumpur, Malaysia	English
Pedagogisk Forskning	Universitetsforlaget, Oslo 3, Norway	Norwegian
Pour	Grep, 13–15 rue des Petites Ecuries, 75010, Paris, France	French
Praxis Schulfernsehen	W Germany	German
Programmed Learning and Educational Technology	APLET, 33 Queen Anne Street, London, W1M 0AL, England	English
Publizistick	W Germany	German
Public Telecommunications Review	National Association of Educational Broadcasters, 1346 Connecticut Avenue, NW, Washington DC 20036, USA	English
Revista del Centro del Estudios Educativos de Mexico	Guliacan 108–4, Mexica 11, DF, Mexico	Spanish
Revista Brasileira de Eustudos Pedagogico	Rue Voluntarios da Patria 107, CP, 1,200 000, Rio de Janeiro, Brazil, South America	Portuguese
Review of Educational Research	AERA, 1126 16 Street, NW, Washington DC 20036, USA *Editorial:* Samuel Messich, Editor, RER, Box 2604, Educational Testing Service, Princeton, New Jersey 08540, USA	English
Rundfunk und Fernsehen	W Germany	German
Tanzanian Educational Journal	Box 9121, Dar-es-Salaam, Tanzania	English
Teaching at a Distance	Open University, Walton Hall, Milton Keynes, MK7 6AA, England	English

Name	Address (where known)	Languages
Trends in Education	HMSO, Atlantic House, Holborn Viaduct, London, EC1, England *Editorial Office:* Department of Education and Science, Room 2/11, Elizabeth House, York Road, London, SE1 7PH, England	English
Unterrichtwissenschaft	Beltz Verlag, 694 Weinheim, Postfach 167, W Germany	German
Vergleichende Paedagogik	Linderstrasse 54a, Berlin 108, Dem Rep of Germany	German

INDEX